The Complete
Systemic Supervisor

D1370230

The Complete Systemic Supervisor
Context, Philosophy, and Pragmatics

Thomas C. Todd
Adler School of Professional Psychology

Cheryl L. Storm
Pacific Lutheran University

Authors Choice Press

New York   Lincoln   Shanghai

The Complete Systemic Supervisor
Context, Philosophy, and Pragmatics

All Rights Reserved © 1997, 2002 by Thomas C. Todd and Cheryl L. Storm

No part of this book may be reproduced or transmitted in any
form or by any means, graphic, electronic, or mechanical,
including photocopying, recording, taping, or by any
information storage retrieval system, without the written
permission of the publisher.

Authors Choice Press
an imprint of iUniverse, Inc.

For information address:
iUniverse, Inc.
2021 Pine Lake Road, Suite 100
Lincoln, NE 68512
www.iuniverse.com

Originally published by Allyn and Bacon

ISBN:0-595-26133-7

Printed in the United States of America

To all the supervisors and supervisors-in-training
we have worked with, who have convinced
us that there is still much to be
learned about supervision

Contents

PHILOSOPHY: PREFERRED IDEAS, VALUES, AND BELIEFS

PRAGMATICS: METHODS AND INTERVENTIONS

19 The Blueprint for Supervision Relationships: Contracts   272
Cheryl L. Storm

20 Live Supervision Revolutionizes the Supervision Process   283
Braulio Montalvo and Cheryl L. Storm

21 Dismounting the Tiger: Using Tape in Supervision   298
Howard Protinsky

22 Case Consultation: Stories Told About Stories   308
Kenneth Stewart

Preface

This book was born out of a mixture of excitement and frustration on both our parts. Both of us regard our extensive involvement with the American Association of Marriage and Family Therapy's (AAMFT) Committee on Supervision as one of the most creative and exciting episodes in our professional lives. In Cheryl's case this included a long stint as the editor of the *Supervision Bulletin,* while Tom developed the learning objectives and model curriculum for the supervision course. Both of us continue to find our work in training and supervising supervisors among our most rewarding professional endeavors.

Our frustration came as we attempted to teach supervision courses, Cheryl in the AAMFT Summer Institute or tutorially and Tom in a mixture of academic and post-degree settings. Existing texts tended to lump supervision and training together, often emphasizing training at the expense of supervision. Much of the controversy and creative ferment in the field, evident in the *Supervision Bulletin,* was lacking in these texts. Supervisors-in-training often felt inundated by all the supplemental readings we assigned to compensate for these deficiencies. They also felt that their readings had not specifically prepared them to write the Supervisory Philosophy Statement and Case Study required for the Approved Supervisor application for AAMFT.

We hope the present book and the accompanying *Resource Guide* remedy these problems and convey a sense of excitement, both through our chapters and those we have commissioned from writers on supervision we admire. Neither we nor they have shied away from controversy or sought to create some safe middle ground.

The Introduction part sets the historical and evolutionary context of supervision and describes one generic framework for conceptualizing goals for supervision that transcends particular models.

The Context part focuses on two distinct meanings of context with regard to supervision: (1) contextual variables, such as gender, sexual orientation, ethnicity and social class, as well as practices supervisors can use to increase contextual sensitivity; and (2) contexts in which supervision typically occurs, including academic contexts, agencies, and private practice.

The authors who wrote for the Philosophy part of this book were instructed to explore the implications of prominent therapy models for *supervision*, while avoiding extensive discussions of training. These models have been grouped into major clusters, with models in a given cluster examined for common assumptions and those assumptions and interventions that were distinctive. For many of these models, such a systematic effort to explore the implications for supervision had not been attempted previously in print, and supervisors should find much stimulating material to expand and refine their personal philosophies of supervision.

The Relationships part highlights aspects of the supervisory relationship which can be controversial and problematic, particularly discrepancies of power, the potential for exploitation of this power and other constraints on supervisees, and the complexities of dual relationships in supervision. Again, our aim is to stimulate responsible thought and dialogue rather than offer simplistic formulas.

Although we believe the whole book is highly pragmatic, the Pragmatics part focuses on the "nuts and bolts" of supervision—supervisory contracts, diverse supervision modalities, and alternative supervisory structures such as individual and group supervision. The reader is offered systematic guidance to enable informed choices about modalities and to circumvent predictable shortcomings.

In the final part, Training Supervisors, we offer specific guidance for those supervisors who are endeavoring to teach and supervise novice supervisors, including advice specific to the requirements for the AAMFT course on supervision.

While throughout the book we seek to put the teaching and learning of systemic supervision on more solid footing, we hope that readers will emerge from the experience sharing our excitement and determined to adapt our recommendations to their unique context, philosophy, and individuality.

In the accompanying guide, we share ways we and others have found to make supervision practices effective and efficient. As a result, the *Resource Guide* contains practical tips such as developing a personalized model for collecting information from supervisees about their cases, easy access to resources like videotapes and readings on supervision, and forms, including everything from tallying supervision hours to evaluation instruments, that can be easily reproduced and adapted to enhance any supervisor's practice.

We would like to thank two reviewers whose comments assisted us in the preparation of this book: Harlene Anderson of the Houston Galveston Institute and Cheryl Rampage of Northwestern University.

We would like to conclude by describing the personal motivation that led us to this project and acknowledging those who contributed to our success in completing *The Complete Systemic Supervisor* and its *Resource Guide*.

TOM: I had no good excuse for writing another book, since I already knew the amount of work that was involved and the competing priorities that would be affected, all for the opportunity to make minimum wage for my efforts, no matter how successful the book was. I definitely owe a huge debt to my wife, Tracy Lewis-Todd and to my daughters, who were most impacted by the book, and to the institutions that knowingly or unknowingly contributed resources to make the book possible. So how do I explain committing to do this?

The easiest level of explanation is that supervising and training supervisors has been my "growing edge" for many years. I love to help supervisors, experienced or not, articulate what they believe about supervision and fully develop the implications for supervision of their therapeutic assumptions and interventions. A close second in importance was my work with the AAMFT Supervision Committee, where I got to work closely with Cheryl and with Anthony Heath, along with others too numerous to list here.

That work led me to believe that there was a distinctive emphasis on many facets of supervision that was missing from current texts in the field, one which supervisors-in-training sorely needed to prepare to write their Philosophy Statements and Case Studies. That vision was enough to help me inspire Cheryl, in turn, as well as Mylan Jaixen at Allyn and Bacon. As for the fruits of our inspiration and our ability to inspire the many writers on supervision we admired, readers can finally judge for themselves.

CHERYL: My investment in writing this book probably began when I was an undergraduate. The day I was to declare my major I solved my internal struggle regarding whether to pursue a career in journalism or social services by flipping a coin. The desire to help others improve their relationships won out over visions of interviewing famous people and traveling to exotic places. The writing bug bit me again when, like many ambitious doctoral students, I wanted to see my name in print and share my thinking about marriage and family therapy (MFT) with others. I owe reaching this goal to three key professors: Janeen Bernard, who quite tactfully suggested that, although I had interesting ideas, my ability to convey them in writing was grossly lacking; Douglas Sprenkle, who unknowingly gave me the same message and under whose tutelage I published my first journal article; and finally a professor whose name I have long forgotten but who taught me to write when I took her course. Since then I have combined my love for supervising and teaching MFT with the journalistic career I almost had, and have published on the topic with my colleagues Anthony Heath and Charles York, who have significantly shaped my thoughts on supervision as well as my educational practices.

When I was given the opportunity to be the editor of the *Supervision Bulletin*, I truly integrated my career interests and also proved to myself that I could write. It was through my interaction with my colleagues on the AAMFT Supervision Committee—individuals such as Marshall Fine, Anthony Heath, Jay Lappin, and Harriet Roberts— and with the many supervisors-in-training and Approved Supervisors I talked with about supervision during my tenure that convinced me there was a need for a book specifically addressing MFT supervision. This book, however, probably still would not have been written if Tom had not drawn the same conclusion and asked me to join him as co-editor. I will be forever grateful to him for this opportunity to satisfy a professional dream. And most important, I could not have completed this endeavor without my husband, John Eckholt, whose technological know-how, pep talks when I was discouraged, and willingness to have our family life disrupted so I could carve out time for the project are behind every page.

About the Authors

Thomas C. Todd received his doctorate in clinical psychology from New York University and did postdoctoral training at the Philadelphia Child Guidance Clinic, where he worked with Minuchin, Haley, Madanes, Aponte, and Montalvo. He has run family therapy oriented psychology internship programs at the Philadelphia Child Guidance Clinic, the Harlem Valley Psychiatric Center, and Forest Hospital; and was director of a post-degree marriage and family therapy (MFT) program at Bristol Hospital, which is accredited by the Commission on Accreditation for Marriage and Family Therapy Education (COAMFTE). Currently, he is coordinator of the MFT program at the Adler School of Professional Psychology and is on the faculty of the Chicago Center for Family Health. Tom served for several years on the American Association for Marriage and Family Therapy (AAMFT) Commission on Supervision (later changed to the Supervision Committee), serving as chair and developing the model supervision course. He is also internationally known for his work with M. Duncan Stanton on family therapy and drug abuse, culminating in their book, *The Family Therapy of Drug Abuse and Addiction*, which received an outstanding research award from the AAMFT. More recently he has integrated solution-focused therapy and other approaches in *Family Therapy Approaches with Adolescent Substance Abusers* co-edited by Matthew Selekman.

Cheryl L. Storm received her doctorate in marriage and family therapy from Purdue University. She has directed two MFT master's degree programs accredited by the COAMFTE, including the one at Pacific Lutheran University where she is currently chair of the Department of MFT and a professor. She chaired and served on the AAMFT Supervision Committee, was the editor of the *Supervision Bulletin*, the only publication in the field that specifically targets MFT supervision; and has taught the supervision course at AAMFT's summer institute. Recently, Cheryl edited the *Journal of Systemic*

Therapies special issue on postmodern supervision. Other publications on supervision include a book chapter on supervisory ethics, numerous journal publications on supervision including teaching supervision and developing a philosophy of supervision, and the *Family Networker* article, "Answering the Call: A Manual for Beginning Supervisors," with Anthony Heath. She also serves on several journal editorial boards, including the *Journal of Marital and Family Therapy*.

Contributors

Contributors were selected because of their previous writings on supervision, experience as supervisors and trainers of supervisors, teaching of supervision, and prominence in the field and in professional supervision organizations. The brief descriptions here merely summarize their primary professional affiliation and supervisory context. The majority of these authors are designated Approved Supervisors by the American Association for Marriage and Family Therapy (AAMFT).

JOAN BIEVER, Ph.D., is an associate professor and chairperson, Psychology Department, Our Lady of the Lake University, San Antonio, Texas. She supervises master's and doctoral students in the program's training clinic.

MONTE BOBELE, Ph.D., is an associate professor, Psychology Department, Our Lady of the Lake University, San Antonio, Texas. He supervises master's and doctoral students in the program's training clinic.

SHIRLEY BRAVERMAN, M.S.W., is an associate professor, Department of Psychiatry, McGill University, Montreal, Quebec. She has supervised psychiatric residents, social workers, psychologists, and nurses in hospital, agency, and private settings.

MARTHA COOK, M.S.W., is the clinical director of the McHenry County Youth Service Bureau, Woodstock, Illinois. She has supervised interns and mental health professionals.

MARSHALL FINE, Ed.D., is an associate professor, Department of Family Studies, MFT Program, University of Guelph, Guelph, Ontario. He is a former member and chair of the AAMFT Supervision Committee. He supervises MFT master's students and therapists in the community.

GLEN T. GARDNER, Ph.D., is a professor, Psychology Department, Our Lady of the Lake University, San Antonio, Texas. He is the director of the marriage and family therapy program and supervises master's and doctoral students in the program's training clinic.

KENNETH V. HARDY, Ph.D., is an associate professor of MFT and chair of Child and Family Studies, Syracuse University, Syracuse, New York. He has provided supervision to doctoral and master's students and community therapists.

INGEBORG E. HAUG, D.Min., is Clinical Director of the MFT Program, Fairfield University, Fairfield, Connecticut and an assistant clinical professor at the University of Connecticut Medical School, Farmington, Connecticut. She supervises master's MFT students and third-year psychiatry residents.

JAY LAPPIN, M.S.W., is the Family Therapy Director for CENTRA—a multidisciplinary group practice, supervises therapists in public and private agencies, and conducts large-scale organizational change projects in the Philadelphia area. He is a former member and chair of the AAMFT Supervision Committee.

JANIE K. LONG, Ph.D., is the Director of Clinical Training of the MFT doctoral program at the University of Georgia, Athens, Georgia. She provides supervision and supervision-of-supervision at the graduate level and has previously supervised clinicians employed at a psychiatric hospital.

TERESA MCDOWELL, M.A., is a supervisor for the MFT Program, Pacific Lutheran University, Tacoma, Washington. She also supervises clinical staff of agencies, mental health centers, and in-home services, as well as postgraduates in private practice.

BRAULIO MONTALVO, M.A., is a staff member at the Senior Health Center, University of New Mexico Medical School, Albuquerque, New Mexico, and a consultant on live supervision. He supervises health care and mental health professionals.

MARILYN PETERSON, M.S.W., is a lecturer at the School of Social Work, University of Minnesota, Minneapolis, Minnesota, and adjunct lecturer at other colleges in the area. She conducts supervision groups in the community.

HOWARD PROTINSKY, Ph.D., is a professor, Department of Family and Child Development, and director of the doctoral program at Virginia Tech University, Blacksburg, Virginia. He supervises doctoral students.

ANNE HEARON RAMBO, Ph.D., is director of the MFT master's program, Nova Southeastern University, Fort Lauderdale, Florida. She supervises interns, fellows, residents, and other family therapists in training.

PETER ALAN REINER, Ph.D., is an instructor Clinical Psychiatry and Behavioral Sciences, Northwestern University Medical School, Chicago, Illinois. He has supervised students, institute trainees, and physician residents in MFT in the Chicago area.

SANDRA A. RIGAZIO-DIGILIO, Ph.D., is an associate professor in the MFT Program and is on the faculty of the Department of Psychiatry, University of Connecticut, Storrs, Connecticut. She supervises MFT students, interns, and supervisors-in-training, as well as post-degree interdisciplinary professionals.

LAURA GIAT ROBERTO, Psy.D., is an assistant professor, Psychiatry and Behavioral Sciences, Eastern Virginia Medical School, Norfolk, Virginia. She provides postgraduate supervision to interns, residents, and family therapy trainees.

JANINE ROBERTS, Ed.D., is an associate professor, School, Consulting, and Counseling Psychology Program, University of Massachusetts, Amherst, Massachusetts. She supervises clinicians, graduate students, school counselors, and psychologists working in mental health centers, outreach programs, schools, and other institutions.

LEE SHILTS, Ph.D., is vice president, The Center for Innovative Solutions, and is on the faculty of both the master's and the doctoral MFT programs at Nova Southeastern University, Fort Lauderdale, Florida.

DOUGLAS SPRENKLE, Ph.D., is a full professor in the MFT doctoral program, Purdue University, West Lafayette, Indiana. He supervises doctoral students.

KENNETH STEWART, Ph.D., is a private practitioner in the Minneapolis/St. Paul area and is an adjunct faculty member at the Minnesota School of Professional Psychology. He supervises master's and doctoral students and psychiatry residents in clinical, academic, and community mental health settings.

TIM SUTHERLAND, M.A., works in conjunction with evangelical Christian churches, Chicago, Illinois, to provide on-site counseling to their communities. He provides supervision to therapists wishing to work within this context, and to therapists working in a wide variety of other settings.

KARL TOMM, M.D., is a professor of psychiatry and director of the Family Therapy Program, University of Calgary, Calgary, Alberta. He supervises students, interns, residents, and postgraduate professionals.

JEAN TURNER, Ph.D., is an assistant professor, Department of Family Studies, MFT Program, University of Guelph, Guelph, Ontario. She provides supervision for students in psychology and MFT training programs, and for therapists in private practice.

CHARLES D. YORK, Ph.D., is a associate professor and director of the clinic, MFT Program, Pacific Lutheran University, Tacoma, Washington. He supervises master's students in an on-site clinic and in community agencies.

The Complete
Systemic Supervisor

1

Thoughts on the Evolution of MFT Supervision

Thomas C. Todd and Cheryl L. Storm

From the outset, we would like to make it clear that we are not offering an objectivist description of the field of supervision, either in this chapter or in the book as a whole. Although we are proud of what we have assembled and confident that it will be extremely valuable to supervisors of any level of experience, we definitely want to acknowledge our own selectivity and subjectivity in organizing this material. As we have each trained and supervised supervisors, we have been continuously reminded that ideas and principles, which we consider obvious, may not be so to others in the field. This chapter should make more explicit what we believe has been important in the evolution of the field of marriage and family therapy (MFT) supervision and what areas will continue to be critical in shaping its future.

SUPERVISION: A DISTINCT ENDEAVOR FROM TRAINING AND CONSULTATION

At some point in our careers, we have both received a version of all of the following three queries from colleagues regarding a potential working relationship:

1. An experienced therapist calls for assistance in learning the solution-focused model of therapy. Several others within her agency are also interested in learning this model of treatment.
2. An agency director is seeking someone to meet with her staff on a monthly basis to discuss "stuck cases" with them.
3. A therapist, in private practice, wants to contract for postgraduate supervision. He is working toward state certification and needs ongoing supervision of his clinical work to qualify.

Although all of these requests have an educational purpose, we have viewed each request as different from the others in the ways described here which have significantly influenced our responses to our colleagues' queries.

In the first example, we view the request as one for training. Training teaches the tools of the trade (Liddle & Halpin, 1978). Liddle and Saba (1982) define *training* as the comprehensive teaching of theories, skills, and techniques that either precedes or occurs alongside the development of clinical skills. In the case here, training involves the teaching of a specific model of therapy to therapists who are already qualified professionals. In other cases, training may occur along with supervision of practitioners striving to become fully qualified.

Trainers accept ultimate responsibility for developing an educational experience targeted

TABLE 1.1. Distinguishing Aspects of Training, Consultation, and Supervision

Aspects	Training	Consultation	Supervision
Definition	Teaching of theories, skills, and techniques	Peerlike exchange between therapists and invited expert	Qualified therapist monitors professional development and socialization of partially qualified clinician
Relationships	Teacher/Student	Invited guest	Professional mentor
Experience	Highly directed	Collaborative	Inherently hierarchical
Accountability	Outcome of therapy	Consultee's satisfaction	Outcome of therapy and gatekeeper of profession
Participants	Postgraduate professionals with related degree	Practicing fully qualified professionals	Students plus novice professionals
Typical Settings	Institute or agency	Agency or workshop	Educational institution, agency, or private practice/contract
Time Period	Usually time-limited	One-shot to extended period	Continuous relationship for extended period
Evaluation	Moderate	None	Required
Follow-up	Some	Little if any	Continuous
Liability	Minimal	Minimal	High

at a specific training request. Their relationship with therapists is one of teacher to student or expert to nonexpert. It is most often time-limited and includes readings, mini-lectures, skill-training exercises, and clinical work. Trainers typically teach theoretical ideas and therapeutic skills; follow up on cases where therapists are applying the ideas they are teaching; and track assignments, suggestions, and directives they have given to therapists (Heath & Storm, 1983b). Training generally occurs in an institute or agency setting, frequently with professionals who have a related degree and wish to learn MFT. Legal liability may be lessened because participants are already embedded in a work context with supervisory support. Because therapists are already qualified professionals, liability is minimal.

We view the second example as a request for *consultation*—a short-term, peerlike exchange usually between qualified therapists and an invited expert (Piercy & Sprenkle, 1986).

The consultant can be metaphorically described as an invited guest. . . . The guest is not an ongoing member of the household and . . . is not responsible for the continuity and outcome of the household. However, the guest is invited into the interior of the house, perhaps into some of the bedrooms. The extent and duration of the invitation depends upon the trust level and the needs/desires of the hosts. If a room needs repair and the guest has the inclination and skills to remedy this problem, then the household may want to show the guest this room. The guest can then determine if he/she has the skill, desire, and time to work with the problem (Haber, 1994, p. 10).

Although consultation can occur over an extended period of time, it frequently is a one-time encounter. A consultation may be requested for the purposes of obtaining ideas for overcoming therapeutic impasses, learning of a new clinical realm in which the consultant has expertise, or promoting personal and professional development (Piercy & Sprenkle, 1986). Consultants address these areas with a sensitivity to the entire consultation system, the relationships between and among themselves, and the therapists, the clients, and the organization (Wynne, Weber, & McDaniel, 1986). Because consultants have no responsibility for evaluating participants nor their work (Nielson & Kaslow, 1980), follow-up and liability are minimal.

In the final example, we view the request as one for *supervision*—a continuous relationship focused on therapists' practice settings and their specific development of competency as they gain practical experience (Liddle & Saba, 1986). Supervision involves the following key elements: "(a) an experienced therapist, (b) safeguarding the welfare of clients by (c) monitoring a less experienced therapist's performance (d) with real clients in clinical settings, and (e) with the intent to change the therapists's behavior to resemble that of an exemplar therapist" (Mead, 1990, p. 4). The supervisor's responsibility is broader and includes the professional development of supervisees and their socialization into the profession. Table 1.1 summarizes the distinguishing aspects of training, consultation, and supervision.

Supervision can be highly tailored to specific needs, goals, and learning styles of supervisees. In general, beginning supervisees tend to seek help in specific intervention techniques, intermediate therapists desire theory development with complex problems, and more advanced clinicians want assistance with integration (Mead, 1990). Whether with beginners or more advanced therapists, supervision generally tends to occur over an extended period of time of regularly scheduled appointments, thus creating more intimate and intensive relationships between supervisors and therapists than between trainers or consultants and therapists. Although supervision is tailored to individual needs, which differ widely for supervisees at

different stages, supervisors are typically guided by a minimal standard that has been agreed on by the profession for independent practice, credentialing, completion of educational programs, and so on, which supervisees are working toward. These standards significantly influence the supervision experience by defining it and framing the overall goals for supervision. Because supervisors are usually expected to evaluate their supervisees, there is an inherent hierarchy in the relationship. Supervisors are legally liable for the work of their supervisees because, in most cases, they are considered the qualified providers and supervisees are viewed as still in training (Engleberg & Storm, 1990; Slovenko, 1980). These factors create a context in which supervisors closely follow cases, tracking the suggestions or directives they give. In fact, "focused attention on specific cases is the hallmark of supervision" (Piercy & Sprenkle, 1986, p. 289).

We define training, supervision, and consultation *as if* they are mutually exclusive. In actuality, they are frequently intermingled. For example, it is not uncommon to conduct training with a group of clinicians while also simultaneously supervising some or all of them. Most of you will have opportunities to do all three at various times during the course of your career.

Careful clarification with those seeking services, whether they are interested in training, consultation, supervision, or a combination, can be extremely helpful before agreeing to work together because these endeavors differ in responsibilities, the relationship between participants, the structure of the process, the degree of evaluation and follow up involved, and legal liability. When agreements reflect these differences, we believe you will be maximally effective. For example in the first example, our training agreement would include: (1) a set number of training sessions with scheduled topics, (2) a packet of readings to be supplied by us for participants, (3) an agreement that each therapist would practice the solution-focused model with a specific number of cases and show their work to us via videotapes, and (4) accessibility of us for guidance on therapists' solution-focused cases. In the second consultation example, our agreements would emphasize: (1) a commitment by agency staff to prepare case presentations in a particular way prior to the scheduled consultation, (2) our willingness to discuss cases with therapists who were practicing from differing theoretical models and with a wide variety of styles, and (3) an understanding that the consultation time did not qualify as supervision and was not being reported to outside credentialing bodies. In the third example, our supervision agreement would include the components described in the next section. Readers are referred to other excellent resources for an in-depth discussion of training (Liddle, Breunlin, & Schwartz, 1988) and consultation (Andolfi & Haber, 1994; Wynne, McDaniel, & Weber, 1986).

VALUES UNDERPINNING MFT SUPERVISION

In the first generation of marriage and family therapists, clinicians who were largely self-taught graduated to become supervisors based on seniority and experience (Liddle, 1991). As they engaged in this new endeavor of supervision, their professional values, as expected, shaped their supervision practices. We believe these values—marriage and family therapists show their work to one another, invite comment from each other, and recognize themselves as an integral part of every interaction—were critical in creating the supervision context of which we are so proud today.

Professional Values: Showing, Commenting, and Influencing

Initially marriage and family therapists showed their work to one another out of their excite-

ment and their desire to learn about the clinical innovation of MFT. It was a natural extension for supervisors to continue to do so with their supervisees. Beavers (1986) argues that there were several other additional factors working in concert to promote showing one's work. There was an aversive reaction to the ideas and supervision practices of psychoanalysis such as the reviewing of process notes during private, confidential supervision interchanges. The change from cognition to an emphasis on interaction "all but necessitated visual instruction and family observation" (p. 16). Finally, improvements in technology allowed for therapy to be easily viewed via videotapes or one-way windows. Early supervisors frequently demonstrated MFT to their supervisees, worked with them as cotherapists, and formed teams with supervisees as they assisted them to become marriage and family therapists. They expected their supervisees to "do as they did," and assumed supervisees would endorse this value of "show and tell" and willingly, even excitedly, pursue live supervision, taping of their work, or working together with supervisors on cases.

As they worked together, early supervisors and supervisees invited each other to comment on their respective work, demonstrating a value of openness about one's work. Supervisors asked supervisees to notice particular aspects of their therapy and were interested in supervisees' general input. Supervisors more directly answered supervisees' pleas regarding what to do than was commonly practiced by supervisors in the psychotherapy community. When supervisors were behind one-way windows, watching tapes, or participating in sessions as co-therapists or team members, it became difficult for supervisors to remain aloof and not be active participants in the therapy process. Thus, together supervisors and supervisees discussed the direction of therapy, decided supervisees' next moves, and created interventions to be tried. Frequently, it was difficult to separate supervisors' and supervisees' ideas from one another because they built synergistically on one another's comments.

Because of the systemic epistemology of the field, from the start, most supervisors acknowledged that they were a critical component in the supervisory process. They realized that what they saw in their supervisees' abilities and their supervisees' work was as much a reflection of their own abilities and their supervision as it was of their supervisees' competency and therapy. This questioning of supervisor objectivity led supervisors to look at themselves and their contribution to the supervisory process. This scrutinizing of the supervision process ultimately created a value that supervision was an endeavor in its own right that required specific training.

These Values Create a Unique Supervision Context

Overall, we believe these values promoted a unique supervision context within MFT in several ways. First, the "show-and-tell" value seems to have led to an emphasis on supervision being based on raw data whereby supervisors have access to therapy sessions either through observation or taping. Hearing about cases from the perspective of supervisees is not generally acceptable as the primary mode of supervision, but is viewed by most supervisors as an ancillary method of supervision. Second, the value of openness about one's work appears to have further promoted supervision based on raw data and also encouraged supervisors to supervise in dyads, groups, and teams, because a climate of commenting about each other's work occurs more easily in groupings of more than one supervisee and a supervisor. Interestingly, the American Association for Marriage and Family Therapy's (AAMFT) definition of *individual supervision*, which is widely used as a guide for state certification and licensure laws, is two supervisees supervised simultaneously by one supervisor which creates a context

where supervisees see and comment on each other's work regularly (AAMFT, 1991). Finally, the value that supervision is an endeavor in its own right that requires specific training resulted in the field taking supervision seriously by designating who is qualified to supervise, defining what supervision is and what it is not, and setting criteria for supervisor training. As can be seen, these values have influenced MFT supervision greatly and are evident in today's supervision practices.

AAMFT'S INFLUENCE ON SUPERVISION

Before we discuss the historical role played by the AAMFT in the development of supervision practices in the field, it is important to describe the role of the American Family Therapy Academy (AFTA)—originally called the American Family Therapy Association—which both of us have belonged to, Tom since its inception. AFTA by definition is comprised of professionals in the field who are not only experienced clinicians but supervisors, trainers, and teachers of MFT. We believe that AFTA has been an extremely helpful support network for supervisors and trainers in the field and that it has been in the vanguard in discussing important issues on the larger systems level (e.g., gender and privilege and culture and political constraints, along with their impact on supervision, training, and education of marriage and family therapists). Since its inception, however, AFTA has taken the stance that it would not attempt to set standards in the MFT field, so it is hard to document and measure the impact of AFTA on MFT supervision. In discussing the standard-setting role and history of AAMFT in this area, we do not intend to minimize the role of AFTA, particularly because many of the key figures in this history belong to both organizations.

Although all of the mental health disciplines are concerned with preparing professionals for practice via supervision and carefully specify the supervision experience, only AAMFT and the American Association of Pastoral Counseling (AAPC) professional organizations designate supervisors, define supervisors' qualifications, and require supervisor training. The steps to becoming designated as a supervisor in the two organizations are somewhat similar, probably because so many of early members belonged to both organizations.

The Creation of the Approved Supervisor Category

Benningfield (1988) concludes, in a historical review of AAMFT's involvement in supervision on which this section is based, that the position of supervisor within the discipline took on more and more prominence and significance within the AAMFT as time went on. The topic of designating supervisors first arose in 1961 when David Mace, the Executive Director of the American Association for Marriage Counseling (AAMC), which later changed its name to AAMFT, suggested a select group of members be named as supervisors to supervise clinicians who were unable to take advantage of the three marriage counseling internship sites in the country. He believed this would improve the quality of marriage counseling and increase membership in AAMC. The idea of designating supervisors was debated within the organization for a decade more before any action was taken. Many in the organization feared that designating supervisors would discourage interested professionals from seeking out more formal education in marriage counseling by supplanting it with supervision from these supervisors.

During the late 1960s, a consensus evolved regarding a need for a clearer definition of supervision and of the qualifications for supervisors. In 1971, the Approved Supervisor designation was established, a definition of supervision was adopted, a grandfathering period created, and the first 67 (20 females and 47 males) Approved Supervisors were named. By 1974, there were 200 Approved Supervisors. Also in 1974 the Board created a separate committee, the Committee on Supervision (COS), with Fred Humphrey as chair, to review applicants and recommend appropriate individuals for the designation of Approved Supervisor.

Setting Supervision Standards for the Field

Setting the standards for the practice of MFT supervision was added to the committee's charge in 1975. As a result, the COS took a leadership role in the discipline for establishing supervision practices as well as determining the policies and procedures for designating Approved Supervisors. For example, in 1976 the COS decided that a family member could not supervise any other family member, essentially discouraging dual relationships within supervision early on. In 1977, the COS agreed applicants for the Approved Supervisor designation had to demonstrate a systemic conceptualization, which supported those who were arguing that MFT was a unique discipline because of our systemic epistemology. Both of these examples illustrate the role COS has had in defining the culture and practice of MFT supervision. In 1983, when the Board of AAMFT moved to change the Committee to a Commission, which could then function semi-autonomously from the Board, the importance of this role was highlighted.

It was during the next decade that the two of us shared an interest and commitment to supervisory training with each other and some of the contributors to this book, notably Marshall Fine and Jay Lappin. It was during this period of time and because of the efforts of many of the members of the COS that we believe major strides were made in promoting supervisory training, in defining the practice of supervision, and in increasing the knowledge of Approved Supervisors in the field. In our opinion, this golden age of supervisory training included the following accomplishments.

First, the numbers of supervisors increased. Several tracks were created with differing requirements for becoming designated as an Approved Supervisor to encourage more experienced therapists, including those with national prominence, to pursue becoming trained as supervisors. Second, a course of supervision was added to the training regime in an effort to improve the breadth of knowledge on supervision of Approved Supervisors. Part of the course requirement was offered at the annual AAMFT conference thus initiating a supervision track at the national meeting. Third, a newsletter, the *Supervision Bulletin* with Tony Heath as the first editor, was launched to provide a forum for the COS and Approved Supervisors to share information and ideas. The newsletter became the only publication in the field on supervision trends and issues. Fourth, forums (i.e., in the newsletter and at the national conferences) were held for controversial discussions, such as on the topic of dual relationships, to build consensus and devise policies consistent with the practices and thinking within the field.

Finally, there was a concerted effort to improve the diversity of Approved Supervisors and to increase supervisor sensitivity to diversity. The COS held applicants to the requirement of demonstrating sensitivity to contextual variables (i.e., gender, race, ethnicity, and so on) out of a concern that marriage and family therapists as well as supervisors were not addressing these influences well. Other efforts included a minority stipend program to support minority supervisors-in-training, personal recruitment of minority supervisors-in-training, and the filling of vacancies on the COS with members that increased the diversity of the group—ultimately resulting in a body at one point in time where there were an equal number of members from the minority and majority cultures.

The governance structure of the AAMFT was reorganized and the COS again became a committee in 1991. Although theoretically the role and functioning of the body was to remain the same, it seemed to us that slowly the mandate from the organization seemed to change. A reorganization of AAMFT governance in 1995 collapsed the COS and the Membership Committee into a new body, the Standards Committee. This new Committee was given the charge of management of review procedures for membership in AAMFT and designation of Approved Supervisors. It appears that the days of the COS as leading the field in its shaping of MFT supervision practice, forecasting of new trends, and highlighting of controversial issues may be ending. Recently this has been coupled with a shift in responsibility to Approved Supervisors for evaluating supervisors-in-training at the local level.

Although this book is aimed at helping therapists fulfill the learning objectives as established by the COS for supervisor training, it is not meant to be the "official" AAMFT view. In fact, some of the ideas in the chapters here challenge the prevailing view. The authors of Chapter 18, for instance, outline the issues and present differing viewpoints regarding the recent controversy in the field about whether multiple relationships should be more readily accepted within the field rather than discouraged. As editors, we purposively do not take a position, but leave the decision up to you. Some chapters, such as the one on ethics (Chapter 3) and the one on teaching a supervision course (Chapter 26), are more influenced by the AAMFT because of their subject matter, while the majority are only affected to the degree to which the COS has influenced the practice of supervision in the field.

CRITICAL AREAS OF SUPERVISION

The major parts of the book address broad areas which all supervisors should be knowledgeable about—context, philosophy, relationships, pragmatics, and supervisor training. The sections that follow describe our thinking about the organization of each part of this book and the rationale used in soliciting chapters for each of the parts.

Context: Multiple Perspectives

Recently, Cheryl asked her supervisees to bring to group supervision a videotaped therapy excerpt in which their clients differed from them in race, gender, ethnicity, culture, religion, socioeconomic status, or in some other way. Her supervision goal was to heighten her supervisees' awareness to the ways that these differences, which have been termed *contextual variables* in the supervision literature, influence their work. After watching five minutes of one of the supervisee's tapes, Cheryl asked: "What did you notice?" One by one the supervisees described the interaction in terms of ways the therapist established a relationship with the client by actions such as smiling, leaning forward to listen, and so on. Frankly, Cheryl was shocked. The first thing she noticed was that she was watching a female, white therapist working with a white mother and her two children of color. At first, Cheryl questioned her attitudes and values. Was she racist? Were her supervisees truly "color-blind"? When it was her turn, she shared what she first noted. There was momentary silence and then several supervisees admitted they too had noticed the differences in race between the therapist and clients. Ironically, when the supervision group turned their attention back to the case, they discovered the presenting problem was that the mother felt her children were being treated un-

fairly by the school because they were of mixed race! In this case, the mother made the contextual variable central.

In another case, a female supervisee showed an excerpt of therapy with a male, middle-aged client who was seeing her to "straighten out" his life. He had no job, nowhere to live, and no money. In the clip she chose to show, he was upset that his previous employer was holding his tools until he repaid a salary advance he had received. During the brief excerpt, the supervisee focused on helping him find a place to live while he kept refocusing their interaction on his tools. Although the difference was subtle, the males in the supervision group noticed it immediately. Once the difference was pointed out, the supervisee acknowledged that as a white, middle-class, female therapist the client's plan to live in his car was quite frightening. Her contextual experience was very different than that of her male, working-class client; it was shaping her therapy session with him.

From this exercise, Cheryl learned that her supervisees were, like her, unsure about whether to directly address the differences between them and their clients or to ignore the differences. She learned that her supervisees were comfortable talking about contextual variables, such as race, when their clients brought it up, but did not feel comfortable introducing these variables as significant influences.

Similarly, there are many instances when contextual variables have influenced our supervision. For example, a lesbian supervisee benevolently corrected Cheryl's language by suggesting Cheryl ask supervisees about their clients' partners instead of inquiring about their wives and husbands. Thankfully Cheryl managed to create an environment where the supervisee felt safe to challenge Cheryl's heterosexual bias in a supervision group. Or in another situation, a male supervisor-in-training asked Tom if he could ever measure up as sensitive to diversity because he worked with supervisees and clients just like himself. When supervision occurs between like individuals, how do supervisors ensure their supervisees are prepared to work with a heterogeneous clientele? Together they addressed this by assessing how the homogeneity of his supervisee's gender, culture, and race influenced his approach to supervision, and how Tom and the supervisor-in-training's similarities in contextual variables were shaping supervision training.

Like many supervisors, Tom had given relatively little thought to the importance of the context in which he supervised. Beginning at the Philadelphia Child Guidance Clinic, he had helped to develop several programs for training predoctoral psychology interns in MFT. When he began training individuals interested in being designated Approved Supervisors by AAMFT and introduced supervisors-in-training who were not psychologists to this context, he began to see many ways in which context made quite a difference. Often nonpsychologists were not valued supervisors when their supervision was not critical for their supervisees' degrees. Similarly, master's-level social workers and marriage and family therapists, who were respected supervisors in other contexts, found themselves devalued because of their lack of doctoral credentials. What had seemed a straightforward context for supervision in MFT clearly had other dimensions.

As we interacted with other supervisors, we began to see wide differences in supervision practices based on the context in which supervision occurred. In an agency context, for example, having a supervisor from another discipline was not uncommon while in other settings, such as academia, supervisees are only supervised by supervisors from their own profession. Tom was surprised to realize that in some contexts supervisees were reassigned supervisors every fifteen weeks as compared to the year he was accustomed to having with su-

pervisees. Cheryl was surprised to discover that in some settings supervisees never show their actual work to supervisors.

In the part on context, authors discuss the influence of contextual variables on supervision. We define contextual variables broadly as the ever-present, unique aspects of supervisors, supervisees and clients, and the unique aspects of the environment in which supervision and therapy occur. Contextual variables can be virtually endless. Supervisor, supervisee, and client variables include aspects such as gender, race, religion, culture, class, ethnicity, and so on. Environmental aspects include setting, ethical guidelines of the profession, the legal context, and others. We have chosen to focus on the contextual variables of gender, sexual preference, race, class, and ethics because these variables are always present in supervision. We have selectively chosen the contextual variables of educational programs, agencies, and privately contracted supervision because these are three predominant settings in which supervision occurs. Many supervisors-in-training in these settings have learned about the importance of context through difficult lessons, which have proved costly to their supervisees and their clients. Issues, such as emergency back-up or policies for handling unsatisfactory evaluations, which might have been taken for granted in one context, needed to be explicitly developed when the supervisory context shifted. We chose supervisors who have worked extensively in each context to offer warnings to less-experienced supervisors of potential pitfalls and to give suggestions for minimizing such problems, while also highlighting the unique advantages of each context.

We are aware that there are many other important contextual variables such as religion, being physically challenged, ethnicity, public agency settings, legality, and so on, that can have as much of an impact on supervision as those we have included. Although we may not be comprehensive, we believe many of the ideas presented here can be translated to those contextual variables not covered, and that much overlap exists in the ways contextual variables influence supervision.

We hope you learn about the ways contextual variables influence supervision, develop an awareness of your personal biases regarding contextual variables, and become appreciative of the contextual differences that exist. Most important, we hope these chapters will expand your ability to help supervisees' learn to be contextually sensitive in their therapy, and your ability to be contextually sensitive in supervision.

Philosophy: Preferred Ideas and Beliefs

How important are supervisors' theories of therapy in determining how they will conduct supervision? Opinions vary considerably. Mead (1990), for example, believes that it is not only possible but desirable to have a general theory of supervision. Others argue that supervision is a separate body of knowledge with distinct skills that are independent from therapeutic skills. Cheryl had been impressed by the potential usefulness of one's theory of therapy for developing a theory of supervision, as she has articulated in her work with Tony Heath (Heath & Storm, 1983a; Heath & Storm, 1985). Having inexperienced supervisors examine their therapeutic approaches for implications for supervision often seemed to reassure them that they were more prepared to "answer the call" to becoming a supervisor than they might have believed initially.

There is general consensus that it is optimal for supervisees' theory of therapy to correspond to that of their supervisors and to have supervisory contracts include further learning of that approach. We noted, however, that combining the topics of training and supervision often obscured the assumptions of supervision.

The theory of paradoxical therapy, for example, can be taught in a straightforward manner. This avoids the question of whether it is possible or desirable to use paradoxical techniques in supervision. In addition, supervision in the trenches often requires supervisors to supervise therapists who are practicing from models different than those of their supervisors because of their education, training, or professional context, or because therapists prefer other models than those of their supervisors.

A major impetus for this book was our desire to have a singular focus on supervision rather than including training. In the philosophy part, each author has been instructed to keep the two topics separate and to focus almost exclusively on supervision, emphasizing the unique assumptions and interventions characteristic of the models covered in each chapter. If we had chapters representing every MFT therapy model as applied to supervision, we could easily have filled several books. Although we are interested in specific theories, and especially in helping you develop your own theoretical approach to supervision, we elected to group models that seemed to share common assumptions together. We then gave chapter authors the opportunity to discuss the ways individual models departed from this common ground. We believe this provides the best opportunity to explore the philosophical underpinnings of supervision and to highlight the similarities and differences between different "schools" of therapy and supervision.

Relationships: Power, Problems, and Complexity

It may seem surprising that any psychotherapist could need reminding that the relationship is at the heart of an intense interpersonal process like therapy or supervision. Painful as it may be, both of us had to admit that at times this was true for us, at least in the arena of supervision. At times both of us proceeded with contracting and conducting supervision as though the supervisory relationship were taken for granted and did not need to be cultivated or examined.

On further reflection, we wonder if this was not an example of some "double standard" in operation. We noted that we held supervisees to a much higher standard of behavior than clinical clients, especially when our supervisees were fully credentialed therapists; we tended to assume that, of course, both supervisors and supervisees were focused on providing better therapy and believed that a no-nonsense, businesslike approach was all that was required. To further complicate this issue, both of us realized that we had a somewhat aversive reaction to any assumption that supervisees needed to be reassured and constantly supported, which seemed to imply that they could not function autonomously.

It seems tempting and all too easy to focus on supervisory techniques, teaching psychotherapeutic skills, concrete details such as contracting, and philosophies of supervision, rather than the risky and uncharted territory of the supervisory relationship. Although this book as a whole certainly reinforces the importance of these areas, the chapters in the third part remind us that these technical issues pale in significance, particularly for supervisees, compared to the supervisory relationship. Supervisees think of little else until a positive supervisory relationship is assured—then, and only then, can they turn their attention to some of these other topics.

The two other issues in the relationship part—power and dual relationships in supervision—have been the subject of much controversy in the recent supervisory literature. We hope that some of this controversy is reflected in these chapters, and trust that supervisors will have strong reactions to some of this material. Again, supervisors should be reminded that, while these issues are important and difficult, it is hard to reassure supervisees that

there is no hierarchy, or that blurred relationship boundaries are safe, unless they experience safety and security in the supervisory relationship.

Can the positive aspects of the supervisory relationship be taught, particularly through a book? Probably not. We hope that the three chapters in the relationship part will provide some cautionary examples, while avoiding simplistic answers. Further, we hope to open the minds of supervisors to the unavoidable complexities of the supervisory relationship, and by so doing also hope to create room for a much more open dialogue with supervisees.

Pragmatics: Methods

One of the authors of the part on pragmatics, Charles York, laments the existence of "Rolodex® therapists"—clinicians who spin Rolodexes to arbitrarily select techniques to use in therapy without therapeutic goals or rationales. We extend this concern to supervisors who similarly choose methods to employ in the context of supervision. For example, we are wary of supervisors who prefer live supervision because they believe it is the "gold card" of supervisory methods rather than thoughtfully selecting live supervision with goals and rationales in mind. For many years, live supervision was viewed as the "best" method for supervision; anything else was second choice. More recently writers have proposed that other methods, such as case consultation, are viable alternatives that offer supervisors and supervisees learning opportunities not offered by live supervision. Because we believe there is no gold card of supervision methods, we propose each method is, in and of itself, an intervention with unique advantages and disadvantages.

As will be seen from the chapters in the philosophy part, we and others have found that methods interface with supervisors' preferred ideas, styles, and values. A supervisor, for instance, who prefers structural ideas will use live supervision very differently than a supervisor who leans toward a psychoanalytic philosophy of supervision. Similarly, experiential supervisors are more likely to volunteer to be co-therapists with their supervisees, while postmodern supervisors are more likely to prefer having their supervisees work in teams.

We also believe that methods interface with the learning goals of supervisors and supervisees. When supervisors wish to assist supervisees in assessing their own family experiences' effect on their therapy practices, using supervisees' genograms during supervision may be the supervisory method of choice. In contrast, if supervisors hope to increase supervisees' awareness of the influence of race on their therapy, case consultation may be the best method for this assessment because it allows time for an in-depth discussion on what is frequently a touchy topic. Finally, we suggest that methods interface with the context in which they are used. Each supervision setting and mix of contextual influences has unique constraints and opportunities. Supervisors contracting privately with supervisees may find videotaping of therapy sessions to be the best way for them and their supervisees to monitor the effect of male supervisors supervising male therapists who are seeing predominantly female clients. Or, supervisors in agency settings may discover that group supervision is the only method their agency can afford because of limited resources.

As a result of these interfaces, we think methods are important choices that supervisors make which either fit or do not fit their supervision philosophies, either accomplish or fail to accomplish supervisors' and their supervisees' learning objectives for supervision, and either promote opportunities or increase constraints on contextual influences. In the pragmatics part, each author was asked to write on a specific method of supervision, and to address the topic in a way that applied to supervisors of many persuasions. However, all

the authors approach the topic from their own preferred ideas, styles, and values; the learning objectives they tend to have for supervision; and their contextual experiences. As a result, for example, the chapter on live supervision (Chapter 20) has a structural slant, the one on case consultation (Chapter 22) has a postmodern perspective, and the one on genograms (Chapter 25) has an intergenerational bias. Even so, we hope the chapters in this part of the book will help you make thoughtful, sophisticated, informed choices about the methods you choose to employ in the context of supervision given your personal slant, bias, or perspective.

Training Supervisors: Teaching and Supervising

"Who needs training as a supervisor anyway? Isn't this something that one just does, learning how to do it along the way?" (Liddle, 1991, p. 642). We believe the answer to these questions is largely influenced by generational membership and by professional allegiance. Liddle (1991), who initially posed the questions, speculates that some therapists and supervisors privately ask these questions because early MFT supervisors were generally self-taught, which may have led to a devaluing of supervisor training. If you are a member of an early generation of the field, you are probably more likely to believe that supervisors can learn by doing and that formal training is unnecessary. We speculate that supervisor training is also viewed as less critical by those marriage and family therapists who are not closely aligned professionally with the AAMFT, whose primary professional identification is with another mental health discipline—psychology, social work, and so on, or who may view MFT as a subspeciality of another mental health discipline rather than a discipline in its own right. As noted earlier, the AAMFT and the AAPC are the only mental health professional organizations that have established a formal supervisory designation which requires completion of a supervisor training program. Those marriage and family therapists who have high allegiance to AAMFT as the professional organization representing the MFT discipline are likely to endorse the supervisory standards established within the field and desire AAMFT's supervisory stamp of approval.

Although Tom is of an earlier generation than Cheryl and we both experienced supervisor training when it was less stringent than it is today, we find ourselves increasingly valuing our supervisor training as we experience the complexity and challenges of doing supervision. We are at times somewhat envious of the quality of formal training available to our colleagues today. Because our professional allegiance is primarily to the discipline of MFT, we are committed to promoting the supervisory standards set by AAMFT. It is in this spirit that this final part of the book focuses on preparing you to contribute to the process of educating the next generation of supervisors.

For many of you, training supervisors may seem a distant or perhaps even unlikely future endeavor, but we believe it may become of interest to you later on. Once you have experience in supervising therapists and have learned to juggle three balls (i.e., the ability to consider client interaction, therapy interaction, and supervisory interaction), you may wish to add another (i.e., supervisor-in-training and supervisor interaction) by training supervisors. You may choose to teach a supervision course, become a supervisor-of-supervision, or both. For the most part, you will be a self-taught educator of supervisors because there is no formal process for this next step. (Who educates the trainers who train the supervisors to train the supervisors? This, of course, can go on to infinity.) In the first chapter, because many supervisors are grateful for a course outline on which they can build, Cheryl suggests ways for teaching a course on supervision. In the second chapter, along with two of our former su-

pervisors-in-training, we offer information and share supervision-of-supervision experiences we have found useful in enabling us to juggle four levels of interaction simultaneously.

SUPERVISORS CARRY THE TORCH FORWARD

Current research, similar to current literature, tends to be more about training of therapists than about supervising of marriage and family therapists. In their reviews of the MFT training and supervision literature, Liddle (1991) and Avis and Sprenkle (1990) conclude that rigorous research on supervision is sorely needed. The following paragraphs briefly summarize what is known about the supervision process in MFT based on these limited findings.

Several surveys (Lewis & Rohrbaugh, 1989; McKenzie et al., 1986; Nichols, Nichols, & Hardy, 1990; Wetchler, Piercy, & Sprenkle, 1989) have assessed supervisory practices and found some general trends. There seems to be an increased use of videotaped supervision, larger numbers of supervisors affiliating with training and educational settings in contrast to supervising within private practices, and more diversity within the ranks of supervisors (e.g., more females, more master's trained supervisors, a greater range in the experience level of supervisors).

Interestingly, even though there is consensus in the field that supervised practice is critical to becoming a competent marriage and family therapist, there is no research evidence to support the conclusion that experiential learning is superior to didactic instruction. In fact, there may be somewhat skimpy evidence to the contrary. In a study of medical students learning MFT, Tomm and Leahey (1980) found no difference in the acquisition of skills between those who were involved in an experiential quasi-supervisory experience and those who were involved in a more traditional instructional format. The authors compared the three training methods of lecture with videotaped examples, small groups with prepared videotaped examples, and small groups where students interviewed families and presented these tapes for discussion. This final method could be viewed as a quasi-supervision process. However, this study is not generalizable to supervision of marriage and family therapists because it was done with medical students, and it was not a study assessing supervision of therapy.

Similarly, Tom encountered an unexpected finding regarding supervision in a therapy outcome study he conducted with Jay Haley in the 1970s (Todd & Haley, 1973). In this study, cases in which the therapist received supervision showed significantly *worse* outcomes than those receiving no supervision! Although this surprising finding probably reflects therapists selecting difficult cases to present in supervision, it also underscores the danger in assuming that supervision is automatically helpful and points to the need for more careful research, particularly linking supervision to therapy outcome. These two studies are far from definitive, but both show that supervisors have no cause to be complacent about the impact of supervision. Like the rest of the mental health field, we can expect more accountability about supervision and more pressure to provide evidence of its cost effectiveness.

Much of the research effort on MFT supervision has been directed at studying supervision methods, particularly live supervision, which is by far the most widely studied. There are surveys of supervisors' use of live supervision (Lewis & Rohrbaugh, 1989; McKenzie et al., 1986; Nichols, Nichols, & Hardy, 1990; Wetchler et al., 1989), supervisees' experiences of live supervision (Liddle, Davidson, & Barrett, 1988; Lowenstein, Reder, & Clark, 1982), family members' experiences with live supervision (Piercy, Sprenkle, & Constantine, 1986), studies of phone-ins during live supervision

(Frankel & Piercy, 1990; Wright, 1986), and supervisory intervention decision making during live supervision (Gorman, 1989)—see Chapter 20 for more information about research findings on live supervision. There is also a recent growing interest in researching videotape supervision. Street and Foot (1989) assessed the impact on supervisees of observing a therapy session versus watching a videotape. Their cautionary results suggest that neither method is superior to the other. Protinsky (Chapter 21) describes an innovative qualitative research approach to the study of videotaped supervision that could help us understand more fully supervisees' experiences in taped supervision.

There is some research that includes the views of supervisees about their experience with supervision. One nonrandom study found that supervisees in programs accredited by the Commission on Accreditation for MFT Education viewed the quality of their supervision as good, but that the majority did not receive the type of supervision they desired (Brock & Sibbald, 1988). In two other studies, MFT supervisors and supervisees reported interpersonal skills in general and respecting supervisees in particular (Wetchler, 1989) and supervisor directiveness (Wetchler & Vaughn, 1991) as important abilities for supervisors to have.

After reviewing the research on supervisor effectiveness in the general psychotherapy literature, Mead (1990) concludes that findings suggest beginning supervisors need help in developing skills, positive supervisory relationships, and a model of supervision to guide their work. Because there is little reason to believe MFT supervisors are any different than their counterparts in the mental health field, training of MFT supervisors seems critical. Overall, however, the research literature on MFT supervisory effectiveness is so scant that the training of supervisors is primarily based on our cherished beliefs, sometimes on historical accidents, and frequently on the pragmatics of the contexts in which supervision occurs. Yet as Liddle (1991) writes:

> Supervisors must be formally trained. . . . Being a skilled therapist is not enough. Clinical skill and knowledge are indispensable for, but no guarantee of, supervisory success. Without exagerration, the success of the family therapy field depends on the next generation(s) of supervisors. Our field can progress no further than do those who define it and teach it to others. . . . It is they who carry the torch (p. 688).

Although there is ever-growing content on MFT supervision, as can be seen, there is precious little research showing the effectiveness of MFT supervision to help supervisors carry the torch forward into the next generation. However, we hope this book will assist you in carrying your torch in three ways. First, we hope you will carry it into new territory because you have learned about others' experiences regarding the influence of context whether that context is a new cultural group or an innovative work setting. Second, we hope you will carry a brighter torch because you are aware of the diversity that exists within the field as well as the tried-but-true philosophies and pragmatics of MFT supervision. Finally, we hope you will carry your torch higher because you are more self-confident in your abilities as a supervisor as a result of our work and that of our contributors.

REFERENCES

American Association for Marriage and Family Therapy (AAMFT). (1991). *AAMFT Approved Supervisor designation: Standards and responsibilities.* Washington DC: Author.

Avis, J., & Sprenkle, D. (1990). Outcome research on family therapy training: A substantive and methodological review. *Journal of Marital and Family Therapy, 16,* 225–240.

Beavers, W. (1986). Family therapy supervision: An introduction and consumer's guide. *Journal of Psychotherapy and the Family, 1,* 15–24.

Benningfield, M. (1988). The commission on supervision: A historical review. Unpublished paper.

Brock, G., & Sibbald, S. (1988). Supervision in AAMFT accredited programs: Supervisee perceptions and preferences. *American Journal of Family Therapy, 16,* 256–261.

Engleberg, S., & Storm, C. (1990). Supervising defensively: Advice from legal counsel. *Supervision Bulletin, 4,* 6.

Frankel, B., & Piercy, F. (1990). The relationship among selected supervisor, therapist, and client behaviors. *Journal of Marital and Family Therapy, 16,* 407–421.

Gorman, P. (1989). Family therapy supervision in an agency setting: An analysis of moments–of–intervention. Unpublished doctoral dissertation, University of Massachusetts.

Haber, R. (1994). Introduction: Consultative resources in family therapy. In M. Andolfi & R. Haber (Eds.), *Please help me with this family: Using consultants as resources in family therapy* (pp. 3–32). New York: Brunner/Mazel.

Heath, A., & Storm, C. (1983a). Answering the call: A manual for beginning supervisors. *The Family Therapy Networker, 7,* 36–37, 66.

Heath, A., & Storm, C. (1983b). Beginning supervision: What to do and what to avoid. Presentation at the American Association for Marriage and Family Therapy, Washington, DC, October.

Heath, A., & Storm, C. (1985). Models of supervision: Using therapy theory as a guide. *The Clinical Supervisor, 3,* 87–96.

Lewis, W., & Rohrbaugh, M. (1989). Live supervision by family therapists: A Virginia study. *Journal of Marital and Family Therapy, 15,* 323–326.

Liddle, H. (1991). Training and supervision in family therapy: A comprehensive and critical analysis. In A. Gurman & D. Kniskern (Eds.), *Handbook of family therapy,* 2nd ed. (pp. 638–697). New York: Brunner/Mazel.

Liddle, H., Breunlin, D., & Schwartz, R. (1988). *Handbook of family therapy training and supervision.* New York: Guilford Press.

Liddle, H., Davidson, G., & Barrett, M. (1988). Outcomes of live supervision: Trainee perspectives. In H. Liddle, D. Bruenlin, & R. Schwartz (Eds.), *Handbook of family therapy training and supervision* (pp. 386–398). New York: Guilford Press.

Liddle, H., & Halpin, R. (1978). Family therapy training and supervision literature: A comparative review. *Journal of Marriage and Family Counseling, 4,* 77–98.

Liddle, H., & Saba, G. (1982). Teaching family therapy at the introductory level: A conceptual model emphasizing a pattern which connects training and therapy. *Journal of Marital and Family Therapy, 8,* 63–72.

Lowenstein, S., Reder, P., & Clark, A. (1982). The consumer's response: Trainees' discussion of the experience of live supervision. In R. Whiffen & J. Byng-Hall (Eds.), *Family therapy supervision: Recent developments in practice* (pp. 115–129). New York: Grune & Stratton.

McKenzie, P., Atkinson, B., Quinn, W., & Heath, A. (1986). Training and supervision in family therapy: A national study. *American Journal of Family Therapy, 14,* 293–303.

Mead, D. (1990). *Effective supervision: A task-oriented model for the mental health professions.* New York: Brunner/Mazel.

Nichols, W., Nichols, D., & Hardy, K. (1990). Supervision in family therapy: A decade restudy. *Journal of Marital and Family Therapy, 16,* 275–285.

Nielson, E., & Kaslow, F. (1980). Consultation in family therapy. *American Journal of Family Therapy, 8,* 35–42.

Piercy, F., & Sprenkle, D. (1986). Supervision and training. In F. Piercy & D. Sprenkle (Eds.), *Family Therapy Sourcebook* (pp. 288–321). New York: Guilford Press.

Piercy, F., Sprenkle, D., & Constantine, J. (1986). Family members' perceptions of live observation/

supervision: An exploratory study. *Contemporary Family Therapy, 8,* 171–187.

Slovenko, R. (1980). Legal issues in psychotherapy supervision. In A. Hess (Ed.), *Psychotherapy supervision: Theory, research, and practice* (pp. 453–473). New York: John Wiley & Sons.

Storm, C. (1993). Defensive supervision: Balancing ethical responsibility with vulnerability. In G. Brock (Ed.), *Ethics casebook* (pp. 173–190). Washington, DC: AAMFT.

Street, E., & Foot, H. (1989). The reliability of video viewing of family therapy interviews. *Journal of Family Therapy, 11,* 297–306.

Todd, T., & Haley, J. (1973). Therapy outcome study of 200 cases at the Philadelphia Child Guidance Clinic. Unpublished.

Tomm, K., & Leahey, M. (1980). Training in family assessment: A comparison of three teaching methods. *Journal of Marital and Family Therapy, 6,* 453–458.

Wetchler, J. (1989). Supervisors' and supervisees' perceptions of the effectiveness of family therapy supervisor interpersonal skills. *American Journal of Family Therapy, 17,* 244–256.

Wetchler, J., Piercy, F., & Sprenkle, D. (1989). Supervisors' and supervisees' perceptions of the effectiveness of family therapy supervisory techniques. *American Journal of Family Therapy, 17,* 35–47.

Wetchler, J., & Vaughn, K. (1991). Perceptions of primary supervisor interpersonal skills: A critical incident analysis. *Contemporary Family Therapy, 13,* 61–69.

Wright, L. (1986). An analysis of live supervision "phone-ins" in family therapy. *Journal of Marriage and Family Therapy, 12,* 187–190.

Wynne, L., McDaniel, S., & Weber, T. (1986). *Systems consultation: A new perspective for family therapy.* New York: Guilford Press.

2

Self-Supervision as a Universal Supervisory Goal

Thomas C. Todd

I suspect that most supervisors would claim that self-sufficiency of their supervisees is one of their ultimate goals as supervisors, yet surprisingly little has been written on this topic. Even more important, there is little guidance regarding the principles and techniques for achieving this worthy goal. I believe that it is possible to develop guidelines for what I prefer to call "self-supervision" which can be embraced by the vast majority of supervisors and which can be adapted to the specifics of a wide variety of supervisory models. Examples utilizing disparate theories are offered in this chapter to provide a sense of how this adaptation can be achieved.

Mead (1990) mentions the term *self-supervision* but does not elaborate on it. Keller and Protinsky (1985) also use the phrase but proceed to a general discussion of self-management within a structural–strategic model. Kagan (1975) probably has come closest to describing self-supervision without ever using the term. In Kagan's model of Interpersonal Process Recall (IPR), therapists use videotapes of their sessions to stimulate recall of options and reactions during the session that could prove useful in improving their therapy. Although a facilitator is used in the process, the facilitator's role is much less directive than that of a traditional supervisor, and it is easy to imagine being able to conduct the inquiry process with oneself.

DEFINING SELF-SUPERVISION

To arrive at a definition of self-supervision, it may be useful to begin with a definition of *supervision*. Mead (1990) defines supervision as follows:

> An experienced therapist safeguarding the welfare of clients by monitoring a less experienced therapist's performance with clients in a clinical setting with the intent to change the therapist's behavior to resemble that of an experienced family therapist (p. 4)

Three components of this definition immediately highlight the self-reflective nature of self-supervision and the inherent difficulties created: a process of self-monitoring; comparison with some ideal model of therapy; the intent to change one's therapeutic behavior.

The following section examines the implications of these three characteristics in developing a model of self-supervision. For present purposes, self-supervision can be defined as a

Note: A briefer version of these ideas appeared in the *Supervision Bulletin* (Todd, 1992).

process whereby therapists self-monitor their therapeutic behavior, comparing this behavior with some model of more effective behavior, with the intent of changing their behavior to resemble this model more closely.

TOWARD A GENERAL MODEL OF SELF-SUPERVISION

An adequate model of self-supervision should give some sense of how the self-reflexive process can be accomplished. What will be proposed is a general model of self-supervision that can be applied to a wide variety of theories of therapy and supervision. Examples from disparate theories are offered as an indication of how a specific model could be developed. To do this, each of the three critical ingredients of the definition are examined.

Self-Monitoring

To achieve self-supervision, therapists must engage in some process of self-monitoring. Presumably, this includes some notion of the kinds of data that are the focus of the process and some technology to achieve collection of the desired kinds of data. Specifics can vary widely, in line with particular theories. For example, therapists could assess their interventions by reviewing videotapes of therapy sessions. Videotapes could also be used as a stimulus to recall process during the session, as in Kagan's IPR model. Steiden (1993) describes the use of discourse analysis with such data for self-supervision. Another source of data could be the internal reactions of therapists, to look for countertransference; similarly, using the Internal Family Systems model of Schwartz (1995), Cook (see Chapter 9) describes how to help supervisees monitor internal reactions and how to know when particular "parts" have been triggered. Braverman (see Chapter 25) de-

scribes the use of a "double genogram" from a Bowenian perspective, which could be used as a tool for self-supervision.

Ideal Model

In self-supervision, therapists also compare their actual therapeutic behavior with some idealized norm. Therapists could compare videotapes of their work with images from training videotapes of master therapists. The "model" also could come from the therapist's own behavior rather than that of a master therapist. For example, in the solution-focused model, the comparison could be to successful excerpts from one of the therapist's own tapes, or even to a fantasied scenario of success (Selekman & Todd, 1995).

Change Toward the Ideal

Different supervisory models embody widely different assumptions about how change toward a more desirable standard of therapeutic behavior takes place. A complete model of self-supervision should make these assumptions explicit. Is it helpful to be embarrassed by watching one's behavior on tape? Would it be more helpful to focus on proximity in therapeutic relationships? How can countertransference patterns be detected in a way that produces change in the therapist?

SELF-SUPERVISION IN CONTEXT

Depending on the context, self-supervision is often a training goal for most mental health professions. Outside of agency contexts, most supervision occurs as a step toward some form of licensure or credentialling. This may be achieving Clinical Membership in AAMFT or becoming licensed in a profession such as social work or psychology. Typically for these purposes, completing supervision successfully requires the supervisor to pass judgement on the readiness of the supervisee for independent private practice, where supervision will no longer be mandated and will usually be at the discretion of the former supervisee. As gatekeepers of marriage and family therapy (MFT) and other mental health professions, supervisors are expected to prepare supervisees for self-supervision or for practicing without supervision. Clearly most supervisors would prefer to think of their task as the former.

In most graduate program contexts and even in postdegree MFT programs, supervisors are not expected to prepare students for complete self-sufficiency. Even if a postdegree student is a fully licensed professional in some other mental health discipline, the MFT field does not expect the student to be fully prepared for independent MFT practice at the completion of the program, as is obvious in the additional hours of supervised MFT casework and supervision required for Clinical Membership and state credentialling. Even when complete self-supervision is not the goal, it may be very useful for supervisors and supervisees to assess the degree of self-sufficiency or the intensity of supervision needed as an indication of successful progress in the program. A beginning student in an MFT program might need to have every session observed live, but it would be a problem if a student nearing graduation still needed such close monitoring.

SELF-SUPERVISION GUIDELINES

The principles offered in the following sections are generic guidelines to help supervisors with the task of preparing supervisees for self-sufficiency. Although they fit some supervisory models better than others, especially those that are problem- and goal-oriented, hopefully any supervisor should find them stimulating.

Make Self-Supervision an Overall Goal

When supervisors are clear with supervisees that they will work together to make supervisees self-sufficient, the process changes dramatically. Supervisees become more equal partners in the supervisory process and are better able to give precise feedback to supervisors. They understand the goals of supervision and realize that supervisors will share responsibility with supervisees so that they can transition to self-sufficiency.

Offering this goal encourages supervisors and supervisees to develop a clear description of the self-sufficient supervisee. How will they know that supervision is no longer needed? What are the characteristics of a competent therapist? What are the standards set for licensure or recognition as an independent practitioner?

Comprehensive lists of skills are available, such as the observational, conceptual, relationship and executive skills of Tomm and Wright (1979), as well as more model-specific lists (Figley & Nelson, 1989, 1990). Depending on supervisors' models, there will be some differences in the knowledge, skills, and attitudes that are considered critical and the concepts used to describe them. The proposed list needs to be negotiated with supervisees, but more important and more difficult, both parties need to agree on how each attribute will be operationalized. For example, a supervisor and a supervisee may agree that it is important to recognize countertransference or to set limits in sessions, but how will they know that the supervisee is skillful enough to be considered self-sufficient? What types of families or presenting problems, or . what kinds of in-session behavior, should the supervisee be able to handle independently? Supervisor and supervisee should agree on benchmarks of progress in these areas, as well as how both will recognize that routine supervision is no longer needed. Few would argue for total self-sufficiency as a goal; for most of us, the definition of self-sufficiency would include having the ability to judge when to seek consultation or supervision as appropriate.

It is also helpful to discuss with supervisees the methodology for achieving self-sufficiency, as well as supervisors' beliefs about how this process will work. I often share the guidelines in this chapter with my supervisees and have found that this has a significant effect on the supervisory process. It leads naturally into a discussion of how this goal will be achieved and how responsibility will be shared. Once supervisors have developed specific ideas for implementing the guidelines in ways that fit their models and beliefs about change, this process can be even more helpful because supervisors will include details about skill measurement, preparation for supervision, contents and focus of supervision, evaluation, and so on, in their initial contracts with supervisees.

A series of examples from the structural model illustrates some of the stages that could be identified and evaluated toward the goal of eventual self-sufficiency. Beginning students might be able to get two family members to interact directly when supervisors phone in and give instructions during live supervision. Later supervisees might be able to conduct this intervention after general discussions in supervision. Self-sufficiency in this area would seem to be achieved once supervisees could perform this intervention with some flexibility so that it did not appear artificial, and when they could critique their own tapes without supervisory input, recognizing that this intervention was appropriate. (Supervisors might go even farther and expect supervisees to be able to identify when the structural model should be abandoned, or at least be able to find other ways to achieve the same purpose as stimulating direct interaction.)

Inventory Supervisees' Assets and Skills

Most supervisors claim that they evaluate the skills of supervisees, although probably not as systematically and explicitly as would be optimal for supervisees' learning. This process needs to be transparent so that supervisees can eventually conduct their own "search" of assets and skills to find the resources to succeed in therapy. For example, a former homemaker who was training to be a therapist initially needed her supervisor's input to see her organizational skills as an asset in therapy. By making the process of identifying skills explicit, she could be encouraged to find other skills, such as flexibility and the ability to juggle conflicting priorities, on her own. Supervisees need to value all their resources, whether they have been developed through formal training, clinical experience, or general life experience. Supervisees need to have a plan for gradually filling in any gaps that remain after formal training and supervision are over.

Understand Supervisees' Learning Styles

Help supervisees understand how they learn best. What do they retain from one supervisory session to the next? What supervisory input leads to behavioral change in the therapy being supervised? Are supervisees willing to experiment with supervisory recommendations without extensive prior discussion, or do they need to discuss concepts first? (See Duhl, 1983.)

In a consultation session conducted by this chapter's author, a therapist was initially surprised to be asked how she learned best, asserting that she had never been asked that question. On reflection, she noted that she learned by having a variety of specific suggestions. At the end of a supervision session she rarely knew which alternative she would choose, often reworking the suggestions to find a new possibility. In contrast, another supervisee typically appeared to be in general agreement with his supervisor. The tape of the next session often showed little impact of the supervision. After further discussion, the supervisee admitted that he learned best under supervision when he was pinned down about specific actions to be taken in the next session.

Supervisees often do not know their own learning styles well enough to provide clear guidance to their supervisors. More typically, supervisors and supervisees need to collaborate together on a plan to learn more about supervisees' learning styles. To do this optimally, supervisors need to offer considerable variety in the supervisory input; this may require supervisors to depart from customary behavior in order to provide a greater range.

Achieve a Coherent, Congruent Therapy Approach

The ability to self-supervise presupposes an adequate theoretical framework within which to function. Using such a framework makes it easier for supervisees to critique their sessions and to look for behaviors that would be considered "errors" within that framework. In the author's formative years at the Philadelphia Child Guidance Clinic, Haley asked students and staff "What is your theory of change?" so often that it was put on his birthday cake. To sharpen their ability to critique their own tapes, he also asked therapists to describe what would be inconsistent or a "mistake" within their frameworks.

This principle implies that an important task of supervisors is to help supervisees articulate their theories of therapy and to test these theories for coherence and completeness (see Piercy & Sprenkle, 1986). Beginning supervisees may not be able to do this initially, but this should definitely be seen as a developmental goal as supervision progresses. More advanced supervisees should be able to do

more than simply apply a prepackaged theory well. With supervisory help, they should be testing theoretical ideas for "fit" with themselves as therapists and with their therapeutic contexts. This includes factors such as beliefs about therapy and life in general, gender and culture, therapeutic style, and characteristic ways of handling conflict.

Encourage Well-Formed Goals and Questions

The less supervisees do to prepare for supervision, the more they depend on their supervisors to structure supervision, ask the right questions, and give sage advice. Conversely, a well-formed question often contains its own answer (Todd & Greenberg, 1987). Initially, supervisees do not always recognize good questions. In addition to helping supervisees shape better questions, supervisors should give feedback about the adequacy of their original questions. Similarly, supervisors can help supervisees develop more useful goals for supervision.

The author uses a summary form for supervision that supervisees are expected to complete before the session (see _Resource Guide_). This form specifically asks for goals for the supervision session. (Supervisors from other orientations presumably differ in the kinds of information they seek and the format requested for the information. A transgenerational supervisor, for example, might ask for formulations in terms of patterns across the generations and request a genogram.) Early in supervision, supervisees ask very general questions such as "Tell me if I'm on the right track" or even "Help!" Supervision should _never_ proceed with such a poorly defined goal. The summary form helps walk supervisees through the process of defining clear goals for supervision. They are asked to identify aspects of their session that seemed to go well, indicators of trouble, desired outcomes, and so on. More advanced supervisees might ask more specifically about suggestions to involve a silent teenager, or handle scapegoating. In my experience, spending a few minutes asking about the genesis of the question and the supervisee's own thoughts often makes watching the tape almost unnecessary. When supervisees can process their own questions in a similar fashion or even brainstorm with a peer, they are well on their way to self-sufficiency.

Have Supervisees Self-Select Material for Supervision

Having made goals and questions explicit, supervisees can be expected to look for clinical material that bears on these issues. Again, once supervisees are able to do this, it is a small step to self-supervision. Supervisees may be asked to select portions of a tape for other purposes. They could be asked to bring in examples of successful application of specific techniques, for instance, or to show how they deal with high levels of conflict. This can help in the assessment process outlined here. Showing successful portions of a taped session may be used to underline assets and resources that supervisees have previously minimized (Selekman & Todd, 1995).

Stay Focused

As supervisees discuss cases or review sessions, supervisors should continue to ask themselves and supervisees how the material presented relates to the goals of supervision. The need for such feedback should diminish as supervisees learn to self-monitor. The same yardstick should apply to other members of a supervision group and to supervisors. Supervisees should be encouraged to ask supervisors how their suggestions or anecdotes apply to the goals of supervision. (One of the author's favorite math professors encouraged students to ask for clarification whenever the professor said, "Obviously . . ." Often, the most valuable

learning occurred when the professor was forced to explain what he had thought was obvious.)

Seek Client Feedback for Fine-Tuning

Help supervisees learn from client feedback. Ask them to reflect on the kinds of feedback that would indicate whether an intervention was on target; then, evaluate actual feedback together. How should supervisees use this feedback to improve services to these clients? Often therapists do not seek specific feedback, or act as though they already know the answer. Clients may need encouragement to be truthful and reassurance that their feedback will help their therapy be more useful to them. One useful practice is for supervisees to serve as interviewers for each other's cases, with the therapist watching or reviewing tapes of such feedback interviews. After a few of these experiences, most therapists can begin to obtain and listen to feedback from their own cases.

Case follow-up is also helpful on a more general level. Storm (1995) routinely sought six-month followup from clients using questions specific to the particular case. Such a practice encourages therapists and supervisors to be curious and open-minded about cases, particularly with respect to their theoretical assumptions about change. Neat "conclusions" about cases are often challenged by subsequent data! Encouraging such an attitude among supervisees helps to reassure supervisors that supervisees will continue to learn from their clients long after supervision is completed.

Encourage Learning Through Small Increments

When supervisees are unrealistic about the learning process, they often blame themselves for not making the rapid strides they expect.

Kagan (1975) stresses the importance of helping supervisees examine changes that are within their grasp during the supervisory session rather than having supervisors engage in "Monday morning quarterbacking." Even self-review can be too critical. Often, supervisees change through small steps and should not condemn themselves for changing too slowly.

Identification of small and specific learning goals can help significantly in goal achievement (see discussion of solution-focused supervision in Chapter 13). General goals sometimes do not suggest what means will be needed to achieve them, although a specific series of incremental goals frequently makes it obvious what needs to be done at each step.

Be Transparent

Supervisors should avoid the temptation of "gee whiz" supervisory interventions. If self-supervision is the ultimate goal, interventions that seem to come out of nowhere will not help achieve this goal and may make self-supervision seem an impossible goal. This principle extends well beyond dramatic interventions to all supervisory behavior such as the rationale for particular lines of questioning. Supervisors should encourage supervisees to ask about any aspect of supervision that is not completely clear so that ultimately they can do something similar themselves. Before intervening, I often ask, "So what do you think I am going to recommend?" or "What do you think I'm going to ask?" As supervisees get better at anticipating the answers, they are well on their way to making the supervisor obsolete!

Generate Alternatives, Not Answers

If a supervisor agrees that no therapeutic question has a single answer (Todd & Greenberg,

1987), then it does not make sense to provide only one answer. Mead (1990) indicates that the research literature consistently shows that advanced supervisees do not want answers. It may be more useful to engage in a mutual process of brainstorming to generate alternatives. Afterward supervisees can be helped to examine the processes they use to choose the alternatives that fit best.

Promote Generalization

Ideally, the goal of supervision is "learning how to learn" (Bateson, 1972). This can create conflicting demands for supervisors to balance the immediate needs of client families with the learning needs of supervisees (Goldenthal, 1994). Even if it is necessary to provide specific help for a supervisee to intervene in an immediate situation, it is still important to move beyond this to more general principles that can be extended to other situations.

Combining supervisory modalities can help achieve both sets of objectives. Live supervision can be used to provide immediate help and support, while delayed review of videotapes, or simply discussing the case after the session, may help ensure generalization.

One of my professors in graduate school (Ben Avi, 1967) was asked how to identify a good therapy session. Ben Avi responded that he was suspicious whenever he believed that he understood the session itself or had a complete formulation of the case. According to him, a good session was one that led to a new understanding of another case or something in his own life. This highlights a problem that is even more seductive in supervision, where it can be tempting to judge supervision by whether supervisees have accepted our supervisory pearls of wisdom rather than whether they have extended supervisory suggestions into their own ideas or generalized to other situations.

Contextualize Recommendations

Although generalization is important, it is equally important for supervisors to articulate those differences that make a difference. What changes in context would result in changes in recommendations? It is particularly crucial for supervisors to address important differences between themselves and their supervisees (e.g., gender, age, ethnicity, status) that could have a bearing on the appropriateness of particular interventions.

Supervisors can model an attitude of genuine curiosity and "not knowing." Beyond the obvious statement that a characteristic such as age matters, it may not be obvious to supervisors how that difference matters. Supervisees' ideas on the subject are at least as valid as those of supervisors. Often supervisees possess some characteristics that may make them a better fit as therapists for certain cases than their supervisors would have been. This is a golden opportunity for supervisors to learn about these differences from supervisees, just as supervisees can begin to learn from clinical families. (See Chapter 7 for other ways to accelerate this learning process.)

Contextually sensitive supervision is difficult in itself, as Chapters 4 through 7 in this book attest. When self-supervision is the goal, contextual sensitivity is particularly difficult. Supervision can provide the crucial second perspective that helps to appreciate context. For therapists to depend on a single set of lenses, they need to become more aware of context as well as inevitable areas of distortion. When distortion is present, therapists need to be prepared to seek consultation or refer cases to therapists who do not share their particular blind spots.

Structure Feedback on the Supervisory Process

It is useful to structure frequent feedback and exploration of the supervisory process. For example, the final five minutes of each supervisory session can be reserved for a discussion of what was useful for the supervisee and why. This not only provides useful feedback for supervisors but also helps supervisees to understand how they learn.

Similarly, both parties can reflect on the process at the beginning of the next supervisory session and after review of case material from the case previously discussed. The process of further reflection leading up to the therapy session and the process of revising ideas from supervision in reaction to clinical feedback are crucial processes on the road to self-supervision.

Develop Other Resources Beyond Supervision

Self-supervision does not have to be a solitary process. It can include the use of peers or less formal resources such as spouses or friends, assuming that confidentiality is not breached. One major advantage of group supervision or shared supervision is that supervisees can learn to make better use of such resources. Once again, the attitude of supervisors can be crucial in accelerating this process. Are other group members treated as valued contributors and collaborators or just as an audience for the brilliance of their supervisors? The group process is aided significantly if other group members are provided with guidelines, such as those in this chapter, and encouraged to apply them to help their peers become more self-sufficient.

REFERENCES

Bateson, G. (1972). *Steps to an ecology of mind.* New York: Ballantine Books.

Ben Avi, A. (1967). Personal communication.

Duhl, B. (1983). *From the inside out and other metaphors: Creative and integrative approaches to training in systems thinking.* New York: Brunner/Mazel.

Figley, C., & Nelson, T. (1989). Basic family therapy skills, I: Conceptualization and initial findings. *Journal of Marital and Family Therapy, 15*, 349–365.

Figley, C., & Nelson, T. (1990). Basic family therapy skills, II: Structural family therapy. *Journal of Marital and Family Therapy, 16*, 225–264.

Goldenthal, P. (1994). A matter of balance: Challenging and supporting supervisees. *Supervision Bulletin, 7*, 1–2.

Kagan, N. (1975). *Interpersonal process recall: A method of influencing human interaction.* Lansing, MI: Michigan State University.

Keller, J., & Protinsky, H. (1985). A self-management model for supervision. *Journal of Marital and Family Therapy, 10*, 281–288.

Mead, D. (1990). *Effective supervision: A task-oriented model for the mental health professions.* New York: Brunner/Mazel.

Piercy, F., & Sprenkle, D. (1986). Supervision and training. In F. Piercy, D. Sprenkle & Associates (Eds.), *Family therapy sourcebook* (pp. 288–321). New York: Guilford Press.

Schwartz, R. (1995). *Internal family systems therapy.* New York: Guilford Press.

Selekman, M., & Todd, T. (1995). Co-creating a context for change in the supervisory system: The solution-focused supervision model. *Journal of Systemic Therapies, 14*, 21–33.

Steiden, D. (1993). Self-supervision using discourse analysis. *Supervision Bulletin, 6*, 2.

Storm, C. (February, 1995). Personal communication.

Todd, T., (1992). Self-supervision: A goal for all supervisors? *Supervision Bulletin, 5*, 3.

Todd, T. & Greenberg, A. (1987). No question has a single answer!: Integrating discrepant models in family therapy training. *Contemporary Family Therapy, 9*, 1–2.

Tomm, K., & Wright, L. (1979). Training in family therapy: Perceptual, conceptual and executive skills. *Family Process, 18*, 227–250.

3

Ethical Issues
Where Do You Draw the Line?

Cheryl L. Storm and Ingeborg E. Haug

Regina Moss describes a marital therapy case to her supervisor, Melanie Davis. She remarks that a colleague in her agency, who was seeing an extended family member of the couple, reviewed the couple's file without her consent. Melanie begins to feel uneasy. Are the couple's and the extended family member's rights to confidentiality violated? She asks about the assurances given to clients with regard to confidentiality. Regina hesitantly replies that she did initially guarantee confidentiality to the couple when they asked if their extended family members would have access to information about their therapy. She also explains that it is common practice in the agency for therapists to review each other's files. Melanie wonders about how comfortable the two therapists seem to be with the exchange of information. Because she would react strongly to a colleague reading a case file without her knowledge, she reflects on the differences in their reactions. Melanie further questions her own response because supervisors at the agency also seem to view sharing of files as no problem. She is alarmed about the implications for the clients of being given assurances regarding confidentiality that have been disregarded.

Melanie considers the possible impact of encouraging Regina to question agency policy especially because this is occurring during the first few months of Regina's first professional job. In addition, Melanie thinks about questions she can ask to assist her supervisee to acknowledge the complexity involved in the situation, to consider possible unintended consequences of what has occurred, and to determine alternative responses. She hopes such supervisory inquiries will contribute to an expansion of Regina's ethical thinking. But most important, she asks herself what steps she should take to ensure that she is acting as an ethically responsible supervisor. What is her supervisory responsibility if there has been a violation of confidentiality? Melanie's position is particularly difficult because she does not have easy access to another supervisor to discuss her dilemma.

Situations like the one described here are not uncommon in supervision. As therapists discuss their cases, supervisors hear warning signals conveying possible ethical concerns. At times, supervisees will bring clearly defined ethical dilemmas to supervision, such as when a supervisee requests guidance regarding accepting a gift from a client. In still other situations, supervisors find themselves in supervisory ethical quandaries; for example, when a supervisee attends supervision erratically but the supervisor is still responsible for providing timely and adequate supervision (Storm, 1993). All of these types of situations require supervisors to consider the additional layer of supervisory ethical responsibility in order to assist their supervisees in becoming professionals who practice consistent with the ethical guidelines of the profession.

SUPERVISORS' ETHICAL RESPONSIBILITIES

Although there is a lack of comprehensive ethical standards for supervisors (Haug, 1994; Newman, 1981; Upchurch, 1985), the following sections describe generally accepted ethical responsibilities of supervisors to clients, to supervisees, and to the profession and public at large. Based on a review of the literature and the interpretation of the Code of Ethics for Marriage and Family Therapists (AAMFT, 1991a), here we describe idealized supervisory ethical responsibilities and behaviors.

To Clients

Because supervision is held out to the community as a way for consumers to receive services from partially trained professionals who require an opportunity to practice so that they can become fully qualified (Slovenko, 1980), supervisors protect clients' welfare, rights, and best interests. They are accountable for ensuring that clients receive informed, reasonable care (Cormier & Bernard, 1982; Engleberg & Heath, 1990; Mead, 1990). Supervisors ensure that their supervisees accurately inform clients about their credentials and their participation in supervision, including names and qualifications of their supervisors. Open disclosure and informed consent minimize the potential for clients to experience fraud, deceit, misrepresentation, invasion of privacy, and breach of confidentiality (Kapp, 1984).

To Supervisees

Supervisors help prevent supervisees from being "in over their heads" (Cormier & Bernard,

1982, p. 488) in several ways. First, they make themselves available and provide timely and adequate supervision so that supervisees are receiving the degree of support and guidance they need, including access to their supervisors in emergency situations (Cormier & Bernard, 1982; Mead, 1990; Tanenbaum & Berman, 1990). Second, supervisors assess therapists' readiness for supervision by screening potential supervisees for their knowledge and competency (AAMFT, 1991b; Tanenbaum & Berman, 1990). Third, they help their supervisees present their abilities (i.e., credentials, training, experience, and skill) honestly and accurately to clients, other professionals, and the community at large. Finally, as their supervisory relationship progresses, they provide timely feedback and evaluations. Supervisors build in procedures for resolving differences and take proactive steps to resolve difficulties when conflicts occur at any point in supervision.

Consistent with informed-consent doctrines (Bray, Shepherd, & Hays, 1985), supervisors inform supervisees about their preferred ideas about supervision and therapy, and the nature of the supervision context. Based on this information, supervisees can select supervisors who fit with their preferred ideas, practices, and values (White, 1989/90). Supervisors do not discriminate by refusing to provide supervision to therapists on the basis of biases or prejudices. Supervisors respect supervisees' uniqueness, dignity, and right to hold different values, attitudes, and beliefs. Supervisors are sensitive to the influence of contextual variables (e.g., race, cultural, gender, religion, and so on) on their relationships with supervisees as well as on their supervisees' clinical relationships.

Although supervisors typically are discouraged by many from engaging in multiple relationships with supervisees (AAMFT, 1991a; Cormier & Bernard, 1982), multiple relationships are ubiquitous and probably most supervisors are involved in them at some point (Ryder & Hepworth, 1990). Supervisors involved in multiple relationships manage them in a manner that maximizes the benefits and minimizes possible exploitation to clients and supervisees. (See Chapter 18 for a full discussion of multiple relationships in supervision.)

The prohibited multiple relationship most supervisors agree should be avoided is becoming sexually involved with supervisees (AAMFT, 1991a; Bernard & Goodyear, 1992). Although the current ethical code prohibits supervisees from conducting therapy with supervisees (AAMFT, 1991a), there is currently a debate on this issue in the field (see Chapter 18 and Storm, 1991b). The other multiple relationship that is prohibited by the professional policies (AAMFT, 1991b) is supervising a family member.

Supervisors focus on their supervisees' clinical work and professional development. They recognize that information that is obtained in supervision, whether about a supervisee's professional or personal life, is confidential except in certain circumstances such as when (1) supervision occurs within a training context, (2) supervisees report potential harm to self or others by clients or themselves, or (3) the law specifies limits to confidentiality. In all other cases, a release of information signed by the supervisee is required.

To the Profession and Public at Large

As highly visible representatives, supervisors protect the reputation of and public confidence in the profession. They ensure that the next generation of marriage and family therapists is adequately prepared and professionally competent to provide quality care to consumers, and that they are socialized professionals who can represent the profession well to the public at large (Storm, 1991). Most supervisors believe they serve as gatekeepers for the profession by evaluating supervisees' competence (AAMFT, 1991b; Bernard & Goodyear, 1992; Mead, 1990). As gatekeepers, supervisors

are direct in their evaluations of supervisees even when it results in uncomfortable supervisory relationships. Supervisors recognize the extent and limit of their own competence and seek consultations and further training as warranted (Tanenbaum & Berman, 1990). Supervisors who regularly solicit feedback from their supervisees and colleagues are in a better position to fulfill this responsibility. In performing these functions, they are mindful and protective of the public's trust in the profession.

ETHICAL DECISION MAKING

Several excellent publications describe the process of ethical decision making in therapy (Kitchener, 1984; Ratliff, 1988; Rest, 1983, 1984; Woody, 1990; Zygmond & Boorhem, 1989). However, for the most part, supervisors have been left on their own to translate and distinguish differences between clinical and supervisory ethics (Storm, 1993). For example, although collaborating with clients on business ventures is decreed unethical, co-authoring publications with supervisees may be appropriate mentoring by supervisors.

Ethical decision making begins with an awareness that all supervisory actions, even seemingly insignificant ones, have ethical consequences because they have the potential of affecting the well-being of supervisees, their clients, and the profession and public at large (Haug, 1994). Ethical behavior emanates from standards that are externally and internally developed. Theories of ethics, professional codes of ethics, theoretical premises of the field, the sociolegal context of supervision, and supervisees' personal/professional identity provide external guidance in critically evaluating the ethical dimensions of supervision. (For an in-depth discussion of each of these areas, see Woody, 1990.)

Ethical decision making, however, also is based on internalized beliefs and values about what constitutes ethical behavior. Are there any fundamental values therapists and supervisors might endorse and use as guidelines for careful ethical reasoning and thoughtful choices? Zygmond and Boorhem (1989), based on a review of the literature, identify five ethical principles that are applicable for helping professions: autonomy, beneficence, nonmaleficence, justice, and fidelity. Applied to supervision, they are defined as follows:

- Whenever possible, supervisors should affirm and guard supervisees' and their clients' rights to make autonomous decisions as long as they do not infringe on the rights of others.
- Supervisory actions should benefit supervisees and their clients.
- Above all, supervisors should do no harm.
- Supervisees and their clients should be treated fairly and equally, without discrimination.
- Finally, it is paramount that supervisors be truthful, loyal, and reliable.

When ethical dilemmas occur, supervisors (and therapists) must use careful and principled reasoning that produces the most benefit and least harm (Zygmond & Boorhem, 1989; Woody, 1990). Ethical dilemmas, such as the one at the beginning of this chapter, evolve when there are competing ethical principles (Kitchener, 1984; Rest, 1983; Woody, 1990; Zygmond & Boorhem, 1989). It is important for supervisors to consider the intended and unintended consequences of their actions for all involved: clients, the profession, the community at large, and supervisees (Haug, 1994).

Ethical Dilemmas

This section contains and discusses vignettes of ethical dilemmas that have been adapted from the authors' actual supervisory experiences. They represent variations of common situations most supervisors will deal with at some time during their career. We purposely pose questions in the hope of stimulating readers' participation and personal consideration of the complexities and options involved. Each situation is discussed in light of the supervisor's ethical responsibilities to clients' welfare, the interests of the profession/public at large, and supervisees' professional development. Because ethical guidelines are by necessity general, they cannot foresee the specific situations practitioners face. Ethical reasoning, therefore, always takes place in a gray zone of competing considerations and requires of us thoughtfulness and the courage to choose one alternative over another. It is not uncommon for supervisors to reach differing conclusions. In the following discussions we have included several possible supervisory alternatives. The actions we chose attempt to balance the supervisor's responsibility to all. These actions, however, are neither the only response nor necessarily the only correct one.

VIGNETTE I: A QUESTION OF ABUSE

Susanne James supervises Sharon Tulley at the agency where Sharon is an intern. They listen to an audiotape of Sharon's session with an exhausted mother of a willful five-year-old girl. The mother describes with frustration and helplessness how her daughter refuses to listen to her, especially when she calls her in from playing in the yard. Suzanne nods approvingly when she hears Sharon tell the mother that she needs to assert her parental authority. Her approval quickly turns to alarm, however, when she hears the therapist and mother plan to lock the child out of the house for an extended period of time to "teach her a lesson" and help her become more compliant. The supervisor wonders whether this qualifies as child abuse and what her responsibilities are.

Client Welfare

Suzanne notes that the mother's initial reaction to her therapist's intervention might be relief at being offered a concrete strategy that empowers her and hopefully will bring about the desired change in her daughter's behavior. The child, however, is by design meant to experience fear and rejection in the hope of motivating her to be more cooperative. In the short run, the daughter would experience the unpleasant consequences of alienating her mother; the long-term effects are uncertain. Is it not also conceivable that the five-year-old might panic at being locked out of the house and endanger herself in an effort to get help? If as a result an accident did happen, who would be responsible? The mother for lack of oversight? The therapist for encouraging neglect? The supervisor for not intervening? If the child did react with fear and hysterics, might the mother feel guilty for what she might come to see as a potentially cruel and dangerous disciplinary act, thereby compounding her presenting problems and harming instead of helping her? The intervention could also lead to further escalation and defiance by the daughter and fortify the destructive pattern.

Interests of the Public/Profession at Large

Further, Suzanne wonders about the reactions of the mother's neighbors and family. Would they view the mother as being neglectful or abusive and the therapist as suggesting abusive behavior? The planned intervention could cause harm and would most likely not engender confidence in the services of family therapists; instead, it could tarnish the professional reputation of family therapists at large.

Supervisee's Professional Development

The supervisee explains that she is applying the accepted and respected therapeutic technique of paradoxical intervention to disrupt the system and support the mother. Sharon has faith in this mother and believes she would not let her child experience too much distress or become endangered. Suzanne validates her supervisee's motives but emphasizes that even well-intentioned actions can produce harmful unintended consequences, which must be considered in order to heed the ethical imperative: First do no harm.

Suzanne also has serious concerns about her supervisee's competence, because this is the third time she has used questionable judgment regarding child discipline. Is she knowledgeable about child development and parenting approaches? Did Suzanne conceptualize the issues systemically and base her intervention on a thorough understanding of the role of the symptom within the larger relationship system? Does Sharon understand paradoxical interventions, interventions generally based on the expectation of noncompliance? Sharon seems to be planning to use what she claims to be a paradoxical technique without awareness of the literature suggesting that it should not be used in situations where there is a potential for harm. Does Sharon understand what constitutes child abuse and her professional responsibilities in that regard? Does she have the knowledge base necessary for performing clinical work? Did Suzanne adequately screen Sharon's clinical readiness before agreeing to assume supervisory responsibilities? Has Suzanne participated in allowing Sharon to practice beyond the limits of her competence? What are Sharon's responsibilities to the clients, to her supervisee, to the degree program where Sharon is a student, as well as to the profession at large?

Possible Actions

On reflection, Suzanne and Sharon agree that the potential for harm overrides the potential benefits of this particular intervention. Sharon will contact the mother and request that she not implement the agreed on plan. Suzanne concludes that the planned actions would have constituted child abuse and that she would have been legally mandated to report her supervisee to the authorities. While acknowledging that other supervisors might interpret this latter conclusion as an isomorphic overreaction of the supervisor and would instead focus on Sharon's personal issues, Suzanne and Sharon agree to focus on her cultural beliefs about appropriate parenting that brought her to suggest such punitive actions. In regard to Sharon's readiness for clinical practice, Suzanne reviews her supervisee's background and, believing Sharon has the basic knowledge needed, resolves to suggest reading materials to her supervisee to supplement her knowledge concerning child development, parenting approaches, paradoxical interventions, and child abuse. She also decides to contact the training institution where Sharon is a student and alert her teachers about the gaps in her knowledge. She further implements a more thorough screening of potential supervisee's knowledge and readiness to practice so that in the future any concerns can be addressed before she assumes supervisory responsibilities.

VIGNETTE II: THE PHANTOM CO-THERAPIST

Ron Meyer contacted Barbara Hadley, a private practitioner and AAMFT Approved Supervisor, for supervision. In his second supervisory session, he presents an audiotape of a marital case. As Barbara listens to the audiotape, she is surprised to hear Ron working with a co-therapist. Ron confirms that he is working with his wife Maria who he claims is a natural, if uncredentialed, therapist.

Client Welfare

To protect clients' rights, Barbara inquires whether the clients are fully informed about the level of Maria's training, experience, and credentials. Are they aware of being seen not only by an untrained individual, but also of the likelihood that Maria may not be bound by a professional code of ethics which guides her practice and holds her accountable? Does Maria hold herself out as being supervised by Barbara? Are clients informed about supervision? After full disclosure, were clients presented with clear choices concerning their treatment? Have they given their informed consent without undue pressure? Are other safeguards needed to ensure that clients' rights are not violated?

Interests of the Public/Profession at Large

Barbara is also concerned whether the Meyers hold themselves out to the public as credentialed therapists and wonders whether they have violated any state laws regulating mental health practice. In an effort to protect the public from incompetent or unscrupulous therapists, some states require mental health professionals who are not licensed or certified to register. Some states accept bachelor's-level therapists in order to impose accountability where otherwise none would exist.

Supervisee's Professional Development

Ron explains that male–female co-therapy teams have been found to be particularly useful in marital therapy, because they provide a model for positive couple interaction. Many well-known therapists work with their spouses, some of whom do not have the education to be credentialed in their own right. He and his wife began working conjointly after they attended several marital enrichment programs. They both feel this arrangement benefits their clients.

Barbara is troubled that Ron had not fully disclosed his typical clinical practices when they formulated a supervisory contract at their first meeting. She is worried about his seeming propensity to be less than candid and truthful and wonders whether this might isomorphically be a factor in the therapy he provides. Ron's behavior appears to her naive at best, and possibly irresponsible and unprofessional as far as therapy and supervision are concerned. Barbara wonders if she was too vague in her supervisory contract with Ron and thus contributed to the confusion. She is glad, however, that she insisted on reviewing raw data of Ron's work, because otherwise Maria could have been involved in providing therapy without anyone's knowledge.

In addition, Barbara questions whether it is ethical to provide supervision to only half of the therapy team because she is only able to listen to and influence half of those responsible for treatment. This is particularly problematic because Barbara knows she is not only ethically but also legally responsible for the outcome of the therapy her supervisees provide. At this point, however, if she decides to refuse supervision, on the grounds that Maria does not have the requisite training and experience, might the couple continue to provide treatment without supervision and quality control? Might they then be more likely to harm clients than they would be if Barbara agrees to supervise on the condition that both co-therapists participate?

Possible Actions

Barbara decides that clients' welfare, the training needs of Ron and Maria, and the interests of the public and the profession are best served by her providing supervision to Ron and Maria conjointly in an ongoing manner. Barbara clarifies her supervision contract with Ron and establishes one with Maria. Supervision will emphasize a review of audio- or videotapes of the sessions the Meyers provide. She discusses Maria's alternatives in obtaining further professional training, and the implications of her relying on her husband's

professional judgment when she is so limited in her own knowledge.

Another supervisor might come to a different conclusion and refuse to provide supervision altogether and strongly recommend that Ron discontinue working with his wife until she has received additional professional training. Barbara also assists the therapists in developing an explicit informed-consent document which clients will sign at the onset of treatment. Some supervisors might look at Barbara's participation in this clinical arrangement as "aiding and abetting" unprofessional behavior with potentially harmful consequences to the public and the profession.

VIGNETTE III: TO SPEAK OR NOT TO SPEAK

The Center for Family Therapy has contracted with Amy Parnass to provide weekly supervision for their staff. During her individual supervision hour, Karen Goldman consults Amy on a case involving sexual abuse of a child. Karen confides that this subject is particularly difficult for her because her sister had been sexually abused by an uncle when she was eight. Amy explores with Karen how she and her family dealt with this traumatic experience. Amy is satisfied with Karen's assertion that this issue will not interfere with her clinical work. Later, Karen and Amy meet with other supervisees in group supervision. The group focuses on another sexual abuse case. Karen becomes increasingly agitated and protective in her responses. She takes the position that the ideas of the other therapists are too harsh and indicate a lack of understanding for the abused child. The other therapists comment that Karen's responses seem inconsistent with her usual ideas about therapy. The next day in a memo, the agency director informs Amy that Karen will be offered a position in the newly created sexual abuse program that will open next month.

Client Welfare

Karen's frankness in revealing her personal issues is viewed by Amy as a positive sign of her desire to prevent her personal issues from interfering with her clinical effectiveness. However, Amy wonders whether Karen's reactions are sufficiently serious to prevent her from working effectively with these clinical situations. Amy carefully reviews Karen's clinical work to determine the appropriateness of her case formulations, treatment plans, and interventions to be sure the quality of client care is not compromised.

Interests of the Public/Profession at Large

Amy wonders about her ethical responsibilities if Karen does accept her new assignment with the sexual abuse unit. Could, or even should, her concern for the welfare of future clients, as well as for the agency's reputation of excellence, override her concern for Karen's confidentiality? Supervision is confidential except in very specific and circumscribed situations, including "to prevent clear and immediate danger to a person or persons" (AAMFT, 1991a). Would it be ethical for her to breach her supervisee's confidentiality and inform the administration of her grave concerns regarding Karen's competence to deal with sexual abuse cases? Might it even be unethical for her not to do so?

Supervisee's Professional Development

In considering the best way to approach Karen, Amy reviews the policies established in Karen's supervision contract for addressing ethical and competency concerns arising in supervision. How clearly are the criteria and the parameters of confidentiality defined? Amy wants to be frank in the way she communicates her concerns to Karen about Karen's clinical work. Amy wonders whether she should only suggest or actually mandate personal therapy for Karen. In responding to Karen's strong re-

actions in group supervision, Amy is careful not to violate her supervisee's right to confidentiality. If she did in fact breach confidentiality and revealed personal information, which she had learned in Karen's individual supervision, in the group setting, what redress would Karen have? Could Karen file an ethics complaint against her supervisor?

Possible Actions

Amy is encouraged by Karen's openness in discussing her personal issues, which mirror those of her clients, in supervision. She recommends that Karen seek personal therapy and not accept further sexual abuse cases without her supervisor's consent. Amy also decides to tell Karen in a private conversation that, given the challenges she admittedly faces in working with child sexual abuse cases, she does not think it appropriate for Karen to accept the new position. Amy informs Karen that if Karen disregarded Amy's recommendation and did accept the new position, she would need to notify the administration of her concerns. Amy documents all of these discussions and actions in order to protect all parties involved, including herself. To clarify her judgments and decisions Amy might also seek peer consultation or supervision-of-supervision as well as legal advice.

Some supervisors might believe Amy should be assigned sexual abuse cases so that she has the opportunity to learn to treat them without personally reacting while she is receiving supervision on them. Still other supervisors could request a release of information to the administrator of the new position so that they could convey their concerns while highlighting Amy's abilities, thus leaving the hiring decision to the agency's discretion.

VIGNETTE IV: A CLASH OF GENDER VALUES

Mary Miller is showing her supervisor, Susan Rush, a videotape of her work with a traditionally oriented couple. One of Mary's therapy goals is to help the couple explore alternative ideas about gender. She is particularly pleased that the wife is considering going to college despite the husband's reluctance to support her on this. As Susan watches the videotape of her work, she becomes increasingly uncomfortable with Mary's comments to the couple. To Susan, they seem to be mini lectures on women's rights which convey the message that choosing to be a traditional homemaker is an inappropriate option for women.

Client Welfare

In reviewing the tape, Susan questions the process of how the therapist and clients arrived at the goals for therapy. Were the clients' goals and issues given primacy? Did Mary impose her own agenda or did clients and therapist decide on therapeutic goals in collaborative conversation? Is this therapy meeting the clients' expressed needs, which might or might not include changing their complementary relationship to a symmetrical one? Is treatment turning into a process of indoctrination where client autonomy is being compromised? Did Mary consider this couple's ethnic and cultural background and expectations? Susan also questions whether the needs of both partners in the client couple are addressed or whether Mary is partial to the wife, and perhaps unfairly dismissive of the husband's concerns? Are there signs that Mary's interventions might create conflict in the marital dyad which could stretch the clients' emotional resources to the breaking point, thereby harming rather than helping the couple?

Supervisee's Professional Development

Mary explains that she sees it as her ethical responsibility to attempt to balance the unbalanced marital relationship and points to literature in support of her therapeutic model.

Issues of power and powerlessness are at the core of problematic couple relationships, she believes, and it is her obligation to support the wife's effort to become more independent. Mindful of her supervisee's right to hold values different from her own as well as the clients' right to make their own decisions, Susan wonders how she might sensitize Mary to identify the line between imposing her values on clients and helping clients identify and transcend their limitations. How might Mary be helped to explore the power dynamics in the relationship between these clients without sounding doctrinaire? Can she set her personal convictions aside and treat this couple fairly and justly even if they should make choices she disagrees with?

Possible Actions

Susan's first step is to review with Mary the clients' therapeutic contract to ascertain that therapy is meeting the clients' goals and needs, and to encourage Mary to also take this step with her clients. Susan also decides to seek consultation from another supervisor to clarify her role as a supervisor, to explore her reactions to Mary, and to find out how her values are impacting the supervisory relationship. Would another supervisor conclude that Mary seemed to be using her position as a therapist to promote her own values or would Mary's responses be viewed as within an acceptable range of exposing the couple to other ideas regarding their gender roles? Susan believes Mary's values are impinging on clients' rights to decide for themselves; another view in terms of potential power differences could be to suggest that Mary bring in another like-minded colleague to help balance the discussion. (See Tomm's comments in Chapter 18.)

VIGNETTE V: THE INSURANCE DILEMMA

Tracey Reynolds, a supervisor and licensed marriage and family therapist, receives an offer to work at the local family therapy agency for four hours each week as a clinical consultant. Tracey enjoys mentoring beginning therapists and welcomes the opportunity to provide more hours of supervision. Her proposed duties are to supervise all unlicensed professionals and student therapists at the agency and to create a weekly case conference for all clinical staff. Her contract specifies that Tracey is to sign all insurance forms for the therapists she supervises, because their clients would otherwise not be eligible for third-party reimbursements.

_____

Client Welfare

Tracey realizes that for most agencies the incentive to hire a person with her credentials has much to do with financial matters, namely an agency's enhanced ability to obtain third-party reimbursement for clients. The Center's clients are mainly interested in their bottom line: to receive third-party payment or reimbursement for therapeutic services at the agency. In all likelihood, they will not lose sleep over the specifics and ethics of who signs their insurance forms. The supervisees, likewise, are probably more focused on improving their clinical skills than on insurance matters.

Interests of the Public/Profession at Large

The resolution of these dilemmas is of vital importance to several larger systems. The agency as well as the nearby training institution would be severely impacted if Tracey could not sign insurance forms for the students she supervises. The agency would undoubtedly suffer financially. It would probably lose part of its clientele and might not be able to continue to offer either services for a minimal fee, practicum sites to students of the nearby university, or employment to beginning therapists.

Tracey is aware that misrepresentation of facts on insurance forms is not only considered unethical, but is illegal and constitutes insur-

ance fraud, a felony by law. Tracey realizes that it would be fraudulent and unethical for her to sign insurance forms without truthfully identifying her role vis-à-vis the clients and the treating therapists. If she signs a form identifying herself as "supervising therapist," how might the insurance companies react? Would they refuse third-party reimbursements? Could she sign as the provider if she switched to live supervision? How would it be different if she decided to see each case personally at least once, possibly in co-therapy with her supervisee?

To a large extent, employers or individuals purchasing insurance contracts can stipulate the medical or mental health conditions they want covered, who they accept as providers, and under what circumstances they will provide reimbursement. In the past, Tracey realizes that some insurance companies accredited an agency as a whole rather than individual providers at that agency; however, policies have changed in the rapidly changing health-care delivery system.

Supervisees' Professional Development

The agency's clientele is primarily made up of couples and families, not individuals. Most insurance policies, Tracey realizes, do not cover relational diagnosis and treatment. Misrepresenting marital or family therapy as individual therapy, with the intent to deceive the insurance carrier to gain reimbursement, can result in ethical, civil, or criminal charges against the therapist as well as the supervisor. It is similarly unethical and fraudulent to intentionally apply an inaccurate diagnosis, including minimizing or overstating existing conditions. Furthermore, as a systemic supervisor, Tracey teaches her supervisees to understand and treat symptoms within their relational and interactional context, not in isolation as individual diagnosis implies. Tracey contemplates how she might reconcile her systemic worldview with the realities of the health-care delivery system and still model responsible ethical behavior to her supervisees. She wonders whether she could instruct her supervisee to accept the family's definitions and diagnose the "identified patient" in a given system and then add the *DSM-IV* "V Code" to the diagnosis, while also indicating the treatment modality as couples or family therapy, as the case may be. Would this be ethical and legal and acceptable to insurance companies?

Possible Actions

Tracey resolves to ask for guidance from the various insurance carriers in question. She also decides to contact the state department where she holds her license to inquire about specific regulations in her state that oversee policies at nonprofit agencies and/or state-licensed agencies that accept Title XIX clients. Tracey also might be well advised to seek legal consultation. Other supervisors might choose to co-sign insurance forms for their supervisees, clearly identifying each party as "treating therapist" and "supervisor," and diagnose the identified patient with both an individual diagnosis and a "V Code," thereby indicating the treatment modality accurately.

VIGNETTE VI: EAVESDROPPING?

John Sumner is the only AAMFT-Approved Supervisor in the rural area where he practices. He accepted Chuck Barras as his supervisee so that Chuck could meet AAMFT membership requirements. Chuck is presenting a case of a local couple torn apart by marital infidelity. As John listens to the tape, it becomes clear to him that the clients are a couple he and his wife have known socially for a long time.

Client Welfare

Realizing the situation he is in, John wonders if he should immediately ask Chuck to stop the tape and request that Chuck obtain supervision on this case from someone else. He considers how the couple would react if they knew he was listening to their therapy session? They may feel betrayed by both their therapist and their friend, and both relationships damaged. The information received so far will already alter his relationship with his friends whether or not they become aware of the situation. John believes that clients' rights to informed consent include being informed not only about the qualifications of their therapist, including his or her student status, but also about the identity and qualifications of the supervisor. Chuck had not disclosed this information to the couple, and the supervisor worries that their confidentiality and right to informed consent have been compromised. How can the present situation best be rectified? Even if John were to discontinue supervising this case, do the clients need to be informed? Are they entitled to this information which clearly will have some subtle or not so subtle repercussions in their private life whether or not they know about it? Which course of action will prevent the clients from greater harm: telling or concealing the facts from them?

Supervisee's Professional Development

Chuck is concerned that he receive supervision to improve his clinical skills in MFT as well as to meet the AAMFT membership criteria. In this rural area, it is impossible for him to find another AAMFT Approved Supervisor specializing in systemic therapies unless he were to travel several hours. Chuck is also very reluctant to inform his clients of the facts and worries about their reaction. John wonders how to best help Chuck through this uncomfortable situation.

Possible Actions

John encourages Chuck to contact AAMFT and describe his ethical dilemma in the hope that he be granted permission to receive credit for supervision from a non-AAMFT colleague in his small town. In the future, Chuck will inform his clients about the identity of his supervisor and continue supervision with John in those cases where he obtains the clients' explicit consent. For all other cases, Chuck will receive supervision from an alternate supervisor. John and Chuck decide that the clients' interests can be best served if they are informed of the situation in a joint meeting with both Chuck and John present, and allowed time to process their reactions.

The issue of whether the client couple needs to be informed retroactively about the breach of confidentiality might be decided differently by different supervisors according to their judgment of what produces the least harm to the couple and the legal context in which they and their supervisees work. Some state laws allow liberal sharing of information if providers can justify their actions as in the best interests of their clients; other state laws have tight restrictions on the sharing of information.

CONSIDERATIONS FOR ETHICALLY INFORMED SUPERVISION

Overall, supervisors are more than passive conveyors of ethical information. They assume a proactive stance to help their supervisees and themselves develop ethical awareness and to make decisions consistent with ethical values, both internal and external, guiding the profession. Supervisors maximize clinical and supervisory effectiveness and minimize vulnerability for clients, supervisees, and themselves.

A chapter by Storm (1993) applied the metaphor of defensive driving to ethically informed supervision. Defensive drivers are always looking down the road for unpredictable events, possible accidents, and ways to prevent harm to all on the road. Similarly, supervisors use their greater professional experience and knowledge to guide supervisees in anticipating possible difficulties in the future and in assessing various possibilities and alternatives. They consider supervisees' past performance, abilities, and background the context in which supervisees work, their prior experiences in supervision, as well as their personal professional experiences in order to anticipate possible issues and dilemmas supervisees may face. Supervisors recognize that clients' perspectives and interpretations may change over time and help supervisees include this consideration in their clinical work (Haug, 1993).

Ethically informed supervision, which upholds the principles of autonomy, beneficence, nonmaleficence, justice, and fidelity in the service of protecting clients' and supervisees' rights and welfare, is primarily intended to ensure high standards of client care. Supervisors help supervisees increase their therapeutic effectiveness while minimizing clients' risk in receiving care from professionals still in training. Supervisors help prevent their supervisees from inadvertently making unethical decisions or acquiring legal liability and sensitize supervisees to the ethical aspects of professional practice. Supervisors do not walk in the shoes of therapists, but they are responsible and accountable ethically and legally for providing supervision consistent with the professions' standard of care for supervision (Engleberg & Heath, 1990; Engleberg & Storm, 1990).

The actions by supervisors cited here increase the likelihood that supervisory responses will be beneficial to supervisees and clients while preventing, as much as possible, harm to all. First, it is prudent for supervisors to ensure that all parties (i.e., supervisees and clients) are informed and consenting consumers of supervision (Kapp, 1984). This includes supervisors' careful initial screening of potential supervisees to determine whether supervisees are ready for supervision, and whether a fit exists between supervisors' and supervisees' preferred ideas, values, and styles.

Second, it is equally important to clearly establish agreed-on goals for supervision and policies guiding the relationship. Agreements regarding remedial work and ways of working with supervisor and supervisee differences (e.g., cultural beliefs, personal style, preferred ideas, and so on) are more easily resolved at the beginning of supervision rather than after supervisees have invested time, financial resources, and energy into the supervision process. Supervisees are better informed about what supervision with this particular supervisor will entail when comprehensive screening has been done.

Third, specific, clearly delineated contracts assist supervisees in making informed decisions, and also contribute to supervisors treating supervisees fairly. Contracts developed collaboratively minimize misunderstandings and maximize agreements (Tanenbaum & Berman, 1990). Contracting also promotes gender-sensitive supervision by minimizing the hierarchy in supervision because they delineate each participant's responsibilities (Wheeler et al., 1989). Contracts, when negotiated between parties, can promote mutual collaboration. (Chapter 19 in this book further describes the benefits of supervision contracts for supervisors and supervisees and presents the various items that can be covered within a contract.)

Fourth, documentation of supervision with supervisees also promotes accountability of all involved. This documentation allows verification of hours and provides specific information regarding supervisees' progress for evaluations and recommendations. When differences or difficulties in supervision evolve, documentation assists supervisors, supervisees and others, who may be called to mediate or investigate, to reach resolution. Documentation helps supervisors to be truthful, loyal, and reliable when asked to recommend supervisees for employment based on their work together.

Fifth, access to raw data, whether through videotapes, audiotapes, or observation of therapy sessions, assists supervisors in obtaining critical information for supervision. Based on information from raw data, supervisors are able to provide adequate and timely supervision, assess supervisees' readiness for clinical work, and ensure that clients receive reasonably satisfactory treatment. Supervisors who are alert to potential crisis situations, dangerous clients, or supervisees' lack of expertise in a given situation protect supervisees and themselves from inadvertently making unethical decisions or assuming legal vulnerability.

Sixth, careful assessment and serious consideration of the complications and potential for confusion and harm in multiple relationships assists supervisors to determine precautionary steps to implement when multiple relationships are contemplated or unavoidable. Supervisors who take the potential negative aspects of multiple relationships seriously and implement preventive measures are also increasing the potentially enhancing aspects of these arrangements for themselves, their supervisees, and clients. Several authors (Storm, 1993; Tomm, 1992) recommend consultation with colleagues, supervision of supervision, and involving third parties of the supervisees' choosing as precautionary steps supervisors can take (see Chapter 18).

Finally, when ethical dilemmas occur, supervisors and supervisees consider together the intended and unintended consequences of actions from multiple perspectives, including that of supervisees, supervisors, consumers, the sociolegal context, and the professional community. Considering multiple perspectives helps supervisors and supervisees decide which course of action is most likely to benefit those involved while minimizing harm.

WHERE DO YOU DRAW THE LINE?

Applying these ideas to the vignette at the beginning of this chapter, Melanie, the supervisor, is balancing the ethical principles of ensuring client confidentiality (i.e., fidelity) with that of ensuring that no harm comes to the clients and supervisee (i.e., nonmaleficence). Complying with one creates conflict with the other. Melanie, aware of the influence of her actions on Regina and her clients, asks herself questions about a variety of intended and unintended consequences. If the couple discovers their therapy file has been reviewed by their relative's therapist and that Melanie and Regina were aware of it, could the couple view the situation as a serious breach of confidentiality requiring legal action? If the couple's trust in Regina is compromised, what is the potential impact on their therapy? How could Regina respond *now* to prevent greater harm and act in the best interests of all involved? If Melanie does not bring the issue to Regina's attention, could she be viewed as failing to act as an ethically responsible supervisor? If Melanie encourages Regina to question her agency's policy, will the agency supervisors view Regina as a troublemaker, possibly affecting Regina's future promotions and salary? Would discussing these issues contribute to Regina's learning or detract from focusing on Regina's treatment concerns? What is the likelihood of these various intended and unintended consequences? What supervisory action would you take?

REFERENCES

American Association for Marriage and Family Therapy (AAMFT). (1991a). *AAMFT Code of Ethics.* Washington, DC: Author.

AAMFT. (1991b). *AAMFT Approved Supervisor Designation: Standards and responsibilities.* Washington, DC: Author.

Bernard, J., & Goodyear, R. (1992). *Fundamentals of clinical supervision.* Needham Heights, MA: Allyn and Bacon.

Bray, J., Shepherd, J., & Hays, J. (1985). Legal and ethical issues in informed consent to psychotherapy. *The American Journal of Family Therapy, 13,* 50–60.

Brock, G., & Coufal, J. (1994). A national survey of the ethical practices and attitudes of marriage and family therapists. In G. Brock (Ed.), *Ethics casebook* (pp. 27–48). Washington, DC: AAMFT.

Cormier, L., & Bernard, J. (1982). Ethical and legal responsibilities of clinical supervisors. *Personnel and Guidance Journal, 60,* 486–490.

Engleberg, S., & Heath, A. (1990). Legal liability in supervision: An interview with AAMFT legal counsel. *Supervision Bulletin, 3,* 2–4.

Engleberg, S., & Storm, C. (1990). Supervising defensively: Advice from legal counsel. *Supervision Bulletin, 4,* 6.

Haug, I. (1993). Dual relationships: Sex, power, and exploitation. Presentation at the Annual Meeting of the AAMFT, Anaheim, CA, October.

Haug, I. (1994). Ethical considerations in family therapy concepts and practices. Paper delivered at the International Conference of the Institute for Systemic Experience, Prague, Czech Republic, September.

Kapp, M. (1984). Supervising professional trainees: Legal implications for mental health institutions and practitioners. *Hospital and Community Psychiatry, 35,* 143–147.

Kitchener, K. (1984). Intuition, critical evaluation and ethical principles: The foundation for ethical decisions in counseling psychology. *Counseling Psychologist, 12,* 43–55.

Newman, A. (1981). Ethical issues in the supervision of psychotherapy. *Professional Psychology, 12,* 690–695.

Mead, E. (1990). *Effective supervision: A task-oriented model for the mental health professions.* New York: Brunner/Mazel.

Ratliff, N. (1988). *A workbook for ethical decision making.* El Paso: Montgomery Methods.

Rest, J. (1983). Research on moral development: Implications for training counseling psychologists. *Counseling Psychologist, 12,* 19–29.

Ryder, R., & Hepworth, J. (1990). AAMFT ethical code: "Dual relationships." *Journal of Marital and Family Therapy, 16,* 127–132.

Slovenko, R. (1980). Legal issues in psychotherapy supervision. In A. Hess (Ed.), *Psychotherapy supervision: Theory, research, and practice* (pp. 453–473). New York: John Wiley & Sons.

Storm, C. (1991a). Supervisors as guardians of the profession. *Supervision Bulletin, 4,* 4.

Storm, C. (1991b). Drawing the line? An issue for all supervisors. *Supervision Bulletin, 4,* 1.

Storm, C. (1993). Defensive supervision: Balancing ethical responsibility with vulnerability. In G. Brock (Ed.), *Ethics casebook* (pp. 173–190). Washington, DC: AAMFT.

Tanenbaum, R., & Berman, M. (1990). Ethical and legal issues in psychotherapy supervision. *Psychotherapy in Private Practice, 8,* 65–77.

Tomm, K. (1992). The ethics of dual relationships. *Calgary Participator, 1,* 11–15.

Wheeler, D., Avis, J, Miller, L., & Chaney, S. (1989). Rethinking family therapy training and supervision. In M. McGoldrick, C. Anderson, & F. Walsh (Eds.), *Women in families* (pp.135–151). New York: W. W. Norton.

White, M. (1989/1990). Family therapy training and supervision in a world of experience and narrative. *Dulwich Centre Newsletter,* 27–38.

Woody, J. (1990). Resolving ethical concerns in clinical practice: Toward a pragmatic model. *Journal of Marital and Family Therapy, 16,* 133–150.

Upchurch, D. (1985). Ethical standards and the supervisory process. *Counselor Education and Supervision, 25,* 90–98.

Zygmond, M., & Boorhem, H. (1989). Ethical decision making in family therapy. *Family Process, 28,* 269–280.

4

Keeping Context in View
The Heart of Supervision

Jay Lappin and Kenneth V. Hardy

Lily:
out of the water . . .
out of itself
NICHOLAS A VIRGILIO

The (re)emergence of reality as a subjective experience (Anderson & Goolishian, 1988; Anderson, 1990; Castanades, 1968; Levenson, 1972; Maturana & Varella, 1980; Pearce, 1988; Reiss, 1981; von Glasersfeld, 1980, 1984; Watzlawick, 1977, 1984; White, 1989; Zukav, 1979) has left many supervisors in a quandary. Should one dive into the chancy waters of political correctness or stay on shore and risk becoming a supervisory dinosaur? In either situation, can the tarpits be far away? The personal comfort supervisors derived from knowing that they saw the world the same way as their supervisees has been replaced by a nervous focus on respecting differences to the point that muted unease can win out over confident supervisory declaratives. How can one expect stability from

the tiny world of couple and family therapy,[1] if the larger world is so unsteady?

As Drucker (1994) notes: "No other century in recorded history has experienced so many social transformations and so radical ones as the twentieth century" (p. 53). But just because society is transforming, does it mean that couple and family therapy supervision must follow suit? Supervision, for many, already feels like being the plate juggler at the circus—an unsteady combination of skill, nerve, and luck. Why would anyone want to add the "context plate" mid-act, during an earthquake? Well, for those in the audience, it's a better show—they get their money's worth. For the juggler, it pushes for new skills, battles complacency, and ensures greater job security. The juggler's apprentice, with basics under her or his belt, and the example of the master's ability to stretch herself or himself, is better equipped for life on the road.

- *"Perhaps we could take a minute to talk about your past supervisory experiences and make a list of your 'Bests' and 'Worsts' so that we will know what to do more of, what to do differently, and what to avoid."*

Note: This chapter is dedicated to Peter Urquhart who always knew the way. The senior author would also like to thank his wife Joyce and sons Jeffrey and Timothy for their love and support, and Matthew McMann for his help with "Reference Bingo." Grateful appreciation to all the families this author has known who have privileged him with their diversity. Special thanks to Braulio Montalvo and his early morning "infograms," and to Cheryl and Ken whose friendship and patience made this possible. Thank you, as always, to Bruce Buchanan. Virgilio poem used with permission.

[1] To acknowledge and respect everyone, the authors have chosen to use the designation "couple therapy" rather than "marital therapy" in order to include committed relationships between heterosexuals, gays, and lesbians.

FIGURE 4.1.   A Supervisor Asks for Feedback . . .

© Tribune Media Services, Inc. All Rights Reserved. Reprinted with permission.

- *"I really want this to be an open process between us. I am inviting you to let me know if there is any time that I say or do something that makes you feel uncomfortable or if you are even wondering why I say or ask you something. I will also check in with you from time to time to see if we are doing OK."*

A balanced practice requires supervisors and therapists to examine the myriad of contextual variables that give meaning to those being supervised and to their clients (Hardy, 1993). Contextual variables, such as race, class, gender, and religion, are just a few of the dimensions of the self that shape reality. Until recently, however, these issues were seldom acknowledged as meaning systems for clients, supervisors, or therapists. It was as if the mind were separate from body, family, community, or society. Fortunately, just as family therapy's paradigm shift challenged traditional psychiatry's segmentation of self from family, the feminist critique challenged family therapy's segmentation of individual and family from the organizing forces of gender and in so doing, opened the field to a wider vista of possibilities (Allen & Laird, 1991; Avis, 1985; Bograd, 1984; Brodsky & Hare-Mustin, 1980; Goldner, 1985a,b, 1987a,b; Good-

rich et al., 1988; Hare-Mustin, 1978; James & McIntyre, 1983; Libow, Raskin, & Caust, 1982; Luepnitz, 1988; Taggart, 1985, 1989; Walters et al., 1988). This attention to gender has fueled interest in the ways that other contextual issues have been ignored. Although the field has begun to devote attention to a broader array of contextual variables, the focus remains scattered, superficial, and marginalized. Nowhere is this more apparent than in the recognition of the influence of these variables on supervision. Given this dearth of navigational guides, it is no wonder that supervisors can feel adrift in the supervisory sea.

SUPERVISION AND CONTEXT: LINKED AT LAST

Although there has been increasing attention to contextual variables in couple and family therapy (Anderson, 1994; Ault-Riche, 1986; Caust, Libow, & Raskin, 1981; Falicov, 1988; Hardy, 1990; Karrer, 1990; Korin, 1994; Libow, 1985; McGill-Roberts, 1991; McGoldrick, Pearce, & Giordano, 1982; Peterson, 1991; Piercy et al., 1982; Preli & Bernard, 1993; Reid et al., 1987;

Saba, Karrer, & Hardy, 1990; Storm, 1991, 1992; Wheeler et al., 1989), the field is still experiencing developmental delay because contextually sensitive supervision has never been truly integrated into theory and practice. Supervisors have, for the most part, been left to extrapolate what contextually sensitive supervision is from what is known about contextually sensitive therapy.

- *"I wonder if part of what is going on between you and the family are your respective different ethnic responses to illness? For example, how does your ethnic group view being sick? Some ethnic groups have very clear ideas about being sick, caretaking, using supports, using food, traditional medicines, and so forth, that you may want to pursue with the family."*[2]

- To a majority supervisee: *"Tell me about some of the experiences you have had where you have felt 'different' or judged before people really knew who you were. What was that like? How did it feel? How often have you had those experiences? If you have not experienced it much, why do you think that is? How do you think it might affect you if you had those experiences every day?"*

The gaps between contextually sensitive theory and practice and between theories themselves have added to supervisors feeling "deskilled," uncertain, and at a loss. Here, loss incorporates not only uncertainty, but also feeling that one's struggles and knowledge are marginalized as irrelevant for the times. Given these powerful feelings, even conscientious supervisors of the majority culture, particularly those with majority culture supervisees, could experience the call for inclusion as another required, but perhaps unnecessary stop as they shepherd their charges toward clinical proficiency. Likewise, majority supervisees, who are

less likely to feel the pinch of context, may also feel that contextually sensitive practice does not resonate with their day-to-day experience; they may see it simply as a technical aspect of their work—a technique to be mastered—rather than a way of thinking.[3] As Bateson (1970) has suggested, given that "a difference is a very peculiar and obscure concept" (p. 1), it is easy to appreciate how it can become even more obscure in a context of sameness. In our culture, this is most true for majority men who are supervising other majority men (especially those of the same race and class). Like skiers in a blizzard, the travelers can become snowblind and lost before they know it. If one is truly sensitive to contextual issues and vigilant, however, a supervisory setting can be created in which *many* differences can emerge and be discussed constructively, including the relevance of context. When one gets right down to it, there is no such thing as a totally homogeneous group, particularly when it comes to theories about something as complex as human systems.

Being conversant in multiple theories is already valued by many supervisors. They know that supervision is enhanced and deepened when models are contrasted and brought to life. Supervisors who are willing to consider issues of difference, whether they be of race, gender, culture, class, sexual orientation, theory, or thinking, create a chain of positive isomorphic consequences. Each link—supervisor, supervisee, clients, and institution—benefits from an environment with greater "requisite variety" (Ashby, 1978, p. 110). The down side, however, is that having everyone's voice heard can get pretty noisy and, it is more work. Opening a system up to greater democracy means that it will have to struggle to get and

---

[2] See outline for cultural formulation and glossary of culture-bound syndromes in the *American Psychiatric Association diagnostic and statistical manual–IV* (pp. 843-849), 1994.

[3] There are signs that this trend is changing. Although publications by Kliman (1994), Coale (1994), and Korin (1994) are not specifically designated for supervisors, they address contextual issues in clear and conceptually sound ways; see also Weingarten (1995).

maintain participation, account for differences, and then continually refine its mechanisms for resolving those differences. To avoid the mess, business, for example, traditionally has relied on paternalistic models of management. The concept of workers as cogs in the industrial machine required that they do things quickly and without thinking—"the brains" were at the top. Now, with competition greater than ever, there is a real need for businesses to "work smarter and be adaptive, intelligent, and evolving" (Wheatley, 1995). Few of us can afford the paternalistic models of old—we need all the brains we have, all of the time. As a result, both business managers and couple and family therapy supervisors are beginning to share a more naturalistic, adaptive, systems-based management paradigm designed to account for a more uncertain and complex environment.

WHY IS CONTEXUALLY SENSITIVE SUPERVISION SO IMPORTANT?

> *No creature can learn that which the heart has no shape to hold.*
> CORMAC MCCARTHY

For Majority Culture Supervisors and Supervisees

Supervisors have been living the life of sailors. Much like a sailor, we plied our trade using our theories to guide us. In good weather and with our destination in view, getting there was its own evidence of success. In turbulent seas, or with objectives beyond the horizon, this form of navigation loses its utility. To locate a position in such circumstances, greater complexity is required—use of constellations, sextants, and radar becomes necessary to remain on course. Just as in other sectors (i.e., air travel with radar and auto safety with seatbelts and airbags), new technologies became available as

consumers and regulators demanded more of providers. In the twenty-first century, both context and consumer (supervisees) will require supervisors to adapt to an increasingly pluralistic environment where people of color will be the majority and whites the minority (Wilson & Gutierrez, 1985; Yutrzenka, 1995).

In the business world, where companies are thriving on chaos (Peters, 1988) and adapting to a "destabilized context" (Vaill, 1989), some managed-care companies are now requiring therapists to document proof of diversity competence in their applications to become providers. Although business may be starting to adopt what family therapists have known for years, therapists and supervisors still have the edge when it comes to challenging and changing one's inner system. It is here, where one's inner constellation guides our way, that contextually sensitive supervision offers explorers the greatest possibilities.

Traveling into uncharted waters is familiar to supervisors who have challenged the stereotypic thinking of supervisees where it *really* counts—at the personal level of experience and values (Christensen, 1989; Corvin & Wiggins, 1989; Lappin, 1983; Leitch, 1992; Parker, 1987; Parker & McDavis, 1979; Parker, Bingam, & Fukuyama, 1985; Pedersen, 1988; Preli & Bernard, 1993; Storm, 1991; Webb, 1983; Wheeler et al., 1989). Discussions of theory and technique can offer a haven of intellectualization and distance. Genuine discussions of race, culture, gender, and class, on the other hand, offer no such refuge. Rather, the intersection of *who* therapists are and *how* they live is open for examination. Meaningful discussions about values should be at the core of the supervisory process. It is the unfolding and growth of the person of the therapist that increases her or his range of responses to clinical situations.

Research tells us that it is the fit *between* therapist and client and the client's perception of that fit that determines successful outcome and is ultimately of greater significance than any specific theoretical orientation (Grune-baum, 1988). In cross-cultural work, therapists who establish better credibility with clients are likelier to have positive treatment outcomes (Sue & Zane, 1987). Fit and credibility find synchonicity in the relationship between supervisee and supervisor. Because it is the therapist's responsibility to accommodate to the client, the ability to reconfigure the self as "a self of many possibilities" (Lifton, 1993, p. 1) increases the probability of improving fit. Or, to the degree that one can change oneself, the likelihood of changing other systems is increased. Engaging supervisees in this process is at the heart's shape of supervision.

By searching for the possibilities of self, especially in a resource poor environment, supervisors convey an invaluable lesson about reciprocity and responsibility. The ability to use oneself creatively yields important dividends of empowerment, self-reliance, and collaboration. In the end, everyone—families, couples, supervisees, and supervisors—benefits from the search for strength (Minuchin & Fishman, 1981). It is this conviction of possibility that sustains hope and provides the foundation for more client-driven practice (Berg, 1994; Colapinto, 1988; deShazer, 1985; Haley, 1963, 1973; Lappin, 1983, 1988; Madanes, 1981; Minuchin & Fishman, 1981; Montalvo, 1983, 1986, 1990; O'Hanlon & Weiner-Davis, 1989).

There is also the issue of the numbers. At the public service level, there are simply not enough minority supervisors or therapists to meet the needs of the populations being served. Consequently, until such time as there are more minority supervisors and clinicians, the likelihood is high that majority supervisors and therapists will encounter minority clients. To the degree that supervisees experience their supervisors ". . . creat[ing] a context within the supervisory relationship that is safe and supportive enough to risk new behaviors" and in which they "honor diversity" (Anderson, 1994, p. 4), the probability is increased that their

work will be that much more successful. For supervisees, it means that the practice of working with and noticing diversity more finely hones their ability to notice and utilize difference(s) with all clinical populations. This is especially important if they wind up working only with their own—where familiarity can blind one to contextual differences. (For an exploration of white privilege, see McIntosh, 1988.)

For Minority Clients

Clients miss out when inclusion is not practiced because their richest resource—themselves—remains untapped. Because the nature of asking for, needing, or being required to seek help automatically puts the client one-down (Lappin & VanDeusen, 1994), it is understandable that clients may feel that the addition of cultural difference creates a chasm too wide to bridge. The result is that minority clients not only underutilize mental health services (Sue, Allen, & Conaway, 1975; Ponterotto & Casas, 1991; Sue et al., 1974; Sue & Zane, 1987; VanDeusen & Lappin, 1979) but also are likely to terminate treatment "at a rate of >50% after only one contact with the therapist" (Sue & Sue, 1990, p. 7). No doubt these statistics contribute to the self-fulfilling myth that minority clients do not do well in therapy. In this situation, the feeling of being disempowered leaches into the entire treatment system. Believing they are not successful with diverse populations, majority culture supervisors and therapists can seek the comfort of treating their own.

For Minority Supervisors and Therapists

The call for inclusion, for minority supervisors and therapists, can feel long overdue. However, it has been heard before. Whites have had "an invisible weightless knapsack of special provisions, assurances, tools, maps, guides, codebooks, passports, visas, clothes, compass, emergency gear, and blank checks" (McIntosh, 1988, p. 2) while minorities have had to fend for themselves. Being a minority means that one is *always* accommodating to the majority. To paraphrase Watzlawick et al. (1967), if there are a lot more of *them* than *you*, then you cannot *not* accommodate. Being steeped in the daily experience of accommodation and marginalization in the larger world, however, could mean that working in the smaller world of therapy with those who are one's own could have understandable appeal. The benefits of same-culture work are obvious and many. But, like majority culture practitioners who work only with their kind, minority therapists can miss enriching experiences by only working with their kind. Supervisors lose an opportunity to highlight inter- and intragroup differences that can be used to expand thinking and challenge stereotypes (Preli & Bernard, 1993).

- *"You were saying that the family seems to be resistant to your work with them. Let's see if we can't put our heads together and think of all the possible reasons that might be so. Perhaps there are other factors—class, race, ethnicity, gender, and so on—at work, not just your skills."*
- *"I'm wondering if you have ever had the experience of working for or being supervised by someone from a minority culture—how was that experience for you? How do you think our differences or sameness may factor into our work together?"*

In public agencies, the combination of the majority culture: (1) not (having to) know the minority culture (McIntosh, 1988), (2) being overly respectful of difference, and (3) lacking experience with minority clients, can result in minorities specializing in minority clients and becoming "house ethnics" (Lappin, 1983, p. 127). In the private practice realm, African American therapists find that it is not uncommon for majority culture colleagues to refer only African American clients. The minority culture practi-

tioner's sense of obligation/comfort of treating fellow minorities can also contribute to this non-variegated referral phenomenon. Although Hunt (1987) echoes the caution that a context of minority therapist/client sameness is not without its dangers, it also holds many possibilities.

Both/And: A Way Toward Co-Evolution

Because supervisors may feel caught between political correctness and extinction, it is necessary to avoid the trap of monolithic thinking. Toward that end, a diverse point of view must account for theoretical models that are not necessarily based in contextually sensitive practice. It serves no purpose to pit the old against their newer counterparts; this is noninclusionary and neither learns from the other. Rather, the question seems to center around how to *both* honor existing models *and* co-create new ones.

One way to use diverse thinking in this process would be to incorporate the traditions of other cultures in the change process. As supervisors contemplate contextually sensitive practice, the African American tradition of honoring "family historians" (Boyd-Franklin, 1989, p. 49) would be a useful metaphor to employ. The internal transition of letting go and "coming to terms with the new situation" (Bridges, 1991, p. 3) needs recognition and support as well. If, in effect, people are being expected to trade-in some of what they know for a newer, yet unproven model, it will be important to respect their wisdom and appreciate the difficulty of change. In a society that is so future-oriented and fast-paced that the idea of a gourmet meal is standing in front of a microwave oven and yelling "Hurry up!," it is easy to reduce our elder's or colleague's experience to a sound bite. What we offer here hopefully will guide, but not dictate, a more reflective journey into the world of contextually sensitive supervision.

RESOURCES AND ISOMORPHS: RACE AND CLASS INFLUENCE SUPERVISION

In the field of counseling, a large body of literature exists on cross-cultural counseling, including journals such as the *Journal of Multicultural Counseling and Development*, the *Journal of Afro-American Issues*, and the *Journal of Non-White Concerns*. In 1982, a seminal work for the field of family therapy was published, *Ethnicity and Family Therapy*, edited by McGoldrick, Pearce, and Giordano. Unfortunately, despite their shared interest in culture, there is little cross-fertilization between the fields of family therapy and counseling. Counseling is almost totally bereft of family therapy literature and family therapy, for its part, has scant counseling references.[4] The reasons for this ironic gap of professional cultures are, no doubt, complex and serve as a humble reminder to the dangers of self-interest. The fact is, family therapy's beginnings are populated with many such cross-cultural excursions—social work, psychiatry, hypnosis, anthropology, mathematics, and cybernetics all played critical roles in the field's early development. In that respect, family therapy theory has traditionally been like the artists described by Levi-Strauss (1966). These were "bricoleurs" who, in creating their art, scavenged a little bit of this and a little bit of that (bric-a-brac) to create a "bricolage." As contextually sensitive practice becomes more prevalent and the notion of diversity begins to include more and more thinking from other fields, couple and family therapy has the opportunity to, while maintaining its roots, create yet another paradigm shift and a whole new aesthetic.

---

[4]The references for cross-cultural counseling are extensive. Two source books with in-depth references are Sue and Sue (1990) and Ponterotto and Casas (1991).

Race, class, gender, age, sexual orientation, or being physically challenged, like all other contextual variables, shape what we see, how we see it, and the significance of what we attach to what we see. Whether they are more or less visible, contextual variables are to clinical practice like the dark side of the moon is to the tide, constants whose influences are unseen, yet inexorable. The vignettes in this chapter will illustrate the point. We recognize that there are many other factors at work in these cases besides race or class, but because race and class are contextual constants and gender and sexual orientation are dealt with elsewhere in this book, we chose to highlight the variables of race and class individually. Our hope is that this singular focus and momentary suspension of a more systemic perspective will provide greater clarity and depth.

Race: Removing the Silence

Although couple and family therapy training in the United States occurs in one of the most race-conscious countries in civilized society today, racial issues remain marginalized in couple and family therapy. The marginalization of race is understandable given the history of the broader social context. The gulf that has divided the races historically is a backdrop to our clinical practices. Racial beliefs and relationships strained by racial practices cannot be forgotten simply by entering into the intimate experience called therapy or supervision. Racially based notions, such as "minorities don't believe in therapy" and "race is not an issue among white clients and therapists," are indications of societal myths that, unacknowledged, can contaminate treatment and supervision. Like a system whose shared denial evolves over time, the power of these myths lies in their subtlety. In effect, these myths and others slip beneath the radar of critical thought. In the world of clichés, universally accepted truths—"stupid is as stupid does"—receive little opposition. Also, in an all-majority context, espousing "benign" racial myths is not likely to exceed the threshold of social propriety. Absent of blatant racism, mild slurs about "them" might simply be considered by the group as part of the normal group process of defining who is in and who is out of the group.

In the field of couple and family therapy, supervisors are given the power to perform the "who's in and who's out" function of determining who does and does not become a therapist. How a supervisor uses this power, models for the supervisee how someone who is in the business of helping others uses power in relation to those who have less power. In the day-to-day on-line ambiguity of the real world, where protocol often fails to match situation, supervisees also absorb their supervisor's ability to improvise her or his values, thinking, and how that thinking is operationalized. (Does the supervisor challenge inappropriate remarks, and if so how does she or he do it and still stay connected?) In therapy, where moments of ambiguity flow together like water on wax paper, it is crucial that therapists internalize their supervisor's capacity for managing the complex clinical and emotional skills of simultaneously joining while challenging.

Although race is one of the principle ways in which the self is defined, it is often ignored in virtually all areas of clinical practice. Clients, trainees, and supervisors alike whose lives are impacted profoundly by skin color and/or racial identity are often expected to deny this dimension of themselves in therapy and supervision. The case that follows illustrates context and culture and the difficult choices therapists and supervisors must make as they juggle the complexities of treatment.

A CASE OF "JUST US"

A white therapist was treating a white couple and was being supervised live by a white supervisor. During therapy, the husband said to the therapist, "Thank God it's just us here so I can talk openly about those damn despicable spics and niggers that I have to work with." The therapist, apparently stunned by the client's openness, remained quiet. The husband broke the silence by proceeding to describe the difficulties he experienced working with his co-workers whom he found to be too loud to suit him. A few minutes later, the supervisor phoned into the therapy room with the directive to the therapist to inquire how this issue was related to the couple's relationship. The therapist agreed and followed the directive. Even as the client attempted to redirect his attention to the couple's relationship, he continued to make racially derogatory references about his co-workers.

During the postsession debriefing, the therapist, supervisor, and the treatment team, which contained one African American member, remained mute regarding the racial aspects of this session. Interestingly, the topic of race was never mentioned.

This case poignantly illustrates how race is a critical issue in therapy and supervision even when all, or in this case, virtually all of the participants are of the same racial group. The client's "just us," comment reveals his contextual and racial assessment. He believes it is permissible for him to talk openly about his co-workers without reprisal. It is difficult to imagine that this same discussion would have occurred with a Latino or African American therapist. Because the client assumed that all participants were of the majority race, he read the environment from a perspective of familiarity—as a majority person. Because he is with majority people most of the time, the all-majority therapy room became a kind of virtual reality for him. In that regard, it is a situation in which he feels safe, and in most cases, would be correct in assuming that his remarks would go unchallenged. If anything, depending on the class (working class, upper, lower, poor) and circumstances (social, work, family gathering, and so on) and gender of the people he was with, it would be likely that he would have had the experience of the others responding to his racial comments with either awkward silence, or by being joined by the other majority members in similar stories. In this instance, he simply assumed that his experiences in most other all-majority contexts would be the same as this one. Unfortunately, the opportunity to elevate the level of clinical discourse for this couple was missed. By pursuing the racial dimensions of the client's self, treatment could have become a broader expanse, encompassing not just the world of the client and his wife, but the larger world in which they live and work (Coale, 1994; Leitch, 1992; Kliman, 1994).

The supervisor's apparent uncertainty about addressing the racial dynamics of the case added to the group's discomfort of witnessing inappropriate racial messages. Dealing with them more openly would have reduced the dissonance between experience and expectation—that *someone* (i.e., the supervisor) needed to act—and it would have established precedent for how to handle such situations in the future. Instead, addressing the racial remarks receded into the margins as the more technical considerations of retaining focus on the presenting problem became headline and text. It is as if the micro-focus on technique occluded the tension created by the husband's racism and the therapist's silence. What was the experience of the African American member and the mixed race supervision group? What was learned by him and by the others? The following questions would have been helpful for the therapist to pursue:

- To the husband: "*I notice you use, what I consider to be, some fairly angry and negative words to describe the men you work with. How did you decide to use these terms?*"

- "*Oh, you probably said that because you think I'm white. That's a mistake people often*

make because I look white" (Ignatiev, 1994, p. 85).[5]

- "*I understand that you have had some unfortunate experiences with the Puerto Rican and African American men you work with, but I have had some rewarding experiences and happen to know that some Puerto Ricans and African Americans are hurt by terms such as spics and niggers. That's why I don't use them.*"

- To the wife: "*Have you heard your husband use these terms before? What do you think this means? Do you share his views about Puerto Rican and African American people?*"

- "*What do you see as the possible connections between how he deals with and talks about these men and how he treats you or other areas of his life that are difficult for him?*"

In the United States, terms such as "nigger," "spic," and so on, are important markers of racially based realities and relationships. These terms, when used by whites with whites in reference to African Americans and Puerto Ricans, are powerful reminders of contemporary racial inequalities and discrimination. In fulfilling the role of leader, a supervisor's actions and inactions are under constant scrutiny. In instances where race is the issue, or when tense disparities exist in the supervisory setting, it is the supervisor's job to help the supervisee understand her or his experience. How are they to make sense of the world if those who they entrust to do so do not? In such situations, the option of responding with silence is not an option. In the long run, what supervisees ultimately remember, as supervisory elders know, is not their pearls of wisdom, but the imperfect process of discovery and those who helped along the way.

In this case, a crucial shift occurs for the African Americans and the rest of the group when the supervisory discussion opens to in-

_____
[5] See also *Race Traitor: A Journal of the New Abolitionism* (Box 603, Cambridge, MA 02140).

clude the racial dimension. Just like any other limiting construction of reality (a parent saying a child is "bad," a supervisee feeling "stupid"), the "narrow framework of racial reasoning" (West, 1993, p. 29) can become grist for the supervisory mill. What is more, by removing the silence, racism's power as a symptom begins to ebb. In this case, the supervisor could have incorporated the racial issues overtly into the supervision process by employing any of the following strategies:

- *"The husband made several references to niggers and spics. What do you think it means that he used those terms so openly? Do you think this behavior is in any way connected to their presenting problem?"*

- *"It has been my experience that in our society we don't usually use racial slurs as openly as he did. What do you think this says about him? His relationship with his wife? His relationship with the therapist? His relationship with his co-workers and with us?"*

- *"I wonder how he would have responded to knowing that one of our members is African American? How do you think this knowledge would have impacted the therapy? How has it impacted our relationship?"*

- *"What might the potential relationship be between the husband's views toward his co-workers, his gender, your gender (to therapist), his relationship with his wife, social class issues, and so on?"*

- *"As a white person standing back here with you (an African American), I am aware that I felt embarrassed because someone of my race used derogatory terms to describe your group. I wanted to protect myself and perhaps you by shutting him up!"*

Any of these responses would have edged the supervisory discussion to a more open conversation about race. Instead, the supervisor and supervisees passively disavowed their racial selves through silence. As a result, the

ways in which their race impacted the supervision and therapy was ignored and a potential opportunity for growth was missed. In many respects, this case was a gift for this supervisory team, ultimately providing them with an opportunity to discuss the racial dimensions of their relationship. Moreover, attending to the context, which in this case was predominantly race, would also empower all the supervisees to break the otherwise culturally prescribed silence regarding sensitive cross-racial issues. Addressing race would create opportunities for the team to explore the ways in which their work is hampered and enhanced by their racial differences. It is only after taking such a risk that this cross-racial supervisory team can begin to genuinely appreciate that their racial differences may be far greater than their skin color or previous interactions might otherwise have suggested.

Class: Unveiling the Complexity

Although often a sensitive, volatile issue that is denied, class is every bit as complex and pervasive as race is (Bernal & Alvarez, 1983; Breunlin, Schwartz, & MacKune-Karrer, 1992; Inclan & Ferran, 1990; Kliman, 1994).[6] In the United States, where the prevailing belief is that "anyone can make it," class becomes a phenomenon that shares the stage with race as one of the great unspokens whose ability to shape attitudes, beliefs, and behaviors is often denied, unaddressed, or oversimplified (Ackerman, 1967; Aponte, 1976; Bernal & Alvarez, 1983; Engels, 1884, 1948; Fulmer, 1988; Inclan & Ferran, 1990; Lewis, 1959; Poster, 1978; Ross, 1995; Sennett & Cobb, 1972, 1993; Zaretsky, 1973). The pervasiveness of class and classism, although denied, still surfaces. Now, for example, *anyone* can wear a beeper—the golden days

---

[6] As Kliman (1994) notes on class and religion and Ellis and Murphy (1994) note on sexual orientation, the literature has been both scant and, at times, conflictual.

of beepers, when you saw a beeper and thought, "Doctor"—are over. Our society's discomfort with, and denial of class, is inextricably tied to broader cultural ideals such as (1) everyone can advance to a different class, and (2) everyone is created equal. As Ross (1995) reminds us: "Class, many in our culture believe, is based on effort, not on power or access or race or ethnicity or gender" (p. 330). It is as if class and effort were interchangeable—because we are all equal and have equal opportunity, then, if we work hard enough, we can move on up to the next class. The notions of hard work, laziness, economics, and who is deserving collide at the intersection of class and race in a messy pile-up. Knowing this, most people take an alternate route.

- *"When you were growing up, what class did you identify with? What class are you now? Do you remember your experiences of being with someone from a class different from your own? How are you passing along messages about class? If you have children, is there anything you would like them to do or think differently from you regarding class?"*

- *"What do you think happens when people marry into different classes? Have you seen any families in which, after divorce, one of the parents changes class? What do you think happens to the parent whose class is lowered? How do you think living in two classes affects the children (Ross, 1995)? What might be some positive consequences for the person who changes class?"*

- *"What do you think happens in a low-income, noncollege-educated home if one of the members does particularly well? For example, if they got a scholarship to a good college or did well in sports" (Ross, 1995)?*

Reductionism, with its appeal of clarity and simplicity, is an understandable alternative to the anxiety and confusion of complexity. Unfortunately, seeing one's way clear through complexity's ambiguity requires a high threshold for pain. Like remodeling one's house or moving, one needs to be able to tolerate the uncertainty and the mess while making the transition. Precisely because class is so complicated and unacknowledged, it is often confused with race. Rubin (1994) makes the case:

> [T]he economic decline of the last two decades coupled with the rising demands of our minority populations have led whites to try to establish a public identity that would enable them to stand against the claims of race. By reclaiming their ethnic past, whites cannot only retell the ordeals of their immigrant ancestors, they can use those stories to document that transcendence is possible for those who are worthy (p. xiv).

Family therapy has also oversimplified and, in most cases, minimized class issues. Although family therapists have devoted some attention to class (Bernal & Alvarez, 1983; Fulmer, 1988; Kliman, 1994; Ross, 1995), the focus has been skewed toward low-income families (Aponte, 1976; Inclan & Ferran, 1990; Lindblad-Goldberg & Dukes, 1985; Minuchin et al., 1967; Simon, 1986, 1987). The clinical consequences of this limited lens are many.

First, the narrow definition of class implies that class and low-income are interchangeable concepts, minimizing the effects of racism (Boyd-Franklin, 1989). Second, other class designations, particularly in terms of class differences between therapists and family, or supervisor and supervisee, may be cast in the interior confines of psychological explanations—*in* the person or the family rather than on the broader plain *between* the individual and the larger social/political system. As a result, instead of following family therapy's tradition of putting problems into context, inattention to class winds up "blaming the victim" (Ryan, 1971)—an unintended consequence. Third, the hidden impact of class on the development of theory and technique is obscured. As the saying goes, "garbage in, garbage out." If theory does not at least attempt to account for some of the more relevant variables within which it is contained, it is fundamentally flawed. The consequent limited scope of its conclusions compromises thinking and practice.

Finally, the minimization of class and its attendantly narrow focus on the culturally bound ideals of independence, artificially sever self from community. As Hillman has explained, "self" is the "interiorization of community" (Orange, 1995, p. 85). "If 'self' includes 'community,' then caring for others *as they live inside us* means that healing ourselves is inseparable from healing whatever small situations we inhabit" (Orange, 1995, p. 85). In this regard, not only is the poor community prevented from greater introspection, accountability, and elevation from victim status (Inclan & Ferran, 1990) all of us—both hurt and helpers, of all classes—are short-changed by limited healing.

- *"What do you think would happen if you had to suddenly immigrate to another country, leaving everything you own behind and had to live in a different class in your new host country? How would it change your relationships to your family and others?"*

- *"What experiences have you had with families from different classes? What does your class say about 'their' class? What do you think their class says about yours? What are your ideas about the class of your clients?"*

- *"Did you know that in 1950 a family of four paid approximately 2% of its annual gross earnings to the federal government in income and payroll taxes? Today, that same family would pay 24% in federal taxes and an additional 8% in state and local taxes (Mattox, 1990). How do you think that has affected families? Who do you think has been most affected by these changes? How do you think race factors into this change?"*

- *"Have you ever noticed that when people first meet one another, they typically ask 'What do*

you do?' Do you think that might be one way people check each other out for class relationships? What are some other ways that people check out class?"

- *"When class comes up in a session, what do you do with it? Let's think together about how we might be able to tie class in with re-thinking the family's situation. Is there a way you can think of to mobilize some of the family's values around class to recast behavior in a different light?"*

The following case vignette highlights the potential impact of class issues in supervision and therapy.

A CASE OF "CLASS WARS"

The husband, Walter, and the wife, Nancy, were being seen by Joanne, their therapist. Joanne spent most of the session disrupting what she considered to be destructive interactional patterns between the partners. They frequently yelled at each other angrily, relying heavily on an array of personal invectives. Joanne's incessant attempts to get the couple to communicate with each other in a less attacking manner appeared fruitless. When the couple did manage to cease insulting each other, Nancy turned her chair away from the therapist and refused to talk.

The supervision team consisted of the therapist, Joanne, the two supervisees, Karen and Bob, and the supervisor, Donna. Joanne has six years of clinical experience. Her family is upper-middle class. Her father is an attorney and her mother is a physician. One of the supervisees, Karen, is a therapist with five years of clinical practice. She is the youngest of a working-class family of eight. Her father is a labor foreman and her mother is an insurance clerk. The second supervisee is Bob, a therapist with four years of experience. He is one of two children of a middle-class family in which both of his parents are college professors. The supervisor, Donna, has over fifteen years of supervisory experience and holds a doctorate in family therapy. She is a middle-class mother of three.

Joanne, using a videotape of the session, presented the case to her team and reported that she felt "stuck and frustrated with this case." After entertaining several laudatory comments from her colleagues regarding the progress Joanne seemed to have made with the family, she appeared unconvinced. Karen observed Joanne's lack of hopefulness about the session and the family and asked in a rather terse voice, "What's wrong, don't you think they are capable of changing?" Joanne, pausing, said, "No I don't . . . they seem so limited!" Donna, the supervisor, then asked, "What do you mean by limited?" Before Joanne could formulate a response, Karen asserted, "Yeah, what do you mean by limited?" Joanne, sensing Karen's affect, seemed bewildered. After reflecting for a few seconds, Joanne explained that she felt the couple was limited in their ability to comprehend abstract ideas. She felt they were extremely concrete, to the point that they were unable to grasp the dynamics she was working so hard to help them understand and change. At that point Donna interceded and asked the team to consider the interaction between Karen and Joanne. Two key issues emerged.

The first issue involved what Karen ultimately referred to as Joanne's classism. Karen felt that it was because the couple was poor and not college educated that Joanne was convinced that they were incapable of understanding what she was explaining. She felt it was these class-based assumptions that made Joanne unwilling to consider the possibility that maybe there was something about how she was communicating that was problematic. Karen further felt it was Joanne's elitism that informed her belief that conceptual sophistication was integral to change rather than exploring other avenues. The second issue involved Karen's affect.

Bob pointed out that he was intrigued that Karen had been sensitive to Joanne's reference to limited while he had been oblivious to it. He wondered if there was something about their respective classes and class-based experiences that was responsible for his lack of awareness of and her sensitivity to this issue.

As the team processed these questions, there were several revelations. Joanne eventually conceded that her expectations of the couple were class-linked. There were certain attributions she made about them based on their class designation. She acknowledged that if they were middle class she would have been much more likely to question herself about the ways in which she might be limited in her approach to them. She also admitted that she assumed the couple was unable to comprehend complex dynamics because they were not college educated, and it was her bias that such comprehension was a necessary part of change. Joanne concluded that perhaps it was her beliefs that were limited, not her clients' abilities. Maybe her narrow ideas about how change could occur were just as problematic as the potential range of the couple's conceptual skills.

Karen's affect initially denied that her reaction was informed by her class designation because she identified herself as middle class. However, as the conversation progressed it became clear that she struggled with class issues. Although she identified herself as middle class, by societal standards, she was from a solidly working-class family. This realization engendered a great deal of emotion from Karen who for the first time in her life talked about some of the stigmas she felt were associated with this designation. Although she now had a middle-class lifestyle, she noted that as a child growing up her family lived a very different type of life. She recalled the painful feelings of shame she endured as a child regarding her family's social standing and how it had driven her to work hard to "improve her lot in life."

CONCLUSION

La necesidad tiene cara de hereje
[The face of neccessity is heresy]
ARGENTINIAN PROVERB[7]

In an essay on "the commons," Snyder (1990) describes the tradition of *commons* use throughout Eurasia as "the undivided land belonging to the members of a local community as a whole" (p. 30). He goes on to say: "The commons is the contract a people make with their local natural system. The word has an instructive history: it is formed of *ko*, 'together,' with (Greek) *moin*, 'held in common.' But the Indo-European root *mei* means basically to 'move, to go, to change'" (p. 31).

Supervision, from our perspective, is "the commons" of the therapeutic community. It is the place where the commerce of ideas co-exist with the people who own them. In this coming together, supervisors and supervisees share in the craft of learning how to change others, and in doing so, are themselves changed. As with other ecologies, interdependence and fragility are not always readily apparent. What is apparent, however, is that the larger context is shifting. Our capacity for adaptation and improvisation will be tested as never before. Weighing in on either side of our evolutionary see-saw are two competing principles, both of which come from the world of living systems. First is the principle of least effort. It states that "a system will try to adapt to its environment or will try to change the environment to suit its needs, whichever is easier" (Umpleby, 1984, p. 32). The second is the principle of equifinality. "According to this principle, a system can reach the same final state from differing initial conditions and by a variety of paths" (Katz & Kahn, 1966, 1978, p. 100).

As a human endeavor, supervision has always contained these two principles. What we as supervisors do with them in the moments and months of our work has to do with the juxtaposition of self/supervisee/setting/theory/client(s), and the larger context. In our ability to self-organize, that is, "the innate capacity to create structures and processes that respond to the needs of the moment" (Wheatley & Kellner-Rogers, 1995, p. 2), we continuously evolve changes in supervisory practice. Although it may *feel* heretical to challenge some of our most cherished theories, we have to believe that without the challenge, or our ability to respond to it, we *would* face extinction. It is incumbent on us as supervisors, in our roles as mentors and leaders in the field, to impart the capacity for self-reflection, integrity, and the ability to transform. In that, we fulfill our purpose and obligation to self and community.

REFERENCES

Ackerman, N. (1967). The emergence of family diagnosis and treatment: A personal view. *Psychotherapy, 4,* 125–129.

Allen, J., & Laird, J. (1991). Men and story: Constructing new narratives in therapy. In M. Bograd (Ed.), *Feminist approaches for men in family therapy* (pp. 75–100). New York: Haworth.

Anderson, H., & Goolishian, H. (1988). Human systems as lingustic systems: Preliminary and evolving ideas about the implications for clinical theory. *Family Process, 27,* 371–394.

Anderson, J. (1994). Supervising in an urban multicultural agency: A supervisor does her homework. *Supervision Bulletin, 7,* 4–5.

Anderson, W. (1990). *Reality isn't what it used to be.* San Francisco: Harper & Row.

Aponte, H. (1976). Underorganization and the poor family. In P. Guerin (Ed.), *Family therapy: Theory and practice* (pp. 432–448). New York: Gardner Press.

Ashby, W. (1978). Self-regulation and requisite variety. In F. Emery (Ed.), *Systems thinking* (pp. 105–124). New York: Penguin.

---

[7] The senior author is indebted to Jorge Colapinto for this and many other bits of wisdom.

Ault-Riche, M. (Ed.). (1986). *Women and family therapy.* Rockville, MD: Aspen.

Avis, J. (1985) The politics of functional family therapy: A feminist critique. *Journal of Marital and Family Therapy, 11,* 127–138.

Bateson, G. (1970). *Form, substance, and difference.* Alfred Korzybski Memorial Lecture, South Beach Psychiatric Center. Paper prepared under Career Development Award (K2–21, 931) of the National Institute of Mental Health.

Berg, I. (1994). *Family based services: A solution-focused approach.* New York: W. W. Norton.

Bernal, G., & Alvarez, A. (1983). Culture and class in the study of families. In C. Falicov (Ed.), *Cultural perspectives in family therapy* (pp. 33–50). Rockville, MD: Aspen.

Bograd, M. (1984). Family systems approaches to wife battering: A feminist critique. *American Journal of Orthopsychiatry, 54,* 558–568.

Boyd-Franklin, N. (1989). *Black families in therapy: A multisystems approach.* New York: Guilford Press.

Breunlin, D., Schwartz, R., & MacKune-Karrer, B. (1992). *Metaframeworks: Transcending the model of family therapy.* San Francisco: Jossey-Bass.

Bridges, W. (1991). *Managing transitions: Making the most of change.* Reading, MA: Addison- Wesley.

Brodsky, A., & Hare-Mustin, R. (Eds.) (1980). *Women and psychotherapy.* New York: Guilford Press.

Castanades, C. (1968). *The teachings of Don Juan: A Yaqui way of knowledge.* Berkeley: Regents of the University of California Press.

Caust, B., Libow, J., & Raskin, P. (1981). Challenges and promises of training women as family systems therapists. *Family Process, 20,* 439–447.

Christensen, C. (1989). Cross-cultural awareness development: A conceptual model. *Counselor Education and Supervision, 28,* 270–287.

Coale, H. (1994). Using cultural and contextual frames to expand possibilities. *Journal of Systemic Therapies, 13,* 5–23.

Colapinto, J. (1988). Teaching the structural way. In H. Liddle, D. Breunlin, & R. Schwartz (Eds.), *Handbook of family therapy training and supervision* (pp. 17–37). New York: Guilford Press.

Corvin, S., & Wiggins, F. (1989). An antiracism training model for white professionals. *Journal of Multicultural Counseling and Development, 17,* 105–114.

deShazer, S. (1985). *Keys to solution in brief therapy.* New York: W. W. Norton.

Drucker, P. (1994). The age of social transformation. *Atlantic Monthly,* 53–80.

Ellis, P., & Murphy, B. (1994). The impact of misogyny and homophobia on therapy with women. In M. Pravder-Mirkin (Ed.). (1994). *Women in context: Toward a feminist reconstruction of psychotherapy* (pp. 48–73). New York: Guilford Press.

Engels, F. (1884, 1948). *The origin of the family, private property, and the state.* Moscow: Progress Publishers.

Falicov, C. (1988) Learning to think culturally. In H. Liddle, D. Breunlin, & R. Schwartz (Eds.), *Handbook of family therapy training and supervision* (pp. 335–357). New York: Guilford Press.

Fulmer, R. (1988). Lower-income and professional families: A comparison of structure and life cycle process. In B. Carter & M. McGoldrick (Eds.), *The changing family life cycle: A framework for family therapy,* 2nd ed. (pp. 545–578). New York: Gardner Press.

Goldner, V. (1985a). Feminism and family therapy. *Family Process, 24,* 31–47.

Goldner, V. (1985b). Warning: Family therapy may be dangerous to your health. *Family Therapy Networker, 9,* 19–23.

Goldner, V. (1987a). Instrumentalism, feminism, and the limits of family therapy. *Journal of Family Psychology, 1,* 109–116.

Goldner, V. (1987b). Generation and gender: Normative and covert hierarchies. *Family Process, 27,* 17–31.

Goodrich, T., Rampage, C., Ellman, B., & Halstead, K. (1988). *Feminist family therapy: A casebook.* New York: W. W. Norton.

Grunebaum, H. (1988). What if family therapy were a kind of psychotherapy? A reading of *The Handbook of Psychotherapy and Behavior Change. Journal of Marital and Family Therapy, 14,* 195–199.

Haley, J. (1963). *Strategies of psychotherapy.* New York: Grune & Stratton.

Haley, J. (1973). *Uncommon therapy: The psychiatric techniques of Milton H. Erickson.* New York: W. W. Norton.

Hardy, K. (1990). The theoretical myth of sameness: A critical issue in family therapy training and treatment. In G. Saba, B. Karrer, & K. Hardy (Eds.), *Minorities and family therapy* (pp. 17–33). New York: Haworth Press.

Hardy, K. (1993). Live supervision in the postmodern era of family therapy: Issues, reflections, and questions. *Contemporary Family Therapy, 15,* 9–20.

Hare-Mustin, R. (1978). A feminist approach to family therapy. *Family Process, 17,* 181–194.

Hunt, P.(1987). Black clients: Implications for supervision of trainees. *Psychotherapy, 24,* 114–119.

Ignatiev, N. (1994). How to be a race traitor: Six ways to fight being white. *Utne Reader, 66* (Nov/Dec), 85.

Inclan, J., & Ferran, E. (1990). Poverty, politics, and family therapy: A role for systems theory. In M. Pravder-Mirkin (Ed.), *The social and political contexts of family therapy* (pp. 193–213). Boston: Allyn and Bacon.

James, K., & McIntyre, D. (1983). The reproduction of families: The social role of family therapy? *Journal of Marital and Family Therapy, 9,* 119–129.

Karrer, B. (1990). The sound of two hands clapping: Cultural interactions of the minority family therapist. In G. Saba, B. Karrer, & K. Hardy, (Eds.), *Minorities and family therapy* (pp. 209–237). Binghamton, NY: Haworth Press.

Katz, D., & Kahn, R. (1966, 1978) Common characteristics of open systems. In F. Emery (Ed.), *Systems thinking* (pp. 86–104). New York: Penguin Books.

Kliman, J. (1994). The interweaving of gender, class, and race in family therapy. In M. Mirkin (Ed.), *Women in context: Toward a feminist reconstruction of psychotherapy* (pp. 25–47). New York: Guilford Press.

Korin, E. (1994). Social inequalities and therapeutic relationships: Applying Freire's ideas to clinical practice. In R. Almeida (Ed.), *Expansions of feminist family therapy through diversity* (pp. 75–98). New York: Haworth Press.

Lappin, J. (1983). On becoming a culturally conscious family therapist. In C. Falicov (Ed.), *Cultural perspectives in family therapy* (pp. 122–136). Rockville, MD: Aspen.

Lappin, J. (1988). Family therapy: A structural approach. In R. Dorfman (Ed.), *Paradigms of clinical social work* (pp. 220–252). New York: Brunner/Mazel.

Lappin, J., & VanDeusen, J. (1994). Family therapy and the public sector. *Journal of Family Therapy, 16,* 79–96.

Leitch, L. (1992). Explicitly recognizing contextual influence broadens our scope of inquiry. *Supervision Bulletin, 5,* 6–7.

Levenson, E. (1972). *The fallacy of understanding.* New York: Basic Books.

Levi-Strauss, C. (1966). *The savage mind.* Chicago: University of Chicago Press.

Lewis, O. (1959). *Five families: Mexican case studies in the culture of poverty.* New York: Basic Books.

Libow, J., Raskin, P., & Caust, B. (1982). Feminist and family systems therapy: Are they irreconcilable? *The American Journal of Family Therapy, 10,* 3–12.

Libow, J. (1985). Training family therapist as feminists. In M. Ault-Riche (Ed.), *Women and family therapy* (pp. 16–24). Rockville, MD: Aspen.

Lifton, R. (1993). *The protean self.* New York: Basic Books.

Lindblad-Goldberg, M., & Dukes, J. (1985). Social support in black, low-income, single-parent families: Normative and dysfunctional patterns. *American Journal of Orthopsychiatry, 55,* 42–58.

Luepnitz, D. (1988). *The family interpreted: Feminist theory in clinical practice.* New York: Basic Books.

Madanes, C. (1981). *Strategic family therapy.* San Francisco: Jossey-Bass.

Mattox, W. (1990). America's time famine. *Children Today,* Nov/Dec., 9–11; 31.

Maturana, H., & Varella, F. (1980). *Autopoesis and cognition: The realization of living.* Boston: D. Reidel.

McCarthy, C. (1992). *All the pretty horses.* New York: Knopf.

McGill-Roberts, J. (1991). Sugar and spice, toads and mice: Gender issues in family therapy training. *Journal of Marital and Family Therapy, 17,* 121–132.

McGoldrick, M., Pearce, J., & Giordano, J. (1982). *Ethnicity and family therapy.* New York: Guilford Press.

McIntosh, P. (1988). *White privilege and male privilege: A personal account of coming to see correspondences through work in women's studies.* Wellesley, MA: Wellesley College Center for Research on Women.

Minuchin, S., & Fishman, H. (1981). *Family therapy techniques.* Cambridge: Harvard University Press.

Minuchin, S., Montalvo, B., Guerney, B., Rosman, B., & Schumer, F. (1967). *Families of the slums.* New York: Basic Books.

Montalvo, B. (1986). Family strengths: Obstacles and facilitators. In M. Karpel (Ed.), *Family resources: The hidden partners in family therapy* (pp. 93–115). New York: Guilford Press.

Montalvo, B., & Gutierrez, M. (1983). A perspective for the use of the cultural dimension in family therapy. In C. Falicov (Ed.), *Cultural perspectives in family therapy* (pp. 15–32). Rockville, MD: Aspen.

Montalvo, B., & Gutierrez, M. (1990). Nine assumption for work with ethnic minorities. In G. Saba, B. Karrer, & K. Hardy, *Minorities and family therapy* (pp. 35–52). Binghamton, NY: Haworth Press.

O'Hanlon, W., & Weiner-Davis, M. (1989). *In search of solutions: A new direction in psychotherapy.* New York: W. W. Norton.

Orange, W. (1995). Millenium madness and psychotherapy. Book review of *We've had a hundred years of psychotherapy-and the world's getting worse* by J. Hillman & M. Ventura. *Tikkun, 10,* 83–85.

Parker, W. (1987). Flexibility: A primer for multicultural counseling. *Counselor Education and Supervision, 26,* 176–180.

Parker, W., Bingham, R., & Fukuyama, M. (1985). Improving cross-cultural effectiveness in counselor training. *Counselor Education and Supervision, 24,* 349–352.

Parker, W., & McDavis, R. (1979). An awareness experience: Toward counseling minorities. *Counselor Education and Supervision, 18,* 312–317.

Pearce, J. (1988). *The crack in the cosmic egg.* New York: Julian Press.

Pedersen, P. (1988). *A handbook for developing multicultural awareness.* Alexandria, VA: AACD Press.

Peters, T. (1988). *Thriving on chaos: Handbook for a management revolution.* New York: Knopf

Peterson, F. (1991). Issues of race and ethnicity in supervision: Emphasizing who you are, not what you know. *The Clinical Supervisor, 9,* 15–31.

Piercy, F., Hovestadt, A., Fennell, D., Franklin, G., & McKeon, D. (1982). A comprehensive training model for family therapists serving rural populations. *Family Therapy, 9,* 239–249.

Ponterotto, J., & Casas, J. (1991). *Handbook of racial/ethnic minority counseling research.* Springfield, IL: Charles C Thomas, Publisher.

Poster, M. (1978). *Critical theory of the family.* New York: The Seabury Press.

Pravder-Mirkin, M. (Ed.). (1994). *Women in context: Toward a feminist reconstruction of psychotherapy.* New York: Guilford Press.

Preli, R., & Bernard, J. (1993). Making multiculturalism relevant for majority culture graduate students. *Journal of Marital and Family Therapy, 19,* 5–16.

Reid, R., McDaniel, S., Donaldson, C., & Tollers, M. (1987). Taking it personally: Issues of competence for the female in family therapy training. *Journal of Marital and Family Therapy, 13,* 157–165.

Reiss, D. (1981). *The family's construction of reality.* Cambridge: Harvard University Press.

Ross, J. (1995). Social class tensions within families. *The American Journal of Family Therapy, 23,* 329–341.

Rubin, L. (1994). *Families on the faultline.* New York: HarperCollins.

Ryan, D. (1971). *Blaming the victim.* New York: Random House.

Saba, G., Karrer, B., & Hardy, K. (1990). *Minorities and family therapy.* New York: Haworth Press.

Sennett, R., & Cobb, J. (1972, 1993). *The hidden injuries of class.* New York: W. W. Norton.

Simon, R. (Ed.). (1986, January-February). Another country: The family therapy of the urban poor. *The Family Therapy Networker, 10,* 1.

Simon, R. (Ed.). (1987, November-December). When the bough breaks: Homelessness in America. *The Family Therapy Networker, 11,* 6.

Snyder, G. (1990). *The practice of the wild: Essays by Gary Snyder.* San Francisco: North Point Press.

Storm, C. (1991). Placing gender in the heart of MFT masters programs. *Journal of Marital and Family Therapy, 17,* 45–52.

Storm, C. (Ed.). (1992). Special issue on contextual variables. *Supervision Bulletin, 5,* 3.

Sue Wing, D., & Sue, D. (1990). *Counseling the culturally different: Theory and practice.* New York. John Wiley & Sons.

Sue, S., Allen, D., & Conaway, L. (1975). The responsiveness and equality of mental health care to Chicanos and Native Americans. *American Journal of Community Psychology, 45,* 111–118.

Sue, S., McKinney, H., Allen, D., & Hall, J. (1974). Delivery of community health services to black and white clients. *Journal of Consulting Psychology, 42,* 794–801.

Sue, S., & Zane, N. (1987). The role of culture and cultural techniques in psychotherapy: A critique and reformulation. *American Psychologist, 42,* 37–45.

Taggart, M. (1985). The feminist critique in epistemological perspective: Questions of context in family therapy. *Journal of Marital and Family Therapy, 11,* 113–126.

Taggart, M. (1989). Epistemological equality as the fulfillment of family therapy with delinquents. In M. McGoldrick, C. Anderson, & F. Walsh (Eds.), *Women in families: A framework for family therapy* (pp. 97–116). New York: W. W. Norton.

Umpleby, S. (1984). *Glossary on cybernetics and systems theory.* Washington, DC: Department of Management Science, George Washington University.

Vaill, P. (1989). *Managing as a performing art: New ideas for a world of change in a chaotic world.* San Francisco: Jossey-Bass.

VanDeusen, J., & Lappin, J. (1979). Indochinese refugee community needs assessment. (Unpublished paper. Research conducted under contract for the Pennsylvania Department of Welfare.)

Virgilio, N. (1988). *Selected Haiku.* Sherbrooke, Canada: Burnt Lake Press.

von Glasersfeld, E. (1980). The concepts of adaptation and viability in a radical constructivist theory of knowledge. In I. Sigel, R. Golinkoff, & D. Brodzinsky (Eds.), *New directions in Piagetian theory and their application to education* (pp. 87–95). Hillsdale, NJ: Erlbaum.

von Glasersfeld, E. (1984). An introduction to radical constructivism. In P. Watzlawick (Ed.), *The invented reality* (pp. 17–40). New York: Guilford Press.

Walters, M., Carter, B., Papp, P., & Silverstein, O. (1988). *The invisible web: Gender patterns in family relationships.* New York: Guilford Press.

Watzlawick, P. (1977). *How real is real?* New York: Vintage Books.

Watzlawick, P. (Ed.). (1984). *The invented reality.* New York: Guilford Press.

Watzlawick, P., Beavin, J., & Jackson, D. (1967). *Pragmatics of human communication: A study of interactional patterns, pathologies, and paradoxes.* New York: W. W. Norton.

Webb, M. (1983). Cross-cultural awareness: A framework for interaction. *The Personnel and Guidance Journal, 61,* 498–500.

Weingarten, K. (Ed). (1995). *Cultural resistance: Challenging beliefs about men, women, and therapy.* Binghamton, NY: Haworth Press.

West, C. (1993). *Race matters.* Boston: Beacon Press.

Wheatley, M. (1995). Self-organizing systems: Creating the capacity for continuous change. Philadelphia: Quality Satellite Network, Inc., Lecture, November 30.

Wheatley, M., & Kellner-Rogers, M. (1995). Breathing life into organizations. *Journal for Quality and Participation,* July/August, 1–4.

Wheeler, D., Myers-Avis, J., Miller, L., & Chaney, S. (1989). Rethinking family therapy training and supervision: A feminist model. In M. McGoldrick, C. Anderson, & F. Walsh (Eds.), *Women in families* (pp. 135–152). New York: W. W. Norton.

White, M. (1989). *Selected papers.* Adelaide, Australia: Dulwich Centre Publications.

Wilson, R., & Gutierrez, F. (1985). *Minorities and the media: Diversity and the end of mass communication.* Beverly Hills: Sage Publications. As cited in Ponterotto, J., & Casas, J. (1991). *Handbook of racial/ethnic minority counseling research.* Springfield, IL: Charles C Thomas, Publisher.

Yutrzenka, B. (1995). Making the case for training in ethnic and cultural diversity in increasing treatment efficacy. *Journal of Consulting and Clinical Psychology, 63,* 197–206.

Zaretsky, E. (1973). *Capitalism, the family, and personal life.* New York: Harper & Row.

Zukav, G. (1979). *The dancing Wu Li masters: An overview of the new physics.* New York: William Morrow.

5

Sexual Orientation
Implications for the Supervisory Process

Janie K. Long

In 1991, Markowitz asked the question: "Gays and lesbians are out of the closet, are therapists still in the dark?" (p. 27). Marriage and family therapy (MFT) supervisors may still be in the dark for at least three reasons. First, Brown (1991) reminds us that much of what we know about the lives of bisexuals, gays, and lesbians and much of what we have been able to do for them as helping professionals, has evolved under the shadow of heterosexism. Second, the mental health professions have viewed issues related to gays, bisexuals, and lesbians as of interest only to those who are themselves lesbian, bisexual, or gay or those who work with gay, lesbian, and bisexual clients. Finally, MFT supervisors have had to rely on literature from other mental health professions as their main source of information. Therefore, this chapter serves only as a starting point in examining the influence of sexual orientation in the MFT supervisory process.

Supervisors should not ignore topics related to sexual orientation because supervisees are likely to encounter lesbian, bisexual, and gay clients. Gautney (1994) suggests that supervisors should talk about sexual orientation whether supervisees or clients are heterosexual, gay, lesbian, or bisexual because sexual orientation is a relevant issue that is easily avoided. Avoidance can lead to not addressing issues, such as heterosexism, with sexual minority clients, which would be equivalent to failing to address racism when working with persons of color. When supervisors fail to introduce supervisees to (1) lesbian, gay, and bisexual issues; (2) the experiences of colleagues, faculty, and clients who are lesbian, bisexual, and gay; (3) self-examination regarding sexual orientation; and (4) consciousness raising regarding sexual minorities, supervisors allow "the development of professionals who are not only deficient in their ability to work with sexual minorities . . . but in the creation of therapists who are uncomfortable with ambiguities and questions regarding sexuality" (Brown, 1991, p. 237). Thus, supervisors who address issues related to sexual orientation encourage supervisees to learn about differences, accept differences, and develop an awareness of their personal biases regarding sexual orientation.

One of the biggest challenges of writing this chapter has been to make it relevant for heterosexual as well as gay, bisexual, and lesbian supervisors. Most of the chapter focuses on heterosexual supervisors and on examples pertaining to heterosexual supervisees. I have chosen this emphasis because most of the population identifies as heterosexual. I, however, include a discussion of issues relevant to lesbian, gay, and bisexual supervisors and supervisees. Regardless of the sexual orientation of supervisors and supervisees, I note issues related to sexual orientation and the treatment of sexual minorities.

SUPERVISORY CHALLENGES

Creating a Safe Environment for Disclosure of Sexual Orientation

Supervisors who have never knowingly supervised gay or lesbian supervisees could ask themselves the following question: "Would gay and lesbian supervisees feel comfortable disclosing their sexual orientation within the environment of my supervision?" This question is not posed to suggest that supervisees should be required to disclose their sexual orientation, but rather to scrutinize the safety of the environment for sharing such information if supervisees choose to do so (Long, 1996). (See the *Resource Guide* for this book for a supervisor's and supervisee's experience in disclosing their sexual orientation.) Supervisees may refrain from revealing information about their sexual orientation because of their perception and/or experience of heterosexism on the part of supervisors, administrators, the institution, or the community.

A supervisor-in-training (SIT) was having a difficult time deciding whether to broach the subject of sexual orientation with her supervisee. The supervisee had given the SIT some clues that she was lesbian, but the SIT was uncertain whether or not to initiate the discussion. The supervisor working with the SIT asked her what her fears were in having this discussion with the supervisee. The SIT responded that she was afraid the supervisee would be angry or devastated to be thought of as possibly lesbian. The supervisor suggested that the supervisee may be relieved or flattered. These observations led to a discussion regarding the heterosexist thinking underlying the SIT's fears.

Gay, bisexual, and lesbian supervisees who do choose to disclose, open themselves to the possibility of lowered status as a result of the stigma attached to their sexual orientation by their supervisors; the burden of "helping" fellow supervisees or supervisors deal with their heterosexism; the possibility of retaliation by administrators who may become privy to this information; unexpected changes in supervisors who may not be as open but who are informed of supervisees' orientations; and concerns about what future employers, who may not be as open and accepting, may discover about their identity. The Commission on Accreditation for Marriage and Family Therapy Education (COAMFTE) does not include sexual orientation in its antidiscrimination clause related to applicants or students, which leaves supervisees in accredited programs unprotected in the event of discrimination (COAMFTE, 1991). Supervisors have a responsibility to make supervisees aware of the potential consequences for public openness and of safe spaces on campus and in the community for sexual minority supervisees to receive support and guidance. Supervisees who do disclose can be put in contact with lesbian and gay professional groups such as the Gay, Lesbian, and Bisexual Caucus in the American Association for Marriage and Family Therapy. (See *Resource Guide* for specific information regarding groups.) In addition to professional validation of their identity, these groups can also provide possibilities for mentoring by other lesbian, bisexual, and gay supervisors.

Lesbian, bisexual, and gay supervisors who consider "coming out" to supervisees also open themselves up to the same kind of potential discrediting. In academic settings, release of this information may jeopardize chances for tenure and promotion. In institutional settings, promotions, salary and benefit increases, and job security may be threatened. In the private practice setting, supervisors who are not publicly "out" may find themselves exposed in the community thus potentially jeopardizing client referrals. Supervisors in any setting, who are out, also open themselves up to instances of discrimination and violence in many communities.

Being open to supervisees about one's sexual orientation can also bring about positive results. Bisexual, lesbian, and gay supervisors can provide heterosexual supervisees with exposure to persons who are different from themselves thus offering supervisees an opportunity to broaden their knowledge base and potentially increasing their level of acceptance as a result of personal exposure. This exposure may provide supervisees with opportunities to confront their own biases and stereotypes (Schrag, 1994). As one male supervisee recently said about his experience with an openly lesbian supervisor: "I never had known anyone who was openly lesbian, and I never would have dreamed a year ago that I would be supervised by one! I was very uncomfortable initially, but now I feel that there is only a very tiny wall that separates us. It makes me sad to say that it exists at all."

Supervisees who are gay, bisexual, and lesbian can also benefit from working with supervisors of like orientation through role modeling and opportunities to discuss how their sexual orientation influences their therapy. These discussions might also occur with a heterosexual supervisor but may lack the understanding of and appreciation of the concerns and contributions of lesbians, bisexuals, or gays. On a personal level, being open about one's bisexual, lesbian, or gay orientation has the potential to model "a method of moving from shame to self-empowerment, from abuse to compassion, and from secrecy to care of self" (Schrag, 1994). In many communities lesbian, gay, and bisexual supervisees and supervisors have an increased chance of interacting in social and professional settings. These interactions are almost inevitable within gay communities outside of large metropolitan areas, and their potential occurrence should be discussed with

agreed-on strategies for handling any ensuing discomfort.

Addressing Heterosexual Bias

Heterosexual bias has been defined as "conceptualizing human experience in strictly heterosexual terms and consequently ignoring, invalidating, or derogating lesbian, gay, and bisexual orientations, behaviors, relationships, and lifestyles" (Herek et al., 1991, p. 958). Heterosexism has been identified as an ethnocentric lens through which much of the culture has traditionally viewed the world (Long, 1996). Historically, this heterosexist lens has been employed by mental health professionals to evaluate, analyze, research, and work in therapy with lesbians, gays, and bisexuals. Specific evidence of the presence of heterosexism in the mental health arena includes the following beliefs:

- The supposition that heterosexuality is "normal" and "healthy" and that gay, lesbian, and bisexual orientations are deviant or pathological (Morin, 1977).
- The assumption that theories and research findings based on studies of heterosexuals are applicable and generalizable to gays, bisexuals, and lesbians (Kitzinger, 1987).
- The presumption that heterosexuality and its accompanying lifestyle provide normative standards against which the lives of lesbians, gays, and bisexuals need to be compared in order to be understood (Goodrich et al., 1988).

Greene (1994) notes that sexual orientation is a topic about which most persons socialized in the United States have intense feelings. Yet, this topic has been carefully avoided in formal training programs for mental health professionals (Brown, 1991; Eldridge & Barnett, 1991; Greene, 1994; Markowitz, 1991). Like other mental health disciplines, the seminal works in the MFT literature are heterosexually biased. It is likely that persons who are not informed regarding issues of sexual orientation will be more susceptible to wearing a heterosexist lens. MFT supervisors are also not unsusceptible to the influence of the pervasive existence of heterosexist bias in the dominant culture. Because of the intensity of feelings related to sexual orientation and the potential for heterosexism, self-examination is a necessary step in preparing supervisors to work with supervisees, including those supervisees who hold different values and opinions than supervisors (Long, 1996). Supervision must be balanced in a way that is respectful and growth-enhancing for supervisees and at the same time advances the welfare of sexual minorities (Long, 1994).

Supervisors' reactions are most likely tied to their level of acceptance of lesbian, gay, and bisexual orientations. Some supervisors may view gays, lesbians, and bisexuals negatively perhaps even as repulsive, immoral, or sick and encourage therapists in establishing the goal of therapy as changing the person's orientation. Other supervisors may consider bisexuals, gays, and lesbians to be stuck in adolescent development. These supervisors focus on ways therapists can encourage their clients to grow out of it. The potential for "becoming straight" is reinforced in supervision. Some supervisors display a pseudo-accepting attitude: "I can work with gays, lesbians, and bisexuals in therapy or supervision as long as it is not the focus of our work." Supervision is characterized by statements such as: "You're not a lesbian to me, you are a person," and "I'm very comfortable in interacting with you so let's not focus on your sexual orientation." These supervisors tend to dismiss sexual orientation as an issue to be addressed.

Supervisors may be accepting of lesbian, bisexual, and gay orientations but, as a result of a lack of knowledge and/or exposure, are unaware of heterosexual bias. Once heterosexism is discovered, they are willing to examine their own attitudes, values, and behaviors to address heterosexism. These supervisors engage in self-examination and encourage supervisees to do the same. Other supervisors value diversity in relationships and see sexual minorities as a valid part of that diversity and as indispensable in our society. They are willing to become allies and advocates to ensure that gays, lesbians, and bisexuals prosper in society. These supervisors encourage therapists to work with and learn from sexual minority clients. They also seek out professional contact with gay, bisexual, and lesbian supervisors.

Supervisors could begin an examination of their biases by asking themselves whether they have ever worked in therapy with lesbian or gay couples; supervised bisexual, lesbian, or gay supervisees; or encouraged the hiring of gay, lesbian, and bisexual colleagues. If the answers are all negative, they should begin to examine ways they may be potentially biased and promote discrimination against these groups. Omission can be a strong form of oppression. Discrimination of supervisees can include lack of inclusion of partners in social functions, lack of recognition of commitment ceremonies between partners, lack of understanding in the event of the illness or death of a partner, and lack of provisions for insurance and benefits to the partner and any co-parented children. Some potential areas of discrimination have previously been addressed, including potential lowered status and benefits and the possibility of job loss. Lowered status can include a demotion, minimal or no salary increases, and being called on to cover holidays because "you don't have a family." Even though supervisors may not be directly responsible for these acts of discrimination, their existence in the work environment can begin to undermine trust in supervisory relationships.

Gay, bisexual, and lesbian supervisors must also monitor their potential bias regarding issues related to sexual orientation. For example, gays and lesbians are sometimes suspect of persons who are bisexual, viewing them as confused, in denial, looking for sexual outlets, or immature in their sexual identity development. These ideas reflect a lack of knowledge and convey negativity toward bisexuals.

Increasing Supervisory Knowledge

Supervisors who allow supervisees to treat gay and lesbian couples and families as though they are heterosexual foster insensitivity and discrimination by denying their possible special concerns (Long, 1996).

A therapist who had previously worked with a lesbian couple in therapy told her supervisor that she had been contacted by the couple to return to therapy. She was puzzled because she felt they had worked through their relationship issues. The supervisor was new to the case and asked the therapist to describe their work together. As the therapist finished her description, she said, "I basically addressed the same issues that I would with heterosexual couples. I don't think lesbian couples should be treated differently." While the therapist was trying to be open and accepting, she was overlooking the differences in same-sex relationships versus heterosexual relationships. The supervisor discussed this possibility with the therapist. When the couple came to therapy, they said that pressures at the job were having a negative effect on their relationship. The therapist inquired whether they were "out" at the office, which she had never considered as a potential issue before. This question led to a discussion on the pressure of remaining invisible in some environments and the discrimination that is dealt with when same-sex couples are "out." These issues became the focus of their work together.

Supervisors can access the growing base of literature related to working with gays, lesbians, and bisexuals and their families in therapy which focuses on ways to minimize heterosexism in therapeutic relationships (Brown & Zimmer, 1986; Levy, 1992; Slater & Mencher, 1991). Heterosexism is present in many of the traditional approaches to family therapy (Ault-Riche, 1986; Goodrich et al., 1988). For example, early popular concepts, such as fusion and boundaries, have been used to pathologize lesbian relationships (Brown & Zimmer, 1986; Burch, 1986; Krestan & Bepko, 1980; Roth, 1989; Sharratt & Bern, 1985). If fusion or enmeshment is understood as the influence of gender-role socialization and the tendency of persons with minority status to bond closely together to provide protection from a hostile environment, the key to promoting growth in the relationship is to allow both parties to find themselves within the relationship, vacillating between connection and separation (Burch, 1985; McKenzie, 1992). Supervisors who are familiar with this literature are equipped to assist supervisees in minimizing heterosexism in the therapy room.

The best way to increase one's knowledge about lesbians, gays, and bisexuals is to seek out personal and professional relationships with members of these groups (Long, 1996). Recently, in speaking with gay and lesbian couples about their therapy experiences, I asked what they would like a therapist to know about being gay or lesbian. Their responses included: the invisibility of our relationship to the majority of persons with whom we come in contact every day; knowledge about the "coming out" process, including dealing with family and friends; "coming out" issues in the work environment; knowledge of the history of the gay rights movement; awareness of the major social battles facing gays and lesbians; and an awareness of the effects of homophobic actions, including the fear of being harmed or killed because of one's sexual orientation (Long et al., 1993). Supervisors' understanding of these issues greatly increases when they do not simply read about them but actually know persons who struggle with these issues on a daily basis.

Relinquishing Stereotypes

Supervisors may hold on to stereotypes of gays and lesbians because they are threatened by the notion that gays and lesbians are more similar to heterosexuals than different, or because the stigma of homosexuality is so great in our society, they want to place themselves as far away from this label as possible (Eldridge & Barnett, 1991). When supervisors are knowledgeable about common stereotypes and the research that refutes them, they can assist their supervisees in ridding themselves of stereotypes. Common stereotypes are refuted by the following research:

1. Gays and lesbians do not desire permanence in relationships. Research indicates that 45% to 80% of lesbians and 40% to 60% of gays are involved in steady relationships at any given time (Peplau & Cochran, 1990), and many lesbians and gays establish lifelong partnerships (Blumstein & Schwartz, 1983; Bryant & Demian, 1994; McWhirter & Mattison, 1984).

2. Gay and lesbian relationships are less satisfactory than heterosexual relationships. When the relationship satisfaction of lesbians and gays is compared to heterosexual couples, few if any differences emerge (Duffy & Rusbult, 1986; Kurdek & Schmitt, 1987; Peplau & Cochran, 1990).

3. Lesbians and gays are not effective parents. Harris and Turner (1985–1986) note that being gay is compatible to effective parenting. Flaks, Ficher, Masterpasqua, and Joseph (1995) found that lesbian couples exhibited more parenting awareness skills than did heterosexual couples. Kirkpatrick, Smith, and Roy (1981) found no differences between lesbian and heterosexual mothers in maternal interests, current lifestyles, and child-rearing practices.

4. Children who are raised by gay or lesbian parents will be psychologically damaged in some way (e.g., poor social adjustment, sexual identity confusion). Several studies have found no evidence of sexual identity confusion (Golumbok, Spencer, & Rutter, 1983; Green, 1982; Kirkpatrick, Smith, & Roy, 1981; Patterson, 1994). Green et al. (1986) found no differences in measures of peer group popularity or social adjustment between children of heterosexual and lesbian mothers. Patterson (1994) found normal social competence among children of lesbian parents and similar levels of behavior problems with children of heterosexual parents.

5. Children who are exposed to gays, lesbians, or bisexuals are more likely to be molested. Riveria (1987) and Finkelhor (1986) indicate that molestation is not related to sexual orientation.

6. All gays are or will be HIV infected. Even though the AIDS epidemic remains a crisis in the gay population of the United States, the percentage of HIV-infected individuals who are gay or bisexual men has decreased approximately 20% in recent years (Gonsiorek & Shernoff, 1991). Initial data from HIV-infection prevention programs indicate substantial behavior change which will likely reduce the number of those infections (Kelly et al., 1989; Swarthout et al., 1989).

Abiding by the Ethical Code

Supervisees approach lesbian, bisexual, and gay clients with varying levels of knowledge, acceptance, and comfort. When supervisees lack knowledge, have difficulty accepting sexual orientations other than heterosexual, or are uncomfortable with gays, bisexuals, or lesbians, supervisors find themselves in an ethical dilemma. On one hand, marriage and family therapists are required to advance the welfare of families and individuals and to respect the rights of those seeking their help (AAMFT, 1991). The ethical code further requires that therapists not discriminate against nor refuse professional service to anyone on the basis of sexual orientation. Yet, recently a supervisee stated: "I can't do therapy with gay or lesbian couples. I believe that what they are doing is wrong. I cannot support their relationships. It would compromise my religious beliefs." Another supervisee, taking a similar position, said: "I don't believe that same-sex couples can ever be happy so I would be doing them a disservice to offer to work with them." From the point of view of clients and some colleagues, these therapists are violating the ethical code.

In addition, marriage and family therapists are aware of their influential position with respect to clients, they avoid exploiting the trust and dependency of such persons and do not use their own professional relationships with clients to further their own interests (AAMFT, 1991). Yet, a supervisee commented: "They choose to be that way which means that they can change, and I want to help them. I've heard that there are types of therapy that work with this problem, and I want to find out more about them." Another stated: "If she is bisexual, I cannot encourage her relationship with a woman. I will try to encourage her in developing a relationship with a man. She has too much to lose by having a relationship with a woman." If supervisees attempt to convert same-sex couples to heterosexuality or convince them that their sexual orientation is a symptom to be cured, they are not complying with ethical principles.

Although therapists are to respect clients' rights to make decisions, help them to understand the consequences of these decisions, and to clearly advise a client that a decision on marital status is the responsibility of the client (AAMFT, 1991), many therapists have difficulty following these ethical standards. For example, one supervisee explained: "My belief about this couple is that they should end their relationship. Having one male in a couple is dysfunctional enough . . . but two! Barry's bisexual so he has a chance to have a *normal* relationship with a woman." Another noted: "I

know they want me to say that they should have a wedding ceremony, but I can't. I do not believe in the validity of a lesbian marriage. What they are doing is against the law."

On the other hand, another ethical principle requires therapists to assist persons in obtaining other therapeutic services if the therapist is unable or unwilling, for appropriate reasons, to provide professional help (AAMFT, 1991). Supervisors and supervisees may be able to resolve dilemmas by turning to this ethical principle. For example, one supervisee stated this as her rationale for referring a client: "I cannot condone their lifestyle, but I want to treat them with respect. I feel that I would do them a disservice or possibly cause them harm so I am going to make a referral." Another supervisee shared her rationale for referral: "I simply cannot work with this couple. I have never known someone who is gay, and I don't have a clue about how to work with them." In the first case, the supervisee was citing a conflict in values, while in the second case the supervisee was acknowledging a lack of knowledge as the reason for referral. However, do both of these reasons constitute "for appropriate reasons" as required by ethical principles? Refusing to work with sexual minorities because one believes their lifestyle is immoral is a very different issue than refusing to work with them because of a lack of knowledge and skill (Long, 1994).

A supervisor in a private, church-affiliated clinic chooses a gay couple as a case for team supervision. Strong opinions are expressed and over half of the team members request another case. The supervisory challenge is heightened by the context. Church doctrine dictates that same-sex relationships are immoral. The beliefs of the supervisor do not coincide with those of the institution; however, he is employed by the institution, and the supervisees have the weight of church doctrine to support their right to refuse service. The issue of what is ethical behavior becomes very context laden.

___

The dilemma for supervisors is to find a way to assist their reticent supervisees to honor the ethical code by respecting clients' rights, refraining from discriminating on the basis of sexual orientation, not exploiting clients for their own interests, and referring when they are unable to provide therapy for appropriate reasons. Thus, supervisors must simultaneously consider clients and supervisees. How can supervisors ensure the best possible services to sexual minority clients while also ensuring that supervisees are being encouraged to broaden and examine their own beliefs, skills, and knowledge?

When supervisees prefer to refer gays, lesbians, or bisexuals because of a conflict in values, supervisors must first consider the welfare of clients (Long, 1996). In a recent pilot study, six persons who self-identified as gay, lesbian, or bisexual participated in interviews concerning their perceptions of the therapy experience (Long et al., 1993). Respondents were asked if they would consider working with therapists who did not condone their lifestyle. Their response was a resounding "NO." In keeping with the tenor of the AAMFT Code of Ethics (1991) and the response of this group of subjects, supervisors are doing a disservice to sexual minority clients by assigning them therapists who are opposed to their sexual orientation (Long, 1996). Although supervisors may believe that exposure to persons who are bisexual, gay, and lesbian would be a good training experience for supervisees who are uncomfortable with sexual minorities, supervisors must find other avenues for supervisees to gain exposure to these populations in arenas outside the therapy room. Options include allowing supervisees who are aversive to these orientations to observe therapy sessions involving gays, lesbians, and bisexuals from be-

hind the mirror or on a videotape (Long et al., 1993) and reviewing audio- and videotapes of sessions for stereotyping and heterosexual assumptions. Hopefully, supervisees will become interested in broadening their own knowledge and skills in working with sexual minorities after their beliefs have been challenged by this exposure. When this occurs, careful supervision is required.

If supervisees are unwilling to work with sexual minorities because of a strong value conflict, supervisors should ensure that supervisees fully understand the standard of care for the treatment of sexual minorities and the ethical code. Supervisors should further assist supervisees in formulating professional goals appropriate to their personal convictions and a method for conveying their beliefs to prospective employers and clients.

When supervisees prefer not to work with lesbians, bisexuals, or gays because of a lack of knowledge, supervisors must decide if supervisees can provide adequate therapy while developing their knowledge base. In the study mentioned before, participants stated the most important quality in a therapist was an openness and acceptance of who they were. All respondents also noted, however, that they expect therapists to have a knowledge base regarding sexual orientation and would not continue to see therapists if a lack of knowledge became apparent (Long et al., 1993). Supervisors who discover a lack of knowledge on the part of supervisees should monitor their cases closely while expanding supervisees' knowledge base.

___

A male therapist was assigned a case of marital discord. The husband refused to come to therapy, and the couple separated. The wife decided to continue therapy and moved in with a female friend. The friend came into therapy with the client to offer a supportive presence The two women eventually became involved in an emotional and physical relationship and were struggling with identity issues. The male therapist had never worked with a lesbian couple and was not familiar with the literature. He wondered if he should transfer the case. The supervisor provided the therapist with some reading material on sexual identity and offered to do live supervision with the clients and supervisee. The therapist continued on the case, learning a lot about sexual identity issues and lesbian relationships.

When supervisors and supervisees agree that supervisees should not see particular clients because of a conflict in values, a lack of knowledge, or a fear of doing harm, the task of supervision is not complete. A problematic area, which supervisees should be invited to examine, has been uncovered. The challenge for supervisors is to provide a safe and informed context in which this exploration can take place.

A supervisee who believes that gays and lesbians should be treated with respect but who does not condone their relationships asks not to see lesbian and gay couples in therapy for fear of doing them harm. The supervisor encourages the supervisee to observe the sessions of another therapist who is working with a same-sex couple from behind a one-way mirror. In supervision the supervisor explores with the supervisee the origin and nature of the fear of doing harm and invites the supervisee to compare his way of thinking about the couple with those of the other therapist. Through this exploration the supervisee begins to identify that his fear is highly related to his lack of exposure and knowledge of same-sex couples. He is forced to confront his stereotypes.

Supervisees who are lesbian, gay, or bisexual also bring their values and biases to supervision. Supervisors should not assume that bisexual, gay, and lesbian supervisees can more easily work with gay, bisexual, and lesbian clients because they have similar life ex-

perience. For instance, supervisees who have "come out" may have strong opinions about how and when clients should disclose their sexual orientation. Those opinions should not, however, interfere with the client's right to make decisions about life choices and the consequences of those choices.

INTEGRATING SEXUAL ORIENTATION INTO SUPERVISION

Supervisors have a commitment to supervisees to ensure that they have adequate knowledge and skills to work with diversity in families. It is not enough to simply say that we recognize multiculturalism; supervisors must take responsibility for ensuring that supervisees have the theoretical knowledge and the clinical skills to work with gays, lesbians, and bisexuals (Long, 1996). We must not give supervisees the message that dealing with these issues will never occur in their therapy by avoiding the topic during supervision. Gautney (1994) writes about her experience as a lesbian supervisee: "Our attempts [in supervision] to demonstrate that my sexual orientation was not an issue led us into a conspiracy of silence" (p. 3). This conspiracy contributed to a lack of richness and depth in her supervisory process. These issues are most effectively addressed when they are integrated into the supervision process. The following are some suggestions for integrating gay, bisexual, and lesbian concerns into supervision (Long, 1996):

1. Supervisors should seek out ways to monitor their own biases and stereotypical thinking on a periodical basis. Taping supervision sessions related to sexual orientation issues and reviewing those tapes for bias and stereotyping is a good place to start. Whenever possible, invite gay, lesbian, or bisexual supervisors to review the tapes with you. Examining tapes for bias in the presence of supervisees is also helpful.

2. Use examples in supervision that include gays, bisexuals, and lesbians. Supervisors must examine their use of language for clues that they may be stereotyping bisexuals, lesbians, and gays as abnormal or dysfunctional. For example, when comparing gay or lesbian couples to other family types, parallel terms should be used (i.e., comparing lesbian couples with heterosexual couples as opposed to "normal" couples). Also, when talking about healthy parental units, couples, or families, do not always refer to them as heterosexual.

3. When assigning readings, include works pertaining to bisexuals, lesbians, and gays. Do not assume that readings related to gay relationships can be applied to lesbian relationships. Even though some similarities exist, McWhirter and Mattison (1988) note the differences between gay and lesbian couples are as distinct as the differences between heterosexual and same-sex couples.

4. Supervisors can take several approaches in training supervisees to be sensitive to bisexual, gay, and lesbian clients including role-plays; review of tapes for insensitive approaches; and use of case materials to determine how they might view the case if the clients were lesbian, gay, or bisexual and vice versa (Dahlheimer & Feigal, 1991; Greene, 1994).

5. Invite openly gay, lesbian, and bisexual supervisors to consult on a variety of cases not just cases related to sexual orientation.

6. Help supervisees become aware of bias in language, both in therapy and in supervision. Supervisors can point out the necessity of monitoring one's language when eliciting information from clients. For instance, suggesting that a supervisee ask a client, whose sexual orientation is unknown, "at what age they first engaged in sexual activity" rather than "at what

age the client first had sexual intercourse." Supervisors should also caution supervisees not to assume that clients are heterosexual if clients say they are married. Many gay and lesbian couples exchange vows and have wedding ceremonies. Supervisees also need to be aware that gays and lesbians often refer to their friendship network as "family" and that for many gays and lesbians this "family" often is just as crucial and influential as their family of origin and at times even more so.

7. Supervisors who value gay, bisexual, and lesbian orientations; who demonstrate to supervisees that they are advocates and allies of sexual minorities; and who become involved in the gay community at some level will likely be sought out by bisexual, lesbian, and gay supervisees. Gay communities in many areas offer opportunities to become involved, including lectures and workshops related to gay concerns and issues; AIDS benefits and support groups; local chapters of the Federation of Parents and Friends of Lesbians and Gays, Inc.; and lesbian and gay parent support groups.

CONCLUSION

The process of becoming a therapist exposes supervisees' vulnerability and challenges them to examine their personal themes (Satir, 1987). These themes arise from their personal background, including their sexual orientation, and will undoubtedly be challenged many times throughout training. Supervisors do not have a choice as to whether supervisees will encounter sexual orientation issues within the therapy room; supervisees can only choose whether or not to participate in the exploration of those issues. The examination of sexual orientation within the supervision process is particularly challenging because of the many cultural and religious taboos surrounding the topic. It is important for supervisors to remember that the supervisory role is not to dictate supervisees' beliefs but rather to provide a safe environment for supervisees to explore their beliefs (Long, 1996). Supervisors can help establish this safe environment for exploration by examining and attending to their own heterosexism and by including content related to gays, bisexuals, and lesbians throughout the supervision process.

REFERENCES

American Association for Marriage and Family Therapy (AAMFT). (1991). *AAMFT Code of Ethics.* Washington DC: Author.

Ault-Riche, M. (1986). A feminist critique of five schools of family therapy. In M. Ault-Riche (Ed.), *Women and family therapy* (pp. 1–15). Rockville, MD: Aspen.

Bell, A., & Weinberg, M. (1978). *Homosexualities: A study of diversity among men and women.* New York: Simon & Schuster.

Blumstein, P., & Schwartz, P. (1983). *American couples: Money, work, sex.* New York: William Morrow.

Bozett, F. (Ed.). (1989). *Homosexuality and the family.* New York: Harrington Park Press.

Brown, L. (1989). New voices, new visions. *Psychology of Women Quarterly, 13,* 445–458.

Brown, L. (1991). Commentary on the special issue of *The Counseling Psychologist*: Counseling with lesbians and gay men. *The Counseling Psychologist, 19,* 235–238.

Brown, L., & Zimmer, D. (1986). An introduction to therapy issues of lesbian and gay male couples. In N. Jacobson & A. Gurman (Eds.), *Clinical handbook of marital therapy* (pp. 451–468). New York: Guilford Press.

Bryant, S., & Demian (1994). Relationship characteristics of American gay and lesbian couples: Findings from a national survey. *Journal of Gay and Lesbian Social Services, 1,* 101–117.

Burch, B. (1985). Another perspective on merger in lesbian relationships. In L. Rosewater & L. Walker (Eds.), *Handbook of feminist therapy: Women's issues in psychotherapy* (pp. 100–109). New York: Springer.

Burch, B. (1986). Psychotherapy and the dynamics of merger in lesbian couples. In T. Stein & C. Cohen (Eds.), *Contemporary perspectives on psychotherapy with lesbians and gay men* (pp. 57–71). New York: Plenum Medical Book Company.

Commission on Accreditation for Marriage and Family Therapy Education (COAMFTE). (1991). *Manual on accreditation.* Washington, DC: Author.

Crawford, S. (1987). Lesbian families: Psychosocial stress and the family-building process. In Boston Lesbian Psychologies Collective (Eds.), *Lesbian psychologies: Explorations and challenges* (pp. 195–214). Chicago: University of Chicago Press.

Dahlheimer, D., & Feigal, J. (1991). Bridging the gap. *The Family Therapy Networker, 15,* 44–53.

Duffy, S., & Rusbult, C. (1986). Satisfaction and commitment in homosexual and heterosexual relationships. *Journal of Homosexuality, 12,* 1–24.

Eldridge, N., & Barnett, D. (1991). Counseling gay and lesbian students. In N. Evans & V. Wall (Eds.), *Beyond tolerance* (pp. 147–178). Lanham, MD: University Press of America.

Finkelhor, D. (1986). *A sourcebook on child sexual abuse.* Newbury Park, CA: Sage.

Flaks, D., Ficher, I., Masterpasqua, F., & Joseph, G. (1995). Lesbians choosing motherhood: A comparative study of lesbian and heterosexual parents and their children. *Developmental Psychology, 31,* 105–114.

Gautney, K. (1994). What if they ask me if I'm married?: A supervisee's view. *Supervision Bulletin, 7, 3,* 7.

Golumbok, S., Spencer, A., & Rutter, M. (1983). Children in lesbian and single-parent households: Psychosexual and psychiatric appraisal. *Journal of Child Psychology and Psychiatry, 24,* 551.

Gonsiorek, J., & Shernoff, M. (1991). AIDS prevention and public policy: The experience of gay males. In J. Gonsiorek & J. Weinrich (Eds.), *Homosexuality: Research implications for public policy* (pp. 230–243). Newbury Park, CA: Sage.

Gonsiorek, J., & Weinrich, J. (Eds.). (1991). *Homosexuality: Research implications for public policy.* Newbury Park, CA: Sage.

Goodrich, T., Rampage, C., Ellman, B., & Halstead, K. (1988). *Feminist family therapy: A casebook.* New York: W. W. Norton.

Green, R. (1982). The best interests of the child with a lesbian mother. *Bulletin of the American Academy of Psychiatry and the Law, 10,* 7–15.

Green, R., Mandel, J., Hotvedt, M., Gray, J., & Smith, L. (1986). Lesbian mothers and their children: A comparison with solo parent heterosexual mothers and their children. *Archives of Sexual Behavior, 15,* 167–184.

Greene, B. (1994). Lesbian and gay sexual orientations: Implications for clinical training, practice, and research. In B. Greene & G. Herek (Eds.), *Lesbian and gay psychology* (pp. 1–24). Thousand Oaks, CA: Sage.

Greene, B., & Herek, G. (Eds.). (1994). *Lesbian and gay psychology: Theory, research, and clinical applications.* Thousand Oaks, CA: Sage.

Harris, M., & Turner, P. (1985–1986). Gay and lesbian parents. *Journal of Homosexuality, 12,* 101–113.

Herek, G., Kimmel, D., Amaro, H., & Melton, G. (1991). Avoiding heterosexist bias in psychological research. *American Psychologist, 46,* 957–963.

Kelly, J., St. Lawrence, J., Hood, H., & Brasfield, T. (1989). Behavioral intervention to reduce AIDS risk activities. *Journal of Consulting and Clinical Psychology, 57,* 60–67.

Kirkpatrick, M., Smith, C., & Roy, R. (1981). Lesbian mothers and their children. *American Journal of Orthopsychiatry, 51,* 545–551.

Kitzinger, C. (1987). *The social construction of lesbianism.* London: Sage.

Koepke, L., Hare, J., & Moran, P. (1992). Relationship quality in a sample of lesbian couples with children and child-free lesbian couples. *Family Relations, 41,* 224–229.

Krestan, J., & Bepko, C. (1980). The problem of fusion in the lesbian relationship. *Family Process, 19,* 277–289.

Kurdek, L. (1994). *Social services for gay and lesbian couples.* New York: Haworth Press.

Kurdek, L., & Schmitt, J. (1987). Relationship quality of partners in heterosexual married, heterosexual co-habiting, and gay and lesbian relationships. *Journal of Personality and Social Psychology, 14,* 57–68.

Laird, J. (1993). Lesbian and gay families. In F. Walsh (Ed.), *Normal family processes,* 2nd ed. (pp. 282–328). New York: Guilford Press.

Levy, E. (1992, January). Strengthening the coping resources of lesbian families. *Families in Society: The Journal of Contemporary Human Services, 73,* 23–31.

Long, J. (1994). MFT supervision of gay, lesbian, and bisexual clients: Are supervisors still in the dark? *Supervision Bulletin, 7,* 1, 6.

Long, J. (1996). Working with lesbians, gays, and bisexuals: Addressing heterosexism in supervision. *Family Process, 35,* 377–388.

Long, J., Lindsey, E., Manders, J., Dotson, D., & Wilson, R. (1993, October). *Training MFTs to work with gay and lesbian couples and families.* Workshop presented at the annual meeting American Association for Marriage and Family Therapy, Anaheim, CA.

Markowitz, L. (1991). Homosexuality: Are we still in the dark? *The Family Therapy Networker, 15,* 26–35.

Martin, A. (1993). *The lesbian and gay parenting handbook: Creating and raising our families.* New York: HarperCollins.

McKenzie, S. (1992). Merger in lesbian relationships. *Women and Therapy, 12,* 151–160.

McWhirter, D., & Mattison, A. (1984). *The male couple: How relationships develop.* Englewood Cliffs, NJ: Prentice-Hall.

McWhirter, D., & Mattison, A. (1988). Stages in the development of gay relationships. In J. DeCecco (Ed.), *Gay relationships* (pp. 161–168). New York: Harrington Park.

Morin, S. (1977). Heterosexual bias in psychological research on lesbianism and male homosexuality. *American Psychologist, 19,* 629–637.

Patterson, C. (1994). Children of the lesbian baby boom: Behavioral adjustment, self-concepts, and sex role identity. In B. Greene & G. Herek (Eds.), *Lesbian and gay psychology* (pp. 156–175). Thousand Oaks, CA: Sage.

Peplau, L., & Cochran, S. (1990). A relational perspective on homosexuality. In D. McWhirter, S. Sanders, & J. Reinisch (Eds.), *Homosexuality/heterosexuality: Concepts of sexual orientation* (pp. 321–349). New York: Oxford University Press.

Riveria, R. (1987). Legal issues in gay and lesbian parenting. In F. Bozett (Ed.), *Gay and lesbian parents* (pp. 199–227). New York: Praeger.

Roth, S. (1989). Psychotherapy with lesbian couples: Individual issues, female socialization, and the social context. In M. McGoldrick, C. Anderson, & F. Walsh (Eds.), *Women in families: A framework for family therapy* (pp. 286–307). New York: W. W. Norton.

Satir, V. (1987). The therapist's story. *Journal of Psychotherapy and the Family, 3*(1). Also in M. Baldwin & V. Satir (Eds.), *The use of self in therapy* (pp. 17–25). New York: Haworth Press.

Schrag, K. (1994). Disclosing homosexuality: A supervisor's view. *Supervision Bulletin, 7,* 3, 7.

Sharrat, S., & Bern, L. (1985). Lesbian couples and families: A co-therapeutic approach to counseling. In

L. Rosewater & L. Walker (Eds.), *Handbook of feminist therapy: Women's issues in psychotherapy* (pp. 91–99). New York: Springer.

Slater, S., & Mencher, J. (1991). The lesbian family life cycle: A contextual approach. *American Journal of Orthopsychiatry, 61*, 372–382.

Swarthout, D., Gonsiorek, J., Simpson, M., & Henry, K. (1989). A behavioral approach to HIV prevention among seronegative or untested gay/bisexual men with a history of unsafe behavior. *Proceedings Fifth International Conference on AIDS*, Montreal, Canada, p. 784.

6

Gender and Supervision
Evolving Debates

Jean Turner and Marshall Fine

Once upon a time there was a beautiful supervisor. She was the fairest supervisor in all the land. She had a thriving supervisory practice and therapists flocked to her from near and far just to be touched by her beauty and wisdom. One day a rugged and handsome therapist, hearing of her wisdom and fairness, left a message on her answering machine. "Ms. Taken, I have heard that you are a very fair supervisor. I would like to talk with you about the possibility of supervising my therapy work."

Ms. Taken returned his call saying that she was open to the possibility of developing a supervision relationship. The appointed time arrived, and he swooped into her office. Any Hollywood fool could see that they were meant for one another. From the moment their words made contact, they simply could not stop from dialoguing about supervision. He knew she was right for him and he proposed that they develop a supervision contract

She hesitated for a moment, smiled, and then told him there was one thing he would

have to know first. She sounded serious so he listened intently. "I have to tell you," she said in a controlled but slightly quivering voice, "like most women I have at various times faced discrimination and have been depreciated especially by some men because I am female. Sometimes my pain and anger about those experiences comes out, even when it is not intended or reasonable under the circumstance. You will have to be prepared for this possibility."

He sat back and looked dazed. After a moment of silent reflection he spoke, "But I have been told that you were so wise and fair." TO BE CONTINUED. . .

The topic of gender and supervision does not fit into any kind of neatly wrapped package. Gender and supervision can be analyzed at multiple levels: the experiences of individual supervisors and supervisees, the dynamics of supervisory relationships, and the sociopolitical structures and processes existing within supervision contexts. There are also various observer standpoints (i.e., men, women, supervisor, supervisees), each of which implies different power and status. Moreover issues of gender and power evoke strong feelings—anger, sadness, guilt, frustration, defensiveness, confusion, to name a few—for both men and women. These feelings relate not only to the long history

---

Note: This chapter is based on an equal sharing of ideas. Mainly, Jean drafted the text and Marshall edited and commented on drafts. Some readers have viewed Jean's decision to write a chapter about gender with a male co-author as problematic because it raises questions about power and authority. We acknowledge that it does.

of women's subordination but also to a lack of consensus, both at societal and interpersonal levels, on how to fairly address these injustices.

In writing this chapter, we intentionally pursued two objectives. The first was to review what we read in the literature and to add comments related to our own experiences. The second objective was to take a "critical," reflexive stance, one that involves analyzing the politics and power relations inherent in all perspectives, including our own and those that are currently seen as politically correct (Flax, 1992). The rationale for this second objective emerges from the fact that gender issues are currently political issues about which there are evolving debates in the field. Taking a critical perspective, we acknowledge power inequities and connect ourselves with issues of social justice. At the same time, we maintain a skepticism about perspectives that involve commitment to any single standpoint (Fine & Turner, 1991). Overall we have attempted to follow the feminist and constructionist practices of making transparent our subjectivity as authors, and of underlining the impossibility of an objective view (Gergen, 1985; Haraway, 1991; Hare-Mustin, 1994).

MAJOR THEMES: PAST AND PRESENT

Almost without exception, female supervisors have been the authors of what has been written in the marriage and family therapy (MFT) field about gender and supervision. The initiative of women, beginning in the early 1980s, is hardly surprising. Concern about gender inequality was introduced to family therapists by feminist authors beginning in the mid-1970s (e.g., Hare-Mustin, 1978). Since that time many authors have pointed out the pitfalls of men supervising women, the likelihood that the contribution of women will be devalued whether they are supervisors or therapists in

supervision, and the difficulties male supervisors face in attempting to work effectively with women therapists given the legacy of patriarchy (Doherty, 1991c).

JEAN: We have hardly begun to talk about gender and I am already in a bad mood! As our discussions and writing of this chapter become more focused, I am increasingly aware of both my personal hurts and the collective pain of women related to the prejudice and discrimination we have faced. Incidents when I knew I was undervalued because of my sex, some long in the past and usually not in my awareness, are permanently etched in my memory. You know, Marshall, I feel such injustices should not be completely dismissed, but I also never want them to run my life or turn my heart to ice. Once revitalized these memories can be dangerous; I start to observe my world with a gender-paranoid gaze. Any man who enters into my field of vision is subjected to scrutiny. Watch out!

MARSHALL: It may take another hundred decades for the simmering anger of countless years of oppression to boil dry—to find peace in shared respect and understanding. So with a mournful appreciation of the historical and contemporary injustices inflicted on women, how shall I watch out, and what should I do if you transfix me in your field of scrutiny? Will it be difficult to separate my maleness from my actions? my thoughts? my being? Is it possible? I am reminded of living as a Jew. I never try to hide my Jewishness but sometimes it lies dormant and I can fool myself into believing that I am just a "regular" person. However, every once in a while someone reminds me, typically in a negative way, that I am Jewish—someone notices and draws conclusions about me. It doesn't seem to matter what I say. And THAT makes me feel powerless and angry.

Empowerment of Women

In our view the most ground-breaking contribution to the literature on supervision has been made by feminist authors. They have strongly expressed what had not been previously acknowledged—that gender/power relations are as consequential in supervision relationships as they are in all other relationships, and that the personal is political. A number of authors point out that women supervisors and women therapists are disadvantaged and, therefore, need to be empowered (see, for example, Ault-Riche, 1988; Avis, 1989; Caust, Libow, & Raskin, 1981; Libow, 1986; Okun, 1983; Reid et al., 1987; Wheeler et al., 1989). These authors suggest that supervisors work toward increasing general knowledge about women and power inequity; ensuring that women therapists are safe and appropriately treated in supervision with male supervisors; and helping female supervisors to confront those male therapists who may not respect a woman's authority and knowledge. Ault-Riche (1988) proposes that women therapists need to apprentice with supervisors who are "healthy and competent" female models. Supervisors are perceived as expert mentors empowering female therapists who will, in turn, empower their female clients.

Executive Skill Building and Androgyny

Instrumentality and authority-taking abilities were initially the most highly valued by supervisors concerned with empowering women (Caust et al., 1981; Libow, 1986; Wheeler et al., 1989). In the 1980s, strong executive skills and assertiveness were assumed to be essential for working competently as a therapist, particularly in the popular, male-oriented structural and strategic models of the time. This was problematic for women, given that females tended to be socialized to be submissive and approval-seeking (Ault-Riche, 1988). Several authors expressed concern that women supervisors might be devalued by therapists of both sexes, given that the profession was male-led and the workplaces were male-dominated (Libow, 1986; Okun, 1983).

JEAN: I remember January 1981. Just in the middle of one client's sentence I hear a sharp knock on the therapy room door. I get up with apologies to the clients, a black family who recently arrived in Canada from Jamaica. With an annoyed look and tone, my supervisor admonishes me to confront the husband. She points out that he not only disrespectfully came late to the session but he has also taken over the therapy conversation. Once again I have been foolishly blind to men's power tactics. In my supervisor's eyes, I am colluding with this guy in silencing his wife. My empathic listening to the man's painful story about searching for employment was detracting from the concerns his wife had earlier voiced about their relationship. What an embarrassment! Will I ever be able to work as the kind of female therapist she is trying to empower me to be? As I head back into the room, she gives a final stern-toned instruction: "Never apologize when you leave a therapy room." I mumble, "I'm sorry."

One strategy for attaining power was to emulate the attributes of the more dominant group. Yet some of the early writers went beyond encouraging women to "catch up" with men by proposing "androgyny" for *both* sexes (Nelson, 1991; Reid et al., 1987; Warburton, Newberry, & Alexander, 1989). Achieving androgyny, according to Okun (1983), would involve men and women in "the development of a full complement of both instrumental and expressive modes of perceiving and behaving" (p. 48). A truly androgynous individual is able to draw on whichever abilities are most appropriate to meet the demands of a particular situation.

From our point of view both the proposal for executive skill building and the proposal for androgynous development are partial solutions with some unintended, contradictory implications. Traditionally feminine attributes (caring, nurturance, flexibility) are implicitly devalued when women are asked to seek equality by developing stereotypically male executive traits. Perhaps as a response to this devaluing, several authors who have published their ideas more recently seem to be granting priority value to traditionally feminine attributes and raising questions about some traditionally male attributes (Bograd, 1991; Doherty, 1991b; Meth & Pasick, 1990). The proposal for androgeny is narrow in its focus on making changes in gendered behavior as individuals. It does not directly challenge the multitude of ways in which the larger social system supports, and is supported by, patriarchal ideologies and practices. The supervision literature does not yet reflect concern in the field about changes in gender and other inequalities requiring both political and personal action (e.g., Avis, 1992; Waldegrave, 1986). An article by Porter and Yahne (1994) on supervision and advocacy is, perhaps, a harbinger of this future direction.

Gender Transformations and Inclusivity

In the fifteen years since gender issues in supervision were first identified, we have witnessed a rapid and continuing transformation in gender relations. In fact, general uncertainty about relationships, personal identity, and political alliances are part of what is termed the "condition of postmodernity" (Gergen, 1991; Harvey, 1989). This has led to both confusion and controversy about what constitutes correct behavior between the sexes, along with greater tolerance for gender fluidity. Considered in this current context, the approaches to dealing with gender/power relations we have reviewed here (male valuing, androgyny valuing, female valuing) appear unnecessarily constraining. Debates have emerged about the underlying assumptions behind these approaches which conceptualize gender as dichotomous; *male* implies a lack of *female*, and vice versa (see Ellman & Taggart, 1993).

A second aspect of the transformation in the gender politics has been greater attention to inclusivity. Authors in various fields argue that gender inequalities cannot necessarily be given priority over other inequalities related to race, class, gender orientation, and so on (e.g., Almeida, 1993; hooks, 1990; Kliman, 1994). These days a supervisor would be very cautious about what to do in a situation where a white female supervisee with a high-level education is working with a male client from a disenfranchised racial group who talks at length about the pain of being unemployed and ignores his wife's concerns. We agree with Watson (1993) when she suggests that supervisors should be considering the *simultaneous* intersect of gender with class, race, and other relationship-organizing principles.

Recently, authors are beginning to identify self-awareness and the development of collaborative therapist–client relationships rather than skill building as the major foci of supervision work (e.g., Sirles, 1994; Storm, 1991; Watson, 1993). This shifts the supervision process toward ongoing reflection on gender self-descriptions, on expectations for the other sex, and on the complex power dynamics related to the multiple identities of the participants (racial, class, religious, and so on).

POWER AND GENDER CONFIGURATIONS IN SUPERVISION

Socially constructed gender inequalities related to the legacy of patriarchy continue to be played out in supervisory relationships, although the script for the interaction is not clearly written. There are inherent complications in supervision arising from the intersect between two different axes of power: power related to role (supervisor and therapist), and power related to gender (male and female). Because the power accorded to supervisors is legitimized by professional accrediting associations, it is more easily acknowledged, discussed, and negotiated by supervision participants (Fine & Turner, 1996). In contrast, power inequities related to gender lack social legitimacy in the current social context where egalitarian values are now endorsed by a majority of men and women. Just how men and women should interact with each other to reflect those values is still at issue. Lack of clarity and legitimacy impede open dialogue about gender/power relations in supervision.

Further contradictions are created by standpoint differences between those with more power (i.e., supervisors, men) and those with less power (i.e., supervisees, women). Goode (1982) argues that, in relations of inequality, the more powerful actors risk being "blind"—unaware of their privileged position especially if it has been inherited rather than intentionally sought after. In contrast, members of subordinate and marginalized groups are highly attuned to power dynamics given that their lives are significantly affected by the actions of the more powerful. Fearing reprisal, members of the subordinate group are unlikely to openly voice their protest about injustices. Also, subordinated individuals begin to devalue themselves in accord with their lower status in the system and question their own experience.

Based on Goode's predictions about the self-silencing of subordinates, we perceive that supervisors have greater responsibility than supervisees for opening up a dialogue about power more generally (Fine & Turner, 1996), and gender inequality more specifically (Kaiser, 1992). It follows that male supervisors who have the possibility to wield power along two axes also carry a double burden of responsibility to be on the look out for any untoward effects, to avoid unintentional exploitation, and to acknowledge collective and personal pain related to marginalization.

In the context of these power relations, the emphasis in the literature on the perils of men supervising women is understandable, but leaves much unsaid. To date only a few writers have commented, albeit briefly, on the opportunities provided by both cross-sex and same-sex supervisory relationships (Okun, 1983; Nelson, 1991; Warburton et al., 1989). In several of the newer explorations of gender and supervision, authors mention both male and female supervisees although they do not comment on gender similarities/differences (Roberts, 1991; Sirles, 1994; Storm, 1991; Mac Kune-Karrer et al., 1994). Each gender configuration of supervisor, therapist, and client offers opportunities and constraints.

Women Supervising Women

For women therapists, the identified empowering aspects of this configuration include working intensively with competent same-sex models, feeling freer to voice their personal experiences and engage in self-disclosure, being able to develop more collaborative supervisory relationships than with male supervisors, and having fewer concerns about personal safety. There are also positive features of the female–female configuration for supervisors: they may expect fewer challenges to their authority from female than from male supervisees; they may find it easier to disclose their own personal experiences thereby developing more trusting relationships; and they may have fewer concerns about female therapists working with female clients who have been sexually abused by men.

Ironically, when women supervise women, there may be particular constraints related to power blindness. For example, both supervisor and therapist may underplay the power of the therapist if they construe women as invariably less powerful participants in any interaction. Female–female supervision may be a struggle when a woman therapist who is accustomed to support and solidarity from women meets up with her female supervisor's expectations that she be independent and able to field challenges from assertive colleagues, clients, and the supervisor herself. Female socialization in mutuality may lead women supervisors and therapists to take overly supportive stances with each other. Finally, women in the female–female supervision configuration need to be vigilant about gender experience gaps when their clients are men.

Men Supervising Men

The male–male configuration is the least visible in the writings to date about gender and supervision. Men working with men brings to mind the traditional apprenticeship or mentoring model in which a younger, less experienced man is "fathered" by an older, more expert man (Osherson, 1986). Whatever the supervision approach, therapist and supervisor have a unique chance to work together in a domain that is not traditionally perceived to be male-oriented—the domain of "caring," "helping," relationship-focused activities (Nelson, 1991).

When all members of the therapeutic system are men, there may be an opening to explore the tender qualities of everyone involved. When the client is a woman, male therapists and supervisors working together are likely to be very conscious of gender differences that may create gaps in empathy. They may, therefore, be more apt to seek extra consultation than a male–female supervision pair who may, mistakenly in some cases, believe that they "have all the gender bases covered."

There are aspects of same-sex male supervision that may make this configuration risky. We question whether the apprenticeship or mentoring model for male–male pairs may create a pernicious blindness to power relations. The supervisor may be quite aware of his greater power in relation to a man he is supervising, seeing him as needful of mentoring. However, conceptualizing the therapist in this way, the supervisor may be blind to the power of that male therapist in relation to his clients, especially those who are women. Plus, the male therapist himself may be hampered in reflecting on his own influence on the interaction with clients (Doherty, 1991c).

A second possible pitfall of the male–male configuration may be therapist–supervisor competition. We have wondered if same-sex supervision is difficult for many men given that the traditional expectation is that they should seek and receive support from women, and display their independence in relation to male authority figures (Bergman, 1991; Stiver, 1991).

MARSHALL: I began to notice that one male therapist in our graduate program would occasionally walk into my office uninvited. When individual supervision began, he was often late, making no excuses for his tardiness. It was only after I made clear my concerns about his "attitude" toward supervision (me!) that I was awakened to a gendered version of the events. He said that he wanted to "show me he was strong and should be considered an equal—a man among men." Much generative discussion ensued, culminating in an agreement that, above all, mutual respect was what mattered.

Men Supervising Women

With the exception of a short comment by Nelson (1991), the advantages of the male supervisor with female supervisee configuration have been virtually ignored, leaving some important positive experiences undocumented. For example, it was a significant eye-opener for Jean, who grew up in a traditional, rural setting, to have a male supervisor who had highly developed skills for observing relationships and the capacity to stay connected with clients when emotions ran high. Working with male supervisors who have nonstereotyped qualities may also enable female therapists to value facets of their own gender identity that are at odds with tradition. Male supervisors who are able to nondefensively acknowledge the anger and pain of women related to their subordination generate hope and break down the barriers of mistrust.

The male–female supervision configuration has understandably been considered the most problematic given that male supervisors are accorded greater power than female supervisees on both supervision gender axes of power. Even the most egalitarian men (and women) cannot escape the legacy of patriarchal influence. Because men are accorded gender power when they personally may not desire it, they may have to remind themselves and be reminded that they have it (Nelson, 1991).

In acknowledging gender inequities, some men have created the possibility for new visions of gender relations. However, well-intentioned, gender-sensitive men are still prone to other, more subtle power blindness. Our experience is that some male supervisors and therapists attempt to "correct" the gender inequities by insistently leading women supervisees and clients toward liberation, or protecting them without first obtaining their permission (Turner, 1993). These men may fail to see that, in their zeal, they have unwittingly exercised (once again) the kind of paternalistic privilege that robs women of voice and personal agency. Whenever the supervision configuration is opposite-sex, it might be worthwhile to increase accountability measures through frequent consultation with supervisors who are the same sex as the supervisee (Tomasese & Waldegrave, 1993).

Women Supervising Men

When women supervise male therapists, there may be useful opportunities for both participants to reappraise gender relationships. The female–male configuration provides an avenue for men to learn to respect female authority figures. It also gives the female supervisor a chance to learn more about men's experience from a position of strength.

Little has been written on the constraints inherent in the female supervisor–male supervisee configuration. Some women supervisors are partial to female-oriented models of caring that highlight empathy and mutual empowerment (Gilligan, 1982; Surrey, 1991). These supervisors may fail to recognize that male therapists may be just as empathic as their female colleagues in different, though equally therapeutic, ways. Another set of possible blinders for female supervisors relates to their not infrequent experience of being the devalued, less powerful party in opposite-sex encounters. Women's history of powerlessness may lead some of them to underestimate their influence and control over male therapists (Turner, 1993). This understandable lack of sensitivity to supervisory power relations can be even more consequential when women are supervising men who have themselves experienced oppression related to other aspects of their identity (e.g., class, race, gender orientation, and so on). In mixed-sex group supervision where men are in the minority position, women supervisors may be inclined toward solidarity with the women therapists in the group, leading to unexpected consequences.

JEAN: After the third supervision meeting with a female and a male therapist I realized that I and the woman were responding to the man's work in a way that, after some initial defensive comments, he would just nod as if in agreement. In contrast, when we talked about the woman's therapy work, she and I became involved in lively, lengthy, and generative dialogues. Over time we paid less and less attention to what the male therapist said. When the three of us finally discussed this pattern, I found out that the man had been searching for a way to protest being marginalized, but had felt silenced by his fear that we would think he was being sexist if he spoke up. I made a commitment to resign from "Women's Clubbing"! I have always abhorred those times when men dominate conversations to the exclusion of the women present—the idea that I had unintentionally contributed to developing a reverse version was intolerable.

TWO UNDERLYING ISSUES

In the process of our literature review and writing the chapter, two ideas surfaced that have not been directly addressed:

1. Gender politics are emotionally charged.
2. Sexuality, gender, and supervision are easily linked.

In our opinion these ideas are implicit, but are generally left unstated in the literature and in many of the arguments about the value of particular gender configurations in supervision.

Voicing Personal and Collective Pain About Gender Oppression

The lack of consensus about gender politics, combined with the continued legacy of structural inequities, tend to generate strong feelings and between-sex conflict. If anger and bitterness regarding the opposite gender are closeted inside or only shared in same-sex groups, there may be little possibility for the kind of debate that promotes change. Providing an opportunity for supervisors and supervisees to voice a range of emotions forestalls the development of direct outrage or indirect expressions of annoyance (e.g., sarcasm, innuendoes, and so on), which can sneak into dialogues with clients or colleagues. We encourage supervisors to initiate discussions about feelings and provide time for emotion-laden dialogues about gender. Just how to best go about this is still open for debate. Same-sex supervision teams may find it easy to converse, but they may also need to set aside extra time so that the discussion moves beyond venting anger to-

ward the opposite sex in general and leads to reflection on alternative personal experiences and "realities." Doherty (1991a) and others (Bergman & Surrey, 1992) optimistically propose dialogue between men and women, leading to mutual understanding and eventual equality, as the most promising direction. However, for open exchanges to happen, women may need to feel safe from the negative influence of men's power, and men may need to feel liberated from political correctness. In opposite-sex configurations, participants may need to accept that their feelings will sometimes offend the other person, who may experience their anger as a personal attack. Time to reflect on the emotions is perhaps the most important factor because the links between feelings and ideas about them may be diffuse and changeable.

MARSHALL: Jean, I did not address my own gender anger directly in our first dialogue in this chapter. A hundred times I have attempted to specifically locate my anger with women and all my thoughts and feelings seem shallow and incomplete, diffuse and complex. My anger when I do feel it appears with both men and women—this makes some sense given my family background. I think I am most angered by people who tell me what I should do and who insist that they know what I feel and think. With these people I feel discounted—I render myself irrelevant. Overall, however, it is important to say that anger in no way predominates my being when I work with women **or** men. My experience is mainly one of appreciation, respect, fun, and curiosity.

JEAN: Looking back at my initial comment, it feels very sharp and antimale. I believe that at the core of any anger that comes up for me about gender is a commitment to fairness for everyone and that this is regardless of sex, race, class, or other differences. Then I ask myself, fairness from whose perspective and who am I to decide? As I start considering each individual's unique personal and collective history, some of the rage subsides and I reevaluate my personal ethics one more time. So I cycle between these contradictory positions—fierce commitment to my view of fairness *and* skepticism about any one point of view, including my own.

Sex, Lies, and Videotape

Who I am as a woman/man, and who are you as a man/woman? These are intensely intimate and personal questions partly because they relate to sexual attraction, vulnerability, and sexual power relations (Goldner, 1991). In North American society, one's particular sexual interests and behavior are kept relatively private. In these times of changing gender politics, talk of sexuality may be misconstrued as a welcome sexual invitation on the one hand or, at the other extreme, sexual harassment. Lacking safety, we believe that both men and women tend to keep quiet, or even lie, about sexual attractions that develop in the context of supervision. Silencing on the topic of sex, gender, and supervision has left much of what could be commented on not necessarily hidden but mainly unspoken (Okun, 1983).

Sex is likely to be discussed in supervision as long as the focus is on the clients' sexual problems, or on a possible sexual attraction between the client and the therapist (Bird, 1993). In this case, viewing videotapes of therapy sessions is particularly helpful to provide feedback to the therapist on aspects of his or her behavior that might be misconstrued by the clients. This gender and sex-focused supervision dialogue is legitimate because its ultimate purpose is the welfare of the client.

Talk about sexual attraction or desire between therapist and supervisor is more risky; the purpose is removed from client welfare and the misuse of power is at issue. We have discussed with each other at length the pros and cons of including the topic of sexual attraction in our general discussion with supervisees about gender/power relations in supervision. However, neither of us have actually gone

ahead with this. Is it this kind of hesitation that sets the stage for confusions later? Are we foolishly hiding our heads in the sand, or are we somehow aware that for everyone this is a topic best left alone unless it is brought up spontaneously?

ABSENT AUTHORS, MISSING KNOWLEDGE, EVOLVING IDEAS

Male supervisors have yet to document their perspectives on gender and supervision, even though women supervisors have been writing on the topic for the past fifteen years. In light of this history, our co-authorship of this chapter as a female–male team appears to be a rather unique event. The voices of supervised therapists, male and female, speaking about issues of gender in supervision are also absent in the literature. Until the field becomes more gender inclusive and the perspectives of direct consumers of supervision are documented, our understanding of how gender/power relations affect and are affected by the supervisory process are seriously restricted (Nutt, 1991). The story of gender and supervision is likely to be unended, unending, and always under revision because a "new order" of gender relations is unlikely to ever replace the old patriarchal hierarchy. As the debates continue, we will be preparing to hear the not-yet-said, and to look beyond our present shortsightedness.

MS. TAKEN AND THE MAN SEEKING SUPERVISION   CONTINUED

She sits back, genuinely concerned for the therapist who seems so confused and disappointed that she might harbor anger—that she might be "human." Her thoughts race, searching for something to say—something that will make him feel more at ease. But, is it her responsibility to help him feel at ease? She feels surrounded by all the external and internal voices categorizing her as wise and fair (whatever that means)—and a woman to boot!

Then, in the midst of this self-reflection, she hears the words leave her lips, "I AM wise and fair." TO BE CONTINUED . . .

REFERENCES

Almeida, R. (1993). Unexamined assumptions and service delivery systems: Feminist theory and racial exclusions. *Journal of Feminist Family Therapy, 5,* 3–23.

Ault-Riche, M. (1988). Teaching an integrated model of family therapy: Women as students, women as supervisors. *Journal of Psychotherapy and the Family, 3,* 175–189.

Avis, J. (1989). Integrating gender into the family therapy curriculum. *Journal of Feminist Family Therapy, 1,* 3–26.

Avis, J. (1992). Violence and abuse in families: The problem and family therapy's response. *Journal of Marital and Family Therapy, 18,* 223–230.

Bergman, S. (1991). Men's psychological development: A relational perspective. *Work in progress, No. 48.* Wellesley, MA: Stone Center Working Paper Series.

Bergman, S., & Surrey, J. (1992). The woman–man relationship: Impasses and possibilities. *Work in progress, No. 47.* Wellesley, MA: Stone Center Working Paper Series.

Bird, J. (1993). Coming out of the closet: Illuminating the therapeutic relationship. *Journal of Feminist Family Therapy, 5,* 47–64.

Bograd, M. (1991). Female therapist/male client: Considerations about belief systems. In M. Bograd (Ed.), *Feminist approaches for men in family therapy* (pp. 123–145). New York: Haworth Press.

Caust, B., Libow, J., & Raskin, P. (1981). Challenges and promises of training women as family systems therapists. *Family Process, 20,* 439–447.

Doherty, W. (1991a). Men's institute. *AFTA Newsletter, Fall,* 38–40.

Doherty, W. (1991b). Beyond reactivity and the deficit model of manhood: A commentary on articles by Napier, Pittman and Gottman. *Journal of Marital and Family Therapy, 17,* 29–32.

Doherty, W. (1991c). Can male therapists empower women in therapy. *Journal of Feminist Family Therapy, 3,* 123–137.

Ellman, B., & Taggart, M. (1993). Changing gender norms. In F. Walsh (Ed.), *Normal family processes, 2nd ed.* (pp. 377–404). New York: Guilford Press.

Fine, M., & Turner, J. (1991). Tyranny and freedom: Looking at ideas in the practice of family therapy. *Family Process, 30,* 307–320.

Fine, M., & Turner, J. (1995). Collaborative supervision: Minding the power. (Chapter 16 in this book.)

Flax, J. (1992). The end of innocence. In. J. Butler & J. Scott (Eds.), *Feminists theorize the political* (pp. 445–463). New York: Routledge.

Gergen, K. (1991). *The saturated self: Dilemmas of identity in contemporary life.* New York: Basic Books.

Gergen, K. (1985). The social constructionist movement in modern psychology. *American Psychologist, 40,* 266–275.

Gilligan, C. (1982). *In a different voice.* Cambridge: Harvard University Press.

Goldner, V. (1991). Sex, power, and gender: A feminist analysis of the politics of passion. In T. Goodrich (Ed.), *Women and power: Perspectives for family therapy* (pp. 86–106). New York: W. W. Norton.

Goode, W. (1982). Why men resist. In B. Thorne & M. Yalom (Eds.), *Re-thinking the family: Some feminist questions* (pp. 131–150). New York: Longman.

Haraway, D. (1991). *Simians, cyborgs, and women.* New York: Routledge.

Hare-Mustin, R. (1978). A feminist approach to family therapy. *Family Process, 17,* 181–194.

Hare-Mustin, R. (1994). Discourses in the mirrored room: A postmodern analysis of therapy. *Family Process, 33,* 19–35.

Harvey, D. (1989). *The condition of postmodernity.* Cambridge: Blackwell.

hooks, b. (1990). *Yearning: Race, gender, and cultural politics.* Toronto: Between the Lines Press.

Kaiser, R. (1992). The supervisory relationship: An identification of the primary elements in the relationship and an application of two theories of ethical relationships. *Journal of Marital and Family Therapy, 18,* 283–296.

Kliman, J. (1994). The interweaving of gender, class, and race in family therapy. In M. P. Mirkin (Ed.), *Women in context: Toward a feminist reconstruction of psychotherapy* (pp. 25–47). New York: Guilford Press.

Libow, J. (1986). Training family therapists as feminists. In M. Ault-Riche (Ed.), *Women and family therapy* (pp. 16–24). Rockville, MD: Aspen.

Mac Kune-Karrer, B., Simmons, V., Stathos, K., & Weigel-Foy, C. (1994). Gender beliefs in training/supervision: Removing constraints. Workshop presentation at the Conference of the American Association for Marriage and Family Therapy, Chicago, October.

McIntyre, D. (1991). Social justice. *Australian and New Zealand Journal of Family Therapy, 12,* 79–84.

Meth, R., & Pasick, R. (1990). *Men in therapy: The challenge of change.* New York: Guilford Press.

Nelson, T. (1991). Gender in family therapy supervision. *Contemporary Family Therapy, 13,* 357–369.

Nutt, R. (1991). Family therapy training issues of male students in a gender-sensitive doctoral program. In M. Bograd (Ed.), *Feminist approaches for men in family therapy* (pp. 261–266). New York: Haworth Press.

Okun, B. (1983). Gender issues of family systems therapists. In B. Okun & S. Gladding (Eds.), *Issues in training marriage and family therapists* (pp. 43–58). Ann Arbor, MI: ERIC/CAPS.

Osherson, S. (1986). *Finding our fathers: How a man's life is shaped by his relationship with his father.* New York: Fawcett Columbine.

Porter, N., & Yahne, C. (1994). Feminist ethics and advocacy in the training of family therapists. *Journal of Feminist Family Therapy, 6,* 29–48.

Reid, E., McDaniel, S., Donaldson, C., & Tollers, M. (1987). Taking it personally: Issues of personal authority and competence for the female in family therapy training. *Journal of Marital and Family Therapy, 13,* 157–165.

Roberts, J. (1991). Sugar and spice, toads and mice: Gender issues in family therapy training. *Journal of Marital and Family Therapy, 17,* 121–132.

Sirles, E. (1994). Teaching feminist family therapy: Practicing what we preach. *Journal of Feminist Family Therapy, 6,* 1–26.

Stiver, I. (1991). The meanings of "dependency" in female–male relationships. In J. Jordan, A. Kaplan, J. Baker, I. Stiver & J. Surrey (Eds.), *Women's growth in connection: Writings from the Stone Center* (pp. 143–161). New York: Guilford Press.

Storm, C. (1991). Placing gender in the heart of MFT master's programs: Teaching a gender sensitive systemic view. *Journal of Marital and Family Therapy, 17,* 45–52.

Surrey, J. (1991). Relationship and empowerment. In J. Jorndan, A. Kaplan, J. Miller, I. Stiver & J. Surrey (Eds.), *Women's growth in connection: Writings from the Stone Center* (pp. 162–180). New York: Guilford Press.

Tamasese, K., & Waldegrave, C. (1993). Cultural and gender accountability in the "just therapy" approach. *Journal of Feminist Family Therapy, 5,* 29–45.

Turner, J. (1993). Males supervising females: The risk of gender-power blindness. *Supervision Bulletin, 6,* 4, 6.

Waldegrave, C. (1986). Mono-cultural, mono-class, and so called non-political family therapy. *Australian and New Zealand Journal of Family Therapy, 6,* 197–200.

Warburton, J., Newberry, A., & Alexander, J. (1989). Women as therapists, trainees, and supervisors. In M. McGoldrick, C. Anderson, & F. Walsh (Eds.), *Women in families: A framework for family therapy* (pp. 152–165). New York: W. W. Norton.

Watson, M. (1993). Supervising the person of the therapist: Issues, challenges and dilemmas. *Contemporary Family Therapy, 15,* 21–31.

Wheeler, D., Avis, J., Miller, L., & Chaney, S. (1989). Rethinking family therapy training and supervision: A feminist model. In M. McGoldrick, C. Anderson, & F. Walsh (Eds.), *Women in families: A framework for family therapy* (pp. 135–151). New York: W. W. Norton.

7

Four Supervisory Practices That Foster Respect for Difference

Anne Hearon Rambo and Lee Shilts

Recent debate (Anderson, 1994; Hardy, 1994; Shields et al., 1994) has focused on the search for a "focal point" (Anderson, 1994, p. 145) in marriage and family therapy (MFT) supervision and training. As the director of a MFT master's degree program, the first author is frequently asked by prospective students what sets MFT apart from other mental health disciplines such as social work, psychology, and mental health counseling. There are many answers to this question, including the historical, the conceptual, and the pragmatic. But sometimes the question is phrased more personally: "Why *did* you become a family therapist?"

To this question, only one answer leaps to mind, but it often is not the answer prospective students expect. Their assumption tends to be that family therapists are not particularly interested in individuals; to the contrary, our experience is that family therapists are most different from other therapists in the very intensity of their respect for individual difference. Like many who now practice MFT, the first author was initially trained in another field. As a clinical social worker, specializing in techniques of individual play therapy, she experienced herself as (regretfully) attempting to mold children to better fit their context—smoothing out the spikey peculiarities their teachers and parents could least tolerate. It was with great relief that she stumbled on MFT and

this way of working, which offered the option of altering the context instead, opening more space for each individual, quirks and all.

This chapter's second author experienced a similar transition. As a cognitive/behavioral individual therapist, he became frustrated with his clients' apparent slowness to change their irrational thoughts and restrictive belief systems. As his perspective shifted to interaction, and the social construction of reality, he marvelled instead at the speed of change in conversation.

MFT's focus on contextual change frees us to respect individual difference and protest overly restrictive contexts. Changing the context, rather than pathologizing the person, is a theme that runs through not just the individual histories of family therapists, but also through the history of the field, from the original family therapists' protest against the acontextual consideration of schizophrenia through the feminist family therapists' advocacy of social change, up to and including the current discussion of multicultural awareness. All fields of psychotherapy share a concern for clients; but we would argue that MFT is unique in its liberating focus on contextual change. It is that liberating aspect of family (systems) therapy that continues to make its practice a joy, and which we suggest as an organizing experience—*A FOCAL POINT*—for socialization into the field.

We propose the following four practices designed to increase appreciation of diversity and particularity: 1) reference to the client as an integral co-creator of the therapy process, 2) awareness of the therapy context, 3) appreciation of language and skill in its use, and 4) concrete experience with cultural diversity and the particularities of others' lives. For each practice, we briefly describe the supervision goals, and suggest specific exercises useful with beginning therapists in a didactic or academic setting, with practicing therapists ready for more case-specific supervision, and with experienced therapists seeking a new challenge. Our assumptions are that beginning therapists have little previous contact with clients; intermediate therapists are in practice, but not independently; and experienced therapists are practicing with minimal supervision. We concur with Mead's (1990) formulation that, in general, supervisees move from a need for more structure to a desire for less. Additional detail regarding the exercises is available in this book's *Resource Guide*.

THE FIRST PRACTICE: PRIVILEGING THE CLIENT'S VOICE

Recent discussion in the field (Anderson & Goolishian, 1990; deShazer & Berg, 1992) has focused on MFT as a collaborative process. Rather than seeing therapists as acting on clients, the proposed picture is one of therapists and clients acting together in conversation. Of equal importance to the authors is the grounding of supervisor's "wisdom"—the additional vision implied by the term—in something other than institutional hierarchy alone. Supervision, also, can be an acting with rather than a unilateral enforcement of the supervisor's style or model. Yet, both in therapy and supervision, in our view it is not useful to be so collaborative and nonimposing that one fails to do one's job, to introduce sufficient difference to meet the client's (and the supervisee's) request for change.

We have found it possible to avoid either imposing a model unilaterally or relapsing into inaction by keeping both therapy and supervision focused on the client's voice. With beginning therapists, with access to live supervision, this goal can be met by positioning the supervisor as the living anchor—the person responsible for keeping the therapy grounded in the particulars of each client situation. The client then becomes the expert, the authority on those particularities. This leaves the supervisee free to try any and all therapeutic approaches, subject to the restraining voice of the client, as encouraged by the supervisor.

In practice, live supervision typically may begin with the supervisor in the room with the supervisee and the client(s). The supervisor is introduced as a sort of "anchor" person who works to keep the therapist and client connected in a unique way. Many of the clients we see at our university clinic are multiproblem families referred by other agencies, and, usually, they enthusiastically agree with the premise that it is possible for therapists and clients to wander in separate directions, to their mutual frustration. Most families can supply an example or two of their own frustrating experiences with helping professionals.

The supervisor then introduces a series of questions, questions asked of clients by the supervisor, to provide that anchoring:

- Do you feel the therapist is hearing and understanding your situation?
- Is there anything he or she seems to be missing?
- Is anything happening differently for you since you've been coming here?
- Would you like to see more difference, less difference, the same?

- Do you have any ideas about how that might happen?
- Do you have any (other) suggestions for the therapist?

As always in therapy, we consider the skillful use of questions to be crucial here; questions that put the client on the spot with respect to approving or disapproving of his or her therapist would clearly be inappropriate. The questions should focus on what the client is finding more and less useful, in a reflective, nonjudgmental way. Such questioning positions the client as a co-author of the therapeutic story. This does not abrogate the supervisor's responsibility, but it includes the client's voice as well.

The supervisor explains that he or she may intervene to stop the process, enter the room, and explore these questions routinely, to begin the second, fourth, sixth, and any subsequent sessions: when requested by the supervisee, when requested by the client, and/or when made uneasy by what the supervisor is seeing. In between these times, the supervisor takes an observing role, either behind a one-way mirror or in a corner of the therapy room. (The authors find that the physical location of the supervisor is best left to the consensus of supervisee and client and should be what is most comfortable for both of them.)

Supervisees who hear directly from their clients that they are not joining well, not introducing sufficient difference, or overwhelming the client with interventions, are likely to be sincerely motivated to seek help with these skills. At the same time, clients have been identified as a potential resource for building these same therapist skills, and so given a corresponding responsibility for their own satisfaction. The therapy remains focused on the client–therapist experience rather than on school of therapy, current fashionable technique, or supervisor–supervisee differences.

When differences between supervisor and supervisee do arise (for example, when a supervisor feels the urgency of the client's complaint is not being heeded, and the supervisee disagrees), the issue can be referred openly to the client for ultimate clarification. This cuts down on the hidden, behind the one-way mirror group processing and occasional tension, which has reportedly been confusing for some clients experiencing live supervision of their therapy (Schwartz, Liddle, & Breunlin, 1988; Wright, 1986). Most important, we hope that such a model exemplifies respect for the individual particularity of the client's voice.

With more experienced therapists, the supervisor's questions of the client may be saved for "stuck" situations, when supervisor and therapist are at variance, or the therapy seems not to be progressing. When ongoing live supervision is not an option, the supervisor may be brought into the room with the client on a one-shot basis, and introduced as a consultant for just this purpose.

For experienced therapists, the challenge may be to move from this kind of impromptu and ongoing inclusion of the client's assessment to a more formal outcome measure, which keeps the virtue of ongoing corrective feedback, yet adds the external credibility of accepted measures. A recent study (Doherty & Simmons, 1995) of MFT practice patterns, utilizing in-depth questionnaires given to MFT clients, is a good step in this direction. Truly "client-driven" (Shilts, Filipino, & Nau, 1994, p. 30) interviews can lead to client-focused assessments of one's practice.

This ongoing assessment and reevaluation, in turn, is our best guard against overgeneralizing and stereotyping. Hartman (1994) comments that the overly glib generalizations she learned in her graduate social work education, such as "Women who give their child up for adoption recover quickly from the experience," were all undone when particular, individual clients provided contradictions from their own experience. Beginning and advanced therapists alike benefit when we remind ourselves that our work is grounded, not in the abstractions of model or theory, but in the concrete individuality of each client's experience with us.

THE SECOND PRACTICE: REMAINING AWARE OF OUR CONTEXT

Recently, as part of a panel, the first author presented a review of MFT history. Some members of the audience persistently mourned aloud over the lost golden days and vanished opportunities for family therapists entering the field. Thinking them simply lacking in information, she happily pulled out facts and figures relating to the burgeoning job opportunities for her program's graduates. For several years now there have been more hospitals, social service agencies, and state facilities wanting MFT professionals than MFT graduates to fill the positions. But, she was told, those jobs do not count: "Those are all jobs *in* places; before we did not have to worry about being *in* someplace else."

If there ever were true family therapists who could practice someplace that was not inside of some larger social entity, who could blissfully ignore the exigencies of context, those days are indeed gone. This has implications for supervision in two ways. First, we will survive better if we train ourselves and the next generation to be aware of our professional context. Second, and more important, we will serve our clients better if we perceive that, for them, our services are a part of the matrix of opportunities and constraints that make up their world. This awareness can be built into our supervision practice in several ways.

For beginning therapists, it can be useful as a didactic exercise to practice budgeting for hypothetical MFT. If they were to seek out

MFT, where would they go? From whom would they seek a recommendation? How much would it cost them, and what else would they have to give up to be able to afford this? We may offer our clients infinitely more than eating out at restaurants twice a week, or taking a vacation, but often we do not cost any less, and may cost quite a bit more. What level of distress would be necessary before the sacrifice was worth it? It is important not to confuse this issue with the free or low-cost, exploratory, family-of-origin work offered by many programs to beginning therapists. The question is: What would it cost, in both pride and financial expense, to seek out a stranger and confess a major family problem, quite apart from one's professional preparation? Often MFT students are surprisingly naive about what their insurance covers, and about the typical cost of therapy services.

With more experienced therapists, and a particular case, especially one that seems to be "stuck," it can be useful for the supervisor to find out, either directly as a consultant or indirectly through the therapist, what this therapy means in the material context of the family. To find this out, it is necessary to ask all the questions therapists are traditionally too polite to ask:

- What would you spend these dollars on if you weren't spending them on therapy?
- What is not happening that would usually happen during the hour you are here?
- Will someone have to work more later to make up (to make up the absence at work, to wash the dishes that weren't washed because of rushing to the appointment, and so on)?
- What is this costing you (in every sense of the word), and what do you expect in return?
- If Dad's employer is letting him have time off from work to come to therapy, what is the employer expecting in return?

Increasingly, these are questions that are asked about *all* participants in the therapy process. Money, time, and loss of privacy are all costs of receiving therapy, and it behooves us to know in detail how much we are costing our clients, and why.

For senior therapists, it may be possible to intervene in, as well as try to understand, the context of the mental health delivery system. Managed care has found a responsive climate in large part because many employers and insurance companies perceive that mental health professionals charge too much, report too vaguely, and perform too little, and it is probable that all too many of the general public agree with this assessment. How could we raise our standards and position ourselves in context in a different way? One approach to strengthening our difference is for MFTs to band together in collaborative ways, with each other and with other professionals. In our regional area, this has meant breakfast meetings of MFTs with MFT students; interest groups around the issues of collaborative family health care and psychotherapy with the terminally ill, which cut across disciplinary lines; and a long-running social/support group for isolated MFTs in private practice. In addition to encouraging supervisees to join professional organizations and pursue appropriate licensure, supervisors can set the example of attention to context by their own attentiveness to colleagues. As we share with and learn from each other, we spin a web of connection that supports our work.

THE THIRD PRACTICE: TRAINING IN LANGUAGE SKILLS

The consideration of what therapy costs, as discussed before, leads us to the consideration of what it is we are selling. Since the 1970s, family therapists, in particular, have become increasingly uncomfortable with a view of the therapist as an hierarchically superior expert, with "correct" answers for family living (Goolishian, 1990). Although epistemological debate around the concepts of second-order cybernetics was a catalyst for this discomfort in the 1970s and 1980s, a distrust of pat solutions was actually imbedded in the field from its inception, given the historical family therapy emphasis on observation and, above all, on continued learning from families themselves (Broderick & Schrader, 1981; Jackson, 1961).

Still our clients clearly come to us, and pay us hard-earned money, based on the belief that we have *some* special skill to offer. It has been suggested that this expertise is best understood as an expertise in conversation (Anderson & Goolishian, 1990), in "the weaving of words" (Keeney, 1990, p. 6), in curiosity about language (Byrne & McCarthy, 1988), in the ambiguation of meaning (Hoffman, 1990)—in short, in language itself. Our clients can remain experts on their lives, authors of their own stories, if you will (White & Epston, 1990), while still finding it useful to consult with a therapist who is practiced in the process of story-making itself. If we can give our clients nothing else, we can always give them a space to play with words, and the company of someone (ourselves) who loves language.

For beginning therapists, this may best involve practice with language outside the therapy room, as well as within it. Supervisees may be too anxious to play with language when they lack experience and skill. Play provides the opportunity to experiment in safety, to launch trial explorations into the not yet familiar. Therapy, like play, exists as a unique context clearly defined as separate and apart from everyday life (Bateson, 1972); thus, it can also become a context in which to explore options. It can embody an enchanted space, like the mythical "third province" of Irish folklore (Byrne & McCarthy, 1988). But, in therapy, the play is primarily with words and their attendant meanings. A supervisee anxious to deliver the "correct" intervention, and/or please the supervisor, may be too constrained to experience this.

Beginning exercises in simple listening and observation are helpful warm-ups. Heath (1993) presents several such exercises, including tracking everyday conversations, counting the number of times you ask questions in a particular way, and noticing details of others' dress. Supervisees may also benefit from visiting day-care centers, crowded shopping malls, hospitals, and other prime sites of interaction, and learning to simply sit and overhear conversations. Novels, movies, and plays provide rich opportunities for hearing talk.

As the beginning therapist learns to listen to the fascinating stories all around us, it becomes useful to consider the nature of "story" itself. In Western culture, the story form is a relatively fixed one. The individual hero is first confronted with, and then vanquishes or is vanquished by, an evil (Rambo, 1993). Outside of therapy, the supervisee can practice constructing and deconstructing stories, both ancient (fairy tales) and thoroughly modern (self-help texts). (Details of these exercises are given in this book's *Resource Guide.*)

In case-specific supervision, the supervisor can use the therapist's new knowledge of the basic story form to assist the therapist to hear the client's story in a new way. What would happen if the focus was not individual, but interactional? What would happen if the evil turned out not to be so evil, or the hero and the villain reached a compromise? (Story deconstructing/transforming questions are given in this book's *Resource Guide.*) The language of story gives supervisor and supervisee a common language across models—where one hears exceptions to the problem, the other may hear family-of-origin issues, but both can hear the familiar cultural theme of a lucky escape from your past (from Cinderella to Horatio Alger).

Finally, experienced therapists can renew their appreciation of language by focusing in at a microlevel. Chenail (1993) discusses one case in detail, using the qualitative research technique of recursive frame analysis. Working from an audiotape of a therapy session, the listener attends to shifts in the talk, from one set of meanings to another, and represents these shifts in visual form. Through this technique, the reader can "hear" at a level of precision not usually experienced. Similarly, Brown and Gilligan (1992) discuss their "voice-sensitive" (p. 25) approach to hearing and rehearing their interviews. They listen to the tape of each session at least four times, attending first to the story; then to voice of self; then to their response as listeners; and finally to their resistance, or objections, as listeners (Brown & Gilligan, 1992).

Such microanalysis can be a fascinating supervision approach with a therapist ready for a challenge and/or with oneself; listening at this close level makes it impossible to hear even a familiar story in quite the same way. For example, one supervisee, hearing herself over and over on tape, recognized how clearly the high pitch of her voice betrayed her discomfort—and how differently her clients responded when her voice relaxed and deepened. In researching her client's talk, she learned something quite specific about her own voice.

Whether being introduced to the sheer multiplicity of voices, telling and transforming stories, or listening like a researcher listens, therapists who are alert to language gain expertise in the basic tools of their trade. Supervision that fosters this expertise fosters more fluid and flexible therapy, less given to constraining language and rigid thought.

The novelist and psychiatrist Percy (1987) writes:

It is a matter for astonishment, when one comes to think of it, how little use linguistics and other sciences of language are to psychiatrists. When one considers that the psychiatrist spends most of his [or her] time listening and talking to patients, one might suppose that there would be such a thing as a basic science of listening-and-talking, as indispensable to psychiatrists as anatomy to surgeons (p. 159).

Such a basic science may be still more essential for MFTs. If and when we can easily engage in conversation, we have what we need to shift contexts.

THE FOURTH PRACTICE: "SHADOWING" OR STANDING IN A DIFFERENT PLACE

Language alone is not enough, however; part of learning about difference is the visceral experience of it. *Planned, concrete exposure* to cultural diversity is the most recent addition to our repertoire of practices, and it may become the most challenging. Jabouin (1994) describes her work with Haitian-American immigrant families, in which she acts as an advocate and a bridge between the Creole-speaking and English-speaking communities, as "shadowing." With recently arrived Haitian immigrants in government offices, she is standing with, not merely translating for, these families. This word fit for us when we began to describe the experiential exercises we were constructing to help our supervisees literally stand in a different context.

For beginning therapists, such experiences may need to be quite structured. Without outside intervention, most of us, however much we may think and talk about others' lives, do not see, hear, touch, taste, and smell much outside of our neighborhoods, our own familiar

contexts. In one exercise, supervisees were challenged to broaden their experience of human diversity through focused participation in a hypothetical "family."

Such hypothetical "families" can be constructed by the supervisor to reflect ethnic, socioeconomic, and cultural groups prevalent in the practice area. Or, supervisees may be asked to create a hypothetical "family" most different from their own family of origin. More advanced supervisees, already in practice, may construct a "family" similar to those families with whom they have the most difficulty joining. The hypothetical "family" constructed out of supervisor-and-supervisee experience could be briefly described as follows:

Marie and Jeanbart Desvarieux emigrated to the United States from Haiti six months ago. They have not yet been able to obtain legal citizenship status. Marie and Jeanbart work together in their own house and office cleaning business. They work as many hours as they can, six to seven days a week and, thus, are able to average an income of $250 a week. They are both fluent in Creole; both understand some English—at present, Jeanbart speaks somewhat more fluently. Their formal education was limited because of warlike conditions in Haiti. Jeanbart suffers from recurring nightmares about his torture at the hands of the military police in Port au Prince. Marie and Jeanbart are practicing Catholics. They are both 22 and are expecting their first child in October.

Other families constructed ranged from low- to high-income levels; spoke English, Spanish, Hebrew, and Creole; were of Cuban-American, African-American, and European-American descent; and were Protestant, Jewish, or Catholic. Once a description is generated, "family" members complete a series of assignments designed to cover the typical developmental tasks of any family with a child: finding child care, dealing with schools, moving through adolescence, and so on. (Assignments, and additional details, are given in the *Resource Guide*.) Typically, extremes of poverty and affluence were difficult differences for our supervisees to experience. Also, supervisees whose families arrived in this country more than twenty years ago found the experiences of more recent immigrant families very different, and vice versa.

In the course of completing their assignments, supervisees dealt with realtors, or walked door to door looking for rooms for rent, depending on their "shadow" family's income level. Among other interesting discoveries, supervisees learned first-hand that grocery store prices are generally much higher in low-income areas, which came as a shock to many of them. Their indignation ("But my family can't afford that!") led them to the understanding that poverty is not simply a lack of money but a lack of options as well. If a gallon of milk costs ten cents more at one suburban store than at another, an affluent family can drive to the store with better prices; a low-income family may be limited to the one store within walking distance of the only housing they can afford. Following such discoveries, supervisors noted more sensitive questioning of families around their life circumstances, and less blithe assumptions about available options.

Inevitably, completing the tasks led supervisees into conversations in the community they would not have otherwise experienced. These out-of-context encounters were sometimes comic, and sometimes sad. One supervisee, by profession and training a rabbi, was asked by the other members of her hypothetical "family" to investigate the "family's" birth control options. When she found herself shouting at the third Catholic priest who explained the church's policy to her, she ruefully reflected that ecumenical dialogue was not as easy when one was personally invested in the fate of a hypothetical nineteen-year-old who is fearful of having too many babies too soon. A group member "shadowing" a hypothetical affluent African-American family became frustrated when realtor after realtor kept showing him affluent suburbs populated primarily by European-Americans despite his stated preference for a more culturally diverse neighborhood. The implicitly still segregated nature of many of the area's suburbs could not be openly discussed with realtors fearful of violating a law, or deviating from their usual practices; instead, he took to questioning affluent-looking African-American couples in the shopping mall about where they lived, an activity understandably viewed with suspicion by the mall security guard. Unlike a classroom-bound didactic exercise, the line between hypothetical and actual blurred quickly in these encounters. Actually standing in line at the immigration office, or waiting for food stamps, provides an empathetic experience no amount of abstract sympathy can provide.

In case-specific supervision, supervisees can be asked to "shadow" the daily life of a particular client family. If a therapist is failing to join with an overwhelmed single mother, perhaps he can set his alarm clock one day to keep the same hours as she does. After one such experience, the therapist not only stopped asking the client to spend more quality time with her children, but congratulated her on surviving; one day of rising at five (when the baby wakes up) and not turning out the light until midnight (when the last load of laundry is done) altered his perspective viscerally. If the therapist does not understand the family's protective insistence on keeping younger children indoors, perhaps she can go after dark to buy a quart of milk at the convenience store in the family's neighborhood and experience the atmosphere of threat they do not know how to convey to her. The clients can be involved in constructing such experiences, as when one of our supervisee's clients taught her how to experience a hallucination (Rambo, 1993).

The last and most difficult experience of difference, of course, is going back to one's own context in a different way. Viscerally experiencing one's half-suppressed biases and limitations can be painful, but it is surely essential to a true understanding of difference. We have found the following questions useful starting points for an in-depth supervisory conversation:

- What kinds of difference are you most comfortable with?
- What kinds of difference are you most uncomfortable with?
- When dealing with difference, and perceiving others as less privileged than yourself, are you more likely to err in the direction of naive colonialism ("I can fix them! I know just the programs to sign them up for") or paralyzing guilt/empathy ("I do not know what to say; I better not say anything; Maybe somebody else can take this case")?

Supervisees will naturally want to say that they do neither, and can perfectly balance appropriate concern with respectful nonintrusiveness. We all wish we could do that; but we all make mistakes, and offend others. It is clinically very useful to know *in which direction* you are likely to err. When dealing with difference, and perceiving others as more privileged than yourself, are you more likely to err in the direction of pretense ("There aren't really any differences here, it's not important; They'll accept me pretty soon anyway") or condemnation ("They're all alike, I hate them")? Again, supervisees should identify their likely direction of error.

In the final analysis, such conversations open our supervision to the world outside. They also return us to what is unique about family therapy, the intense consideration of individual difference in context.

A UNIFYING GOAL ACROSS MODELS

Historically, MFT supervision corresponds isomorphically to the various models of MFT its supervisors represented (Schwartz, Liddle, & Breunlin, 1988). We concur with Anderson (1994) that, in the complex reality of modern delivery systems, MFT will need a unifying "magnet" (p. 147) to hold together its diverse practitioners. We suggest one possible magnet is the celebration of difference, a celebration enriched by the constant, poignant awareness of context, with all its constraints. MFT supervision, then, would need to incorporate practices across models that foster both respect for individual difference and awareness of context. Such supervision should itself incorporate respect for individual difference, in adapting to the differing needs of beginning, intermediate, and advanced supervisees (Mead, 1990). The four practices presented here are a step toward that goal; we invite discussion of other, similar practices others may have evolved.

REFERENCES

Anderson, H. (1994). Rethinking family therapy: A delicate balance. _Journal of Marital and Family Therapy, 20,_ 145–150.

Anderson, H., & Goolishian, H. (1990). Supervision as collaborative conversation: Questions and reflections. In H. Brandau (Ed.), _Von der supervision zur systemischen vision._ Salzburg: Otto Muller Verlag.

Bateson, G. (1972). _Steps to an ecology of mind._ New York: Random House.

Broderick, C., & Schrader, S. (1981). The history of professional marital and family therapy. In A. Gurman & D. Kniskern (Eds.), _The handbook of family therapy_ (pp. 5–35). New York: Brunner/Mazel.

Brown, L., & Gilligan, C. (1992). _Meeting at the crossroads: Women's psychology and child development._ Cambridge: Harvard University Press.

Bryne, N., & McCarthy, I. (1988). Moving statutes: Re-questing ambivalence through ambiguous discourse. _The Irish Journal of Psychotherapy, 9,_ 173–182.

Chenail, R. (1993). Making maps. In A. Rambo, A. Heath, & R. Chenail (Eds.), *Practicing therapy* (pp. 155–265). New York: W. W. Norton.

deShazer, S., & Berg, I. (1992). Doing therapy: A post-structural re-vision. *Journal of Marital and Family Therapy 18*, 71–81.

Doherty, W., & Simmons, D. (1995). Dealing with who we are and what we do: Clinical practice patterns of marriage and family therapists in Minnesota. *Journal of Marital and Family Therapy, 21*, 3–16.

Goolishian, H. (1990). Family therapy: An evolving story. *Contemporary Family Therapy, 12*, 173–180.

Hardy, K. (1994). Marginalization or development? A response to Shields, Wynne, McDaniel, and Gawinski. *Journal of Marital and Family Therapy, 20*, 117–138.

Hartman, A. (1994). Speech given at the New Voices in Human Systems conference, Northhampton, MA, October.

Heath, A. (1993). Reading signs. In A. Rambo, A. Heath, & R. Chenail, *Practicing therapy: Exercises for growing therapists* (pp. 89–153). New York: W. W. Norton.

Hoffman, L. (1990). Constructing realities: An art of lenses. *Family Process, 29*, 1–12.

Jabouin, F. (1994). Personal communication, November 2.

Jackson, D. (1961). Interactional psychotherapy. In M. Stein (Ed.), *Contemporary psychotherapies* (pp. 256–271). New York: The Free Press of Glencoe, Inc.

Keeney, B. (1990). *Improvisational therapy.* St. Paul, MN: Systemic Therapy Press.

Mead, D. (1990). *Effective supervision: A task-oriented model for the mental health professions.* New York: Brunner/Mazel.

Percy, W. (1987). *The message in the bottle: How queer man is, how queer language is, and what one has to do with the other.* New York: Farrar, Strauss, & Giroux.

Rambo, A. (1993). Hearing stories. In A. Rambo, A. Heath, & R. Chenail, *Practicing therapy: Exercises for growing therapists* (pp. 13–85). New York: W. W. Norton.

Schwartz, R., Liddle, H., & Breunlin, D. (1988). Muddles in live supervision. In H. Liddle, D. Breunlin, & R. Schwartz (Eds.), *Handbook of family therapy training and supervision* (pp. 183–193). New York: Guilford Press.

Shields, C., Wynne, L., McDaniel, S., & Gawinski, B. (1994). The marginalization of family therapy: A historical and continuing problem. *Journal of Marital and Family Therapy, 20*, 117–138.

Shilts, L., Filipino, C., & Nau, D. (1994). Client-informed therapy. *Journal of Systemic Therapies, 13*, 39–52.

White, M., & Epstein, D. (1990). *Narrative means to therapeutic ends.* New York: W. W. Norton.

Wright, L. (1986). An analysis of live supervision "phone-ins" in family therapy. *Journal of Marriage and Family Therapy, 12*, 187–190.

8

The Ivory Tower and
the Institute
Supervision in Educational Programs

Cheryl L. Storm and Douglas H. Sprenkle

Supervised practice is a significant component of all marriage and family therapy (MFT) educational programs. Because of the demand for supervisory services by a growing number of MFT educational programs, many supervisors will have the exciting opportunity of affiliating with doctoral, master's degree, or postgraduate educational programs sometime in their supervision careers. In fact, a recent study of Approved Supervisors designated by the American Association for Marriage and Family Therapy (AAMFT) found supervisors are increasingly affiliating with educational programs and practicing their craft within them rather than in their private practices (Nichols, Nichols, & Hardy, 1990). Although there are literally dozens of articles describing MFT educational programs at universities (Bardill & Saunders, 1988; Berger, 1988; Combrinck-Graham, 1988; Cooper, Rampage, & Soucy, 1981; Everett, 1979; Garfield & Lord, 1982; Meltzer, 1973; Nichols, 1979, 1988; Sprenkle, 1988; Winkle, Piercy, & Hovestadt, 1981), and in postdegree training institutes (Berman & Dixon-Murphy, 1979; Herz & Carter, 1988; LaPerriere, 1979; Van Trommell, 1982; Wright & Leahey, 1988), the unique aspects of supervising within these contexts are only fleetingly mentioned. In this chapter, you learn about supervising in educational programs and the tradeoffs to make when supervising in this

setting, rather than contracting privately with supervisees.

DIFFERENCES BETWEEN THE IVORY TOWER AND THE INSTITUTE SETTING

In this section, supervision in entry-level, degree-granting programs is compared with postgraduate programs. Because the master's degree has evolved as the entry-level credential for the MFT profession, the number of master's degree programs exceeds doctoral programs, and the greatest growth in MFT university programs is at the master's level (Joanning, Morris, & Dennis, 1985; Sprenkle, 1988); the major focus of this chapter is a comparison of supervision in master's programs to supervision in postgraduate programs. Because more postgraduate programs are affiliated with free-standing institutes rather than with universities, supervision is discussed as it tends to occur in free-standing institute programs. Criteria for the comparison include: influence of the wider context, supervisor and supervisee characteristics, the learning goals, the supervision format, supervisee clinical practice, the supervisory relationship, and evaluation of supervision (see Table 8-1). Because entry-level, degree-granting programs

TABLE 8-1. Comparison of Supervision in Academic and Institute Contexts

	University Setting	Institute Setting
Influence of Wider Context	University culture	Marketplace
Supervisors	Generalists	Multidisciplinary specialists
	More percent of time in teaching and research	More percent of time in clinical work
	Diversity among supervisors in program	Similarity among supervisors in program
	Higher accountability for supervisees' work	Shared accountability for supervisees' work
Supervisees	Novices	Novices at MFT, but seasoned professionals
	Younger, with less life experience	Older, with more life experience
Learning Objectives	The basics	Additional learning
	Development of supervisees' unique models	Expertise in institutes' preferred model
	Socialization as MFT professionals	MFT identity added to existing professional one
Supervision Format	Within shorter academic course	Longer supervision contract
	Theory precedes clinical work	Simultaneous emphasis on theory and clinical work
Clinical Practice	More often on-site	More often off-site
	Focus on many cases	Can focus on fewer clinical cases
Relationship	Emphasis on experiencing variety	Emphasis on fit
	Multiple roles around educational activities	Multiple roles around professional activities
Evaluation	Highly structured and formally documented	More fluid and informal

and institute programs vary widely and no two programs are alike, the comparisons here are tentative generalizations offered to entice you to consider the unique aspects of supervising in these different educational programs.

The Influence of the Wider Context: University Culture versus Marketplace

Degree-granting programs are heavily influenced by university culture, structure, policies, and procedures. These ultimately determine matters such as who can be hired as supervi-

sors, where and when supervision occurs, and the overall role of supervision within the curriculum. In contrast, supervisors in institute programs are greatly influenced by the marketplace and "what works" given the available trainees, faculty, and their respective backgrounds (Herz & Carter, 1988). Employed professionals, the typical institute supervisees, are highly interested in gaining cost-effective, quality training without adding to their overloaded schedules (Herz & Carter, 1988). Consequently, institute supervisors must find creative ways to deliver quality supervision that fits with their supervisees' worklife.

When considering the specifics of supervision (e.g., what constitutes supervision, how much, ratio of individual to group formats, size of membership in group supervision, and so on), all educational programs are influenced to a large degree by licensing laws and credentialing requirements. Many also are influenced by accreditation standards developed by the Commission on Accreditation for Marriage and Family Therapy Education (COAMFTE), the nationally recognized accrediting body for MFT. Accreditation standards are highly developed and specific for doctoral, master's, and postgraduate programs (COAMFTE, 1996). Historically, the majority of educational programs accredited by the COAMFTE grant degrees. This is not surprising given the history of and acceptance of accreditation within universities and the challenges that exist in developing a postgraduate program. (See Herz & Carter [1988] for their experience in starting and maintaining a free-standing institute.)

Supervision practices are mandated when a program is accredited. For example, current accreditation standards for master's programs specify criteria such as the following: programs must offer 100 hours of supervision by AAMFT-Approved Supervisors or the equivalent, fifty percent must be videotaped or live supervision, group supervision can include up to six supervisees, supervised practice must occur over one calendar year, and so on. (COAMFTE, 1996). Those postgraduate programs that choose to become accredited must balance "what works" with the constraints of meeting accreditation standards. Nonaccredited MFT programs have more flexibility. In the remainder of the comparison, readers familiar with postgraduate programs accredited by the COAMFTE should consider supervision in them as more similar to degree-granting programs in their learning goals and similar to institute programs on the other criteria.

When degree-granting programs in a related discipline, such as social work, psychol-ogy, nursing, or medicine, have an MFT training component, supervision is defined by both disciplines. Some of these programs aim to grant a degree in both MFT and the parent discipline, others provide their students with a specialization in MFT, and some offer MFT as one of several electives (Fennell & Hovestadt, 1985; Hovestadt, Fennell, & Piercy, 1983). Supervision in the first type of program usually complies with national standards for the field of MFT and the parent discipline. When MFT is a program specialization, supervisees are supervised by a qualified MFT supervisor on a limited number of cases presenting marriage or family problems with the goal of supervisees' learning basic MFT skills. When MFT is an elective course of study, supervisees frequently are supervised on a few cases by a qualified psychotherapist with no formal training in MFT, with the goal of exposing supervisees to the practice of MFT and broadening their abilities. A major goal for supervisors affiliated with the latter two types of programs is to encourage their supervisees who are interested to become fully qualified marriage and family therapists by seeking additional MFT training and supervision. For a more in-depth discussion of MFT training in educational programs in other disciplines, see the section on Training Contexts in the *Handbook of Family Therapy Training and Supervision* by Liddle, Breunlin, & Schwartz (1988).

Supervisors: Generalists versus Specialists

In the university context, supervisors are expected to be generalists (Sprenkle, 1988). Although they may emphasize their preferred ideas about therapy, as generalists they are expected to be knowledgeable about the major theoretical approaches in the field and to be able to supervisee master's students practicing from a wide range of theories of therapy, as in the following example.

Sue, a supervisor who leans toward strategic ideas in her model of therapy, is currently overseeing the work of four supervisees. Two of them are novice therapists who have just begun practica. They are learning intergenerational approaches in their coursework and are unfamiliar with other models of therapy. Her other supervisees, who are half-way through their practica, are excited about the narrative approach and have previously studied structural and brief therapy models. One of them wishes to focus exclusively on applying the narra-tive approach to her cases while the other wants to integrate narrative ideas with structural and brief ways of working. Sue's university context re-quires her to adapt to her supervisees' models of therapy and assist them in developing their pre-ferred ways of working.

Supervisors affiliated with master's programs, therefore, must either have a philosophy of su-pervision that allows them to supervise thera-pists who are practicing from a range of models, change their philosophy of supervi-sion to fit with supervisees' preferences and curriculum (e.g., use a structural philosophy of supervision with supervisees learning struc-tural therapy, a narrative philosophy of super-vision with supervisees learning narrative therapy, and so on), or contract with master's programs to selectively supervise students practicing from particular therapy approaches.

Most institutes, in contrast, are well known for a specific approach to therapy. For example, the Family Therapy Institute of Washington, DC, is renowned for the strategic approach, while the Brief Therapy Institute of Milwau-kee is the prime site for solution-focused ther-apy training. Because supervisors specify their theoretical preferences more clearly (Henry, Sprenkle, & Sheehan, 1986), supervisees essen-tially adapt to supervisors' models via selecting to train at the institute. It would be highly un-likely for a trainee at the Mental Research In-stitute training program to have a supervisor

who has a psychodynamic philosophy of ther-apy and supervision! Supervisors and super-visees practice from the same set of ideas, allowing supervisors to develop a philosophy of supervision to fit a particular approach to ther-apy. For example, Cantwell and Holmes (1995), in describing their institute's supervision phi-losophy, base their underlying assumptions and accompanying methods on social con-structionist theory. Their assumption that there is no right way of doing therapy leads them to prefer that supervision occur in teams and in groups where multiple views are expressed.

Because supervisors affiliated with univer-sity programs are expected to be generalists while those in institutes can be more special-ized, supervisors attached to university pro-grams may be more diverse from one another while those in institutes may be more similar to each other in their preferred ideas, methods, and styles. Supervisors who hold full-time fac-ulty positions in master's programs usually have the same professional degree because of the discipline/culture of the university, while institute supervisors tend to be multidiscipli-nary (Colapinto, 1988). Institute supervisors have more freedom to specify and to practice their preferences. A study comparing MFT training practices in universities with institutes found university faculty and students viewed their programs as more theoretically diverse while institute faculty and students cited their training as based on clearly expressed theoret-ical ideas (Henry, Sprenkle, & Sheehan, 1986). University supervisors who are full-time fac-ulty are also expected to be competent teachers and researchers, and they typically spend a smaller percentage of their time in the clinical realm. Although supervisors in institutes may also be involved in teaching and research, they tend to spend a much larger portion of their time in clinical practice. Supervisors affiliated with master's programs, but not full-time fac-ulty, tend to be more similar to institute super-visors.

Supervisees: Novices versus Seasoned Professionals

Generally, supervisors in master's programs work with more inexperienced therapists, frequently including supervisees who have never stepped into therapy rooms. Postgraduate program supervisors practice with more seasoned professionals, supervisees who already have a master's degree (Bloch & Weiss, 1981; Henry, Sprenkle, & Sheehan, 1986). Their supervisees frequently have counseling degrees and may even be credentialed mental health professionals. Often they are also professionals in a related profession, such as education, the ministry, or nursing, with significant professional experience.

Jan, a typical supervisee in a MFT master's program, has an undergraduate degree in psychology, interned at a battered women's shelter, and worked for a year as a residential counselor coordinating the daily living activities of adolescents in a group home. Although she has some professional experience, the role of therapist is entirely new to her. In contrast, Maria is the prototype for institute programs. She has a master's degree from a counseling psychology program and worked for eight years in several social service positions, including group worker and individual therapist for women with eating disorders. Her current position is as a therapist within the family and children's unit of a mental health center.

In master's programs, supervisees tend to be younger with less life experience. Sometimes supervisors find themselves indirectly helping their supervisees mature as young adults, perhaps even "leave home."

Twenty-three-year-old Tony was living at home with her parents who were also financing her graduate degree. Chris, her supervisor, received a call from her father inquiring about Tony's progress. After informing him that supervisee confidentiality prevented Chris from answering him, she helped Tony process ways to respond to her father's call as an adult rather than from her triggered "adolescent defiance" stance.

Supervision is different with this novice group; it requires more attention to professional socialization and supervisees' understanding of life experiences that most older supervisees have by the mere act of living longer. The one exception is the older supervisee who is making a career shift. For example, Brian, in his early forties, worked for years in the trades before returning to school for his undergraduate degree in psychology and his graduate degree in MFT. Interestingly, better consumer ratings of therapy have been found to be correlated with less life experience of supervisees (Anderson, 1992; Lyman, Storm, & York, 1995).

Supervising seasoned professionals with extensive professional and life experience gives supervision a flavor of its own. Supervisors can readily tap life experiences sometimes resulting in immediate empathetic responses of supervisees to clients. The increased professional experience can result in less attention in supervision to referral options and community resources.

Karl, a pastor participating in an institute program, is presenting the Clark family during group supervision. Originally, the family sought therapy because the fifteen-year-old girl was disobeying her parents. Recently, the girl was killed in a car accident by a drunk driver. Karl is at a loss regarding how to proceed. Stan, the supervisor, suggests Karl draw on his pastoral experiences to help the family come to terms with their grief.

Learning Objectives:
The Basics versus
Additional Learning

Because supervisees in master's programs tend to be obtaining their first professional degree, their supervisors focus more on basic competencies while ensuring that clients are receiving adequate services. Because postgraduate supervisees usually have previous professional experience in a helping profession, supervisors help them learn ways of practicing that challenge supervisees' traditional ways of working; essentially supervisors may be helping them to relearn some of the basics! Consider the two different supervision scenarios that follow. In the first case example, the supervisor assists the supervisee learn the basics of assessing for child abuse.

Bob is supervising Sam, a first-semester, master's-level, unmarried supervisee in his mid-twenties. As Bob is watching a videotaped session of Sam's work with a family, the father states he has spanked the six-year-old out of total frustration. The mother joins in saying the father is far too harsh with the child. Sam notes that he was uncomfortable with the father's remark and asks for guidance. He tentatively explored the potential of child abuse, however, Bob felt he had not gone far enough. Fortunately, the clients are scheduled to come again the same afternoon. The remainder of supervision is spent in reviewing ways to conduct the interview, including specific questions Sam could ask to check out child abuse, procedures for reporting child abuse, and planning therapeutic alternatives based on possible family members' responses.

In the second scenario, the supervisor is helping the supervisee relearn by bridging her past training to her present goals.

Michelle, a licensed clinical psychologist midway through an institute program in structural family therapy, is being supervised by Jack Michelle develops relationships well with clients one on one and has excellent interviewing skills. However, even with the best of intentions, she has difficulty allowing and directing family members to interact with each other. She understands the theoretical principle underlying enactments, but finds herself redirecting clients to talk with her rather than each other. When Jack inquires about her experience, Michelle explains that she learned to create an intense, intimate relationship with clients in her doctoral training which she misses when therapy focuses on family members' interaction with one another. Jack's supervisory challenge is to help Michelle feel useful and a part of the change process when she is not so central.

The overall learning objective for the supervision process in master's programs tends to be the application of several MFT models with an end goal of supervisees developing their own unique approach (Everett, 1979; Henry, Sprenkle, & Sheehan, 1986; Nichols, 1979). In fact, some educational programs require that supervisees do an "epistemological declaration" (Liddle, 1982) of their model before completing the program. In postgraduate programs, the encompassing supervision goal is for supervisees to become proficient in the approach offered by the institute (Berman & Dixon-Murphy, 1979; Bloch & Weiss, 1981; Henry, Sprenkle, & Sheehan, 1986). Supervisors in both settings focus on supervisees' professional socialization as marriage and family therapists. However, supervisors affiliated with master's programs are more often helping supervisees develop their first professional identity while postgraduate supervisors are encouraging the addition of another professional affiliation to their supervisees' existing ones (Sutton, 1985–86).

Supervision Format: Academic Course versus Supervision Contract

Although supervisors in both settings work toward supervisees' integration of theory and practice, they differ in their methods (see Piercy & Sprenkle, 1984; Colapinto, 1988; Papero, 1988; Pirotta & Cecchin, 1988 for examples of differing educational methods). In master's programs, classroom learning typically precedes clinical work. Thus, supervised practice takes the form of an academic course, which is believed to be optimal when it is begun at the midpoint of the student's first year (Keller, Huber, & Hardy, 1988). Because supervision is embedded in a course, the university calendar predetermines the length of supervisory relationships. It is not uncommon for supervisees to be assigned a new supervisor at the beginning of each term. Course requirements outlining supervision criteria (i.e., frequency, hour quotas, preparation, and so on) are applied similarly to all students enrolled in practica.

In contrast, supervision in postgraduate settings tends to begin almost immediately with theory integrated into clinical experience. Supervision takes the form of a more personalized supervision contract between supervisors and supervisees for a longer period of time, particularly when trainees receive supervision of cases in their own clinical practices. Although the supervision contract must meet overall program requirements, it allows for more flexibility. Supervision also often comprises a greater proportion of the curriculum in institutes (see Colapinto, 1988; Fisch, 1988; Mazza, 1988; Pirrotta & Cecchin, 1988 for curriculum designs); essentially it is the "core component" (Herz & Carter, 1988) for many programs. Trainees are less willing than students to participate in traditional learning activities such as reading, listening to lectures, written assignments, and so on. Thus, institute supervisors must frequently find ways to embed learning of theoretical concepts within the supervisory process.

Clinical Practice: On-site, Off-site, or a Combination

Supervision of clinical work generally occurs in one of three places: on-site, off-site, or at a combination of both. In the first model, supervisees receive supervision of their clinical work conducted at the site of the program. This model is frequently used in degree-granting programs, particularly in accredited programs, where an educational program operates a fully functioning on-site clinic. Supervisees may practice with a highly educated, homogeneous population if the clinic serves primarily the university community. Or, supervisees may work with a more diverse clientele if the site serves the general community. Because the program operates the clinic, supervisors have input into every aspect of supervisees' clinical experiences.

Phil, a supervisor affiliated with a master's program, is assigned to supervise Debbie, a first-year practicum student. Phil requested to work with Debbie because she had an interest in working with young children, an area he specializes in. Because he also assigns cases to her, he can ensure that he supervises Debbie treating families experiencing difficulties with young children.

In the second model, supervisees receive supervision on their practice which occurs off-site in community agencies where they are placed by the program or where they work. This model is most often associated with institute programs when trainees are already practicing mental health professionals or master's programs structured to accommodate working older adult students. When supervisees practice in agencies, this arrangement requires supervisors to maintain ongoing cooperative relationships with agency-designated supervisors. It is important to delineate responsibilities to minimize confusion for supervisees regarding whose supervisory input, on what issues, and when it should be given priority (Bernard & Goodyear, 1992).

Don is receiving supervision from Denise, the MFT program supervisor, and Tom, the agency supervisor. Denise and Tom have a working agreement that Denise is responsible for the ongoing clinical supervision of Don while Tom is responsible for administrative supervision (i.e., recordkeeping, agency policies and procedures, and assignment of cases). Don wonders if he should help a client advocate for additional services by challenging an administrative decision of the agency. Denise and Tom view the situation differently—Denise sees Don's proposed intervention as therapeutic for the family while Tom disagrees. Because Denise and Tom have clearly defined roles, Denise is able to assume the central supervisory position in assisting Don to determine what he wants to do and how to do it in a manner that supports his clients and gains the agency's backing.

In this model, the clientele supervisees work with is as varied as the agencies and practices involved.

In the third model, a combination of the previous two exists. A program may have supervisees practice on-site for a period of time followed by placement in the community or practice on-site and off-site simultaneously (see Nichols, 1988; Papero, 1988; Sprenkle, 1988 for examples of this model). When this model underlies an institute program, supervisees frequently receive supervision from program supervisors on a limited number of their cases.

Barbara supervises Joan, a certified chemical dependency counselor employed in a residential drug treatment program who is just beginning the MFT institute program. As part of the requirements, Joan is to provide family therapy to six families at the treatment program. Barbara will supervise these cases. On the remainder of the cases, Joan will continue services as she always has done. During her training, Joan will also receive live supervision on two cases for services provided to institute clientele.

The degree to which supervisors are accountable for the cases they do not supervise and are treated by their supervisees from a non-MFT approach is somewhat unclear because it is uncharted legal territory (Engleberg & Storm, 1990). Supervisors are advised to inquire about "at risk" clients in supervisees' entire caseloads (Storm, 1994). Supervisors sometimes attempt to divorce themselves from responsibility for these cases by defining their supervisory responsibilities in supervision contracts as only for specific cases and in descriptions of their training programs.

Supervisory Relationships: Prevention of Clones or In-Depth Knowledge

Although supervisors in both types of programs endorse supervisees experiencing a variety of supervisors (Henry, Sprenkle, & Sheehan, 1986), switching of supervisors in shorter time spans occurs more frequently in master's programs. When the change occurs, supervisees may experience more variety of supervisory philosophies and methods because of the theoretical diversity practiced by supervisors and taught by university programs. This emphasis on diversity has important implications for supervisory relationships. On one hand, it prevents the development of relationships that promote graduating "clones of supervisors" and promotes supervisees' development of their novel approaches to therapy, an important learning objective of master's program supervisors. On the other hand, it inhibits the development of more intimate, personal, trusting supervisory relationships. Supervisors are limited in their knowledge of supervisees' abilities simply by the constraints of time for obtaining information and getting to know their supervisees. The longer, supervisory relationships common to institute supervisors allows supervisors to learn about their supervisees' competencies in-depth and see more of the subtleties of supervisees' clinical work; it also allows time for long-range, broader supervisory interventions.

Sally, an institute supervisor, makes a note to herself to find an opening to talk again with David, her supervisee, about his professional demeanor. They are currently meeting with school personnel regarding a case of David's. Per his typical stance, David is saying little, hesitant in his contributions, and letting his co-therapist take the initiative. Although they talked previously about his tentativeness in his relationships with other professionals, David still seems to be holding back. Sally thinks to herself, "What a shame it will be if David can't communicate his competency as a therapist to other professionals." Fortunately, Sally and David will be working together for several more months so they will have time to focus on David becoming more confident in his relationships with other professionals.

Supervisees may become more comfortable sharing their struggles, insecurities, and personal reactions when they have a longer relationship history with supervisors.

Multiple supervisory relationships are ubiquitous in educational programs (Ryder &

Hepworth, 1990). At universities, supervisors are frequently also classroom teachers, research chairs, advisors, and/or collaborators on publications. These multiple roles have at their center educational endeavors. Supervisors, for the most part, have multiple contacts with supervisees within their educational programs. At institutes, supervisors may serve on professional committees together, have employment affiliations with the same organizations, and/or collaborate on community projects. These multiple roles are grounded in chosen collegial activities which occur in the wider professional community. In either case, the legitimate and necessary supervisory function of socialization of supervisees as marriage and family therapists encourages multiple relationships. Supervisors, then, must maintain a heightened sensitivity to the ethical responsibilities and complexities involved in managing multiple relationships (see Chapter 18 for a full discussion of the issues).

Evaluation: The Academic's Achilles Heel and the Trainer's Herculean Efforts

The Achilles heel of many university supervisors is evaluating students' progress during the clinical sequence in the program. In the usual university scenario, faculty members use papers, tests, and various other written assignments as a means to accumulate information for student evaluations. Although supervisors can use these methods, they do not tap supervisees' progress well. The supervision process, including observation of therapy, discussion about cases and therapeutic issues, co-therapy or team experiences with supervisors, and so on, becomes the source of data for the evaluation process. Unfortunately, supervision is also often misunderstood or considered "nonacademic" in the university context, frequently lacking credibility as a justifiable faculty activity

(Sprenkle, 1988). The challenge, then, for supervisors at universities is to evaluate supervisees' progress in the clinical sequence in a manner that translates clinical training into language and processes understood by academicians and that is consistent with the larger university culture. This results in evaluation becoming highly structured, formal, and documented (see the *Resource Guide* with this book for supervision recordkeeping instruments).

Bill supervised John who was in his third of four semesters of practicum. During John's previous semesters, he impressed his supervisors, receiving high ratings on his evaluations. However, his previous supervisors and Bill noted a subtle change in John's therapy and attitude at the beginning of this semester. John's demeanor shifted from seeking out opportunities for learning and input to impatience, even perhaps annoyance, when faculty, his peers, or Bill made comments about his cases. Over the semester John made several decisions about cases that concerned Bill: he talked openly about clients in a class that included nontherapists, omitted mentioning that he was a therapist-in-training to outside referral sources, and assumed a "supervisory" stance with his peers. On each occasion, Bill discussed these issues with John during supervision. John was also experiencing a difficult divorce, which he cited as a reason for the changes that were noted in him. Bill and John discussed the potential value of John obtaining personal therapy; but he subsequently decided not to pursue this resource.

Near the end of the semester John dealt with an emergency situation without following clinic procedures, failed to contact a supervisor about the situation, made decisions that the supervisory team believed were not in the best interests of the clients, perhaps even harmful to them, and placed the supervisor and program in legal jeopardy. When Bill discussed John's rationale for his decisions, John felt his actions were being questioned unfairly. He believed Bill

should unconditionally accept his judgment and support him. His response reaffirmed Bill's growing concerns about John's professional development and level of competence.

Bill agonized over the situation and John's evaluation. He consulted with the other supervisors and they concluded John was not ready to advance on to the next and final semester of practica. In talking with John about this decision, John strongly felt the decision was unfair because he believed he had no indication there was a serious concern. Although Bill agreed they had not discussed the possibility of repeating the semester, Bill reminded him of the several instances when he had expressed concern about John's progress. John decided to challenge the decision within the wider university context.

Bill found it difficult to justify the decision because he had only documented some, but not all, of the concerns in his supervision notes; and he had not given John the university required mid-semester warning or notification of concerns and specific remedial steps in writing with adequate time and full opportunity to complete them. Although many of these actions had been done informally within supervision, they were not easily demonstrated to the university community. In the end, a compromise was worked out for John. The experience led the supervisory team to develop a more formalized evaluation process that emphasized providing therapists-in-training with specific information in writing about concerns, documenting of supervision sessions, developing plans with supervisees to address concerns, and proactively taking action when concerns emerge.

Free-standing institutes can tailor their evaluation process more easily to their specific training goals, schedule their evaluations after a longer span of time or after a specific component or number of hours is reached, and be somewhat less formal (see *Resource Guide* for evaluation and recordkeeping instruments).

Although the university calendar determines the scheduling of evaluations for supervisors working in universities, institutes tend toward end-of-year evaluations. Because they have fewer institutional constraints, the wider professional community in which institutes are embedded significantly shapes the evaluation of trainees. The true evaluation is probably whether supervisees' practice in their work setting changes (Herz & Carter, 1988). Supervisors frequently make "Herculean" efforts to assist supervisees in becoming skilled in MFT because the consequences to clients, the program, and the profession of dismissing a trainee from an institute program may be greater. The following example illustrates the supervisory dilemma.

Sara has been supervising Clara, a second-year trainee of a two-year institute program, for the past year and a half. Clara has a master's degree in social work and is employed at an agency serving children with school problems and their families. Although Clara is enthusiastic about MFT, she struggles with involving parents in therapy. Clara admits that she is most comfortable working one on one with children using methods of play therapy learned in her social work program. Sara and Clara have spent many supervision sessions focusing on ways to increase Clara's comfort level. They have role-played ways to engage parents in therapy, watched sessions of other therapists successfully involving parents, and brainstormed specific steps Clara could take with her cases. Occasionally Clara meets with a mother and a child but infrequently talks with fathers. On a couple of occasions, Clara has started with a family unit but quickly therapy turns into individual sessions with the children and the mother. Clara voices a desire to meet with families and an understanding of its importance, but offers many reasons for her inability to do so. She notes that she is already fully licensed; therefore, this training is voluntary.

Sara wonders if an MFT approach simply runs counter to Clara's values, beliefs, and preferences. Should she suggest that Clara leave the program? None of the other supervisors have seen Clara's work. Would they view it similarly? Should she recommend Clara extend her time in the program because she is still at a beginning level of ability? Because Clara will continue to work with families at her agency regardless of whether she completes the training, should Sara, for the good of the families, devote more time and effort to help Clara gain these skills? Should she arrange to do co-therapy with Clara or conduct more live supervision so Clara can learn by having the positive experience of involving parents? This alternative would require Sara to engage in unpaid supervision of Clara. If Clara agrees to additional training, does she join the incoming class of six or is a special arrangement made? Who bears the cost? If Clara receives her certificate, how will this affect the credibility of the program in the community?—Clara's MFT skills could be negative advertisement.

After Sara discusses the issues with the other faculty, she and Clara agree that Clara will continue in the program by participating in some of the sessions with the incoming group and receive live supervision with other supervisors at no expense to Clara. In the faculty's opinion, the potential benefit to Clara, clients, the program, and the profession offset the greater costs in supervisory time and effort.

When supervisors work for master's or institute programs, the evaluative responsibility is integral to their supervisory role and has far-reaching implications. A low evaluation can mean supervisees do not advance to the next step in their program or are dismissed, and it can have a significant impact on their educational and career goals. For university supervisors, it may mean working diligently to assist supervisees to change careers (Mead, 1990). For institute supervisors, it may mean helping supervisees assess their strengths and define professional goals outside the realm of MFT. Not surprisingly, one study of faculty and supervisees found supervisors in both settings were reluctant to expel supervisees lacking competencies, preferring remediation (Henry, Sprenkle, & Sheehan, 1986). When supervisors develop plans to address concerns about supervisees' lack of competence or consider dismissing supervisees from programs, supervisors must balance fairness to supervisees with supervisory accountability to clients and the profession. Mead (1990) recommends supervisors in educational settings ensure there is clarity of expectations within the program; early, regular, and frequent evaluations; and documentation at the first hint of a concern. When supervisors are considering developing remedial steps, Mead further recommends that supervisors consider the cost and time to be invested by supervisees, the time needed and opportunity supervisees have to address problem areas, and the consequences if the plan fails.

SPECIAL CONSIDERATIONS FOR DOCTORAL PROGRAMS

As noted before, growth in degree-granting graduate programs has occurred primarily at the master's level. In 1988, there were seven accredited doctoral programs (Sprenkle, 1988). A decade later, there are only 12 MFT doctoral programs (compared to a shift from 17 to 42 master's programs). This relatively slower growth (and smaller numbers) is probably because the master's degree remains the entry-level degree for the profession. An MFT doctorate is typically only required for those who want to teach in an MFT program in a university context. Students whose goals are exclusively clinical often choose doctorates accredited by the American Psychological Association to become eligible for licensure as a psychologist. However, there certainly are clin-ically oriented students who choose MFT programs over psychology programs because the nature of the training program in the former is appealing.

There is really no way of knowing how many nonaccredited doctoral MFT programs exist. This is because the term "program" (if not defined by an external accrediting agency) can mean anything from a few courses offered by well-intentioned, if not necessarily well-qualified faculty, to something approximating the COAMFTE standards. We know of a small number of well-developed programs in family psychology. There are also a few doctoral programs, primarily in schools or departments of education, with primary allegiance to the American Counseling Association rather than to AAMFT. Because of the variability among the non-COAMFTE-accredited programs, what will be said about doctoral programs in the remainder of this chapter applies to those that have the endorsement of the COAMFTE.

The context in which supervision occurs is both similar to and different from the master's context. Like master's programs, doctoral programs are heavily influenced by the university culture—perhaps even more so (as will be noted here). For doctoral programs as well, the rather demanding supervision requirements of COAMFTE and AAMFT are ever-present challenges to both students and their supervisors. Doctoral faculty supervisors also wear multiple hats; they divide their time as supervisors with roles as teachers, researchers, and advisers of research (along with the committee and administrative demands that are always part of academic life). As with master's programs, supervision typically occurs within the context of clinical practica. Frequently, students enroll in different practica taught by different faculty to broaden their range of supervisory experiences. Evaluation is also highly structured and formally documented. Finally, the methods of supervision that are emphasized (live, video, team) tend to be similar. There are at least three major differences in the supervisory context in doctoral programs. They are described in the following sections along with some related advantages and disadvantages.

Specific Training in Supervision

Clinical and academic requirements include specific training in supervision and the doctoral curriculum must include a supervision course. This makes sense because almost all MFT doctoral graduates find themselves in positions where their job descriptions include the role of supervisor. It also has the advantage of creating a group of students who are conscious that there is a supervision subspecialty and who are therefore more likely to take on responsibility for representing the field as a whole. Senior doctoral students take the course and, for example, at Purdue University it is considered the "capstone" of the student's clinical careers. Most students are heavily invested in the course and all want to be considered a "good supervisor." At most institutions, the course typically includes a didactic and clinical component. Students seem to appreciate the opportunity to integrate theory and practice within the same course—a goal given lip service in doctoral education but rarely carried out so explicitly. A detailed description of one course (at Purdue University) can be found in Sprenkle (1988) and Heath and Storm (1985). (See also Chapter 26 regarding methods for teaching such a course in a variety of settings and the *Resource Guide* for an example of a course outline.)

In the clinical component of the course, the student or supervisor-in-training (SIT) does supervision with master's or beginning doctoral-level trainees. This supervision is itself supervised ("metavised") by (most typically) the faculty member in charge of the supervision course. (Student supervision does not "count" as part of the supervision therapists must receive in their programs and only supplements the supervision offered by faculty. Student supervision also does not usually count for state licensing or credentialing bodies such as AAMFT.)

In Purdue University's course, for example, up to three SITs are assigned to one of the clinical practica, which meets from 2:30 to 9:30 P.M. one night a week and includes three slots for live supervision of cases. Each of the SITs may supervise live up to three cases that night and at least one of these cases will be metavised by the faculty member in charge of the supervision course. The metavisor will observe the SIT conduct a pretherapy session meeting with a supervisee, will watch the session itself with the SIT from behind the mirror and discuss call-ins or other forms of during-session interventions, and will also observe the SIT conduct a posttherapy session feedback meeting with a supervisee. Sometimes reflecting teams, cotherapy, or other modalities will be utilized as part of the process. At the end of the evening, the metavisor meets with the SITs for extensive discussion and feedback on their work with supervisees. As part of the didactic seminar, SITs also present edited videotapes of some of their other sessions.

Students supervising other students can also be a disadvantage. This has led at least one accredited doctoral program to decide not to include a clinical component in its supervision course.

Martha was a member of her doctoral program's supervision class. She was assigned to supervise Sara. Although Martha was a third-year student, and Sara was in her first year of doctoral studies, the two became close friends during the semester. Martha helped Sara through a difficult marital separation and the two frequently went out for lunch during the week and socialized on weekends. Sara was struggling with a difficult marital case and the client (husband) triggered many of Sara's issues with her own estranged husband. Martha had a hard time separating what she knew about Sara outside of the SIT–supervisee relationship and was not clear just what she was comfortable saying in front of the faculty metavisor. Sara also resented her friend taking on what seemed like a quasi-evaluative role vis-à-vis her therapy. The two requested a special meeting with the metavisor to try to sort out these conflicting roles and to determine whether a SIT–supervisee relationship was still possible. The three mutually agreed that these dual relationship issues, while part of the learning process, were inhibiting Sara's growth as a clinician and Martha's as a supervisor. Sara was assigned to another SIT.

Extensive Practice Requirements in the Internship

Doctoral students are expected to complete not only the clinical requirements of an accredited master's program, but also 500 (minimum) face-to-face client-contact hours during a nine- to twelve-month internship. The internship is designed to approximate the intensity of full-time clinical practice. By the time doctoral students begin this experience, their skill level is often quite high. Their internship supervisors may experience them as more like supervisees from postgraduate institutes than like graduate student supervisees. In fact, there sometimes is an incongruent hierarchy where the doctoral supervisees are more up-to-date clinically than the internship supervisors who work with them. It is typically the case that the doctoral intern supervisees (because they have taken the supervision course) are more current in their knowledge of the supervision literature. These role reversals are not necessarily a problem if supervisors offer perspectives that are new to supervisees and/or are themselves highly skilled in their preferred orientations, and the doctoral supervisees are open to this new input.

Doctoral supervisees also experience supervision in a context that is substantially different from the university setting, where it is not uncommon for supervisees to receive almost as many supervision hours as client-contact hours. Interns rarely receive more than the required minimum of one hour of supervision for five hours of client contact. Receiving supervision is now more a part of an overall job that includes not only greater client contact but also extensive paperwork, staff meetings, and so on. Doctoral supervisees have less flexibility in their schedules in their internships than they did back at the university and fewer opportunities to seek out guidance on their cases. Although this can be frustrating for supervisees, the advantage is that it is good preparation for the transition to the real world of postuniversity life.

Balancing the Clinical and Research Emphasis

University requirements for research loom large in doctoral programs. Although some students do not fully comprehend its meaning when they "sign on" for doctoral studies, the PhD (the only degree offered by the accredited doctoral programs) is a research degree. Beyond the specific requirements of the MFT program, virtually all universities require rigorous training in research methodology and statistics as well as completion of a scholarly dissertation. Because most programs are in departments of Child or Human Development and Family Studies (or related titles like Human Ecology), they frequently also require coursework on these themes, and students are examined on this material, as well as research skills, by comprehensive examinations. This has the advantage of producing supervisors with broad knowledge beyond MFT. It also has the advantage of creating supervisors with the skills to do original research about supervision—something that is sorely needed as a review of the supervision research literature attests (Avis &

Sprenkle, 1990). We have the impression that a growing number of scholarly dissertations are being written about supervision themes and some of these are finding their way into print (e.g., Sells et al., 1994; Wetchler, Piercy, & Sprenkle, 1989; White & Russell, 1995).

One disadvantage of this research emphasis is that a few students, drawn to the field by its clinical thrust, are not well matched in temperament or interest for the rigors of the research enterprise. They may not fully realize this incompatibility until well into their program.

John was one of the strongest clinicians his doctoral program had ever produced. He was clearly the "star" in his clinical practica. He also was the most sought after SIT in the supervision class. In fact, many of the students preferred his supervision to that of the faculty, which was a humbling experience for many of them. However, John showed little interest and motivation in his research courses and failed one of his comprehensive examinations on research. He also did not successfully defend his dissertation proposal before leaving for his internship. Furthermore, John got so caught up in the clinical work in his internship setting (where his talents were so warmly received) that he never could seem to find time to revise his proposal. John's advisor (who was also one of his supervisors) came to believe that John would probably never pass his exams or complete his dissertation and was probably not suited for doctoral studies. He decided to try to counsel John to pursue a clinical career.

This is a good example of the stresses of the "multiple hats" worn by doctoral supervisors who are also faculty. Unlike virtually all institute supervisors, and unlike some supervisors in clinically oriented master's programs, they must keep one eye focused on their supervisee's competence as a researcher. It was painful for John's supervisor to see him "succeed clinically" yet "fail" in the program.

Diverse, But Mature Supervisees

Supervisees are more mature but highly diverse in their clinical orientations, skills, and wants from supervision. Not surprisingly doctoral students are much less likely than their master's counterparts to be young and inexperienced because most have a previous graduate degree and many have worked in a clinical setting after getting a master's degree. However, there is considerable diversity because their prior graduate work many not have been in MFT but rather in social work, clinical psychology, counseling, ministry, or even family studies. Although the day may come when doctoral MFT programs will recruit mostly from MFT master's programs, that is not currently the case. This means that some students are very knowledgeable about MFT theory and practice while others are relatively "green" even though the program may have chosen them because of highly developed talents in other areas such as research. In this sense, then, some MFT doctoral supervisees are like supervisees in institutes who are novices in MFT but seasoned professionals in some other arena. Some students enter their doctoral programs with highly developed theoretical orientations to MFT while others have only a vague awareness of theoretical preferences. The former are much less likely to be malleable to the faculty supervisor's preferred clinical approach. The presence of students who already know their theoretical preferences, combined with the faculty supervisor's awareness that there is no compelling evidence for the superiority of one approach over another, leads to an appreciation of and tolerance for differences. The advantage of this diversity is that it can create an exciting environment in which students are exposed to a variety of approaches and have the opportunity to integrate them. A potential disadvantage for supervisors is that one often has supervisees in the same practica or supervision groups with very disparate wants.

Frank, supervisor for the doctoral practica, has six students in his group, three of whom are graduates of MFT master's programs. One has an MSW, one has a degree in counseling psychology, and the other has a master's in family studies. One of the MFT master's supervisees was trained rather exclusively in contextual family therapy and is a strong proponent of this approach; another is well grounded in a structural–strategic orientation; and the third became quite enamored with the solution-focused model during the second year of his master's program. In addition to the weekly practicum group, Frank meets with the first two, Sue and Tom, for supervision.

Sue prefers to look at all of her cases from an historical perspective and wants feedback from Frank around things like patterns of intergenerational indebtedness. Tom's approach is ahistorical and he wants feedback about organization and pattern. Frank personally leans toward an emotion-focused emphasis. Although there is often good natured bantering among the three, sometimes things get tense, especially when Sue questioned the ethics of a paradoxical intervention Tom had tried with a client and sought Frank's support. Frank also struggles with balancing, on the one hand, trying to empower Tom and Sue to do their best work within their theoretical orientations and, on the other hand, believing that they may have prematurely ossified in their views, pushing them to look at alternatives.

Frank also has Steve, the family studies graduate, in individual supervision with Mary who is a solution-focused devotee. While bright and reflective, Steve has had very little "in-room experience" with couples and families and needs a lot of attention to case management skills. Mary knows just what to do to keep a case moving and, if anything, needs to be encouraged to be less structured and to have less of a "cookie-cutter" approach to her work. Frank struggles with their almost diametrically opposed needs and wonders if it is possible to make their weekly meetings productive for both Steve and Mary.

Although Frank's final supervisory pair, Len (the MSW) and Stacey (the counseling psychologist), are similar in that they have had relatively little clinical training specifically in MFT, Len wants lots of attention given to larger systems issues and Stacey is much more focused on the microsystems of clients, therapists, and supervisors. Frank is challenged by this diversity but, in his honest moments, he admits to his colleagues that it is also frustrating. He comments that, ironically, in his "structural–strategic" days, he supervised a student who went on to be Tom's professor and clinical mentor. Frank's former supervisee had taught Tom a lot of things that he, Frank, no longer believes. "What goes around, comes around," Frank murmurs.

SUPERVISING IN EDUCATIONAL PROGRAMS: TRADEOFFS

In educational settings, supervisors tend to supervise more teams, co-therapists, and groups because therapists-in-training are part of a predetermined structure, simplifying scheduling and the numbers of therapists needed for teamwork, co-therapy, and groups. More live supervision and videotaped supervision is conducted; educational programs invest the resources in required technology and prefer these methods of supervision (Sprenkle, 1988). Because the opportunity for and feasibility of varying supervision structures and methods are more easily accomplished, supervision can be more tailored to supervisees' learning needs and interests. For example, Teresa, who was supervising therapists learning the narrative approach, easily formed reflecting teams. As Roberts (see Chapter 24 in this book) notes, a supervisor who is working with supervisees in a private contract arrangement may have considerably more difficulty creating reflecting teams and may need to be more creative. Because supervisees are beginning a new educational endeavor their interest, investment, and enthusiasm are usually high. Consultation about supervision occurs more frequently because ethical standards for supervisee confidentiality allow discussion with other supervisors within the same educational program. (Delivering a quality supervision experience may, in fact, require consultation among supervisors.) When multiple relationships exist there is more safety created within educational contexts for supervisors and supervisees as a result of the open dialogue that can occur within programs among supervisors and supervisees.

There are a number of tradeoffs when supervising privately contracted supervisees rather than affiliating with educational programs (see Chapter 10 for an in-depth discussion of supervising in this setting). There may be a better match between supervisors' and supervisees' treatment philosophies, styles, and values because supervisees select their supervisors, rather than being assigned to them, in privately contracted supervision. In educational settings, supervision is divided among the faculty of the degree-granting or postgraduate program based on programmatic responsibilities. There is a tendency for privately contracted supervision to be with individuals or dyads and to occur over a greater span of time. This one-on-one or two-supervisees-to-one supervisor structure and the greater length of time of the supervisory relationship is more likely to facilitate an intimate, mentoring supervisory relationship. However, supervision is sometimes permeated with a sense of "just clocking hours" because supervisees are anxious to transcend the status of being in training to being a fully accomplished professional.

Some supervisors may prefer affiliations with educational programs because they offer ease in using a variety of supervision structures and methods, an embedded organized supervision process, and collegiality. Other supervisors may prefer the selectivity, intimacy, and personal flexibility of supervision that is privately contracted. Many supervisors will create supervision practices where they experience both—trading one set of advantages for another depending on whether they are supervising in ivory towers, institutes, or their private practices.

The differences between the Ivory Tower and the Institute are powerful witnesses to the influence of context on supervision. Even within a single context, such as a university, whether the program is for a master's or a doctorate degree, context has a major impact on the supervisory enterprise. Whatever the context in which the reader receives or gives supervision, we hope the eight dimensions described in this chapter will be useful lenses for you to consider how the unique requirements of your own setting impacts your work.

REFERENCES

Avis, J., & Sprenkle, D. (1990). A review of outcome research on family therapy training. *Journal of Marital and Family Therapy, 16,* 225–240.

Anderson, S. (1992). Evaluation of an academic family therapy program: Changes in trainees' relationship and intervention skills. *Journal of Marital and Family Therapy, 4,* 365–376.

Bardill, D., & Saunders, B. (1988). Marriage and family therapy and graduate social work education. In H. Liddle, D. Breunlin, & R. Schwartz (Eds.), *Handbook of family therapy training and supervision* (pp. 316–330). New York: Guilford Press.

Berger, M. (1988). Academic psychology and family therapy training. In H. Liddle, D. Breunlin, & R. Schwartz (Eds.), *Handbook of family therapy training and supervision* (pp. 303–315). New York: Guilford Press.

Berman, E., & Dixon-Murphy, T. (1979). Training in marital and family therapy at free-standing institutes. *Journal of Marital and Family Therapy, 5,* 29–42.

Bernard, J., & Goodyear, R. (1992). *Fundamentals of clinical supervision.* Needham Heights, MA: Allyn and Bacon.

Bloch, D., & Weiss, H. (1981). Family therapy training: Institutional base. *Family Process, 20,* 133–146.

Cantwell, P., & Holmes, S. (1995). Cumulative process: A collaborative approach to systemic supervision. *Journal of Systemic Therapies, 14,* 35–46.

Cooper, A., Rampage, C., & Soucy, C. (1981). Family therapy training in clinical psychology programs. *Family Process, 20,* 155–156.

Colapinto, J. (1988). Teaching the structural way. In H. Liddle, D. Breunlin, & R. Schwartz (Eds.), *Handbook of family therapy training and supervision* (pp. 17–37). New York: Guilford Press.

Combrinck-Graham, L. (1988). Family therapy training in psychiatry. In H. Liddle, D. Breunlin, & R. Schwartz (Eds.), *Handbook of family therapy training and supervision* (pp. 265–277). New York: Guilford Press.

Commission on Accreditation for Marriage and Family Therapy Education (COAMFTE). (1996). *Manual on Accreditation.* Washington, DC: Author.

Engleberg, S., & Storm, C. (1990). Supervising defensively: Advice from legal counsel. *Supervision Bulletin, 3,* 2–4.

Everett, C. (1979). The master's degree in marriage and family therapy. *Journal of Marital and Family Therapy, 5,* 7–14.

Fennell, D., & Hovestadt, A. (1985). Family therapy as a profession or professional speciality: Implications for training. *Journal of Psychotherapy and the Family, 1,* 25–40.

Fisch, R. (1988). Training in the brief model. In H. Liddle, D. Breunlin, & R. Schwartz (Eds.), *Handbook of family therapy training and supervision* (pp. 78–92). New York: Guilford Press.

Garfield, R., & Lord, G. (1982). The Hahnemann master's of family therapy program: A design and its results. *American Journal of Family Therapy, 10,* 75–78.

Heath, A., & Storm, C. (1985). From the institute to the ivory tower: The live supervision stage approach for teaching supervision in academic settings. *American Journal of Family Therapy, 13,* 27–36.

Henry, P., Sprenkle, D., & Sheehan, D. (1986). Family therapy training: Student and faculty percep-

tions. *Journal of Marital and Family Therapy, 12,* 249–258.

Herz, F. & Carter, B. (1988). Born free: The life cycle of a free-standing postgraduate training institute. In H. Liddle, D. Breunlin, & R. Schwartz (Eds.), *Handbook of family therapy training and supervision* (pp. 93–109). New York: Guilford Press.

Hovestadt, A., Fennell, D., & Piercy, F. (1983). Integrating marriage and family therapy within counselor education: A three-level model. In B. Okun & S. Gladding (Eds.), *Issues in training marriage and family therapists* (pp. 31–42). Ann Arbor, MI: ERIC/CAPS.

Joanning, H., Morris, J., & Dennis, M. (1985). An overview of family therapy educational settings. *American Journal of Family Therapy, 13,* 3–6.

Keller, J., Huber, J., & Hardy, J. (1988). What constitutes appropriate marriage and family therapy education? *Journal of Marital and Family Therapy, 14,* 297–306.

LaPerriere, K. (1979). Family therapy training at the Ackerman Institute: Thoughts of form and substance. *Journal of Marital and Family Therapy, 5,* 53–58.

Liddle, H. (1982). On the problems of eclecticism: A call for epistemological clarification and human scale theories. *Family Process, 4,* 243–250.

Liddle, H., Breunlin, D., & Schwartz, R. (1988). *Handbook of family therapy training and supervision.* New York: Guilford Press.

Lyman, B., Storm, C., & York, C. (1995). Rethinking assumptions about trainee's life experience. *Journal of Marital and Family Therapy, 21,* 193–203.

Mazza, J. (1988). Training strategic therapists: The use of indirect techniques. In H. Liddle, D. Breunlin, & R. Schwartz (Eds.), *Handbook of family therapy training and supervision* (pp. 93–109). New York: Guilford Press.

Mead, D. (1990). *Effective supervision: A task-oriented model for the mental health professions.* New York: Brunner/Mazel.

Nichols, W. (1979). Education of marriage and family therapists: Some trends and implications. *Journal of Marital and Family Therapy, 5,* 19–28.

Nichols, W. (1988). An integrative psychodynamic and systems approach. In H. Liddle, D. Breunlin, & R. Schwartz (Eds.), *Handbook of family therapy training and supervision* (pp. 110–127). New York: Guilford Press.

Nichols, W., Nichols, D., & Hardy, K. (1990). Supervision in family therapy: A decade restudy. *Journal of Marital and Family Therapy, 16,* 275–286.

Papero, D. (1988). Training in Bowen theory. In H. Liddle, D. Breunlin, & R. Schwartz (Eds.), *Handbook of family therapy training and supervision* (pp. 62–77). New York: Guilford Press.

Piercy, F., & Sprenkle, D. (1984). The process of family therapy education. *Journal of Marital and Family Therapy, 10,* 399–408.

Pirrotta, S., & Cecchin, G. (1988). The Milan training program. In H. Liddle, D. Breunlin, & R. Schwartz (Eds.), *Handbook of family therapy training and supervision* (pp. 38–61). New York: Guilford Press.

Ryder, R., & Hepworth, J. (1990). AAMFT ethical code: "Dual relationships." *Journal of Marital and Family Therapy, 16,* 127–132.

Sprenkle, D. (1988). Training and supervision in degree-granting graduate programs in family therapy. In H. Liddle, D. Breunlin, & R. Schwartz (Eds.), *Handbook of family therapy training and supervision* (pp. 233–248). New York: Guilford Press.

Sells, S., Smith, T., Coe, M., Yoshioko, M., & Robbins, J. (1994). An ethnography of couple and therapist experiences in reflecting team practice. *Journal of Marital and Family Therapy, 20,* 247–266.

Storm, C. (1994). Defensive supervision: Balancing ethical responsibility with vulnerability. In G. Brock (Ed.), *Ethics casebook* (pp. 173–190). Washington, DC: AAMFT.

Sutton, P. (1985/86). An insider's comparison of a major family therapy doctoral program and a leading nondegree family therapy training center. *Journal of Psychotherapy and the Family, 1,* 41–51.

Van Trommell, M. (1982). Training in marital and family therapy in Canada and the United States. *Journal of Strategic and Systemic Therapy, 1,* 31–39.

Wetchler, J., Piercy, F., & Sprenkle, D. (1989). Supervisor and supervisee perceptions of the effectiveness of family therapy supervising techniques. *American Journal of Family Therapy, 17,* 35–47.

White, M., & Russell, C. (1995). The essential elements of supervising systems: A modified Delphi study. *Journal of Marital and Family Therapy, 21,* 33–54.

Winkle, C., Piercy, F., & Hovestadt, A. (1981). A curriculum for graduate level marriage and family therapy education. *Journal of Marital and Family Therapy, 7,* 201–210.

Wright, L., & Leahey, M. (1988). Nursing and family therapy training. In H. Liddle, D. Breunlin, & R. Schwartz (Eds.), *Handbook of family therapy training and supervision* (pp. 278–289). New York: Guilford Press.

9

Systems-Oriented Supervision in an Agency Setting

Martha Cook

Supervision in an agency context presents challenges and learning opportunities for supervisors and supervisees. In an agency context, both must contend with multiple roles and multiple realities. Supervisors need to be aware of their own roles at different agency levels such as administration, supervision, and the provision of direct service. They must also be cognizant of supervisees' different roles, and at what systemic levels those roles are played out. For example, supervisees play the role of therapist with their clients, the role of supervisee with supervisors, and the role of employee with administrators. Supervisors must notice when there are problems or conflicts between these roles and make them "grist for the mill" in supervision.

The agency supervisor has to contend with the realities of the client, referral sources, the agency, the supervisory relationship, the supervisee, plus the supervisor's own reality. With all these realities to juggle, isomorphism becomes a key concern for the systemic agency supervisor. Juggling multiple realities also places the systemic agency supervisor in the sometimes uncomfortable role of having to decide which reality will prevail to provide the best client care.

The complexities of agency life heavily influence supervisory relationships and frequently make supervisory guidelines and boundaries difficult to establish and maintain. In an agency context, systemic supervision requires continually evaluating the supervisory relationship, as well as assessing how the supervisory relationship fits into the larger agency context. It is the nature of social service agencies to constantly grow and change, so the supervisory relationship must do likewise.

DISTINCTIVE ASPECTS OF SUPERVISION IN AGENCIES

Funding sources may require an agency to be accredited by national organizations or licensed by the state. Thus, the more programs of different types that an agency operates, the more complex the systems necessary to maintain the programs. Social service agencies are generally embedded in the communities in which they exist. They receive referrals from other community institutions such as schools, court systems, police departments, hospitals, child welfare agencies, and sometimes by word of mouth. Most often, social service agencies have been established to meet the needs of clients who cannot afford to obtain services in the private sector. As the following sections discuss, this type of supervisory context has several distinctive aspects.

Accountability to Multiple Funding Sources

When an agency has multiple funding sources and treatment programs, it also has accountability to all these constituencies. Funders usually differ in their documentation requirements, and in the types of client populations for which they will fund services. This places responsibility on supervisors to ensure that clients are being treated in the appropriate programs, with funded services. Agencies differ in their mission statements and target populations. Agencies may offer multiple services, targeted for birth-to-grave programs, or they may be more specialized in their target populations such as youth and family, battered women and children, residential treatment for substance abuse, and so on.

The type of agency and its mission partially define what focus clinical supervision will take. For example, the mission of a youth and family service agency may be to improve the quality of life for children and their families while keeping children at home. The mission of an agency serving battered women may be to protect the woman and her children from an abusive husband, with a longer term goal of reuniting the family. Supervisors in these two agencies would need to start with different supervision foci. In the first case, supervisors might focus on assisting supervisees with planning interventions to strengthen the parental subsystem and improve parenting, thus working toward preventing the children from being removed from the home. In the second case, supervisors could assist supervisees in planning interventions to develop the mother's abilities to protect herself and her children from abuse, and then work toward her making decisions about her marital relationship.

Attention to Isomorphism

In an agency context, supervisors must pay attention to isomorphism, because there are multiple systemic layers within which client-therapist-supervisor issues can be played out. Understanding and applying the concept of isomorphism is central to supervision in an agency context. The multiple levels and realities of the agency context make isomorphism easier to observe. *Isomorphism* refers to the replication of similar patterns at all levels of a system (Liddle & Saba, 1985). Numerous writers have noted how the dynamics of families in treatment in various agency contexts can be reenacted throughout the client-therapist-supervisor-agency community system. Harbin (1978) notes that structural arrangements of families may be repeated by hierarchical structures in hospitals where "personnel lower in the administrative hierarchy have multiple supervisors and so there are no clear lines of authority" (p. 1497).

Schools have also been found to replicate the family dynamics of children. Aponte (1976), in a discussion of "context replication" between school and home, describes how a child's relationships with classmates, teachers, and the principal replicate relationships with brothers, sisters, and parents.

Minard (1976) observes a parallel between the triangulation process that occurs in families (Bowen, 1978; Haley, 1980) and the triangulation process that occurs in a variety of organizational systems. She used Bowen's approach to look at triangulation problems in a day-care center for preschool children. Montalvo and Pavlin (1966) and Ebner (1979) also note the prevalence of triangulation and other faulty communication patterns in child care agencies and residential treatment programs.

Schwartzman and Kneifel (1985) observe that "family problems will not be resolved by a treatment/service system that repeats these problems at the helping level" (p. 104); they point out:

> The first step toward correcting service system replication of family problems is obviously recognizing that such replications exist. This

means that it is crucial for service providers to assess not only the state of the family, but also that of the service system treating the family (p. 104).

As Montalvo and Pavlin (1966) comment:

> It should be obvious that the social system of the treatment center must be better than that of the children's own homes if it is to evoke improvement in the children under its roof. A counselor, as overwhelmed as a mother with a disorganized collection of ten or more children, all demanding individual attention, nurture, and protection, can hardly do more than that mother was able to do (p. 711).

What follows is a case example of isomorphism in a residential treatment center.

Mike, an appealing twelve-year-old, was in residential placement at the center. His older siblings had been under the guardianship of child welfare. One younger sibling lived at home. Multiple unfounded reports of neglect had been filed against the mother. The mother, 43, had multiple health problems, was illiterate, and came from an extremely abusive and chaotic background. Mike's natural father was chemically dependent and frequently violent in the home. Of all the children, Mike was the most protective of the mother, attacking his father when he became violent with Mike's mother.

In school, Mike frequently was in fights, disruptive, and often cut classes. After he was placed in special education, he continued to have numerous problems, including fighting, throwing rocks at school buses, and being disobedient. His behavior continued to escalate to include aggression toward school personnel, for which he was charged with assault.

Mike's family members appeared emotionally entangled. Although the mother was not effective in her parenting of the children, the family was strongly loyal. This was illustrated by the

mother harboring the children when they ran away from placement. The mother could also be very insensitive to her children, as seen in her giving away Mike's beloved dog while her son was at the treatment center. The mother had tried many ways to control her children, including arguing, threatening, and making deals.

Treatment and management of Mike in the residential treatment center posed many challenges, in part because of the replication of the family's patterns of loyalty and disengagement within the residential treatment center. The center was part of a larger agency with several departments. Several of these were involved in Mike's care. As in many institutional settings, the center experienced problems with internal communications. Separate departments, such as the cottage program, therapeutic recreation, prevocational training, and individual/family therapy, failed to notify other involved staff of developments in the case. Each department tended to operate as if it were the dominant one in the case, forgetting the larger system. In addition, this case inspired strong feelings in the staff, which may have interfered in the treatment. Helpers seemed to ally with particular treatment approaches rather than seeing the needs of the family.

The isomorphism of this case becomes clear when examining the similarities between the institutional and family systems, specifically the formation of triangles, loyalty issues, and lack of clear communication. Mike expressed a great loyalty to his mother and became enraged at anyone who even hinted that she was not a good parent. Staff easily became triangulated between Mike and mother; multiple other triangles emerged in this case. For example, a teacher, siding with Mike, became angry with the therapist. The teacher thought that more steps should have been taken to put Mike in the custody of child welfare and to engage the mother in therapy. The intense loyalty this teacher felt toward Mike appears to have been an isomorph of the intense family loyalty.

In the cottage program and at school, Mike continually challenged authority. Clearly, this was learned in his family, and worked when he did it with his mother. A conflict emerged when the school and the child care staff argued over disciplinary measures for Mike. The staff appeared triangulated into "good parent" and "bad parent" roles with Mike, each believing that they were doing the right thing for him. Just as in his home environment, the conflict between caretakers increased Mike's acting-out behavior.

For Mike to be treated successfully at the residential treatment center, it became essential for the entire staff to communicate frequently about his case. A major task of the supervisor was to ensure that this type of communication occurred. Other supervisory tasks included helping caretakers to have empathy for the mother, whom they often found repulsive and undermining of their work with Mike. The supervisor needed to refrain from being drawn into the loyalty issues the case inspired, or else supervision would become ineffective.

Managing Multiple Realities

Agency supervisors must deal with multiple realities. Supervisors assist supervisees in negotiating clients' realities, as well as managing the documentation and case-management realities called for in agency guidelines. If conflicts arise within these realities, supervisors must determine which reality will prevail. For example, the executive director of an agency received a call from a reporter who had interviewed her for a newspaper article about agency services. The reporter complained that when she brought her daughter in for an initial assessment the intake worker had asked leading questions of the child and had appeared incompetent. The reporter also complained she had waited so long for services that she took her daughter elsewhere for therapy. The exec-

utive director brought this situation to the clinical supervisor, who was in a dual role as clinical supervisor/director. In handling this situation, the supervisor's role was to reassure the executive director that steps would be taken to prevent similar situations from occurring, assess the situation to determine what had probably occurred between the client and intake worker, and then to intervene accordingly. This included carefully interviewing the intake worker about the incident and determining what new skills the worker might need to learn.

COMMON ASPECTS OF SUPERVISORY RELATIONSHIPS

Although specific parameters of the supervisory relationship may vary from agency to agency, the following sections describe some of the commonalities that can be found.

Sanctioning of Supervision

When formal supervisory relationships are sanctioned by an agency, regular meeting times can be openly established and supervisors are granted certain authority over supervisees, such as responsibility for supervisees' evaluations and overall clinical performance. In most agency contexts, supervisors hold ultimate responsibility for clinical decisions that are made on cases, especially those that are high risk. Often, there are occasions when clients cannot wait for supervisees to learn the necessary intervention skills, and supervisors must take charge of a case temporarily to ensure that it is properly and ethically managed. For example, supervisees may be afraid to confront an abusive parent in order to protect the children.

In contrast, supervisory relationships that are not sanctioned by an agency remain informal.

Administrators may conclude that the relationship is destructive in some fashion, particularly if the informal supervisory relationship is somehow perceived as detracting from formal, agency-sanctioned supervision. For example, clinicians frequently supervise each other informally by discussing cases over coffee, at the water cooler, in each others' office doorways, and so on. If these discussions lead supervisees to arrive at interventions that supervisors deem inconsistent with client need, this can cause tension in supervisory relationships and challenge lines of authority in the agency.

Supervisors are sometimes hired from outside the agency, although they may also be chosen from within the ranks of existing agency employees. When supervisors are hired from outside the agency, they face multiple challenges. First, they must deal with the usual problems of learning a job in a new agency. To be effective supervisors, they must also work their way into a position of trust with their new staff. Depending on the legacy left behind by previous supervisors, this may be a difficult task. If previous supervisors were extremely well-liked by the staff, the incoming supervisor may find it difficult to follow in their footsteps and will have to live through staff mourning the loss of their previous supervisors. If a previous supervisor was disliked by the staff, the new supervisor may be met with suspicion and distrust from staff. Supervisors coming from the outside may be perceived by the staff as having been hired by the administration to "whip them into shape." They may also be perceived as an arm of the administration. Thus, supervisors in this position may find themselves unable to enter the staff group easily because they may be perceived as "hired guns." The staff may take some time to adjust to new supervisors, who need to earn staff respect and trust to enable them to truly assume the supervisory role.

A supervisor who is assigned from within the agency also faces challenges. Frequently, therapists are promoted and/or assigned additional duties as supervisors. Whereas they were originally part of the peer group of other therapists, new supervisors may find themselves in an isolated or lonely position. Newly promoted supervisors also may find themselves being tested by staff who were previously their peers. These staff members may still think of new supervisors as part of their peer group and may not have learned to see them as authority figures yet. Staff members who were once more open and friendly may become more closed and distant. Supervisors promoted from within may need training in new supervisory skills and require assistance in making the transition.

Multiple Supervisors Complicate Supervision

In general, agencies assign one supervisor per supervisee, but in larger agencies with multiple services, supervisees may be working in more than one program area and have different supervisors for different programs. Obviously this can greatly complicate supervision. Supervision becomes even more difficult if there are significant theoretical differences among supervisors or disagreements between them. For example, if supervisees have one supervisor with a family systems orientation and another with an individual orientation, supervisees can easily become confused in their thinking about therapy.

How the supervisor and supervisee relate to the rest of the treatment team depends, in part, on what authority is placed with the supervisor. If the supervisor is in charge of the entire team (e.g., a family preservation program team), then case decisions made with one team member may be enforced through sanctioned agency lines of authority. If the supervisor were from a different program area and supervising only one team member, then it would be more difficult to gain the cooperation of the entire team because that particular supervisor may have no authority over them.

A case manager for a funding source disagreed that phone calls to a sick child just prior to the child going into surgery were therapeutic. The case manager thought they were unnecessary and should not be part of the treatment plan, nor paid for by the funder. The clinical supervisor supported the therapist's treatment plan to the case manager. The case manager then agreed to support the phone calls as a therapeutic intervention for the client. In this case, the supervisor's role was to act as an advocate for the therapist by supporting the treatment plan, which had been developed with the guidance of the supervisor and was in the best interest of the client.

Wearing Two Hats: Administrative and Clinical Supervisory Roles

Agency supervisory relationships frequently are "dual" relationships. One member of a clinical team may also be assigned supervision responsibilities and actually be supervising other team members. This clinical supervisor is being asked to be both a peer and a supervisor to other team members. To be able to function adequately in both roles, the agency needs to include supervisors, when appropriate, in administrative decisions that affect supervisors and their supervisees. If this does not occur, supervisors may not be perceived as having authority sanctioned by the agency.

Supervisors in administrative and clinical roles are in "dual" relationships with their supervisees. In their supervision, these supervisors, wearing two hats, need to be very clear which hat they are wearing. If this is left unclear, supervisees may end up relating only to supervisors as administrators, or clinical supervisors may become stuck in their administrative role. For example, supervisors and

supervisees may feel constrained in their degree of openness with each other and the material each feels comfortable bringing to supervision sessions. Supervisees may be concerned about the ability of a supervisor/administrator to fire them or recommend raises and promotions. Supervisors in administrative roles may also have access to considerable information from outside the supervision process and may feel unsure what and/or how much information to share with supervisees. For example, a supervisee may be upset over the behavior of another agency employee. The supervisor, in the role of administrator, has access to personal information about this employee. In the role of supervisor, this information must be kept out of the meeting with the supervisee. The job of supervisors is to listen to supervisees and help them problem solve.

Assigning Staff to Supervisors

There are several ways in which supervisors are assigned. A supervisor may be assigned based on the supervisory needs of the staff. For example, a supervisee seeking to become certified may require a supervisor with particular credentials. A staff member may wish to learn a particular model of intervention (e.g., solution-focused treatment). Supervisors may also be chosen based on programmatic needs; for example, the agency crisis intervention team may be lacking in teamwork and sound assessment skills. A supervisor possessing the ability to bring the team closer together and teach them assessment skills may be assigned to the program.

Supervisors and supervisees are generally assigned to each other at an administrative level, according to the structure of the agency and agency needs. "Informed consent" of supervisees is probably rare because many agency supervision arrangements are forced on supervisors and staff. This may have a negative impact on supervisory relationships, especially if there are personality conflicts or major differences in theoretical orientation between supervisors and supervisees. Both can feel trapped, dreading the supervisory experience. Thus, supervisors who are flexible and open to supervising all types of staff with various theoretical orientations are in a better position to be effective.

Problems that arise in supervisory relationships are best addressed through a willingness by supervisors to be open about issues and discuss them directly with supervisees. For example, I use the Internal Family Systems Model (Schwartz, 1995) as a guide to understanding the parts of myself that are being activated in the supervisory relationship and how they might be interfering with the relationship's progression. After this self-examination, I share what I feel is relevant to the supervisory relationship with supervisees. I also ask that supervisees explore the parts of themselves that are being activated in the supervisory relationship and how they might be interfering with the relationship's progression. Initial supervision meetings are best spent openly discussing the supervisory relationship, including internal and external constraints that exist in the relationship. Internal constraints may be any negative or difficult feelings supervisees and supervisors have about their relationship. External constraints may be difficulties that exist in having supervisory relationships accepted in the agency, or problems in supervisees' specific program areas.

Frequently, agency supervisors supervise staff who have different clinical orientations. Because it is generally easier to supervise staff who share a supervisor's clinical orientation, providing supervision to those who do not presents new challenges.

_____

One supervisee, who was newly assigned to me, waited some time before scheduling her first su-

pervision session. She was an individual therapist, trained in a psychodynamic framework. When we met, she explained to me that she had been hesitant to meet with me out of fear that I would expect her to know my model and want her to use it as the sole approach in her therapy. We had a lengthy discussion about my supervisory style being collaborative and respectful of a therapist's approach to treatment. It was also very helpful, in reassuring her, that I had been trained in a psychodynamic framework and would be able to understand her approach. She stated she did want to learn more about family therapy and was pleased to have this opportunity to learn.

_____

In this example, as the clinical supervisor, if the staff member had not raised the issue of our different approaches to treatment, it would have been my responsibility to do so.

Because of the complexity of many agency cases, and their strong tendency to create isomorphism in the agency that serves them, supervisors need to recognize when therapists' personal issues are being triggered. Personal issues can be viewed as an isomorph of the family system and can give therapists diagnostic information about cases. If supervisors believe therapists' personal issues appear to be detrimental to therapy, supervisors may want to recommend personal therapy. Supervisors often feel constrained in presenting their concerns about therapists' personal issues. To some degree, this depends on the quality of the supervisory relationship and the degree of administrative support supervisors feel. If supervisors feel they should confront an issue with a supervisee, but believe they will be criticized by the administration, then they are less likely to do so.

One of the benefits of supervising in an agency is that most agencies have established internal procedures for handling difficult situations in supervision. Hopefully, supervisors will recognize such situations and seek consultation, either from a superior or a peer, then take the responsibility for attempting to resolve it with their supervisees. Supervisors may need to carefully document their efforts in case a supervisee files a grievance, or in the event that the supervisee's job performance becomes unacceptable. If intervention at the lowest possible level, between the staff member and supervisor, fails, then the staff member can follow the agency's procedures.

MULTIPLE INFLUENCES ON THERAPY AND SUPERVISION

Multiple Clients: Families and Referral Sources

Because agency clients are frequently poor, they tend to have multiple problems, many associated with lack of financial resources. These problems may include inadequate medical care, insufficient food and/or clothing, substandard housing, crowded living quarters, and increased family and marital stress. Therapists usually find themselves confronted with multiple issues to sort through as treatment plans are developed. When therapists work with multi-problem families, they can be drawn into a crisis orientation. Family crises become crises for therapists. The task of supervisors is to help supervisees maintain enough distance to see families' larger patterns and not become focused on only one aspect of families thereby ignoring others.

When involuntary clients are referred, referral sources usually have goals they expect from the agency, the therapist, and the clients. These goals need to be incorporated into the treatment contract, along with any goals the therapist may set with the client. Obviously, this can create dilemmas for therapists, especially if clients are angry with referral sources for mandating treatment or if therapists disagree with the goals of the referral source. The

supervisory role is to help therapists take a broader view of cases and understand the perspective of the other agencies involved. Supervisors guide therapists toward integrating the goals into treatment. If necessary, supervisors help therapists process their feelings about other agencies to avoid becoming adversarial with them. For example, in a case referred by the juvenile court, one goal for the youth was performing community service, an idea that the youth resisted. The treatment plan for the youth needs to address the goal of helping the youth accomplish the community service. In this case the "client" is the juvenile court and the therapist must cooperate with them.

Agencies deal with a variety of treatment populations. Most states have laws pertaining to these different clients. For example, there may be specific state laws pertaining to the rights of people identified as "mentally ill." States enact laws pertaining to juveniles, the elderly, domestic violence, substance abuse, and so on. Agency supervisors need to be knowledgeable about laws pertaining to the agency's treatment populations, and especially those pertaining to the cases they supervise.

The Medical Model Constraint

Social service agencies commonly use the medical model to identify an individual family member as symptomatic, and then diagnose them using the *Diagnostic and Statistical Manual of Mental Disorders* (American Psychiatric Association, 1994). In the typical treatment plan, the role of marital and family therapy is generally one part of a larger plan, which could include multiple modalities. Supervisors can assist therapists in making systemic diagnoses of cases while working within a linear context. If marriage and family therapists feel unsupported in their approach to treatment by others in the agency, they may feel frustrated, begin to doubt themselves, or feel they cannot stay in an agency where they perceive themselves as isolated. As a supervisor, it is important to offer therapists a framework for thinking about psychiatric diagnosis. For example, clinicians can think of the diagnosis as a working description of the identified patient's reactions to the family system.

Because multiple modalities of treatment are frequently used, including psychiatric assessment and medication, individual therapy, family therapy, and group therapy, supervisors function most effectively if they are familiar with multiple theoretical models. Many agencies claim to have a dominant theoretical model, and in fact, some use one model exclusively. However, in most agency settings, it is unusual for a supervisor to be able to supervise only MFT cases. Agency supervision challenges supervisors to be flexible and creative while working within the constraints imposed by the agency's internal structure and funding sources.

OPPORTUNITY FOR VARIETY IN SUPERVISORY METHODS

Most agency contexts offer opportunities for a wide variety of supervisory methods, which can fit different supervision needs. For example, novice therapists may require individual supervision, while with more experienced therapists, group supervision may be more useful and expedient. In an agency providing outpatient therapy services, therapists may have autonomy to set their own schedules, but as a result, they may feel isolated from other staff members. Group supervision can serve to help clinicians feel supported and promote teamwork, as well as assist them in navigating difficult agency cases. Group supervision can be useful for the agency supervisor because it is an efficient use of time, while maximizing the training benefits to the staff through their exposure to ideas from other colleagues.

The practicality of live team supervision in an agency may depend on funding sources as well as direct service requirements for the staff. Live supervision is not a financially sound practice in many agencies because the agency can only bill for one therapist's time spent on the case. Other team members cannot receive credit toward their direct service goals. Video- and audiotaping are often the most practical methods of supervision. If clinicians have access to equipment, and clients have consented by signing the proper release forms, audiotaping can be easily accomplished by most clinicians.

For maximum supervisory results, a combination of methods is best. This maximizes learning opportunities for therapists and offers supervisors expanded opportunities to assess therapists' skill levels and to determine how to make supervision beneficial.

EVALUATION OF SUPERVISEES' PROGRESS

In most agencies, supervisors must oversee the clinical work of staff members and their case management skills. In evaluating successful supervision from a clinical perspective, the measure of success is partly based on achieving clinical goals related to the mission of the agency. For example, a child protective agency may have as its mission protecting the welfare of children, while seeking to reunite children with their families. The success of all cases would be measured against this goal.

Monitoring clinical progress of cases is typically a joint undertaking of supervisors and supervisees. Through the use of various supervision methods, supervisors and supervisees can assess the needs of cases, therapist–client interactions, and the usefulness of particular interventions. Monitoring is also frequently achieved through supervisees' verbal reports of case progress. In a collaborative effort to provide the best service for clients, supervisors may set clinical goals with their supervisees. In each supervision session, the supervisor and supervisee can track the goals, determining which ones have been achieved, which ones may need to be revised, and which ones are no longer appropriate and need to be discarded.

Goals are also used in monitoring the progress of supervision. Often, these goals are written, although they are sometimes just verbal agreements. Written goals are included in the yearly performance evaluation of the supervisee. Goals may be developed for supervisees as they work with various types of cases and need to develop new skills. Goals can be tracked on a weekly, monthly, or yearly basis. Supervisors and supervisees can refer to them to track supervisees' progress in achieving them.

Broadening the clinical abilities and theoretical understanding of supervisees is greatly valued in agencies because of the wide variety of cases clinicians must learn to treat. To survive as a successful therapist in an agency environment, a particular set of case management skills is required. One important skill is the ability to think critically and thoroughly throughout a case. Therapists need to assess clients at many different levels (i.e., social, educational, medical, financial, family relationships, and so on). Another important skill supervisors seek in supervisees is the ability to make sure nothing critical is being missed in a case. Supervisors want their supervisees to be independent in their case management skills. This increases the therapists' autonomy and decreases their dependence on supervisors for direction.

Agency life can move at such a fast pace that it is very important for therapists to know how to manage their cases on a day-to-day basis. Caseloads can be high and supervisors may not always be readily available to answer questions. A third important skill that supervisors want in their supervisees is the ability to set boundaries for themselves with clients and with staff members. For example, if a client is frequently canceling or changing appointments, a therapist needs to know how to ad-

dress this directly, appropriately, and in a timely manner. A staff member also needs to know how to say "no" to other staff members, because by saying "yes" too often, they may become overextended and possibly burn out.

As supervision progresses, supervisors hope supervisees will become less concerned with what to do, and more interested in understanding their role in the client-therapist-supervisor-agency system. Next, as supervisees progress, supervisors hope they will be increasingly able to hypothesize about cases and develop interventions based on their hypotheses. With more advanced supervisees, supervision can be more about thinking about clinical concerns and less about management issues.

The success of supervision is also measured by whether it helps therapists broaden their perspective about cases. Successful supervisory interventions help supervisees remove constraints to the therapy. For example, in group supervision, a therapist presented a case of a sixteen-year-old sex abuse victim who lived with her mother. The mother expressed intense anger and hatred toward her daughter. The therapist had been working with the case for about a year, with no change in the mother–daughter relationship although other family relationships had improved.

The therapist could not see any reason for the mother to continue to be so angry with her daughter. Discussion with other group members revealed that the parents were divorced. The perpetrator of the abuse was the daughter's seventeen-year-old brother who now lived with the father. Historically, the parents had a very violent and angry marriage. The father had physically abused the mother. The mother had turned to her son for support and elevated him to the role of her confidant. In this case, the therapist needed help in seeing the possibility that the mother was angry with the daughter because the mother saw her daughter as having taken away her confidant by accusing him of sexual abuse. The therapist noted she had been constrained in her thinking by not being able to consider the mother–daughter relationship in the family context.

A CASE EXAMPLE

The following supervision case example highlights the most important aspects of the supervisory contract that are distinctive to an agency setting, while also highlighting some common dilemmas of agency supervision.

Peter worked in a substance abuse treatment program providing therapy to youth and their families. Because of the specialized nature of the program in which Peter worked, he received consultation on an as-needed basis from the supervisor of the substance abuse treatment program, who reported to me in my role as clinical director of the agency. As a result of this arrangement, there were times when Peter came to supervision having already consulted on cases. I welcomed this additional input because the consultant was a specialist in substance abuse and knew more on the subject than me. All three of us recognized, however, that, in cases of disagreement, I was ultimately responsible for clinical decisions on Peter's cases.

Because I was both Peter's supervisor and the clinical director of the agency, we had a dual relationship. This sometimes constrained us in our degree of openness with each other, as well as limiting the content of supervision. Peter appeared very concerned with pleasing me, partly out of recognition of my power to fire him or recommend raises or promotions. In my role as clinical director, I had access to considerable information from outside the supervision about Peter and his cases. At times I felt unsure about what kind of information or how much information from other levels of the agency to share with Peter. My ethical responsibilities to Peter were to avoid exploiting his trust and dependence on me; I had to be

very aware of my dual roles. This was kept an open topic for discussion, initiated by either Peter or myself, to ensure I would use good judgment and not exploit my relationship with him. I also had the ethical responsibility of maintaining the confidentiality of personal material Peter disclosed to me.

Many of Peter's cases were court-involved and involved Child Welfare. Because of the complexity of Peter's cases, and because this was his first professional position, there were times when I had to be explicit and directive to exercise my legal/ethical responsibilities to Peter's clients. In the early stages of Peter's development as a therapist, I had to offer step-by-step guidance and direction. As Peter's level of skill became more advanced, less supervisory direction was needed. The supervisory relationship originated in the agency requirement for every clinical staff to receive weekly supervision. We agreed to keep administrative issues to a minimum. When this became impossible, we agreed to schedule additional time for clinical supervision.

Peter's learning goals and my assessment were incorporated into the following goals and objectives: to become less activated by his clients; to set boundaries with his clients; to identify parts of himself that played a role in his therapy, and to learn how to take charge of those parts by being centered in himself; to share more of himself with clients and colleagues, as appropriate; to relate theory and technique; to learn case management skills; and to further develop his sense of professional competence.

Peter had a strong tendency to want to help his clients, which interfered with working collaboratively and empowering them to take charge of themselves. From the beginning of my work with Peter, he acknowledged having this strong and active "helper" part; he seemed to feel responsible for changing his clients and making them well. Peter felt he was not doing his job if he was not being helpful. When this part of him was activated, Peter appeared compulsively helpful and overly responsive. As Peter's supervisor, I also had an active "helper" part. Initially, this part of me was easily activated when Peter was struggling to find direction with his clients. I worked on being less activated by Peter's struggles. I learned how to quiet the helper part of me so she would not take over the supervision process.

By doing this, I modeled for Peter what he needed to learn to do with his clients. When I became more quiet in supervision and stopped filling in the blanks for Peter, he had to turn inward and rely on himself for answers to his concerns. Through my role-modeling and supervisory discussions, Peter began to integrate the concept that being less helpful is more helpful to clients. In his therapeutic work, he began to have pre-session and insession internal dialogues with his helper part, asking him to trust that Peter could make good clinical decisions, and to move aside and not take over the therapy session. Clients usually responded to this by being able to talk about their own parts.

Peter had an intense need to please and to look good to others. This seemed to contribute to his anxiety. As Peter's supervisor, I took steps to help diminish his high level of anxiety. One step was to share positive feedback from others about Peter's work. I also used selective self-disclosure about my own internal struggles. I asked Peter to explain how he might teach other therapists about calming down their own parts because if Peter could teach it, then he could understand how to do it for himself.

The example of my work with Peter highlights a few unique issues to be considered when making supervision contracts in an agency setting. When dual relationships exist, supervisors should be clear with supervisees about what issues are to be addressed in any given meeting. If nonclinical issues interfere with clinical supervision, more supervision time will be needed. It is also important for supervisors to be open to hearing supervisees'

concerns regarding how the administrative relationship may affect clinical supervision. Supervisors must also be clear with themselves about the role they assume during a supervision meeting. One time a therapist came to supervision upset with the behavior of the agency's executive director during a staff meeting. The therapist ventilated her feelings with her supervisor who was in the dual role of being clinical director and clinical supervisor. In this case, the supervisor had to work to keep her feelings and concerns originating in her role as clinical director out of her interaction with the therapist. The supervisor's job was to help the therapist sort through her own reactions, not to defend the executive director or his behavior.

REFERENCES

American Psychiatric Association (1994). _Diagnostic and statistical manual of mental disorders—DSM-IV._ Washington, DC: Author.

Aponte, H. (1976). The family-school interview. _Family Process, 15,_ 303–311.

Bowen, M. (1978). Theory in the practice of psychotherapy. In M. Bowen, _Family therapy in clinical practice_ (pp. 337–388). New York: Aronson.

Breunlin, D., Schwartz, R., & Mac Kune-Karrer, B. (1992). _Metaframeworks._ San Francisco: Jossey-Bass.

Ebner, M. (1979). Hard hats vs. soft hearts: The conflict between principles and reality in child and adolescent care and treatment programs. _Child Care Quarterly, 8,_ 36–46.

Haley, J. (1980). _Leaving home._ New York: McGraw-Hill.

Harbin, H. (1978). Families and hospitals: Collusion or cooperation? _American Journal of Psychiatry, 135,_ 1496–1499.

Liddle, H., & Saba, G. (1985). The isomorphic nature of training and therapy: Epistemological foundations for a structural-strategic training paradigm. In J. Schwartzman (Ed.), _Families and other systems: The macro systemic context of family therapy_ (pp. 27–47). New York: Guilford Press.

Minard, S. (1976). Family systems model in organizational consultation: Vignettes of consultation to a day care center. _Family Process, 15,_ 313–320.

Montalvo, B., & Pavlin, S. (1966). Faulty staff communications in a residential treatment center. *American Journal of Orthopsychiatry, 36,* 706–711.

Schwartz, R. (1995). *Internal family systems theory.* New York: Guilford Press.

Schwartzman, H., & Kneifel, A. (1985). Familiar institutions: How the child care system replicates family patterns. In J. Schwartzman (Ed.), *Families and other systems: The macrosystemic context of family therapy* (pp. 87–107). New York: Guilford Press.

10

Privately Contracted Supervision

Thomas C. Todd

Privately contracted supervision is one of the most common supervisory contexts, according to a survey by McKenzie et al. (1986). Given the widespread nature of this practice, it is somewhat surprising how little literature is devoted specifically to this topic. A partial exception is Kaslow (1986) who has written about supervision of private practice. This chapter has the broader title of "privately contracted supervision," rather than "private practice supervision," because the crucial characteristic is the private and voluntary relationship between supervisor and supervisee. The supervisor is functioning privately in the supervisory contract but may work in an agency or an academic institution. Similarly, there can be great variability in the clinical practice context of the supervisee, who may see clients privately or in an agency context. Although it is probably unusual for a student in a degree program to be seeking private supervision, it is not uncommon for a supervisee who is a trainee in a post-degree program to contract for private supervision.

Depending on the structure of the private practice, supervision of therapists in private practice may not exhibit all the qualities outlined in this chapter. If supervision is performed by the head of a group private practice, this supervision tends to be a hybrid of privately contracted supervision and agency supervision (see Chapter 9). Many of the issues outlined in this chapter may be present, including contractual ambiguities, lack of safeguards for the supervisee, and heightened legal liabilities and responsibility for the supervisor (Storm, 1990). Key differences, which make it similar to agency supervision, include the lack of choice of supervisor and the multiple hats, such as employer, case assigner, and supervisor, the supervisor wears.

As will be seen throughout this chapter, much of what is distinctive about privately contracted supervision flows from (1) the voluntary nature of the relationship, (2) the relative privacy of the relationship, and (3) the direct financial reimbursement that is usually involved. The typical preventive and remedial measures that are recommended are intended to minimize the impact of one or more of these qualities—to make the relationship more structured and formal, to build in measures of outside accountability, and to make the financial parameters of the relationship clearer.

THE INSTITUTIONAL CONTEXT

Privately contracted supervision, which will be called "private supervision" hereafter, describes a relationship in which a supervisee voluntarily enters into a private contract for supervision with a supervisor. With rare exceptions, the supervisee usually pays the supervisor directly for this service.

Several factors can have a significant impact on this supervisory relationship. More often than with other supervisory contexts, private supervision may involve a supervisee who has little or no advance knowledge about the supervisor; however, this is less likely if both work in the same agency or are part of the same academic institution. This means that the initial contracting period tends to take longer and involve more self-disclosure by the supervisor, because the supervisee may not know the theoretical orientation of the supervisor or what the expectations of the supervisor may be.

Supervisors-in-training (SIT) may feel that they have a particularly difficult task of "selling" themselves, especially when the supervision arrangement has been brokered by a third party such as the person who is supervising the SIT. It may be tempting to offer to supervise free, meet at the supervisee's location, and so on, to attract supervisees, but these concessions have a way of coming back to haunt the relationship. In such situations, both parties may feel that the supervisee is doing the SIT a favor, creating a position of reverse dependency that is problematic. The SIT is indeed getting something extra from the experience and may be comparatively inexperienced as a supervisor, so it may be reasonable to set a lower fee for supervision. On the other hand, the supervisee is also receiving valuable supervision from a more experienced colleague; some payment should be expected. When such payment is not part of the contract, this can obscure the lack of value placed on the supervision by the supervisee, resulting in lateness and missed sessions, failure to tape sessions or do assigned readings or paperwork, and so on.

The private supervisor also may know relatively little about the supervisee—skill level, theoretical orientation and sophistication, expectations for supervision—or about the supervisee's caseload or practice setting. Because of the degree of potential legal exposure of the supervisor, the initial contract should be considered tentative until such factors have been assessed.

Private supervision can include a surprisingly wide range of skill levels, which can be problematic if the supervisor begins to believe that the supervisee is seeing clients that are beyond the supervisee's skill level or is receiving inadequate supervision in the supervisee's work context. As will be seen in later discussions of ethical and legal issues, this may put the supervisor in an ethical quandary or expose the supervisor to significant legal risk. Liability may be reduced, but typically not eliminated, if the supervisee is already a fully licensed professional.

Inherent in the private supervision arrangement is some reason why additional or alternate supervision is attractive or necessary. It is critically important to understand these reasons and the nature of other supervisory relationships in order to develop an adequate contract for private supervision. It makes considerable difference whether the marriage and family therapy (MFT) supervisor is the only supervisor of a case, or whether there is another supervisor with a significantly different orientation. Similarly, it is important to know whether key figures, such as the other supervisor, an agency administrator, or a psychiatrist in charge of a private practice, recognize the need for the private supervision arrangement (and may even pay for it!), or whether they merely tolerate this arrangement because of the supervisee's wish for professional advancement.

THE NATURE OF THE SUPERVISORY RELATIONSHIP

Typically in private supervision, the supervisor is hired by the supervisee so that the supervisee can work toward some training objective, most often American Association for Marriage and Family Therpay (AAMFT) Clinical Membership (or designation as an Approved Supervisor) or state licensure as a marriage and family therapist. Often, there is a further credentialing objective in a second profession, such as pastoral counseling, social work or psychology, which necessitates a supervisor with both sets of credentials. Two other parameters—cost and the degree of expertise or status of the supervisor—can operate to an unusual degree in private supervision. In some cases, the cost of supervision is a dominant factor that influences the choice of supervisor. In others, where cost is less of an issue, the supervisee may have the option of choosing a supervisor based almost exclusively on reputation, with a spectrum of choices much wider than is available in an agency or educational context (Kaslow, 1986).

As noted before, the practice of supervision on a fee-for-service basis is extremely common in MFT training (McKenzie et al., 1986). Supervisors should be warned, however, that state licensing statutes may place limits on the practice of having the supervisor "hired" by the supervisee. For example, practitioners seeking licensure as marriage, family, and child counselors in California are expected to have a supervisor who is employed by an agency rather than the student, presumably because of concerns about conflict of interest (State of California, 1996). Furthermore, in California supervisees must be employed in an agency or institution and cannot be in private practice except as an employee in a group practice. Few states have such carefully drawn regulations about supervision, but supervisors functioning privately would be well advised to research state regulations carefully.

In those states and professions where it is considered legal and ethical for the supervisor to receive payment from the supervisee, there is little question that such payment has the potential to color and influence the relationship. Few supervisors are economically dependent on the income from supervision, yet few supervisors want to be "fired," even when the money is insignificant. Monetary issues can also be awkward when dealing with issues such as late cancellations by the supervisee.

Because the private contract presumably can be dissolved by either party, contracting should explicitly cover the consequences of such termination. There has been particular ambiguity about the possibility of a negative evaluation, with some supervisees believing that firing the supervisor eliminates the possibility of a negative evaluation to the credentialing body. The position of most supervisors, credentialing bodies, and probably the lay public, is that the supervisor has not only a right but a duty to provide such a negative evaluation, with both parties given opportunity to explain their respective views. Because it is not necessarily obvious how this possible situation would be handled, this contingency should be covered in the initial supervisory contract. On the other side, supervisors who have unilaterally terminated supervision have sometimes refused to provide an evaluation to the credentialing body, a stance that is rarely upheld if challenged by the supervisee.

The contract should make clear what the supervisee is "buying" for his or her money. At times supervisees have believed that there was an implied contract that they would obtain their credentialing goal automatically after completion of a specified number of hours of supervision, yet supervisors have the ethical responsibility of requiring additional supervision if the competency level of the supervisee does not meet minimal standards. This is particularly awkward when significant amounts of money have changed hands. Careful contracting and ongoing evaluation help avoid such ugly surprises. (See Chapter 19 for an in-depth discussion of supervisory contracts.) The handling of negative evaluations should be addressed, as well as the issue of future financial arrangements. Will the supervisor continue to see the supervisee free until the goal is achieved? For a reduced fee?

Other economic factors may further complicate private supervision. Historically, there is considerable precedent for clinicians to seek supervision for purposes of obtaining third-party reimbursement, which they could not obtain based on their qualifications. This practice is receiving much more ethical and regulatory scrutiny. Thus, it should be done carefully, if at all, and with thoughtful attention to the ethical guidelines of the professions involved, as well as relevant state regulations. Primarily this requires being precise about the nature of the supervisory relationship, being careful not to mislead either clients or third-party payers about who is performing the treatment or the training and credentials of the therapist. Because one or both of the parties may receive considerable financial gain from this relationship, the supervisory relationship can be easily distorted. The supervisee may be less critical about the quality of supervision, because the economic purpose is still being fulfilled and might be jeopardized by complaints. Similarly, a well-paid supervisor may be less inclined to be very critical or give an unfavorable evaluation of a supervisee.

The remaining potential problem area arises from the "private" nature of the supervisory relationship. In privately contracted supervision, the private nature of the supervisory relationship is accentuated and institutional safeguards usually are lacking (Storm, 1990). It seems that this would be less true when a SIT is being supervised, but this is usually experienced by the supervisee as only a partial safeguard. When problems develop in supervision, there is still a need for a third-party mechanism to resolve extreme disputes; the supervisor-of-supervision is not necessarily regarded by the supervisee as such an objective third party. When difficulties develop, it is typically too late to work out such a conflict-resolution mechanism without that issue becoming contentious; therefore, it is preferable to make this part of the initial contract.

Problems can develop in the opposite direction as well because the private nature of the relationship can also allow a "mutual admiration" relationship to develop unchecked. Although the quality of the supervisee's therapy may suffer, complaints are unlikely unless there is a third party, such as a supervisor-of-supervision or an agency supervisor, to provide a contrasting view. (This problem, and ways of counteracting it, are discussed in more detail in Chapter 17.)

THE NATURE OF SUPERVISEES' WORK SETTINGS

The Clinical Population

Private supervision does not presuppose a particular clinical setting or population. There is no real limit to the kinds of cases that can potentially appear in private supervision, other than the limits inherent in the particular practice setting. Two kinds of problems, which are particularly troublesome when they occur together, may arise. At times, a case may be assigned to a supervisee that the supervisor believes is dangerously beyond the ability and training of the supervisee. The supervisor would never have assigned such a case to this supervisee, yet this has occurred in the clinical setting beyond the supervisor's control. Such cases may even be so difficult that the supervisor would never have personally undertaken the case without psychiatric backup, the ability to hospitalize, and so on. Naturally, it is best to anticipate such nightmare cases beforehand, both when contracting with the supervisee and when discussing case responsibility and backup with agency supervisors, psychiatrists, and other treatment team members.

Unfortunately, it is not unusual to recognize such situations after the fact, when it can be difficult to deal with them adequately. For example, I was presented in supervision with a case of significant lethal potential in which the supervisee, in solo private practice, allowed a depressed patient to leave an individual session without a clear no-suicide contract. The therapist attempted to telephone the patient after the session but received no answer. Although the presenting question for supervision was what the supervisee should do at this point, obviously much of the problem lay in the contract between therapist and client, and secondarily between supervisor and therapist.

Many issues need to be confronted before a crisis occurs (because crises typically occur at eight o'clock at night in a nearly deserted building!):

- How would the therapist assess suicide risk responsibly?
- What if a patient were suicidal yet refused to be hospitalized voluntarily?
- What if there were no insurance?
- Which psychiatrist or hospital does the therapist have a relationship with?
- At what point in the process would the supervisor be called?
- What if the supervisor was unavailable?

This list of questions is by no means exhaustive but is an illustration of the kinds of factors that should be anticipated long before a suicidal crisis is encountered, especially when the therapist works in a clinical setting that provides little backup. Although it may be tempting to say that the therapist and others involved in the case should have thought of these things before taking on the case, this unfortunately does not limit the liability of the supervisor once involved in the case.

The Treatment Team and the Structure of Treatment

Because clinical settings differ widely in private supervision, it is difficult to generalize about the nature of the treatment team. Although the supervisee's role on the team may vary, the supervisor's role does not vary nearly so much. Almost by definition, the supervisor is not a member of the treatment team, at least not without considerable effort on the part of the supervisor to establish a working relationship. In my experience, the bulk of the effort to develop such a relationship must come from the MFT supervisor. Often, the rest of the team does not even acknowledge the supervisor's existence, or does so only after the supervisee does something clinically that the rest of the team considers a mistake.

Many MFT supervisors in private contexts are remarkably naive about the treatment team and organizational structure of the clinical settings in which their supervisees operate. This conveys an unfortunate message to the supervisee, especially one who is comparatively inexperienced, that having the "correct" treatment plan is all that matters, rather than that it is important to negotiate the plan with one's colleagues, particularly those with clinical responsibility in the setting. In our substance abuse research, for example (Stanton, Todd & Associates, 1982), we found the role of the medical director critical in determining whether a recommendation of family therapy would be supported by the treatment program. Even having as sophisticated and well known a supervisor as Jay Haley did not eliminate the need to handle such relationships diplomatically. (See Haley, 1980, for his discussion of this aspect of the project.) In this setting, because of the importance of methadone and other medications, the role of the psychiatrist was extremely important; in other settings the clinical director or immediate supervisor may be more important and psychiatrists may play a somewhat peripheral consulting role.

THE "IDEOLOGY" OF THERAPY AND SUPERVISION

It is equally important for the supervisor to become aware of the prevailing treatment ideology in the supervisee's treatment setting and to help the supervisee become equally sophisticated. Many settings are multimodal, with no dominant ideology (other than eclecticism). In other settings, even those with multiple views, there may be a clear "pecking order" of points of view, with some having much higher status than others. In most cases it is wise for the MFT supervisor to be appropriately humble, because the MFT supervisor's peripheral position is often an indication of the status of MFT in that setting.

For example, I have supervised and consulted in clinical contexts in which conjoint therapy was fine as long as the identified patient and family members sought it but where there was little institutional support if patient or family objected and asked for individual therapy. Similarly, many settings support conjoint treatment as long as it is part of a multimodality treatment plan, but not if the MFT therapist argues that only conjoint treatment should be provided.

The work setting also may limit the "clout" of the private supervisor in determining what supervisory modalities, such as videotaping, live supervision, or co-therapy, will be employed. Although the private supervisor needs to avoid stipulating a modality that is unworkable in the clinical setting, it is equally important to avoid settling for a less direct form of supervision than will be satisfactory to the AAMFT or some regulatory body. For many private supervisees, the path of least resistance in their clinical settings is to avoid taping or live supervision. Often agency settings initially

react negatively to such requests, and supervisees may be reluctant to force the issue. Fortunately, AAMFT is quite adamant about the need for direct access to clinical material, so MFT supervisors can insist on the need for taping or live supervision. Often agencies find ways to cooperate when approached directly by supervisors.

MFT supervisors in private supervision may be low on the totem pole of supervisors, especially if they are supervising students. For example, I have supervised many SITs who were "add-ons" in the lives of psychology interns. They had little relevance for the intern's primary concern, namely completing the internship successfully. If the ideology of those in charge of the training program is antagonistic or incompatible to a systems orientation, it can be counterproductive for the student to be perceived as an MFT zealot. Although this is by no means universally true, it behooves the MFT supervisor to have a realistic sense of the receptivity of key figures in the clinical setting to MFT.

Of all the contexts for MFT supervision, private supervision is the context in which marriage and family therapy occurs without institutional sanction. This is not a problem in MFT training settings, or in agency settings where the MFT supervisor is an employee; however, private supervision is apt to be handicapped by this lack of institutional support. This can take the form of uncoordinated treatment plans, or can take other forms such as a lack of MFT cases. The supervisor's lack of institutional standing limits the power of the supervisor to do anything about this situation. The supervisor can attempt to hold the supervisee accountable, but often the supervisor suspects that the fault does not really lie with the supervisee. It might seem that this difficulty could be circumvented by discussing individual cases from a systemic framework, depending on the theoretical stance of the supervisor. This is rarely satisfactory when there are institutional obstacles to conjoint therapy. Among other difficulties, it makes it problematic to "turf" cases as suggested in the next paragraphs.

In private supervision, the supervisee often has a "real" supervisor who is more accountable than the MFT supervisor for the case in the clinical setting. Usually this supervisor is not a marriage and family therapist, or at least not an Approved Supervisor; otherwise, the services of an additional private supervisor would not be necessary. Therefore, much depends on the relationship between the MFT supervisor and other supervisory or administrative figures in the life of the supervisee. The supervisor is always well advised to clarify the actual contract, as much as possible, to avoid clinical confusion and to avoid creating unnecessary difficulties for the supervisee.

Wherever possible, the MFT supervisor should divide the clinical turf with other supervisors so that MFT cases are supervised primarily by the MFT supervisor. Depending on the nature of the clinical setting, there may be limits to this purity, but this is usually the ideal to be sought. Supervisees in private supervision often receive supervision concerning other modalities, but this does not need to be confusing if the different supervisors are dealing with distinct cases.

RELATIONSHIP TO OTHER INSTITUTIONS, THIRD PARTIES, AND THE LAW

In private supervision, usually the achievement of some goal, such as Clinical Membership or state licensure, is explicit from the beginning. This is often not true in agency supervision, where supervisees may only decide to seek these goals long after supervision has been initiated. However, I have encountered numerous examples in which supervisees were initially uninterested in credentialing or state

regulation yet ultimately decided to pursue it. Rather than taking a simple "No" at face value, it seems preferable to describe in detail what is additionally required to pursue these goals, or what would be the consequences of having the supervisee change his or her mind at a later date. A partial list of questions to consider includes the following:

- What is required by credentialing or regulatory bodies?
- What are the stipulations regarding the types of cases or types of clinical contact that will receive credit?
- What records will be kept, and by whom?
- Are there any stipulations, such as the need for taping or live supervision, concerning supervisory modalities?
- What is the nature of the evaluation process, including time frame and format?
- What is the process whereby a supervisee can deal with an unsatisfactory evaluation?

Anyone who has supervised in multiple contexts or for a variety of purposes will quickly recognize that, typically, the answers will differ for different situations. If confronted early, there is no inherent reason why supervision cannot achieve more than one purpose, but if this is not planned from the beginning, major discrepancies may be encountered at a later date.

Private supervision can expose the supervisor to considerable liability and place the supervisor in unique ethical and legal quandaries. Two competing forces are at work. First, the private context may mean that the supervisor is the most senior and credentialed professional dealing with the case, implying that the supervisor has the most knowledge and authority (and is therefore a prime candidate for a lawsuit!). On the other hand, as has been detailed before, the supervisor often lacks the power to select or screen cases, dictate agency policy, and so on. It is small wonder that supervisors who correctly perceive this situation develop clear policies regarding dangerous or suicidal cases and duty to warn, among others.

Legal opinions vary about the possibility of limiting one's legal liability in private supervision. The optimal situation is to be supervising a fully licensed professional who has a clearly designated supervisor in the work setting. In this situation, the private MFT supervisor may have a role that is primarily for education and consultation purposes rather than supervision. (Of course, this limited relationship, therefore, would not qualify as supervision in the eyes of AAMFT and some regulatory bodies!)

Many supervisors attempt to limit their liability by contracting to work with only a subset of the clinical cases being seen by a supervisee. This is probably a successful strategy when there is another supervisor who is responsible for the supervisee's other cases. If there is no such other supervisor, it is unsafe to assume that the supervisor has no responsibility for the other cases, even when there is a written agreement to that effect.

The commercial nature of private supervision makes the situation additionally awkward because adequate supervision for the supervisee's entire caseload may be quite expensive. "Reasonable and customary" guidelines for ratios of supervision hours to therapy hours apply here and depend on the level of expertise of the supervisee, as well as standards set by credentialing and regulatory bodies. Rather than accepting a ratio of supervision-to-therapy based on the supervisee's finances, it is best for the supervisor to imagine having to justify the extent of supervision in court should a case go badly. Would a layperson or a colleague consider it possible to have adequate oversight of the supervisee's caseload, given the frequency and duration of supervision, and given the experience level of the supervisee? If there are emergency "triage" procedures built in to the supervision whereby the supervisee is expected to alert the supervisor to potential danger with a case, is it reasonable to believe that the supervisee has sufficient clinical judgment to carry them out?

Recordkeeping and documentation of supervision can provide protection for the supervisor, but unfortunately they are often a weak link in the system. Unlike agency or training contexts, private supervision does not automatically entail particular forms of recordkeeping. Two levels of recordkeeping are important to safeguard the supervisor. One is documentation of the content of supervision, to show that issues of dangerousness have been considered, and to detail supervisory recommendations and followup. The second level is documentation of statistical parameters of supervision such as hours of supervision received and clinical hours of therapy conducted by the supervisee, which will be required by AAMFT or some other body at a later date.

EVALUATION

Private supervision often mirrors the strengths and weaknesses of therapy conducted in a private setting, at least before the advent of managed care. Nowhere is this more obvious than in the area of evaluation. Many, if not most, private supervisors approach each session with a focus on the supervisee's immediate needs. Both parties tend to judge the success of supervisory input based on meeting those needs. In this respect short-term feedback from the supervisee is very important. This is probably accentuated by the tenuousness of the contract, compared to training or agency contexts, and the commercial nature of the transaction. (Did the supervisee get his or her money's worth?)

In my experience as a supervisor and a trainer of supervisors, apparently positive supervisory relationships can come tumbling down like a house of cards when a more formal evaluation is required for Clinical Membership or professional licensure if this evaluation has not been anticipated and systematically related to session-by-session progress. To relate this to analogous situations in therapy, therapists are rarely required to make a formal evaluation of the success of therapy for some third party. When judged on their own merits, therapy sessions may seem productive, yet the therapist may be unwilling to say in absolute terms that therapy has been so successful that the patient will not drink and drive or that parents will not abuse their children. Hopefully the need for such an evaluation has been part of therapy from the beginning, and the therapist will have shared her or his sense of progress toward the goal on an ongoing basis. Even so, when important outcomes are at stake, it should be expected that differences in perspective can become the source of heated debate and hard feelings, especially if therapy has been expensive.

UNIQUE ADVANTAGES OF THE PRIVATE CONTRACT

By now the reader may have concluded that the private supervisory contract is fraught with potential liability and contracting problems and should be avoided at all cost. That is definitely not the conclusion that I wish to promote—like many supervisors, I supervise extensively in this context, and many of my most gratifying supervisory experiences occur in private supervision. Although I do believe that supervisors should take my cautions seriously, I would also like to highlight the unique advantages of the private supervisory context.

The most obvious advantage is choice. Unlike other settings, private supervision allows the participants in supervision to choose each other freely (Kaslow, 1986). This often means a better theoretical match, and also that other variables deemed important can weigh heavily in the selection process. For example, a supervisee who has never had a strong female supervisor

can deliberately choose one. Supervisors, in turn, can highlight variables that matter to them. At this point in my career, for example, I am comparatively uninterested in supervising absolute beginners in MFT and tend to refer them to other supervisors (where I am sure they receive better supervision!). Supervisors who have primary jobs in one sector can add supervisees who will round out their list of supervisees.

Freedom of choice can extend to other areas as well. There is often considerable latitude in the supervisory contract, allowing more flexibility of scheduling and caseloads. A single case may be the exclusive focus, or particular types of cases, or initial sessions, and so on. This, however, does depend on the nature of other supervisory relationships, as well as third-party considerations, such as counting hours for AAMFT. Finally, both parties are presumably free to terminate the relationship through a process that, hopefully, has been spelled out in advance. Because supervisees often feel constrained in supervision (see Chapter 17), this factor can be particularly empowering for supervisees. The combination of these factors can have a dramatic effect on the climate of supervision, compared to supervision in other contexts. Both parties often feel less pressure and constraint, especially if the supervisor feels that responsibility for the case is shared with other supervisors. The supervisor can brainstorm ideas with the supervisee without feeling the need to come up with a single "perfect" recommendation. The supervisee, in turn, feels free to entertain new ideas without feeling pinned down.

As repeatedly emphasized throughout this chapter, the supervisory contract is absolutely critical to structure supervision and protect both parties. Contingencies, which routinely might be part of the larger institutional context in an agency or training program, must be covered in such a contract. This would include evaluation methods, grievance procedures, and so on.

Supervisee selection and screening for appropriateness are crucial for the private supervisor. In the private setting, little screening is done for the supervisor, so she or he needs to consider carefully the proposed contract. Any new supervisory relationship should be considered exploratory and the contract nonbinding for a preagreed period until the supervisor has had an opportunity to assess the knowledge and skills of the supervisee directly, as well as to develop an in-depth understanding of the clinical setting in which the supervisee is operating (Kaslow, 1986). Financial parameters should be clearly specified. This goes well beyond simple fee-setting to include the cost of missed sessions, what the supervisee has "bought" for his or her money, what the economic consequences will be of a negative evaluation or a recommendation for additional sessions.

Expectations of both parties should be spelled out in advance. What is the supervisee expected to do to prepare for supervision? Are there requirements, such as taping of sessions, that must be fulfilled? What can the supervisee expect in return? How will feedback and evaluation be provided, and will the feedback be two-directional or focused exclusively on the supervisee?

Case responsibility and lines of supervisory authority must be clear to all concerned, including other supervisors and agency administrators. Procedures for handling dangerous situations and emergencies should be spelled out in advance. Necessary consent for taping and sharing of information also must be obtained.

REFERENCES

California, State of (1996). Business and Professions Code: Marriage, Family and Child Counselors, Section 49.

Haley, J. (1980). _Leaving home: The therapy of disturbed young people._ New York: McGraw-Hill.

Kaslow, F. (1986). Seeking and providing supervision in private practice. In F. Kaslow (Ed.), _Supervision and training: Models, dilemmas, and challenges_ (pp. 148–157). New York: Haworth Press.

McKenzie, P., Atkinson, B., Quinn, W., & Heath, A. (1986). Training and supervision in marriage and family therapy: A national survey. _American Journal of Family Therapy, 14,_ 293–303.

Stanton, M., Todd, T., & Associates (1982). _The family therapy of drug abuse and addiction._ New York: Guilford Press.

Storm, C. (1990). Striking the supervision bargain. _Supervision Bulletin, 4,_ 3–4.

11

Psychoanalytic Approaches to Supervising Couple and Family Therapy

Peter Alan Reiner

In the broadest sense, a *psychodynamic* approach to human behavior is any approach that focuses on the interactions of mind, body, and environment with specific emphasis on the interplay among an individual's internal (intrapsychic) experiences, conflicts, structures, functions, and processes (Fenell & Weinhold, 1989; Paolino, 1978; Sperry & Carlson, 1991). *Psychoanalytic* approaches are a *subset* of psychodynamic approaches that are characterized by ideas set forth by Freud and his followers and which can be grouped in a variety of ways (Pine, 1990; Summers, 1994). Here, I will consider three: "classical" psychoanalytic, self psychological, and object relations.[1] When contrasted with nonanalytic approaches, there is a great deal of commonality among them, which is emphasized in this chapter. For example, all share the beliefs that unconscious mental activity and motivation are extremely important and that early experience, especially with parents or parental figures, has a strong influence on later experience and behavior. The differences among the psychoanalytic approaches, significant and important as they are, are noted rather cursorily.[2,3,4]

The central components of psychoanalytic treatment of families and couples are described at some length for several reasons. They comprise the model that the supervisor must teach; they highlight important skills, attitudes, and understandings that the supervisee must master; and, because of the significant overlap between psychoanalytic family therapy and psychoanalytic supervision, many are common to both processes.

CRITICAL CONCEPTS THAT SUPERVISORS TEACH

At the beginning of therapy, the psychoanalytic therapist negotiates a frame for the therapy. The *frame* (or "structure") of therapy refers to the formal arrangements such as the frequency, time, and length of sessions; the setting; the participants; the fee; the arrangements for billing and payment; and so forth (Auld & Hyman, 1991; Langs, 1979). For two key reasons, maintaining a consistent frame, that is, avoiding any non-negotiated deviation in these areas, is championed. First, establishing and maintaining a consistent frame helps to create a *holding environment* for the client system (Scharff & Scharff, 1987; Winnicott, 1960/1986). Second, if the therapist maintains a consistent frame, any attempts to "bend" or to deviate from it are construed as meaningful communications from, or about, the client system that may reflect transference (Auld & Hyman, 1991; Greenson, 1967; Scharff, 1995; Scharff & Scharff, 1987). These beliefs contrast sharply with the stance that frame issues—or their collaborative negotiation or renegotiation—are peripheral issues or "administrative details." Flexibility may be helpful in negotiating frame issues such as who is expected to attend sessions, whether one or more clients receives additional concurrent therapy, and so forth; the nature of these negotiations and the maintenance of appropriate boundaries between or among concurrent therapies are key.

By adhering to the negotiated frame, the therapist creates a "protective barrier" or holding environment within which clients can grow and develop psychologically, free from outside intrusions or "impingements" (Langs, 1973; Summers, 1994; Winnicott, 1960/1986). Further, the holding environment (or "holding") provided by the therapist serves to *contain* clients' emotions and experiences. The therapist's ability to tolerate clients' anxieties and tensions, while remaining solidly empathic with their internal experiences, helps clients to feel deeply understood, soothed, and "held" (Elson, 1986; Kohut, 1984; Solomon, 1989; Winnicott, 1960/1986). The therapist generally does not contain or "manage" clients' emotions by interrupting or limiting their expression. Rather, the therapist tracks affect, allows it to develop, and helps the client system to tolerate the experience of it. The reactions of individuals and of the family system as a whole to *both* the holding environment and the person of the therapist compose their transference reactions.

Central to psychoanalytic family therapy is the belief that understanding transference and countertransference is critical to treatment. Most broadly, *transference* refers to clients' (often unconscious) *displacements* or *projections* onto others, usually therapists, of feelings, impulses, defenses, and fantasies from important past relationships or conflicts (Freud, 1912/1958a; Greenson, 1967; Weiner, 1975).[5] In part these projections help to "create" or to recapitulate in the therapy important (and often problematic)

aspects of clients' earlier significant relationships or conflicts (Meissner, 1978; J. Scharff, 1992).[6] Not coincidentally, this "re-creation" of aspects of earlier relationships or conflicts may also occur in clients' current relationships with significant others (Dicks, 1967; Malan, 1976; Scarf, 1987). *Countertransference* analogously refers to therapists' reactions to clients' transferences, as well as to the therapists' own (usually unconscious) displacements, projections, or other "distortions" that arise in therapy and which stem from the therapists' early relationships, unresolved conflicts, and so forth (Auld & Hyman, 1991).

From an object relations perspective, the matrix of transference and countertransference develops, in part, through *projective* and *introjective identification* (Ogden, 1994; Racker, 1957, 1968; Tansey & Burke, 1989; J. Scharff, 1992; Segal, 1964). Through the process of projective identification, the therapist may be induced to feel, or to behave, as the client (or client system) has in the past or as significant others have felt, or behaved, toward the client (or client system). Thus, the therapist's awareness of her or his own feelings and thoughts during sessions may illuminate transference and, countertransference phenomena, and, by extension, the client system's unconscious processes, impulses, conflicts, and so on (D. Scharff, 1992; Scharff & Scharff, 1987, 1991; Slipp, 1995).

The attention paid to the therapist's understanding of the client system reflects the key goal of helping clients to develop *insight* into their internal and interpersonal processes (Langs, 1973; Malan, 1976; Weiner, 1975). Explicitly championed is the notion that it is helpful for clients to become aware of the unconscious forces that govern their experiences and interactions. Therapists promote such understanding or insight, and develop the *therapeutic alliance* (Greenson, 1967; Langs, 1974; Pinsof & Catherall, 1986; Reiner, 1978, 1988; Zetzel, 1956; *cf.* Brenner, 1979) by making *interpretations*. Interpretations give meaning to intrapsychic or interpersonal events by illuminating their previously unconscious sources, motivations, causes, and so forth (Auld & Hyman, 1991; Dare, 1986; Greenson, 1967). Bringing previously unconscious conflicts, needs, wishes, and impulses into conscious awareness (i.e., undoing _repression_) decreases their "power," their influence on the present. In family therapy, for example, insight gained through interpretation may serve to reduce clients' projections or displacements that have influenced their views of one another. Rarely does a single interpretive comment have such a dramatic effect; rather, this comes about through elaboration of the insights gleaned from repeated interpretation—a process called _working through_ (Greenson, 1967; Weiner, 1975). In addition to fostering insight, interpretations serve as metacommunications to the client system that the therapist is present, is listening, and values understanding (Scharff & Scharff, 1987).

Adhering to the principle of _nondirective listening_ (Langs, 1974; Scharff & Scharff, 1987; Scharff, 1995), or maintaining what Freud (1912b/1958) called "evenly-suspended attention," facilitates the therapist's understanding of the client system's unconscious dynamics as well as the clients' experience and expression of transference reactions (Greenson, 1967). When the therapist maintains therapeutic neutrality and follows the family's lead—rather than directing, advising, or prescribing—attention can be devoted to the sequence of the clients' associations, to what is mentioned and what is avoided, and to changes in affect, all of which serve as bases for inference about clients' unconscious mental processes.[7] As noted, unconscious processes can also be inferred from transference reactions and informed by countertransference reactions (Scharff, 1992); they may also be revealed by careful exploration of clients' resistances.

Resistance refers to all the forces in the client system that oppose the procedures or processes of the therapy, often in service of avoiding anxiety associated with allowing unconscious material into conscious awareness (Greenson, 1967; Langs, 1973). Clients may manifest resistance nonverbally such as by chronically arriving late or with family members other than those negotiated with the therapist; or verbally such as by frequent lapses into silence or by restricting conversations to a highly limited group of topics or feelings (Scharff & Scharff, 1987; Weiner, 1975). Exploring impediments to clients' willingness to participate fully or to speak freely facilitates inference about what they may be trying to avoid and why. Thus, analyzing clients' inevitable resistance, as with transference, generates insight into clients' unconscious processes, which can be shared with (or interpreted to) the client system.[8] Although clients' past individual and family experiences may manifest indirectly through transference or resistance, they may be explored more directly.

From the perspective of this _historically based_ approach, _the past matters_, and knowledge of the past informs the understanding of the present (Nichols, 1988). In general, the focus is not so much on obtaining factual and complete chronologies as on understanding clients' (conscious and unconscious) experiences of their important relationships. Particular attention is also paid to issues of actual or potential loss or abandonment; this is further reflected in an emphasis on _planned terminations_. Once obtained, individual and collective histories can be connected to, or integrated with, specific present situations or difficulties in a way that enhances meaning and insight (Scharff & Scharff, 1987). As with any other material, clients' histories are allowed to emerge spontaneously as they are elicited by issues in the present, with relatively little guidance from the therapist. Although the therapist may at times ask about experiences in clients' families of origin (or with each other) that may influence current attitudes or behaviors, she or he does not unilaterally decide to utilize one or more sessions exclusively to "gather history," to construct a genogram, and so on.

The individual and family histories that emerge are one source of information about the client system's and individual members' *developmental phases* or *levels*. These are important foci of psychoanalytic couple and family therapy, given the goals of facilitating both the system's further developmental growth and its management of developmental stress. Of interest are the developmental levels of each individual and of the family system as a whole, as well as their interactions. Each person's developmental level or stage is conceptualized from the psychosexual perspective of Freud and extended to the psychosocial arena, reflecting the influence of Erikson (1950) among others (Scharff & Scharff, 1987). The nature and quality of the children's relationships with their parents is especially important, and is viewed through the lens of the children's stages of development (Scharff & Scharff, 1987). Put simply, how do the children characteristically relate to their parents and to their family, and how appropriate are these ways given the children's developmental levels?

The family system's developmental level or stage may be thought of from two vantage points. First, there is the aspect that has to do with the family's journey through the "family life cycle" (Carter & McGoldrick, 1980, 1989; Gerson, 1995; McGoldrick & Carter, 1982; Pittman, 1987). The family's developmental stage can be located in the matrix of important internal and external transitions such as the birth of the first child, the launching of the last child, and so on. Of course the nature and the timing of such developmental stages is best understood within various larger contexts, including ethnicity (Boyd-Franklin, 1989; Breunlin, Schwartz, & Mac Kune-Karrer, 1992; McGoldrick, 1989), sexual orientation (Scrivner & Eldrige, 1995), and so on. Second, there is the aspect of family developmental level that has to do

with a shared underlying mode of relating, problem solving, or experiencing (Scharff & Scharff, 1987). That is, the *interpersonal system* may be functioning at a particular psychosexual or psychosocial level or in ways described by various psychoanalytic writers who have illuminated developmental issues (Bowlby, 1958/ 1986; Mahler, 1972/1986). The "fit" among these various aspects of development may explain why a client system manages certain developmental tasks, phases, or transitions more successfully than it does others (Scharff & Scharff, 1987). Further, the couple's or family's (psychological, psychosexual, or psychosocial) developmental levels have implications for the anticipated length of treatment, the nature of the work, and the responses of the therapist that might prove especially helpful or problematic (Scharff & Scharff, 1987).

As it is described here, the psychoanalytic model of marital and family treatment is a complicated one. How the task of learning to apply this model is conceptualized and guided in supervision is discussed in the following section.

CRITICAL ASPECTS OF PSYCHOANALYTIC SUPERVISION

Traditionally, therapists who work with individuals and are training to become psychoanalysts present clinical material to their individual supervisors from memory or from "process notes" written after therapy sessions. In formal psychoanalytic training, taking notes during therapy sessions is strongly discouraged, in part because it may interfere with "hearing" the clients (Freud, 1912/1958b). So, too, is audiotaping or videotaping sessions; the recorder is viewed as an intrusion into the session, or in Langs's parlance (1979), as a violation of the therapeutic "frame." Given these attitudes, it is obvious that in traditional, formal psychoanalytic training situations observed or "live" interviews are not conducted. However, as the contexts change from formal psychoanalytic training to less formal situations in which psychoanalytic or psychodynamic therapy is taught, and from training devoted to work with individuals to that focused on work with couples or families, more latitude is allowed. Thus, for example, sessions may be recorded or observed; yet interrupting a therapist with suggestions during an observed interview or a consultant's entrance into the therapy room would be viewed as inappropriate. These latter activities are still seen as overly intrusive and as detracting from the importance placed on the therapist's experiences and internal processes during sessions.

Just as the psychoanalytic psychotherapist establishes and maintains a frame with the client system, the supervisor establishes and maintains the frame with the supervisee (Langs, 1994). Thus, frame issues—meeting frequency, time, and place; freedom from interruption; and so on—are not considered incidental or "administrative" details. Unplanned deviations from the supervisory frame are given thoughtful consideration, much as are unplanned deviations from the therapeutic frame. Within the established frame, the psychoanalytic supervisor listens to the therapist's presentation of clinical material, regardless of method, with several key aims. A central supervisory function is *teaching* the supervisee, as opposed to treating the couple or the family through the supervisee (Lothane, 1984; Muslin & Val, 1989); the supervisor assesses the therapist's understanding of psychoanalytic principles and skill in their application in order to determine what to teach. Just as the psychoanalytic psychotherapist must form a "therapeutic alliance" with the client system, the psychoanalytic supervisor must form a *learning alliance* with the supervisee (Fleming & Benedek, 1966; Wool, 1989).

The establishment of a collaborative learning alliance may be more difficult because of a second central supervisory function, the *evaluation* of the therapist's ability or potential to function as a therapist, which is often required by a training institution, a credentialing or licensing organization, or the like (Ekstein & Wallerstein, 1958; Zaphiropoulos, 1984). The supervisor also pays particular attention to the therapist's countertransference, both as the therapist reports (or analyzes) it and as it may be inferred from various aspects of the therapist's presentation (Jacobs, David, & Meyer, 1995). Just as the psychoanalytic psychotherapist listens to the client system in the particular manner previously discussed, the supervisor listens to the therapist and draws inferences about the therapist's unconscious processes, conflicts, dynamics, and so on (Langs, 1994). In addition, the supervisor examines her or his reactions to, or experiences of, the therapist and of the supervisory relationship with the therapist.

Sorting through this cluster of experiences, thoughts, and inferences—drawn directly from the therapist and the supervisor and indirectly from the client system—is a central and complex task for the supervisor and the supervisee (Jarmon, 1990). One goal is to identify the "transference-countertransference situation" in the therapy, that is, to understand the client system's transference to the therapist and the therapist's corresponding countertransference to the client system (Gill, 1994; Mitchell, 1993; J. Scharff, 1992; Tansey & Burke, 1989). In addition, the supervisor helps the therapist to determine what this situation suggests about the client system, or the therapist, or their interaction. To the degree to which the supervisor believes that the therapist's responses to the client system are not idiosyncratic, are not indicative of the therapist's unresolved issues or conflicts, they are taken to have substantial meaning about the client system. The supervisor, as necessary, guides the therapist in using countertransference responses to understand the client system and in translating the understandings into interpretations to be shared. To the degree that the supervisor perceives the therapist's responses to be derived from the therapist's unresolved issues or conflicts, they are taken to have substantial meaning about the therapist rather than about the client system.

The "Teach" or "Treat" Controversy

When the supervisor believes that the therapist's personal issues are substantially influencing the perception and the treatment of the couple or family, several important issues are raised: the degree to which, if at all, this should be explored in supervision; and whether therapists are expected to have had (or to be in) personal therapy. From the beginning of the psychoanalytic movement, the major experience that was deemed essential—the *sine qua non*: to prepare an individual to function as a psychoanalyst—was her or his personal psychoanalysis, the so-called "training analysis" (Fleming & Benedek, 1966). That is to say, having successfully completed treatment *as a client* with a recognized psychoanalyst was a necessary, although not clearly a sufficient, condition for beginning practice; it was the "major training vehicle" (Ekstein & Wallerstein, 1958, p. 243). Soon added to this requirement was that of receiving supervision on one's early attempts to provide psychoanalysis to others, the so-called *controlled analyses*.

Initially, there was a difference of opinion about whether a single analyst, or different analysts, should provide one's training analysis and supervise one's first control analysis. Should one's therapist—more or less as a continuation of ongoing therapy—provide supervision on one's first case(s) or should one find a different analyst to provide supervision, generally after one's training analysis was complete? Embedded in this difference of opinion were issues about matters of timing, and more importantly, the so-called "treat" or "teach"

controversy. That is, were the primary difficulties of a fledgling psychoanalyst the result of unresolved personal issues that created "blind spots" (i.e., "countertransference problems") that were in need of further analysis, or was there more to be gained from exposure to a different analyst who would provide needed instruction and direction and who would refer the beginner back to the training analyst for further treatment only if personal problems arose? Eventually, it was agreed that the training and control analyses—the treatment and the supervision of a novice analyst—should not be conducted by the same person and that the practical supervised work should begin while the training analysis was still being conducted (Fleming & Benedek, 1966).

Not only were the supervision and the treatment of a beginning analyst to be provided by different analysts, but the boundary between the two was to be rigidly maintained. This was thought to be essential to maintain the integrity of both enterprises. The complete separation ensured the confidentiality of the novice's own therapy; allowed the novice's analyst and the novice's supervisor to have clearly defined, distinct roles; and so on. Over time, however, many (Ekstein & Wallerstein, 1958; Racker, 1957; Searles, 1955) found this rigid boundary to be overly restrictive, even counterproductive, and ofttimes not maintained (Issacharoff, 1984); particularly objectionable was the prohibition of considering any of the novice's personal issues (or countertransference) in any way in supervision (Sarnat, 1992; Tansey & Burke, 1989). As a result, despite some strong objections, *supervisors* began to address novice therapists' personal issues in limited and carefully defined ways rather than immediately and categorically referring the novices for further treatment.

This specific issue—whether and how to respond to a supervisee's countertransference problems—has been addressed repeatedly, though intermittently, in the psychoanalytic literature (Issacharoff, 1984; Jarmon, 1990; Tansey & Burke, 1989). It remains an area of active controversy.[9] In general, a discussion of the novice's countertransference issues that arise at a particular point in treatment with a specific couple or family is thought to fall within the purview of supervision (Jacobs et al., 1995; Weiner & Kaplan, 1980). In contrast, counter-transference (or "family-of-origin") issues that arise repeatedly, both within and across a therapist's cases, might be more appropriately explored primarily in the therapist's personal psychotherapy. Perhaps more important than the issue of whether a therapist's personal issues are circumscribed or pervasive is the consideration of the key purpose of exploring them.

As Ekstein and Wallerstein (1958) note, the therapist's personal problems are addressed in supervision with the primary goal of enhancing the therapist's ability to treat the client system rather than of resolving the therapist's inner conflict. Sarnat (1992) makes a cogent case for expanding the consideration of countertransference issues in supervision; she notes that all therapists experience countertransference and that to limit its discussion in supervision may "pathologize" the supervisee.

What is *not* questioned in discussions of the controversy is the need for the supervisee's personal issues to be addressed in some setting. However, as the focus shifts from the formal psychoanalytic candidate to the therapist-in-training who wishes to practice couple and family therapy from a psychoanalytic perspective, the need for personal analysis or psychoanalytic psychotherapy is not taken as an absolute. It is, though, strongly encouraged; virtually all psychoanalytic supervisors believe that few people who have not had personal psychotherapy can function adequately and openly as couple and family therapists. Underpinning this belief is the notion that the therapist must be open to receiving ("holding" or "containing") anxiety and other potentially disturbing affects, conflicts, or experiences from the

client system. To the extent that the therapist cannot remain open to this material, couples and families cannot be encouraged to experience and to explore it (Moldawsky, 1980).

Parallel Process

Just as the psychoanalytic psychotherapist must remain open to receiving potentially disturbing affects, conflicts, or experiences from the client system, the supervisor must remain open to receiving the like from the supervisee (Langs, 1994). *Supervisors*, as well, are therefore urged to have completed personal therapy. To the degree that their personal issues do not interfere, supervisors' perceptions of supervisees and of the supervisory relationships may provide valuable insight not only into the supervisees, but into client system–therapist relationships as well.[10] Succinctly put, aspects of the client system–therapist relationship may be replicated in the therapist–supervisor relationship, a phenomenon known as *parallel process* (Caligor, 1984; Doehrman, 1976). Incidentally, although clinicians from nonanalytic orientations may note such isomorphism, it is the psychoanalytic literature that is rife with discussions of its meanings and underlying processes, following its description by Searles (1955) and its labeling as "parallel process" by Ekstein and Wallerstein (1958).

As an example, consider a supervisor who feels briefly overwhelmed by the chaotic, complex, or pressured presentation of a therapist who has emerged from a session with a chaotic, complex family that the therapist experienced as overwhelming. Optimally, the supervisor understands that aspects of the relationship between the family and the therapist have been "re-created" in the supervisory relationship and can share this insight with the therapist. The supervisor's aim of developing insight or understanding in the therapist corresponds to the therapist's task of fostering insight in the couple or family. To state this important point more generally, the manner in which the supervisor responds to the therapist may serve as an explicit or implicit model for the manner in which the therapist responds to the client system. In this sense, then, the relationship between therapist and family may replicate aspects of that between supervisor and therapist; if this is an unconscious phenomenon, it is another aspect of parallel process (Grey & Fiscalini, 1987).

Modeling

Such modeling by the supervisor is an important method used to teach the therapist the skills, the knowledge, and the attitudes of psychoanalytic therapy. It should be clear by now that most of the skills and attitudes the supervisor wishes to enhance in the therapist are used and modeled in the supervisory relationship. Teaching and maintaining the *analytic attitude* (Schafer, 1983) is especially important (Langs, 1994). As characterized by Moldawsky (1980, p. 127), this "attitude" includes the following elements: a genuine interest in clients and a respect for their autonomy; awareness that the therapy process involves discovering rather than knowing in advance; an empathic, but neutral, stance with intrapsychic or interpersonal conflicts; a nondirective, but involved, position that allows for the development or the expression of transference; an awareness of the inevitability and the power of resistance; and the fundamental assumption that there are unconscious forces at work that can be inferred and articulated. In addition to teaching this attitude, the supervisor tries to enhance various skills: establishing and maintaining the therapeutic frame, gathering individual and family histories, assessing individual and family development, tracking and "containing" affect, exploring resistance, fostering insight by providing well-timed interpretations, and so on.

Supervision Concepts Highlighted by Each Model

The supervisory model described here is consistent with the "classical" psychoanalytic treatment model and has been championed in several classic books (*viz.*, Ekstein & Wallerstein, 1958; Fleming & Benedek, 1966). However, just as concepts from self psychology have informed the treatment of couples and families, so too have they influenced its supervision (see Endnote 3). Brightman (1984), for example, highlighted the *narcissistic vulnerability* of the supervisee, the need for the supervisor to function as a *selfobject* for the supervisee, the need for the supervisee to give up a grandiose version of a professional self, and so on. Analogously, concepts that are central to object relations thinking (see Endnote 4) have been applied to the supervisory situation (Jarmon, 1990). Watkins (1990) applied Mahler's (1972/1986) model of the *separation-individuation process* to the development of the relationship between supervisor and supervisee. Each subphase of the separation-individuation process is explored with emphasis both on typical supervisee characteristics and on helpful supervisor behaviors (*cf.* Holloway, 1987).

Evaluation

Under ideal circumstances, the supervisor has a chance to evaluate the supervisee's work on an ongoing basis both by observing it directly and by listening to accounts presented during supervision. Observing sessions from behind a one-way mirror (or attending to audio- or videotapes of sessions) allows the supervisor to more readily gauge observable skills such as maintaining the frame or managing the session. What is not revealed in these arrangements is a vital component of understanding psychoanalytic couple or family therapy: the therapist's internal experience. In part to this end, the supervisee describes the ongoing therapy to the supervisor, often on the basis of "process notes" written immediately following sessions. Speaking broadly, the supervisor evaluates the degree to which the description "makes sense" (i.e., reflects coherence in the supervisee's understanding of the internal and external processes in the family session). The supervisor also evaluates the supervisory relationship in a somewhat analogous way: Does the supervisee interact with the supervisor in an understandable, coherent manner that makes sense? If the therapist's interactions with the supervisor or accounts of sessions reveal difficulties, the supervisor gauges their nature, their extent, if and how they can be addressed, and so on.

In addition, there are more widely accepted aspects of evaluation that reflect attempts to demystify or to concretize the process. Supervisors may periodically negotiate specific, explicit therapy (or supervision) goals with their supervisees, which may be used as bases for evaluation. Furthermore, in the service of safeguarding supervisees, the supervisees are required to evaluate themselves, and their self-evaluations are compared to the supervisors'; the supervisees also evaluate the supervisors; the process for resolving substantial differences in opinion is clearly defined; and so forth (Jacobs et al., 1995).

A Recent Example

I periodically lead seminars on psychoanalytic marital therapy in which I present videotapes of my own work and respond briefly to questions about others' ongoing cases. Near the end of a recent meeting, a psychology intern, who had been an enthusiastic participant in earlier meetings, appeared to become more and more restless and uncomfortable. I had the sense that she wanted to leave immediately, but I couldn't tell if she were responding to something that had occurred in the seminar or to anxieties about extraneous matters. I found myself growing increasingly solicitous; for example, I repeatedly emphasized the keen insights that she and other interns had articulated in earlier meetings. This did not seem to ameliorate her distress, and when the meeting ended, she virtually flew out of the room. I left her a note asking her to call me.

We spoke the evening of the same day, and she immediately commented that she was relieved that I had asked to speak with her. She confirmed that she had become highly uncomfortable near the end of the seminar; she explained this in the following way. Prior to the meeting, she had been feeling overwhelmed by the difficulty of one of her marital cases, and she had been eager to consult me about it, especially since she had found me helpful in the past. Although at the meeting she found my ideas about the case useful, she experienced my tone as offensive and one comment, in particular, as frankly devaluing. I had apparently said that I was presenting my ideas about her case in an oversimplified form but that this was "good enough for intern work." After my comment, she wanted to leave immediately and it required a great deal of effort for her to stay; she was unable to concentrate on the discussion and blamed herself for not being more attentive.

As she described how she had felt, I realized immediately that I had recently had two comparable experiences that had generated similar feelings in me. Ironically, each had occurred as I sought consultation in writing _this_ chapter. Each had essentially the same components as her experience with me. Specifically, I had felt somewhat overwhelmed or daunted by my writing task; I had sought consultation from recognized authorities in the field; the authorities had given me answers that they acknowledged were "oversimplified" but "good enough" for my purposes; I had felt devalued and wanted to end the conversations immediately; and I had attacked myself for not being able to remain attentive to the consultants.

I apologized to the intern for my devaluing comment and tone, and I shared these recent experiences and my understanding that I had "done to her what had been done to me." I was relieved that we were talking together before she met with the couple again; otherwise, I would have been extremely concerned that she would bring residue from our interaction into the therapy. As we ended, I obtained her permission to discuss the incident and our conversation about it at the next meeting. At that meeting, I noted that she and I had spoken, that she had called my attention to a comment she found offensive, and that she had given me permission to share our discussion. When I asked how others had felt, several noted that they had also been put off by my tone or by the particular comment. After they elaborated on their reactions, I apologized to them as well. And then I asked them to join me in trying to make sense of what had occurred.

For the next twenty minutes, we discussed my experience and the interns' experiences, essentially as noted before. Both experientially and conceptually, two aspects stood out to the interns: the *parallel process* through which conflictual aspects of my interactions with consultants were (unconsciously) recreated in my interactions with the interns; and, of course, the *projective identification* that had occurred. (I did not address the issue of the particular intern's valency, nor mine, other than to note that she had felt overwhelmed by her task, as I had by mine.) I *modeled* the *analytic attitude*, that is, I conveyed my beliefs that our intrapsychic and interpersonal processes were worth exploring and that the *insight* would be useful. I believe that the "repair" to our *learning alliance* was highly successful: Several interns commented in subsequent meetings that they were very pleased to have a professor or a supervisor to whom they could express anger, who took responsibility for his behavior as I had, and who could talk about the interaction in a way that promoted learning.

TYPICAL SUPERVISION ISSUES

Psychotherapists who have been trained either to practice marital or family therapy from theoretical orientations other than psychoanalytic (e.g., structural/strategic, functional) or to conduct individual, but not marital or family, psychotherapy have the advantage of being "seasoned." To whatever degree there are commonalities among all therapies, regardless of theoretical orientation or of modality (*viz.*, individual, marital, family, or group), seasoned therapists have had similar experiences. Each has functioned in a professional role; negotiated meeting times, places, and payment; and, usually, intervened with clients for specified lengths of time. However, previous learning and experience that is inconsistent with the theory or practice of psychoanalytically oriented couple or family therapy may actively interfere with the transition to working in this new way. Naturally, the difficulties that arise in attempts to make this transition may reflect attitudes or skill "deficits" from previous training and experience, therapists' personal issues, various constraints in the system or "context" in which the transition is attempted, and so forth (Ekstein & Wallerstein, 1958; Scharff & Scharff, 1987; Wachtel, 1979; Will & Wrate, 1989). To illustrate issues that typically require attention in supervision, let us consider two situations: that of the psychoanalytically (or psychodynamically) oriented therapist who has been trained to work only with individuals and that of the marital and family therapist who has been trained from a theoretical orientation other than psychoanalytic.

Supervision of Psychoanalytically Oriented "Individual" Therapists

Psychoanalytically oriented psychotherapists who have worked primarily, if not exclusively, with individuals, face myriad characteristic challenges as they begin to work with couples and families. Highly salient, for example, are the needs to think "systemically" (in the interpersonal sense); to develop new, and sometimes more active, systemically based interventions; to resist the pulls and tugs of older, more familiar ways of working; and to manage the intense anxieties or other countertransferential feelings that may arise. Ellen Wachtel (1979), who practiced long-term, psychodynamically oriented psychotherapy with individuals and then trained as a family therapist, describes her experiences with these issues in an article that is useful reading for therapists who are undergoing similar transitions. Also useful in this regard is a thoughtful chapter by David and Jill Scharff (1987) entitled "Resistance to Beginning Object Relations Family Therapy."

It is not unusual for individually focused, psychoanalytically oriented psychotherapists (henceforth referred to as *individual psychotherapists*) to encourage, or at least to allow, individual clients to attribute their difficulties to early experiences in their families (often with their parents). Such blame assignment may serve various therapeutic goals, including enhancing therapists' alliances with clients, alleviating clients' guilt, boosting clients' senses of self-worth, and providing a context in which clients' problematic behaviors once might have been adaptive. In work with families or couples, there are certainly myriad interventions and perspectives that can be used to accomplish these goals (e.g., discussion of powerful transgenerational patterns, or focus on circular or "mutual" causality). Such techniques and the interpersonal systemic orientation that underpins their use must be understood, practiced, and incorporated while the tendency to encourage clients to blame the previous generation is resisted.

In part by their responses and silences, individual therapists inadvertently or deliberately exert control over the content, the process, and the emotional tone of sessions. These methods of control are less effective in conjoint sessions, because members often respond to each other more strongly than to the therapist. When they want to exert control during family sessions, individual therapists frequently must use interventions that are more active and directive than those they are accustomed to and often more comfortable with (Will & Wrate, 1989). Thus, for example, individual therapists who are beginning to work with families and couples often comment on the "chaos" or "noisiness" of sessions; on the difficulties staying "focused" during sessions; on the lengths they had to go to "to get the family" to stop arguing or interrupting; or on how they felt "unimportant" or "incidental" to the client system. Characteristic of the difficulties encountered by individual therapists is their reluctance to be assertive enough to redirect the process or the content in order to manage or to facilitate the session. For example, many are loathe to interrupt clients or to raise their voices enough to be heard with louder client systems. These and similar issues, in part, may be the result of countertransference or "interface" issues that arise forcefully in the context of conducting family, but not individual, therapy.

In fact, many seasoned individual therapists, who have undergone personal psychoanalysis or psychotherapy and can work with individuals without undue countertransference difficulties, experience unexpectedly strong, and at times problematic, reactions in work with families or couples. Wachtel (1979) attributes this phenomenon to two factors: first, that therapists' own psychoanalyses or psychotherapies often do not resolve their issues with their own families of origin, and second, that the potential for therapists to be "stirred up" emotionally by the playing out of family conflicts and dynamics may be greater with a family present than it is in merely listening to an individual client describe her or his family circumstances and issues.[11] Thus, for example, an individual therapist who begins to work with chaotic or contentious larger systems and who fails to intervene assertively may not only lack experience being assertive during therapy sessions but may be reexperiencing a sense of helpless from her or his own childhood experiences. In part to address therapists' anxieties caused by these and other reasons, David and Jill Scharff (1987) suggest that therapists who are making the switch from individual to couple and family work begin not only with couples before working with families but also begin by working with a more experienced co-therapist.

Often, individual therapists must change their existing beliefs and attitudes about issues of confidentiality and privacy, which may interfere with their ability to lead family therapy sessions effectively or their willingness to use audio- or videotapes or to arrange for live supervision. In their experience, exploration of personal feelings, conflicts, fantasies, and so forth, has taken place in a highly controlled, explicitly bounded, dyadic situation. They are often reluctant to encourage clients to self-disclose with any "depth" in family sessions, either because of a lack of experience or because of their own, possibly exaggerated, fears of other family members' responses to this sensitive material. They may fear, for example, that the family's collective impulses (or drives) will somehow overwhelm the family's collective ego (Scharff & Scharff, 1987). As individual therapists allow themselves more license in exploring feelings and going for "depth" in family therapy sessions, they often become confused with process issues such as how long to talk to one person without including others in the discussion and how (or if) to encourage responses

by other family members (Will & Wrate, 1989). That is to say, they may feel they are facilitating or participating in individual work and are unsure of how to integrate this with the family context.

In addition to their concerns about the vulnerability of a family member who reveals confidential or highly personal information in a family session, therapists may feel extremely anxious or self-conscious about their own participation in helping a client to explore such issues with others present. That is, there may be an affront to the *therapist's* own sense of privacy or even propriety. To deliberately exaggerate to make the point, participating publicly in what has previously been a private, dyadic interaction may evoke only slightly less anxiety, squeamishness, and self-consciousness than having a sexual encounter in front of others. In a similar vein, but more broadly and delicately stated, the Scharffs note several "comforts" that therapist may find in individual, but not in family, work. "The dyadic treatment format of individual therapy may be chosen to protect against anxieties of family work: competition and sharing, being observed at work, being taken over or excluded" (1987, p. 32).

Few families, although perhaps more couples, enter treatment with a clear belief that family or couple treatment, as opposed to individual treatment, will be the most helpful. It is often necessary to convince clients of this, which is understandably more difficult for therapists who are uncertain themselves. Even when they believe the problems of the identified (index) patient arose in, reflect, or regulate, the larger interpersonal system, therapists may or may not believe that psychoanalytic family or couple therapy is the treatment of choice; that is, there may or may not be consistency among their explicit or implicit theories of problem formation, problem maintenance, and problem resolution (Feldman & Pinsof, 1982; Pinsof, 1983, 1995). Making a clear and unequivocal recommendation for couple or family therapy requires individual psychotherapists to manage their well-ingrained tendency to focus on the individual as the unit of analysis and treatment. As Wachtel notes, once therapists learn to see family interactions, they may be more effective in engaging clients in family treatment (1979, p. 130).

The supervisor helps individually focused family psychotherapists begin to *see* characteristic and important interpersonal sequences in a way that both illuminates the context, function, or meaning of specific behaviors and supports the decision to work at the family level. Although at times such therapists may not understand the implications or importance of what they are seeing, at other times their experiences are surprising, or even jarring, to them and leave them searching for nonindividually focused, non- (or not exclusively) intrapsychic explanations. Especially when discussed in supervision, these latter instances prove extremely valuable in helping them make the transition to psychoanalytic work with families and couples. For example, it is sometimes only when one family member "becomes" symptomatic right after (or while) another is becoming asymptomatic that the individually oriented therapist may take a longer look at interpersonal systemically based explanations and ways of intervening. With couples, analogously, although a sophisticated psychoanalytic clinician who has worked primarily with individuals may be able to describe the processes and nuances of projective and introjective identification that underlie some aspects of "role" assignments (Barnett, 1971; Dicks, 1967; Scarf, 1987; Zinner, 1976/1989), it may be only when members "trade roles" that she or he focuses more sharply on interpersonal systemic concerns. If, for example, "overadequate" and "underadequate" partners change roles, or "pursuers" trade places with "distancers," this engenders tremendous confusion in therapists who implicitly or explicitly believe that feelings and "self-experiences" are located *only* (or primarily) on an individual level. After

a number of such role reversals, therapists are much more likely to suggest that an individual is verbalizing or "carrying" a feeling or an aspect of experience *for the system*.

A final challenge that faces individual therapists has to do with their difficulties in valuing their previous experience as they make the transition to psychoanalytic work with couples and families (Scharff & Scharff, 1987). Often, they have perceived family therapy to be an "entirely different animal" (or even to be conducted by "entirely different animals"!) with little in common with the individual therapy they have been trained to practice. Family therapy may be viewed as having inappropriately high or low goals, as using "manipulative" or "nongenuine" methods (e.g., use of paradox), as requiring an entirely different skill set, and so on (Scharff & Scharff, 1987; Will & Wrate, 1989). Thus, ironically, although some difficulties arise from therapists' allegiance to previous training and experience, a major supervisory challenge is highlighting the similarities among psychoanalytic individual, couple, and family work (Kaslow, 1977). Explicitly focusing on their highly refined and essential skills, such as nondirective listening, may help to address their anxiety. This issue of valuing previous experience and training tends to be less problematic for nonpsychoanalytic therapists who have been trained to work with couples and families. They encounter other difficulties, however, which the following section describes.

Supervision of Systems-Oriented, Nonanalytic Therapists

Marital and family therapists who work from nonpsychoanalytic theoretical orientations encounter a number of characteristic challenges in learning psychoanalytic theory, concepts, and interventions. To gain a clear understanding of the fundamentals, it is often useful for them to read introductory level books about psychoanalytically oriented psychotherapy. While such books concern psychotherapy with individuals, they define and illustrate the basic building blocks of the theory, the general strategy for treatment, and the associated methods of intervention; as noted, these also apply, in the main, to work with couples and families. For clinicians who have had little exposure to psychoanalytic therapy, good places to start are books by Auld and Hyman (1991) and Weiner (1975). Within the first few pages of their book, Auld and Hyman provide a discussion of other readings that may be useful. The Scharffs (1992) have written an introductory book on object relations therapy, which may also help to orient the nonanalytic clinician.*

If lengthy readings cannot be pursued, it is often helpful for nonanalytic therapists to read two approachable articles by Maggie Scarf (1986a, 1986b). These articles introduce the layperson to object relations thinking; and they describe concrete interventions ("tasks") for use with couples in a way that facilitates understanding of the intrapsychic meanings or consequences of their use. Somewhat analogous functions can be provided to the more sophisticated clinician by examination of articles that highlight the integration of intrapsychic and interpersonal understandings and techniques, such as Feldman (1979) and Feldman and Pinsof (1982). Finally, Jill Scharff's (1995) chapter is valuable reading for virtually all therapists; it summarizes the goals, tasks, and termination criteria of psychoanalytic marital therapy.

Couple and family therapists who have not been psychoanalytically or psychodynamically trained may struggle with the needs to relinquish some control over both the process and the content of sessions. Such therapists may have well-developed managerial skills that

---

*Clinicians who have had some prior exposure to psychoanalytic theory and approaches will find that there are many good choices such as Greenson (1967) and Langs (1973, 1974).

hinder their efforts to be less active or directive. As noted previously, psychoanalytic work with couples and families does involve management skills, but these are thought of in terms of managing *the session* rather than the participants, of "holding" rather than managing anxiety (Scharff & Scharff, 1987; Siegel, 1992). So, although there may be a need for the therapist to remain relatively active, especially at first, there is rarely a need for the therapist to remain particularly directive. That is to say, the therapist must learn to avoid imposing her or his "agenda," to curtail giving directives or advice, and so on. For many, such a stance is in direct conflict with that developed through earlier training; frequently, the therapist feels that she or he is not "doing enough" or "doing anything" for the system; and it may be even more difficult to champion this stance when ministering to a client system that is requesting immediate solutions. Of course, the adoption of a nondirective approach serves many functions such as allowing the development and the exploration of the family's themes, which may derive from individual or collective unconscious processes or conflicts; leaving the responsibility (or power) for determining session content in the clients' hands; and so forth.

In addition, the utilization of a nondirective, less active stance often results in an increase in clients' experiences and expressions of affect. Nonanalytic therapists may have been encouraged to regard affect as incidental to, or as even a manipulative or undesirable force in, couple or family therapy. They may have been trained either to discourage the development or expression of affect or to develop and highlight (only) specific affects in service of circumscribed aims. In addition to their theoretically based reasons for discouraging the development of affect, therapists may have personal reasons as well. They may be quite uncomfortable with clients' strong affective expressions, especially when discouraged from reacting in a prescriptive or directive manner that might divert the session focus, provide them with emotional distance, and so on. Thus, it may be difficult—or at the very least, a new experience—for characteristically active and directive therapists to "sit with" (to hold or to contain) clients' affects and to tolerate the uncertainties about their conscious and unconscious meanings. Yet developing tolerance for both affect and ambiguity and achieving a balance between engagement and neutrality are central to adopting a psychoanalytic orientation to couple or family therapy (Scharff & Scharff, 1987) or for that matter, to individual therapy (Greenson, 1967; D. Scharff, 1992).

Learning to value affect is but one component of learning to discern and to value clues about unconscious processes. As noted, psychoanalytic therapists believe that affects often signal unconscious meanings, processes, and conflicts (Scharff & Scharff, 1987). Listening for changes in affect, for possible meanings underlying sequences of associations, for incongruities between content and affect, and so forth, is a learned skill that often needs to be more fully developed by nonanalytic therapists. In this sense, nonanalytically oriented therapists must learn to *hear*, just as Wachtel (1979) notes that analytically oriented individual therapists must learn to *see*. It may be useful for nonanalytically oriented supervisees to read Reik's (1949) book, *Listening with the Third Ear*. In addition to valuing and attending to clients' affects, therapists making the transition to psychoanalytic work may need to enhance their abilities to attend to and to use their own affects.

Nonanalytic couple or family therapists may devote some attention to their feelings during sessions, but may not have developed the complete openness to their inner experiences championed by psychoanalytic therapists. At the same time, they may need supervisors' encouragement to *use* their feelings, that is, to alternate experiencing them with reflecting on them in service of learning about conscious and unconscious aspects of the client system. In addition, they may need explicit instruction and practice in providing clients with interpretations and in modeling an emphasis on understanding or insight. Implicit in these notions is the idea that the relationship between the therapist and the client system is a vital source of information about the client system. The relationship and its dynamics must be understood regardless of whether the understanding is made explicit at any particular point in therapy. Thus, instruction and guidance in all the aspects of the therapeutic relationship that are highlighted in psychoanalytic work, but less so in work from other theoretical orientations, are essential. These include the now familiar list: establishing the frame, understanding unplanned deviations from it, exploring transference and resistance, and so on.

CONCLUSION

Psychoanalytic approaches derive from ideas set forth by Freud or his followers and focus on the intrapsychic and interpersonal influences of unconscious factors. In psychoanalytic couple and family therapy, the therapist establishes a frame for the therapy and maintains a neutral, nondirective stance. Unconscious conflicts, wishes, aspects of past relationships, and so on are suggested by the sequence of clients' topics, revealed in transference reactions, manifested in resistance, and may be inferred from countertransference reactions. The therapist's understanding of the unconscious material is shared with clients by making interpretations, a process designed to foster insight and to facilitate the working through of unresolved conflicts or situations. As a result, clients' projections and displacements that have influenced their views of one another are reduced; the family system's capacity to hold or to contain all members' experiences is increased; each person's autonomy is enhanced; and further family development is facilitated.

The supervisor plays an important role in familiarizing the apprentice therapist with the techniques, values, and attitudes that are particular to psychoanalytic treatment of couples and families. Within the frame of the supervisory relationship, the supervisor explicitly and implicitly teaches the supervisee in ways that reflect the supervisee's current skill level. The supervisor models a way of working that is based on the analytic attitude, carefully attending to the supervisee's and the family's affects, unconscious communication, degrees of understanding, and so on. In addition, the supervisor is alert to parallels (based on projective and introjective identification) between the family's relationship with the therapist and the therapist's relationship with the supervisor. In such cases—and more generally—the tone, manner, or content of the supervisor's response to the supervisee may serve as a model for the supervisee's response to the family.

Endnotes

1. In this chapter, the "classical" psychoanalytic model includes both drive theory and ego psychology (cf. ego analysis, Wile, 1993, 1995). Self psychology is treated as distinct from object relations theory; their interrelationship has been addressed elsewhere (e.g., Murray, 1995; Scharff & Scharff, 1992; Summers, 1994). The relational and interpersonal (psychoanalytic) models (e.g., Greenberg & Mitchell, 1983) are not specifically addressed, nor are distinctions between "one-person" and "two-person" psychologies (e.g., Aron, 1990). Gill (1994, 1995) and especially Summers (1994) provide percipient analyses of these issues.

2. The "classical" psychoanalytic model focuses on resolving unconscious conflicts from early childhood that cause discord when *acted out* in family relationships. Biologically based aggressive or libidinal (*id*) impulses or drives are highly defended against (by the *ego*), in part because of their (real or imagined) social unacceptability (which is represented intrapsychically in the *superego*). Although some (*viz.*, Meissner, 1978; Nadelson, 1978) imply that the classical model is applicable to the treatment of couples and families, many (Scharff & Scharff, 1987) have expressed reservations about the limited applicability and utility of drive theory and of the *structural model* in this work. Because of the intensely intrapsychic focus of the classical model, family therapists who have used it have incorporated techniques derived from other approaches; have reconceptualized selected key components (Lachkar, 1992; Solomon, 1989); or both (e.g., Feldman, 1992; Slipp, 1984).

3. To the "classical" model described in Endnote 2, self psychology adds a co-equal focus on the environmental conditions that shape inner experience as well as the key concept of *selfobject* experiences (Wolf, 1988). Selfobject experiences are one's experiences of others that provide the self with psychological sustenance, guidance, mirroring, strength, and so on (Elson, 1986; Kohut, 1984) and which can be gradually replaced by self-functions or self-structure (through a process called *transmuting internalization*). Incomplete or distorted selfobject experiences may leave the self unduly susceptible to fragmentation when self-esteem is threatened; this susceptibility is referred to as *narcissistic vulnerability* (Feldman, 1982). The self psychological model has been applied to work with families (Brighton-Cleghorn, 1987; Donaldson-Pressman & Pressman, 1994) and especially to work with couples (Feldman, 1982; Finkelstein, 1987; Lansky, 1981, 1986; Nelsen, 1995; Solomon, 1989). Therapy with couples aims to reduce each partner's narcissistic vulnerability, to reduce cognitive distortions about the relationship, to enhance partners' empathy for each other, and so on (Feldman, 1982; Solomon, 1989).

4. Object relations couple and family therapy is the most robustly articulated psychoanalytic approach. Two classic books by the Scharffs (1987, 1991) present this treatment model; they detail its forerunners (Skynner, 1976) and evolution. As in this chapter, central object relations concepts—*holding environment, containment, projective identification*, and so on—have been woven into virtually all contemporary psychoanalytic writings on the treatment of couples and families (Catherall, 1992; Finkelstein, 1987; Mallouk, 1982; Siegel, 1992; Slipp, 1995). The unconscious, collusive forces involved in *mate selection* have been emphasized (Dicks, 1967; Gurman, 1978; Sager

& Hunt, 1979; Sager et al., 1971; Zinner, 1976/1989), as has each partner's predisposition to participate in specific ways (*valency*) in the underlying processes of projective or introjective identification (Bion, 1959). Projective identification has been highlighted in families, in part to illuminate *shared family assumptions* (Skynner, 1981; Zinner & Shapiro, 1972/1989); and between the client system as a whole and the therapist (Scharff & Scharff, 1987, 1991).

5. Defined in this way, not all reactions to therapists would be considered transference, but rather only those that were "inappropriate" to the situation (Greenson, 1967; Murray, 1995; *cf.* Gill, 1994). Greenson (1967) would provide an entirely analogous definition of countertransference that centers on the therapist's "inappropriate" reactions to the client.

6. In work with families and couples, David and Jill Scharff (1987, 1991) emphasize the client system's reactions to the provision of the holding environment (*contextual holding*), which they label *contextual transference*. This emphasis contrasts with that often found in psychoanalytic treatment of individuals, in which more emphasis is placed on *focused transference*, which is individual clients' reactions to the person of the therapist (*centered holding*).

7. To be sure, the psychoanalytic therapist may need to be active in managing or organizing the session, making certain that each family member has a chance to speak, facilitating the conversation, and so on (Scharff & Scharff, 1987).

8. This perspective stands in marked contrast to those whose associated methods of treatment, often labeled "supportive" or "covering up," aim to strengthen resistances (Weiner, 1975). Still other therapies seek to circumvent or to "manage" resistance in a variety of ways; these are not truly psychoanalytic (Greenson, 1967).

9. See Sarnat's (1992) article "Supervision in Relationship: Resolving the Teach-Treat Controversy in Psychoanalytic Supervision," for example, for a succinct history of the controversy and the issues involved. In addition, the Sarnat (1992), Jarmon (1990), and Gediman and Wolkenfeld (1980) discussions of the two- (or three-) person nature of the supervision process are interesting reading.

10. The proviso that the supervisor is contributing little, if any, to the parallel process allows us to circumvent a variety of issues. For example, omitting consideration of the supervisor's contributions, that is, unresolved issues or *valencies* (Bion, 1959), permits a discussion of parallel process—when used in the context of individual supervision of therapy with an individual—that ignores its complex, triadic nature (Gediman & Wolkenfeld, 1980; Jarmon, 1990). (Note, however, that the example provided later in this chapter illustrates difficulties that arise from the supervisor's contributions to the supervisory relationship.) The current discussion is also limited in that group supervision of marital and family therapy (a fairly common procedure) is not considered at any length. Of course through parallel process, various aspects of the family's (or client's) experience may be induced in, or experienced by, different members of a supervision group (Caligor, 1984; Grey & Fiscalini, 1987). Bion's work (1959) may be particularly helpful in understanding the family's and the supervision group's processes.

11. In keeping with her contention that individual psychotherapies generally encourage clients to blame their parents, Wachtel believes that most clients leave individual psychotherapy or psychoanalysis with powerful unresolved issues with their families of origin. This may not be the case for clients who have been treated individually from a systemic perspective, or from any perspective that encourages enhancing relationships with family members in the present as opposed to working through intrapsychic conflicts and managing the *internalized* parents or family dynamics (i.e., introjects and object relations) derived from the past. It is clear that Wachtel believes that to focus only on the intrapsychic, at times at the expense of current interpersonal relationships, is a mistake. In fact, she suggests that perhaps psychoanalysis or individual psychotherapy should "routinely" be followed by family therapy!

REFERENCES

Aron, L. (1990). One-person and two-person psychologies and the method of psychoanalysis. *Psychoanalytic Psychology, 7,* 475–485.

Auld, F., & Hyman, M. (1991). *Resolution of inner conflict: An introduction to psychoanalytic therapy.* Washington, DC: American Psychological Association.

Barnett, J. (1971). Narcissism and dependency in the obsessional-hysteric marriage. *Family Process, 10,* 75–83.

Bion, W. (1959). *Experiences in groups and other papers.* New York: Basic Books.

Bowlby, J. (1986). The nature of the child's tie to his mother. In P. Buckley (Ed.), *Essential papers on object relations* (pp. 153–199). New York: New York University Press. (Reprinted from *International Journal of Psycho-Analysis,* 1958, *39,* 350–373.)

Boyd-Franklin, N. (1989). *Black families in therapy: A multisystems approach.* New York: Guilford Press.

Brenner, C. (1979). Working alliance, therapeutic alliance, and transference. *Journal of the American Psychoanalytic Association, 27,* 137–157.

Breunlin, D., Schwartz, R., & Mac Kune-Karrer, B. (1992). *Metaframeworks: Transcending the models of family therapy.* San Francisco: Jossey-Bass.

Brightman, B. (1984). Narcissistic issues in the training experience of the psychotherapist. *International Journal of Psychoanalytic Psychotherapy, 10,* 293–317.

Brighton-Cleghorn, J. (1987). Formulations of self and family systems. *Family Process, 26,* 185–201.

Caligor, L. (1984). Parallel and reciprocal processes in psychoanalytic supervision. In L. Caligor, P. Bromberg, & J. Meltzer (Eds.), *Clinical perspectives on the supervision of psychoanalysis and psychotherapy* (pp. 1–28). New York: Plenum.

Carter, E., & McGoldrick, M. (Eds.) (1980). *The family life cycle: A framework for family therapy.* New York: Gardner Press.

Carter, E., & McGoldrick, M. (Eds.) (1989). *The changing family life cycle,* 2nd ed. Boston: Allyn and Bacon.

Catherall, D. (1992). Working with projective identification in couples. *Family Process, 31,* 355–367.

Dare, C. (1986). Psychoanalytic marital therapy. In N. Jacobson & A. Gurman (Eds.), *Clinical handbook of marital therapy* (pp. 13–28). New York: Guilford Press.

Dicks, H. (1967). *Marital tensions.* New York: Basic Books.

Doehrman, M. (1976). Parallel processes in supervision and psychotherapy. *Bulletin of the Menninger Clinic, 40,* 3–104.

Donaldson-Pressman, S., & Pressman, R. (1994). *The narcissistic family: Diagnosis and treatment.* New York: Lexington Books.

Elson, M. (1986). *Self psychology in clinical social work.* New York: W. W. Norton.

Ekstein, R., & Wallerstein, R. (1958). *The teaching and learning of psychotherapy.* New York: Basic Books.

Erikson, E. (1950). *Childhood and society.* New York: W. W. Norton.

Feldman, L. (1979). Marital conflict and marital intimacy: An integrative psychodynamic-behavioral-systemic model. *Family Process, 18,* 69–78.

Feldman, L. (1982). Dysfunctional marital conflict: An integrative interpersonal-intrapsychic model. *Journal of Marital and Family Therapy, 8,* 417–428.

Feldman, L. (1992). *Integrating individual and family treatment.* New York: Brunner/Mazel.

Feldman, L., & Pinsof, W. (1982). Problem maintenance in family systems: An integrative model. *Journal of Marital and Family Therapy, 8,* 295–308.

Fenell, D., & Weinhold, B. (1989). *Counseling families.* Denver, CO: Love Publishing.

Finkelstein, L. (1987). Toward an object-relations approach in psychoanalytic marital therapy. *Journal of Marital and Family Therapy, 13,* 287–298.

Fleming, J., & Benedek, T. (1966). *Psychoanalytic supervision.* New York: Grune & Stratton.

Freud, S. (1958a). The dynamics of transference. In J. Strachey (Ed. and Trans.), *The standard edition of the complete psychological works of Sigmund Freud* (Vol. 12, pp. 97–108). London: Hogarth Press. (Original work published 1912.)

Freud, S. (1958b). Recommendations to physicians practising psycho-analysis. In J. Strachey (Ed. and Trans.), *The standard edition of the complete psychological works of Sigmund Freud* (Vol. 12, pp. 109–120). London: Hogarth Press. (Original work published 1912.)

Gediman, H., & Wolkenfeld, F. (1980). The parallelism phenomenon in psychoanalysis and supervision: Its reconsideration as a triadic system. *Psychoanalytic Quarterly, 49,* 234–255.

Gerson, R. (1995). The family life cycle: Phases, stages, and crises. In R. Mikesell, D. Lusterman, & S. McDaniel (Eds.), *Integrating family therapy: Handbook of family psychology and systems theory* (pp. 91–111). Washington, DC: American Psychological Association.

Gill, M. (1994). *Psychoanalysis in transition: A personal view.* Hillsdale, NJ: Analytic Press.

Gill, M. (1995). Classical and relational psychoanalysis. *Psychoanalytic Psychology, 12,* 89–107.

Greenberg, J., & Mitchell, S. (1983). *Object relations in psychoanalytic theory.* Cambridge: Harvard University Press.

Greenson, R. (1967). *The technique and practice of psychoanalysis* (Vol. 1). New York: International Universities Press.

Grey, A., & Fiscalini, J. (1987). Parallel process as transference-countertransference interaction. *Psychoanalytic Psychology, 4,* 131–144.

Gurman, A. (1978). Contemporary marital therapies: A critique and comparative analysis of psychoanalytic, behavioral and systems theory approaches. In T. Paolino, Jr. & B. McCrady (Eds.), *Marriage and marital therapy: Psychoanalytic, behavioral, and systems theory perspectives* (pp. 445–566). New York: Brunner/Mazel.

Holloway, E. (1987). Developmental models of supervision: Is it development? *Professional psychology: Research and practice, 18,* 209–216.

Issacharoff, A. (1984). Countertransference in supervision: Therapeutic consequences for the supervisee. In L. Caligor, P. Bromberg, & J. Meltzer (Eds.), *Clinical perspectives on the supervision of psychoanalysis and psychotherapy* (pp. 89–105). New York: Plenum.

Jacobs, D., David, P., & Meyer, D. (1995). *The supervisory encounter: A guide for teachers of psychodynamic psychotherapy and psychoanalysis.* New Haven: Yale University.

Jarmon, H. (1990). The supervisory experience: An object relations perspective. *Psychotherapy, 27,* 195–201.

Kaslow, F. (1977). Training of marital and family therapists. In F. Kaslow & Associates, *Supervision, consultation, and staff training in the helping professions* (pp. 199–234). San Francisco: Jossey-Bass.

Kohut, H. (1984). *How does analysis cure?* A. Goldberg (Ed.), with P. Stepansky. Chicago: University of Chicago Press.

Lachkar, J. (1992). *The narcissistic/borderline couple: A psychoanalytic perspective on marital treatment.* New York: Brunner/Mazel.

Langs, R. (1973). *The technique of psychoanalytic psychotherapy* (Vol. 1). Northvale, NJ: Jason Aronson.

Langs, R. (1974). *The technique of psychoanalytic psychotherapy* (Vol. 2). New York: Jason Aronson.

Langs, R. (1979). *The therapeutic environment.* New York: Jason Aronson.

Langs, R. (1994). *Doing supervision and being supervised.* London: Karnac.

Lansky, M. (1981). Treatment of the narcissistically vulnerable marriage. In L. Lansky (Ed.), *Family therapy and major psychopathology* (pp. 163–182). New York: Grune & Stratton.

Lansky, M. (1986). Marital therapy for narcissistic disorders. In N. Jacobson & A. Gurman (Eds.), *Clinical handbook of marital therapy* (pp. 557–574). New York: Guilford Press.

Lothane, Z. (1984). Teaching the psychoanalytic method: Procedure and process. In L. Caligor, P. Bromberg, & J. Meltzer (Eds.), *Clinical perspectives on the supervision of psychoanalysis and psychotherapy* (pp. 169–192). New York: Plenum.

Mahler, M. (1986). On the first three subphases of the separation-individuation process. In P. Buckley (Ed.), *Essential papers on object relations* (pp. 222–232). New York: New York University Press. (Reprinted from *International Journal of Psycho-Analysis,* 1972, 53, 333–338.)

Malan, D. (1976). *The frontier of brief psychotherapy.* New York: Plenum.

Mallouk, T. (1982). The interpersonal context of object relations: Implications for family therapy. *Journal of Marital and Family Therapy, 8,* 429–441.

McGoldrick, M. (1989). Ethnicity and the family life cycle. In E. Carter, & M. McGoldrick, (Eds.), *The changing family life cycle,* 2nd ed. (pp. 69–90). Boston: Allyn and Bacon.

McGoldrick, M., & Carter, E. (1982). The family life cycle. In F. Walsh (Ed.), *Normal family processes* (pp. 167–195). New York: Guilford Press.

Meissner, W. (1978). The conceptualization of marriage and family dynamics from a psychoanalytic perspective. In T. Paolino, Jr., & B. McCrady (Eds.), *Marriage and marital therapy: Psychoanalytic, behavioral, and systems theory perspectives* (pp. 25–88). New York: Brunner/Mazel.

Mitchell, S. (1993). *Hope and dread in psychoanalysis.* New York: Basic Books.

Moldawsky, S. (1980). Psychoanalytic psychotherapy supervision. In A. Hess (Ed.), *Psychotherapy supervision: Theory, research, and practice* (pp. 126–135). New York: John Wiley.

Murray, J. (1995). On objects, transference, and two-person psychology: A critique of the new seduction theory. *Psychoanalytic Psychology, 12,* 31–41.

Muslin, H., & Val, E. (1989). Supervision: A teaching–learning paradigm. In K. Field, B. Cohler, & G. Wool (Eds.), *Learning and education: Psychoanalytic perspectives* (pp. 159–179). Madison, WI: International Universities Press.

Nadelson, C. (1978). Marital therapy from a psychoanalytic perspective: (Marital therapy). In T. Paolino, Jr., & B. McCrady (Eds.), *Marriage and marital therapy: Psychoanalytic, behavioral, and systems theory perspectives* (pp. 101–164). New York: Brunner/Mazel.

Nelsen, J. (1995). Varieties of narcissistically vulnerable couples: Dynamics and practice implications. *Clinical Social Work Journal, 23,* 59–70.

Nichols, W. (1988). An integrative psychodynamic and systems approach. In H. Liddle, D. Breunlin, & R. Schwartz (Eds.), *Handbook of family therapy training and supervision* (pp. 110–127). New York: Guilford Press.

Ogden, T. (1994). *Subjects of analysis.* Northvale, NJ: Jason Aronson.

Paolino, T., Jr. (1978). Marital therapy from a psychoanalytic perspective: (Introduction: Some basic concepts of psychoanalytic psychotherapy). In T. Paolino, Jr. & B. McCrady (Eds.), *Marriage and marital therapy: Psychoanalytic, behavioral, and systems theory perspectives* (pp. 89–101). New York: Brunner/Mazel.

Pine, F. (1990). *Drive, ego, object, self.* New York: Basic Books.

Pinsof, W. (1983). Integrative problem-centered therapy: Toward the synthesis of family and individual psychotherapies. *Journal of Marital and Family Therapy, 9,* 19–35.

Pinsof, W. (1995). *Integrative problem-centered therapy: A synthesis of family, individual, and biological therapies.* New York: Basic Books.

Pinsof, W., & Catherall, D. (1986). The integrative psychotherapy alliance: Family, couple and individual therapy scales. *Journal of Marital and Family Therapy, 12,* 137–151.

Pittman, F., III. (1987). *Turning points: Treating families in transition and crisis.* New York: W. W. Norton.

Racker, H. (1957). The meanings and uses of countertransference. *Psychoanalytic Quarterly, 26,* 303–357.

Racker, H. (1968). *Transference and countertransference.* New York: International Universities Press.

Reik, T. (1949). *Listening with the third ear.* New York: Farrar & Straus.

Reiner, P. (1988). The development of the therapeutic alliance (doctoral dissertation, University of North Carolina at Chapel Hill, 1987). *Dissertation Abstracts International, 48,* 2466.

Sager, C., & Hunt, B. (1979). *Intimate partners: Hidden patterns in love relationships.* New York: McGraw–Hill.

Sager, C., Kaplan, H., Gundlach, R., Kremer, M., Lenz, R., & Royce, J. (1971). The marriage contract. *Family Process, 10,* 311–326.

Sarnat, J. (1992). Supervision in relationship: Resolving the teach–treat controversy in psychoanalytic supervision. *Psychoanalytic Psychology, 9,* 387–403.

Scarf, M. (1986a, November). Intimate partners: Patterns in love and marriage (Part 1). *Atlantic Monthly,* 45–54, 91–93.

Scarf, M. (1986b, December). Intimate partners: Patterns in love and marriage (Part 2). *Atlantic Monthly,* 66–76.

Scarf, M. (1987). *Intimate partners: Patterns in love and marriage.* New York: Random House.

Schafer, R. (1983). *The analytic attitude.* New York: Basic Books.

Scharff, D. (1992). *Refinding the object and reclaiming the self.* Northvale, NJ: Jason Aronson.

Scharff, D., & Scharff, J. (1987). *Object relations family therapy.* Northvale, NJ: Jason Aronson.

Scharff, D., & Scharff, J. (1991). *Object relations couple therapy.* Northvale, NJ: Jason Aronson.

Scharff, D., & Scharff, J. (1992). *Scharff notes: A primer of object relations therapy.* Northvale, NJ: Jason Aronson.

Scharff, J. (1992). *Projective and introjective identification and the use of the therapist's self.* Northvale, NJ: Jason Aronson.

Scharff, J. (1995). Psychoanalytic marital therapy. In N. Jacobson & A. Gurman (Eds.), *Clinical handbook of couple therapy* (pp. 164–193). New York: Guilford Press.

Scrivner, R., & Eldrige, N. (1995). Lesbian and gay family psychology. In R. Mikesell, D. Lusterman, & S. McDaniel (Eds.), *Integrating family therapy: Handbook of family psychology and systems theory* (pp. 327–345). Washington, DC: American Psychological Association.

Searles, H. (1955). The informational value of the supervisor's emotional experience. *Psychiatry, 18,* 135–146.

Segal, H. (1964). *Introduction to the work of Melanie Klein,* 2nd ed. New York: Basic Books.

Siegel, J. (1992). *Repairing intimacy: An object relations approach to couples therapy.* Northvale, NJ: Jason Aronson.

Skynner, R. (1976). *Systems of family and marital psychotherapy*. New York: Brunner/Mazel.

Skynner, R. (1981). An open-systems, group analytic approach to family therapy. In A. Gurman & D. Kniskern (Eds.), *Handbook of family therapy* (pp. 39–84). New York: Brunner/Mazel.

Slipp, S. (1984). *Object relations: A dynamic bridge between individual and family treatment*. Northvale, NJ: Jason Aronson.

Slipp, S. (1995). Object relations marital therapy of personality disorders. In N. Jacobson & A. Gurman (Eds.), *Clinical handbook of couple therapy* (pp. 458–470). New York: Guilford Press.

Solomon, M. (1989). *Narcissism and intimacy*. New York: W. W. Norton.

Sperry, L., & Carlson, J. (1991). *Marital therapy: Integrating theory and technique*. Denver, CO: Love Publishing.

Summers, F. (1994). *Object relations theories and psychopathology: A comprehensive text*. Hillsdale, NJ: Analytic Press.

Tansey, M., & Burke, W. (1989). *Understanding countertransference: From projective identification to empathy*. Hillsdale, NJ: Analytic Press.

Wachtel, E. (1979). Learning family therapy: The dilemmas of an individual therapist. *Journal of Contemporary Psychotherapy, 10*, 122–135.

Watkins, C., Jr. (1990). The separation-individuation process in psychotherapy supervision. *Psychotherapy, 27*, 202–209.

Weiner, I. (1975). *Principles of psychotherapy*. New York: John Wiley & Sons.

Weiner, I., & Kaplan, R. (1980). From classroom to clinic: Supervising the first psychotherapy client. In A. Hess (Ed.), *Psychotherapy supervision: Theory, research, and practice* (pp. 41–50). New York: John Wiley.

Wile, D. (1993). *After the fight: Using your disagreements to build a stronger relationship*. New York: Guilford Press.

Wile, D. (1995). The ego-analytic approach to couple therapy. In N. Jacobson & A. Gurman (Eds.), *Clinical handbook of couple therapy* (pp. 91–120). New York: Guilford Press.

Will, D., & Wrate, R. (1989). Pragmatics and principles: The development of a family therapy training programme. *Journal of Family Therapy, 11*, 149–168.

Winnicott, D. (1986). The theory of the parent–infant relationship. In P. Buckley (Ed.), *Essential papers on object relations* (pp. 233–253). New York: New York University Press. (Reprinted from *International Journal of Psycho-Analysis*, 1960, 41, 585–595.)

Wolf, E. (1988). *Treating the self: Elements of clinical self psychology*. New York: Guilford Press.

Wool, G. (1989). Relational aspects of learning: The learning alliance. In K. Field, B. Cohler, & G. Wool (Eds.), *Learning and education: Psychoanalytic perspectives* (pp. 747–770). Madison, WI: International Universities Press.

Zaphiropoulos, M. (1984). Educational and clinical pitfalls in psychoanalytic supervision. In L. Caligor, P. Bromberg, & J. Meltzer (Eds.), *Clinical perspectives on the supervision of psychoanalysis and psychotherapy* (pp. 257–273). New York: Plenum.

Zetzel, E. (1956). Current concepts of transference. *International Journal of Psycho-Analysis, 37*, 369–376.

Zinner, J. (1989). The implications of projective identification for marital interaction. In J. Scharff (Ed.), *Foundations of object relations family therapy* (pp. 155–173). Northvale, NJ: Jason Aronson. (Reprinted from H. Grunebaum & J. Christ, Eds., *Contemporary marriage: Structure, dynamics, and therapy*, pp. 298–308, 1976.)

Zinner, J., & Shapiro, R. (1989). Projective identification as a mode of perception and behavior in families of adolescents. In J. Scharff (Ed.), *Foundations of object relations family therapy* (pp. 109–126). Northvale, NJ: Jason Aronson. (Reprinted from *International Journal of Psycho-Analysis*, 1972, 53, 523–530.)

12

Supervision
The Transgenerational Models

Laura Giat Roberto

Time present and time past
Are both perhaps present in time future,
And time future in time past. . . .
What might have been and what has been
Point to one end, which is always present.

ELIOT (1943, p. 13)

Transgenerational (TG) models of family functioning and marriage and family therapy (MFT)—also called *intergenerational* and *multigenerational*—focus not only on current patterns of interaction, emotional dynamics, and organizational structure in clinical families, but also on those of supervisees (Roberto, 1992). Transgenerational schools are distinguished from other schools by marriage and family therapy supervisors and educators primarily by (1) their valuing of historical information, (2) the belief that past patterns of relating and behavior influence present and future patterns, and (3) their pursuit of therapy outcomes beyond discrete symptom control or reduction. Transgenerational dynamics and family of origin are thus the unit of analysis (Nelson, Heilbrun, & Figley, 1993).

CENTRAL PRINCIPLES OF TRANSGENERATIONAL MODELS

Transgenerational models of family functioning are based on current behavior, but also *relational dynamics* over long spans of time, as well as *implicit values, cultural inheritances,* and *beliefs*. They hold that current interactional patterns not only reflect *past* events, but also "feed forward" into childrearing and thus shape the behavior and values of *future* family generations (Boszormenyi-Nagy & Krasner, 1986; Roberto, 1992).

Transgenerational models of therapy are "time-sensitive" rather than circular. They view the evolution of twenty- to forty-year relational patterns as an unfolding rather than as a closed loop, constructing a "layered" map of the family system over time (usually beginning two generations back, working up to present minor children). This theoretical layering of events over time distinguishes TG models from all other models. Like a three-dimensional chessboard, the "pieces" of a family are viewed over the context of at least three lifetimes. As cited in Carter and McGoldrick (1980, p. 10):

> It becomes imperative, therefore, for the
> family therapist to assess not only the dimen-

sions of the current life cycle stress, but also its connections to family themes, triangles, and labels coming down in the family over historical time (Carter, 1978).

Triangles

Triangling, one of four central principles in the TG models, is the process by which situational or developmental family challenges are transmitted across generations. Triangles are persistent emotional tensions, focused around the behavior of certain members or painful historical (nodal) family events. These tensions are contained to a specific group of three or more family members (usually one being a child), and may expand to include additional persons when the stresses are unresolved (Friedman, 1991; Kerr, 1981).

According to TG models, pathological triangles do not develop fortuitously, but stem from chronic anxiety underpinned by persistent deficits or unresolved stressors such as traumatic loss. In well-functioning families, triangling of tensions is transient, and does not become "fixed." Instead, members have the self-direction, or differentiation, necessary for problem solving (Scharff & Scharff, 1987); empathy; tolerance of conflict; and tolerance of autonomy in others (Bowen, 1978/1988; Friedman, 1991; Kerr, 1981); mutuality and willingness to advance "due consideration" (Boszormenyi-Nagy & Krasner, 1986); and flexibility in family and social roles for everyone (Boszormenyi-Nagy & Krasner, 1986; Roberto, 1991; Whitaker & Keith, 1981).

In dysfunctional couples or families, members have difficulty creating and maintaining these conditions for each other. TG models hold that such problems are especially influential if the dysfunction is present in a parent or grandparent (i.e., dysfunction has more powerful consequences the farther one goes up the "family tree"). In these families, problems in mutuality and intimacy, tolerance of differences, and

self-awareness/self-control create emotional intensity during stressful periods such as life-cycle transitions. One or several members become the recipients of this anxiety and are identified as "the problem," and one or several others are triangled in to diffuse the intensity. In TG models of therapy, such problem dynamics are viewed as reactions to relational imbalances or unresolved conflicts from family-of-origin experiences and those of past generations.

Triangles can lead to fusion of several members around a symptom, cutoff of the family by one member, and implicit triangles maintained by secrets. Most TG models, however, recognize that many triangles are culturally relative. For example, in the Middle Eastern family, certain personal information, such as childrearing concerns, is shared between mother and daughter rather than husband and wife (Baker, 1993); in Western culture, this would be considered a pathological "husband–wife–mother-in-law" triangle.

Differentiation

Differentiation with connectedness, the second coherent principle, is viewed as the basis for health and resiliency in families. However, throughout much of the 1980s, TG supervision emphasized differentiation within family systems without explicitly acknowledging its embeddedness in "normal connectedness." For example, Bowen's writing tended to overfocus on male-socialized expressions of differentiation such as self-directedness, and pathologized the functions of emotionality in development of the intimate self (Knudson-Martin, 1994; Luepnitz, 1988). Contributions by feminist theorists, such as Gilligan (1982), have addressed these limitations in our understanding of differentiation-with-connectedness, pointing out that a definition of self *evolves through attachment to others.* In the 1990s, TG models place more emphasis on how family health requires integrating one's subjective experience with inclusion of others, and learning through emotionality/empathy as much as through rational analysis.

Unresolved Conflict and Symptom Formation

A third classic principle of TG models is that each family contains unique areas of *unresolved conflict* from past events that have been traumatic, disruptive to family cohesion, or environmentally dangerous. These conflict areas are significant because they cannot be easily integrated into a family's belief system, and continue to generate anxiety, secretkeeping, and other blocks to problem solving unless they are openly addressed.

The "vertical" axis of unresolved stress, which may be combined with problematic family beliefs and traditions, intersects the "horizontal" axis of marital/family life cycle stages and transitions, loading them with anxiety or "reactivity" in Bowen's terms, and distorting the ability of members to adapt well (Carter & McGoldrick, 1980; Friedman, 1991; Roberto, 1992).

Four Dimensions of Family Experience

The fourth coherent principle of TG models is that family experience is not simply behavioral. There are *four areas of family experience*: transgenerational patterns of relationships, transgenerational beliefs and values, current interactional patterns, and current family metaphors. TG models are complex, tracking data from all four areas of family experience. Other MFT models tend to choose and work with one area of family experience more than others.

The role of the TG therapist is to join with family members to increase accountability for self, evolve missing or damaged attachments, free up skills and ways of relating that have been blocked off because of triangles and "liv-ing in the past," draw on family values that will increase resiliency, build on strengths, and increase intimacy and cohesion. Thus, it can be seen that the unique aspect of TG therapy is its *locus of intervention*—session goals move beyond alleviation of transitory presenting symptoms (Roberto, Keith, & Kramer, 1987).

Role of the Transgenerational Therapist

There are a number of unique basic TG therapy skills (Nelson, Heilbrun, & Figley, 1993). Of these skills, many could be considered attributes of the therapist's person rather than therapeutic behaviors; hence, *use of self* is a distinct class of tools in TG therapies. Use of self means becoming aware of one's own embeddedness of "self-in-family-system," and using this contextual awareness as a filter in the evaluation of clinical families and the systemic hypothesizing that is necessary to family treatment. This is considered the *most important skill* for beginning TG therapy therapists to have (Nelson, Heilbrun, & Figley, 1993).

Behavioral skills for TG therapy include generic family therapy skills such as self-awareness, helping clients maintain a change focus, and an "I" position, maintaining boundaries, tracking symptomatic cycles, joining, clarifying family relationships, reframing symptoms, interrupting patterns, role-modeling, using insights, integrating theory into interventions, facilitating intense emotional expression and having teaching skills. Unique, theory-specific therapy skills include understanding one's own family-of-origin dynamics; recognizing triangles; using historical data in therapy, as well as genograms; diffusing clinical triangles; coaching clients in family-of-origin change; assessing family loyalties; identifying sources of intergenerational conflict; assessing individual differentiation; relating past behavior to present behavior; expanding the family system in care; desensitizing families to past events and addressing unresolved grief; and using transgenerational assignments (Nelson, Heilbrun, & Figley, 1993).

CENTRAL PRINCIPLES IN SUPERVISION

Contextual Awareness

To understand the differentiation process (self-in-context), TG supervisors encourage identification of TG patterns and family-of-origin work to give supervisees an experiential awareness of their own *contextual self*—habitual roles, affects, values, and beliefs—as it reflects personal family history. At the same time, the novice therapist's personal learning must be free of anxiety in order to be of use (i.e., not related to current problems). Whitaker and Ryan (1989) point out that contextual awareness is actually never an anxiety-free experience: "As [the process of becoming a therapist] evolves, it is important to recognize that there are some roles that are not natural to a psychotherapist; there are some roles that he finds more difficult" (p. 212). Wynne (1965) advocates family-of-origin work in beginning therapists. Consider the following case, in which family-of-origin work *in itself* appeared to change a supervisee's behavior in MFT:

A psychiatry resident participated in a genogramming exercise near the end of her introductory family therapy practicum. In the process of constructing a four-generational genogram, she conversed at length with her mother on the subject of her mother's family history in the South as the daughter and granddaughter of poor rural farmers. As she became aware of the poverty her family had experienced and their consequent need for mutual support and cooperation, she became less focused on the scientific explanation behind interventions, and more

skilled at providing empathy and support to clinical families.

Self-Delineation and Personal Authority

Developing contextual awareness leads to a change process which can be called *self-delineation* (Boszormenyi-Nagy & Krasner, 1986) or "personal authority" (Williamson, 1981, 1982). Williamson defines personal authority as a step into the mature use of autonomy and decision making, a movement away from being acted upon to acting on, a type of power usually allocated to the parental generation.

It is an increase in one's personal agency in making choices and being accountable for them. Self-delineation and personal authority are two crucial elements in a therapist's professional performance as an expert in healthy human relationships. The ability to risk making errors, formulate decisions in therapy, advance a position with a client family, maintain an "I" position, and be accountable for the results of intervention are basic substrates of responsible caregiving.

The Supervisory Triangle

In teaching personal context in supervision, the TG supervisor forms a *transformational triangle*, in which therapists experience themselves and their work in relation to both clients and supervisory team. The transformational triangle of supervision provides a forum in which the supervisee "first *learns about* psychotherapy, then *learns how to do* psychotherapy, and then, if all goes well, moves to the next step of *becoming* a psychotherapist" (Whitaker & Ryan, 1989, p. 211). The supervisory triangle has unique properties even when the training team is a dyad (one therapist plus supervisor). It is a safe context in which to experiment, apply new skills, assess personal reactions and concerns, and move into creative care planning (Roberto, 1992; Whitaker & Ryan, 1989). TG supervisors prefer an apprenticeship relationship with supervisees rather than encouragement in the studying of masters. In an apprenticeship, the supervisor commits to work toward a lateral rather than hierarchical position with supervisees over the course of the supervision contract.

Supervisees often take on the techniques, values, and style of their supervisors during early work. This outcome will not produce the inventive, self-delineated clinician desired; some writers have commented that modeling per se can be particularly problematic for female therapists with male supervisors (see, for example, Caust, Libow, & Raskin, 1981; Turner, 1993). Apprenticeship-oriented supervision ensures that the therapist moves into more autonomous planning and technique through a deliberately increasing collegial, egalitarian, and open-ended stance on the part of the supervisor, such that the trainee must increasingly take responsibility for the direction of therapy and the methods selected. If a supervisee shows difficulty making the transition to self-delineated plans and opinions by the late stage of supervision, this may be a sign that personal issues or previous life challenges are interfering with learning (Furlong, Smith, & Goding, 1986). Impasses in personal authority in supervision should be addressed through appropriate discussion and, if indicated, referral for psychotherapy with a family therapist.

Diversity

TG supervision highlights and speaks to the cultural, gender, and situational factors that make the supervisee's learning unique. This requirement follows TG models' emphasis on uniqueness and historical evolution in family systems. Within each individual reality is a specific set of values, life cycle issues, personal metaphors, developmental challenges, and gender and cultural filters that shape a supervisee's goals and style of learning.

In one supervisory group, when questioned about personal views on the well-functioning family, members (second-year psychiatry residents) expressed almost universal belief in the importance of marital permanence. This group of young physicians, most of whom were married or in long-term partnerships, have an especially gruelling and isolative work week, and are on call twenty-four hours a day to inpatient units for the severest emotional disorders. The wish of these young physicians for marital permanence for their clients could be seen as a reflection of their own life stage as young marrieds, and of their own anxiety about separation and isolation under the stress of training.

SPECIFIC TRANSGENERATIONAL MODELS

Bowen Model

Bowen's model, also called *natural systems theory*, puts emphasis on differentiation of the self within the family emotional field. The theory did not address the *reciprocal* nature of individuality and togetherness, and as a result must be applied with modifications to therapy with female clients. Bowen theory does not focus on "the possibility of integrating the other into the definition of self in the way connected selves do" (Knudson-Martin, 1994, p. 39). Supervision, as described by trainees of Bowen, is highly theory-focused and action-oriented; it does not utilize affect in therapy, supervision, or coaching (see the comments of Guerin, 1991).

In Bowen theory, *emotional systems* are the field of tensions surrounding poorly differentiated family relationships. What pass for intense emotions (*distinguished from feelings,* which are seen as conscious and under voluntary control) are problematic stress responses, anxiety-driven reactivity. *Feelings,* in contrast, are more like sensibilities: affectively laden responses to significant events. The primary driving force in the emotional system is anxiety, which reflects extreme dependency, or fusion. Supervisees are taught to distinguish between reactivity, or emotionality, in clients and themselves, and feelings or affect, which are one's personal responses to important experiences.

The *intellectual system* is one's capacity to observe, to understand, and to choose processes believed to be basic to differentiation. In Bowen theory, it has often been opposed to the concept of emotion (i.e., the less developed the intellectual system, the more thinking is overwhelmed by intense emotional behavior). Bowenian supervision can allow for exploration of a supervisee's feelings regarding difficult cases or problem sessions but is more likely to refer deeply disconcerted reactions to more formal coaching or personal therapy (see the following).

Family projection process refers to intergenerational transmission of symptoms—an implicit flow of tensions between elders and children in which one or more children are triangulated into unresolved relational problems and become more likely to develop symptoms. In the therapy relationship, families with a strong projection process tend toward pulling a novice therapist into one more emotionally loaded triangle. The Bowenian supervisor watches for recurrent cycling of interactions between the therapist and one or several family members, especially if this cycling is outside of the therapist's awareness and puts the therapist in "the middle of the action" too often. If so, such cycles are pointed out for further study. In Bowen theory, persistent cycling between therapists and family members is believed to reflect

the therapists' own family-of-origin experiences, which places them in anxiety-provoking positions.

The natural systems model emphasizes interaction between family members rather than from family to therapist, to facilitate self-awareness and problem solving in those who desire change. Similarly, supervision focuses on interaction between supervisees and client families to increase therapists' understanding of their own behaviors in sessions, personal responses to problem triangles and painful issues, and anxiety stirred up by therapeutic impasses. Techniques taught follow the generic TG listing of skills, but the priority in supervision is on differentiation of the therapist's self—the ability to hold an "I" position, clearly understand personal abilities and limitations, and move in and out of family triangles without forming self-defeating coalitions. To remain differentiated from the emotional tensions of clients, Bowen supervisors believe the most powerful training ground is family-of-origin work for therapists-in-training.

Symbolic-Experiential Model

Family symbolic process is symbolic-experiential (SE) theory's term for the way that a well-functioning family "as a three- to four-generational whole is longitudinally integrated" (Whitaker & Keith, 1981, p. 190). Members, subgroups, and families as a whole are able to relate in an internalized, symbolic way to this continuous line of persons and their life histories (Connell, Mitten, & Whitaker, 1993). The symbolic process of families has an affective component—it involves deep emotional responses as well as metaphoric ideas about the family (its "myths"). Family symbolic process may be worked with in a current marriage or nuclear family rather than in three-generational therapy. This is a major difference with Bowen theory, and resembles similar emphases in psychodynamic and contextual theories.

In supervision, therapists are encouraged to accept and use emotionality and conflict as a healthy aspect of relational engagement. This stance may require therapists to examine and become comfortable with their own range of emotions. Further, SE supervision pays more attention to symbolic process in treatment planning and debriefings. Supervisees learn to "use the self"—personal stories, metaphors, affective responses, and fantasies—in therapy sessions to increase the therapeutic alliance and aid in emotional expression by clients.

Differentiation is also an important intervention for the SE therapist. However, the SE model, more explicitly than the Bowen model, holds that emotional connectedness and separation are a flux that moves back and forth in intimate relationships and involves intensity and stress. In supervision, supervisees are asked to look beyond such issues as hierarchy and authority in families and to evaluate family potential for individuality and self-expression *along with* intimacy. Strengthening family attachments and cohesion by increasing intimacy between parents and from parents to children is a central goal in SE therapy. The SE supervisor focuses on, more than the Bowen supervisor does, mentoring therapists, developing a close collegial bond, and aiding therapists-in-training to bring their own emotionality into the supervision hour.

Triangles, the emotionally laden groups that form in response to family stress, are given much attention in the SE model just as they are in Bowen theory. They are viewed as the mode of transmission of stress. SE therapy requires the ability to identify, understand, and diffuse triangles. However, because of the central importance of affect and use of self in this therapy, therapists are encouraged to *enter into and engage with* triangular relationships, an especially proximal position for therapists. "Working in close" with families is a quite unique and challenging skill in SE MFT, and supervisors offer active encouragement, humor, and messages that

supervisees are competent to handle the intensity of a symptomatic couple or parent–child problem.

SE theory addresses the problem of *reification* in its techniques. Problems, relational tensions, and interactional patterns, when reified, become "fixed." Reifying a problem involves ceasing to explore its meaning, or to evolve alternatives, instead of overfocusing on symptom-bearers in a way that pathologizes them. Reification leads to *delegation* or *scapegoating*. "The symptom choice includes not only both the families of origin and . . . family network, but also the historical family of previous generations. . . . Symptom choice may even result from projected demands" (Whitaker & Keith, 1981, p. 196). Or, one family member is idealized as the "hero" or the "perfect one"—the *white knight* phenomenon (Whitaker & Keith, 1981). SE supervisors teach therapists to identify the presence of reification in client families, and to share their own thinking so that family members can "think systemic" themselves. For this reason, SE therapists are encouraged not to focus on a symptom for the entire length of therapy.

In the 1970s and 1980s, the body of literature on SE theory referred to therapeutic "battles" to be "fought" between therapist and family, and "won" by the therapist. This metaphor has been widely misunderstood as a stance in which the therapist disregards family concerns, "battling" over which members to include and what should be the locus of change. The terms *battle for structure* and *battle for initiative* actually referred to the process by which the therapist, whose view of problems is systemic, engages with a family whose experience of problems begins as linear. SE supervisors encourage therapists to structure who attends therapy sessions so that clients can see a *connection between* symptom and family structure (the battle for structure). In later sessions, the role of the therapist is to join with the family enough to help them face the challenge of creating change (the battle for initiative). It becomes the task of couples or families to choose and face consequences of change, and therapists to support and empower their choices from a less proximal position with supervisors' help. In this sense, SE therapy is a "staged" therapy that requires supervisors to keep in mind that the therapist's role will change over time.

Contextual School

The contextual model, formulated by Boszormenyi-Nagy and colleagues, particularly focuses on how transgenerational obligations and unresolved parent–child tensions play a role in the appearance of emotional symptoms. Its foremost principle is *relational ethics*, or how intimacy and balance are built through justifiable and trustworthy acts (Boszormenyi-Nagy, 1976; Boszormenyi-Nagy & Ulrich, 1981). In comparison to the other two TG models, the contextual school is actually a microtheory which defines the emotional processes that prevent self-development, cohesion, and conflict tolerance in dysfunctional families. One key element in building relational ethics is *trustworthiness*: a willingness to be accountable for things that are done and said over time. Contextual therapy, therefore, gives special attention to accountability and trustworthiness in the therapist so that family members can safely confide their painful experiences and relational problems.

Earned merit describes how family members earn consideration from each other by making contributions and showing interest in each other's needs and welfare. In children, consideration is simply owed because of the natural trust and dependency of the child (Boszormenyi-Nagy & Krasner, 1986) without being earned. In families that do not show trustworthiness, merit, consideration for each other's efforts, or acknowledgment of loyalty, there are enormous destructive consequences such as lack of self-awareness, behavioral symp-

toms, and missing empathy. Contextual supervision focuses on teasing out the status of these "relational ethics" in client families by aiding the therapist to weigh the fairness, mutuality, and balance of family interactions with clients. It is a less affective or metaphorical, and more symbolic and reflective, type of therapy. Contextual therapists use themselves chiefly as a source of respect and trustworthiness—a process called *multidirectional partiality* (Boszormenyi-Nagy & Krasner, 1986). Supervisors track supervisees' joining behavior with family members to ensure that members receive the "partiality," or unique concern, that will enable them to build trust and perhaps correct past injustices.

Self-delineation is the contextual school's term for self-awareness—the ability to understand and separate self from others while maintaining connection and trust. In families where self-delineation has been constrained or abused, extended family consults may be necessary. All the TG models describe a version of *rejunction*, or reconnection, with cut off or distanced families. Contextual supervisors, like SE supervisors, are prepared to aid supervisees in planning and executing extended family meetings, which may involve parents or siblings who reside far away and often means scheduling far in advance. Supervisees require considerable confidence and perseverence in planning for extended family consults, because client families experience almost intolerable anxiety over the prospect of speaking directly with significant others who have been cut off or held at bay for up to a lifetime. In some cases, instead of family reunions, therapists focus more on the *exoneration* process: as in coaching, clients are helped to reconsider and find the thread of redeeeming value in parents' or relatives' past behavior and "take a new chance" (Boszormenyi-Nagy & Krasner, 1986; Boszormenyi-Nagy & Ulrich, 1981; Roberto, 1992). Contextual supervisors monitor exoneration work with a theory emphasis, much like supervisors of Bowenian coaches.

SUPERVISORY INTERVENTIONS AND MODALITIES

Experiential Interventions

"Education is derived from the Latin word educare, to draw forth" (Duhl, 1983, p. 89). In supervision, we assume that supervisees bring worldviews that color the way they assimilate information. These assumptions are taken for granted and thus guide thinking and in-session behavior until challenged and explored. The TG supervisor strives to promote learning "from the inside out," encouraging trainees to examine their life experiences and metaphors for them.

Experiential exercises provide an opportunity for trainees to integrate parts of the self into their work before taking on the therapist role alone. Experiential interventions "demonstrate and catalyze in trainees the facility to track and evolve inner images and awarenesses into externalized, interpersonal . . . transactions" (Duhl, 1983, p. 103).

Exercises include role-playing within supervisee groups, sharing of personal stories and observations on issues of family distress and family change, exercises that demonstrate TG concepts *in vivo*, conceptual tasks such as watching clinical videotapes and examining personal responses, and question periods in which supervisees are asked to make judgments about clinical material and then deduce the value inherent in those judgments.

A group of pastoral counselors discussed the case of one member. This therapist felt confused about how to set goals for a gay couple; they were experiencing considerable conflict around one partner's distant and unsupportive behavior. Despite their awareness that this partner came from a family of origin that was also distant and reserved, the supervision group kept returning to the fact that this couple was gay in a closed Christian community, and felt that their conflict

was inevitable. The supervisor handed out the genogram of a heterosexual married couple in a similar situation and asked for treatment goals. After correctly defining goals for the heterosexual couple, the therapists then saw and discussed how their own discomfort with this couple's homosexuality led them to disregard what they knew about addressing distance and conflict. Several therapists also commented on silence and reserve in their own families of origin, on issues of sexuality and personal emotion, and the difficulties this had created in working with sexuality in families.

Experiential exercises must be followed by "debriefing" dialogues in which supervisees move from being "in" an exercise to being "outside" of it in order to reflect. "It is both during exercises themselves and during the debriefing process that dialogue between trainees or between trainees and trainers takes place" (Duhl, 1983 p. 93).

Supervision Groups as Intervention

Dell, Sheely, Pulliam, and Goolishian (1977) suggest that supervision groups move through stages of development just as families do. They described these stages as beginning with an initial "battle for structure," in which therapists resist learning systemic thinking. This stage is followed by "naive enthusiasm," where therapists work on technique, looking for a "magic bullet"; and then a "conflictual frustration" stage when the magic bullet skills do not erase family symptoms. The group then moves into "task orientation" where it begins to use creativity and timing; and finally to "mutuality" in which learning, and therapy, are truly circular and equal. This description of group behavior suggests that *participating* in a supervision group is an *intervention* in itself—that supervisees learn systems by participating in the supervisory system.

Some writers have noted that supervision groups have particularly transgenerational symbolism for therapists:

> The dynamics of the group of colleagues with whom one is being trained almost always carry echoes of the competitive struggles that took place in one's family of origin. . . . Often these fantasies and inner struggles are not acknowledged until well into the year (Simon & Brewster, 1983, p. 27).

Diversity

To develop their personal skills and talents in a maximally effective way, the supervision contract established, and resulting interventions, must be tailored to the cultural, gender-specific, and situational needs of supervisees. The supervisor practices *multidirectional partiality* (Boszormenyi-Nagy & Krasner, 1986)—attention to the individual reality of each supervisee. Partiality in supervision develops the unique "voices" of therapists, builds their confidence in what they know from experience about marriage and family life, and increases comfort level with their own metaphors for family living. Attention to cultural and gender differences is an important element in teaching use of self in supervision.

Several times in supervision, a Filipino therapist mentioned that in her culture, husband–wife relations were characterized by a tension around the husband's tendency to allocate home duties to the wife in a stereotypical way, while maintaining his own independence and controlling financial resources. She joked and laughed in a mischievous way about these tensions, indicating that wives tended to cope with the marital disparity by negotiating carefully with husbands and maintaining a sense of humor whenever possible. She was encouraged to use this humor

and lightheartedness in her work with conflictual couples, and her mischievous wit was pointed out as a valuable tool in giving feedback and directives in delicate clinical situations.

Training for Use of Self

Aponte (1994) points out that supervision of therapists must always include training to use "personal selves" (p. 3)—to identify, master, and work on personal issues in relation to clinical cases. *Use of self* is part of the therapist's individual character or style, and has grown so valued in the field that it was recently named as a critical supervisory function *independent of supervisor's orientation* (White & Russell, 1995).

In training for use of self, supervisors maintain a lateral, person-to-person, respectful stance as supervisees build a conscious awareness of their unique qualities, skills, and personal resources. As a preparation for sharing personal reactions with client families, supervisees are asked to share reactions to events in the therapy room. These responses are framed by the supervisor as reflections of the therapist's position in the family therapy, and are highlighted and encouraged.

A male supervisee had great difficulty addressing upset clients, yet had the ability to listen so carefully that he was able to understand and remember their positions on many important issues. He reported to the supervisor that in his family of origin, there was significant alienation between his parents, because his mother showed intense emotions frequently under stress and his father responded with helplessness which was rebuffed. He felt that his position in his family had been to listen to his mother's dissatisfaction with his father, and felt great caution about showing concern and being rebuffed. In therapy, he felt he "froze up" whenever a family member became agitated.

The supervisor pointed out the therapist's position in his parental triangle, and the covert concern about competition that probably had led him to refrain from giving the comfort his father could not. She encouraged the therapist to tell distressed clients that he heard them and to use his excellent recall to repeat painful material back, as well as to assure insecure intimates that they could deliver comfort and advice effectively

Supervisor–Supervisee Interaction Effects

There is a relational aspect to supervision that is particularly of interest to TG trainers who view supervisor–supervisee interchange as *isomorphic with* transgenerational family process. Four relational issues have been identified using contextual principles: accountability, contextual awareness, trust, and power/authority (Kaiser, 1992). Accountability demands that supervisors monitor supervisees for their ability to act in the clients' best interest from the "metaposition" behind the screen.

Contextual awareness, described earlier, requires that supervisors observe themselves for biases, reactivity, or prejudices based on personal history that may impact on treatment of supervisees. Trust reflects both perceiving respect and experiencing safety in the way that supervisees are received by supervisors. Power and authority issues include the need to examine to what extent hierarchy is practiced in training, whether autonomy is encouraged in supervisees, and the ability to tolerate disagreement and experimentation in supervisees.

Coaching

There is little use of indirect or strategic techniques in TG therapy so that the boundary between therapist, clinical family, and supervision is very permeable. The foremost example of this permeability is *coaching*: the use of family-of-origin tasks by supervisors to help therapists understand and modify their own family relationships. Coaching helps supervisees diffuse personal emotional triangles, understand the emotional process of triangulation, and improve the quality of intimate relationships (Kerr, 1981). Awareness of personal values and relational conflicts, ability to avoid relational triangles, personal differentiation, and clear relational boundaries are all considered basic family therapy skills (Nelson, Heilbrun, & Figley, 1993). Coaching is a midway supervisory tool between skill-oriented supervision and personal therapy.

Bowen coined the term "coaching" while at Georgetown University in the 1960s; he created precedent by presenting his own family-of-origin work at a conference in Philadelphia in 1967 (Bowen, 1972). Bowen's attempts at coaching supervisees appeared to him to result in both personal progress and increased clinical effectiveness (Bowen, 1988). Coaching is action-oriented, utilizing a succession of visits and personal contacts with the family to explore and resolve long-term relational tensions (Roberto, 1992).

Supervisees are asked to explore antecedents for their current intimate behavior patterns in the family of origin, beginning with parents and later researching the grandparental generation. The research includes interviews, reading archives and memorabilia, visiting family homes, and even regions of origin, increasing supervisees' understanding of cultural, economic, and gender inheritances and clarifying the source of patterns and rules in their generation (Roberto, 1992).

One excellent description of coaching divides the process into five stages: forming the coaching alliance, a psychoeducational stage, reentering the family of origin, reworking family relationships, and following-through (Carter & McGoldrick, 1980). In the process, supervisees are directed to observe that they are not "outside" family systems, but "inside" their own family system, which is rule-bound in specific and unique ways. Visits and tasks are not generally assigned until the reentry stage. These tasks are quite personal, requiring that supervisees own their own anxiety or confusion over specific family issues rather than pressuring other family members.

A child psychiatry resident in her fifth year of study elected to concentrate in the area of transgenerational therapy and family systems medicine. As she built up her caseload of ill children and their families, she became increasingly concerned with understanding her decision to become a physician, her tendency to caretake others at her expense, and possible connections to her rearing in a household with a terminally ill parent. She entered into a coaching relationship with a family therapist for three months in order to revisit the final illness and death of her parent, to discuss with her sibling and surviving parent her grief, and to shift herself into a more "equal" and less caregiving role in her family of origin. Although the coaching was assignment-oriented and did not focus at length on affective or relational problems in the here and now, she found that she enjoyed her work more and intervened in a less authoritarian manner.

Genogramming

TG supervisors include several entry points for genogram work (see Shirley Braverman's Chapter 25 on genogramming in this book): elective family-of-origin seminars for beginning therapists, advanced family-of-origin seminars for postgraduates where group coaching may take place, and special formats in live supervision. The classic genogramming assignment was described by Guerin and Fogarty in 1972. Supervisees draw and examine their own genograms in small groups, identifying repeating patterns, unresolved conflicts and resulting triangles and

coalitions, and formative events. They examine themes and myths that have been built over four family generations, and distinguish which ones have most guided their choices from those which have created discomfort. Cultural, economic, national, religious, and gender-related issues are brought forth in the exercise.

Videotape Supervision

TG supervision groups rotate presentation of ongoing MFT cases recorded on videotape, using case presentation with three- or four-generational genogram, systemic mapping, hypothesis formation, treatment planning, and construction of assignments. The review and discussion are centered on strengthening clinical skills, monitoring family response to interventions, and examining the therapist's response to supervisory interventions.

Videotape supervision groups allow therapists to discuss their affective responses to events in therapy as well. Positions that are personally new or controversial, alliances that are difficult, confrontations that are taxing, can all be processed in the supervisory dialogue. According to Aponte (1994):

> As clinicians, we must perform professionally. The training context allows a trainee . . . to feel all the personal emotions operating in her in a therapy session because the trainers and group take care of her while watching out for her clients. It opens up the doors between the personal and the professional while strengthening boundaries. It helps achieve permeability while maintaining clarity and control. It helps achieve integration with differentiation (p. 14).

Live Supervision

Although a historically sensitive treatment model might not seem to value live supervision, this modality is necessary to TG supervision. In watching live sessions, supervisor and supervision group observe not only skill level but also information about "triggers" that cause discomfort for therapists in session (McDaniel & Landau-Stanton, 1991, p. 462). Supervisors can discuss triggering events in relation to family material that is at odds with the supervisees' experiences or values. If necessary, persistent discomfort can be examined in light of therapists' family history. Supervisors can catch first-hand signs of unresolved personal problems interfering with therapy skills. These signs are especially clear to supervisors who observe therapists over time, and can thus identify departures of various sorts. Signs that a case is triggering unresolved familial issues include: therapists become anxious, less responsive in sessions, or "shut down" affectively or cognitively; supervisees show implicit signs of distress; therapists show premature closure on important topics; therapists are under- or overintense in focus; therapists have difficulty setting or following up on therapeutic assignments (McDaniel & Landau-Stanton, 1991).

Supervisory Co-Therapy

The co-therapy dyad of supervisor–supervisee is most extensively discussed in the symbolic-experiential literature (Napier & Whitaker, 1978; Roberto, 1992). In this venue, there is a hierarchical but fairly permeable relationship between supervisors and novice therapists, in which supervisors take the lead in making clinical interventions in-session and supervisees watch for effects and facilitates. Supervisory co-therapy requires a debriefing period after a clinical session so that the supervisee can question interventions, and clarify supervisors' intentions or direction. In this form of supervision, it is expected that the middle and late stages will be less hierarchical, more guided by the interventions of both therapists, and more peerlike in nature.

Evaluation

In TG training, crucial skills are (1) attention to the self of the therapist, (2) understanding the impact of family-of-origin dynamics on the conduct of therapy, and (3) identifying theoretical concepts as they are demonstrated in family behavior in therapy and addressing them through technique (Nelson, Heilbrun, & Figley, 1993).

Three kinds of instruments have been used to measure progress and outcome of TG supervision. They include observational measures of supervisees' skill; ratings of supervisees' progress; and self-report evaluations by therapists of their learning experiences. These evaluations tend to utilize Likert formats for skill acquisition and brief essays on personal growth. Supervisory instruments have not been standardized across programs and have appeared in different outcome studies only in the past five years.

BOUNDARIES BETWEEN THERAPY AND SUPERVISION

Supervision begins with dual personal/professional goal setting by therapists to encompass both skill learning and contextual learning; dual goal setting also serves to inform supervisors of developmental challenges facing each therapist (McDaniel & Landau-Stanton, 1991). Supervisees are informed that TG training will require their willingness to share personal reactions to clinical material. The issue is not *whether*, but *how much* personal information will be utilized in the process of integrating technical and clinical information. Supervisees choose the extent to which they will work on a unique style, comment on personal progress and the progress of others, engage supervisors in individual concerns, and report on pertinence of therapeutic events to their own life history.

Supervision and Dual Relationships

Learning personal context is not therapy because it does not address personal distress. The focus is on skill development and improving professional performance. When family-of-origin issues are raised, it is for the purpose of understanding unique formative challenges and experiences. "The notion that the trainee needs both to understand and to resolve her own family-of-origin issues is integral to the philosophy of particular family therapy models" (Ryder & Hepworth, 1990, p. 284). For example, in Aponte's (1994) person–practice model, supervisees identify personal issues for the purpose of identifying resulting professional life patterns.

Aponte takes the position that there is a difference between relational *dual qualities* and *dual relationship*. In Aponte's person–practice model, consultations may be held by the supervisor with a therapist's family of origin to address professional performance problems. Because the object of the consultation is improvement of performance, Aponte labels this as a personalized supervisory relationship or a "dual quality" supervisory experience.

There is a growing controversy in the field that this process constitutes "therapy" as opposed to "training," and thus should be outside and separate from supervision to avoid boundary diffusions and dual relationships. In addition, it should be noted that the concept of personal therapy as a supervision component per se has declined in popularity over the last decade (Nichols, Nichols, & Hardy, 1990).

Tomm (1993), commenting on his own evolving supervisory model, notes that many supervisors in the field find the current *Code of Ethics* of the American Association for Marriage and Family Therapy to be unduly restrictive in its prohibition of discussing therapeutic issues with trainees. A number of theorists and educators have contributed to this growing debate,

and it is highly questionable at this time whether it is always desirable to set a rigid boundary between therapeutic discussion and supervisory (case-related) discussion. As Prosky (1992) comments: "The resonance between trainees' personal/familial issues and their clinical work is an innate part of the systems field under study. . . . [E]xamination . . . produces the sharpest learning curve" (p. 4).

Friedman (1991), commenting on Bowenian training, states the following:

> [T]he differentiation of the therapist is technique. . . . Here, Bowen theory again makes continuous what other theories would catagorize separately, that is, the distinction between a therapist's supervision and his or her own "therapy" as an essential part of training in the Bowen school involves the therapist's working on his or her own differentiation (p. 138).

In other programs, "family of origin issues need to be addressed when other avenues for teaching, such as pre-session planning, telephone call-ins during a session, and role-playing needed skills, fail" (McDaniel & Landau-Stanton, 1991, p. 465).

Boundaries in Supervision

"The question of where to draw the line between training and therapy is sufficiently complex that it is unlikely that anyone can develop a simple boundary that will win universal agreement" (Aponte, 1994, p. 5). Perhaps for this reason, some theorists believe that a therapist's personal life is too complex to be intervened in by supervisors who are attending to instruction at the same time. A second objection is that supervisees doing family-of-origin work will be vulnerable to scrutiny by other supervisees. Lastly, it is difficult to maintain a clear boundary between family-of-origin work and personal therapy in a supervisory model which possesses the dual qualities of skill acquisition and personal development. Specific risks with family-of-origin work have been detailed (Aponte, 1994; McDaniel & Landau-Stanton, 1991):

1. Focusing on supervisees' *unresolved personal issues,* including recent family deaths, intense conflicts, family secrets, and uncovering unexpected information, can create an unexpected, intense emotional reaction that can make supervisees feel exposed, and increase their vulnerability to stress.

2. *Confidentiality* can pose risks such as blurring boundaries between supervisees who work together outside supervision and breaches in storage of genograms, records, and videos.

3. *Abuse of power* can occur if supervisees do not feel free to enter into or refuse any aspect of the training relationship.

4. *Intent to exploit* must be thoroughly examined. Specifically, supervisors must be certain that there is no personal gain motivating supervisors to enter into the dual training relationship (e.g., theoretical interest, personal research).

5. *Harm to supervisees,* whenever it occurs, indicates entry into a dual relationship (i.e., moving beyond Aponte's dual quality relationship into a boundary violation). Such an event calls for a reevaluation and remediation of any dual supervisory contract.

CONCLUSION

Supervisees need an opportunity to identify, track, and resolve personal concerns when they interfere with flexibility, responsiveness, and resourcefulness in therapy. Impasses are considered to reflect challenges in supervisees' current life stages, emotional triangles in their kinship networks, and previous experiences. Typical stressors for beginning family therapists include family coalitions, affectively loaded triangles, delegations, and "revolving slates," three-generational fusions or cutoffs, and implicit and unresolved family "secrets."

A therapist presented his genogram and family-of-origin information at mid-year in a one-year marital/family therapy practicum. Although he and his supervisory group had worked together for four semesters, he had not disclosed to them the fact that his nearest sib, whom he felt quite protective toward, had a chronic major psychiatric disorder. After choosing to disclose this information in his presentation, he found himself describing a profound feeling of guilt for his own state of health. It was suggested afterward that he seek counseling with a local family therapist to explore and resolve these intense feelings of guilt and his parentified position within his family of origin.

It is TG supervisors' task, and privilege, to preside over and later consult in the development of a systemic view in novice TG therapists. The emphasis of the TG model on both historically sensitive intervention skills, and growth of therapists' unique "voices" and sense of selves in MFT, produces supervision that is rich, diverse, and quite powerful. It is expected that these supervision techniques will continue to evolve as the transgenerational models of MFT, and our understanding of transgenerational family process, evolve into the next decade.

REFERENCES

Aponte, H. (1994). How personal can training get? *Journal of Marital and Family Therapy, 20,* 3–15.

Baker, A. (1993). *The Jewish woman in contemporary society: Transitions and traditions.* New York: New York University Press.

Boszormenyi-Nagy, I. 1976. Behavior change through family change. In A. Burton (Ed.), *What makes behavior change possible?* (pp. 227–258). New York: Brunner/Mazel.

Boszormenyi-Nagy, I., & Krasner, B. (1986). *Between give and take: A critical guide to contextual therapy.* New York: Brunner/Mazel.

Boszormenyi-Nagy, I., & Ulrich, D. (1981). Contextual family therapy. In A. Gurman and D. Kniskern (Eds.), *Handbook of family therapy* (pp. 159–186). New York: Brunner/Mazel.

Bowen, M. (1972). Toward the differentiation of a self in one's own family of origin. In J. Framo (Ed.), *Family interaction: A dialogue between family researchers and family therapists* (pp. 171–173). New York: Springer.

Bowen, M. (1988). The use of family theory in clinical practice. In M. Bowen, *Family therapy in clinical practice*, 4th ed. (pp. 147–181). Northvale, NJ: Jason Aronson. (Original work published in 1978.)

Carter, E. (1978). The transgenerational scripts and nuclear family stress: Theory and clinical implications. In R. Sagar (Ed.), *Georgetown family symposium* (Vol. 3, 1975–1976). Washington, DC: Georgetown University.

Carter, E., & McGoldrick, M. (1980). *The family life cycle: A framework for family therapy.* New York: Gardner Press.

Carter, E., & Orfanidis, M. (1976). Family therapy with one person and the family therapist's own family. In P. Guerin, Jr. (Ed.), *Family therapy: Theory and practice* (pp. 193–219). New York: Gardner Press.

Caust, B., Libow, J., & Raskin, P. (1981). Challenges and promises of training women as family systems therapists. *Family Process, 20,* 439–447.

Connell, G., Mitten, T., & Whitaker, C. (1993). Reshaping family symbols: A symbolic-experiential perspective. *Journal of Marital and Family Therapy, 19,* 243–251.

Dell, P., Sheely, M., Pulliam, G., & Goolishian, H. (1977). Family therapy process in a family therapy seminar. *Journal of Marriage and Family Counseling, 3,* 43–48.

Duhl, B. (1983). *From the inside out and other metaphors: Creative and integrative approaches to training in systems thinking.* New York: Brunner/Mazel.

Eliot, T. (1943). *Four quartets.* New York: Harcourt, Brace & World, Inc.

Friedman, E. (1991). Bowen theory and therapy. In A. Gurman & D. Kniskern (Eds.), *Handbook of family therapy, Vol. II* (pp. 134–170). New York: Brunner/Mazel.

Furlong, M., Smith, J., & Goding, S. (1986). Some constraints in the learning of family therapy. *Australian Journal of Family Therapy, 7,* 61–67.

Gilligan, C. (1982). *In a different voice.* Cambridge: Harvard University Press.

Guerin, P., & Fogarty, T. (1972). Study your own family. In A. Ferber, M. Mendelsohn, & A. Napier (Eds.), *The book of family therapy* (pp. 445–467). NY: Science House.

Guerin, P. (1991). The man who never explained himself. Family *Therapy Networker, 15,* 45–46.

Kaiser, T. (1992). The supervisory relationship: An identification of the primary elements in the relationship and an application of two theories of ethical relationships. *Journal of Marital and Family Therapy, 18,* 283–296.

Kerr, M. (1981). Family systems theory and therapy. In A. Gurman & D. Kniskern (Eds.), *Handbook of family therapy, Vol. 1* (pp. 226–264). New York: Brunner/Mazel.

Knudson-Martin, C. (1994). The female voice: Applications to Bowen's family systems theory. *Journal of Marital and Family Therapy, 20,* 35–46.

Luepnitz, D. (1988). *The family interpreted: Feminist theory in clinical practice.* New York: Basic Books.

McDaniel, S., and Landau-Stanton, J. (1991). Family-of-origin work and family therapy skills training: Both-and. *Family Process, 30,* 459–471.

Napier, A., & Whitaker, C. (1978). *The family crucible.* New York: Harper & Row.

Nelson, T., Heilbrun, G., & Figley, C. (1993). Basic family therapy skills, IV: Transgenerational theories of family therapy. *Journal of Marital and Family Therapy, 19,* 253–266.

Nichols, W., Nichols, D., & Hardy, K. (1990). Supervision in family therapy: A decade restudy. *Journal of Marital and Family Therapy, 16,* 275–285.

Perelsz, A., Stolk, Y., and Firestone, A. (1990). Patterns of learning in family therapy training. *Family Process, 29,* 29–44.

Prosky, P. (1992). Support for Kantor Family Institute (Letter to the editor). *Supervision Bulletin, 5,* 4.

Roberto, L. (1991). Symbolic-experiential family therapy. In A. Gurman & D. Kniskern (Eds.), *Hand-*

book of family therapy, Vol. II (pp. 444–476). New York: Brunner/Mazel.

Roberto, L. (1992). _Transgenerational family therapies._ New York: Guilford Press.

Roberto, L., Keith, D., & Kramer, D. (1987). Breaking the family crucible: Symbolic-experiential family therapy. Workshop presented to 45th annual meetings of American Association for Marriage and Family Therapy, Orlando, October.

Ryder, R., & Hepworth, J. (1990). AAMFT ethical code: Dual relationships. _Journal of Marital and Family Therapy, 16,_ 127–132.

Scharff, D., & Scharff, J. (1987). _Object relations family therapy._ Northvale, NJ: Jason Aronson.

Simon, R., & Brewster, F. (1983). What is training? _Family Therapy Networker, 7,_ 25–29, 66.

Tomm, K. (1993). Editorial: Defining supervision and therapy—A fuzzy boundary? _Supervision Bulletin, 6,_ 2.

Turner, J. (1993). Males supervising females: The risk of gender-power blindness. _Supervision Bulletin, 6,_ 4–6.

Whitaker, C., & Keith, D. (1981). Symbolic-experiential family therapy. In A. Gurman & D.

Kniskern (Eds.), _Handbook of family therapy_ (pp. 187–224). New York: Brunner/Mazel.

Whitaker, C., & Ryan, M. (1989). _Midnight musings of a family therapist._ New York: W. W. Norton.

White, M., & Russell, C. (1995). The essential elements of supervisory systems: A modified Delphi study. _Journal of Marital and Family Therapy, 21,_ 33–53.

Williamson, D. (1981). Personal authority via termination of the intergenerational hierarchical boundary: A "new" stage in the family life cycle. _Journal of Marital and Family Therapy, 7,_ 441–452.

Williamson, D. (1982). Personal authority via termination of the intergenerational hierarchical boundary": Part II—The consultation process and the therapeutic method. _Journal of Marital and Family Therapy, 8,_ 23–37.

Wynne, L. (1965). Some indications and contraindications for exploratory family therapy. In I. Boszormenyi-Nagy & J. Framo (Eds.), _Intensive family therapy: Theoretical and practical aspects, with special reference to schizophrenia_ (pp. 289–322). New York: Harper & Row.

13

Purposive Systemic Supervision Models

Thomas C. Todd

It has been difficult to categorize and name the group of models in this chapter. Several of them have been grouped under the rubric of "strategic" (Stanton, 1981) even though a recent conference used the label "interactionalist" to describe them (Keim, 1995). The title here reflects two dominant characteristics. First, these are models that have been categorized as "systems purists" (Madanes & Haley, 1977); although most of the developers of the supervision models elsewhere in this part of this book would probably consider themselves "systemic," they presumably would emphasize other aspects as well. Second, these models emphasize purposive action on the part of the supervisor. Hence the chosen title—purposive systemic models.

These systemic models have accounted for much of the theoretical ferment and debate of the 1970s and 1980s, so it is easy to overemphasize the differences between them. It is also my belief that many of the differences between systemic models, which have been the source of so much controversy in the arena of therapy, are much less significant in the domain of supervision. For example, much has been made of the "function of the symptom," which is thought to differentiate structural therapy and strategic therapy from the Mental Research Institute (M.R.I.) brief therapy and solution-focused therapy. My as-

sumption is that most systemic supervisors rarely assume that problematic supervisee behavior serves a "function" for the supervisee, so these differences would be less significant in supervision.

Although my intention is to focus exclusively on the model of supervision rather than therapy, the models considered in this chapter present some unique difficulties in this regard. As will be seen, all emphasize supervisory responsibility, and all show a preference for live supervision in some form. This combination often leads supervisors to intervene fairly directly with cases, which can obscure the difference between intervening with families and with supervisees.

MODELS TO BE COVERED: STRUCTURAL/STRATEGIC, SOLUTION-FOCUSED, AND MILAN

Most of the models discussed here fall within the structural/strategic continuum, when strategic is taken in its more generic sense. These include structural (including Haley's work in the era of *Problem-Solving Therapy* and *Leaving Home*), Haley strategic, Madanes, M.R.I. Brief Therapy, and Solution-Focused Therapy. Also included is the early work of the Milan team, and the closely related work of Tomm (1987a,b; 1988). I believe the reader will concur that the generalizations made in the Common Assumptions section also apply to these latter models, even though they also helped set the stage for reflecting teams, narrative therapy, and other postmodern methods (see Chapter 15). Perhaps a case could be made for the inclusion of other hybrid models such as Provocative Supervision (Andolfi & Menghi, 1982) and Problem-Centered Systems (Epstein & Bishop, 1981). There was no intention to be exclusive in developing this chapter or even to fully develop the implications for supervision for any single model; instead, I hope readers will see how supervisory implications can be drawn and interventions can be developed from these familiar models, so that they will be able to continue this process independently with any similar models.

As has frequently been true elsewhere in this part, the implications of most of these models for supervision have not been fully developed, and I take full responsibility for my efforts in extending the therapy models to supervision. I am quite familiar with several of the therapy models, having trained extensively at the Philadelphia Child Guidance Clinic with Minuchin, Haley, Madanes, and others. I have also worked closely and published papers with Selekman on ways to apply the solution-focused model to substance abuse problems (Todd & Selekman, 1991) and to supervision (Selekman & Todd, 1995). Although I have taught all the remaining models on a graduate level, I may not have done them full justice. Similarly, I have drawn supervision case examples from my own supervision practice over the past twenty years, and some examples fit the selected model more closely than others. All share my penchant for examples that are dramatic and even outrageous, humorous, and often somewhat paradoxical.

COMMON SUPERVISORY ASSUMPTIONS AND THEIR IMPLICATIONS

The following sections describe supervisory assumptions that were developed primarily from Todd and Selekman (1991) based on several review articles that articulate common assumptions for therapy models (see Stanton, 1981).

Emphasis on Present Interaction

As noted previously, supervisors utilizing these models can be considered "systems purists" who care only about the characteristics of the current system of interaction and what maintains the behavior of the system. This is equally true of the supervisor/therapist/client family system, which is the focus of supervision. Historical explorations are kept to an absolute minimum, consistent with the systemic principle of equifinality—that there are myriad ways to get to the final state, and that one cannot proceed backward to a unique set of preconditions.

This suggests clearly that the supervisor's task is to discover what current factors are maintaining the present situation. For the current situation to be of supervisory concern, there is also an assumption that the situation is somehow "stuck" or problematic. Without concern for history, the supervisor's task is to devise, together with the supervisee, some form of intervention that will resolve this situation or at least unblock it.

The Key Is Small Changes in Interactional Pattern

All these models tend to be optimistic and incorporate the belief that comparatively small changes can ultimately have major impact on the system. This implies that a small change in the behavior of the supervisee (or the supervisor!) can ultimately create significant and lasting changes throughout the system. Although this change may be described differently in the different models, this principle nevertheless unifies all these models. The solution-focused model is clearest in describing a positive snowballing of change, in which small changes produce increasingly larger positive changes.

I once supervised a therapist who was an excellent observer of her own behavior. She sought supervision on a stuck individual case that had considerable lethal potential. Whenever the client, who had made significant suicide attempts in the past, became symptom-free and began to describe positive changes, she would suddenly shift dramatically and talk seriously of suicide. Reflecting on her own behavior, the therapist noted that she experienced considerable tension concerning the potential for suicide. When the client became less suicidal, the therapist relaxed noticeably and sat back in her chair. When the client returned to threats of suicide, she suddenly got the therapist's rapt attention, with the therapist sitting forward and focusing on every word.

After collaboration with the supervisor, the therapist adopted a posture of feigned indifference to talk of suicide, which was somewhat genuine because she had heard it all before. When the client described new healthy behavior, such as new leisure or social activities, the therapist would sit forward and respond with interest. The client's response was dramatic, with the expected result of positive snowballing rather than backsliding. Termination was handled consistently, with the therapist emphasizing strongly that she would welcome continued news of the interests and accomplishments of the client, while implying that she might not be able to take her on again as a client if there were renewed suicidal behavior.

Goal-Directed with Negotiated, Observable Goals

Models in this cluster have at worst been considered "gimmicky" and heavily interventionistic, a charge that is not without merit. The primary safeguard within these models is a commitment to work toward client goals with clearly observable indicators of progress. In supervision the use of indirect and even paradoxical techniques can be justified, provided there is the protection of clearly negotiated goals with explicit measures of success.

Positive Reframing Emphasized Instead of Insight

This group of models takes a strong stance against the importance of insight in therapy, with insight seen as irrelevant or at best a by-product rather than a cause of change. This extreme position is presumably softened somewhat in supervision because it is more important for therapists to be able to understand what led to change so that they can generalize to other situations and other cases. These models are also more likely to combine teaching with supervision than with therapy.

Positive reframing can be an effective and efficient mode of intervention in supervision. In supervision, the "consumer" is more likely to know that the supervisor is deliberately reframing supervisee behavior, while similar efforts in therapy are more likely to go undetected. Although knowing that the supervisor is reframing can make this intervention less potent, this may be counterbalanced by the increased impact of modeling.

Keep It Simple

As a group, these models pride themselves on simplicity, with the M.R.I. model the most extreme. Because these models are so heavily change-oriented, they place a premium on simple and immediately useful hypotheses and case formulations. In supervision, as in other clinical discussions, simple ideas do not automatically prevail; the various models offer a variety of techniques for combating excessively complex or negative ideas of supervisees or their colleagues.

Build on Strengths

All these models attempt to elicit client and supervisee strengths. All tend to try to potentiate existing strengths rather than assuming that everything useful for a therapist must be taught.

Consistent with the previously mentioned mistrust of insight, these models tend to rely on changes in context to remove constraints and create situations in which strengths will become manifest. In supervision, these positive changes would often be followed by a discussion about how the changes took place.

Stuckness Framed as Well-Intentioned Problem Solving

Although this position is most clearly identified with the M.R.I. model, all these models attempt to find ways to positively reframe stuckness to avoid stimulating resistance. The explicit assumption is that supervisees are trying their best to be helpful, and that many "mistakes" are normal and typical of supervisees at their level.

Active and Directive Role of Supervisor

All these models presume an active role on the part of the supervisor, particularly in contrast to the psychoanalytic model of supervision (Chapter 11) and postmodern models (Chapter 15). The nature of this activity may vary, as is shown in the separate sections that describe characteristic supervisory interventions of each model.

Interventionistic

Specific actions of both therapist and supervisor are seen as highly important. Again, particularly in contrast to other models, preplanning and deliberate interventions are seen as possible and useful. There is also an assumption that interventions can be categorized and taught. (This makes it possible to suggest interventions in an economical manner during live supervision phone-ins.) Supervisors also devote considerable energy to devising or selecting supervisory interventions and delivering them in an optimal manner.

Supervisor Responsibility for Effective Intervention

Haley is probably the theorist most noteworthy and most extreme in his views on responsibility, but all theorists in this cluster tend to emphasize the instrumental role of the supervisor. As will be seen, there are some important differences regarding supervisee-generated versus supervisor-generated solutions to supervisee difficulties, with M.R.I. and solution-focused models emphasizing the facilitative role of supervisors, and structural and strategic models seeing supervisors as providing directives or other interventions.

All these models take a strong stance against "resistance" as a useful concept, whether attributed to family members or supervisees. In these models, the responsibility always ultimately resides with the supervisor. For this reason, any description of a difficulty that resides in the supervisee should be recast as a challenge for the supervisor rather than a justification for lack of progress.

Pragmatic

Each model has its own unifying framework, but within that framework all these models tend to be highly pragmatic or opportunistic.

Relatively few possible supervisory interventions would be ruled out categorically, as long as the supervisor can justify the intervention in terms of intended effect and can specify indicators of success or failure.

Change Can Be Rapid

This group of models tends to incorporate a belief in discontinuous change, as opposed to continuous or gradual change (Hoffman, 1989). Perhaps this is less true in supervision where gradual learning may also be emphasized, but there is little question that dramatic interventions and sudden "Aha" experiences are not only considered possible but are highly valued.

SPECIFIC MODELS

Structural Model, Including Early Haley

Primary Goal: Correcting the Hierarchy

Minuchin and Haley both emphasize the importance of correcting the hierarchy and the destructiveness of cross-generational coalitions. This can certainly include correcting an incorrect position of the therapist such as being overly aligned with a child or favoring one spouse over the other. Supervisors must also be alert to their own behavior and their own tendency to undermine the hierarchy and enter into covert alliances that constrain the therapy.

Unique Assumptions of the Structural Model

Joining

In structural therapy, Minuchin and colleagues have emphasized the deliberate use of joining (Minuchin, 1974; Minuchin & Fishman, 1981). This may be less necessary in supervision, because the supervisee has received a good deal of

professional socialization to the process. In group supervision, deliberate manipulation of nonverbal behavior can be quite useful to balance relationships in the group or to counterbalance the effects of a supervisory intervention.

Supervisor's Use of Self

The structural model also can make heavy use of personal influence to achieve particular goals (Aponte, 1994). (In this respect, this is a much "hotter" model than most of the others in this chapter or the remainder of the book. Andolfi and Menghi [1982] is probably most similar.) The supervisor can make deliberate use of self, including the supervisor's affect or selective self-disclosure, to motivate a supervisee to act.

Seeing Is Believing

More than any other model in this chapter, the structural model exemplifies "seeing is believing." Live and videotape supervision are trusted much more than verbal reports, and enactment is frequently recommended. Similarly, the structural supervisor typically wishes to test the system's response to straightforward requests for change. This is particularly important before making a supervisory decision to move in a more strategic direction (Stanton, 1981; Todd, 1981).

Typical Structural Supervisory Interventions

Boundary-Making

In the structural model supervisors, like therapists, need to be alert to potential problems of boundaries and hierarchy and be prepared to intervene to correct them. Given the complexity of the supervisor/supervisee/client system, such problems are common. Interventions are often quite simple, as long as the supervisor remains conscious of communication patterns. When doing supervision-of-supervision in a situation utilizing live supervision with phone-ins, for example, I have resorted to the simple expedient of never touching the telephone. This ensures that all communication will flow through the supervisor-in-training and prevents any short-circuiting of communication.

Enactment

Structural theory is well known for its emphasis on enactment; ideally this takes the form of live supervision, because this allows both observation of the pattern and direct intervention to change it. In supervision, it is also possible to use various analogues of the problem; least desirable is allowing the supervisee merely to talk about the problem, because the assumption is that supervisees often are not consciously aware of the sources of difficulty, especially their own contribution. Role-playing of a stuck therapeutic situation in supervision can be helpful, especially because it allows the supervisor to intervene. Review of videotapes is more helpful from the standpoint of generating data about the supervisee's participation in the problem, although it does not allow direct supervisory intervention.

Intensifying

Deliberate intensification of situations in supervision can be quite effective, particularly when supervisees seem to be underreacting. This can include therapy situations—supervisees seeming too tolerant of out-of-control behavior in sessions—or supervision situations in which there is a lack of appropriate affect from supervisees such as supervisees seeming blasé about their failure to tape sessions or prepare adequately for supervision.

Typical Structural Supervisory Modalities

Live Supervision with Phone-Ins, Walk-Ins

Minuchin, Haley, and Montalvo were among the original pioneers in developing live supervision (see Chapter 20). When used by a struc-

tural supervisor, live supervision with phone-ins takes on a distinctive flavor. Most supervisory interventions are action-oriented directives such as "Tell Father to talk to Mother," "Get the little sister more involved," "Move closer to Mother." All these are similar to interventions—requests for specific action with little or no explanation—a structural therapist would make.

Minuchin also developed a characteristic style of the supervisory "walk-in" in which he would walk into a therapy session with little warning and deliver a dramatic intervention such as "Your therapist isn't telling you that your protectiveness is killing your son." When the parents would begin to respond, he would say "You need to discuss that with your therapist," and leave the room. Although such an intervention sounds unsettling to the supervisee as well as the family, it is characteristically structural.[1]

My belief is that such an intervention is much less destructive than the seemingly similar supervisory practice of coming in and taking over the remainder of the session. With the Minuchin maneuver, the underlying message is still, "You and the therapist can work this out," in contrast to taking over the session, which can be interpreted as an expression of lack of confidence in the supervisee.

Case Example: Realigning the Therapeutic System

The following example shows the influence of Minuchin and early Haley and occurred when I was helping develop a program for hospitalizing whole families at the Philadelphia Child Guidance Clinic (Combrinck-Graham et al., 1982).

_____

A single mother, who had allegedly abused her only child, was hospitalized together with him. On the staff/family level, a familiar dynamic hap-

_____

[1]See Minuchin (1981) for a good example of starting a controversy and shifting it to the parents to resolve.

pened fairly quickly, in which various team members idealized the child and quickly concluded they would be better parents than the mother; they were hostile toward her and acted to displace her.

In supervision, it became obvious that this dynamic was being repeated on other levels. The inpatient therapist (the author) showed, through his actions, that he believed it was unfortunate that mother and son were being seen by an outside outpatient therapist who was not one of the PCGC elite. The supervisor[2] pointed out that this attitude would swamp the clinic with cases and antagonize referral sources. The treatment plan was completely reorganized to change channels of communication and correct the hierarchy. In preparing for discharge, my primary job was to reinforce the outpatient therapist, whose main task was to find actions of the mother to reinforce, who in turn was to reinforce the child.

The assumption was clear that at each level the participants had the skills necessary to emit behavior that could be reinforced. It was assumed that correcting the hierarchy would lead to rapid behavioral change, which it did. All relationships quickly became much more positive, and other behavioral changes followed soon after.

Haley Strategic and Paradox

Primary Goal: Disrupting Dysfunctional Cycles

Haley is well known for careful analysis of cycles of behavior in which symptoms and other dysfunctional behavior are embedded. In his writings, he has offered many examples that illustrate how therapists can unwittingly become part of such sequences (Haley, 1976, 1980). When a supervisor encounters such a situation, Haley considers the supervisor responsible for

[2]The supervisor was Lee Combrinck-Graham, M. D., the Clinical Director of the program.

finding methods for disrupting this cycle, utilizing techniques such as paradoxical supervisory directives, ordeals, or reframing (Haley, 1984). Mazza (1988) offers a wide variety of indirect supervisory interventions in this model.

Assumptions of the Haley Strategic Model

Unique Strategies

Haley's definition of "strategic," based on his work with Erickson, includes developing a unique strategy for every case (Haley, 1973). Presumably, this is equally applicable to supervision. Haley has made clear that he considers the direct teaching function of therapy to be comparatively unimportant and even potentially insulting and countertherapeutic. In this view, most of what is interesting in supervision demands a unique strategy to help the supervisee access new alternatives.

Ericksonian Utilization

Closely related to the above assumption is the importance that Erickson and Haley place on "utilization," in which whatever is brought to therapy or supervision is incorporated and defined as cooperation (Haley, 1973). Although Haley has not formalized this in supervision to the extent done by deShazer (see section of this chapter on solution-focused supervision), Haley's work also implies the advantage of going with supervisees rather than struggling with them.

Importance of Directives

Haley (1976) places particular emphasis on the design and delivery of directives. The clear implication is that the content of the intervention is only one component; the specific wording and the precise mode of delivery are seen as at least equally important. Perhaps it is more common in supervision than in therapy for the content of the intervention to be dominant; however, there are instances in supervision in which supervisory directives merit the same degree of careful attention to wording and delivery. The supervisor needs to take responsibility for the success of the supervisory directive and needs to be willing to take a close look at the language and delivery of the directive should it fail to have the desired impact.

Supervision in Stages

Haley (1984) makes the interesting contention that in most stuck situations it is impossible to get from an initial "abnormal" situation directly to the desired goal. Instead, a supervisor needs to plan an intermediate goal, which is also "abnormal" and which would be undesireable if it became the final outcome. For example, rather than asking a too talkative therapist to talk less, which is difficult to operationalize, a strategic supervisor might develop a rationale for asking the therapist to be completely silent for a period of time in the session.

Typical Strategic Supervisory Interventions

The Paradox Controversy and Paradoxical Techniques

Storm and Heath (1982) offer a commonly voiced position on the use of strategic (paradoxical) interventions in supervision—in essence, "don't get caught!" Presumably there are many strategic therapists who would be even more cautious about strategic intervention in supervision. These concerns about strategic supervision seem to be based on three assumptions:

1. Supervisees are more likely than therapy clients to detect paradoxical interventions.
2. Being aware of the strategic nature of an intervention destroys its effectiveness.
3. Getting caught being strategic will jeopardize the supervisory relationship.

As I have observed elsewhere (Todd, 1981; Todd & LaForte, 1987), clients on the receiving end of paradoxical techniques almost invariably detect that something extraordinary is going on, and eventually the therapist needs to acknowledge this on some level. In supervision, there can be added utility from a learning standpoint of discussing a strategic intervention *after* the intervention has had the desired effect (Protinsky & Preli, 1987). A survey on the use of paradoxical techniques in therapy found that their acceptability (not necessarily their impact) was heightened by increased knowledge about the use of paradox (Sexton et al., 1993). Finally, much of this dilemma disappears, at least in my experience, when one appreciates paradoxes based on contradictory truths.

I received a written communication from a group of supervisees I had been training in the use of written paradoxical directives. The form of the communication made me appropriately suspicious. The carefully crafted message asked me to be cautious when praising them in front of clinical staff and spelled out several potentially negative consequences of such praise. Although I am considered consistently positive and amazingly diplomatic, I have rarely been accused of effusive praise, so this message simultaneously implied "Praise us more" and "Don't praise us so much." When I accused them of being paradoxical, they denied this appropriately, while simultaneously revealing through their nonverbal behavior that they were extremely proud of their efforts. Knowing full well that this intervention was paradoxical did not help me to avoid dealing with this dilemma regarding praise and taking responsibility for its consequences.

In the reference cited here on the acceptability of paradox (Sexton et al., 1993), there was a clear difference in acceptability between techniques that were defiance-based (Rohrbaugh et al., 1981; Todd, 1981) and the more cooperative ones. Two particular techniques, which are not defiance-based, seem particularly well suited to supervision.

(1) Restraining from Change. When applied to supervision, the technique of restraining from change (Haley, 1976; Todd, 1981) involves warning the supervisee of the dangers of changing too fast. The inclusion of the time factor in this technique is crucial. A strategic supervisor might challenge a supervisee about whether the supervisee was ready to take credit for success as a therapist and go on to list some of the dangers. Although the supervisor might incorporate some of the same material as a supervisor working from a psychodynamic or Bowenian perspective, such a gentle challenge would have a different flavor than a suggestion to explore the roots of the supervisee's self-defeating behavior.

(2) Positioning. In supervision, the use of positioning (Todd, 1981) consists of the supervisor deliberately taking a stance diametrically opposed to the stance typically expected of a supervisor. This technique is appropriate in order to maintain supervisory flexibility, especially when the supervisor is being "type cast" or the supervisor and supervisee have developed a counterproductive polarization on some issue.

Most examples of positioning call into question some basic tenet of supervision rather than merely representing a different opinion on a topic on which there are many divergent opinions. For example, the supervisor could argue against the supervisee being too clear about the direction and goals of therapy or suggest that a clear contract might be undesireable. A special case would be situations in which the supervisor's stance is presumably predictable. For example a Haley-oriented supervisor might argue against being in charge of

the therapy. Although such interventions may have a slightly tongue-in-cheek quality, and supervisees should always wonder whether the supervisor believes the position, effective positioning requires drawing on some truth in the situation such as the dangers of clarity or being in charge.

Benevolent Ordeals

Although Haley has written extensively about the use of "ordeal therapy" with therapy clients (Haley, 1984), this approach has rarely been applied to the supervisory arena. (See Protinsky and Preli [1987] and the Case Example that follows for two examples.) Supervisory ordeals would appear to have considerable utility in supervision, because they can turn an unproductive supervisory impasse into a "win-win" situation, and because the process of negotiating an appropriate ordeal appears to be straightforward, especially compared to paradoxical techniques.

As is true of all strategic techniques, supervisory ordeals are only appropriate when there are clearly identified, agreed-on goals, because achieving such goals allows the supervisee to escape from the ordeal. As a last resort, when some important supervisory goal is not being achieved and movement toward that goal appears to be blocked, the supervisor can propose a benevolent ordeal. An ideal ordeal in supervision has certain important features:

1. The alternative behavior should be appropriate to the context of supervision and training (e.g. reading, note-taking, tape review).
2. This behavior is "benevolent" in the sense of being helpful to supervisees.
3. The alternative behavior is clearly under conscious control, in contrast to the problematic behavior, which the supervisee usually characterizes as somehow being

beyond the supervisee's control. ("I don't know why I talk so much." "I can't seem to remember to do that.")

4. The supervisor has reason to believe that the alternative behavior will be an unattractive ordeal for the supervisee, either because anyone would resent the extra work, or because the particular supervisee will find the alternative unpalatable, as in the ordeal supervision example on the next page.

5. Although both parties typically recognize that the proposed contract is an ordeal (especially if the supervisee has read Haley), it is not framed as a punishment but as a useful alternative to get beyond a stuck situation.

If anything, the supervisor should apologize for the ordeal quality of the suggested behavior, implying that it is being recommended in spite of being somewhat distasteful to the supervisor. Both parties usually recognize that it is a distasteful ordeal and that the supervisee's lack of achievement of agreed-on goals makes it hard for the supervisee to avoid agreeing to the ordeal. Often the mere suggestion of the possible remedy may be enough to unblock the situation.

Because appropriate supervisory ordeals may be difficult to imagine, some examples may stimulate the reader's creativity. I have either used or threatened to use the following examples on occasion, although I have rarely needed to resort to a full-blown supervisory ordeal.

1. A supervisee who is much too long-winded in therapy and seems unable to control this can be asked to write down each statement made by the supervisee and describe the rationale for that statement.

2. A supervisee who somehow seems unable to bring in videotapes can be asked to make nearly verbatim "process notes" like a beginning social work student as an alternative. (An example that proves the adage "One man's meat is another man's poison!")

3. A supervisee who has a particular unexplained "block" in supervision or therapy could be asked to do an exhaustive literature review on the topic.

Typical Strategic Supervisory Modalities

Live Team, Final Directives

As noted earlier, strategic supervision, particularly in the Haley model, usually consists of live team supervision of therapy sessions. As Roberts (1983) observed, such a team is often supervisor-dominated in a clearly hierarchical way, in contrast to other models in which team input is more highly valued and the hierarchy is flattened (see Chapter 24). Although Roberts (1983) and several authors in this present book (Chapters 6, 15, and 16) argue for the advantages of flattening the hierarchy, a case can also be made for a more hierarchical model. This can include situations where supervisees are comparative novices, at least beginners in applying a particular therapy model. Even when therapists are experienced, I have encountered many situations in which "leaderless" teams have developed unproductive interactions and have had difficulty extricating themselves from them.

Strategic teams often develop paradoxical final directives or "prescriptions" (Todd & LaForte, 1987), which may or may not be written. It is often best to exclude the therapist from developing the prescription and include the therapist as an object of it. If a directive were to focus on the dangers of rapid change, for example, the therapist could also be warned of these dangers or congratulated for going slowly.

CASE EXAMPLE: ORDEAL SUPERVISION

A supervisor-in-training (SIT) had tried numerous interventions to get a supervisee to bring in videotapes for supervision. A live supervision-of-supervision session was set up, and the supervisee indicated that he was bringing a videotape for the first time in six months. The supervisor (the author) preplanned with the SIT how the supervisee would receive validation for bringing a tape. The session did not go exactly as planned—the supervisee did bring a tape, but it was an inaudible tape of an individual session with a girl with cerebral palsy, with whom therapy had already been terminated! The therapist was given an ambiguous message from behind the mirror congratulating him for finding "the perfect tape," without further elaboration.

During subsequent discussion with the SIT, I realized this was a rare opportunity to apply "ordeal supervision." I suggested that the SIT and I had overlooked the obvious—that because all his supervision sessions were videotaped, there would never be a lack of videotapes to discuss with the supervisee. (Both of us knew that the supervisee hated process discussions.) As agreed, he relayed this realization to the supervisee, noting further that "If we had to, at the next session we could watch the video of us discussing the supervision videotape, and so on." It appeared that the supervisee quickly got the point, but it took a couple of supervisory sessions for the intervention to have the desired effect. In these two sessions the SIT played the videos of supervision, commenting on body language and every nuance of the supervisee's behavior, while communicating nonverbally that he knew this was torture and that he did not take his interventions seriously, yet was willing to continue as long as necessary. The supervisee realized there was only one easy way out, and he even produced two videos at the next session. From then on, videotaping was not a problem.

Contrary to all the fears about being caught making strategic interventions in supervision, the therapist knew exactly what was happening; nevertheless, the intervention still had a powerful effect. He had read Haley extensively and recognized my hand in the intervention. (He subsequently became a SIT with me!) In retrospect, he describes himself as having dug himself into a hole around videotaping and being unable to extricate himself from this. Although the intervention made him very uncomfortable, he thought it was fair and was grateful that it helped supervision move forward.

Madanes

Primary Goal: Correcting "Helpful" Reversals of Hierarchy

In Madanes's therapy model (1981, 1984), it is assumed that symptoms have a helpful function in interpersonal relationships. Children's symptoms and behavior, for example, are seen as benevolent efforts to help their parents solve a problem that cannot be addressed more directly. Similarly, a symptomatic spouse may be "helping" the nonsymptomatic partner. Under what conditions might supervisors assume that similar benevolence occurs in the relationship between supervisor and supervisee? While Madanes does not address this issue, there are three factors that presumably would make this more likely: (1) when the supervisory relationship is long term, (2) when the relationship extends beyond the supervisory hour (e.g., agency supervision, faculty/student), and (3) when one or both of the parties feel "stuck."

Unique Supervisory Assumptions in the Madanes Model

Who Is Helping Whom?

It becomes crucial to address the question of who is helping whom in two extreme supervisory situations. The first occurs when there is reason for one or both parties to believe that the supervisee is helping the supervisor (e.g., the supervisor needs the supervisory hours to become an Approved Supervisor). The second potentially problematic situation is when the supervisee has never acknowledged the need for supervisory help, at least not from this supervisor.

Neither of these situations necessarily dooms the supervisory relationship, and often they can be ameliorated through straightforward contracting. Madanes's unique contribution is to suggest that if the straightforward approach does not work, the supervisor may need to pretend to need the supervisee's help. As Madanes notes (1981, 1984), pretending to need help is not the same as actually needing it, and the pretense can block other "helpful" dynamics. For the intervention to have the desired effect, the supervisor needs to be prepared to exaggerate the situation. In one supervisory situation in which the supervisee never accepted help, I deliberately adopted a posture of incompetence and helplessness. Unfortunately, when the supervisee became reassuring and patronizing, I initially became furious. My internal reaction was, "You fool, I don't need your reassurance to feel effective as a supervisor!" I needed to swallow my pride and exaggerate my helpless stance more dramatically to liberate the relationship from the previously stuck dynamic.

Power and Incompetence

Like Haley, Madanes makes much of power dynamics in important relationships. Seeming incompetence can often serve a function in rebalancing power imbalances that cannot be addressed or resolved in other ways. Although Madanes and Haley downplay the importance of instruction and skill training and emphasize the problems this top-down situation can create, most other models of therapy and supervision allow for the possibility of deficits of skill or knowledge. When skill training and education

have little effect, it is reasonable to wonder whether the "incompetence" of the supervisee has some functional value in the supervisor/supervisee/client system. (See the discussion of "collusive games" in Chapter 17.) Here also it may be helpful for the supervisor to act like Columbo. [It is not obvious what a nonsexist female version of this stance would be.] This often eliminates the potential for power struggles and creates space for competence to emerge.

Therapy (and Supervision?) in Stages

Although Haley and Madanes often provide dramatic and unorthodox interventions in their writings, both emphasize that stuck situations are rarely resolved through a single intervention. When the initial situation is stuck, therapy and presumably supervision need to proceed through a series of stages, often with unusual transitional stages prior to reaching the ultimate goal. To use the previous example, it is possible that the supervisee might need to go through a period of feeling helpful to a confused supervisor before a more balanced relationship could emerge.

Typical Supervisory Interventions

As is true with Haley, Madanes makes extensive use of live supervision, with the therapist often a vehicle for delivering interventions from behind the mirror, which makes it difficult to distinguish between supervisory interventions and therapeutic interventions. Little has been written on using Madanes-style interventions specifically as interventions on the therapist, so these illustrations are somewhat speculative.

Rituals

Madanes (1981) describes several rituals that she has given to supervisees as therapeutic interventions. Often these seem to be more playful versions of Haley's ordeals, such as having a family enact a ritual with the whole family in the middle of the night when a child wakes up with a nightmare. These rituals are always based on hypotheses about the meaning and function of the symptom, particularly in rebalancing power in the family.

While, hopefully, such interventions are needed less often in supervision, in theory there seems to be no particular obstacle to making use of them to rebalance power or unblock a stuck situation. These can be "rituals" for the therapist without the family ever knowing of the therapist's assignment. For example, the supervisee could be instructed to start all sessions in a particular one-down manner, or always to ask the mother for advice on some subject.

I noted a particular stuck pattern during supervision-of-supervision in which an optimistic female SIT kept trying to encourage a male therapist to no avail. Several characteristics of the therapist seemed to interfere with the success of such encouragement, particularly that he was a pessimistic Irishman and former Jesuit seminarian. To deal with this impasse in supervision and to lighten up the mood, the SIT was told to get the therapist to religiously bring in an Irish joke to every supervision session that would help her to understand pessimism and the relationship between the sexes in the Irish culture. (Both of them followed this directive without fail!)

Pretending

Madanes offers many creative examples of blocking problems by having someone pretend to have the problem. Extending this to supervision, a supervisor could pretend to have the supervisee's problem and ask the supervisee for help in dealing with it. Alternatively, a supervisor might prescribe that the supervisee pretend to have the problem the supervisee already has, even though neither supervisor nor supervisee has openly acknowledged this problem. These interventions are complex and potentially confusing, and it is important to

heed the earlier warning that clear supervisory goals are the best safeguard against indirect supervisory interventions that are off the mark and create unnecessary trouble.

CASE EXAMPLE: PRETENDING INCOMPETENCE

As a beginning supervisor, I asked Madanes to consult on a supervisory problem. One of my supervisees was experiencing little success relative to peers and was unresponsive to routine encouragement from me or his fellow students. He seemed demoralized, and it was affecting his therapy.

Madanes responded that this was a predictable problem at this point in the training year, and that there was a pretending intervention which invariably had the desired effect. All that was required was for the supervisee to throw himself on the mercy of his clients. He needed to promise to go into the next session with each of his cases and confess that he felt totally inadequate and was considering changing professions. She anticipated that most clients would be surprised and would quickly point out changes they had made in therapy with him. The supervisory intervention had an effect frequently encountered with pretending interventions: The therapist smiled and said emphatically that he knew that he did not need to perform the experiment. The previously stuck dynamic was unblocked by this single intervention (or the threat of it!).

The M.R.I. Brief Therapy Model

Many of the modernist and postmodern models owe a heavy debt to the classic writings of the M.R.I. Brief Therapy Model. This is most obviously true of the solution-focused model and postmodern language-based theories. Many of the simple ideas of this model have obvious applicability for supervision, as articulated by Fisch (1988) and Storm and Heath (1982).

Primary Goal: Reversing Attempted Solutions

The M.R.I. model posits that well-meaning attempted solutions become the problem. This assumption appears to be a good fit for supervision, because it presupposes good intentions rather than pathology or even that the supervisee's behavior has a "function" in the supervisory system.

Unique Assumptions of the M.R.I. Model

Customership

As Storm and Heath (1982) correctly observe, the notion of "customership" (Fisch, Weakland, & Segal, 1982) can be extended from therapy to supervision. They note that many supervisees do not come to supervision with a supervisory problem to be worked on; other indicators include vagueness, lack of specific goals, and lack of any sense of accountability for follow-through on supervisory recommendations. Supervisees may want other things from supervision, including support and validation, alternative ideas, or simply credit for time spent in supervision. Such motivations, while creating some difficulties for problem-focused supervision, can produce different degrees of customership (Alderfer & Lynch, 1986).

Typical M.R.I. Supervisory Interventions

Avoid Doing More of the Same

The most basic M.R.I. intervention follows directly from the assumption that attempted solutions become the problem—avoid doing "more of the same" ineffective behavior. Often the prescription is to do a 180-degree shift and do the virtual opposite of what has failed to work.

Supervisors are not immune to this more-of-the-same dynamic, and should be aware of the possible need for a supervisory U-turn. Storm and Heath (1982) posit that most stuck supervisory situations come from a failure to notice lack of customership on the part of the supervisee. If this lack of customership is detected early, stuck patterns can be avoided. Targeting the lack of customership by examining the motivation of the supervisee may also make it possible to make genuine customers out of such supervisees.

Tailoring Supervisory Interventions

In the M.R.I. model, the stuck pattern often seems obvious, as does the remedy. M.R.I. theorists caution that one should never assume that implementation will be easy. New interventions need to fit the supervisee's worldview or deviate from it as little as possible. This is crucially important because the aim is never to convert the supervisee to a "better" view of the problem. In this model, supervisors develop interventions in such a way that they do not appear to contradict supervisees' previous actions and beliefs, allowing them to save face. Use of the supervisee's own language and metaphors also makes an intervention more palatable.

Typical Supervisory Modalities

Supervision Between Sessions

Fisch (1988) has emphasized a comparatively unique supervisory modality favored by the M.R.I. model—supervision between sessions, which is actually favored over live supervision. This seems to follow from the model's simplicity and its emphasis on "big-picture" changes in the supervisee's behavior, and changes in the underlying beliefs and assumptions.

The following case, while having paradoxical overtones, is an example of a supervisory 180-degree reversal.

CASE EXAMPLE: THE PERFECT THERAPIST

The supervisor, a SIT with me, was a middle-aged female faculty member whose husband was also on the faculty. The therapist, a much younger woman, had approached the husband sexually but had been rejected. The therapist reframed the experience as the supervisor keeping her husband on a short leash, otherwise he would never have resisted her sexually.

As luck would have it, the case being supervised was a sixteen-year-old boy with a single mother who had a highly sexualized relationship with her son, who appeared to be having considerable difficulty dealing with this. According to the SIT, the therapist was also very seductive with the boy, but she rejected this observation by the SIT and accused her of jealousy. This power struggle had reached a stalemate and the SIT sought my guidance.

I responded that I knew the appropriate intervention but doubted the SIT would appreciate it. Actually I knew the SIT was a well-trained strategic therapist who could easily reverse her position, given sufficient motivation. I explained that she needed to recognize that this woman was the perfect therapist for this particular case, because she was uniquely qualified to teach the young man about seductive women. The SIT immediately appreciated the possibilities of this intervention and readily agreed to use it.

Not surprisingly, the therapist resisted the SIT's directive to use her sexuality in therapy. The competition between therapist and SIT, and between the therapist and the mother, was greatly diminished and the case moved forward.

Solution-Focused

Primary Goal: Identify and Amplify Exceptions

There is little question that the most distinctive goal of solution-focused supervision is the identification of exceptions to problems identified by supervisees. Such exceptions are then amplified to help supervisees develop their own solutions.

Solution-focused supervisors often ask supervisees to locate places in advance on videotape where they think they had done a particularly good job (Selekman & Todd, 1995). If appropriate, they can also be asked to contrast these segments with places where they felt stuck. Supervisors should be particularly alert to the issue of personal agency and amplify statements by supervisees that describe how they produced the more successful segments and how they can do more of this in the future. Although supervisors can also identify exceptions, it is preferable to stick closely to the exceptions supervisees recognize.

Unique Assumptions of the Solution-Focused Model

Supervisees Inevitably Cooperate with Supervisors

The solution-focused model places particular emphasis on the notion of cooperation. Initially I thought this was a semantic exercise to avoid the notion of resistance, but I began to see the importance of this mindset for supervision. Just as in therapy, it is useful to assume that supervisees will cooperate with us in supervision; the main task of the supervisor therefore becomes the identification of the supervisees' unique cooperative response patterns (deShazer, 1985). There is potentially a wide range of supervisee cooperative response patterns, such as supervisees who respond straightforwardly to supervisory directives, those who modify the supervisor's suggestions, those who do the opposite of what has been recommended by the supervisor, and so forth. The supervisor needs to consider the particular response pattern when making future recommendations.

Supervisors Keep Change Talk Happening

In their research, Gingerich et al. (1988) have found that there is a direct relationship between therapist use of change language and positive treatment outcome. When these ideas are applied to supervision, the assumption is that supervisors who use change-oriented language, such as presuppositional words like *when* and *will* and who pay particular attention to change-talk by their supervisees, will have a significantly positive impact on the supervisees' therapy. Specific techniques for doing this are presented in the interventions section that follows.

Supervisees Take the Lead in Defining the Supervisory Goals

Even more than other supervisors in this chapter, solution-focused supervisors see their task as assisting supervisees in identifying small, achievable goals for themselves in their supervisory learning contract and in their therapy sessions.

Solution-Focused Supervisory Interventions

Compliments and Cheerleading

In supervision, compliments (deShazer, 1985) and cheerleading (deShazer, 1988) are interwoven into every aspect of supervision—while reviewing videotape material, at the beginning of phone directives in live supervision, at consultation breaks, and when having postsession discussions. Complimenting supervisees on their therapeutic strengths and their performance in sessions provides helpful encouragement and contributes to professional self-confidence.

Scaling Questions

Scaling questions (deShazer, 1985, 1988, 1991; deShazer et al., 1986) can be used to establish small and realistic supervisory goals, maintain a clear focus in supervision, and serve as a useful quantitative measure of progress. After supervisees identify goals, they can be asked to rate themselves on a scale of goal-achievement, then asked what they would need to do to move a small increment on the scale (Selekman & Todd, 1995).

Pretend the Miracle Happened

deShazer's Miracle Question sequence (deShazer 1985, 1988, 1991) is quite useful with supervisees to operationalize their goals and generate new behaviors. For example, a supervisee could be asked: "Suppose prior to your next session with the Smith family a miracle happened and your impasse with them is solved. How will you be able to tell that the miracle really happened?" "What will you be doing differently with the Smiths in the session?" "How did you get that to happen?" "What will you need to continue to do to make that happen more often?" Such questions can successfully elicit the supervisee's expertise in finding alternatives with their stuck cases.

The miracle question can be extended by asking the supervisee to pretend to engage in a particular miracle behavior and notice how the clients respond (deShazer, 1991; Gingerich & deShazer, 1991). With this supervisory task, it is useful for the supervisee to videotape the session to make it possible to microanalyze differences in therapist–family interaction.

If It Does Not Work, Do Something Different

The previous discussion of the M.R.I. Brief Therapy Model highlights the importance of obtaining information on attempted solutions (Watzlawick, Weakland, & Fisch, 1974) to resolve their presenting problem or achieve supervisory goals. In the solution-focused model, obtaining such information can often be bypassed by using the skeleton key intervention—"If it does not work, do something different." Supervisors need to be alert to ways they may be delivering supervisory directives that have already proven to be ineffective in changing a supervisee's behavior. Conversely, if a particular supervisory cooperative mode of intervention is working with a supervisee, the supervisor needs to do more of what works. When supervision or therapy is stuck, however, *any* change in behavior is likely to be an improvement on doing more of the same ineffective behavior.

Typical Solution-Focused Supervisory Modalities

Final Interventions and Session Structure

Training in the solution-focused model usually incorporates the use of a team for live observation and development of final interventions. Some supervisory phone-ins may occur, but these are liberally laced with compliments. During a consultation break, the therapist receives further encouragement and the final intervention, to be delivered by the therapist to the family, is developed. It is possible for the supervisor to make use of consultation breaks and deliver final supervisory interventions in situations other than live supervision, such as individual supervision with video case review, but I know of no published examples of this extension.

Videotapes also fit well in solution-focused supervision, either as an adjunct to live supervision or as an alternative. Using some of the techniques outlined before, the supervisor typically uses the tapes to identify and highlight strengths rather than becoming a "problem detective."

CASE EXAMPLE: A PLAYFUL SOLUTION

When I was consulting on a case as part of a seminar on solution-focused supervision, I was somewhat surprised when the therapist, an MFT graduate student, asked for help in devising a Madanes-style pretend intervention. Because one of the major tenets of solution-focused supervision is to work on the supervisee's goals, it seemed consistent to honor this request.

Discussion revealed that the therapist was in a considerable bind in this court-referred case. The father of the primary patient, a twelve-year-old girl, was being released from prison for child molestation (not of her or any other family member). The therapist had been instructed to inform the court when the girl had "fully understood her father's crimes" so that visitation could begin. Unfortunately, the girl showed little interest in talking in therapy. Her mother and half-sister showed some embarrassment but were more willing to talk about topics such as sex and sexual abuse. When they talked about these topics in front of the patient, she would hold a magazine in front of her face. Straightforward efforts to get her to put down the magazine and talk were unsuccessful, and the therapist was beginning to feel time pressure to communicate with the court.

When asked to imagine succeeding with the case, the therapist described no longer being in a power struggle with the girl and having a more playful atmosphere. She also shared a Madanes-informed hypothesis that the girl was protecting her mother and half-sister. Soon she said, "Maybe we should all have magazines!" We agreed that she should validate the girl's behavior as protective and helpful toward everyone, including the therapist, and should encourage her to hold up a magazine whenever she sensed that anyone was uncomfortable. After the next few sessions, the therapist wrote to me and reported that she had carried out the pretending intervention as planned and that it had had the desired effect on the atmosphere of the therapy.

_____

The Early Work of the Milan Team

Primary Goal: Multiple Viewpoints Through Questioning

As Nichols and Schwartz note, it is difficult to characterize the work of the Milan associates because there have been several very different Milan models (Nichols & Schwartz, 1995, p. 431). In this section, I confine my analysis to the work of the original Milan team (Selvini Palazzoli et al., 1978, 1980), as well as the work of Boscolo and Ceccin following the split between the men and women on the team (Boscolo et al., 1987; Cecchin et al., 1993). The work of Tomm (1987a,b, 1988) in popularizing and developing Milan-style questioning is also included. Although this work has become progressively less interventionist, from its inception the Milan team has emphasized the use of unusual forms of questioning to develop multiple views of reality and to examine and change hypotheses about systemic behavior.

Unique Assumptions of the Milan Model

In the Milan model, there is a particularly fine line between assumptions and interventions. In their classic paper on "hypothesizing-circularity-neutrality" (Selvini Palazzoli et al., 1980), the original Milan team made these three assumptions central to their emerging model, while also noting that the acts of hypothesizing or asking circular questions, were important interventions.

Hypothesizing

The Milan associates emphasize that supervisors cannot avoid making hypotheses, and that these hypotheses inevitably shape supervision. In this model, it is important for supervisors to articulate their hypotheses about the supervisor/supervisee/client system, and to be alert to the impact these hypotheses can have on supervision.

Circularity

The Milan team placed great emphasis on Bateson's (1979) ideas concerning "news of a difference," that only differences are perceptible. Differences in perception were seen as much more important than any search for a single underlying "truth." Supervisors should pay strict attention to their language in supervision, using phraseology that reinforces that supervision discusses multiple perspectives and hypotheses, not truth.

Neutrality

Although critics of the Milan team have questioned the possibility of true neutrality in therapy, and others have pointed out situations in which moral neutrality seems undesireable, the assumption of neutrality is a cornerstone of the Milan approach. The supervisor should convey an attitude of detached curiosity, of working together to develop more complex hypotheses and views. Facts are seen as enriching understanding rather than proving a particular point of view.

Typical Interventions

Purposive Questioning

Tomm (1985, 1987a,b, 1988) expands the work of the Milan team, particularly their focus on circular questioning, into a typology of questions. This typology includes the assumptions underlying the type of question, the intent behind the question, and the probable effect on the questioner and the receivers of the question. Two forms of questions addressed by Tomm, circular questions and reflexive questions, seem most consistent with the Milan model. Supervisors should find his full typology helpful in analyzing their intentions in asking particular types of questions and the likely effects on supervisee and supervisor.

Circular Questions.   Supervisors use circular questions to orient themselves to the clinical situation with a predominantly *exploratory* intent. Guiding presuppositions are interactional and systemic, embodying the assumption that everything is interconnected. Asking supervisory questions to identify patterns for a systemic understanding tends to have a *liberating effect* on supervisees who, presumably, will be listening to the answers and making connections themselves. Because of their circular nature, these questions tend to have an *accepting effect* on the supervisor who can see multiple views of the situation.

Reflexive Questions.   Reflexive questions are intended to influence the supervisee in an indirect or general manner based on circular assumptions about therapy and supervision. The intent is predominantly *facilitative*, treating the supervisee as an independent individual who cannot be instructed directly, particularly against the supervisee's will. Supervisees, like members of client families, are encouraged to mobilize their own problem-solving resources, with the supervisor operating to open up space for new possibilities. These questions are intended to have a generative effect on supervisees and client families. Accepting the supervisory task of opening up space is seen as having a creative effect on the supervisor.

Resolving Paradoxical Dilemmas

In *Paradox and Counterparadox* (Selvini Palazzoli et al., 1978), the Milan theorists place emphasis on the natural occurrence of paradox in human relationships. Following the work of the "Double Bind" theorists (Bateson et al., 1956; Sluzki & Ransom, 1976), they assume that contradictory demands are placed, which cannot be escaped or addressed directly. In their interventions, they emphasize resolving such paradoxical

dilemmas by separating the contradictory demands in time. A supervisee in some dilemma about success, for example, might be instructed to fail deliberately at certain times while succeeding at other scheduled times, usually with some accompanying rationale.

The Greek Chorus

The "Greek Chorus" (Papp, 1990) and similar uses of the split team can be extremely effective tools for the supervisor and supervisee. Split opinions can be used to advantage whether or not live supervision is used. The general format is straightforward: Two sides of an issue are expressed, with the therapist/supervisee siding with the client family and typically taking an optimistic "pro-change" position, while the supervisor or the team behind the mirror express more skepticism and warn of the dangers of change. Over time, opinions can shift in response to clinical feedback. If there is progress, the nay-sayers should gradually give ground. If there is lack of progress or a setback, the supervisee can say, "Now I see what my supervisor was warning me about!"

Many other splits are possible, such as a split along gender lines (see Case Example at the end of this section) or between an adolescent and parents. Most counselors, probation officers, school personnel, and so on are familiar with the "Good cop, bad cop" routine from TV; the only caveat is that the "Bad cop" needs to agree to the role and needs to be reassured that the split is a healthy disagreement rather than toxic conflict.

_____

My colleague Matthew Selekman and I orchestrated such a split when I was supervising his work in a drug project. He argued that the progress shown by an adolescent drug abuser and his family was real, while reporting that his supervisor, a famous expert on substance abuse, claimed that it could not be sustained. As is typical in such cases, the adolescent took particular delight in siding with the underdog and confounding the experts. Each week he and the therapist would exchange "high fives" and gloat over Dr. Todd's probable reaction. Even though live supervision was not used, everyone was extremely satisfied because the supervisee reported that the whole family had amazed the experts and made believers of them.

Such splits can be taken up another level and used purely in supervision. Often, the other polarity can be attributed to "conventional wisdom" or other abstract sources rather than necessarily being linked to another figure. "I believe that what you (the supervisee) are doing could work, even though most books (or other supervisors) would probably disagree with me." Real splits can also be highlighted in group or shared supervision, with peers usually supporting the supervisee and the supervisor being more skeptical.

Typical Supervisory Modalities in the Milan Model

Uses of the Team

The Observing Team. Uses of the team have reached creative complexity in the work of the Milan team (Pirrotta & Cecchin, 1988). This has included creating an additional team to supplement the usual setup of therapists in the room and team watching behind the mirror. The additional team is introduced purely as an observing team to offer their observations on the team/therapist system.

Orgy of Linear Thinking. A useful intervention from the *Paradox and Counterparadox* era is the "orgy of linear thinking." The Milan team note that it was often difficult to move directly to a neutral, systemic view of a session. They found that a useful warmup was for the team to indulge in unabashed, even exaggerated, linear

"blaming." Team members would take different positions to develop extreme versions of who "caused" the problems. After this, it was typically much easier to move to a multicausal systemic view.

CASE EXAMPLE: A CHAUVINIST/ FEMINIST SPLIT

The author was conducting a Milan-style team in a rural clinic with a case of the "Eternal Triangle." The primary patient, a middle-aged man with alleged panic attacks, used his symptoms to perpetuate the sexist dynamics of his marriage and to pit his wife against his mistress. Rather than being angry at his manipulations, the wife was apologetic. She had also lost twenty-five pounds in an effort to be more attractive.

As these events were reported during a session with husband and wife, gender issues threatened to split the team. The women on the team were furious and wanted to make a direct appeal to the wife that she did not need to tolerate her husband's behavior. The men on the team objected that such an appeal would be too radical for the wife, but the conservative tone of this objection further inflamed the gender split.

As the supervisor of the team, I assumed that feeding back the team dynamics would be therapeutic for the team and for the case; the women were therefore encouraged to write a separate feminist prescription, while the men wrote a prescription supporting the status quo. The two therapists in the room, who both happened to be men, read both written prescriptions. When they came to the women's prescription, they read it in an exaggeratedly condescending manner and then engaged in a mock argument about whether they should follow usual procedure and allow the women's prescription to be mailed along with the men's prescription. The wife interrupted assertively and said, "I want that one!" The team split was no longer toxic, except for some good-natured rivalry between the sexes about who should receive credit for the success.

CONCLUSION

As stated earlier, the purpose of this chapter is not to provide definitive or complete statements of the supervisory implications of the purposive therapy models that have provided the stimulus for this chapter. Instead, distinctive supervisory assumptions of each model have been highlighted and some typical therapeutic interventions have been extended into the domain of supervision. Hopefully these efforts and the case examples provided will stimulate readers to make similar efforts to expand their repertoire of supervisory interventions. By emphasizing common assumptions across models, I hope the stage has been set for more cross-fertilization between models, at least in the domain of supervision.

REFERENCES

Alderfer, C., & Lynch, B. (1986). Supervision in two dimensions: What can be expected from the supervisor-supervisee relationship? *Journal of Strategic and Systemic Therapies, 4,* 70–73.

Andolfi, M., & Menghi, P. (1982). Provocative supervision. In R. Whiffen & J. Byng-Hall (Eds.), *Family therapy supervision: Recent developments in practice.* New York: Grune & Stratton.

Aponte, H. (1994). How personal can training get? *Journal of Marital and Family Therapy, 20,* 13–15.

Bateson, G. (1979). *Mind and nature: A necessary unity.* New York: E. P. Dutton.

Bateson, G., Jackson, D., Haley, J., & Weakland, J. (1956). Toward a theory of schizophrenia. *Behavioral Science, 1,* 251–264.

Boscolo, L., Cecchin, G., Hoffman, L., & Penn, P. (1987). *Milan systemic family therapy.* New York: Basic Books.

Cecchin, G., Lane, G., & Ray, W. (1993). From strategizing to nonintervention: Toward irreverence in systemic practice. *Journal of Marital & Family Therapy, 19,* 125–136.

Combrinck-Graham, L., Gursky, E., & Brendler, J. (1982). Hospitalization of single-parent families of disturbed children. *Family Process, 21,* 141–152.

deShazer, S. (1985). *Keys to solution in brief therapy.* New York: W. W. Norton.

deShazer, S. (1988). *Clues: Investigating solutions in brief therapy,* New York: W. W. Norton.

deShazer, S. (1991). *Putting difference to work.* New York: W. W. Norton.

deShazer, S., Berg, I., Lipchik, E., Nunnally, E., Molnar. A., Gingerich, W. & Weiner-Davis M. (1986). Brief therapy: Focused solution development. *Family Process, 24,* 207–222.

Epstein, N., & Bishop, D. (1981). Problem-centered systems therapy of the family. In A. Giurman & D. Kniskern (Eds.), *Handbook of family therapy* (pp. 444–482). New York: Brunner/Mazel.

Fisch, R. (1988). Training in the brief therapy model. In H. Liddle, D. Breunlin, & R. Schwartz (Eds.), *Handbook of family therapy training and supervision* (pp. 78–92). New York: Guilford Press.

Fisch, R., Weakland, J., & Segal, L. (1982). *Tactics of change.* San Francisco: Jossey-Bass.

Gingerich, W., & deShazer, S. (1991). The briefer project: Using expert systems as theory construction tools. *Family Process, 30,* 241–251.

Gingerich, W., deShazer, S., & Weiner-Davis, M. (1988). Constructing change: A research view of interviewing. In E. Lipchik (Ed.), *Interviewing* (pp. 21–32). Rockville, MD: Aspen.

Haley, J. (1973). *Uncommon therapy: The psychiatric techniques of Milton H. Erickson, M. D.* New York: W. W. Norton.

Haley, J. (1976). *Problem-solving therapy.* San Francisco: Jossey-Bass.

Haley, J. (1980). *Leaving home: Therapy of disturbed young people.* New York: McGraw-Hill.

Haley, J. (1984). *Ordeal therapy.* San Francisco: Jossey-Bass.

Hoffman, L. (1989). The family life cycle and discontinuous change. In B. Carter & M. McGoldrick (Eds.), *The changing family life cycle,* 2nd ed. (pp. 91–105). Needham Heights, MA: Allyn and Bacon.

Keim, J. (1995). Personal communication.

Madanes, C. (1981). *Strategic family therapy.* San Francisco: Jossey-Bass.

Madanes, C. (1984). *Behind the one-way mirror.* San Francisco: Jossey-Bass.

Madanes, C., & Haley, J. (1977). Dimensions of family therapy. *Journal of Nervous and Mental Disease, 165,* 88–98.

Mazza, J. (1988). Training strategic therapists: The use of indirect techniques. In H. Liddle, D. Breunlin, & R. Schwartz (Eds.), *Handbook of family therapy training and supervision* (pp. 93–109). New York: Guilford Press.

Minuchin, S. (1974). *Families and family therapy.* Cambridge: Harvard University Press.

Minuchin, S. (1981). "Anorexia is a Greek word" (Videotape). Cambridge: Boston Family Institute.

Minuchin, S., & Fishman, H. (1981). *Family therapy techniques.* Cambridge: Harvard University Press.

Nichols, M., & Schwartz, R. (1995). *Family therapy: Concepts and methods,* 3rd ed. Needham Heights, MA: Allyn and Bacon.

Papp, P. (1990). The Greek chorus and other techniques of paradoxical therapy. *Family Process, 19,* 45–57.

Pirrotta, S., & Cecchin, G. (1988). The Milan training program. In H. Liddle, D. Breunlin, & R. Schwartz (Eds.), *Handbook of family therapy training and supervision* (pp. 38–61). New York: Guilford Press.

Protinsky , H., & Preli, R. (1987) Intervention in strategic supervision. *Journal of Strategic and Systemic Therapies, 6,* 18–23.

Roberts, J. (1983). Two models of live supervision: Collaborative team and supervisor-guided. *Journal of Strategic and Systemic Therapies, 2,* 68–78.

Rohrbaugh, M., Tennen, H., Press, S., & White, L. (1981). Compliance, defiance, and therapeutic paradox: Guidelines for strategic use of paradoxical interventions. *American Journal of Orthopsychiatry, 51,* 454–467.

Selekman, M., & Todd, T. (1995). Co-creating a context for change in the supervisory system: The solution-focused supervision model. *Journal of Systemic Therapies, 14,* 21–33.

Selvini Palazzoli, M., Boscolo, L., Cecchoin, G., & Prata, G. (1978). *Paradox and counterparadox.* New York: Jason Aronson.

Selvini Palazzoli, M., Boscolo, L., Cecchoin, G., & Prata, G. (1980). Hypothesizing-circularity-neutrality. *Family Process, 6,* 3–9.

Sexton, T., Montgomery, D., Goff, K., & Nugent, W. (1993). Ethical, therapeutic, and legal considerations in the use of paradoxical techniques: The emerging debate. *Journal of Mental Health Counseling, 15,* 260–277.

Sluzki, C., & Ransom. D. (Eds.) (1976). *Double-bind: The foundation of the communicational approach to the family.* New York: Grune & Stratton.

Stanton, M. (1981). Strategic approaches to family therapy. In A. Gurman & D. Kniskern (Eds.), *Handbook of family therapy* (pp. 361–402). New York: Brunner/Mazel.

Storm, C., & Heath, A. (1982). Strategic supervision: The danger lies in discovery. *Journal of Strategic and Systemic Therapies, 1,* 71–72.

Todd, T. (1981). Paradoxical prescriptions: Applications of consistent paradox using a strategic team. *Journal of Strategic and Systemic Therapies, 1,* 28–44.

Todd, T. (1986). Structural-strategic marital therapy. In N. Jacobson & A. Gurman (Eds.), *Clinical Handbook of Marital Therapy* (pp. 71–105). New York: Guilford Press.

Todd, T., & LaForte, J. (1987). *Paradoxical prescriptions: The use of written prescriptions in strategic family therapy.* Paper presented at the Annual Meeting of the American Association for Marriage and Family Therapy, Orlando, October.

Todd, T., & Selekman, M. (1991). Beyond structural-strategic family therapy. In T. Todd and M. Selekman (Eds.), *Family therapy approaches with adolescent substance abusers* (pp. 241–274). Needham Heights, MA: Allyn and Bacon.

Tomm, K. (1985). Circular interviewing: A multifaceted clinical tool. In D. Campbell & R. Draper (Eds.), *Application of systemic family therapy: The Milan method* (pp. 33–45). New York: Grune & Stratton.

Tomm, K. (1987a) Interventive interviewing: I. Strategizing as a fourth guideline for the therapist. *Family Process, 26,* 3–13.

Tomm, K. (1987b) Interventive interviewing: II. Reflexive questioning as a means to enable self-healing. *Family Process, 26,* 167–183.

Tomm, K. (1988) Interventive interviewing: III. Intending to ask lineal, circular, strategic, or reflexive questions? *Family Process, 27,* 1–15.

Watzlawick, P., Weakland, J., & Fisch, R. (1974). *Change: Principles of problem formation and problem resolution.* New York: W. W. Norton.

14

Integrative Supervision
Approaches to Tailoring the
Supervisory Process

Sandra A. Rigazio-DiGilio

Although interest in synthesizing individual, systemic, and ecosystemic approaches into integrative models of therapy has been growing (Case & Robinson, 1990; Duhl, 1987; Feixas, 1990; Feldman, 1985, 1989; Grunebaum & Chasin, 1982; Ivey, 1986; L'Abate & Frey, 1981; Lebow, 1984, 1987; Rigazio-DiGilio, 1994a; Sluzki, 1983; Stanton, 1981; Worthington, 1987, 1992), less has been written about the supervision models necessary to facilitate this process (McCollum, 1990; Piercy & Sprenkle, 1986; Saba & Liddle, 1986; Taibbi, 1990). Integrative therapy models require clinicians to incorporate a wide repertoire of relational, conceptual, perceptual, and executive skills from discrete theories, therapies, and techniques and to know which skills to access to address the needs of clients.[1] Supervision models that support the construction of such approaches not only introduce supervisees to different theories, therapies, and strategies, but also provide broad organizational schemata that clinicians can use to orchestrate assessment and treatment efforts.[2] Additionally, as with integrative

therapy models, these approaches tailor supervisory efforts that are sensitive to the unique needs of the supervisee and the client, and to the dynamics of the therapeutic and supervisory relationships.

Four approaches to integrative supervision, based on their corresponding therapy models, are presented in this chapter. Each offers alternative methods to reorganize existing theories, therapies, and techniques into an integrative framework that provides a broader, alternative perspective on therapy and supervision. In this regard, integrative supervision models represent an advanced form of professional growth for practitioners (Anderson, Rigazio-DiGilio, & Kunkler, 1995).

A challenge that must be addressed within integrative models is the identification of variables used to conceptualize the essential aspects of individual, systemic, and ecosystemic development, therapy, and supervision. Each model presented in this chapter provides a unique set of variables that is used to decipher the work of therapists and supervisors.

The first model is based on the *metaframeworks perspective* developed by Breunlin, Schwartz, and Mac Kune-Karrer (1992). Translated into supervision, this model provides five variables to frame supervision: management of complexity, work with families, work with individuals, focus on gender, and focus

---

[1] The term *clients* is used to refer to individuals, couples, families, or networks engaged in the therapeutic process.

[2] The four models highlighted are advanced and quite complex, and cannot be covered in detail in one chapter. As such, the author refers those readers interested in any or all of the models to the reference list noted at the end of this chapter.

on culture (Breunlin, Rampage, & Eovaldi, 1995).

The second model is derived from *systemic cognitive-developmental therapy* (Rigazio-DiGilio, 1994a,b, 1995; Rigazio-DiGilio & Ivey, 1991, 1993). The corresponding supervision model uses a metaphorical reinterpretation of neo-Piagetian cognitive-developmental orientations to identify supervisee and client worldviews and to sequence questioning and intervention strategies aimed at enhancing and expanding these worldviews (Rigazio-DiGilio, 1994c; Rigazio-DiGilio & Anderson, 1991, 1994; Rigazio-DiGilio, Daniels & Ivey, 1995).

The third model represents a proposed translation of *integrative problem-centered therapy* (Catherall & Pinsof, 1987; Pinsof, 1983, 1988, 1989, 1992, 1994a,b) to the supervisory domain. This proposed model could help supervisors work with therapists to consider interventions from various theories and therapies (e.g., psychodynamic, cognitive, strategic, structural) and to form organized treatment plans aimed at one of three therapeutic contexts (e.g., family/community, couple/dyadic, individual).

The final model is based on a *mythological perspective* conceived by Bagarozzi and Anderson (1989a). The companion supervision model (Anderson & Holmes, 1994; Bagarozzi & Anderson, 1989b) identifies self-awareness and affect as key variables influencing supervisee and client growth.

CORE ASSUMPTIONS OF INTEGRATIVE THERAPY MODELS

Each integrative therapy model, while unique in its own right, shares common core assumptions. When extended to supervision, these assumptions have implications for su-

pervisee development and for the supervisory process.[3]

Therapeutic Assumptions

1. Understanding human, systemic, and ecosystemic development and functioning requires a holistic and recursive perspective. The four positions are built on unique overarching perspectives for understanding development and functioning. For example, the *metaframeworks perspective* focuses on the biopsychosocial continuum to understand development and functioning. *Systemic cognitive-developmental therapy* (SCDT) focuses on how worldviews of individuals, systems, and ecosystems are co-constructed within a person–environment dialectic transaction over time. *Integrative problem-centered therapy* emphasizes how individuals and systems develop an understanding of the world through a progressive process of learning that leads to increasingly accurate approximations of reality. Finally, the *mythological perspective* focuses on the personal themes and stories that individuals, systems, and ecosystems construct over the life span.

2. Nonadaptation is viewed from a health and/or developmental perspective. Each model is based on a nondeficit perspective regarding growth and adaptation. Pathological assumptions, as well as interventions based on such assumptions, are eschewed. Breunlin et al. assume that clients want to behave adaptively and only fail when they are constrained or blocked from doing so. Rigazio-DiGilio views nonadaptation as a natural and logical consequence of devel-

---

[3]Because Breunlin and Pinsof work closely together, you will note their mutual and recursive influence on one another throughout this listing of therapeutic assumptions and supervisory implications, as well as within the explanations of their models.

opmental and contextual history. In Pinsof's words, "until proven otherwise, the patient system can solve its problems with minimal and direct intervention from the therapist system" (1994a, p. 114). Finally, Anderson and Bagarozzi view client mythologies as natural outcomes of family-of-origin experiences.

These models do not rely on deficit-based terminology. Each represents a positive perspective of human and systemic functioning and connotes this to clients through therapist interactions. For example, Breunlin et al. (1995) state that their model "enables therapists to enlist clients in a collaborative effort to identify blocks and constraints and to lift them so the healthy parts of people can solve the problem" (p. 24). Similarly, Rigazio-DiGilio (1996) states that SCDT "recasts the traditional superior and separate role of the clinician to an equal partner engaged in the co-construction of therapeutic environments and client worldviews" (pp. 3–4).

3. School-specific models are insufficient to deal with the wide variety of presenting issues or client types encountered by therapists. The authors of these approaches recognize the limits of school-specific models. They contend that even clients presenting with similar treatment issues will require different therapeutic approaches, depending on developmental, historical, and sociocultural factors. Each of their models offers a classification schema that can empower therapists to coherently select, from among diverse therapeutic perspectives and interventions, those that best fit the needs of the client. In effect, the ongoing needs of the client take center stage, while strict adherence to school-based theories moves to the background.

Supervisory Implications

1. Understanding supervisee growth and functioning requires a holistic and recursive perspective. Integrative supervisors do not possess a preconceived map regarding what speed and direction supervisee progress should take. However, they do possess a metatheoretical framework that guides their interactions. How this interaction plays out is based on the exchanges that occur between the supervisor, the supervisee, and the client. Whether labeled _perspectivism_ (Breunlin et al., 1992), _coconstructivism_ (Rigazio-DiGilio, 1994a), _interactive constructivism_ (Pinsof, 1994a), or _interactive personal myths_ (Bagarozzi & Anderson, 1989a), each model asserts the dialectic reality of the supervisory process. The implications of this position require supervisors to move out from behind static models of school-specific supervision and enter into the ever-changing world of the therapist, the client, the supervisory relationship, and the wider contextual climate. In effect, the assimilative stance of traditional supervision gives way to a more balanced assimilative/accommodative stance.

For example, _systemic cognitive-developmental supervision_ (Rigazio-DiGilio, 1994c; Rigazio-DiGilio & Anderson, 1991, 1994; Rigazio-DiGilio et al., in press) focuses on the potentialities and limitations of the supervisor's and supervisee's orientations, and how these influence experiences, interpretations, and interactions, as well as the fit between supervisor and supervisee. The supervision approach associated with the _mythological perspective_ (Anderson & Holmes, 1994) stresses the importance of recognizing and understanding the stories supervisors and therapists tell themselves and one another to understand, adapt to, or change experience.

2. Supervisory impasses are reflective of incongruities between supervisee need and supervisory context. A core premise of each model is that therapists enter supervision with a repertoire of therapeutic competencies that they wish to enhance or modify. The initial repertoire holds a unique set of potentials and constraints that can be accessed during the supervisory process. When the constraints are activated in therapy or supervision, this is seen as an essential part of the growth process. At these times, it is incumbent on the supervisor to provide an environment tailored to encourage a dialectic transaction that will facilitate the examination of constraints and the identification of avenues for change.

For example, rather than focusing on the deficits inherent in gender constructions, Breunlin et al. (1995) look toward enhancing a supervisee's awareness of their constraints and resources. These authors state that gender awareness is a developmental process that must be woven into the fabric of supervision and addressed over a long period of time. Likewise, Rigazio-DiGilio (1994b) states that supervisees can become constrained within the parameters of one orientation. When this occurs, it is incumbent on the supervisor to co-construct environments where supervisees are encouraged to examine these constraints and explore alternative resources that serve to enhance their repertoire of skills over time.

3. Integrative frameworks organize various therapeutic perspectives, affording supervisees multiple reference points and options for growth. Integrative models assist therapists to organize and access many assessment and treatment strategies to understand clients and to facilitate client growth. Whatever integrative framework is used, supervisees have the opportunity to learn, apply, and refine a comprehensive, broad-based method in their work with clients. Whether using the Breunlin et al. (1995) *multiple frames of supervision*, Anderson & Holmes's (1994) *windows of self*, Pinsof's (1994d) *problem identification matrix*, or Rigazio-DiGilio's (1994a) *cognitive-developmental profiles*, supervisors and supervisees are looking past traditional schools and moving into new ground that tests the borders of their own competence. Additionally, supervisees can organize their own familiar theories, therapies,

and approaches using classification systems provided by each supervisory approach as a backdrop. In effect, when participating in integrative supervision, supervisees learn both a specific unifying framework as well as a unique art of constructing, enhancing, and refining these frameworks over time and in response to their environments.

INTEGRATIVE MODELS OF SUPERVISION

Even though these models share common assumptions, each offers a unique metatheoretical framework that guides supervision. Differences focus on the particular frameworks used to understand therapists, clients, therapeutic relationships, and supervisory alliances, and the heuristics used to guide the selection of supervisory interventions. The structural components of each model are briefly described before moving on to the common elements contained within interventions, modalities, contracting, and evaluation.

The Metaframeworks Supervisory Perspective

According to Breunlin et al. (1995), integrative supervision "requires supervisors not only to facilitate a therapist's work with individuals, families, and their larger systems, but also how to move among these units and the various therapy orientations that apply to each" (p. 553). To accomplish this, their model relies on five conceptual components: management of complexity, work with families, work with individuals, focus on gender, and focus on culture. These components provide heuristics supervisors can use to assist supervisees to consider the entire *biopsychosocial continuum* when assessing clients. These same components also are used by supervisors to assess the needs of therapists.

Managing Complexity

Informed by the constructivist assumption that therapists never fully understand a client's reality, supervisors help therapists recognize the constraints imposed when relying on a limited range of perspectives and strategies for assessment and treatment. In terms of assessment, supervisors help therapists view their evolving clinical hypotheses as *partial explanations*, which highlight the intrapsychic, physical, and/or interpersonal domains of the client. Therapists are guided to examine each of these domains to gain a fuller understanding of the client-in-context. Supervisors guide therapists through this process by providing an alternative set of reactions, insights, and questions that move the therapist within and among each domain, and that guide the therapist to use different theoretical vantage points.

In addition to co-constructing robust hypotheses with the supervisor, the therapist is also assisted to select treatment modalities and interventions consistent with these hypotheses. At times, these selections may require the therapist to enhance her or his existing therapeutic repertoire, providing opportunities to master unfamiliar interventions.

Supervisors also recognize the constraints imposed when they rely on limited frames to understand and work with therapists. Therefore, when assisting therapists' mastery of alternative perspectives and approaches, the supervisor selects from a myriad of supervisory practices and modalities to find the best fit for the needs of the supervisee.

For example, to build a supervisee's commitment to a systems perspective, the supervisor may insist that the entire family come in, may plan, with the therapist, how to accomplish this, and may use live supervision to ensure a good outcome. Later, the supervisor may use video review to facilitate the therapist's comprehensive understanding of information obtained. As such, the supervisor provides a directive, yet collaborative experience for the therapist.

Working with the Family Level

Therapists are requested to initially see the entire family and to gather information about the action constraints surrounding the family, subsystems, and individuals. The initial treatment focus is to examine ways to break through these constraints. Supervisors assist therapists to focus on a family's interactions, guide them to generate testable hypotheses about how such patterns are connected to the presenting problem, and advise them about what interventions might successfully alter these patterns.

Therapists also are guided to examine their client's meaning-making and emotional constraints. In this way, supervision helps therapists find a balance between action-oriented interventions and those that help families integrate new meaning and effect. For example, supervisors might work with therapists to generate a list of questions to ask a family that could uncover their thoughts and feelings. Once uncovered, the therapist would be guided to relate empathically and to collaborate with the family to initiate action.

In a similar vein, supervisors also are interested in the action, meaning-making, and emotional constraints that influence therapists, the therapeutic relationship, and the supervisory process. For example, should a therapist be consistently unsuccessful in securing permission to videotape clients, supervisory questions would focus on the feelings and beliefs the therapist has regarding videotaping. The supervisor also would model empathic listening and collaborative planning aimed at initiating action.

The Individual in the System

Supervisors assume that internal processes also can contribute to problem development and maintenance, and encourage therapists to address these individual dynamics when methods to solve the problem at the family level fail.

There are four degrees of complexity regarding individual dynamics. Beginning with a communication perspective, the therapist is asked to hypothesize what impact each individual's display of feelings, thoughts, and behaviors has on other members as well as on the therapist. If attempts at this level fail, the therapist is guided to incorporate internal processes into their hypothesizing.

At the second level, the therapist is encouraged to more directly examine the thoughts and feelings that are readily accessible to family members. If these attempts fail, the supervisor advises the therapist to initiate a third level of complexity aimed at helping families understand how intrapsychic dynamics can constrain each individual's thoughts and feelings, and the family system as a whole. Treatment, aimed at lifting these constraints and creating new experiences, can be facilitated within the family or in individual sessions that occur as an adjunct to family therapy. If the previous three levels of complexity do not ameliorate individual constraints, the supervisor and supervisee enter into collaborative discussions regarding the initiation of intensive, long-term individual psychotherapy, either in adjunct to or in lieu of family treatment.

Supervisors also are cognizant of these four levels of complexity when assessing and directing supervisee development. Supervisors first help therapists actively master therapeutic competencies. At the second level, therapists are encouraged to identify what professional and personal thoughts and feelings might be contributing to therapeutic or supervisory impasses. They also might be expected to share their beliefs about human and family development and adaptation, and to examine how these beliefs influence their interactions with clients and supervisors. The third level of complexity would be evoked if supervisee development was blocked, or if similar impasses in treatment or supervision occurred over time. Therapists might be assisted to examine the portions of

their intrapsychic processes that are constraining further development. Individual therapy might be encouraged at this time, to assist therapists to examine how their own internal processes affect self and self-in-context. Finally, if constraints cannot be lifted or impasses cannot be broken, then the fourth level of complexity would be evoked by the supervisor. The supervisor and supervisee would enter into discussions regarding the initiation of intensive psychotherapy, either as a compliment to or in lieu of supervision.

Gender-Sensitive Supervision

The gender-socialized personal and professional belief supervisees hold are of primary importance. Therapists are asked to reflect on feminist critiques of family therapy, and to explore their own beliefs about gender-sensitive practice. Supervisors help therapists to recognize the biases and predispositions that may privilege or oppress either gender. Additionally, supervisors help therapists identify the degree of gender balance and gender awareness within any family. Five transitional positions along this continuum have been described—traditional, gender-aware, polarized, in transition, and balanced (Breunlin et al., 1992). The therapist's clinical impressions of the family's gender interactions can also be described using these same five descriptors, giving the supervisor an understanding of the therapist's degree of gender awareness. Finally, therapists are assisted to examine how their own gender impacts treatment. Ideally, supervisors using the model also would examine their own degree of gender awareness, as well as their ability to translate a gender-balanced perspective to their supervisees.

Culturally Sensitive Supervision

The supervisor encourages the exploration of cultural fit between therapist and client, and between client and the dominant culture. An examination of the interface between therapist and client may indicate the need for more general information about the client's cultural heritage, and about the interface between the clients' beliefs and the beliefs of the dominant culture. Supervisors might also encourage therapists to examine their beliefs about diversity, their thoughts about conducting practice as a social intervention, and their abilities to assist families to be successful in their sociocultural interchanges. This same culturally sensitive reflection can be extended to the supervisory alliance. Supervisors must recognize how each individual's cultural heritage affects and is affected by the heritage of the other throughout the supervisory relationship.

The Metaframeworks Perspective in Action

In the metaframeworks perspective, Breunlin suggests that therapy consists of four interrelated processes: hypothesizing, planning, conversing, and reading feedback. Translated to supervision, hypothesizing employs the five metaframework components to frame and interpret the interaction between supervisor and therapist. Based on tentative hypotheses, supervisors will plan specific tasks and events that will transpire over the course of supervision. Within sessions, as the conversation unfolds, supervisors are aware of what statements, questions, and directives will best generate a wider view of the therapist, the therapeutic context, and the supervisory relationship within the working hypothesis. Concurrently, the supervisor reads the feedback emanating from these three domains. The supervisor's interpretation of the feedback in terms of the working hypotheses is checked with the therapist to corroborate or refute the supervisor's impressions. When consensus is reached, the feedback is then incorporated into further hypothesizing and planning. By modeling this process for the therapist, supervisors provide a direct experience for the therapist to emulate this four-pronged process with their clients.

Systemic Cognitive-Developmental Supervision

Systemic cognitive-developmental supervision (SCDS) (Rigazio-DiGilio, 1994c; Rigazio-DiGilio & Anderson, 1991, 1994; Rigazio-DiGilio et al., in press) represents a coconstructive approach that directly links developmental theory (Piaget, 1955; Vygotsky, 1987) to the supervisory process. It was conceived in accordance with Ivey's developmental therapy (1986), 1991), which has been extended to systemic (Rigazio-DiGilio, 1993, 1996, in press; Rigazio-DiGilio & Ivey, 1991, 1993) and ecosystemic (Rigazio-DiGilio, 1994a, 1994b) models. These extensions are comprised within a theory identified as systemic cognitive-developmental therapy.

SCDS posits supervisee growth to be an idiosyncratic journey that transcends stage-specific, developmental conceptualizations. This perspective takes into account the nonlinear changes in cognitive, affective, and interactional complexity that accompany supervisee growth.

SCDS offers an assessment framework that is used to classify supervisee worldviews as these occur in the natural language of the supervisory encounter. These worldviews are categorized into four cognitive-developmental orientations that therapists can access to experience, interpret, and interact within therapeutic and supervisory contexts. Further, the model outlines supervisory environments that correspond with these orientations and serve to enhance therapeutic competence. These environments are constructed through the use of developmentally organized questions, interventions, and modalities that are accessed to tailor supervision to the immediate needs of supervisees and their clients.

As an alternative model of supervision, SCDS offers specific *assessment and questioning strategies*. As a metatheoretical framework, SCDS offers a developmental classification schema that integrates various supervisory interventions and strategies for supervisors to draw on in a theoretically coherent fashion. This schema also allows supervisors to incorporate their own practices into the overarching framework of the model. SCDS is based on six basic dimensions: holistic development, cognitive-developmental orientations, SCDS assessment and intervention strategies, supervisory environments, style-matching, and style shifting.

Holistic Development

"Therapists enter supervision with a unique background of experiences that organize the way they conceptualize and approach clinical and supervisory information" (Rigazio-DiGilio & Anderson, 1994). A therapist's worldview is derived from the degree to which she or he can access and utilize various resources within four cognitive-developmental orientations. Therapists who access resources within several orientations can construct comprehensive conceptualizations of clients, therapeutic relationships, and supervisory alliances. As such, they have access to a wide array of perspectives and interventions. Therapists who access resources within a limited set of orientations, or who superficially access resources within several orientations, will be more limited in their approach to assessment and treatment. Therefore, the goal is to empower therapists to access and master the primary cognitive, affective, and behavioral resources found within each of the orientations so as to enhance therapeutic competencies and personal awareness.

Cognitive-Developmental Orientations

Empirical evidence supports that clients' cognitive-developmental orientations can be identified within the clinical interview (Rigazio-DiGilio & Ivey, 1991). Furthermore, observation of videotaped supervision sessions indicates that the primary and ancillary cognitive-developmental orientations used by therapists to conceptualize clients can be identified in their natural language (Rigazio-DiGilio & Anderson, 1991, 1994). This information is used to tailor the supervisory environment.

Each of the four orientations is represented by a characteristic mode of conceptualizing and elicits a series of competencies and constraints. In general, competencies tend to be available to therapists who can access a variety of orientations, whereas therapists unable to do so can become blocked by the constraints of any one orientation.

Therapists who access the *sensorimotor/ elemental orientation* use immediate sensory experiences to make sense of clients and therapeutic encounters. Competencies include the ability to directly experience and track emotional exchanges and to identify personal feelings in therapy and supervision. If constrained within this orientation, therapists tend to be overcome by emotional interactions, which inhibits conceptual and executive competencies.

Therapists who access the *concrete/ situational orientation* can describe actions and events, and think and act with predictability. Competencies include increasingly accurate if/then reasoning and the ability to anticipate client reactions. Constrained therapists rigidly adhere to specific theories or techniques, and have difficulty with abstract and affectual perspectives.

Therapists who access the *formal/reflective orientation* can articulate recurring patterns of interaction. Competencies include multiple perspective taking, synthesizing ideas from various theories and therapies, and refining treatment plans. Therapists who overintellectualize, minimize, or neglect affectual and behavioral data, or who have difficulty transferring their abstractions into effective interventions, are constrained within this orientation.

Finally, access to the *dialectic/systemic orientation* is represented by therapists who recognize the influence of intrafamilial, historical, sociocultural, and political contexts. This information can be used to conceptualize clinical phenomena from wider contextual and temporal perspectives, and to challenge preconceived notions of self and others (e.g., assumptions regarding gender, culture, power, age, status, education, and so on). Competencies include the ability to remain aware of contextual influences and to seek solutions aimed at the client and the wider environment. Constrained therapists can become overwhelmed by this multiplicity of perspectives and be unable to commit to an effective course of action.

SCDS Assessment and Intervention Questioning Strategies

At the beginning of supervision, the therapist is asked a series of open-ended questions in order to access primary and ancillary orientations. A second set of questions can be used for both assessment and intervention. These questions assist therapists to explore resources within each specific orientation throughout the course of supervision. Questions specific to each orientation are targeted to four specific domains of experience: the client, the self-as-therapist, the therapeutic process, and the supervisory process.

Questions that target the four domains of experience from the vantage point of one orientation are aimed at establishing a firm foundation within that orientation. For example, sustained explorations within the dialectic/systemic orientation are accomplished by asking questions such as: "What cultural/gender influences are impacting on this family's rule-making process?" (client); "What cultural/gender influences are impacting on your assumptions?" (self-as-therapist); "How are these assumptions impacting your interaction with this family and the family's interaction with you?" (therapeutic process); and "How do our cultural/gender similarities or differences come to bear on this relationship?" (supervisory process).

Questions that target the four orientations from the vantage point of one domain of experience are aimed at assisting therapists to tap resources within each orientation. For example, exploratory questions regarding the self-as-therapist might include: "What feelings are triggered as you sit with this family?" (sensorimotor/elemental); "Can you describe what you were doing?" (concrete/situational); "Have you behaved in similar ways with other clients at this stage in therapy?" (formal/reflective); and "What could you do to challenge your assumptions about gender when faced with an intense power differential such as this?" (dialectic/systemic).

Style Matching: Using Supervisory Environments to Establish a Strong Base

According to SCDS, therapist growth is facilitated by using appropriate supervisory environments. Before movement to ancillary orientations can be successful, therapists must demonstrate facility within their primary orientation. To accomplish this, supervisors utilize *style-matching* and *supervisory environments* that correspond to the target orientation.

For therapists within a sensorimotor/elemental orientation, a *directive environment* is recommended. Supervisors provide secure parameters within which therapists can develop professional and personal competencies. Issues that might be emphasized include directing perceptual and/or executive skill development and working through emotional issues of transference and countertransference. Supervisory modalities consistent with this environment are co-therapy teams, live supervision with "bug-in-the-ear" guidance, and role-plays.

Therapists working within the concrete/situational orientation work well in a *coaching environment*. Here, supervisors help therapists gain an understanding of the thoughts, feelings, and behaviors of self, family, and supervisor from a linear, interactive frame. Issues germane to this environment include developing treatment plans, mastering new interventions, and forming therapeutic alliances. Live supervision with pre-, mid-, and postsession processing, video play back, and behavioral exercises represent supervisory modalities used within this environment.

Corresponding to the formal/reflective orientation is the *consultative environment* that is used to encourage therapists to examine the patterns of thoughts, feelings, and actions that occur for self and clients, and that are elicited within therapeutic and supervisory contexts. This environment is also used to help therapists recognize prevalent themes emerging within self, clients, the therapeutic encounter, and the supervisory encounter. Edited video segments illustrating significant themes across sessions or clients, case presentations that focus on patterns of difficulty across therapeutic encounters, and self-analytic inventories represent appropriate supervisory interventions for this environment.

Therapists who possess a strong understanding of one or two theories or who effectively integrate several approaches require a *collaborative* supervisory environment to sustain personal and professional development. The focus is on the core cognitive and metacognitive processes undergirding a therapist's belief system. An examination of contextual and historical influences leads to a deconstruction of therapist's (and supervisor's) assumptions regarding treatment, supervision, and development. Such introspection results in alternative conceptualizations about therapy and supervision. Typical modalities are audio/video and case presentation focused on epistemological and ontological issues, peer consultation, and direct sharing of the supervisor's thoughts.

Style-Shifting: Using Supervisory Environments to Expand Supervisee Development

Helping therapists extend their understanding of clinical, professional, and personal data into new orientations is accomplished by a process of *style-shifting*. After sufficient competency is developed within a therapist's primary orientation, the supervisor assumes a style-shifting position to encourage explorations of issues in underutilized orientations. As supervisees indicate that they are able to access and use resources associated with a new orientation, the supervisor resumes a style-matching posture so that sustained practice can occur.

Over the course of supervision, the style-shifting process enables therapists to journey through all four orientations in a fashion that best fits the needs of the client, the therapist, and the supervisory relationship. It is not unusual to reenter a previous orientation as the needs of client and therapist change. To accomplish this smooth transition from one orientation to another, supervisors must be proficient in accessing and sustaining in-depth analyses of issues at all four orientations.

Integrative Problem-Centered Supervision

Integrative problem-centered therapy (IPCT) represents a clinical–theoretical model for coherently integrating individual and family therapies (Catherall & Pinsof, 1987; Pinsof, 1983, 1988, 1989, 1992, 1994a,b). IPCT is based on a synthesis of theory construction, clinical practice, and research that has implications for clinical and supervisory practice. In this section, an isomorphic extension of IPCT to the supervisory domain is proposed.

The central objectives of *integrative problem-centered supervision* (IPCS) are to assist therapists become proficient at constructing therapeutic alliances with various clients and at employing an organizing schema to direct the course of treatment across therapeutic approaches and modalities. Therapists "must recognize that different families require different types of alliances and, as therapy progresses, different dimensions of the alliance may need to be emphasized in order to accomplish different therapeutic objectives"

(Catherall & Pinsof, 1987, p. 156). Additionally, therapists must "interrelate different pure form therapies to take maximal advantage of their strengths and minimize their weaknesses" (Pinsof, 1994a, p. 104).

Alliance Theory

According to Pinsof, the therapeutic alliance represents the interactive and bidirectional relationship between the patient system (i.e., all human systems involved in the maintenance and/or resolution of the presenting problem), and the therapist system (i.e., all human systems involved in providing psychotherapy to the patient system). This definition of the alliance includes those individuals directly engaged in the therapeutic encounter as well as those indirectly connected to the presenting problem and the treatment. Indirect patient system members might be grandparents who provide child care for the identified patient, but are never seen in treatment. Indirect therapy system members might include supervisors and managed-care review panels. Using IPCS, supervisors would assist therapists to examine the implications of all direct and indirect members of the patient and therapist systems and to consider when and how to include indirect members in treatment (i.e., asking grandparents to attend, engaging with the supervisor in in-session supervision).

Pinsof further distinguishes between four types of mutually influential alliances: individual, interpersonal subsystem, whole-system, and within-system. *Individual alliances* pertain to relationships between individuals in the patient–therapist system. At the *interpersonal subsystem* level, more than one person from either the patient or therapist system forms an alliance with the other system. The *whole-system alliance* targets issues between the whole patient–therapist system. *Within-system alliances* address relationships between individuals and/or subsystems within the patient system or the therapist system.

Supervisors assist therapists to examine how each type of alliance might influence the presenting problem, ongoing treatment, and reactions to the therapeutic process. To do so, supervisors would use Pinsof's therapeutic alliance schema to help therapists chart the composition and impact of the various alliances that are directly or indirectly operating within the therapeutic context. This type of examination would help to determine which therapeutic modalities, interventions, and techniques to draw on and what alliances to target over the course of treatment. For example, while in family therapy, a communications impasse might occur between spouses (interpersonal subsystem alliance) that cannot be addressed in family treatment. The supervisor and supervisee might therefore design an adjunctive treatment plan that includes approaches designed for marital therapy.

The Formation of Alliances

The formation of a therapeutic alliance is built on three content dimensions: agreement about tasks, goals, and the level of emotional bonds between members of the therapist and patient systems. Translating these ideas to supervision, *tasks* are the activities that supervisors and therapists engage in during supervision. The degree of agreement about supervisory tasks is postulated to be directly related to the comfort level evinced by the therapist and supervisor during supervision. *Goals* pertain to the level of agreement and investment in the outcomes of supervision. Establishing a clear understanding about the goals of supervision is an important component of the contracting procedures regarding this model. *Bonds* address affective and relational aspects of the supervisory alliance. Issues of trust, respect, caring, and transference all fall under this category. Supervisors must be aware of these issues and be knowledgeable about how to develop and maintain a positive sense of connectedness with supervisees.

Pinsof's model can be used to demonstrate the interrelatedness of these three components over the course of supervision. For example, it might be possible for a well-respected supervisor to prompt therapist discussion regarding family-of-origin issues even if this was not agreed on initially. The level of trust and respect (bonds) would compensate for the lack of task agreement. Conversely, an unknown supervisor may raise the same issue without success. In the absence of strong bonds, clear tasks and goals will be needed to establish the course of supervision. Over time, supervisor and supervisee may be permitted to deviate from agreed-on tasks and goals if sufficient caring and trust exists.

The Person-of-the-Therapist

The supervisor's and therapist's family life exerts strong influence on the supervisory relationship. Supervisors assist therapists to examine, for example, how issues (e.g., past and current family roles, unresolved interpersonal conflicts, and coping styles) influence the course and outcomes of therapy and supervision. By extension, supervisors must be involved with parallel examinations of self and self-in-context so that they are aware of how their personal life affects their work. For example, roles learned in families of origin can be recreated within the supervisory context. Unless conscious efforts are made to avoid this, these roles can influence the goals, tasks, and bonds developed between supervisor and therapist, and, in turn, among other components of the therapeutic alliance. As such, supervisors and therapists must become aware of how their roles are reenacted within supervision and therapeutic alliances. Although "there is no absolute freedom from roles . . . an informed therapist [supervisor] can have greater choice over which roles to assume, when to assume them, and with whom" (Catherall & Pinsof, 1987, p. 145).

The Problem-Centered Orientation/Modality Matrix

Pinsof has constructed a problem-centered orientation/modality matrix that can be used to inform clinical decisions. The first axis identifies what treatment modalities and what treatment focus will resolve client problems most efficiently. These modalities include family/ community, couple/dyadic, and individual therapeutic contexts. The second axis represents what therapeutic perspectives and approaches can be considered in assessing problems and constructing treatment plans. In descending order, these orientations are behavioral, experiential, and historical approaches.

Using the entire matrix, IPCT initiates therapy by focusing on the behavioral patterns that prevent the system from solving the issues that promoted treatment. If intervention at that level is not effective, the therapist moves to experiential interventions. Historical interventions are accessed only if work within the first two orientations fails to ameliorate the presenting problem. "The progression within IPCT is from the here and now and the interpersonal, to the there and then and the intrapsychic" (Pinsof, 1994a, p. 113).

Supervision could follow the same sequence of strategies. Supervisors might begin with behavioral expectations of therapists, such as asking them to develop therapeutic alliances or to enact particular interventions across the matrix. If movement among these different assignments is positive, then perhaps no other supervisory interventions would be warranted. However, when therapists experience difficulties with the enactment of particular therapeutic competencies, the focus of supervision might move toward an experiential orientation that would focus on examining the cognitive and affective components of, for example, developing and sustaining particular therapeutic alliances. If further difficulties emerge, supervisors might help therapists examine historical issues regarding the impact of personal life experiences on the development of these therapeutic alliances.

Of course, this progression is not to be rigidly adhered to. Rather, the matrix should serve as a heuristic to inform supervisory decisions. Although Pinsof's overarching framework provides an overview for decision making, the importance of the alliance between supervisor and supervisee should always take precedence in determining supervisory interventions.

The Mythological Supervisory Perspective

The *mythological supervisory perspective*, constructed by Anderson and Bagarozzi (Anderson & Holmes, in press; Bagarozzi & Anderson, 1989a,b), is a developmentally oriented approach aimed at assisting therapists to advance their therapeutic skills, to develop an understanding of their *personal myths*, and to design their own integrative therapeutic theory and practice. The model is based on a mythological therapeutic perspective to individual, couple, and family treatment (Anderson & Bagarozzi, 1983; Bagarozzi & Anderson, 1989a), and represents a narrative approach constructed from a coherent synthesis of behavioral, symbolic-experiential, systemic, psychodynamic, and transgenerational theories.

Development of Therapeutic Competencies

As a prerequisite to engaging in advanced supervision from a mythological perspective, therapists must have established basic competencies in four areas: relational, perceptual/conceptual, executive, and personal awareness skills. Regarding *relational skills*, therapists must be able to establish and maintain trusting therapeutic environments. In terms of *perceptual/conceptual skills*, therapists must be able to track and observe relevant clinical data; translate clinical observations into meaningful language reflective of

at least two theoretical approaches; and share observations, feelings, and experiences in a nonthreatening manner. Although therapists are not expected to have mastered a wide variety of *executive skills* before embarking on mythological supervision, they are expected to be able to assume an active role with clients and to demonstrate basic executive competencies such as reframing, clarifying communications, and assigning tasks. Finally, therapists must be committed to their own personal growth and have the capacity for self-awareness. Self-disclosure, comfort with ambiguity, and the ability to take risks are considered central to developing heightened levels of *personal awareness*.

During the prerequisite phase of supervision, therapists might experience difficulty in developing some of these basic therapeutic competencies. If this occurs, supervisors attempt to uncover the *personal themes* that are connected to the impasse. In this way, the development of therapeutic skills goes hand in hand with the personal development of the therapist (Bagarozzi & Anderson, 1989b). At these points, supervisors focus on the personal themes that are reenacted with clients and within the supervisory relationship. Examination of these themes is meant to stimulate deeper personal awareness and therapeutic competency. Once therapists have established these basic competencies, supervisors assist them to incorporate a mythological perspective into their work.

Personal Mythologies

Based on the assumption that individuals experience, interpret, and interact with others in ways that are congruent with their preexisting personal mythologies, supervisors assist therapists to explore how personal myths impact on therapeutic and supervisory encounters. For example, therapists may reenact familiar personal roles when working with specific clients or presenting problems.

Personal myths are those cognitive structures that serve to explain, make sense of, and guide functioning. Multiple personal mythologies are activated during the supervisory process—the supervisor's; the therapist's; the client's; myths emanating from the wider work context; and prevailing cultural, gender, and societal myths. These personal myths are composed of three structural components: the self, the self-in-relation-to-others (interpersonal style), and the internalized ideals of significant others.

The *self* is the coordinating agent that perceives, interprets, and responds to the actions and statements of self and others so as to establish order and meaning to one's experience. While the self seeks full integration and actualization, traumatic historical events and less-than-supportive sociocultural and emotional environments may render the self fragmented and ineffective in certain situations. In supervision, examining the components of personal myths that represent the self helps supervisors and therapists become aware of the blindspots that may exist in the therapeutic and supervisory context.

Through struggles with developmental tasks and interpersonal conflicts, clients, therapists, and supervisors develop a sense of *self-in-relation-to-others*. Individuals use this component of personal myths to anticipate, experience, and interpret interpersonal situations.

In supervision, exploration of a therapist's family of origin, initial work experiences, and other significant life tasks takes on a crucial aspect. Personal mythologies built on these experiences may directly impact intrapsychic processes of projection, introjection, transference, or modeling within the therapeutic or supervisory relationship. A key question to be processed is "Who does the client (supervisor) represent in the therapist's own personal mythology?" (Anderson & Holmes, in press). Isomorphically, supervisors need to be alert to how their interpersonal styles might influence and distort the supervisory encounter, asking

the question, "Who does this therapist (client) represent in my own mythology?"

The *idealized self* represents an enduring, cognitive image of one's desired mate, child, friend, client, therapist, or supervisor that becomes the template against which actual relationships are compared (Anderson & Holmes, 1994). The discrepancy gap between ideal and actual can become the source of unfulfilled expectations, frustration, and interpersonal conflict. In supervision, the exploration of such discrepancies may serve to identify and modify personal mythologies that interfere with therapist, therapeutic, or supervisory progress.

Identification of Personal Mythologies

One objective of this supervision model is to help therapists experience "a greater sense of freedom, spontaneity, flexibility, and creativity in responding to client needs" (Anderson & Holmes, in press). To accomplish this, supervision focuses on four indicators of the major themes embedded in the personal myths of therapists. First, what are the *recurrent topics of concern* expressed by the therapist? Often the repetitive content across cases and sessions is directly related to a major theme in the therapist's personal mythology. Second, what *redundant interactional patterns* are evident in therapy or supervision? Has the style of interacting taken on a rigid and predictable pattern? Third, what specific, *affect-laden conflicts* continuously surface in supervision? The major emotional themes expressed in supervision can be used as a bridge back to the personal mythology of the therapist. The predominant *affective tone* of the supervisory session presents yet another path to explore the implications of personal myths for therapists and supervisors. Further, the level and type of affect experienced in supervision might also be mirrored in members of the client system. Exploration of these feelings can empower therapists (and supervisors) to approach affect-laden situations in a new, more productive fashion.

Use of Personal Mythologies at the Client/Therapist Interface

Supervisors assist therapists in using the assessment strategies listed here to access and assess client mythological themes. Once identified, therapists are assisted to select appropriate treatment modalities and therapeutic interventions to modify central themes in client mythologies. For example, if the themes are constraining (e.g., Expressing anger is dangerous and should be avoided at all costs.), therapists are assisted to develop treatment plans that initially will lift such constraints and later promote the identification and practice of alternative stories.

The therapeutic myths clinicians create with clients "will inevitably reflect their own underlying assumptions about the world, their definitions of family health and functioning, and about how individuals and family systems change, grow, and develop over time" (Bagarozzi & Anderson, 1989b, p. 274). As such, it is essential for supervisors to help therapists examine how their own mythologies affect the development of the therapeutic system. Therapists need to explore whether their unresolved intrapersonal or interpersonal conflicts are influencing their perceptions of and interactions with their clients. To assist supervisees in this process, supervisors can select from a variety of exercises, assignments, and tasks predesigned to alert therapists to the inhibiting effects of their mythologies, and guide them to see their clients without the constraining filters inherent in their myths.

Finally, supervisors lead supervisees to analyze the inhibiting effects and/or positive potentials that surface as a result of the meshing of therapist and client mythological themes. It is assumed that "the supervisor's ability to identify relevant themes and to sensitize the thera-pist to his or her own contribution to the collusive therapist–client pact can help tip the balance in the direction of progress and growth as opposed to stagnation for both client and therapist" (Bagarozzi & Anderson, 1989b, p. 298).

Use of Personal Mythologies at the Therapist/Supervisor Interface

How the personal myths of supervisors and therapists are triggered by the supervisory context also must be understood. To accomplish this, supervisors and therapists must be willing to enter into a relationship that is based on trust, self-disclosure, and risk-taking. Supervisors and therapists also must be willing to share their personal mythologies about the self, each other, the client, and the therapeutic and supervisory relationships.

For supervisors, each therapist and client bring with them a unique history and interactional style that can stimulate myths within the supervisor. Supervisors need to be alert to these reactions. Depending on the intensity of the response, external assistance, in the form of supervision-of-supervision, peer consultation, or individual therapy, may need to be accessed to inhibit any deleterious effects on therapists or clients.

For therapists, the potential to construct an idealized version of the supervisor can lead to overdependency or frustration as a result of unfulfilled expectations. In this regard, therapists need to be willing to reflect on and describe these idealized versions in order to gain a more realistic view of the supervisory encounter.

Finally, supervisors and therapists would do well to acknowledge the constraining and facilitating aspects of the mutual mythology they co-create during supervision. By identifying and examining these interactive mythologies, each participant can take personal responsibility for revising those themes that are interfering with therapeutic and supervisory progress.

The Construction of an Integrative Framework

A primary aim of this approach is to assist therapists to integrate their own conceptual model of therapy and to link this directly to their practice. As supervisees develop the capacity to have a sense of their therapeutic self, it is anticipated that their degree of genuineness, honesty, openness, and courage will increase. By accessing such qualities, therapists are more free to competently and confidently construct a unique way of understanding, experiencing, and relating to clients.

CONVERGENCE AND DIVERGENCE ACROSS MODELS

Supervisory Interventions

Each integrative supervision model is based on an alternative *overarching framework* that informs supervisors how to incorporate various theories and therapies into a more comprehensive understanding of supervisory practice. These frameworks provide specific assessment strategies that supervisors can draw on to construct multidimensional understandings of supervisees, clients, and therapeutic and supervisory relationships. Based on these assessments, supervisors can then select from a wide range of supervisory interventions using the criteria of *best-fit* (i.e., which interventions are most consistent with the needs of the therapist and the client, and the wider contexts of therapy and supervision?).

In addition to being proficient with an extensive array of assessment skills and intervention strategies, what separates integrative supervisors from eclectic supervisors is the ability to use a coherent metatheory to organize the various skills and strategies across therapeutic and supervisory encounters. The heuris-

tic metatheory can be used to guide the work of both therapists and supervisors.

Each integrative model has a specific *firing order* for interventions that is meant to stimulate and advance therapeutic competencies and self-awareness. For example, IPCS, as proposed, offers a sequential set of strategies premised on the belief that more complex, sophisticated, time-consuming, and expensive interventions should be accessed only after direct and inexpensive interventions have proved ineffective. SCDS provides a series of assessment and intervention strategies that are initially used to identify and work within a supervisee's primary orientation, and are later used to identify and explore ancillary orientations, with the ultimate objective being to ensure that supervisees learn to access the most developmentally appropriate orientation over time and under different circumstances.

The metaframeworks perspective helps therapists manage the complexity of treatment by using a variety of available frames to help develop workable hypotheses. Finally, within the *mythological perspective*, supervisors work within two wide domains. First, they select interventions that help therapists advance their therapeutic competencies, and then they employ supervisory interventions that help supervisees articulate the personal myths that might be affecting therapy and supervision.

Supervisory Modalities

Integrative models draw from the full spectrum of supervisory modalities. Again, the criteria of best-fit are employed to guide the selection of modalities; that is, the needs of therapists and clients will inform the decision as to which modality to employ.

It is possible to consider the use of similar modalities across the four models. For example, live supervision could be employed to help a therapist manage the complexity of therapy (metaframeworks perspective) to assist a therapist, constrained within the formal/reflective orientation, to enact therapeutic interventions in the immediacy of the session (SCDS), to support a therapist requiring assistance in constructing a therapeutic alliance (IPCS), or to facilitate a therapist's ability to tolerate and work with ambiguity (mythological perspective). Although the modality is the same, the reasons for selecting it vary across supervisory models.

Because of the multidimensional complexities of integrative models, opportunities to observe directly (e.g., live or co-therapy) or indirectly (e.g., electronic recordings) are easily incorporated, particularly when therapists are trying new interventions and methods. However, other modalities, such as individual or group case presentation, can be used to help therapists acquire new skills, and to help therapists enhance their understanding of self-as-therapist.

Contracting

An essential component of integrative supervision contracts is that therapists will incorporate and combine discrete parts of theories and treatment methods into a coherent metatheoretical framework that provides a multidimensional understanding of human and systemic development and of the therapeutic process. A second contractual component is the expectation that therapists begin with a basic background in some systemic approaches and with previous experience using individual treatment methods.

A third component of an integrative contract informs the therapist that issues of a personal and professional nature will be considered appropriate material for supervision. The personal concepts of self-awareness, personal family experience, and dispositions toward gender and cultural awareness all may be addressed. Professional issues would include the ability

to form therapeutic alliances; manage complexity; and define individual, system, and ecosystemic dynamics from a variety of theoretical and treatment perspectives. In most instances, some access to raw clinical data (i.e., live supervision, co-therapy, electronic recordings) would be a requirement of the contract. Additionally, within an integrative framework, there is wider latitude for therapists to suggest their own unique goals for supervision.

As in all forms of supervision, therapists would be expected to become aware of the ethical, contextual, and legal issues that emerge in clinical practice. Another general issue would address the willingness of the supervisee to seek personal therapy, if indicated, during the course of supervision.

A final consideration of the contract concerns the content of the supervision. Will supervisees be expected to learn a specific integrative model or will the supervisor use their integrative perspective to guide supervisees within particular systemic models or to develop their own integrative perspective? Integrative supervisors have two choices concerning the explicitness of the theoretical constructs of their metamodel. The first position, primarily represented by the mythological perspective and SCDS models, is personified by supervisors who use their metamodel as a lens through which they tailor strategies and interventions to best meet the needs of their supervisee. The second position, primarily represented by the Pinsof and Breunlin models, is typified by supervisors who teach their particular model of supervision and therapy. Of course, all four models can be used in either position depending on the contextual needs of a particular situation. Therefore, it is imperative that an explicit discussion of which position will be adopted first, and if, how, and when to switch to another position needs to be part of any supervisory contract.

Evaluation

Within the domain of integrative supervision, where the particular combinations of interventions is not preordained, success must be gauged in terms of three variables: personal meaning, theoretical connectedness, and clinical utility. Regarding *personal meaning*, supervisory experiences must be situated within the working knowledge base of supervisees. Supervision must have meaning for therapists. If interventions are beyond therapists' conceptual understanding, they will be unable to integrate new information or insight into their repertoire of therapeutic competencies, or into their sense of self-as-therapist. As such, integrative supervision consistently takes into account the constraints, resources, needs, and capabilities of therapists.

In terms of *theoretical connectedness*, a primary aim of integrative supervision is to help therapists make informed decisions about the selection of therapeutic interventions across schools and approaches. All supervisory interventions should therefore facilitate an understanding of how various perspectives and strategies are theoretically connected within the rubric of the wider framework.

Supervisory interventions can have direct or indirect *clinical utility*. Some interventions will be directly applicable to the therapeutic domain and can be readily transferred. Other supervisory interventions will have indirect clinical utility, yet still be important for the development of the therapist. In either case, the ultimate goal is to increase the efficacy and self-knowledge of the therapist.

Specific evaluative tools and strategies, which can be used to monitor therapist, client, and supervisory progress, have been developed for each of the models presented in this chapter. For example, the authors of the metaframeworks perspective have developed a scale to assess the degree of gender-balance reflected in therapist perspectives. The author of SCDS has developed a set of questioning strategies and a companion classification system that can be used to assess supervisee range and flexibility within and across orientations. For IPCT, Pinsof and Catherall (1986) have developed therapeutic alliance scales that can be used to monitor therapist growth in the ability to establish positive therapeutic relationships. Finally, the authors of the mythological perspective (Anderson & Holmes, in press; Bagarozzi & Anderson, 1989b) have developed family relationships history and personal myths assessment guidelines to track supervisee growth.

The acceptability of the supervisee's work can be judged by combining the data from clinical instrumentation developed for each model and the supervisor's ongoing assessment of the therapist's progress in terms of selecting interventions that are meaningful to the client, understanding theoretical connectedness, and demonstrating clinical utility. Beyond this general evaluation, notions of the "complete systemic therapist" differ for each model.

In terms of IPCT, the "good enough" therapist would be able to establish a positive working alliance and be able to access strategies and interventions from systemic and individual frameworks to address client needs. A therapist working within the metaframework perspective would be deemed successful if she or he were able to demonstrate how to read clinical feedback about the effectiveness of interventions and to develop comprehensive hypotheses based on familial, individual, cultural and gender-sensitive understandings. For a therapist working within a mythological model, basic competency within the relational, perceptual, and executive areas of conducting successful therapy would be the first criteria. The second area of competency would require evidence that the therapist can identify and enhance the client's personal mythologies as well as demonstrate an openness to exploring their own personal myths.

Finally, a "complete" therapist within the SCDS model would demonstrate a strong understanding of the co-constructive, developmental paradigm. The therapist would know how and when to identify and access client worldviews; would display the ability to use strategies from various systemic, individual, and network approaches from all four cognitive-developmental orientations; and would demonstrate a capacity to co-construct developmentally appropriate, culturally aware, and gender-sensitive therapeutic environments with their clients.

The Complete Systemic Supervisor

Similar isomorphic statements based on the criteria for "the complete systemic therapist" would also be appropriate to describe "the complete systemic supervisor." In addition, integrative supervisors should demonstrate a thorough understanding of the recursive and complex nature of supervision. For example, according to Anderson and Holmes (in press), the supervisory system is a powerfully charged, fluid, and dynamic patchwork of contributions from clients, therapists, supervisors, and the wider contexts. In this regard, supervisee and supervisor enter their relationship with unique presuppositions that elicit and constrain certain aspects of self and others. The implications of taking this recursive position requires integrative supervisors to go beyond the content-driven nature of school-specific supervision models and to work directly in the multidimensional, highly human arenas of therapy, supervision, and wider contexts. In this sense, a complete integrative supervisor knows how to use and enhance opportunities within multiple contexts to engender mutual personal and professional development.

In one way, supervisors influence supervisee growth by helping them to develop competence in using the overarching integrative framework to construct multiple perspectives, and to draw from a variety of theories, therapies, and strategies to design organized treatment plans that are tailored to specific client needs. As such, the integrative supervisor must demonstrate a capacity to continually synthesize theories, therapies, and techniques to design a coherent set of experiences for the therapist. Integrative supervisors must be willing to assume stances within particular theories or therapies, to integrate various approaches, or to guide the supervisee to construct broader, more comprehensive perspectives. In this fashion, the supervisor must be willing to explore new ideas and material, either within an approach or across approaches to meet the supervisee's needs.

Professional development also entails a continual process of personal understanding for both the supervisee and the supervisor. Domains of personal understanding include awareness of socially or culturally constructed worldviews, and of how these worldviews both constrain and facilitate the sense of self and self-in-relationship.

The complete systemic supervisor will know how to help therapists reflect on the personal issues affecting therapy. The integrative supervisor will know how to make their thinking explicit and will be able to assist the therapist in doing the same in supervision and therapy.

Finally, "complete" integrative supervisors accept the fundamental "incompleteness" of their models. They accept the idea that the "perfect" therapy model for all clients, or the "perfect" supervision model for all therapists, does not exist and that integrative models represent only one path on the journey toward more effective forms of treatment. The search for new strategies and interventions, the openness to revise cherished beliefs and models, and the willingness to learn and synthesize new theories are at the heart of the concept of the "complete" integrative supervisor.

CONCLUSION

Integrative models of supervision provide a multitude of perspectives that, when taken together, offer a robust understanding of supervisee and client development and adaptation. These models offer supervisors organized access to a variety of diverse theoretical perspectives and approaches that can be used throughout the course of supervision. Thus, supervisors can be flexible in supervision; can tailor the supervisory relationship to meet the specific needs of the therapist, the client, and the therapeutic relationship; and can provide service to a wide range of supervisee types. Each supervisory model presented in this chapter provides an alternative and coherent set of dimensions and strategies that can help supervisors access the benefits associated with integrated approaches.

REFERENCES

Anderson, S., & Bagarozzi, D. (1983). The use of family myths as an aid to strategic therapy. *Journal of Family Therapy, 5,* 145–164.

Anderson, S., & Holmes, S. (in press). Personal mythologies: A framework for dealing with therapeutic and supervisory impasses. (Available from the authors at the University of Connecticut, Storrs.)

Anderson, S., Rigazio-DiGilio, S., & Kunkler, K. (1995). Training and supervision of family therapy: Current issues and future directions. *Family Relations, 44,* 489–500.

Bagarozzi, D., & Anderson, S. (1989a). *Personal, marital and family myths: Theoretical formulations and clinical strategies.* New York: W. W. Norton.

Bagarozzi, D., & Anderson, S. (1989b). Training and supervision in marital and family therapy. In D. Bagarozzi & S. Anderson, *Personal, marital and family myths: Theoretical formulations and clinical strategies* (pp. 274–298). New York: W. W. Norton.

Breunlin, D., Rampage, C., & Eovaldi, M. (1995). Family therapy supervision: Toward an integrative perspective. In R. Mikesell, D. Lusterman, & S. Mc-

Daniel (Eds.), *Integrating therapy: Handbook of family psychology and systems theory* (pp. 547–560). Washington, DC: American Psychological Association.

Breunlin, D., Schwartz, R., & Mac Kune-Karrer, B. (1992). *Metaframeworks.* San Francisco: Jossey-Bass.

Case, E., & Robinson, N. (1990). Toward integration: The changing world of family therapy. *The American Journal of Family Therapy, 18,* 153–160.

Catherall, D., & Pinsof, W. (1987). The impact of the therapist's personal family life on the ability to establish viable therapeutic alliances in family and marital therapy. *Journal of Psychotherapy and the Family, 3,* 135–160.

Duhl, B. (1987). Uses of the self in integrated contextual systems therapy. *Journal of Psychotherapy and the Family, 3,* 71–84.

Feixas, G. (1990). Approaching the individual, approaching the system: A constructivist model for integrating psychotherapy. *Journal of Family Psychology, 4,* 4–35.

Feldman, L. (1985). Integrative multi-level therapy: A comprehensive interpersonal and intrapsychic approach. *Journal of Marital and Family Therapy, 11,* 357–372.

Feldman, L. (1989). Integrating individual and family therapy. *Journal of Integrative and Eclective Psychotherapy, 8,* 41–52.

Grunebaum, H., & Chasin, R. (1982). Thinking like a family therapist: A model for integrating the theories and methods of family therapy. *Journal of Marital and Family Therapy, 8,* 403–416.

Ivey, A. (1986). *Developmental therapy: Theory into practice.* San Francisco: Jossey-Bass.

Ivey, A. (1991). *Developmental strategies for helpers: Individual, family, and network interventions.* Pacific Grove, CA: Brooks/Cole.

L'Abate, L., & Frey, J. (1981). The E-R-A model: The role of feelings in family therapy reconsidered: Implications for a classification of theories of family therapy. *Journal of Marital and Family Therapy, 7,* 143–150.

Lebow, J. (1984). On the value of integrating approaches to family therapy. *Journal of Marital and Family Therapy, 10,* 127–138.

Lebow, J. (1987). Integrative family therapy: An overview of major issues. *Psychotherapy, 24,* 584–594.

McCollum, E. (1990). Integrating structural-strategic and Bowenian approaches in training beginning family therapist. *Contemporary Family Therapy, 12,* 23-34.

Piaget, J. (1955). *The language and thought of the child.* New York: New American Library (originally published in 1923).

Piercy, F., & Sprenkle, D. (1986). Family therapy theory building: An integrative training approach. In F. Piercy (Ed.), *Family therapy education and supervision* (pp. 5–14). New York: Haworth Press.

Pinsof, W. (1983). Integrative problem-centered therapy: Toward the synthesis of family and individual psychotherapies. *Journal of Marital and Family Therapy, 9,* 19–35.

Pinsof, W. (1988). The therapist-client relationship: An integrative systems perspective. *Journal of Integrative and Eclective Psychotherapy, 7,* 303–313.

Pinsof, W. (1989). A conceptual framework and methodological criteria for family therapy research. *Journal of Consulting and Clinical Psychology, 57,* 53–59.

Pinsof, W. (1992). Toward a scientific paradigm of family psychology: The integrative process systems perspective. *Journal of Family Psychology, 5,* 432–447.

Pinsof, W. (1994a). An overview of integrative problem-centered therapy: A synthesis of family and individual psychotherapies. *Journal of Family Therapy, 16,* 103–120.

Pinsof, W. (1994b). An integrative systems perspective on the therapeutic alliance: Theoretical, clinical, and research implications. In A. Hovath & L. Greenberg (Eds.), *The working alliance: Theory, research and practice* (pp. 173–195). New York: Wiley.

Pinsof, W., & Catherall, D. (1986). The integrative psychotherapy alliance: Family, couple and individual therapy scales. *Journal of Marital and Family Therapy, 12,* 137–151.

Rigazio-DiGilio, S. (1993). Family counseling and therapy: Theoretical foundations and issues of practice. In A. Ivey, M. Ivey, & L. Simek-Morgan, *Counseling and psychotherapy: A multicultural perspective,* 3rd ed. (pp. 333–358). Needham Heights, MA: Allyn and Bacon.

Rigazio-DiGilio, S. (1994a). A coconstructive-developmental approach to ecosystemic treatment. *Journal of Mental Health Counseling, 16,* 43–74.

Rigazio-DiGilio, S. (1994b). Beyond paradigms: The multiple implications of a coconstructive-developmental model. *Journal of Mental Health Counseling, 16,* 205–212.

Rigazio-DiGilio, S. (1994c). Systemic cognitive-developmental therapy: Training practitioners to access and assess cognitive-developmental orientations.

Simulation and Gaming: An International Journal of Theory, Design, and Research, 25, 61–74.

Rigazio-DiGilio, S. (1996). Systemic cognitive-developmental therapy. *Directions in Clinical and Counseling Psychology: National Program of Continuing Education and Certification Maintenance* (pre-approved APA, NBCC CEU Lesson Plans), Vol. 6 (pp. 3-1–3-19). New York: The Hatherleigh Company, Ltd.

Rigazio-DiGilio, S. (in press). Systemic cognitive-developmental therapy: A nonpathological, integrative approach to partner and family therapy. *International Journal for the Advancement of Counseling.*

Rigazio-DiGilio, S., & Anderson, S. (1991). Supervisee-focused supervision: A cognitive-developmental model. Presentation at the Annual American Association for Marriage and Family Therapy Conference, Dallas, October.

Rigazio-DiGilio, S., & Anderson, S. (1994). A cognitive-developmental model for marital and family therapy supervision. *The Clinical Supervisor, 11,* 93–118.

Rigazio-DiGilio, S., Daniels, T., & Ivey, A. (in press). Systemic cognitive-developmental supervision: A developmental-integrative approach to psychotherapy supervision. In C. Watkins (Ed.), *Handbook of psychotherapy supervision.* New York: Wiley.

Rigazio-DiGilio, S., & Ivey, A. (1991). Developmental counseling and therapy: A framework for individual and family treatment. *Counseling and Human Development, 24,* 1–20.

Rigazio-DiGilio, S., & Ivey, A. (1993). Systemic cognitive-developmental therapy: An integrative framework. *The Family Journal: Counseling and Therapy for Couples and Families, 1,* 208–219.

Saba, G., & Liddle, H. (1986). Perceptions of professional needs, practice patterns and critical issues facing family therapy trainers and supervisors. *The American Journal of Family Therapy, 14,* 109–122.

Sluzki, C. (1983). Process, structure and world views: Toward an integrated view of systemic models of family therapy. *Family Process, 22,* 469–476.

Stanton, M. (1981). An integrated structural/strategic approach to family therapy. *Journal of Marital and Family Therapy, 7,* 427–439.

Taibbi, R. (1990). Integrative family therapy: A model for supervision. *Families in Society: The Journal of Contemporary Human Services, 71,* 542–549.

Vygotsky, L. (1987). *Thought and language* (A. Kozulin, trans.). Cambridge: MIT Press.

Worthington, E. (1987). Treatment of families during life transitions: Matching treatment to family response. *Family Process, 26,* 295–308.

Worthington, E. (1992). Strategic matching and tailoring of treatment to couples and families. *Topics in Family Psychology and Counseling, 1,* 17–20.

15

Postmodern Models of Family Therapy Supervision

Glen T. Gardner, Monte Bobele, and Joan L. Biever

Postmodern approaches in family therapy are relatively new. Presently the core of the existing literature focuses on applications of postmodern concepts to the practice of psychotherapy (Cecchin, 1992; Coale, 1992; Fish, 1993; Gergen, 1985; Hoffman, 1991; Hoyt, 1994; McNamee & Gergen, 1992; Neimeyer, 1993; Owen, 1992; Polkinghorne, 1992; Sluzki, 1992; Weingarten, 1991; White, 1986). Only recently has literature begun to emerge which addresses postmodern approaches to supervision (Hardy, 1993). As a starting point for this chapter, we will briefly describe some of the ideas that orbit in the world of postmodernism.

Postmodernism is a term that is frequently employed to describe the movement away from a quest for, and belief in, ultimate foundations in any areas of our lives. This movement can be seen in many aspects of the world in the latter part of the twentieth century: There has come to be an expanding appreciation of multitude of points of view and realities, an increasing awareness of the worth of differing cultural values, a dissatisfaction with inflexible norms in all areas of life, a heightened awareness of the effects of our own and others' psychological makeup on our perceptions and beliefs, and an expanded realization of the influence of individual points of view and their usefulness. Modern technology has contributed to these changes by facilitating instantaneous contact with others in a worldwide web.

Social scientists and therapists, in particular, find themselves searching for new metaphors for what they do as the scientific metaphor becomes increasingly less satisfying. One of the more useful metaphors that has materialized recently in family therapy is that of the "narrative." A postmodern sensibility in the world of psychotherapy will mean that therapists will pragmatically apply metaphors, techniques, stories, or narratives that fit particular clients.

A number of applications of postmodernism to supervision are emerging. This chapter relies most heavily on the work of Goolishian and Anderson (Anderson, 1992b; Anderson & Goolishian, 1988, 1992; Anderson & Rambo, 1988; Anderson & Swim, 1993, 1994; Goolishian & Anderson, 1992), White and Epston (White, 1986, 1989/1990; White & Epston, 1990), Doan and Parry (Amundson, Stewart, & Parry, 1994), and Biever, Gardner, and Bobele (Biever & Gardner, 1995; Bobele, Gardner & Biever, 1995) in describing supervisory applications of postmodernism. Moreover, several social constructionist ideas that have emerged from postmodernism are the ones we most specifically describe in addressing supervision issues.

COMMON ASSUMPTIONS INFLUENCING SUPERVISION

Although there are several different expressions of postmodern therapies, they share some common assumptions that influence therapy and supervision. Social constructionism has provided an epistemological foundation for many of the postmodern therapies. According to social constructionism, meanings are developed through social interaction and social consensus (Gergen, 1985; Saleebey, 1994). Generally speaking, all understandings are socially negotiated and are related to the context within which they are embedded, especially the immediate conversation. An implication is that meanings are not static and unchangeable, but are the product of social interaction over time. There is an emphasis on the criss-crossing of ideas and meanings in our conversations with one another. Anderson and Goolishian (1988) talk about this crisscrossing as *intersubjective*, which they define as ". . . an evolving state of affairs in which two or more people agree (understand) that they are experiencing the same event in the same way. . . . It is understood that agreement is fragile and continually open to renegotiation and dispute" (p. 372). Anderson and Goolishian (1990) have, in another context, characterized such ideas as a *collaborative language systems* approach to training:

> The training system, like the therapy system, is one kind of meaning-generating or language system. In such a language or learning system, the teacher and the student create meaning with each other. In this sense, both are learners. The teacher (the supervisor) and student (the therapist) create narratives and stories with each other around which they organize the learning task. Implicit in this learning system description is the idea that it is a collaborative, egalitarian, and horizontal system in which their expertise (teacher's and student's) is shared (p. 1).

Along similar lines Gergen (1985) asserts: "From a constructionist position, the process of understanding is not automatically driven by forces of nature, but is the result of active, cooperative enterprise of persons in relationship" (p. 267). Conversations are dynamic processes that evolve over time. One of the implications of this dynamism is that meanings are transitory. No word or communication is ever complete, clear, or enduring because there are always potential new interpretations that may be expressed (Anderson & Goolishian, 1988). Meanings then, are always "on the way." Clients, therapists, supervisees, and supervisors are always in the process of constructing new meanings about themselves and those with whom they are in conversation. The focus for the supervisee, then, is the creation of shifting meanings. "Supervision from a postmodern perspective invites the supervisee to pay attention to the ways in which therapeutic 'realities' are created through language that is ever shifting in meaning. No one story tells the whole story" (Stewart, 1994, p. 6).

Most social constructionist positions value the adoption of a "not-knowing" position (Anderson & Goolishian, 1988, 1992) with respect to supervisees' situations. From this perspective, there is no privileged information; rather, knowledge comes about as a result of the social interactions between people. Supervisory expertise, then, is understood to lie in the manner in which the supervisory conversation is managed. The nonexpert position does not deny the experience and expertise that supervisors possess, but ". . . that there is no 'pre-knowing,' no drawing of irrevocable conclusions which are substantiated by selectively gathering and attending to data which support the theory" (Allen, 1993, p. 40). Supervisors expect that there are different perspectives that supervisees have which are valuable. Stewart (1994) describes the value of supervisees' expertise: "We encourage supervisees to use a lot of ideas gained from years of experience by others, but we also encourage them to travel lightly—to not let any one set of ideas or practices define the therapeutic moment" (p. 6).

A postmodern supervision process has as its goal the enhancement of supervisees' ability to appreciate multiple perspectives and to develop new meanings for supervisees, which can be used to facilitate their clients' therapy. One approach to the development of new meanings is to help supervisees develop alternate meanings from the therapeutic conversation they have participated in: "The goal of the supervision system is the development of a context for co-evolving new meaning, and thus learning and change" (Anderson & Swim, 1994, p. 2). Several other postmodern supervisors (Davis, Gorman, & Lockerman, 1994; Parry & Doan, 1994; Roberts, 1994; White, 1989/1900) focus directly on changing supervisees' own meanings about themselves in the supervisory process through "co-construction with the supervisee of new self-stories that are about competence and growth rather than incompetence and stuckness" (Davis et al., 1994, p. 2). In general, many postmodern supervisors strive to make use of experience and knowledge gained from training, education, and clinical experience while at the same time appreciating and nurturing the uniqueness of supervisees' experiences and knowledge.

SUPERVISION DILEMMAS

For the supervisor who is attempting to apply postmodern concepts to supervision, a number of dilemmas initially arise that are unique to a postmodern perspective (Bobele et al., 1995). The postmodern supervisor must rethink notions of hierarchy, expertise, "truth," classification, and evaluation.

Expansion of Hierarchy

Under social constructionism, the notion of hierarchy is expanded. The training, legal, and ethical contexts in which supervision takes place inevitably create hierarchies. Supervisees generally perceive supervisors as having more expertise, having more experience, and as having professional gatekeeping functions. Supervisors must, at times, suggest alternative ways of behaving in the therapy room, write evaluations, or assign grades in a training setting. In spite of how a supervisor defines a relationship, supervisees and others will often define it as hierarchical. Atkinson (1993) addresses this issue as follows: "I assume that I am in a position of elevated influence. I assume that I often cannot avoid being in a position of elevated influence. I assume that it is possible to abuse my position of influence" (pp. 167–168). Postmodern supervision aims to reduce the unhelpful, limiting consequences of hierarchical relationships as much as possible. Two ways this can be accomplished are to present ideas to supervisees in a tentative language, or to use teams whenever possible to present multiple points of view (Bobele et al., 1995).

Adoption of a Nonexpert Position

Postmodern supervision prescribes the adoption of the "non-expert" position (Anderson & Rambo, 1988; Anderson & Swim, 1994; Goolishian & Anderson, 1992). If the supervisor is no longer an "expert" about therapy, what roles do supervisors perform? Supervision is not based on the assumption that supervisors have access to privileged information about the therapy, the client, or the supervisee. It is a given that supervisors usually have knowledge, skills, and experiences to draw on to facilitate supervisees' progress. The social constructionist recognizes that supervisors and supervisees may effectively use these different skills and knowledge. The emphasis is on the collaborative, cooperative, mutual generation of ideas (Anderson & Swim, 1994). The previously cited description by Allen (1993) of the therapist's position applies as well to the supervisor's position:

> Questioning the position of the therapist as expert does not mean that the therapist abandons all knowledge and expertise. . . . It means that there is no "preknowing," no drawing of irrevocable conclusions which are substantiated by selectively gathering and attending to data which support the theory (p. 40).

Entertainment of Multiple Truths

Perhaps the most bothersome dilemma is the implication that there are many useful ways to approach any particular situation or problem. Supervision is regarded as the entertainment of multiple, contradictory, and mutually exclusive ideas at the same time. The goal becomes the generation of helpful ideas supervisees can use in therapy. Supervisors may present their preferences about "good" therapist behavior while at the same time acknowledging that other approaches might be equally useful. This encourages supervisees to appreciate the validity of the different points of view presented by clients as well.

Balancing of Classification and Nonlabeling

Postmodern supervision finds normative conceptions of supervisees and the supervision process to be unhelpful. We have made it a goal of supervision to avoid the use of pathological or normative labels that tend to close off the expansion of meanings. Frequently, supervisees have normative understandings of clients as a consequence of their training, so a postmodern supervisor helps supervisees look for a balance between commonly understood

information about a family or problem type and the uniqueness of clients. In addition, a postmodern supervisor strives to facilitate an appreciation for the contextual factors supervisees encounter in their work with clients.

Local Rather Than Universal Meaning of Evaluation

Many postmodern supervisors believe supervisees have natural skills, abilities, and talents that can be focused and enhanced to encourage positive changes in clients. The supervision process is one that promotes the effective use of these behaviors in supervisees. It is the responsibility of a supervisor to provide an assessment of the supervisees' refinements of these natural skills, abilities, and talents, to the supervisee, as well as the professional context in which the training is conducted, and, when appropriate, to the larger professional community.

The responsibility of performing evaluations is common for supervisors, and we have come to recognize that evaluations are locally constructed and have local meaning rather than universal meaning. Most social constructionist supervisors draw different distinctions (e.g., Efran & Clarfield, 1992; Turner & Fine, 1995) than supervisors from other frameworks, but, nonetheless, distinctions are drawn. So, for the social constructionist, evaluations are based on standards or criteria that the supervisor believes are important in practicing the craft of psychotherapy. All such evaluations are subjective. Turner and Fine (1995) describe the way that the locality of meaning can shift hierarchically between three contexts. Interpersonally situated realities evolve out of face-to-face conversations with the supervisor. Locally situated realities emerge out the particular training context the supervisor and supervisee participate in. Centrally situated realities result from the formal criteria, standards and laws that the profession and society prescribe for professional practice.

We endeavor to cocreate with our supervisees mechanisms for helpful evaluation that are satisfactory for them and other important parts of the professional ecology. This means that supervision goals are frequently established by the supervisee and supervisor, but are always contextualized by the supervision context, the supervisor's and supervisee's experiences and expectations, and the expectations of the larger professional context. Turner and Fine (1995) provide several excellent examples of the collaborative process in postmodern supervision.

Frequently supervisors use live supervision with one-way mirrors, which provide the capacity for ongoing monitoring of supervisees' progress (Hardy, 1993; Kaplan, 1987; Lewis & Rohrbaugh, 1989; McKenzie et al., 1986). Video- and audiotapes are also valuable tools to evaluate progress (McKenzie et al., 1986). Flemons et al. (1996) have devised a rationale and checklist to identify important skills and abilities for supervisees to demonstrate in postmodern therapy. The ongoing use of such a checklist can provide some information about supervisees' progress. Supervisee reports, in and after sessions, are perhaps the most important instrument the supervisor has, because they provide an opportunity to pay attention to their narratives about their own progress.

INTERVENTIONS BASED ON POSTMODERN IDEAS

There has been some criticism in the field recently about therapeutic, and, by extension, supervision models that are interventive in nature. Some would advocate that deliberate intervention into an ongoing system is to be avoided (Cecchin, Lane, & Ray, 1993; Goolishian & Anderson, 1992; Hoffman, 1991), while others would argue that it is impossible to avoid intervention (Atkinson, 1992; Bobele et al., 1995). Most postmodern approaches to supervision and therapy avoid deliberate intervention into a system to bring about a particular change in supervisees consistent with supervisors' "expert" knowledge. Some postmodern therapists do still intervene, but, ideally, only to manage therapeutic conversations (Anderson & Goolishian, 1988, 1992; Anderson & Swim, 1993). The difference in the two styles of intervention is that a postmodern "intervention" derives from a position of "not knowing" or curiosity. Interventions are designed to expand the universe of ideas that can be brought to the therapeutic conversation. Interventions from the modern perspective may be seen as limiting options and ideas instead of expanding them.

Although there are no supervisory modalities that are uniquely characteristic of this model, live supervision and reflecting teams are frequently used by supervisors who have access to the appropriate facilities (Kaplan, 1987; West, Bubenzer, & Zarski, 1989). Most supervisory modalities can be readily adapted to a postmodern perspective because it is not the modality, but the theoretical grounding that distinguishes this approach. Frequently supervisors prefer group supervision, therapy teams, and live supervision because these all have the potential for creating multiple points of view and enriching the supervisory experience (Anderson & Swim, 1993; Biever & Gardner, 1995; Davis et al., 1994; Parry & Doan, 1994; Prest et al., 1990; Roberts, 1994).

Live supervision, especially with teams, is a preferred method of supervision. Some supervisors still find the use of the telephone to communicate directly with the supervisee helpful. The use of treatment teams comprised of several supervisees and a supervisor is not unique to postmodern supervision (Bernstein, Brown, & Ferrier, 1984; Cade, Speed, & Seligman, 1986; Ferrier, 1984; Green & Herget, 1989a,b, 1991; Quinn et. al., 1985), but the use of such teams can contribute to the goals of postmodern therapy and supervision. Team members provide a variety of perspectives, values, suggestions, and alternative stories that can be considered in working with clients. More recently, Andersen has described a method of using therapeutic teams that has become widely used (Andersen, 1987; Bobele et al., 1989; Feixas, 1990; Griffith & Griffith, 1992; Griffith et al., 1992; Kaslow, 1981; Miller & Lax, 1988; Prest, Darden, & Keller, 1990; Young et al., 1989). The reflecting team, as a therapeutic/supervisory strategy, is an excellent example of a technique directly derived from the postmodern sensibility (see Chapter 24; Biever & Gardner, 1995; Prest et al., 1990). The use of the team enables a number of voices to be heard by the clients as well as supervisees.

The Houston-Galveston Institute has frequently demonstrated their use of the "as if" exercise in supervision and consultation (Anderson, 1992a). In this exercise, a supervisor conducts an interview with the supervisee while other supervisees listen. Each of the listeners is directed to listen to the interview *as if* they were one of the various participants in the system being described. For example, one might listen as if they were the father in the therapist's client family, another as the mother, still others as the children, grandparents, probation officers, teachers, other health-care providers, and so on. Following the conclusion of the supervisor's interview with the supervisee, the listeners share ideas that they had about what the person whose position they were listening in might have. During this phase of the exercise, the supervisor and supervisee simply listen. Conversations between the listener and the supervisory dyad are discouraged at this point. Following the listeners' input, the supervisory dyad processes what was heard, paying special attention to what had been said that was helpful by providing unheard stories to the supervisor and supervisee.

Rambo (1989) describes a supervisory exercise that helps therapists develop multiple perspectives of problems. In this exercise a

group of supervisees is asked to tell someone the story of Cinderella in an interesting and entertaining manner. Next, they are asked to tell the story to someone else from the stepmother's perspective. Next, the supervisee is asked to write up the Cinderella story using medical terminology and a *DSM* diagnosis. In a variation, we have used this exercise with groups asking that the story be told to the group by each supervisee in turn from the perspective of the stepmother, the stepsisters, the prince, and so on, depending on the number of participants available.

Parry and Doan (1994) describe a number of exercises they designed to help supervisees develop "new stories." Sometimes the supervisee is encouraged to create a new story about the client that has some potential for new ways of thinking and acting in therapy with that client. Other exercises are focused on helping supervisees change the stories they have about themselves as therapists. These new stories open up new possibilities for action for supervisees.

To help supervisees develop a sense of the structure of "good stories," White (1989/1990) has developed an exercise that asks a supervision group to select a novel to read. After everyone has had time to read the novel, the group meets to discuss various aspects of their experience with the story. The discussions focus on how the reader became engaged in the story, the different understandings supervisees formed about the story and its characters, how the structure of the story contributed to the reader's experience of the story, and other ideas about the literary merit of the novel.

As indicated earlier, many postmodern supervisors attempt to help supervisees appreciate multiple possibilities and understandings of clients' situations. We try to ask questions, such as the following, that do not have preconceived answers.

- What do you think the client(s)' understanding is?

- What understandings do you have?
- What possible new understandings might be useful?
- What other questions could have been asked that you didn't ask?

Ideas are presented to supervisees in tentative language that allows for the inclusion of other ideas. Live supervision, teams, and group supervision provide the supervisor with multiple voices and points of view that help reduce the perceived differences in expertise and "power." We ask, "What is there about this family, or individual, that is different from what the research and theories tell us?" We work with supervisees to do resource-focused assessments, identifying strengths and assets rather than deficits. We ask about what has been successful for clients as well as what has been successful for supervisees.

We ask questions of supervisees about the context of the therapy that supervisees are providing. We also ask about the clients' socioeconomic situation, and ask about the constraints on possibilities provided by the treatment environment. We ask about these things to help supervisees become sensitized to the contextual influences on therapy and the perceptions of the problem that can be generated. We also encourage supervisees to become sensitive to their own expectations regarding effective therapy and how these views also constrain the generation of other possibilities.

To help supervisees look at conventional diagnostic and casework material from a narrative perspective, it is sometimes helpful for the supervisor to ask, "What is the diagnostic *rumor* that is being spread about this client?" Or "What rumors have you heard from other mental health professionals about this client?" Asking about "factual" information in this way sometimes helps supervisees see that conventional psychiatric explanations are only one source of information about clients, and occupy no privileged status.

AVOIDING CONSTRAINTS TO EFFECTIVE SUPERVISION

Supervision models that highly prize developmental stages in the understanding of the supervision process may be a poor fit with postmodern ideas. Although some postmodern supervisors speak about "beginning supervisees" and "experienced supervisees," they are less likely to adhere to strict models of supervisee development like those described by Stoltenberg and his colleagues (Loganbill, Hardy, & Delworth, 1982; Stoltenberg & Delworth, 1988). Postmodern supervisors may feel constrained by the preexisting assumptions about what supervisees at one particular stage or another might be capable or incapable of doing. At least one empirical study (Fisher, 1989) concludes that trainee level of development may not determine how supervision is actually conducted. Further, level of development was not related to supervisees' perceptions of helpful supervisory behaviors.

Anderson and Swim (1994) attest to the implicit variability and differential categories of supervisees when they write:

> We prefer diverse, heterogeneous learning systems. . . . The ideal learning group would be composed of participants who bring a broad range of experiences, and represent a variety of work settings, professional experience levels, degrees, personal life experience, cultures, and races (p. 149).

It is clear, however, that the value of understandings of different levels, or categories, is that it enriches the diversity of voices and points of view in the supervision group. The modernist practice of "staging" supervisees is to keep them grouped, which may limit an expansion of understandings.

Models that advocate the specification of sets of skills that supervisees should demonstrate (*cf.* Shaw & Dobson, 1988) can be troublesome to some postmodern supervisors because, in such models, the tendency in the supervision is to focus on skill development. The notion of "skill" carries with it the implication of expertise in ways that postmodern supervisors do not always find useful. An attempt to specify, from a postmodern perspective, useful skills for supervisees to demonstrate has been made by Flemons and his colleagues (Flemons, Green, & Rambo, 1996). Their intent is to provide supervisors a rationale for evaluating the progress of the supervisee, not to specify a curriculum.

Another supervisory expectation, which is not necessary from a postmodern perspective, is one that requires the supervisee to claim to adhere to the same theoretical school of thought as the supervisor. The aim of a postmodern supervisor is similar to the postmodern therapist in this regard: the opening up of new possibilities within the other's worldview. With this in mind, it becomes explicit that supervisors and supervisees will always have differences in points of view. It is more apparent when supervisees and supervisors conduct therapy from different models. In any supervisory context, the nature of the contract must be made explicit. White (1989/1990) argues that the degree of comfort experienced by the supervisee depends on how well the expectations of all of the participants are met. He recommends that all supervisees be provided sufficient information to make an informed choice about the supervisory relationship. There are supervision contexts where supervisees attempt to learn a particular approach to therapy and want supervisors to assist in the attainment of that goal. In other contexts, supervisees are not interested in learning to do therapy from the supervisor's theoretical orientation. Postmodern supervisors work within the contract and theoretical models that supervisees prefer.

To some extent, many postmodern supervisors would hold little sacred. To assist on absolutes would contradict the spirit of the postmodern supervisory conversation. Even so, there are pragmatic aspects of the relationship that are usually maintained as inviolate. Supervisors must prepare supervisees for a collaborative approach to supervision. Supervisees must provide at least implicit consent to participate in the supervisory process and be open to entertaining new ideas and practicing new behaviors. Supervisors are obliged to keep the conversational space open for all ideas. Supervisors must have access to information to evaluate supervisees' progress. For example, it is possible that a supervisee who was unwilling to permit live or taped supervision might still be operating under an "evaluative" model of supervision, expecting that the supervisor was going to use the material to negatively evaluate the supervisee.

Often writers propose an isomorphism between therapy and supervision. To the extent both practices aim at changing behaviors and/or cognitive operations, there are similarities, but not necessarily isomorphic processes. *Supervision is not therapy.* Although some postmodern supervisors employ specific training exercises with their supervisees that can also be used with clients (Parry & Doan, 1994; Roberts, 1994), different assumptions about the goals of the relationship are made. In therapy, postmodern therapists assume that clients are experts on their lives. In supervision, it is not necessarily the case that supervisees are experts on therapy. Supervisors from postmodern perspectives tend to focus the content of supervision on the therapeutic relationship the supervisee has with the client. It is helpful as well for the supervisor to make the boundaries of the supervisory relationship explicit with supervisees. Further, the frequent use of teams in postmodern therapies helps deter discussion of personal issues in psychotherapy.

Supervisors are acutely aware of what social psychologists call the fundamental attribution error—"the tendency to overestimate the importance of personality or dispositional factors relative to situational or environmental influences when describing and explaining . . . behavior" (Aronson, 1995, p. 159). Postmodern supervisors are inclined to focus more on contextual variables that are unique to the therapeutic and supervisory contexts than on personal issues of the supervisee. The personal issues of the supervisee addressed in supervision are those that are unmistakably impinging directly on the supervisee's ability to provide effective therapy.

It is certainly the case that if a supervisee's personal issues are interfering with therapy, or if a supervisee requests personal psychotherapy, a referral to a third party would be appropriate. If the supervisee seems unable to avoid conceptualizing client problems in ways that pathologize clients, or demonstrates little potential for generating alternate possibilities, personal therapy might be seen as helpful if attempts to resolve this issue had not been successful—for instance, if a supervisee were to indicate that personal problems, biases, and so on were persistently interfering with their clinical work.

Supervisors often find that focusing on personal issues shuts down discussions and restricts the space for future conversations. Supervisory modalities that emphasize the personal growth of the supervisee through personal therapeutic experiences (*cf.* Watson, 1993) are less evident in postmodern supervision. Professional, and perhaps personal growth, are often seen as inevitable outcomes of successful postmodern supervisory experiences.

Supervisors have clinical, ethical, and legal responsibilities to clients, which may take precedence over supervisees' learning needs. There is no doubt that there are competing goals in the supervisory context, however, the supervisory relationship should also be explicit with the client. Postmodern supervisors often avoid the practice of assigning cases to supervisees based on supervisees' purported level of expertise. Likewise, cases are rarely assigned

on the basis of a presumed diagnosis or problem brought by clients. This practice may set up expectations about the assets and limitations of both supervisees and clients.

SUCCESSFUL POSTMODERN SUPERVISION

Changes in supervisees are seen as resulting from changes in the internal, cognitive processes that are applied to therapy, and are evident in behavioral changes demonstrated by supervisees. It has long been recognized that lasting cognitive changes are most effectively promoted with noncoercive direction: "Allowing people the opportunity to construct their own internal justification can be a large step toward helping them develop a permanent set of values" (Aronson, 1995, p. 211). Collaborating in the generation of multiple ideas and approaches facilitates supervisees' ownership of those ideas.

Supervisees' ability to manage conversations in a therapeutic manner is a broad goal of postmodern supervision. A postmodern supervisor strives to enhance the supervisee's ability to generate new information (Anderson & Swim, 1994; Davis et al., 1994; Shilts & Aronson, 1993; Thomas, 1994). Although the focus is generally on the client, supervisees are frequently also encouraged to generate new information and new views about themselves and their competencies (Parry & Doan, 1994; Roberts, 1994; White, 1989, 1990). Supervisees are expected to spend more time in their therapeutic interactions with clients in a "not knowing" position. A postmodern supervisor looks for supervisees to maintain a position of curiosity (Cecchin, 1987) rather than a noncollaborative, "expert," stance with clients. It is believed such changes promote interactions in such a way that clients identify strengths and competencies and develop more generative understanding of themselves and their situations.

From the supervisor's standpoint, supervision can be seen as successful if supervisees are able to articulate their work or plan for therapy in a way that involves more options for continuing and expanding possibilities with clients. If supervisees feel confounded initially, then leave unstuck, with multiple new understandings of the client system, the supervision has been successful. Often supervisees will have difficulty understanding or listening to a particular person in the client system. If the supervisee can come to a new, nonpejorative understanding of the least-liked person in the system, supervision has been successful.

REFERENCES

Aderman, J., & Russell, T. (1990). A constructivist approach to working with abusive and neglectful parents. *Family Systems Medicine, 8*, 241–250.

Allen, J. (1993). The constructivist paradigm: Values and ethics. In J. Laird (Ed.), *Revisioning social work education: A social constructionist approach* (pp. 31–54). New York: Haworth Press.

Amundson, J., Stewart, K., & Parry, A. (1994). Whither narrative? The danger of getting it right. *Journal of Marital and Family Therapy, 20*, 83–88.

Andersen, T. (1987). The reflecting team: Dialogue and meta-dialogue in clinical work. *Family Process, 26*, 415–428.

Anderson, H. (1992a). Languaging systems consultation. Paper presented at the Annual Conference of the American Association for Marriage and Family Therapy, Dallas, October.

Anderson, H. (1992b). Therapeutic impasses: A breakdown in conversation. (Unpublished manuscript: Houston-Galveston Institute.)

Anderson, H., & Goolishian, H. (1988). Human systems as linguistic systems: Preliminary and evolving ideas about the implications for clinical theory. *Family Process, 27*, 371–393.

Anderson, H., & Goolishian, H. (1990). Beyond cybernetics: Comments on Atkinson and Heath's "Further thoughts on second-order family therapy." *Family Process, 29*, 157–163.

Anderson, H., & Goolishian, H. (1992). The client is the expert: A not-knowing approach to therapy. In S.

McNamee & K. Gergen (Eds.), *Therapy as social construction: Inquiries in social construction* (pp. 25–39). London: Sage Publications.

Anderson, H., & Rambo, A. (1988). An experiment in systemic family therapy training: A trainer and trainee perspective. *Journal of Strategic and Systemic Therapies, 7*, 54–70.

Anderson, H., & Swim, S. (1993). Learning as collaborative conversation combining the student's and teacher's expertise. *Human Systems: The Journal of Systemic Consultation and Management, 4*, 145–160.

Anderson, H., & Swim, S. (1994). Supervision as collaborative conversation: Connecting the voices of supervisor and supervisee. (Unpublished manuscript, Houston-Galveston Institute.)

Aronson, E. (1995). *The social animal*, 7th ed. New York: W. H. Freeman.

Atkinson, B. (1992). Aesthetics and pragmatics of family therapy revisited. *Journal of Marital and Family Therapy, 18*, 389–393.

Atkinson, B. (1993). Hierarchy: The imbalance of risk. Special section: Four views on the construct of hierarchy. *Family Process, 32*, 167–170.

Bernstein, R., Brown, E., & Ferrier, M. (1984). A model for collaborative team processing in brief systemic family therapy. *Journal of Marital and Family Therapy, 10*, 151–156.

Biever, J., & Gardner, G. (1995). The use of reflecting teams in social constructionist training. *Journal of Systemic Therapies, 14*, 47–56.

Bobele, M., Chenail, R., Douthit, P., Green, S., & Stulberg, T. (1989). An interacting team model. *Zietschrift für Systemische Therapie, 3*, 146–153.

Bobele, M., Gardner, G., & Biever, J. (1995). Supervision as social construction. *Journal of Systemic Therapies, 14*, 14–25.

Cade, B., Speed, B., & Seligman, P. (1986). Working in teams: The pros and cons. Special Issue: Supervision and training: Models, dilemmas, and challenges. *Clinical Supervisor, 4*, 105–117.

Cecchin, G. (1987). Hypothesizing, circularity, and neutrality revisited: An invitation to curiosity. *Family Process, 26*, 405–413.

Cecchin, G. (1992). Constructing therapeutic possibilities. In S. McNamee & K. Gergen (Eds.), *Therapy as social construction. Inquiries in social construction* (pp. 86–95). London: Sage Publications.

Cecchin, G., Lane, G., & Ray, W. (1993). From strategizing to nonintervention: Toward irreverence in systemic practice. *Journal of Marital and Family Therapy, 19,* 125–136.

Coale, H. (1992). The constructionist emphasis on language: A critical conversation. *Journal of Strategic and Systemic Therapies, 11,* 12–26.

Davis, J., Gorman, P., & Lockerman, G. (1994). Collaborative supervision in a hierarchical world: Pragmatics of narrative supervision. Paper presented at the Annual Conference of the American Association for Marriage and Family Therapy, Chicago, October.

Efran, J., & Clarfield, L. (1992). Constructionist therapy: Sense and nonsense. In S. McNamee & K. Gergen (Eds.), *Therapy as social construction: Inquiries in social construction* (pp. 200–217). London: Sage Publications.

Feixas, G. (1990). Approaching the individual, approaching the system: A constructivist model for integrative psychotherapy. *Journal of Family Psychology, 4,* 4–35.

Ferrier, M. (1984). Teamwork: Process, problems, and perspectives. *Journal of Strategic and Systemic Therapies, 3,* 17–23.

Fish, V. (1993). Poststructuralism in family therapy: Interrogating the narrative/conversational mode. *Journal of Marital and Family Therapy, 19,* 221–232.

Fisher, B. (1989). Differences between supervision of beginning and advanced therapists: Hogan's hypothesis empirically revisited. *Clinical Supervisor, 7,* 57–74.

Flemons, D., Green, S., & Rambo, A. (1996). Evaluating therapy: A justification and a scheme. *Family Process.*

Gergen, K. (1985). The social constructionist movement in modern psychology. *American Psychologist, 40,* 266–275.

Goolishian, H., & Anderson, H. (1992). Strategy and intervention versus nonintervention: A matter of theory? *Journal of Marital and Family Therapy, 18,* 5–15.

Green, R., & Herget, M. (1989a). Outcomes of systemic/strategic team consultation: I. Overview and one-month results. *Family Process, 28,* 37–58.

Green, R., & Herget, M. (1989b). Outcomes of systemic/strategic team consultation: II. Three-year follow-up and a theory of "emergent design." *Family Process, 28,* 419–437.

Green, R., & Herget, M. (1991). Outcomes of systemic/strategic team consultation: III. The importance of therapist warmth and active structuring. *Family Process, 30,* 321–336.

Griffith, J., & Griffith, M. (1992). Speaking the unspeakable: Use of the reflecting position in therapies for somatic symptoms. *Family Systems Medicine, 10,* 41–51.

Griffith, J., Griffith, M., Krejmas, N., McLain, M., et al. (1992). Reflecting team consultations and their impact upon family therapy for somatic symptoms as coded by Structural Analysis of Social Behavior (SASB). *Family Systems Medicine, 10,* 53–58.

Hardy, K. (1993). Live supervision in the postmodern era of family therapy. Issues, reflections, and questions. *Contemporary Family Therapy: An International Journal, 15,* 9–20.

Hoffman, L. (1991). A reflexive stance for family therapy. *Journal of Strategic and Systemic Therapies, 10,* 4–17.

Hoyt, M. (Ed.). (1994). *Constructive therapies.* New York: Guilford Press.

Kaplan, R. (1987). The current use of live supervision within marriage and family therapy training programs. *Clinical Supervisor, 5,* 43–52.

Kaslow, F. (1981). Group therapy with couples in conflict: Is more better? *Psychotherapy Theory, Research and Practice, 18,* 516–524.

Lewis, W., & Rohrbaugh, M. (1989). Live supervision by family therapists: A Virginia survey. *Journal of Marital and Family Therapy, 15,* 323–326.

Loganbill, C., Hardy, E., & Delworth, U. (1982). Supervision: A conceptual model. *The Counseling Psychologist, 10,* 3–42.

McKenzie, P., Atkinson, B., Quinn, W., & Heath, A. (1986). Training and supervision in marriage and family therapy: A national survey. *American Journal of Family Therapy, 14,* 293–303.

McNamee, S., & Gergen, K. (1992). *Therapy as social construction: Inquiries in social construction.* London: Sage Publications.

Miller, D., & Lax, W. (1988). Interrupting deadly struggles: A reflecting team model for working with. *Strategic and Systemic Therapies, 7,* 16–22.

Neimeyer, R. (1993). Constructivist psychotherapy. In K. Kuehlwein & H. Rosen (Eds.), *Cognitive therapies in action: Evolving innovative practice* (pp. 268–300). San Francisco: Jossey-Bass.

Owen, I. (1992). Applying social constructionism to psychotherapy. *Counseling Psychology Quarterly, 5,* 385–402.

Parry, A., & Doan, R. (1994). *Story re-visions: Narrative therapy in the postmodern world.* New York: Guilford Press.

Polkinghorne, D. (1992). Postmodern epistemology of practice. In S. Kvale (Ed.), *Psychology and postmodernism: Inquiries in social construction* (pp. 146–165). London: Sage Publications.

Prest, L., Darden, E., & Keller, J. (1990). "The fly on the wall" reflecting team supervision. *Journal of Marital and Family Therapy, 16,* 265–273.

Quinn, W., Atkinson, B., & Hood, C. (1985). The stuck-case clinic as a group supervision model. *Journal of Marital and Family Therapy, 11,* 67–73.

Rambo, A. (1989). Cinderella revisited. *Journal of Marital and Family Therapy, 15,* 91–93.

Roberts, J. (1994). *Tales and transformations.* New York: W. W. Norton.

Saleebey, D. (1994). Culture, theory, and narrative: The intersection of meanings in practice. *Social Work, 39,* 351–359.

Shaw, B., & Dobson, K. (1988). Competency judgments in the training and evaluation of psychotherapists. *Journal of Consulting and Clinical Psychology, 56,* 666–672.

Shilts, L., & Aronson, J. (1993). Circular hearing: Working through the muddles of supervision. *Journal of Family Psychotherapy, 4,* 57–67.

Sluzki, C. (1992). Transformations: A blueprint for narrative changes in therapy. *Family Process, 31,* 217–230.

Stewart, K. (1994). Postmodernism and supervision. *Supervision Bulletin, 7,* 6.

Stoltenberg, C., & Delworth, U. (1988). *Supervising counselors and therapists: A developmental approach.* San Francisco: Jossey-Bass.

Thomas, F. (1994). Solution-oriented supervision: The coaxing of expertise. *The Family Journal: Counseling and Therapy for Couples and Families, 2,* 11–18.

Turner, J., & Fine, M. (1995). Postmodern evaluation in family therapy supervision. *Journal of Systemic Therapies, 14,* 57–69.

Watson, M. (1993). Supervising the person of the therapist: Issues, challenges and dilemmas. Special Issue: Critical issues in marital and family therapy education. *Contemporary Family Therapy: An International Journal, 15,* 21–31.

Weingarten, K. (1991). The discourses of intimacy: Adding a social constructionist and feminist view. *Family Process, 30,* 285–305.

West, J., Bubenzer, D., & Zarski, J. (1989). Live supervision in family therapy: An interview with Barbara Okun and Fred Piercy. *Counselor Education and Supervision, 29,* 25–34.

White, M. (1986). Negative explanation, restraint, and double description: A template for family therapy. *Family Process, 25,* 169–184.

White, M. (1989/1990). Family therapy training and supervision in a world of experience and narrative. *Dulwich Centre Newsletter, Summer,* 27–38.

White, M., & Epston, D. (1990). *Narrative means to therapeutic ends.* New York: W. W. Norton.

Young, J., Perlesz, A., Paterson, R., O'Hanlon, B., et al. (1989). The reflecting team process in training. *Australian and New Zealand Journal of Family Therapy, 10,* 69–74.

16

Collaborative Supervision
Minding the Power

Marshall Fine and Jean Turner

TWENTY YEARS AGO THIS DREAM:
I was standing in front of my first family therapy supervisor. I knew nothing and was anxious to soak up knowledge and rush in any stated direction. I looked sheepish as she informed me that as my supervisor she had no desire to feed me answers or to direct my actions. Rather, she preferred to use both of our knowledges and experiences in the supervision of my work with clients. I panicked, "I have nothing to offer! I will be left awash! Families will be depending on what I know to be an empty vessel." I broke into a sweat, gathered what little energy I had left, and fled from the office into a state of confused awakedness. Accountancy sounded like a good alternate career path!

One could speculate that there exists a perfectly collaborative supervisor who stands out among (and above) the others. This supervisor has a constant concern for issues of equality, an unlimited capacity for mutual engagement, and an absolute tolerance for diversity of view. Naturally, there is no such person. Supervision is practiced along a continuum with respect to

Note: This chapter is based on an equal sharing of ideas—mainly, Marshall drafted the text and Jean edited and commented on the drafts.

collaborative endeavors, regardless of the supervisor's favored approach. Over the past decade, since *collaboration* has increasingly come into favor, the term has been used idiosyncratically by supervisors of different persuasions (e.g., Anderson & Swim, 1996; White, 1989/90). In our work we find the following definition serves as a useful guide for distinguishing the various threads in the strand of collaborative practice—collaborative supervision in marriage and family therapy (MFT) involves:

> *Face-to-face ongoing dialogues between a supervisor and therapist where goodwill prevails; the learning is mutual and intense; the power relations are transparent; and the emphasis is on meeting standards of the profession, ensuring the well-being of clients served by the supervisory participants.*

In this chapter, we refer to *supervision* in the legitimizing sense: promoting standardization within the profession; ensuring conformity to the goals and ethical practices; and transmitting skills, knowledge, and attitudes of the profession to the therapist (Bernard & Goodyear, 1992). These goals of legitimization traditionally have been advanced by specific activities of supervisors in unidirectional or hierarchical ways (Hardy, 1993; Hart, 1982). In this traditional framework, the supervisor is viewed as possessing particular specialized skills and knowledges that are "superior" to those persons "under" supervision (Beavers, 1986; Piercy & Sprenkle, 1986). The supervisor is the master therapist—the person with the answers, with the vision, and with the rightful power to normalize and discipline. In contrast, thinking critically about collaborative supervision has led us to pay particular attention to issues of leveling hierarchy and making the power relations between supervisor and therapist transparent.

POWER IN SUPERVISION RELATIONSHIPS

In our view collaboration does not imply equality of input or status in working together, rather it means "to work with" (Anderson & Roberts, 1993). Power is an ever-present ingredient of all relationships, whether they are collaborative or noncollaborative (Foucault, 1979). Supervisory relationships can be more or less level but never flat. The central question, therefore, is: *How* are power relations constructed and played out between the supervisory relationship participants?

Evaluation

All supervisors, regardless of their particular point of view, examine therapists' work in order to ensure conformity to professional standards. The idea of examination as a function of supervision is not foreign (Keller & Protinsky, 1986). Examination involves two main modern practices of power, hierarchical observation and normalizing judgment (Foucault, 1979). *Hierarchical observation* involves the surveillance, or "looking over" by the person with authorized power (the supervisor) of the person seeking legitimization (the therapist) in an effort to control the knowledge and practice of the therapist so that these meet the essential norms of the profession. The power of the su-

pervisor's "observing gaze" is enhanced to the extent that (1) the "gaze" is perceived by the therapist to be constant and encompassing of all clinical work, and (2) the therapist does not know when or how the supervisor is observing. For example, when the supervisor does not clearly indicate to the therapist *how* extensively she or he will be reviewing client records or *when* she or he might be observing from behind the mirror, the therapist is likely to feel the effects of the supervisor's power even more and begin to self-supervise in accordance with the supervisor's expectations.

Normalizing judgments involve ranking and classifying individuals with respect to how well or poorly they have met the normative expectations of those in power. These judgments are enacted through "micro-penalties" for the less powerful that are used as disciplinary measures when standards are not met. In the context of MFT supervision, for example, a supervisor may bring to the attention of a therapist an occasion when she or he acted in an unprofessional way with a client. The supervisor does this to provide a warning that similar behavior in the future may have more serious consequences.

In the examination or evaluation process, ever-present observation and standard-setting judgments are combined into the "normalizing gaze" (Foucault, 1979), which typically involves documentation—supervisors write texts (reports) that describe their observations and classifying judgments of therapists. The "power of writing" is that a classifying report constitutes the person who is the subject of the documentation. Reports provide a more or less permanent trail of evidence that then risks becoming the dominant or unchangeable description that the less powerful person may have difficulty refuting. In this way, the writer of the examination texts becomes a partial "author" of the subject's life and personhood (White, 1989/90). The power of supervisors and of evaluation reports are heightened when

(1) the standards to be met are less visible and explicit, and (2) the therapist has little input into the evaluation process and final documentation.

Position Power and Knowledge Power

More collaborative supervisors who desire to work *with* rather than *over and above* have been critiqued for what some see as their naive notions regarding the possibility of leveling the hierarchy (Efran & Clarfield, 1992; Golann, 1988). Some supervisors find the leveling idea foolish, if not intolerable (Minuchin, 1993). We believe there, in fact, may be an inherent contradiction in the notion of collaborative supervision (Fine, 1993; Turner & Fine, 1996). However, this contradiction may dissolve when the location of different types of power is identified.

Any supervisor is, by definition, in a more powerful position through legitimization by a profession. This kind of supervisory *position power* is real; acting on it is consequential for the person who is supervised. It is necessary because someone must be held ethically responsible for what happens in therapy and supervision so that the welfare of clients is protected (Hardy, 1993). When we, as more collaborative supervisors, speak of leveling the hierarchy, it is not based on this particular power dimension; we always see ourselves in a more powerful position.

A second type of power is exercised when a person is perceived to have specialized and valued knowledge. This *knowledge power* dimension is the one we perceive to be more open to question and to a leveling between supervisor and therapist. Our social constructionist stance leads us to view knowledge as partial, locally situated, socially constructed and, therefore, eminently mutable (see Bobele, Gardner, & Biever, Chapter 15; Gergen, 1994). This represents a paradigm shift from the modernist notion that there is foundational knowledge that applies across contexts and forms a base to which new information is added in a cumulative fashion leading eventually to a truthful representation of reality. From a modernist perspective, supervisors should be teaching therapists practices originating from expert therapists who have garnered renown for their effective interventions. Indeed, Haley (1993) is concerned that there are too many supervisors who do not have knowledge to help therapists change their clients.

As postmodernists and constructionists, we take a different position. We are not anti-knowledge, but we do question the positivist belief in foundational or universal "truth." This position is problematic because it ignores the contexts, which provide unequal constraints and opportunities, within which clients, as well as therapists, are embedded. As others have pointed out, these include differences related to social class, culture, gender, race, and so on (see, for example, Goldner, 1993; Hare-Mustin, 1994; Kliman, 1994; Tamasese & Waldegrave, 1993; Wark, 1994). Further, we challenge the notion of scientific objectivity that underlies so-called expert knowledge because it obfuscates the always present but not evident political intentions of those who are involved in knowledge production. In contrast, taking a "critical" or power analytic position with respect to knowledge increases the choice of those in less powerful positions by making the politics transparent. In our work as supervisors, it is important to ask ourselves and others the following knowledge/power questions:

- *Whose* knowledge is being privileged?
- *How/when/where* was it generated?
- *What does it leave unsaid?*

Therapist Power

When the bright light of the more powerful is shining directly in our eyes, we can be blinded to our own power. Averting one's gaze, the transfixion created by the beam softens and we can observe the light play or see subtleties of gradation. It is erroneous to think that therapists are merely passive objects or "docile bodies" under the normalizing gaze of the supervisor (McNay, 1992). In fact, all relations of power are unstable and changeable. Each person has a capacity to *self-reflect* (constitute their own personhood) even in the face of powerful others, and then to act on their moral preferences.

At the interpersonal level, those with less power have an opportunity to influence any set of relations as long as they remain in dialogue with the more powerful (Marlaire & Maynard, 1993). We view supervision conversations as much more than vehicles for supervisors to reinforce their power. They also expose the supervisor's preferred discourse and, in so doing, open up possibilities for the therapist to protest, even if silently in less collaborative relationships. Finally, at the institutional level, therapists are accorded rights of appeal by the certifying association or regulatory body; these protect them from unfair supervisory practices.

COLLABORATIVE ENVIRONMENT: A VENTURE IN GOODWILL

Looking at supervision relationships only through the lens of power is narrow and misleading. It diminishes other elements and distorts the idiosyncratic, intersubjective aspects that are part of all ongoing relationships. We want to underline here the human connection entailed in working together as supervisor and therapist. This connectedness is enhanced by the focus of providing good service to clients. The rest we consider to be part of an environment of goodwill.

We believe it is the continual nurturing of goodwill that leads to generative and beneficial

supervision for all participants, including clients. Goodwill and collaboration cannot develop unless all participants feel *relatively* free and willing to voice their ideas and opinions. We emphasize relatively because, unlike Habermas (1987), we do not envision the possibility of an ideal speech situation where there is "wholly uncoerced discussion among completely free and equal human agents" (Greene, 1994, p. 443). We suspect that the extent to which an individual expresses an opinion is mediated by the amount of power located within the context and by the sense of trust the therapist and supervisor each have in the words and actions of the other. Naturally, goodwill is not unique to collaborative supervision. Most forms of supervision depend to some extent on goodwill. However, as we shall now detail, the more leveled nature of the collaborative relationship appears to require a demonstration of trust and reciprocity that goes beyond the traditional, more unidirectional supervisory relationship.

COLLABORATIVE PRACTICES

Transparency: Deconstructing the Power Relations of Supervision

Being transparent about the nature and impact of power within the supervision context is inherent to the work we do (Turner & Fine, 1996). This "reciprocal visibility" deemphasizes the power of hierarchical observation in that supervisor and therapist are able to observe each other work in their respective roles. We believe the more hidden and mystical power practices are, the more uncertainty there is for the supervised therapists and the less free they feel to engage in an open dialogue. One of our regular practices in the beginning of supervision is to have therapists hear us acknowledge our power—its jurisdiction, its limits within the entire supervision system, and how we see it entering the specific relationship we hope to develop with them. Making visible the power relations makes it clear that power in the supervision relationship is a topic that is open for dialogue. We introduce the topic of power by situating ourselves with respect to locations within the territory of the supervision system. This system includes, at a minimum, the clients, the therapist, the clinical setting, the supervisor, and the professional association. At each location in the supervision system, there are socially constructed *realities*—negotiated meanings and shared habits arrived at through dialogues between participants (Turner & Fine, 1996). Naming these reality sets identifies the influences that affect the decisions made in supervision. The reality sets are outlined briefly in the following paragraphs.

The ethical standards and criteria for belonging to the professional association, such as the American Association for Marriage and Family Therapy (AAMFT), we call *centrally situated realities*. This reality set is co-constructed by important members of an association. Centrally situated reality sets are the least flexible and most removed from individual supervisors and therapists; they are overarching in the sense that they sit at the top of the professional hierarchy. If a therapist seriously abrogates the guidelines for behavior that represent the centrally situated reality, such as the AAMFT Code of Ethics, supervisors are obliged to close the association gate and deter that therapist from entering the inner circle of legitimated professionals. Although there may be occasional challenges from individual members that association standards are no longer fair, they are slow to change.

Locally situated realities develop through dialogues between supervisors practicing in any given geographical location; for example, the supervisors in a training program or in a local professional chapter that meets frequently. The locally situated realities emerging from their dialogues will, of necessity, have elements that are congruent with the centrally situated real-

ity set. They will also include agreements and habits that are in line with the particular constraints and opportunities of the local context. For example, the four supervisors within the MFT training program where we work tend to practice within social constructionist, narrative, and feminist frameworks. Our preferences are conveyed to the therapists we supervise who are invited to at least attempt some of the practices associated with these approaches. If supervisors deviate at some point from the locally situated group consensus, there may be tension or conflict, but their legitimate status within the profession will not be affected as long as the new approach is within the professional and ethical parameters of the centrally situated reality. On the other hand, a therapist who chooses not to adhere to the joint preferences of the group of supervisors may experience more difficulty, depending on the local supervisors. In cases of serious conflict between program supervisors and a particular therapist-in-training, the therapist's future status might be in jeopardy. This scenario is less consequential for the therapist who is receiving private postgraduate supervision. This therapist can choose a supervisor who works in a preferred way, and the therapist is usually an independent, responsible professional already practicing from recognized approaches within the profession.

Interpersonally situated realities arise from the ongoing conversation and interaction between the supervisor and therapist. These are the most flexible and idiosyncratic realities, given that they typically involve only a few people who, through lengthy and intimate dialogue, develop an agreed-on and unique set of meanings/habits. Here the therapist has the greatest opportunity to influence how supervision is charted, particularly within a collaborative supervision environment. One cannot, for example, phone professional association executives and expect them to change, even just a tiny bit, one of their criteria on certification requirements because one therapist or supervisor would like it so. However, a therapist can attempt to convince a supervisor to make a change in the way supervision is conducted, and even in the means by which the therapist is evaluated.

Personally situated realities spring from internal conversations regarding personal ethical meanings and practices that are connected to the integrity of the individual supervisor or therapist—sets of meanings and habits that each person holds dear. These reality sets are unique because they emerge in the context of one's relationship with self. They may supersede any other reality set if a therapist's or supervisor's personal code of conduct is threatened. For example, a therapist might wish to use a technique with a client that is perfectly acceptable to the centrally situated reality, but is against the supervisor's "ethics of self." Personally situated realities may have been evoked for some supervisors concerned about the gender inequity inherent in many family therapy approaches prior to the feminist critique.

Consumer situated realities may develop when there is dialogue among the therapists in supervision with a particular supervisor, and when clients who are in therapy with a supervised therapist provide feedback to the therapist. Consumer situated realities among therapists-in-supervision with the same supervisor are most likely to develop in training and education programs where the therapists engage in dialogue as a group separately from their supervisors. When consumer situated realities do emerge among therapists, there is a possibility that by sheer number they gain power in voicing their opinions to the supervisor. Clients of therapists-in-supervision can also influence the supervision process (Woodruff, 1993). However, given confidentiality guidelines, they would rarely have the opportunity to dialogue with each other and develop a consensual perspective about their experiences. Feedback from individual clients about the way therapy is going is also feedback to the supervisor. As such, it is a situated reality that can influence the supervisory process and that can be used in the evaluation of therapy and supervision. Mead (1993) argues that supervision should be evaluated by all the consumers of supervision. This ensures social validity—current acceptability of the program of intervention to all consumers, both direct and indirect (therapists, clients, insurance companies, government agencies, and so on).

When we make the location of reality sets visible, we join with therapists in deconstructing the normalizing gaze of the association and demystifying all the associated power relations. In this process, the power hierarchy is tempered, not eliminated. Within a context of reciprocal visibility, both supervisor and therapist work more openly and more collaboratively while still adhering to proscriptions related to the centrally situated reality set.

Evaluation: Practices of Proportion

The power relations of the supervision relationship are most obvious in the evaluation process (Turner & Fine, 1996). The final evaluation report written by the supervisor provides the ultimate indication as to whether the evaluated therapist has conformed (become normalized) with respect to the standards of the profession. Given the potency associated with evaluation, we have developed several *practices of proportion*—practices intended to adjust for the exaggerations of the power imbalance that are out of line with more collaborative supervision, and to clarify the jurisdiction of our normalizing gaze as supervisors. We disclose, from the beginning, not only exactly what it is the therapist is being evaluated on but also how the situated realities are influencing the evaluation process. This type of ongoing transparency about power relations increases therapists' personal agency, and they seem more free to challenge our evaluative judgments. In the unlikely circumstance of a challenge developing into a dispute, therapists are enjoined to use their power by choosing a consultant to add to the supervisory discussion. This consultant, typically another supervisor, acts not as an ally with either therapist or supervisor but as a resource to both. Therapists might also choose to bring in one of their colleagues to help them express their point of view clearly and with strength.

All our written reports contain disclaimers that set boundaries around the context in which the report is written, the limits of its content, and the time-specific, partial view of the supervisor. We dialogue with therapists prior to drafting evaluative reports and refrain from adding comments that have not been discussed in supervision, or that are outside of the agreed-on criteria for evaluation. To proportion the voices of the therapist and supervisor in the written report, some evaluation reports are written in a parallel fashion, allowing supervisor and therapist to state their views in the same document. In other reports, therapists arrange for their colleagues to add to the supervisor's evaluative account. (See Turner and Fine, 1996, for a detailed account of these practices and this book's *Resource Guide* for examples of disclaimers and evaluations.)

Space Making for Circulation of Ideas

We and others (e.g., Anderson & Roberts, 1993) view all opinions, as well as our own, as having merit and deserving of attention in the supervision dialogue. We have become very conscious of the amount of dialogical space we leave for this to happen. We currently engage in space-making practices of proportion by adjusting aspects of our own supervisory voice relative to the voice of therapists.

The tone supervisors use when expressing their ideas is a key aspect of proportional spacing. If the opinions of the supervisor are stated forcefully or with great certainty, most therapists begin to devalue the alternative views

they bring to supervision and eventually shy away from expressing their differences. Everyone, but especially the supervisor, is enjoined to express their views tentatively so as to leave room for dialogue and questioning.[1]

A second important feature of proportional spacing involves *relative talk time*—the relative amount of time each participant has the floor. Working collaboratively involves reflecting internally and/or publicly to make adjustments to the apparent lack of proportionality between our supervisory voice and the voices of therapists. For example, in group supervision, we openly raise the issue of proportional talk time for discussion whenever we perceive significant differences in participation among group members. Intense mutual learning, a defining feature of collaborative supervision, requires participation in the dialogue.

Mutual Mapping of the Supervision Context

A hallmark of a collaborative stance to supervision is the ongoing discussion with therapists about the supervision process, including revisiting past supervision experiences, examining the present, planning the future, and, paradoxically, attempting to ensure that our enthusiasm for collaboration is not imposed. We are mindful of the concern expressed by some therapists that supervisors, given their preferred patterns of supervision, do not always take the idiosyncratic needs of those they supervise into account (Prest, Schindler-Zimmerman, & Sporakowski, 1992).

_____

[1] It is important to note that more collaborative supervisors are not always tentative. In upholding the centrally situated realities, we end up expressing strong opinions on matters of ethics and client welfare. In addition, there are times when a personally situated reality leads us to express our feelings passionately. In these instances, we own these views as idiosyncratic to our personal experience and invite others to own their views in the same manner.

The content, process and structure of supervision meetings are open for negotiation. We are willing to dialogue about whatever content the therapist proposes (e.g., current personal issues, family-of-origin dynamics, direct observations from a videotape), as long as the focus is related to the therapist's development as a clinician. For example, based on the preferences of supervision group members, a therapist may choose to receive feedback on their work through a reflecting team format, a supervision consultation, or a direct critique from the group.

Parallel, Emergent Goal Setting

DeChilio, Koren, and Schultze (1994) define professional/client collaboration as participants "working together in the pursuit of a common goal" (p. 565). Common goals in supervision include concern for the welfare of clients and for the therapist's ability to meet ethical and professional practice standards (Mead, 1990). However, beyond these shared primary concerns and the goal of acquiring legitimized hours that emerge from a joint connection to centrally situated realities, more collaborative supervisors leave it up to therapists to set their own supervision goals. Obviously supervisors need to understand therapists' intentions and to provide consultation on whether the goals fall within what is possible given the constraints of the supervision context. We take this therapist-centered position on goal setting regardless of the therapist's level of professional development. Therapists with little experience may have barely enough information to articulate specific goals for supervision; thus, we expect their initial goals to be less specific and more subject to later revision. By taking this therapist-driven position on goal setting, we extend the therapist's opportunities for meeting personally developed standards within the interpersonal context of the supervision system.

As supervisors we often set our own goals and "go public" about them with therapists. For example, Marshall informed therapists in group supervision that he was working on less readily backing down from ideas he thought would be useful to try out with supervision groups. This goal was not negotiated with therapists and was not necessarily of common interest. By making our own goals transparent, therapists observe us attempting to change and develop. As a result, supervision is more of a parallel than hierarchical process. We view all goals, theirs and our own, as emergent and subject to revision over time as the supervision dialogue progresses. This therapist-driven, revisionary stance to goal setting is a substantial change from traditional supervisory practice of setting goals at the beginning of supervision and basing the final evaluation on the extent to which the goals have been met.

Who Decides and When?

Questions have been posed regarding whose opinions should be given priority if the therapist and supervisor disagree during live supervision (Schwartz, Liddle, & Breunlin, 1988). Berger and Dammann (1982) suggest that the therapist should have the final decision regarding the direction of the therapy process. Hardy (1993) notes that this particular position privileges the special in-room, participatory position of the therapist over the more distant, observing position of the supervisor. Working in a more collaborative framework, we prefer that the therapist and clients together make the final decision.

The only exception to this therapist-centered practice is when we think that the direction of the therapist could be unethical or unprofessional. For example, in one live supervision situation, observers noticed that a therapist was continually, forcefully putting a client's ideas down until she eventually burst into tears. The supervisor consulted with the therapist. Although he first claimed that he did not see anything problematic about his actions, he quickly realized that he was personally reacting negatively to the client. Once having regained his self-awareness he talked with the client about each of their experiences of what had happened.

Unless therapists are outside of the professional margins, we invite them to make their own decisions irrespective of the developmental stage of the therapist. This is not always easy because we may find our own preferences more appealing. We neither hide our views and preferences from therapists nor pretend that we lack a desire to influence them. We can be quite upfront. However, we keep our opinions within a tentative, personally situated frame.

Certainty within Uncertainty

Our uncertainty about knowing is not always welcomed. Many beginning therapists, like novices in any profession, appreciate not only clarity but also some unquestionable guidelines when they are forging into new territory (Loewenstein & Reder 1982; Rosenblatt & Mayer, 1975). They particularly want to reduce uncertainty when they experience themselves as responsible for the welfare of other human beings. Rosenblatt and Mayer (1975) suggest that "trainee anxiety" stems from this kind of *amorphous supervision*. We highlight that therapists will never be left in a position of uncertainty in a client-related situation where immediate action is required. Thus, the uncertainty generated by our preference for dialogical decision making is balanced by a certainty about the supervisory relationship and our commitment to be available for dialogue.

Although uncertainty provokes some initial unease, it also encourages novice thera-

pists to think for themselves within a relatively protected environment. They progressively trust themselves and their capability to develop interesting ideas and options. They are unlikely to find themselves (as we sometimes did in the past) in the anxious situation of trying to come up with answers they think the supervisor expects or will appreciate most (Fine, 1992). Rather, therapists experience the supervisor co-laboring with them in constructing new therapy paths—everyone wearing the same yellow hard hats as they jointly forge through the brush and maneuver across uncharted ground.

Humility and Mutual Perturbation

Our constructionist perspective as supervisors induces us to take humble positions with respect to our gathered professional–personal learnings. We recognize that they are partial in two senses; they are incomplete and they are also the learnings to which we find ourselves partial. Humility seems particularly appropriate given that the knowledges and experiences we are addressing in family therapy are associated with human relationships—a domain in which we are all very active and, therefore, are partial experts.

Traditionally, novice therapists, as the persons least embedded in the family therapy culture, are expected to be the most "perturbed" by new knowledge transmitted from the supervisor because the information is "strange" (Duhl, 1983). As more collaborative supervisors, tentative about our own partial knowledge, we also expect to be perturbed by the therapist's knowledge. Part of our collaborative position is to disclose these stimulations, hopefully indicating to therapists that we are being affected by what they say—an openness others have seen as helpful for therapists-in-supervision (Bernard & Goodyear, 1992).

EFFECTIVENESS OF COLLABORATIVE SUPERVISION

Prior to ending this chapter, it is important to comment on issues of accountability/effectiveness. There are at least three questions to address. First, to what extent is the therapist acting in accordance with the principles and ethical standards of the profession to which he or she wishes to belong? This is effectiveness as viewed from the centrally situated reality set. Second, to what extent is the therapist acting in ways that suggest a correspondence to the approach preferred by the supervisor, and third, to what extent is this correspondence important? These last two questions are based more on local and interpersonal situated reality sets.

With respect to the centrally situated reality set, speculations about the effectiveness of supervision can be developed by observing how closely the therapist appears to be acting in concert with the expectations and ethical standards of the professional association from which she or he wishes to obtain certification. Specifically, are the small professional and ethical "slips" the supervisor observed, and provided corrective feedback on, at the beginning of supervision, still apparent near the end of supervision?

A more collaborative supervisor might add another aspect, not typically noted. Collaborative supervision centers around reciprocal visibility and the notion of encouraging *both* space for the ideas and feelings of therapists *and* vigilance regarding ethical and professional issues on the part of supervisors. Therefore, we include in our effectiveness evaluation observations regarding the amount of feedback we receive from therapists about our own conduct with regard to these centrally located reality sets. That is, we look for whether therapists are

themselves developing a normalizing gaze—are they noticing how we and their colleagues are behaving ethically and professionally, and calling attention to concerns they have?

The second question about effectiveness of supervision falls within the locally and interpersonally situated reality sets. Searching for congruence of approach, Milan supervisors would be interested in observing how fully therapists have integrated systemic thinking into their work (Pirrotta & Cecchin, 1988). Bowenian supervisors might be interested in looking at how well a therapist deals with emotional reactivity in therapy situations (Papero, 1988). Following this logic one might expect collaborative supervisors to look for how closely the therapist's work matches their own leveling preferences. If therapists did not match up, would this indicate "failure" or ineffective collaborative supervision? We hope not! What we do look for is the willingness of the therapist to entertain our perspective in some fashion; to engage intensively in a dialogue with us. If the therapist is not open to trying our preferred therapy practices and discovering whether they fit or not, is she or he open to using ideas related to our preferred approach to clarify and refine another set of practices? Given our appreciation of multiple perspectives, the therapist's openness would be one indication to us that the dialogue between supervisor and therapist was generative and effective.

We have spoken earlier about the importance of goodwill and the collaborative environment. If we have effectively facilitated the construction of this environment, we expect to observe that therapists, over the course of supervision, freely and frankly voice their opinions. If we have developed our own openness to diversity and the partial realities of therapists, we will find ourselves "disrupted" and feeling anxious more frequently than we did in our less collaborative days as supervisors. This disruption would be an indication of mutual, intense learning and, in our view, a sign of effective collaborative supervision.

Finally, we have no "hard measure" of effectiveness. We observe and attempt to place these observations in perspective, utilizing our experiences and preferences for supervision. However, along with most supervisors, we depend heavily on the feedback we receive from therapists. The consumer situated reality is nurtured and encouraged to be brought forth. Here we see the advantage of group supervision, where therapists have the opportunity to dialogue among themselves about the supervisor's practices. We attempt to bring forward our self-critique in the hope that by so doing therapists will feel free to express their likes and dislikes regarding our approach. However, we keep in mind that we can never predict the effect that unequal position power has on the willingness of therapists to critique our work. In light of this power difference, we invite therapists to write an evaluation of our work that we will read only after our evaluative responsibility and obligations with them are completely over. Taking the collaborative approach outlined in this paper leads us to keep in mind that, even with this safeguard and the most collaborative of environments, all accountability/effectiveness evaluations are partial and situated in the context of supervisor/therapist power relations. So, in conclusion, we don't mind the power as long as we _mind_ the power!

REFERENCES

Anderson, H., & Roberts, H. (1993). Collaborative practice within a child protection agency system. *Supervision Bulletin, 7,* 1, 6–8.

Anderson, H., & Swim, S. (1996). Supervision as collaborative conversation: Connecting the voices of supervisor and supervisee. *Journal of Systemic Therapies, 14,* 1–13.

Beavers, R. (1986). Family therapy supervision: An introduction and consumer's guide. In F. Piercy (Ed.), *Family therapy education and supervision* (pp. 15–24). New York: Haworth Press.

Berger, M., & Dammann, C. (1982). Live supervision as context, treatment, and training. *Family Process, 21,* 337–344.

Bernard, J., & Goodyear, R. (1992). *Fundamentals of clinical supervision.* Needham Heights, MA: Allyn and Bacon.

DeChilio, N., Koren, P., & Schultze, K. (1994). From paternalism to partnership: Family and professional collaboration in children's mental health. *American Journal of Orthopsychiatry, 64,* 564–576.

Duhl, B. (1983). *From the inside out and other metaphors: Creative and integrative approaches to training in systems thinking.* New York: Brunner/Mazel.

Efran, J., & Clarfield, L. (1992). Constructionist therapy: Sense and nonsense. In S. McNamee & K. Gergen (Eds.), *Therapy as social construction* (pp. 200–217). Newbury Park, CA: Sage.

Fine, M. (1992). Family therapy training: Part 2—Hypothesizing and story telling. *Journal of Family Psychotherapy, 3,* 61–79.

Fine, M. (1993). Collaboration in supervision. *Supervision Bulletin, 7,* 1, 7.

Foucault, M. (1979). *Discipline and punishment: The birth of the prison.* New York: Springer-Verlag.

Gergen, K. (1994). Exploring the postmodern: Perils or potentials? *American Psychologist, 49,* 412–416.

Golann, S. (1988). On second order family therapy. *Family Process, 27,* 51–65.

Goldner, V. (1993). Power and hierarchy: Let's talk about it! *Family Process, 32,* 157–162.

Greene, M. (1994). Epistemology and educational research: The influence of recent approaches to knowledge. In L. Darling-Hammond (Ed.), *Review of research in education,* Vol. 20 (pp. 423–464). Washington, DC: AERA.

Habermas, J. (1987). An alternative way out of the philosophy of the subject: Communicative versus subject-centered reason. In F. Lawrence (trans.), *The philosophical discourse of modernity: Twelve lectures* (pp. 294–326). Cambridge: MIT Press.

Haley, J. (1993). How to be a therapy supervisor without knowing how to change anyone. *Journal of Systemic Therapies, 4,* 41–52.

Hare-Mustin, R. (1994). Discourses in the mirrored room: A postmodern analysis of therapy. *Family Process, 33,* 19–35.

Hardy, K. (1993). Live supervision in the postmodern era of family therapy: Issues, reflections, and questions. *Contemporary Family Therapy, 15,* 9–20.

Hart, G. (1982). *The process of clinical supervision.* Baltimore: University Park Press.

Keller, J., & Protinsky, H. (1986). Family therapy supervision: An integrative model. In F. Piercy (Ed.), *Family therapy education and supervision* (pp. 83–90). New York: Haworth Press.

Kliman, J. (1994). The interweaving of gender, class, and race in family therapy. In M. Mirkin (Ed.), *Women in context: Toward a feminist reconstruction of psychotherapy* (pp. 25–47). New York: Guilford Press.

Loewenstein, S., & Reder, P. (1982). Part I: Trainees' initial reactions to live family therapy supervision. In R. Whiffen & J. Byng-Hall (Eds.), *Family therapy supervision: Recent developments in practice* (pp. 115–125). New York: Grune & Stratton.

Marlaire, C., & Maynard, D. (1993). Social problems and the organization of talk and interaction. In J. Holstein & G. Miller (Eds.), *Reconsidering social constructionism* (pp. 173–198). New York: Aldine de Gruyter.

McNay, L. (1992). *Foucault and feminism: Power, gender and the self.* Boston: Northeastern University Press.

Mead, D. (1990). *Effective supervision: A task-oriented model for the mental health professions.* New York: Brunner/Mazel.

Mead, D. (1993). Assessing supervision: Social validity and invalidity of evaluation. *Supervision Bulletin, 7,* 4, 8.

Minuchin, S. (1993). Supervisors as social engineers. Treating family therapy friendly organizations: An interview with Salvador Minuchin. *Supervision Bulletin, 7,* 1–2.

Papero, D. (1988). Training in Bowen theory. In H. Liddle, D. Breunlin, & R. Schwartz (Eds.), *Handbook of family therapy training & supervision* (pp. 62–77). New York: Guilford Press.

Piercy, F., & Sprenkle, D. (1986). Family therapy theory building: An integrative training approach. In F. Piercy (Ed.), *Family therapy education and supervision* (pp. 5–14). New York: Haworth Press.

Pirrotta, S., & Cecchin, G. (1988). The Milan training program. In H. Liddle, D. Breunlin, & R. Schwartz (Eds.), *Handbook of family therapy training and supervision* (p. 38–61). New York: Guilford Press.

Prest, L., Schindler-Zimmerman, T., & Sporakowski, M. (1992). The initial supervision session (ISSC): A guide for the MFT supervision process. *The Clinical Supervisor, 10,* 117–133.

Rosenblatt, A., & Mayer, J. (1975). Objectionable supervisory styles: Students' views. *Social Work, 20,* 184–189.

Schwartz, R., Liddle, H., & Breunlin, D. (1988). Muddles in live supervision. In H. Liddle, D. Breunlin, & R. Schwartz (Eds.), *Handbook of family therapy training and supervision* (pp. 183–193). New York: Guilford Press.

Tamasese, K., & Waldegrave, C. (1993). Cultural and gender accountability in the "just therapy" approach. *Journal of Feminist Family Therapy, 5,* 29–45.

Turner, J., & Fine, M. (1996). Postmodern evaluation in family therapy supervision. *Journal of Systemic Therapies, 14,* 57–69.

Wark, L. (1994). Client voice: A study of client couples' and their therapists' perspectives on therapeutic change. *Journal of Feminist Family Therapy, 6,* 21–39.

White, M. (1989/90). Family therapy training and supervision in a world of experience and narrative. *Dulwich Centre Newsletter, Summer,* 27–38.

Woodruff, A. (1993). Considering the "customer" in supervision. *Supervision Bulletin, 7,* 3.

17

Problems in Supervision
Lessons from Supervisees

Thomas C. Todd

The present book has been written predominantly for supervisors and contains myriad recommendations intended to prevent difficulties in supervision, including explicit contracting with the supervisee, careful recordkeeping, periodic evaluation, and ongoing feedback from supervisor to supervisee and vice versa. The need for this chapter is twofold. As might be expected, there are times when straightforward mechanisms are not sufficient to prevent significant problems from developing in the supervisory relationship, problems that are often hard to resolve. The second reason for this chapter was less obvious, at least to the author. Somewhat to my surprise, when discussing the projected supervision book with a group of student supervisees[1] what was noteworthy in my discussions with them was that they were skeptical and cautious about the degree of protection offered by the formal mechanisms mentioned here. They had little faith in some of the mechanisms, while with others they believed that the consequences of invoking them might be much more negative for the supervisees than for the supervisor.

The purpose of this chapter is to help the supervisor appreciate the position of the supervisee, particularly if the supervisee is a student, employee, or someone else for whom the stakes of supervision are high and power differences are great. Topics include how to strengthen the formal supervisory mechanisms, how to know whether they are trustworthy, and how to reassure supervisees that the supervisory process is not biased against the supervisee.

As Bernard and Goodyear (1992) note, there is little research concerning the effectiveness of supervision in mental health. Although most supervisors can offer their own personal experiences or those of colleagues to indicate that supervision can be harmful, this topic has not been analyzed systematically. Perhaps the best way to begin to approach this is by an analogy with therapy. Gurman and Kniskern (1978), who have been concerned about this phenomenon in marriage and family therapy (MFT) have offered a composite prototype of harmful relationships in MFT. When transposed to supervision, the picture is the following:

> A supervisor with poor relationship skills directly attacks "loaded" issues and defenses early in the supervision process, fails to intervene to interrupt dysfunctional patterns in the supervisee's therapy, and does little to structure supervision or support the supervisee. Such a style is apt to be most

---

[1] The author wishes to acknowledge the contributions of numerous current and former supervisees and students in writing this chapter. Unfortunately, for reasons that the chapter makes obvious, most of them were ambivalent at best about being credited by name, so all will remain anonymous.

destructive when the supervisee is inexperienced or highly anxious (Gurman & Kniskern, 1978, p. 14).

The one missing ingredient in the Gurman and Kniskern scenario, which tends to increase the risk and magnitude of harmful effects in both supervision and therapy, is having the relationship be largely involuntary: the supervisor has significant evaluatory responsibility with potentially serious consequences of an unfavorable evaluation.

Most supervisors typically seem concerned about the quality and impact of supervision—how their interventions can be more appropriate, how they can have greater impact on the supervisee and on the therapy conducted by the supervisee, and how to deal with resistance to supervision. Conversations with supervisees reveal that their concerns are often much more basic. Although supervisees worry about the quality of supervision, they are generally more concerned about how to deal with gross neglect of the supervisory contract (e.g., failure of the supervisor to meet for supervision), about sexual harassment, and about supervisory processes that are experienced as destructive or demeaning. Even in such extreme cases, supervisees are frequently reluctant to act, especially when they see themselves as having a lot to lose and when they have little faith that supervision will be improved as a result of their complaints.

WHY SUPERVISEES REMAIN SILENT

Supervisors may be surprised to learn how fearful many supervisees are about potential negative consequences of criticizing or complaining about their experiences in supervision. Sometimes the potential consequences are quite explicit and extremely significant for the supervisee, particularly for a student. A fre-

quently voiced reason for failure to complain to sponsoring academic institutions in which students are enrolled is the fear that the student will not get credit for the supervised clinical experience. Students also are concerned that they may be removed from their clinical sites and may be required to redo the supervised clinical experience, potentially losing significant time in the process. Supervisees are also worried about negative evaluations or poor grades; in the case of students, these may affect academic standing or the chances of getting a desired internship or job. In the case of employed staff members, negative evaluations can have consequences later when they are seeking raises or promotions.

Often supervisees are cautious even when such obvious consequences are not part of the structure of the supervisory relationship. For example, students may be more candid after they have received their final evaluations from clinical training sites. There may still be reluctance, however, because students recognize that their former supervisors can also be sources of employment or recommendations after graduation. Especially in these less-structured situations, students often do not fear conscious retaliation on the part of the supervisor. Much more typically, they express concerns about coloring the relationship, not wanting to be perceived as complainers or troublemakers or as being difficult to supervise.

RECOMMENDATIONS FOR BREAKING THE SILENCE

Conduct a Mutual Assessment of Potential Consequences

The concerns outlined here are difficult to dispel, and it is rarely sufficient for the supervisor to offer simple reassurance. It is necessary to hear the concerns of supervisees and help them to assess potential negative consequences accurately. Examples of positive outcomes for supervisees in similar positions are particularly helpful. For students in academic programs, it is also important to stress that time is of the essence, and that they should deal promptly with any failure to receive promised supervision or training or any other components of the supervisory and training contract. (For example, it is not unusual for clinical sites to have difficulty providing the promised number or types of clinical cases, which can be problematic for students at the end of the training period, when it will be too late to remedy the problem.) Dealing with such contractual difficulties early helps students minimize the potential for resulting loss of time and progress. If an alternative or additional site can be arranged quickly, or a change in supervisors made when needed, usually there is no significant impact on students' progress. Waiting until well after the training period has begun may result in some of the negative consequences feared by students.

Assess Institutional Support Carefully

Both supervisees and supervisors are well advised to consider whether they are likely to obtain desired institutional support for contemplated complaints or negative evaluations. Under the best of circumstances, it is difficult and unpleasant to take strong negative action such as filing a complaint of sexual harassment, recommending that an internship experience be disapproved, or recommending that a supervisee not become a Clinical Member. It is easy to imagine, however, how disappointing and frustrating it would be to take such a step only to have the institution responsible for taking action fail to take the complaint of the supervisor or supervisee seriously or fail to take action despite the merit of the complaint.

Although few of us would knowingly place ourselves in such a "no win" situation, it is not always easy to obtain an accurate assessment of the situation in advance. Supervisees sometimes have the additional worry that even asking hypothetical "what if" questions could trigger negative consequences. Official requests are uniformly answered reassuringly, but such reassurance may be misleading. Any institution will obviously claim that sexual harassment will not be tolerated and will be dealt with or that unqualified students will not be approved. Only informal confirmation from trusted sources will be of real value. Positive examples of how similar complaints have been dealt with in the past will be most reassuring.

Formal inquiries before taking action do have value, however. Most institutions have procedural guidelines for handling complaints and negative allegations. When such guidelines are not followed (e.g., by having required documentation or proceeding through proper channels), the desired outcome may be jeopardized.

Obviously there is also a cost of failing to take action in a seriously negative situation. Before either acting or deciding not to act, the supervisor or supervisee would do well to consider their projected action should the initial complaint fail to bring about the anticipated outcome. Especially if the initial institutional action seems to be self-serving or collusive, the person initiating the complaint needs to consider the merits of taking the complaint outside of the initial institutional framework, such as complaining to a licensing board or to the agency responsible for accrediting the original institution. Taking or even threatening such action can be fairly drastic, but a willingness to see the complaint through to completion often results in a positive outcome.

Ask for Feedback—And Mean It!

Chapter 2 in this book recommends that supervisors seek feedback at the end of supervision sessions to find out how helpful supervision has been and to get a sense of what factors have contributed to the success or difficulties of that particular session. When I asked a group of recent supervisees about their experience with supervisors asking for feedback, they were almost universally astonished at the idea and could rarely recall instances where they were asked explicitly for feedback on a routine basis. (They did recall instances where they had the opportunity to offer formal evaluation of supervisors at the end of a semester or supervisory experience such as a practicum.) On further discussion, we developed a crude typology of supervisors. No estimates will be made of how many supervisors fall into each category. These estimates probably differ radically depending on whether the estimate is made by a supervisee or supervisor, although the estimates of more cynical and jaded supervisors probably approach those of supervisees. Unfortunately, as this chapter discusses later, there is reason to suspect that supervisors may not be terribly accurate at categorizing themselves.

The first category, as described by supervisees who have experienced a variety of supervisors, are supervisors who never ask for feedback and who are described by supervisees as being oblivious to subtle or not so subtle nonverbal cues. At least in stereotypic form, these supervisors appear confident that they know exactly what their supervisees need and therefore have no need to ask. This also seems correlated with supervisors who have concluded that there is one ideal universal method of supervision (which of course is their own) that is equally applicable to all supervisees. As one could well imagine from this description, the experience of the supervisee is being part of a closed system. For reasons that are discussed elsewhere in this chapter, supervisees often elect to remain in this situation. There is no intention to claim here that such supervisory experiences are never helpful or are always harmful and destructive. Instead, the point being made is that supervision conducted in this way is a procrustean bed which

all supervisees are made to fit and that the experience is a "take-it-or-leave-it" experience rather than one of negotiation and fine-tuning.

Supervisors in the second category do ask for feedback from their supervisees but, at least in the eyes of the supervisees, this is done purely to receive reassurance on the adequacy of their performance as supervisors. They compare supervisors in this category to anxious sexual partners who ask "How was that for you?" but who only want to hear positive reassurance. Certainly most supervisors do not wish to be considered in this category, yet this is one of the most frequent experiences supervisees have had when the supervisor asks for feedback. For this reason, it is imperative that the supervisor ask for feedback in such a way that it is obvious that both positive and negative feedback are desired. Recommendations for how to accomplish this will be presented later.

Most healthy supervisory behavior probably falls into the third category. As supervisees describe this category, they say in essence: "The supervisor rarely asked specifically for feedback but was so attuned to the behavior of the supervisee that such questions were not necessary." Probably most supervisors would like to believe their failure to ask for explicit and detailed feedback falls into this category. They hope that they correctly perceive themselves to be sensitive supervisors who probably would not be surprised by anything the supervisee would say about the supervision experience.

The final category consists of supervisors who actually *seek* to be surprised. Rather than assuming they know what is going on in supervision or asking global evaluative questions (e.g., "Was that helpful?"), supervisors in this category ask for detailed feedback in such a way that there is a high probability that the supervisor will learn something new. Examples of detailed supervisory feedback forms are offered in this book's *Resource Guide*. Ideally the supervisor should ask for the feedback that the supervisor considers most relevant to the supervisor, given the model of supervision employed, while leaving enough questions open-ended and unstructured to allow feedback expressed from the point of view of the supervisee. Some questions may be generic (e.g., "What in today's session did you find most helpful?" "Least helpful?") although other questions may relate to specific events in a particular supervisory session (e.g., "What was your reaction when I asked you to present a hypothesis explaining the symptom?"). It is not expected that all supervisors will decide to employ written supervisory feedback forms, but it does seem useful to routinely ask for feedback at the end of each supervision session as well as in more formal periodic evaluations.

What Is the "Book" on You as a Supervisor?

As a long-time director of psychology internship programs in various settings, it has been fascinating for me to see the process whereby outgoing interns transmit the really important information to their incoming peers. New interns value this candid information much more than glossy internship brochures or pages of policies and procedures. I am often reminded of the "slam books" of my grammar school years in which the truth was told anonymously—everyone was always curious about unedited descriptions of themselves yet apprehensive about learning the truth.

One thing that seems obvious to me in this process is that variables of crucial importance to supervisees are rarely described in printed material. Supervisees would probably say that many supervisors are unaware of important characteristics of their performance as they impact on the supervisory relationship (Dellorto, 1990). Most of these characteristics have to do with personal and supervisory style ("All you will ever hear is everything you are doing

wrong." "He'll tell you are doing a great job but that is just because he doesn't want to be bothered."). Other important issues concern the content of supervision ("She's a really supportive supervisor, but she has very conservative values, so don't ever tell her anything that would offend her." "You can do things like that in therapy—for example, take crisis phone calls from patients—but don't ever tell him about it in supervision.").

Given all the difficulties with candor mentioned elsewhere in this chapter, it is obvious that getting feedback about one's personal qualities is an extremely difficult task. It is probably possible to get feedback of this sort from supervisees with whom one has a good supervisory relationship, but these are not the supervisees one typically needs to hear from. Some supervisees are willing to tell an approximation of the truth, particularly when they can attribute it to other supervisees ("I'm not scared of you, but many of the other students find you intimidating."). In a large setting with multiple supervisees, such as an MFT program, it may be possible to get group data that preserve individual supervisees anonymity. The only other avenue that shows some promise is to ask questions in areas where the supervisor already suspects the answer. This will be unsuccessful if the supervisee believes the supervisor is merely seeking reassurance, as discussed in the previous section. If the supervisor really wants to know the truth, this will probably require pressing the issue and not accepting initial reassurances at face value; for example:

SUPERVISOR: "Do you ever find my stories boring or wonder what the point is?"
THERAPIST: "Oh no!"
SUPERVISOR: "I know some of my stories are less relevant than others. How would I know that you didn't see the point?"
THERAPIST: "I would tell you."
SUPERVISOR: "I'm not sure everybody would. In group supervision I often have the feeling that some of the supervisees are spacing out."

THERAPIST: "They probably are. I know some of the students have said after supervision that they wished you would say things more directly."

Because these characteristics of the supervisor are so ingrained and characterological, the supervisor would do well to honestly ask himself or herself two questions: "Do I really want to hear the truth?" "Even if I do hear the truth, will it affect my supervisory behavior and how I approach the supervisory relationship?" Unless the supervisee believes there are positive answers to both these questions, it is unlikely that the supervisor will ever hear the truth directly. Even when there is a good relationship and the supervisee feels confident that the supervisor will listen, supervisees often are reluctant to tell the truth if it is unlikely to produce change, feeling that this would be cruel to the supervisor and serve no constructive purpose.

Be Sure Contracts Are Real

Having a formal supervisory contract has been stressed throughout this book as an important form of consumer protection (see Chapter 19). Standard supervisory contracts suffer from two major limitations:

1. Many issues that are important to the supervisee are omitted from typical contracts.
2. Supervisees do not always believe important aspects of the contracts.

In the spirit of the rest of this chapter we will attempt to look at supervisory contracts from the point of view of the supervisee.

Supervisory contracts typically are most explicit about what the supervisor expects from the supervisee. This usually includes expected preparation for the supervision sessions, issues about audio- or videotaping of sessions and of supervision, what will be covered during supervision, and so on. Supervisees often would like clearer specification of what *they* can ex-

pect from the supervisor. Some of this material is factual, such as who keeps what kinds of records, while other material may be less well defined, such as whether the supervisor will make recommendations, whether the supervisor will suggest readings, how collaborative the process will be, and so on.

Statements of expectations by themselves have limited meaning. Supervisees want to learn how seriously the expectations are meant and what actual contingencies relate to them. These issues may be addressed explicitly in a written contract, but whether or not they are in writing, the most important question is what does the *behavior* of the supervisor say? For example, the author takes seriously having supervisees prepare a written case summary for each supervision session. In the course of almost every supervisory relationship, a supervision session will occur in which the supervisee has not prepared this form, often claiming to have run out of forms or to have misplaced them. If I have additional forms readily at hand, that conveys one message, while if I say, "Don't worry about it," that conveys another. A sterner behavioral message, which rarely needs to be repeated, is to give the form to the supervisee with instructions to fill it out while I busy myself with other tasks.

Paying careful attention to behavior concerning expectations often reveals important contingencies on the supervisee's part. I am unfortunately notorious for being chronically late, especially in the early morning. In response to my guilt, I recently offered to reduce the supervisory fee because of greater than customary lateness. This prompted one of my supervisees to raise the issue of credit for the supervision time. The supervisee stated quite explicitly that getting credit for the full supervision time was more important than a reduced fee and that she was quite willing to pay the full fee if that meant getting credit for the entire time. This example raises the more general issue of verbal and behavioral messages concerning the supervisee's right to complain. Does the supervisor give a clear message that the supervisee has the right to complain about an issue such as chronic lateness? Equally important, are there indications that such feedback will make a difference in the behavior of the supervisor?

Collusion Between Supervisor and Supervisee

Thus far the material in this chapter has assumed that one or both parties in the supervision process were experiencing problems. This may create overt conflict, although many situations described in this chapter do not result in open conflict because of the fears of the supervisee. It is also possible that supervision may become problematic at the opposite extreme, in which there is too little conflict because of a pattern of collusion between supervisor and supervisee. Other examples in this chapter may seem to be examples of the supervisee colluding with the supervisor to protect the supervisor's ego or to avoid retaliation. This section deals with situations in which conflict is avoided with the participation and collusion of both supervisor and supervisee.

Reasons for Collusion

Reasons for this collusion may take a multitude of forms and may be conscious or unconscious. The chapter on privately contracted supervision (Chapter 10), discusses economic factors that may prompt one or both parties to ignore problems or difficulties such as lack of learning by the supervisee, poor clinical performance, or inadequate preparation or participation in supervision. In that chapter and elsewhere in this book, dual relationship issues, which can similarly constrain both parties from a full and honest discussion of negative factors, are considered. Other forms of collusion may also be problematic, even if they are less extreme. The supervisor can avoid bringing up conflictual material because of a personal distaste for con-

flict, which may be buttressed by a philosophical belief and a model of supervision that only emphasizes positives and collaboration. Finally, both supervisor and supervisee who share common beliefs in a particular therapy model or who have strong similarities, such as religion, ethnic background, or gender, may fail to notice issues related to these common characteristics.

Collusive "Games"

Kadushin (1968), using the framework of "games" developed by Berne (1964), lists a variety of anxiety–avoidant maneuvers adopted by supervisors and supervisees. The supervisor and supervisee, with the unspoken acquiescence of both, take on complementary roles that help both parties avoid the anxiety of a more candid and less ritualized relationship. A wide variety of such complementary roles are possible and are probably common in many supervisory relationships; these patterns are destructive when they become rigid and interfere with corrective feedback. Common examples include a supervisee who flatters the supervisor, who in turn accepts the praise; a supervisee who comes with a list of questions, playing to the strengths of the supervisor, who becomes the "answer man" (or woman); a supervisee who is extremely self-critical, coupled with reassurance from the supervisor.

Recognizing Collusion

Few supervisors would like to believe that they are guilty of such collusion, yet who among us can state with confidence that this never occurs in their supervision? I have noted typical patterns which are tipoffs that some degree of conflict avoidance is occurring. These patterns transcend particular supervision models, although some models can exacerbate these problems. These patterns have been easiest to observe in supervision-of-supervision; it is much more difficult to observe one's own patterns, although reviewing video- or audiotapes can make it much easier.

Probably the most common form of collusion, albeit a mild form, is when supervisor and supervisee focus exclusively on the clinical case. This pattern is much more obvious when they take this process a step further and spend considerable time blaming clients for lack of progress rather than taking some responsibility themselves or seeing that the lack of progress is a problem to be solved by the therapist with the aid of the supervisor. Naturally there are times when it is appropriate to discuss cases in considerable depth, but frequently it would be obvious to an outside observer that important issues in supervision are not being addressed or that the supervisee is not being held accountable for the therapy. If the supervisee describes problems in the therapy, it is appropriate for the supervision to focus on a plan for dealing with these problems. Similarly, if the supervisee describes some characteristic of a client, such as co-dependence, or of a system, such as enmeshment, a natural question is how the treatment plan should be revised to take this characteristic into account. When such discussion is not occurring, this suggests that some degree of collusion may be operative. This impression is underscored if there is an atmosphere of pseudomutuality between supervisor and supervisee and when this unity between supervisor and supervisee appears to occur at the expense of clients.

Another common pattern is when supervisors allow supervisees to hide behind safe generalities and abstractions (Therapist: "I'm going to work on their co-dependence." Supervisor: "Good."). When concepts and operations are vague, there is little substance to the supervision and little sense of accountability. The antidotes to this pattern are straightforward: The supervisee should be pinned down to clarify what is meant by abstract terms and to commit to a specific form of action in therapy. It is often important to obtain more primary data on events in therapy, usually through taping or live supervision.

Such interventions to break collusive patterns are not difficult, but they sometimes arouse anxiety in the supervisor, particularly novice supervisors. Because this chapter places such a heavy emphasis on the perspective of the supervisee, it is useful to note that supervisees often recognize this collusion on a subconscious level. They have the sense that something is not quite real about the supervision or that the supervisor is holding back for some reason, even though supervisees may have difficulty pinpointing exactly what is going on or may have a wide variety of explanations for this phenomenon. Most typically both parties are relieved when supervision is placed on a more solid basis.

SUPERVISEES REACT TO SUPERVISORY MODALITIES

The existing literature does offer some guidance to the supervisor seeking a better understanding of the supervisee's perspective on various supervisory modalities. This is especially true of supervisees' reactions to live supervision (Gershenson & Cohen, 1978; Liddle, Davidson, & Barrett, 1988; Lowenstein, Reder, & Clark, 1982). It seems safe to assume that supervisees have reactions to any supervisory modality, especially modalities that differ dramatically from their expectations. This can apply equally to being asked to present a genogram or being asked to bring in a case for live supervision.

It is also safe to assume that supervisees have different needs at different points in their learning (Friedman & Kaslow, 1986; Hess, 1986; McDaniel, Weber, & McKeever, 1983; Miars et al., 1983), with a general tendency for supervisees to need more direct help and direction early in their training, and more autonomy later. At every stage, however, it is likely that the supervisee may have mixed feelings about any modality or any other component of training. For example, a beginning MFT student may find live supervision reassuring but may also experience a lack of ownership of the case; a more advanced supervisee may recognize that group supervision is cost-effective and appropriate for the supervisee's stage of development but may also miss one-to-one supervision.

As has been stressed throughout this chapter, supervisors need to find ways to obtain accurate feedback. Although a preferred supervisory modality may not be abandoned just because the supervisee reacts negatively to it, some accommodation and custom-tailoring is usually possible and desirable. Getting such accurate feedback can be problematic, especially if there is a prevailing orthodoxy. This can be just as true when the supervisory orthodoxy is a time-honored technique, such as process notes, as when it is a newer technique such as the use of reflecting teams. Supervisors need to ask for feedback in an open-ended, neutral manner. Although it helps to reassure supervisees how the feedback can be helpful, it is equally important for supervisors to convey through their attitudes and nonverbal behavior that they expect to learn something useful from this feedback.

In view of the difficulties with candor emphasized throughout this chapter, it is also important for supervisors to be alert to nonverbal feedback about supervisory modalities and techniques (e.g., How does the behavior of the supervisee change when a supervisory session is not being taped? Are significant topics brought up before the tape goes on, or in the hall after the supervisory session is over?). Similarly, how is supervision different when there is no tape to watch, or when a live family does not show up? All of these differences can be noted and then discussed during supervision, again with a stance of genuine supervisory curiosity.

RESOLVING STUCK PATTERNS OR SEEKING DIVORCE

Supervisory Standoffs

Extensive experience in supervision and supervision-of-supervision leads me to caution supervisors that they should not assume that therapists they supervise feel stuck whenever the supervisor feels stuck. It is surprising how often supervisees are satisfied with progress when supervisors feel impatient or unhappy with what they experience as lack of progress. This is often more than a simple difference in perception or even using different "yardsticks" of progress; frequently the two parties are working on different goals and need to discuss these differences.

In the spirit of this chapter, it is important to underscore the opposite situation: Just because the supervisor is satisfied with a supervisee's progress, especially if it is progress toward goals defined largely by the supervisor, there is no guarantee that the supervisee feels similarly satisfied. Especially when factors such as those outlined elsewhere in this chapter are operative, it is important for the supervisor to seek honest feedback diligently.

Obviously, when one or both parties feel stuck, it is important to talk about the situation. This includes examining any differences in perception and the explanations both parties have to account for the standoff. Supervisors should assume that supervisees *always* have some ideas to account for the lack of progress, and that these ideas should be taken seriously rather than dismissed as defensiveness. When ideas differ, is it possible to find a larger frame of reference in which both views could be "correct"?—for example, the supervisee may feel unsupported although the supervisor may have been operating under the belief that the supervisee should not need such extensive support at the supervisee's level of training. Even when it is impossible to find a unifying framework, it may be possible for the supervisor to put the supervisee's ideas to an operational test even though the supervisor does not believe the supervisee's explanation of what is wrong (e.g., a supervisor accused of lack of clarity might take the complaint at face value and put supervisory recommendations in writing or have the supervisee do so).

When Divorce Seems Unavoidable

Like many marital couples, supervisor–supervisee dyads have often failed to consider the possibility of divorce. A good supervisory contract, like a prenuptial agreement, considers this eventuality. Even with careful contracting, a supervisory "divorce" can be emotionally messy and can leave scars (or legal consequences) for both parties.

The "No-Fault" Divorce

By far the easiest form of early termination is ending supervision by mutual consent, on grounds of lack of progress and incompatibility. Ideally, this situation has been recognized early; in more longstanding relationships, the implications and consequences may be more difficult—Will the supervisee receive full credit for the hours? Will the supervisor send in an evaluation? Even in relatively painless "divorces," such questions need to be considered and resolved.

Terminating Supervision

As Mead (1990) notes, the literature offers little guidance concerning the process of termination in supervision. Mead lists four supervisory tasks in this regard: (1) summarize progress made by supervisee, (2) discuss further needs for training and supervision, (3) promote generalization from supervision, (4) resolve interpersonal issues between supervisor and supervisee and bring supervision to closure (Mead, 1990, p. 127). As the reader may al-

ready have concluded, achieving these goals can be extremely problematic when supervision is being terminated for lack of supervisee progress or more extreme reasons, such as unethical behavior of the supervisee, or if the supervisee has initiated termination because the supervisee is dissatisfied with supervision.

Although a graceful termination of unsuccessful supervision may be as unlikely as an immediately happy divorce, it is generally helpful for both parties to avoid an abortive ending no matter what the circumstances. Some effort toward the four goals listed previously is worthwhile even if it is unlikely that any of them will be fully achieved. Depending on the circumstances, it may be possible for the supervisor to help the supervisee to place this supervision experience in a larger context and see it as a step in a long-term process, which might be continued after personal therapy, or with another supervisor. Even under the worst of circumstances, it is usually possible to underscore some achievements in supervision, although a high level of conflict may make it difficult for the supervisor to focus on them or for the supervisee to hear them.

"Premature" termination of supervision usually makes the supervisor rely more on a written final evaluation, which can be a subject of considerable controversy. Although supervisees may have been reminded of their rights for written rebuttal, it is almost always useful to have a face-to-face discussion to see if there are areas in which alternative wording might be negotiated. Often the wording that supervisees happen to find the most objectionable does not deal with areas supervisors regard as critical for the evaluation.

Recommending Dismissal from the Profession

More drastic outcomes of supervision are possible, including recommending that a supervisee not receive credit for a supervision experience or even be counseled out of the profession. Mead (1990) deals with this latter possibility at some length. It is somewhat surprising how rarely this contingency is addressed even though such gate-keeping functions are clearly among the obligations of supervisors. Mead is careful to point out the need for clear contracting in advance, including expectations and evaluation methods, as well as ethical standards. Policies and procedures for dismissal must be clear and followed carefully. It seems safe to say that these will never allow one supervisor to single-handedly remove a trainee from the profession.

If such a development occurs at a late stage in a student's clinical training, it is unlikely that a student will accept such a recommendation without objection and even legal challenges. Considering that students routinely challenge dismissal for such objective reasons as repeated failure on comprehensive examinations, and even there can succeed in getting academic institutions to grant exceptions, the case for dismissal for failure to achieve minimal levels of clinical competence must be exceptionally strong to withstand expected challenges. Dismissal on ethical or legal grounds can be less controversial. In any event, attempting to work through a lengthy process to a peaceful outcome is always to be desired. This requires a painstaking, gradual process where there are periodic benchmarks and detailed discussions of progress and possible means for remediation. When handled with such care, it may be possible to have students reach the desired conclusion that they do not belong in the field or need to take extensive time off for personal therapy.

CONCLUSION

Although this chapter has been replete with horror stories, that is not intended to be its major thrust. Instead, I hope to have instilled more interest in and respect for the perspective of students and other supervisees, along with an appreciation of some of the difficulties in getting them to be candid with supervisors. Even though there are many potential problems to be avoided, particularly through anticipating these problems and contracting carefully to minimize them, the primary safeguard remains a good supervisory relationship and an open process between supervisor and supervisee.

REFERENCES

Berne, E. (1964). *Games people play*. New York: Grove Press.

Bernard, J., & Goodyear, R. (1992). *Fundamentals of clinical supervision*. Needham Heights, MA: Allyn and Bacon.

Dellorto, M. (1990). Family therapy supervisory matches: Factors that contribute to goodness in fit. Unpublished doctoral dissertation, Illinois School of Professional Psychology.

Friedman, D., & Kaslow, N. (1986). The development of professional identity in psychotherapists: Six stages in the supervision process. In F. Kaslow (Ed.), *Supervision and training: Models, dilemmas, and challenges* (pp. 29–49). New York: Hawthorne Press.

Gershenson, J., & Cohen, M. (1978). Through the looking glass: The experiences of two family therapy trainees with live supervision. *Family Process, 17*, 225–230.

Gurman, A., & Kniskern, D. (1978). Deterioration in marital and family therapy: Empirical, clinical, and conceptual issues. *Family Process, 17*, 3–20.

Hess, A. (1986). Growth in supervision: Stages in supervisor and supervisee development. In F. Kaslow (Ed.), *Supervision and training: Models, dilemmas, and challenges* (pp. 51–67). New York: Hawthorne Press.

Hutt, C., Scott, J., & King, M. (1983). A phenomenological study of supervisees' positive and negative experiences in supervision. *Psychotherapy: Theory, Research, and Practice, 20*, 118–123.

Kadushin, A. (1968). Games people play in supervision. *Social Work, 20*, 184–189.

Liddle, H., Davidson, G., & Barrett, M. (1988). Outcomes of live supervision: Trainee perspectives. In H. Liddle, D. Breunlin, & R. Schwartz (Eds.), *Handbook of family therapy training and supervision* (pp. 386–398). New York: Guilford Press.

Lowenstein, S., Reder, P., & Clark, A. (1982). The consumer's response: Trainee's discussion of the experience of live supervision. In R. Whiffen & J. Byng-Hall (Eds.), *Family therapy supervision: Recent developments in practice.* New York: Grune & Stratton.

McDaniel, S., Weber, T., & McKeever, J. (1983). Multiple theoretical approaches to supervision: Choices in family therapy training. *Family Process, 22,* 491–500.

Mead, D. (1990). *Effective supervision: A task-oriented model for the developing professions.* New York: Brunner/Mazel.

Miars, R., Tracey, T., Ray, P., Cornfield, J., O'Farrell, M., & Gelso, C. (1983). Variation in supervision: Process across trainee experience levels. *Journal of Counseling Psychology, 30,* 403–412.

Rosenblatt, A., & Mayer, J. (1975). Objectionable supervisory styles: Students' views. *Social Work, 20,* 184–189.

18

Multiple Relationships in Supervision
Stepping Up to Complexity

Cheryl L. Storm, Marilyn Peterson, and Karl Tomm

A supervisor and a supervisee meet frequently at the supervisor's home to work on a paper they are co-authoring. After a supervision session, a supervisor and therapist share ideas for coping with the effects of managed care on their practices over lunch. A supervisor, noting that a supervisee's response to a particular family seems to be unusual, refocuses supervision on the therapist's family-of-origin issues. All of these scenarios have a commonality—participants are involved in multiple relationships with one another. They all have a dual agenda (Peterson, 1992). Multiple relationships are prevalent and inevitable in supervision (Goodyear & Sinnett, 1984; Ryder & Hepworth, 1990), perhaps evolving naturally from the nature of the supervisory context. At the heart of supervision is the goal of assisting supervisees in becoming supervisors' peers, thus supervisors frequently perform multiple roles and interact with supervisees in several settings.

SUPERVISORY MULTIPLE RELATIONSHIPS

Multiple relationships in supervision seem to be of three types (Storm, 1992). The first type, probably the most prevalent, is a mentoring relationship. Supervisors, involved in multiple roles with their supervisees, enrich or expand professional horizons of supervisees. In addition to functioning as supervisors, they also may be teachers, collaborators, or co-workers of their supervisees. Supervisees have opportunities to discuss other professional issues (e.g., developing a practice, publishing, and so on) with experienced colleagues who are willing to extend their contact beyond the supervision hour. In these relationships, more experienced professionals assist less qualified ones in developing into fully participating colleagues with professional identities of marriage and family therapists. Supervisors engaging in these multiple relationships perform critical and necessary professional socialization.

The second type of multiple relationships overlaps personal and professional relationships (Bograd, 1992; Storm, 1992) by combining a mixture of social, business, or other personal connections with the supervisory role. Sexual relationships with supervisees, prohibited by the American Association for Marriage and Family Therapy (AAMFT) Code of Ethics (1991a), fall into this category. Although there seems to be support in the mental health field

Note: Cheryl organized, edited and wrote the beginning and concluding sections. Marilyn and Karl responded to the vignettes.

for this prohibition (Brock & Coufel, 1994; Bernard & Goodyear, 1992), most supervisors agree there is a distinction between those relationships that constitute sexual harassment and those that stem from mutual caring on the part of both participants (Bernard & Goodyear, 1992). When the average therapist knows of at least one couple who began their relationship in a training context, it is more difficult to label the latter as inappropriate. Another prohibited relationship of this type is providing supervision to current or former family members.

The third type of multiple relationships combines supervision and therapy. This frequently evolves because some supervisors believe focusing on supervisees' personal issues is critical to therapists' development and competency (see Chapters 11 and 12). Because personal issues are intricately woven throughout the supervision process, supervision can easily become a therapeutic encounter. This challenges the definition of supervision as a sustained, intense learning experience focused on professional development clearly distinguishable from personal psychotherapy of the supervisee (AAMFT, 1991b). Although the ethical code prohibits supervisors from providing therapy to supervisees, a recent survey of Clinical Members of AAMFT found that just over one-fourth of participants approved of providing therapy to supervisees in some situations (Brock & Coufel, 1994). Almost 18% of those sampled had done so.

BOOBY TRAPS OR BENEFICIAL?

There are two positions debated in the field regarding nonsexual multiple supervisory relationships (Bograd, 1992). Consistent with the ethical code, one side argues supervisors should avoid multiple relationships whenever possible because of inherent dangers.[1] Essentially, multiple relationships are seen as "booby traps" (Bograd, 1992, p. 35). The other side believes multiple relationships can be mutually rewarding for participants. The first position focuses on the danger for exploitation of supervisees while the second position emphasizes the potential for enrichment of supervision. Both positions may be naive because all multiple relationships have the possibility for harming and enhancing supervisory relationships.

Dangers to Supervision

Most supervisors agree that engaging in a multiple relationship adds complexity to the supervisory process and can carry with it the potential for exploitation. *Exploitation* refers to participants taking advantage of the supervisory relationship for another purpose beyond that of the training agenda, which, in some way, results in harm to supervisees, clients, or the profession. Supervisors can take advantage of supervisees to further their own careers, informal lunches can turn into romantic trysts, and supervisors can focus on supervisees' lives to the extent that irresponsible supervision occurs because clinical work of supervisees is ignored. In some cases, supervisees feel trapped and used by their supervisors. In others, supervisors and supervisees may mutually collude so that they both personally benefit, and compromise professional training and clinical services.

Because of the hierarchical nature of the supervisory relationship, many believe supervisees are unable to freely and equally consent to the nonprofessional aspect of multiple relationships. Supervisee silence may prevail if supervisees find it difficult to comment on their

_____

[1] All further references to the ethical code are to the AAMFT Code of Ethics (1991). Ethical codes of the other mental health professional organizations address multiple relationships to varying degrees. Readers are referred to them for nuances.

perspective when it is different than that of their supervisors. Peterson (1992) notes the most problematic relationships are those situations in which a dual agenda develops and one agenda is kept covert, under the guise of the official relationship. In these cases, supervisees cannot use their perceptions to monitor safety in the relationships. "Once clarity of professional relationships has been muddied, there is a good chance for confusion, disappointment, and disillusionment" (Bograd, 1992, p. 34). Others who believe the supervisory hierarchy is critical, because of the evaluative functions of supervision, are concerned that multiple relationships can reduce supervisors' power and alter supervisors' capacity to perform this function (Cormier & Bernard, 1982; Pope, 1991). Once the supervisory hierarchy is altered there is no way to go backward and begin again.

Enhancements to Supervision

Supervisory multiple relationships can enhance supervision by increasing the connectiveness and personal responsibility of participants (Bograd, 1992; Tomm, 1991). "Dual, or even triple or quadruple, relationships are accepted as part of the inevitable and potentially beneficial complexities of human life" (Bograd, 1992, p. 35). Supervisors and supervisees are able to be more honest, more authentic, and more egalitarian in their relationships (Tomm, 1991). This can lead to personal growth by both as they learn to manage complexity in relationships. "A good supervisory relationship might be one that emphasizes ambiguity, contradiction, and complexity, and that avoids oversimplifying relationships" (Ryder & Hepworth, 1990, p. 127).

Several authors (Tomm, 1991; Ryder & Hepworth, 1990) feel supervisory multiple relationships can reduce the power differential in supervision. Supervisees who relate to their supervisors in multiple roles and contexts have more information about their supervisors, demystifying them in the process (Bograd, 1992).

Tomm (1991) suggests supervisors are required to demonstrate more integrity and mindfulness. Ryder and Hepworth (1990) contend that multiple relationships "move away from exploitation, not toward it, to the extent that they are moving genuinely toward collegiality and equality" (p. 130). Many believe multiple relationships are essential to increase access for minority therapists to mentors within the field (Committee on Racial and Ethnic Diversity, personal communication, 1992). An invitation to dinner at a supervisor's home may be the encouragement a minority supervisee needs to continue pursuing a career in a profession dominated by the majority culture.

DUAL RELATIONSHIPS INTRODUCE COMPLEXITY

As Bograd (1992) notes, there is little written regarding when to engage in or to avoid multiple relationships. Serious consideration is critical to avoid possible complications and the potential for exploitation and to introduce enrichment into supervisory relationships (Storm, 1992). Pope (1991) contends that professionals too easily define multiple relationships as necessary or unavoidable without seriously pursuing creative alternatives. Supervisors are well advised to approach multiple relationships by attempting to differentiate those that are cause for little concern from those that carry a high degree of risk for exploitation (Goodyear & Sinnett, 1984). Kitchener (1988) suggests guidelines for differentiating between such relationships. Applied to the supervision context, they are the following:

1. As incompatibility between supervisor and supervisee roles increases, so will the potential for misunderstanding and harm from the relationship.
2. As obligations of the supervisor and supervisee diverge from one another, the potential for divided loyalties increases.

3. As the power and prestige of the supervisor increases, the potential for exploitation of the supervisee increases and the ability of the supervisee to remain objective about his or her best interests decreases.

Factors supervisors may consider that can tip the scales in deciding to engage or avoid multiple relationships include: benefits to supervisees, benefits to supervisors, age and status differences, professional autonomy of supervisees, gender configuration, existence of safeguards for processing complaints, reasons supervisees are seeking supervision, degree of isolation involved, and access to consultation for both participants. If there is more potential benefit to the supervisor than the supervisee and both participants are private practitioners with little access to consultation, the decision may be very different from a situation in which the supervisee is already professionally credentialed or employed in an agency setting or there is little status difference between the participants in the professional community.

Prior to engaging in multiple relationships, supervisors can consult with other supervisors for additional input regarding ways multiple relationships serve their self-interests. Supervisors may find it helpful to hypothesize about the supervisee's perspective with other uninvolved therapists and about the clients' perspectives with nontherapist colleagues and friends. Fully discussing the potential benefits and costs of the specific situation with supervisees adds information for both participants. Precautionary steps, aimed at preventing exploitation of supervisees and at maximizing the benefits to supervisees, can be agreed on before supervision begins. For example, private practice supervisors may wish to build in a second opinion as a normal step in their supervision because there are no grievance procedures available to supervisees in their setting. When difficulties arise once supervisors are involved in multiple relationships, supervisors can obtain supervision-of-supervision or consult with others (Preister, 1991; Storm, 1992). Because he believes that adding supervisors to the relationship system increases the power differential between supervisors-and-supervisees, Tomm (1991) prefers to add power to the supervisee side of the relationship by having supervisees select third parties to review or monitor difficulties. A balanced assessment from multiple perspectives helps all participants make informed choices, but it is especially important for supervisors who bear the responsibility for the final decision.

When intimacy occurs between mutually consenting supervisory participants, Bernard and Goodyear (1992) recommend obtaining a new supervisor, or if replacement is not an option, asking another supervisor to monitor the supervision. If neither of these alternatives is possible, careful documentation of the supervision and the supervisee's work is important. At the time of evaluation, audio- or videotapes of the supervisee's therapy can provide data for a second opinion from another supervisor. If the format is group supervision, they advise participants to disclose their relationship and request that other members tell them if preferential treatment of the supervisee is occurring. Overall, consult, consult, consult!

In the next sections, MFT supervisors, Marilyn Peterson and Karl Tomm, respond to supervision scenarios. These cases illustrate the decision-making process of engaging in a multiple relationship.

CASE SCENARIO: TOO CLOSE TO HOME

You are supervising David, a family therapist who has a masters degree from an MFT program and has been obtaining post-degree supervision for the past six months. David works for a mental health center that has no staff formally trained in MFT. Thus, he contracted with you, a private practitioner, for supervision with his agency's blessing. During supervision, David expresses frustration with a case that involves a young child's behavioral problems. He notes: "This is too close to home." He asks you to provide therapy to his eleven-year-old son who is having some school difficulties. He states that he and his wife are aware of your reputation in the community as being highly skilled in working with children and their parents, and they want the best therapy for their son. The other trained family therapist they know is over 250 miles away. What is your response? Would your response be different if you and David worked for the same agency?

Marilyn's Response: Too Much Risk for All Participants

Combining the role of supervisor and therapist reinforces the power arrangement and widens the power differential between supervisor and supervisee. When supervisors become therapists, supervisees may feel trapped by the power of supervisors who control their professional futures. They may be hesitant to question or complain and feel unable to end supervision without serious consequences. If the supervisor were to work at the same agency as the supervisee, the power multiplies because the supervisor probably has influence over the supervisee's livelihood, evaluations, advancement, and/or salary.

David, who wants the best help possible for his son, probably cannot anticipate all the possible difficulties that might arise for him as client and supervisee, the supervisor in both his roles, his wife, and his child. It is up to the supervisor to grasp how the situation could impact David's learning. To do so, as the supervisor, I would pose the following questions: How does having a dual relationship with David impact my interventions as supervisor and therapist? If I confront David on his parenting, how does my confrontation impact the supervisory relationship? If I have personal information about David obtained during therapy, am I tempted to use that information when David presents a case in supervision that has similar dynamics to his own situation? Similarly, if I have information about how David operates with clients, can I (should I) use that information in therapy? Would my attempt to screen out what belongs where inhibit my responses in either supervision or therapy? If I believe there should be no artificial divisions and, therefore, freely take information from one situation into the other, what do I do with that information when I formally evaluate David's performance? How might the difficulties that occur in supervision increase David's anxiety and the dependency he feels on me for his son's therapy? How might that anxiety express itself in David's relationship with his son (after all, it is the son's difficulties that necessitated the need for therapy)? Given my awareness of these possibilities, how free would I feel as either supervisor or therapist to respond as I would to other supervisees and clients and operate without reservation in supervision and therapy?

If I see David's son alone or with his parents, how would the son feel seeing the person who is supervising his father? How would the supervisory arrangement I have with his father impact the power the child would accord me? How free would the child be to confide in me? Would the child feel free to criticize his father? What would I do if there were an allegation of abuse? How would an allegation against either the mother or father impact the supervision? Although therapists are usually concerned about how reporting abuse could change the therapeutic relationship, the concern would be heightened because this potential information could also endanger the supervisory relationship. How might my prior and ongoing supervisory relationship with David impact the couple, the wife, and the therapy? Does the supervisory relationship with David place the wife at a disadvantage? Given societal prescriptions about mothers, women commonly blame themselves for their children's difficulties. Does the supervisory relationship with David contribute to the powerlessness the wife may already feel?

How does the gender of the supervisor affect these dynamics? If I am a male supervisor, does the wife feel more vulnerable to the influence of two men who are both therapists? If I am a female supervisor, what competitive dynamics might be present? While it would be important to monitor and address these gender dynamics with any couple in therapy, the prior and ongoing supervisory relationship emphasizes all aspects of the supervisor's power and influence. Because the wife is "excluded" from the supervisory relationship, what is unknown to her might function as a "secret" in the therapy, which again contributes to whatever powerlessness she may already feel. I would also question my motivation in becoming a therapist to this family. I would ask myself what motivates me to respond to David's request. How am I influenced by my own grandiosity and need to be the "special" one? What invites me into the arrangement?

If I were the supervisor, I would decide that I could not be a supervisor to David at the same time I was a therapist to his family. I would talk with him about other possibilities for help that exist in the community for his family (e.g., pediatricians, ministers with a counseling background, childhood educators). I would also explore with him the possibility that I could be the therapist if we formally terminated the supervision, agreed that a return to supervision in the future might not be possible, and said goodbye. If David chose to proceed with me as therapist, he and I would need to accept the loss that inevitably accompanies the hard decisions around boundaries, and the sadness that he and I cannot have it all.

Karl's Response: Accepting Supervisory Complexity

My first response would be to affirm David for recognizing the possibility of a connection between his frustration in treating a family with childhood behavioral problems and his concern about his son's difficulties. After expressing appreciation for his openness, I would encourage him to carefully reflect on the following questions: What are the similarities and differences in the relationship dynamics of the two situations? How could positive changes in his personal situation influence his clinical work? How could improvements in his clinical skills with families enable his own effectiveness as a parent?

My second response would be to address his request for therapy by strongly supporting David's desire for outside input to address his personal situation. Such input could be a significant learning opportunity, regardless of whether it was provided by me, someone else, or both. Therapists, like many others, tend to be hesitant to seek therapy for themselves yet this personal experience contributes enormously to their capacity to appreciate clients' experiences in therapy. I would then inquire about what resources he, his wife, and son have drawn on in the past and what other resources they considered for their present situation. If I was aware of additional resources other than those he mentioned, I would raise them for him and his wife to consider. Assuming that alternative resources were not readily available, were not suitable, and/or he had a strong preference to work with me, I would remind him that the current ethical code prohibits a supervisor from providing therapy to a supervisee. However, I would also indicate that I do not agree with a rigid and blind application of this standard and that some colleagues, including myself, have already taken some steps to try to rescind this prohibition. I would explain my understanding of the rationale behind the standard, namely, the potential for confusion about roles and responsibilities, and the increased risk of exploiting the vulnerability of the supervisee/client by virtue of the cumulative power differential in the two relationships. I would also briefly explain the rationale for my disagreement with the standard, namely, that the person of the therapist and the doing of therapy are inextricably interrelated and that a dual involvement offers unique opportunities for identifying isomorphic patterns that may be manifested in both contexts and for enabling a transfer of constructive changes from one context to the other.

I would engage David in an open and frank discussion of the inherent complexities of multiple relationships and invite him to join me in identifying the potential complications that could arise in our specific situation. This would include a review of our history with each other, an exploration of the current supervisory and therapeutic issues needing attention, and speculation about possible future difficulties. For instance, would seeing him in therapy make it more difficult for him to raise problems in his clinical work with me as a supervisor? Would the supervisory relationship make it more difficult to be open in therapy? To what extent would his wife and son feel disadvantaged in therapy given our separate supervisory relationship? How would his increased vulnerability to evaluation in supervision affect him? If it became too confusing or difficult to move forward in both relationships and one or the other or both had to be relinquished, how would he and his family be affected by the disruption? There could be complications related to turning down his need for personal help as well. How would David and his family feel about themselves, me as a person, and family therapy as a field, if I unilaterally rejected his request for therapy? How would he feel if I cited the Code of Ethics to insist he give up his supervision before offering any therapy? After exhausting our initial joint exploration of possible consequences, I would suggest that he discuss the possibility of therapy as fully as possible with his wife and with anyone else who he felt might help. I would ask for his consent for me to confer with one of my colleagues about it as well.

If we both anticipated greater potential benefits than risks and decided to proceed, I would propose we build in a safeguard of having third parties involved to monitor either or both of our evolving relationships. For instance, it would be important for us not to drift into personal therapy during supervision times and vice versa. The monitoring could be done on a regular ongoing basis or on an ad hoc basis when significant concerns or conflict arose between us. To restrain any further increase in my advantage of power and privilege, I would explicitly commit myself to give priority to David's choices of who these third parties would be and how and when they would be involved. I would propose that we agree to respect each other's freedom to discontinue either or both involvements should any major or unexpected difficulties arise.

I would explain to David my need to try to counter the bias that I probably held in favor of his perspective compared to that of his wife and son. I would ask him to recognize their inevitable disadvantage in not having a prior relationship with me and encourage him to give his wife and son the option of seeing me without him initially, if they wanted to, in order to meet me, ask questions, and begin forming a relationship. However, I would be open to starting therapy with them all together if his wife and/or son felt no need for separate meetings. At the beginning of the first interview I would ask the son and wife about their feelings regarding my dual relationship with David to be sure they are aware of the complexities involved. If either of them had any serious concerns, I would reconsider the whole issue with David. If they did not, I would proceed by declaring everyone's entitlement to raise concerns about alignment imbalances at any time as the therapy evolved. Given my ongoing supervisory relationship with David, it would be important for me (and them) to continuously monitor the strength of my alignment with him in comparison to other family members. Where

I would go from here would depend on David's responses, those of his family and my colleagues, and on the kinds of issues that came up in the subsequent supervisory and therapeutic meetings.

If David and I worked for the same agency, the complexities would be considerably greater. Not only would we have a confounding relationship as co-workers but other members of the agency could be influenced by changes in our relationship as well. This would make the process of exploring possible consequences much more cumbersome and difficult. Indeed, the burden of monitoring for possible negative effects among us as colleagues in the agency could outweigh the potential benefits. Nevertheless, complexity alone would not constitute sufficient reason to deny David's request for personal help, and I would remain receptive to the possibility.

My personal decision to accept or decline David's request for therapy would depend on the degree of congruence I anticipated in my roles as supervisor and as therapist. If my intentions to help David develop as a professional, to help him develop as a person and family member, and to help his son and wife develop as well, felt authentic and consistent with one another, I would be open to proceed. If, for whatever reason, I did not experience such congruence, I would be reluctant to go beyond an exploration of the possibility of therapy. If I could foresee unresolvable conflict or anticipated significant contradiction between the two roles, I would decline the request. For instance, if I experienced my supervisory task as primarily one of evaluating his competence to practice, rather than one of enhancing the development of his clinical skills, I would not be comfortable proceeding. My primary orientation to supervision, however, gives priority to the learning and development of supervisees. Any assessment that occurs along the way is secondary and is applied toward supervisees' professional development, including the possible identification of certain limitations.

My willingness to proceed despite the inevitable increase in risks for complications and exploitation relates partly to my readiness to address these dangers at the outset and all along the way. I orient myself, David, his family, and others to note and raise any problematic developments. I try to monitor the consequences of my own behavior, acknowledge my mistakes, and take action to correct them. I commit myself in both professional roles to give priority to David's needs over mine. For instance, if he felt the dual involvement was becoming too much of a strain while I felt exciting new opportunities were emerging, I would defer to his desire to discontinue. I also try to remain open to insights and intervention from third parties, particularly when I cannot see or appreciate the nature or magnitude of my own involvement in problematic events, patterns, or situations. However, my willingness to proceed is grounded more strongly in my recognition of the unique advantages and benefits that can accrue through multiple relationships.

One advantage is the possibility of making more coherent, rigorous, and balanced distinctions about a supervisee's patterns of responding to others and to analogous situations because my experiential database is much richer when I know David in both contexts. For instance, the probability of clearly identifying a supervisee's unrealistic expectations for children, which might support patterns of frustration and abuse when a child misbehaves, is lower in a supervision context alone. Unrealistic expectations in a parent are, however, relatively easy to distinguish in the therapy context. If such expectations did become apparent in therapy, I would assume David's response to a misbehaving child and the child's parents would be significantly influenced in his work context. Indeed, the probability is high that David would be supporting (covertly, if not overtly) unrealistic expectations of the father in the clinical case. Given my knowledge about David from the domain of therapy, the issue would be taken up with more rigor (and perhaps more vigor) in supervision. Recognizing and working on such similarities and overlaps in the two contexts could enable progress in both.

Although learning from example is always useful, there is a unique manner in which such learning is especially effective when David, as a developing clinician, can learn from me as a therapist also working with him as a client. Not only can he experience the moment-to-moment effects (beneficial or otherwise) of my therapeutic initiatives with him and his family, he can connect them to the specific skills we have been working on in supervision. This makes it possible to work toward greater "lived" congruence and more integration between theory and practice. It, of course, would be incumbent on me (as therapist) to be as consistent as possible with myself (as supervisor) and to acknowledge my difficulties and limitations when this does not happen. Such acknowledgment would also contribute to a reduction of the cumulative hierarchy and power imbalance.

Another distinct advantage is that strengths and resources evident in one context can be drawn on and applied in the other. For instance, if I noticed David as therapist being particularly attentive to a child's experience at crucial moments, I could try to bring forth these skills during the therapy with his family. I would have greater confidence that this competence existed because I had actually witnessed it in supervision and I could probably cue him more easily during the therapy by introducing similar language. Thus, the isomorphism between David's professional and personal situations offers an excellent opportunity to mobilize the synergistic effects of learning similar skills in different domains. Changes in awareness, understanding, attitude, feeling, and action in one area may be transferred to and even enhance new learning in the other and vice versa. The results of such developments are often mutually reinforcing; con-

sequently, the positive changes in both areas are more liable to be enduring.

A Dialogue Between Respondents

Marilyn's Response to Karl: Concern About David's Vulnerability

Karl's initial sensitive response demonstrates a deep appreciation for David and respect for his courage. He innately understands David's apprehension about himself as father and clinician and how the expression of these concerns increases his vulnerability. In response, he builds a "container of safety" that mitigates against shame, encourages David's efforts for himself and his son, and fosters an acceptance and pride in what he has elected to do. I would hope that my response to a supervisee could be as loving and complete as Karl describes.

Karl's discussion of the ethical code, however, is fraught with difficulties. Although Karl's frank discussion about his position, his actions to rescind the prohibition, and the rationale for his position ostensibly gives David information he needs to make an informed choice, Karl tends to minimize the inherent power differential and the extent of his influence on David's decision making. How free is David to truly make this decision? He feels an urgency about his situation. He wants Karl to be his therapist. Karl believes in what David is trying to do for himself. Karl is even willing to go against the Code of Ethics to give David what he wants. The criteria for giving informed consent customarily includes no undue influence. Given this set of circumstances, I question whether David has free choice. More important, Karl's attempts to inform David about the ethics code and the current political milieu have the effect of inviting David to join in what amounts to collusion against the present standard. To be in therapy with Karl, David also has to turn against the proscribed code of the profession. I question the impact this alliance would have on supervision and therapy, and how the experience of this alliance teaches David to behave with his clients. Moreover, I am concerned about David's increased professional vulnerability because of his participation in this arrangement.

Karl is concerned about David's and his family's feelings if he declines to see them or insists that David stop his supervision before receiving therapy. Although I concur that David may feel cheated, it is also possible David would grow. For example, I would explain to David that he deserves the best possible help for his personal situation and the family he loves. He also deserves the best possible supervision I can give. If I were to see him as a client *and* supervisee, I would feel responsible for protecting his increased vulnerability. I might also put a lot of energy into monitoring myself so as not to misuse the increased advantage I would have by knowing him in two separate roles. Consequently, I probably would not be as free to give all I could in either situation. He would be deprived of what otherwise would be available if this complication were not present. Instead of using the Code of Ethics to substantiate my decision, I would share my sadness about my limitations and my wish that it could be otherwise. I would want him to understand that my response grows out of my wanting him to have more than I could provide. I would hope I was giving him permission to not be all things to all people. I would be aware that this might be particularly important to David whose male socialization might equate inability to perform with failure to provide. Besides exploring his feelings to my response, I might mark this experience as pivotal in helping David examine his expectations of himself in response to his clients.

Karl would clearly go in another direction. He would use the input from others and third-party involvement to monitor possible difficulties between himself and David. This move is important because it makes the arrangement overt, assumes the need for close protection of David's increased vulnerability, and isolates the management of the dual relationship. Although expanding the field serves as a check on Karl's increased power in the relationship, this preventative measure unfortunately becomes a delegation and abdication of responsibility. It should only be used in situations where there is no other option. Moreover, if I were asked to serve as the third party by either David or Karl, I would want the full authority to monitor the duality. I therefore would want to be in charge of where, when, and how monitoring would proceed.

I have questioned Karl's willingness to see David as a client, but his appreciation of David's request, focus on giving David a full explanation of the hazards and benefits involved, and use of a third party to safeguard the arrangement is laudable and creative. However, Karl's decision does not just impact David's life. It affects the lives of David's wife and son and potentially the lives of agency staff. How free, for example, is David's wife to refuse to participate in an arrangement that has already been worked out by "the experts"? How free is an eleven-year-old son, who may already feel ashamed of his school performance and responsible for his parent's emotions, to raise objections or do anything other than what is expected? In an agency setting, Karl would likely be the equivalent of David's boss. Would David's son or wife do anything that might jeopardize David's job? These questions demonstrate that the decision to proceed potentially disempowers others and could victimize those who are "innocent" of the arrangement but forced to participate. Again, the question of whether informed consent is possible must be examined.

Moreover, if this situation were to occur in an agency setting, problems could be more extreme. An agency supervisor's decision to see David and his family as clients potentially disturbs and even harms those who again are "innocent" of the arrangement but forced to participate. This "imposition" potentially creates alliances between those who know and those who do not, and between those who support the dual relationship and those who do not. This "imposition" potentially distorts the interaction between David and his colleagues and skews the relationships between the supervisor and his other supervisees who are not clients. The important dynamic is not complexity but the harm, inadvertent or otherwise, that could be done to others.

Dual relationships are common and necessary to the functioning of rural communities, communities of color, and small social communities. Without question, the ability to draw material from a variety of "real-life" contexts gives an advantage to the person doing the job. Unfortunately, it is that advantage that is commonly misused. Solutions for managing dual relationships cannot wipe out the inherent power differential and its debilitating potentials. Karl's response minimizes his personal influence and therefore the significance of the power differential and restricts the options of those who are in lesser power positions. Making certain that David is fully aware of the risks and benefits inherent in the arrangement, and using a third party to help monitor their relationship and address any problems that might arise, only appears to reduce Karl's increased power and David's vulnerabilities. I contend these efforts remove the constraints so Karl can use his power more freely. This freedom has the potential to endanger whoever is on the receiving end.

Karl's Response to Marilyn: More Priority to Ethic of Caring

Marilyn and I come to opposite conclusions in our responses to David. One of the underlying reasons for this difference could be that she gives relatively more priority to an ethic of

rights, while I give more priority to an ethic of caring. An *ethic of rights* is based on the human right to noninterference, while an *ethic of caring* is based on human connectedness. When acting within a frame of rights, a supervisor should not interfere with any aspect of a supervisee's life outside the domain of supervision, particularly if such intervention is liable to be harmful and/or is unwanted. When acting within a frame of caring, a supervisor should be ready to respond to the needs of a supervisee outside the supervision on the basis of human relatedness and compassion. The expectations and demands of these ethical frames sometimes overlap and are congruent; at other times they diverge and become contradictory. A dilemma arises when the ramifications of these differing orientations conflict. Professionals need to find their own compromise or balance between them in making choices. By raising selective questions in the manner she does, Marilyn tends to bias herself toward the conservative side of not interfering in David's personal life and thus she does not respond directly to his personal pain. In other words, she gives her professional responsibility priority over her humanity. She has the current Code of Ethics on her side, but in my opinion, professionalism is given too much status.

The ancient medical dictum, *primum non nocere* (first do no harm), is consistent with an ethic of rights to noninterference. Implied in this is, of course, a concern about the ultimate welfare of the other. However, concern and caring are not what is focused on in the dictum. When the statement is taken literally, the caring recedes into the background and can be overlooked entirely. The most obvious route to be certain that one is doing no harm, is to do nothing at all. The decision to not accept David's request for help can be justified in this manner. My preference would be to revise the dictum to read: "First be honest in your caring, then do no harm." Greater honesty in our concerns about the welfare of others would make it more likely that we would recognize anticipated losses and the possible harm done by not responding. In other words, I would prefer to also hold myself accountable for not taking action in situations where direct action may be called for.

Another basis for our contrasting conclusions may evolve from the different ways we look at and handle power. Although the consensuality in the social situation of supervision creates the fundamental power differential, much can be done to increase or decrease the expression and enactment of power differences depending on the propensities and activities of the parties involved. Marilyn and I acknowledge the importance of the power differential between supervisor and supervisee, and between therapist and client. Both of us take this differential into consideration in our decision making. However, my impression is that Marilyn tends to handle professional power as an objective reality: it exists in the form of real authority and as professionals we are stuck with it. Consequently, she exercises the power of her professional position with clear authority. For instance, she unilaterally enacts her supervisory power by saying "no" to therapy or "goodbye" to supervision. I suspect David would experience some disempowerment by such action. In contrast, I tend to regard professional power largely as a social construction and orient myself to manage the differential socially by sharing power wherever possible. I try to enact this by giving David some say in the decision about therapy. From my point of view, she remains relatively unaware of her own activity in producing the very power she is concerned about. For instance, Marilyn's strong emphasis on the dangers of professional power and on client vulnerability has the social effect of constructing an even greater power differential. Fortunately, however, her deep concern about its abuse would tend to mitigate against such dangers of professional misuse in her hands.

CASE SCENARIO, PART 1: MENTORING A GIFTED THERAPIST

You are supervising a group of therapists who are half-way through obtaining the hours of supervision required for credentialing. Your practice has decided to add another therapist. Sandy, one of the supervisees, is a particularly gifted therapist and could make a significant contribution to your practice. Your partners ask you to talk to her about the position. How do you respond? Would your response change if the supervision was occurring as part of a degree-granting program? How do you respond when supervision group members learn about the opening and several others express an interest?

Karl's Response: A Concern Regarding Conflict of Interest

When my partners first asked me to talk to Sandy about the new position, I would decline because it would only be fair to the rest of the group and to other therapists in the community if we organized an open competition. Everyone should be appraised of the employment opportunity. If Sandy and/or other members of the group then applied, I would disqualify myself from the selection process and trust my colleagues to make an appropriate choice. My personal need to have a congenial partner should not take priority over my supervisees' needs to be treated fairly and to have an equal opportunity to apply for the job. I would also inform the group of my stance on this to minimize the possibility of fostering favoritism, competition, and jealousy among group members.

If my partners insisted that I participate in the selection process or if I had strong personal reasons for wanting to be involved, I would request that we wait until after the course of supervision is over before the position is advertised. If waiting was not an option, I might consider raising the issue with the whole group of supervisees to see if a negotiated consensus on my participation in the selection process is possible. If group members did not want me to be involved, or some did but others did not, I would remain firm in disqualifying myself as a participant in the selection process. If the supervision was part of a degree-granting program, I would be more insistent that the position not be offered until after graduation. I would be in a conflict-of-interest situation if Sandy was hired as a partner before my supervision evaluation was completed; my personal desire to have her be a successful partner could unduly influence my evaluation of her competence. If there was an urgent need in our practice for more staff, then the offering should be limited to those who have already graduated. In this case, Sandy would not qualify as an applicant for the position.

Marilyn's Response: A New Agenda Is Introduced

There is an inherent duality created because the supervisor and supervisees are colleagues. The incongruity, for these supervisees, of being less experienced yet colleagues, is simultaneously resolved because supervision is a mentoring process. The power differential structuring the supervisory interaction is congruent with this mentoring role. Customarily, supervisees outgrow the need for supervisors. Their evolving status as peers symbolically acknowledges supervisees' growth and their professional maturity. While each may continue to learn from the other, their interaction now is principally defined by their collegial relationship. Supervision can become problematic if either supervisors or supervisees alter the inherent and necessary power differential, equalizing their positions prematurely. In this situation, the power differential that structures supervision is blurred by the supervisor's col-

leagues. Their request, if acted on by the supervisor, thrusts a new agenda into the supervision. This new agenda competes for the supervisor's attention to the supervisees' learning. The introduction of a new agenda also double-binds participants, because their responses to the new agenda have repercussions for the original one. Going through the supervisor rather than approaching the supervisees themselves results in using the supervisory relationship to get what the colleagues want for their practice. They take advantage of Sandy's vulnerable position as a supervisee and of the knowledge they have of her abilities gleaned through the supervisory relationship. When the colleagues ask the supervisor to represent their interests, they capitalize on the supervisor's influence and use the advantage created by the supervisory relationship to fulfill their agenda. The supervisor is double-bound: (1) If the supervisor refuses to fulfill the colleagues' request and suggests that they look elsewhere, the supervisor may be acting against the best interests of the practice. (2) If the supervisor complies, the supervisee is moved into a potential peer relationship with the supervisor and elevated as "special" within the supervision group. Sandy's ability to make a free-and-informed decision may also be tainted by the flattery of having been "chosen" by her supervisor.

If I were the supervisor, I would first address my colleagues' expectation that I approach Sandy. Although I might be concerned about their reactions, I would discuss their insensitivity to my position as supervisor, Sandy's vulnerability as supervisee, and the impact their request might have on the other supervisees and the group process. I would discuss with my colleagues the ramifications of hiring a supervisee. I would share my concerns about becoming a peer to someone I was supervising.

If the practice still wanted to hire from within the supervision group or if other supervisees seemed interested in applying, I would publicly declare that I was excluding myself from the entire hiring process. I would explain that I was taking this action so that I could protect the supervisory relationships and remain available for the group processing that might be necessary if one of the supervisees were hired. I would suggest several ways to keep the boundaries clear. First, if Sandy was hired for the job, she could find another supervisor outside the practice. This option allows Sandy to move fully into a peer status and not jeopardize her supervision. Although this arrangement might inconvenience Sandy and lengthen the time spent in supervision, she would be informed of this restriction before applying for the job and, therefore, would know what to expect if she accepted the position. Second, if Sandy was hired, the permanency of the hiring could be provisional and dependent on the supervisor's evaluation and Sandy's successful completion of the supervision. The agency, in effect, would join the supervisor in maintaining the intergenerational boundary, support rather than confuse the supervisor's authority, and prioritize the supervisee's learning. Again, Sandy would be informed of a "conditional" hire before applying for the job. While this option makes the boundaries clearer and reduces some of the predicaments raised by the intrusion of a second agenda, this arrangement is still problematic. How free is Sandy to question and challenge a supervisor who has power over the permanency of the position? How free is the supervisor to challenge the supervisee or to negatively evaluate the supervisee's performance when the supervisor knows that colleagues are invested in the supervisee becoming a permanent staff member? I would use an independent consultant to keep the supervisory process open and honest and to help me with the issues that could arise between my colleagues and myself.

CASE SCENARIO, PART 2: PROFESSIONAL RESPONSIBILITY OR JEALOUSY?

Sandy is hired and continues to attend group supervision. Over time, you become concerned about Sandy's professionalism. Specifically, she seems to be presenting herself to clients as having more experience and training than she has. You raise your concern with her. She wonders if your concern is "professional jealousy." Your caseload has been unusually low while Sandy has turned away referrals because she has no openings. How do you respond now?

Karl's Response: Supervisor Responsibility in Contributing to the Problem

Because we hired Sandy, we regarded her as "superior" to all other applicants. As a result, she could legitimately regard us as seeing her as special. Indeed, as a supervisor and as partners, we may have become so enamored by her creative gifts that we recruited her into a pattern of admiring her own competence to the point that she became overconfident. If this is what has happened, my partners and I should take partial responsibility for her behavior. We should acknowledge this and apologize for our complicity in creating the problem. I have encountered several situations where young family therapists have been actively "promoted" beyond their maturity on the basis of their giftedness only to face greater pain later as their inflated expectations of themselves were punctured.

I would take Sandy's implication of my professional jealousy very seriously. Despite my discomfort with the suggestion, there is probably some truth to it. Given the significant differential in our caseloads, it is quite likely that I would be envious of her success. If, after reflection, I could see the truth in what she implied, I would acknowledge this and validate her entitlement to have doubts about the legitimacy of my concern about her professionalism. If, by this point, she too has reflected on her behavior and could acknowledge that she has erred in her presentation of herself to clients, I would express appreciation that we could have such a useful clarifying conversation and leave it at that.

If Sandy steadfastly denied any impropriety, while I remained deeply concerned about her professional conduct (in the presence or absence of some professional jealousy on my part), I would suggest we meet with a third party to discuss the situation. I would give her priority in choosing who the third party should be and where we should meet; it would be helpful, for instance, to avoid meeting "on my ground," such as in my office, to help reduce the hierarchy and to minimize impositional overtones. My intention in pursuing the meeting with a third party is not to apply further pressure for her to accept my perspective, but to create a context where she would feel less intimidated by my authority and hence somewhat safer in expressing her frustration with me and the supervisory process. With a third party mediating our discussion, I would feel less responsible for managing the process and thus could devote more of my attention to listening to her and to stating the basis of my concerns more clearly. There is a significant probability that both of us would learn a great deal from such a process. Engaging a third party to participate in clarifying the issues would expand our social field. Hopefully it would enable the deconstruction of some old perceptions and meanings and the reconstruction of some new ones that would be more coherent and consensual. This development would constitute a systemic enactment which could not only help us get over our impasse but also contribute to some unique experiential learning in a method for transcending interpersonal differences.

If our respective positions happened to polarize during the third-party discussion and our disagreement escalated, I would seriously consider relinquishing my role as her supervisor. If I found myself too angry or too anxious to even allow a third party to meet with the two of us in the first place, I would assume that I was having some personal difficulties that needed attention. I would then take initiative to seek a personal consultation, obtain supervision of my supervision, and/or get some therapy for myself.

Marilyn's Response: Peer Relationships Create Difficulty in Processing Conflict

If Sandy were hired, I would be sensitive to the feelings of the other supervisees and the concerns that would need to be addressed in the group supervision. Group members might feel jealous of their colleague, angry with the practice, and/or shamed by rejection. Because I removed myself from the hiring process, I would be more available to respond as a supervisor, instead of a member of the practice, to their reactions, which, if not attended, might block or disrupt their learning.

Exploring how motivation and personal experiences impact clinical decisions makes the relationship between supervisor and supervisee an intimate endeavor. Conflicts are to be expected and used to help supervisee learning. When the power differential is blurred by an agenda that proscribes a peer relationship, it is more difficult to assess which reality has led to the conflict and which reality should be used as the basis for a response. In this vignette, the supervisor's concern about the supervisee's practice perhaps may be a cover for peer competition and professional jealousy. The supervisee's accusation that the supervisor is jealous may be a cover to deflect the criticism and control of the supervisor. If I were the supervisor and Sandy had been hired on a provisional basis subject to my recommendation, I would first examine her accusation to determine if I were jealous of her "success." If I were envious, I would need to ascertain whether I could continue to supervise without my reaction interfering with her learning. I would also need to ascertain if my jealousy, though present, was motivation for my concerns about her professionalism and possible misrepresentation. I might need to acknowledge with her and/or in the supervision group the truth of her allegation. We might need to see a consultant together or ask a consultant to help us discuss this situation in the group.

If I felt that my concern was valid, I would identify our conflict as Sandy's struggle with my authority. I would ascertain whether she is open to learning about herself, her motivation, my concern (besides jealousy), and what she has to change as a result of this exploration. Because the professional's role embodies authority and power, Sandy's ability to "own" this struggle would be critical to responsibly handling her authority with clients. If Sandy was not able to learn from this situation and we were not able to resolve the conflict, I might decide: (1) I could not recommend her credentialing; (2) I could not recommend she be hired by the practice; (3) she needs therapy about her authority issues; (4) she needs to stay in supervision for a longer period than is normally required for credentialing; and/or (5) she needs to enter supervision with someone else. I would expect the practice, which hired her only provisionally, to support my recommendation.

A Dialogue Between the Respondents

Karl Responds to Marilyn's Response: Rely on Personal Authenticity and Sapiential Authority

Marilyn and I appear to be in substantial agreement in our responses. Both of us recognize the

compromising position that our colleagues place us in, give priority to the needs of our supervision group over the needs of our colleagues, entertain withdrawing from the selection process, and acknowledge the potential validity of Sandy's claim that we could be jealous and would openly acknowledge this if there were some truth to it. In this case, probably my greatest difference with Marilyn revolves around her expectations for her colleagues to support her supervisory authority. I would not ask my colleagues to make Sandy's appointment provisional and contingent to my decision regarding Sandy's competence in supervision. Nor would I expect them to avoid splitting with me in my final recommendations. Such agreements unnecessarily increase the supervisor's power over the supervisee. I would prefer to leave space for Sandy to seek other opinions and alternative sources of support. Whenever possible, I prefer to rely on personal authenticity and sapiential authority rather than authority ascribed by social role and/or status. In other words, if I had difficulty convincing Sandy of an issue in supervision that I was concerned about, I would prefer to gather more relevant information and knowledge and seek explanatory power to support me rather than to recruit more people with social power to support me. If I was unable to adequately identify and describe the pertinent behaviors and events to persuade her or to develop a sufficiently coherent explanation that Sandy could understand, I would invite her to explore my concerns about her work and perhaps elicit my underlying assumptions and presuppositions in the process. In so doing, hopefully we would work toward a more collaborative supervisory process.

Marilyn Responds to Karl's Response: Rely on Integrity of Colleagues

Although our conclusion is the same, Karl and I emphasize different concerns. Karl would decline because his involvement would interfere with the need for a fair and open process. Although I would decline for the same reason, my primary concern would be the integrity of my colleagues whose agenda for my involvement already prejudices the hiring process. Even though our differences may appear inconsequential, I believe they could be determinative of what ultimately occurs. Openly addressing my colleagues' behavior might illuminate and subsequently preclude the competition, false promotion, jealousy, and mistrust that erupts between me and Sandy.

If Karl decided to participate in the hiring process, he would try for a "negotiated consensus" with the group. Although this solution might give supervisees a significant role in determining their fate, they also might feel responsible for the process and, therefore, unjustified in addressing the anger about the final outcome, shame of rejection, or the supervisor's part in the decision. Some supervisees might feel confused because they cannot reconcile their ongoing feelings of vulnerability with the illusory control they have been given. Unable to accurately assess the true size of their power, they are apt to feel double-bound and unsafe.

Karl recognizes the power differential and the potential for conflicted loyalties when he is given the line authority and responsibility to evaluate Sandy, now a partner, for a degree-granting institution. Although the formal power to evaluate certainly highlights the disparity of power between supervisors and supervisees, I contend that the power differential is inherent to the relationship and supervisors need to be aware that they have significant influence in supervisory relationships that do not have a formal evaluative function.

I concur with Karl's ideas about how to address Sandy's possible misrepresentation and the implication of professional jealousy. The need for critical self-reflection, use of a third party, and establishment of a safe environment brings an authenticity and vulnerability that could allow for mutual exploration and healing. If these procedures were not effective, Karl would relinquish his role as supervisor. Because Sandy would still need supervision, I assume she would be passed on to someone else. I have seen a number of supervisees "passed on" when conflicts with their supervisors became irreconcilable. Indeed, these problems were often redefined as "personality clashes." To be fair to these supervisees, new supervisors often were not informed about the problems that had occurred. Unfortunately, the supervisees' same problems surfaced again when these individuals again behaved inappropriately with clients. I, therefore, would not relinquish the gatekeeping aspect of the role so quickly. Instead, supervisors should carefully monitor what might need to happen next.

SUPERVISORS STEP UP TO THE COMPLEXITIES

As can be seen, there are many factors to consider and weigh when making the initial decision to participate in a multiple relationship. In the above examples, Marilyn and Karl were assisted in making their decisions by considering and weighing the following factors:

- They identified the potential complications *and* enhancements. A biased decision was likely if only complications *or* enhancements were assessed.
- They considered the gender configuration of the participants, which altered significantly the possible complications and enhancements.
- They took inventory of their philosophy of supervision, emphasis on the gatekeeping function of their supervisory role, and beliefs about addressing supervisory power. Both discussed the situation with supervisees and turned to other colleagues to

help them expand their view of the complexity involved. "If this, then this" scenarios forced the consideration and weighing of alternatives.

- Once involved, supervisors must be willing to step up to the complexities. Pretending they do not exist increases the likelihood of the complexities leading to harm; stepping up to them allows for minimizing the potential harm.
- Marilyn and Karl cited self-reflection, making a commitment to honor their supervisees' needs over their own, monitoring of relationships by supervisors and others, and recognition of the inherent power differential in supervision as helpful in warding off difficulties and identifying the initial signs of complications.
- Fall back plans and safeguards were a must. They outlined alternatives ranging from supervisees changing supervisors to seeking therapy/consultation regarding their personal reactions.

Because multiple relationships are inevitable in supervision, supervisors must develop a process for deciding when to engage or avoid them and how to manage those they become involved in. Each situation includes unique factors to be considered and weighed. Supervisors, in the same situation, may ultimately come to differing decisions as Marilyn and Karl did. However, it is the thoughtful and in-depth consideration and weighing of the possible complications, risks, and enhancements that assist supervisors (and supervisees) to make informed decisions and develop safeguards when they proceed with multiple relationships. It is supervisors "who must carry the lion's share of responsibility for misunderstandings and complications, false moves or confusing developments, regardless of the progress toward equality between the two parties" (Bograd, 1992, p. 37). Supervisors should also remember, as the American author Nancy Thayer wisely stated, "It's never too late—in fiction or life—to revise" (cited in *Women's Wit and Wisdom*, 1991).

REFERENCES

American Association for Marriage and Family Therapy (AAMFT) (1991a). *AAMFT Code of Ethics.* Washington, DC: Author.

AAMFT (1991b). *AAMFT Approved Supervisor designation: Standards and responsibilities.* Washington, DC: Author.

Bograd, M. (1992). The duel over dual relationships. *Family Therapy Networker, 16,* 33–37.

Bernard, J. & Goodyear, R. (1992). *Fundamentals of clinical supervision.* Needham Heights, MA: Allyn and Bacon.

Brock, G., & Coufal, J. (1994). A national survey of the ethical practices and attitudes of marriage and family therapists. In G. Brock (Ed.), *Ethics casebook* (pp. 27–48). Washington, DC: AAMFT.

Cormier, L., & Bernard, J. (1982). Ethical and legal responsibilities of clinical supervisors. *Personnel and Guidance Journal, 60,* 486–490.

Goodyear, R., & Sinnett, E. (1984). Current and emerging ethical issues for counseling psychologists. *The Counseling Psychologist, 12,* 87–98.

Kitchener, K. (1988). Dual role relationships: What makes them so problematic? *Journal of Counseling and Development, 67,* 217–221.

Peterson, M. (1992). *At personal risk: Boundary violations in professional-client relationships.* New York: W. W. Norton.

Pope, K. (1991). Dual relationships in psychotherapy. *Ethics and Behavior, 1,* 21–34.

Preister, S. (1991). AAMFT Code of Ethics changes. *Family Therapy News, 22,* 20.

Ryder, R., & Hepworth, J. (1990). AAMFT ethical code: "Dual relationships." *Journal of Marital and Family Therapy, 16,* 127–132.

Storm, C. (1991). Supervisors as guardians of the profession. *Supervision Bulletin, 4,* 4.

Storm, C. (1992). Nonsexual dual relationships examined. *Family Therapy News, 24,* 12, 29.

Storm, C. (1994). Defensive supervision: Balancing ethical responsibility with vulnerability. In G. Brock (Ed.), *Ethics casebook* (pp. 173–190). Washington, DC: AAMFT.

Thayer, N. (1991). *Women's wit and wisdom*. Philadelphia: Running Press.

Tomm, K. (1991). The ethics of dual relationships. *The Calgary Participator: A Family Therapy Newsletter, 1*, 11–15.

19

The Blueprint for Supervision Relationships

Contracts

Cheryl L. Storm

Recently, when my husband and I decided to remodel our house, I was reminded of the importance of a specific, detailed contract. After hearing many remodeling horror stories, we carefully sought out a contractor in whom we felt we could place our trust and then painstakingly discussed every aspect of the project. Together we planned the logistics, mutual expectations, evaluation process, and procedures for resolving difficulties should they occur. Like most homeowners who remodel, our job was not perfect nor problem free. However, unlike many homeowners, we were relatively satisfied and our contractor left on good terms. In retrospect, the hours spent hammering out the terms of our written contract were well spent. Essentially, it was the contract that provided all of us with the working blueprint for our relationship.

Similarly, the working agreements between supervisors and supervisees, *supervision contracts*, can be mutually beneficial. Initially, supervision contracts help supervisors and supervisees clarify their expectations of one another and outline the responsibilities of each participant within the relationship. Developing a contract "promotes genuine collaboration in exploring needs and identifying goals" (Fox, 1983, p. 39) by supervisors and supervisees. Thus, contracting sets the context for a reciprocal relationship because the terms of the agreement are made explicit. For all supervisors and supervisees, but especially for women and minority supervisees, formal supervision contracts can promote shared responsibility for learning that occurs (Wheeler et al., 1989). For example, Kay, an African American supervisee, felt comfortable requesting more time from Ted, her supervisor, to deal with a challenging case because they had discussed Ted's desire to tailor supervision to Kay's specific needs during their contracting session.

As supervisory relationships evolve, adjustments, which become apparent over time, can be made in supervision contracts to allow for the unique needs and desires of participants. For example, John, a supervisor, and Sharon, a supervisee, altered their contract so that Sharon could have increased live supervision of her cases when it became clear to them that Sharon could benefit from supervisory guidance in structuring sessions with highly interactive families. As in this case, contracts can be altered to fit supervisees' growth and learning curves.

Later, contracts can provide direction at key moments. When supervisors and supervisees begin working together, they commonly assume the best about their upcoming supervision experience. If unforeseen complications occur, both participants can find solace in having made some prior agreements about how they will proceed in their relationship if difficulties evolve. For instance, Brian, a supervisor, and Kevin, a supervisee, were relieved to have guidelines to turn to when a difference of opinion arose between them regarding Brian's evaluation of Kevin.

Contracts can maximize the fit between supervisors and supervisees, ensuring the attainment of goals established by the participants (Prest, Schindler-Zimmerman, & Sporakowski, 1992). Fran, a supervisor, and Betty, a supervisee, concluded another supervisor was a better match for Betty based on their discussion about what Betty was looking for from supervision during their contracting meeting and what Fran could offer her as a supervisor.

Contracts provide supervisors and supervisees with a concrete means for measuring and documenting progress and performance of supervisors and supervisees (Fox, 1983). Dan, a supervisee in private practice, was not surprised when his supervisor, Charlie, noted that he needed to tape more of his therapy sessions for supervision because taping was a condition of their original supervision contract. Likewise, Charlie, was not surprised when Dan reminded him that he had hoped to integrate narrative theoretical ideas into his predominantly strategic approach, and wanted to refocus supervision to accomplish his goal. As can be seen, contracts increase the potential for a successful supervision experience while protecting both participants by decreasing the margin for misunderstandings that exists (Storm, 1991).

COMPONENTS OF SUPERVISION CONTRACTS

All supervisors and supervisees negotiate some form of a supervision contract with one another. Variation occurs, however, in the degree of formality, specificity, and mutuality of the process. For example, some supervisors develop a formal, businesslike contract while others cover the basics in an informal conversation with new supervisees. Some supervisors use contracts to highlight only the major agreements while others carefully explain the specifics of their supervision agreements in detail. Some supervisors, clear about the terms on which they will agree to supervise, use standardized contracts to outline the parameters of their supervision.

Other supervisors, wishing to mutually negotiate the terms, leave extensive room for supervisees' input, with some supervisors even creating a unique contract for each new supervisee. In my experience, I have found that written contracts formalizing supervision agreements with relatively specific information about each area have proved invaluable to me and my supervisees. Although I encourage input from supervisees and incorporate unique aspects of our agreements into contracts, I have concluded over time that certain information and terms are important for me to always include in my supervision contracts. Some information is based on my personal situation. For example, because my work schedule changes frequently, I work out of three geographical locations, and I travel frequently on weekends; therefore, it is critical to have specific agreements spelled out about what to do in the event my supervisees' need an immediate supervisory response. Other information seems to be important to include because it contributes to an effective supervision experience for supervisees and myself. For instance, I have found it important to have any supervision requirements that must be fulfilled for credentialing, licensing, or professional organizations defined up front.

Regardless of the degree of formality, specificity, and mutuality involved, all effective supervision contracts outline logistics, clarify the supervisory relationship, identify goals, describe supervision methods, review clinical issues, comply with credentialing requirements, and specify evaluation procedures. In the sections that follow, I discuss each of these areas and use illustrations from the practices of supervisors to highlight effective contracting.

Outline of Logistics

The specific arrangements for supervision are usually one of the first areas negotiated, including fees; frequency of supervision; time, place, and length of meetings; and overall schedule. Contracts specify the terms of individual and/or group supervision because the pragmatics and logistics may differ. Of particular importance is how fees are set. Many supervisors charge a different fee for individual versus group supervision. In group supervision, does the supervisor have a set rate regardless of the number of supervisees who participate? Or, is there an hourly fee divided amongst those who participate?

Specific arrangements based on the context in which supervision occurs are important to address such as when supervision occurs at a different site than where supervisors work—will supervisors make a site visit and, if so, how frequently? Some therapists will have other supervisors involved in their work. For example, an agency therapist may have two supervisors (a superior who does not meet credentialing standards and a privately contracted supervisor whose credentials are acceptable). Discussion of the hierarchy of supervisory responsibility and legal liability of each can be important to avoid supervisees being caught in a supervisory crossfire (Prest, Schindler-Zimmerman, & Sporakowski, 1992).

For supervisors and supervisees, cancellations by either can have important consequences. Supervisors may find themselves legally responsible for supervisees' work, which

they may know very little about.* In private practice settings, supervisors may be left with costly free time in their schedules. Supervisees' progress toward credentialing can be significantly slowed down if supervisors cancel too often. Both can become frustrated and be inconvenienced. As a result, many supervisors include a cancellation clause in their contract. Jeske (1994) agrees to provide a free session of supervision if he cancels without adequate notification and requires full payment by supervisees if they do.

Consistent with informed-consent doctrines (Bray, Shepherd, & Hays, 1985), supervisors require their supervisees to notify their clients that they are receiving supervision (Kapp, 1984). Similarly, supervisors-in-training notify their supervisees of their supervisors' names and credentials, and the process of supervisory training. McDowell (1991), seeing advantages to involving agency supervisors in the contracting process, discusses the effect of supervision on the work system with agency supervisors. By collaborating with agency administrators, she also believes it is easier to ensure that the effect of outside supervision is beneficial. The ethical codes and standards of practice adhered to can be specified by the participants. For example, Bob, an AAMFT Approved Supervisor, supervises Jim, a licensed social worker. It was important for both of them to be familiar with and understand each other's professional obligations and ethical guidelines. Although similar in many ways, there were some differences. Access to raw data was critical to Bob, who was supervising according to the standards of the marriage and family therapy (MFT) field, but less important to Jim whose profession does not require raw data in supervision. All parties affected by the supervision arrangement—clients, supervisees,

---

*See the case example cited in Storm (1993) for an extensive discussion of supervision implications.

supervisors, and agencies—are thereby informed consumers.

Clarification of the Supervision Relationship

The initial contracting process begins with an exploration of the *fit* in working together. A discussion of supervisors' and supervisees' preferred therapy and supervision ideas, methods, and style of working is an important starting place (White, 1989/1990) as well as supervisors' and supervisees' preparation for the supervision process (Mead, 1990). One important area to discuss is flexibility and the desire to explore ideas, methods, and styles other than their preferred ones. On more than one occasion I and a potential supervisee have foregone working together after thoroughly exploring our fit with one another.

Supervisors often include their views about the inherent hierarchy and power differential embedded in the supervisory relationship. As Fox (1983) notes, with most other contracts, negotiations occur between equal partners. If supervision occurs within an agency by a superior, a supervisee cannot easily withdraw from supervision. If supervision occurs between a therapist and a privately contracted supervisor, the supervisee's power is increased resulting in initial negotiations between individuals who are more equal. However, once an agreement is made, the supervisee is frequently dependent on the supervisor for endorsement into the profession. Some supervisors highlight the beneficial aspects of hierarchy by emphasizing the expertise they bring to supervisory relationships. Others prefer to underscore the potential negative influences of supervisory power and describe their supervisory efforts to minimize the power (see Chapter 16).

An agreement regarding the procedures for renegotiating the contract or resolving supervision disagreements can be a "God send" if the worst happens. Some supervisors commit to making a concerted effort to achieve an amicable closure and ask supervisees to do the same. For example, Stoner (1994) includes in his contract:

> While a friendly atmosphere between us is advocated and will be fostered in our supervisory process, we will be aware of issues and professional boundaries involving our biases, friendships, gender, personality, race, sexual orientation, values, and/or differences regarding philosophy and conduct of the therapy process. If differences or power struggles arise, and/or boundary issues become problematic, we will commit ourselves to try to resolve separating issues in a professional and mutually beneficial manner.

Many supervisors suggest that third parties, sometimes agreeing in advance to specific persons, be invited to help in conflict resolution. If a premature termination of supervision occurs (for any reason including logistics), some supervisors advise their supervisees that they will want permission to consult with supervisees' next supervisors. Hanson (1993) stipulates a two-week notification period to allow for adjustments to be made by both parties.

When dual relationships are present, an in-depth discussion of the complexity involved is strongly recommended, including potential complications, exploitation, and enhancements to supervision. Because these situations can be tricky when problems occur, it is critical to include procedures for processing problems. Inclusion of the issues discussed may prove helpful to both parties. (See Chapter 18 on multiple relationships in supervision.)

Identification of Supervision Goals

Supervisors vary philosophically with regard to their goals for supervision. For example, some emphasize skill building while others stress personal growth (McDaniel, Weber, & Mc-Keever, 1983). For those supervisors who emphasize personal development experiences, several authors (Braverman, 1984; Munson, 1984) recommend therapists be fully informed to avoid potential abuses of this way of supervising and that therapists should enter into such a supervisory process voluntarily. Many supervisors of this ilk require supervisees to do family-of-origin genograms thus sharing personal information. Some supervisors stipulate that supervisees must participate in therapy for themselves while in supervision. Others forewarn supervisees that, if personal issues intrude on the learning process, supervisors may refer them to therapy.

Specific learning objectives can include perceptual, conceptual, and executive skills; theoretical, practical, or technical application of a therapy model; expertise with a specific symptom or population; or particular developmental objectives such as developing one's style or integrated model (Rigazio-DiGilio, 1994). Some supervisors believe it is critical to assess supervisees' cognitive and learning styles and tailor learning objectives accordingly (Duhl, 1986). Therapists also seek supervision for specific reasons unique to them such as support, nurturance, or personal growth (Alderfer & Lynch, 1986). Because some therapists are hoping to repeat a past supervision experience while others are committed to avoiding one, an exploration of supervisees' previous supervision experiences can help supervisors be more effective.

Description of Supervisory Methods

The supervisory methods to be used, whether co-therapy with supervisors, live supervision, review of video- or audiotapes or case presentations, are integral to the supervisory agreement. These supervisory methods are different avenues of intervention for supervisors. Jane, a supervisor, and Kevin, a supervisee, selected videotaped supervision as a primary method because Kevin was having trouble assessing family patterns. In contrast, Jane focused heavily on case presentations with her other supervisee, Susan, because Susan had many questions about a wide variety of cases and this method allowed them to cover the issues within the time allotted for supervision. The various methods also require different preparation on the part of the participants. For example, some supervisors prefer to watch supervisees' entire videotapes prior to supervision meetings while others expect their supervisees to select excerpts, which illustrate the issues they would like to address, in advance to show during supervision. By determining the methods, supervisors and supervisees can take the appropriate steps so they are ready to make the most of supervision meetings.

Including some methods that involve observation of supervisees' therapy (i.e., raw data) into supervision contracts is a widely endorsed standard for MFT supervision. Live supervision and/or video- or audiotaped therapy sessions allows supervisors to determine if they are providing an appropriate amount of supervision in a timely manner, assess therapists' readiness for supervision and progress over time, make sounder evaluations because they are based on therapy data, and ensure that clients receive at least minimally satisfactory treatment (Storm, 1993). Access to raw data can be one of the stumbling blocks in supervision because of the extra permissions required from supervisees' work settings and clients. Transporting of case records and tapes to supervision when it occurs at a different site than where supervisees are employed has to be conducted discreetly with an eye toward confidentiality.

Review of Clinical Issues

Because supervisors and supervisees are both responsible for supervisees clinical work (Engleberg & Storm, 1990; Slovenko, 1980), it is critical to discuss their respective responsibilities. Supervisors explain their legal accountability regarding treatment provided to clients, noting they are ultimately responsible. Clear procedures are important to include for when clients are in danger to themselves or others, and when abuse or neglect of children or the elderly is occurring. Most supervisors outline step-by-step actions supervisees must take in these cases, particularly if their supervisees are not employed by institutions with defined procedures for crisis cases. Supervisors identify the limitations of their supervision. Some supervisors inform their supervisees of their malpractice coverage and require that supervisees provide documentation regarding theirs. For MFT supervisors, it is important for supervisees to agree to emphasize an MFT perspective in their practice.

The mechanisms for sharing clinical information are determined, which allow supervisors and supervisees to make the most of their time together by keeping supervision focused. Supervisors advise therapists of their preferences regarding the organization of case information by supervisees in preparation for supervision. Supervisees generally are appreciative of knowing in advance what information supervisors need to enable them to discuss their cases. Some supervisors ask for written or oral summaries of cases based on specific criteria, some for genograms, some for case files, and so on (see *Resource Guide* for examples of case presentation forms). Whatever the mechanism, supervisors and supervisees prevent supervision from rambling by agreeing on the case material that is useful.

There should also be a mechanism for the overall review of supervisees' cases because supervisors are typically responsible for supervisees' entire caseloads. Supervisors must also judge whether the amount of supervision done is sufficient to cover supervisees' cases. If a supervisee is seeing forty clients per week, is an hour of supervision adequate? Because supervisors are responsible for verification of therapy hours later on, supervisors and supervisees who develop a method for recordkeeping of clinical contact hours provided by supervisees are prepared to provide required documentation.

Compliance with Requirements of Credentialing Bodies, Employers, and Educational Institutions

Because supervision can be significantly influenced by credentialing bodies, employers, or educational institutions, supervisors frequently review the criteria that supervision is to fulfill with supervisees and use these requirements to shape their final supervision contract. State, professional organizations, employers, or educational program requirements can easily dovetail or significantly differ with each other and with participants' notions of supervision.

When supervision is being obtained because it is required, supervisors are advised to pay attention to the specific criteria and structure supervision accordingly. Supervision usually is defined by those mandating supervision; for example, AAMFT does not accept didactic instruction as supervision. Supervisors working with supervisees interested in obtaining Clinical Membership in AAMFT may want to forewarn supervisees that if they agree to focus on a new clinical area requiring supervisees to obtain some background knowledge, time for instruction and discussion of assigned readings may be needed and will be scheduled in addition to supervision. Some supervisors inform supervisees of their evaluative role for credentialing bodies and educational institutions and outline their typical responses, such as requiring coursework, readings, tape reviews, and so on, if a weak area surfaces.

Specification of Evaluation Procedures

An evaluation process specifies who gets what information when and identifies the sources of information. Whether supervisors and supervisees evaluate their work on an ongoing basis or at specific points in time, describing the evaluation process initially in a contract and providing copies of any evaluation forms keeps both participants accountable to a critical process that either can launch or delay supervisees' careers.

Supervisors may wish to think ahead regarding the information they will need to enable them to speak meaningfully about their supervisees' competency and build these information sources into their contracts. Will they only be asked to discuss supervisees' therapeutic abilities? Or, will they be asked about their compliance with state laws, case management abilities, or general professionalism? In the latter case, supervisors may wish to request ongoing contact with employers and access to records. When credentialing bodies or educational programs are mandating supervision, it is standard for a written evaluation to be required at the conclusion of supervision. Supervisors frequently invite supervisees to review their ongoing documentation of their supervision sessions.

Evaluation is highly influenced by supervisors' philosophies of supervision. If supervisors' philosophies encourage the sharing of personal issues by supervisees, supervisors may wish to explain the ways these will be handled during evaluations. Some supervisors place the emphasis of evaluation on supervisees' progress toward their unique goals while others critique therapists' work against an outside standard. Some supervisors believe supervisees should be maximally involved in the process; thus, evaluation is based primarily on supervisees' self-perceptions. Others use standardized evaluation instruments (e.g., Pinsof's 1979 Family Therapist Behavioral Scale or the 1983 Family Therapist Rating Scale by Piercy, Laird, and Mohammed).

Some supervisors remind therapists that their gatekeeping function may result in their requiring supervisees to seek additional clinical training and supervision. As Stoner (1994) states:

> Verification of hours of supervision does not necessarily mean endorsement or recommendation. Such a recommendation is based on the successful completion of the supervision process in an ethical and professional manner, as well as the assessment of supervisee competence by the supervisor.

Most supervisors build in ways for the evaluation of the overall supervision process and their work as supervisors. Some encourage ongoing feedback regarding supervisees' experience with supervision while others formalize the process via specific feedback forms at specific points in time (see examples in *Resource Guide*).

THE EVOLUTION OF AN EFFECTIVE SUPERVISION CONTRACT

The Initial Supervision Contract

A therapist, Cindy, who recently moved to Washington from California, is seeking a supervisor to help her attain credentialing as a marriage and family therapist in both states. Although residing in Washington, she hopes to return to California in a year or two. She is currently employed part-time for a family therapy agency and has begun a private practice. Although she receives supervision at her agency, her current supervisor is unable to talk with her about her private practice cases or to provide enough hours of supervision to meet the state regulations. In addition, the agency supervisor is qualified as a supervisor in Washington, but not in California. Cindy has a degree in counseling with a specialization in MFT. Based on recommendations from agency colleagues, she contacts Melissa by telephone for supervision.

After establishing that Melissa has openings for supervisees and that she qualifies as a supervisor in California, Melissa and Cindy briefly discuss logistics and Melissa's general goals. Based on this exchange, they tentatively agree to work together and set up a time for a contracting meeting to discuss the specifics of their supervision arrangement.

During the meeting, Melissa structures a discussion that covers the contracting areas described here. They agree to meet once every other week for two hours at Melissa's office for a fee of $60 per hour. Cindy expresses an interest in sharing supervision with another therapist because she would like to reduce the cost of supervision and because she feels professionally isolated—there is only one other therapist in the small agency where she works. However, she does not know of anyone. Melissa notes that she may have another supervisee who would be interested in such an arrangement, and says she will check out this possibility for Cindy.

They move on to a discussion of each of their backgrounds, MFT training, and supervision experiences. Melissa includes her background and preparation as a supervisor as well. They seem to be a good match. Cindy's preferred therapy model is structural and her goal for supervision is to become better at structural interventions. Melissa, although more of a solution-focused therapist, feels competent in the structural approach and in her ability to help Cindy reach her goals. Melissa also concludes that Cindy seems to have an ad-

equate educational background in MFT because she elected to specialize in it during her counseling degree.

The one area that is a stumbling block is Melissa's lack of familiarity with California's licensing law and Cindy's lack of familiarity with Washington's credentialing law. If Cindy wishes to become regulated under both laws, they agree it will be important to have supervision comply with both state's requirements. Melissa gives Cindy a copy of the Washington requirements, and Cindy commits to bringing a copy of the California requirements for Melissa to review.

Melissa inquires about the agency's knowledge of Cindy's seeking outside supervision. Cindy has already checked with her agency supervisor and received permission for her to obtain additional supervision on agency cases. In fact, the agency supervisor wishes to talk with Melissa so he can support Cindy's undertaking. Although the idea of bringing videotapes of therapy to supervision is new to Cindy, she does not think there will be problem. Cindy seems hesitant to be supervised live, but enthusiastic about bringing tapes of her therapy sessions for supervision.

They also discuss Cindy's private practice cases. Cindy sees four cases that were referred to her by her pastor. She is unsure regarding how these clients will react to being told she is in supervision and to being asked to be taped. Cindy is visibly uncomfortable as Melissa insists that they be told and that she have access to raw data on these cases also. Melissa attributes Cindy's reaction to the newness of their supervision relationship, to Cindy's lack of experience with supervision based on raw data, and to Cindy's concern about establishing a private practice in a new locale. She believes they will be able to work through Cindy's discomfort. After their meeting, Melissa formalizes their agreement in writing. She and Cindy review it at the beginning of their next meeting.

Reevaluation of the Initial Supervision Contract

Initially supervision goes well. Cindy seems committed to the experience—she brings issues about her cases to supervision, is interested in Melissa's input, and tries out intervention strategies discussed in supervision. Melissa and Cindy's supervision relationship develops and both enjoy working together.

A pattern emerges whereby Cindy complains of having difficulty meeting with families. Melissa notes that Cindy tends to bring tapes of her therapy sessions with mothers or adolescents from the agency, but rarely sessions where they are together. However, her goals for these sessions seemed appropriate to Melissa so she had not questioned Cindy's decision to meet individually with family members. On exploring Cindy's tendency to meet individually with family members, Cindy admits she is hesitant to meet with the entire family. She states that she had only met with one family during her training; all her therapy had been done with individuals.

Shortly after Melissa learns of Cindy's lack of experience with families, she receives a call from Cindy's agency supervisor because Cindy has had several complaints from parents who felt she sided with their adolescents and were not appreciating their concerns. The agency supervisor is concerned and he hopes Melissa will be able to help Cindy be more successful with parents.

When Melissa and Cindy discuss the situation, Cindy states she is extremely uncomfortable when there is parent–child conflict and prefers to separate the family members when conflict emerges rather than help them work out their disagreement with one another. Melissa, puzzled about Cindy's original goals for supervision, asks Cindy about her goal of becoming a more competent structural therapist—a model that can be intense and involves encouraging family members to interact with one another. Cindy states that she once saw Minuchin at a conference and liked his way of doing therapy, had read an article on his work which appealed to her, and believed the approach would work well in her current setting. Once she tried to practice it, however, she found it to be more difficult for her than she had expected. She has become increasingly anxious about her therapy as she has tried to work structurally and has avoided discussing it with colleagues, which has only increased her professional isolation.

A Renegotiated Supervision Contract

Although Melissa and Cindy initially discussed Cindy's therapy experiences and training, Melissa realizes she was lax in not pursuing the topics in depth. She had not asked specifically about Cindy's work with families or her knowledge about structural therapy (or family therapy for that matter). She had assumed more background, education, and experience than Cindy actually had. Because she did not ask for specifics, Cindy did not know what was relevant information for Melissa to know. If she had known of Cindy's lack of experience, she would have structured their initial agreement differently. Melissa decides to talk with Cindy about renegotiating their agreement.

Melissa proactively discusses with Cindy her knowledge and experience in detail so that they can tailor their supervision to her needs. They decide to include readings on the structural family therapy model and to schedule separate meetings for them to review the material. They determine that Cindy could benefit from live supervision and make the appropriate arrangements. They further redefine Cindy's goals to reflect her level of ability. Together they agree that Cindy's goals will be to learn the basics of structural family therapy and to engage families in therapy. To counter some of Cindy's isolation, Melissa suggests that Cindy join a supervision group of therapists with similar experience because they had not been able to find another supervisee to share supervision time.

Cindy excitedly joins the group. After discussing the responsibilities of having a private practice, Cindy voluntarily decides she is not ready and refers her families to someone else.

Although the initial supervision was based on a thoughtful contracting process, it was only through the process of being in supervision together that Melissa and Cindy could create a supervision arrangement that was tailormade. The initial contract acted as the foundation on which they could build.

CONTRACTING TIPS

The following are several tips I have found helpful to keep in mind when contracting. First, determine whether requests are for training, supervision, consultation, or some combination thereof. (See Chapter 1 for a discussion of the similarities and differences between training, supervision, and consultation.) Trainers, like contractors, assist clinicians in building a new theoretical structure for therapy. Consultants, similar to interior designers, work with therapists' existing preferred ideas, styles, and values to pull them together so that they complement rather than detract from each other, and to decide what new to add. Supervisors, akin to remodelers, help therapists rework, expand, and add to a preexisting therapy model. Once you have determined if training, consultation, supervision, or a combination is being requested, be sure to underscore your responsibilities, structure for the process, goals to be attained, degree of evaluation, and follow-up involved.

To develop a contract that reflects your philosophy, preferred ideas, methods, and supervisory interventions, be prepared to discuss this information clearly and succinctly with potential supervisees. For example, I highlight to potential supervisees my commitment to focusing on the influence of contextual variables on supervision; my underlying constructivist and systemic beliefs; and my structured, active style of supervising. As you discuss your preferences, be sure to gain an understanding of your supervisees' preferred ideas, methods, interventions, and style of therapy and supervision. This will allow you both to determine the potential for satisfying supervision experiences.

Outline expectations for yourself and your supervisees. Fox (1983) suggests discussing the following questions to facilitate a match between supervisees' needs and supervisors' knowledge and skill: "What do we expect from each other? What can we each give to each other? Are our goals the same? Can we achieve them? How can we achieve them? What constraints exist? and How will we know when we have achieved the goals?" (p. 39). By doing so, Fox believes supervisees become active self-directive, invested learners who define their needs and move beyond "tell me what to do" to assertively assuming responsibility for their professional development.

It is important to include all relevant areas. Typical contracts include an outline of the logistics; clarification of the supervisory relationship; identification of supervisory goals; description of supervisory methods; review of clinical issues; compliance with credentialing, employers', and educational requirements; and specification of evaluation procedures. The *Initial Supervision Session Checklist* developed by Prest, Schindler-Zimmerman, and Sporakowski (1992) outlines the many topics that can be covered (see *Resource Guide*).

To facilitate clarity and provide documentation of agreements, supervisors are encouraged to formalize contracts in writing. Written contracts can incorporate the unique philosophies and personal styles of supervisors and supervisees (see the *Resource Guide* for several styles of written contracts). A major advantage to written contracts is that they can remind participants of the original commitments made to one another.

Although it is important to tailor supervision contracts to individual supervisees, pay attention to requirements and limitations defined by credentialing bodies and educational institutions that mandate supervision. This ensures that supervisees are receiving the type of supervision they need to reach their professional goals.

Finally, always leave room for reconsideration and renegotiation of the contract. A contract done initially, but long forgotten and tossed in a drawer, does not fulfill its potential usefulness. In contrast, a worn contract that changes with the evolving supervisory relationship can create satisfied supervision consumers.

REFERENCES

American Association for Marriage and Family Therapy (AAMFT) (1991). *AAMFT Approved Supervisor designation: Standards and responsibilities.* Washington, DC: Author.

Alderfer, C., & Lynch, B. (1986). Supervision in two dimensions. *Journal of Strategic and Systemic Therapies,* 5, 70–73.

Braverman, L. (1984). Family of origin as a training resource for family therapists. In C. Munson (Ed.), *Family of origin applications in clinical supervision* (pp. 37–48). New York: Haworth Press.

Bray, J., Shepherd, J., & Hays, J. (1985). Legal and ethical issues in informed consent to psychotherapy. *The American Journal of Family Therapy,* 13, 50–60.

Duhl, B. (1986). Toward cognitive-behavioral integration in training systems therapists: An interactive approach to training in generic systems thinking. In F. Piercy (Ed.), *Family therapy education and supervision* (pp. 81–108). New York: Haworth Press.

Engleberg, S., & Storm, C. (1990). Supervising defensively: Advice from legal counsel. *Supervision Bulletin,* 4, 6.

Fox, R. (1983). Contracting in supervision: A goal-oriented process. *The Clinical Supervisor,* 1, 37–49.

Hanson, E. (1993). Supervision contract. Unpublished document.

Jeske, J. (1994). Supervision contract. Unpublished document.

Kapp, M. (1984). Supervising professional trainees: Legal complications for mental health institutions and practitioners. *Hospital and Community Psychiatry,* 35, 143–147.

McDaniel, S., Weber, T., & McKeever, J. (1983). Multiple theoretical approaches to supervision: Choices in family therapy training. *Family Process,* 22, 491–500.

McDowell, T. (1991). Contracting from the top down. *Supervision Bulletin,* 6, 3–4.

Mead, D. (1990). *Effective supervision: A task-oriented model for the mental health professions.* New York: Brunner/Mazel.

Munson, C. (1984). Uses and abuses of family of origin material in family therapy supervision. In C. Munson (Ed.), *Family of origin applications in clinical supervision* (pp. 61–70). New York: Haworth Press.

Piercy, F., Laird, R., & Mohammed, Z. (1983). A family therapist rating scale. *Journal of Marital and Family Therapy,* 9, 49–59.

Piercy, F., & Sprenkle, D. (1986). Supervision in training. In F. Piercy & D. Sprenkle (Eds.), *Family Therapy Sourcebook* (pp. 288–321). New York: Guilford Press.

Pinsof, W. (1979). The Family Therapist Behavioral Scale (FTBS): Development and evaluation of a coding system. *Family Process,* 18, 451–461.

Prest, L., Schindler-Zimmerman, T., & Sporakowski, M. (1992). The initial supervision session (ISSC): A guide for the MFT supervision process. *The Clinical Supervisor,* 10, 117–133.

Rigazio-DiGilio, S. (1994). Supervision contract outline. Unpublished document.

Slovenko, R. (1980). Legal issues in psychotherapy supervision. In A. Hess (Ed.), *Psychotherapy supervision: Theory, research, and practice* (pp. 453–473). New York: John Wiley & Sons.

Stoner, A. (1994). Supervision contract. Unpublished document excerpts reprinted with permission.

Storm, C. (1991). Striking the supervision bargain. *Supervision Bulletin,* 4, 3–4.

Storm, C. (1993). Defensive supervision: Balancing ethical responsibility with vulnerability. In G. Brock (Ed.), *Ethics casebook* (pp. 173–190). Washington, DC: AAMFT.

Wheeler, D., Avis, J, Miller, L., & Chaney, S. (1989). Rethinking family therapy training and supervision. In M. McGoldrick, C. Anderson, & F. Walsh (Eds.), *Women in families: A framework for family therapy* (pp. 135–151). New York: W. W. Norton.

White, M. (1989/1990). Family therapy training and supervision in a world of experience and narrative. *Dulwich Centre Newsletter, Summer,* 27–38.

20

Live Supervision Revolutionizes the Supervision Process

The discussion of live supervision that follows has three parts. In the first section, the historical development of live supervision is traced from the early days to the present. Special attention is devoted to highlighting the advantages and disadvantages as they have been viewed over time. In the second section, an interview with Montalvo, one of the inventors of live supervision as we know it today, describes its beginnings, answers critics, and poses a new direction. In the final section, Montalvo illustrates multiple ways of using live supervision to promote therapists' development in numerous case examples.

_____ Back to the Future: A Review Through Time _____

Cheryl L. Storm

THE INVENTION OF LIVE SUPERVISION

Initially, therapists experimenting with family therapy demonstrated their work to one another and taught each other their methods by conducting therapy while being observed by their colleagues from behind one-way mirrors. These pioneers justified violating the sacrosanct private relationships of therapists and clients because of the newness of what they were doing. They became intensely interested and involved in each other's work, frequently making comments about their observations and suggesting interventions.

Live supervision was a natural outgrowth of the ways these pioneers worked with one another; essentially, they were conducting live supervision with each other. When Haley concluded that a directive given to a therapist during therapy could be simultaneously a supervisory and therapeutic intervention (Liddle, 1991), live supervision as we know it today was born. Haley, Minuchin, and Montalvo developed live supervision as a method of supervising in the early 1950s. They broke many of the traditional rules of supervision by observing from behind one-way mirrors and guiding clinicians' work by interrupting sessions with helpful hints. As supervisors they were active, directive, and intervened in the ongoing therapeutic interaction.

Montalvo (1973) describes, in a now classic paper, ground rules for supervisors practicing this new method of live supervision. He recommends the following guidelines: Supervisees are forewarned that they may initially feel they are under remote control. To minimize this feeling, supervisors act in ways consistent with supervisees' styles and preferred ways of working. Supervisors and supervisees agree, prior to sessions, to the terms of their working arrangement. Supervisors agree to call supervisees out of sessions and supervisees agree to leave sessions to obtain feedback on their work. All supervisory input is a suggestion unless supervisors say supervisees "must do something," which is done rarely and usually only as a result of client danger. Mutual consent and collaboration is maintained by both participants, believing it is the right of supervisors to make demands and of supervisees to question those demands. The majority of case planning occurs in pre- and postsession discussions, with supervisors using restraint during therapy sessions. These recommendations remain as important guidelines for supervisors today.

THE REFINEMENT OF LIVE SUPERVISION

For many, live supervision became the *sine qua non* of supervision. In fact, almost half of the literature on marriage and family therapy (MFT) supervision methods is on live supervision (see bibliography of articles in the *Resource Guide*). Several authors have expanded on Montalvo's original suggestions (Berger & Dammann, 1982; Birchler, 1975; Liddle & Schwartz, 1983; Schwartz, Liddle, & Breunlin, 1988). Over time, supervisors have become increasingly aware of the complex decision making involved in live supervision. When time constraints exist, how do supervisors intervene in such a way that their actions benefit therapy and promote supervisees' growth? Supervisors are called on to make intervention decisions during presession preparations, ongoing therapy, mid-session breaks, and postsession meetings. According to Liddle and Schwartz (1983), there are specific

considerations for each of these points in time. They further believe that when supervisors intervene during sessions, before acting they should consider the urgency of the situation, the probability that supervisees will be successful without supervisory intervention, the probability that supervisees can implement the suggestions, and the degree their supervisory intervention balances supervisees' dependence on them versus supervisees' autonomy. When differences occur between supervisors and supervisees, Berger and Dammann (1982) strongly recommend supervisees' perspectives take precedence because they have access to the in-session context that supervisors lack.

Others have focused on a specific aspect of live supervision such as observer messages (Breunlin & Cade, 1981), the bug-in-the-ear (Byng-Hall, 1982), assessment (Heath, 1983), and phone-ins (Bistline, Mathews, & Freiden, 1985; Coppersmith, 1978; Wright, 1986). Specific guidelines for using these methods in live supervision are offered by these authors.

PROMOTERS AND CRITICS OF LIVE SUPERVISION

Supervisors who endorse live supervision assume supervisees can best learn some therapy skills by practicing them during therapy sessions with supervisory support. Because opportunities are created for therapists to try out new behaviors suggested by supervisors in the immediate moment when the behavior is the most therapeutically appropriate, supervisors believe supervisees' learning is accelerated. They can help supervisees who are stuck or signaling for help by suggesting alternatives otherwise not considered by supervisees. Supervisors also believe therapists' self-report of their work can leave out some critical information about their responses, clients reactions, or therapeutic interaction that is overlooked by supervisees or unintentionally deleted. Supervisors gain this information from observing sessions. If there are other supervisees also observing sessions, these supervisees can study cases without the pressure of being responsible for therapy and with the luxury of time to assess cases and consider possibilities. Supervisors can supervise them by selectively commenting on aspects of the session, requesting that observers pay attention to the session in a particular way, and/or asking for their opinions to tap into their perspective and thinking. Finally, supervisors argue live supervision provides quality control for clients because clinical errors can be avoided or corrected. Supervisors can interrupt and redirect the session at critical moments. Proponents further contend that clients benefit, rather than being harmed, from the insertion of supervisory input. In fact, the only research study of families' reactions to live supervision found that clients were generally positive about the experience, feeling it provided better services because two heads are better than one (Piercy, Sprenkle, & Constantine, 1986).

Some supervisees are excited by being so intensely involved in therapy with their supervisors during live supervision. Essentially, supervisees and supervisors have an experience in common on which to base their work. Some supervisees report liking the safety net provided by live supervision. They note it allows them to be more creative and increases their comfort in trying new behaviors. Others note it is reassuring to know that supervisors have seen their work and have had the opportunity to take over sessions, but chosen not to do so. Some supervisees believe excellent learning opportunities are created when supervisors join their sessions and demonstrate alternatives.

From the start, however, some supervisors (particularly those preferring psychodynamic, intergenerational, and experiential ideas) were less likely to use the live supervision method. They viewed it as intrusive, pushy, and dehumanizing for supervisees and clients. They were troubled by the viola-

tion of therapist–client privacy and the effects of live supervisory input on therapeutic relationships. Over time other critics emerged (Beroza, 1983). Some supervisors noted that they felt overly responsible for their supervisees' therapy. These supervisors found it difficult to allow their supervisees to proceed at their pace and conduct therapy their way when they believed clients could be helped more expediently if supervisees would follow the supervisors' instructions. Without the pressure of the moment and the presence of clients, these supervisors could relax and allow their supervisees the time and freedom to conduct therapy according to supervisees' preferred style, ideas, and interventions.

Some supervisees complained they became "puppets" who could not differentiate their clinical abilities from those of their supervisors. Some supervisees became less confident about their work rather than more self-assured because they found themselves increasingly relying on their supervisors for ideas and instructions. Some supervisees even became reluctant to practice without the presence of a supervisor. Other supervisees experienced themselves as caught between supervisors and clients, or between their preferred ways of working and their supervisors' ways (Elizur, 1990). As can be seen, supervisees' development can be constrained by overdependence on supervisors, a lack of opportunity to practice independently, encouragement of supervisees' passivity, and deskilling of supervisees.

Although descriptions of supervisees' experiences with live supervision exist in the literature (Gershenson & Cohen, 1978; Lowenstein, Reder, & Clark, 1982), there is only one study that assesses them empirically. Liddle, Davidson, and Barrett (1988) found there were differences in the responses of novice and experienced supervisees to live supervision. Novice supervisees were worried about being judged as incompetent, thus, they were preoccupied with their performance and supervisory evaluation.

These reactions rapidly disappeared once they participated in live supervision. More experienced supervisees were apprehensive about potential power and control issues with their supervisors. These reactions dissipated once supervisees felt respected by their supervisors. Both groups viewed the mid-session consultation break favorably, wanted to be active participants in intervention planning, and preferred therapist initiated over supervisor initiated consults as time went on.

In a review of the limited research on live supervision, Liddle (1991) concludes that there is no empirical support for "the adverse opinions about and the emotional claims made for the harmful effects of live supervision" (p. 658). The decision to practice live supervision cannot currently be based on research. Rather, it is a decision supervisors make based on their theoretical leanings, supervision philosophy, and access to one-way mirrors. Most important, if live supervision is conducted, there are clearly ways to do so that promote supervisees' development and autonomy and ways that do not.

THE FUTURE OF LIVE SUPERVISION

Recently, Hardy (1993) argues that the feminist, social constructionist, and cultural relativism movements will transform live supervision in family therapy. Overall, these ideas challenge the traditional hierarchical structure of live supervision and the idea that supervisors' observations about therapy are at least equally if not more important than supervisees' perspectives. As a result, supervisors are experimenting with ways of making the mirror more permeable or removing it. These include reflecting team approaches (see Chapter 24); in-home live supervision without a mirror (Zarski et al., 1991); and approaches where supervisors talk directly to clients on the telephone, share their ideas with supervisees in front of clients, or invite clients to join them behind the mirror (Furman & Ahola, 1992). In the next section, Montalvo takes us back to his original recommendations and then brings us up to date with current trends that are sure to be part of the future of live supervision.

REFERENCES

Berger, M., & Dammann, C. (1982). Live supervision as context, treatment, and training. *Family Process, 21,* 337–344.

Beroza, R. (1983). The shoemaker's children. *Family Therapy Networker, 7,* 31–33.

Birchler, G. (1975). Live supervision and instant feedback in marriage and family therapy. *Journal of Marriage and Family Counseling, 1,* 331–342.

Bistline, J., Matthews, C., & Freiden, F. (1985). The impact of live supervision on supervisees' verbal and nonverbal behavior: A preliminary investigation. *Journal of Marital and Family Therapy, 11,* 203–205.

Breunlin, D., & Cade, B. (1981). Intervening in family systems with observer messages. *Journal of Marital and Family Therapy, 7,* 453–460.

Byng-Hall, J. (1982). The use of the earphone in supervision. In R. Whiffen & J. Byng-Hall (Eds.), *Family therapy supervision: Recent developments in practice* (pp. 47–56). New York: Grune & Stratton.

Coppersmith, E. (1978). Expanding uses of the telephone in family therapy. *Family Process, 19,* 411–417.

Elizur, J. (1990). "Stuckness" in live supervision: Expanding the therapist's style. *Journal of Family Therapy, 12,* 267–280.

Furman, B., & Ahola, T. (1992). Glasnost supervision: Removing the mirror in live supervision. *Supervision Bulletin, 5,* 1–8.

Gershenson, J., & Cohen, M. (1978). Through the looking glass: The experiences of two family therapy trainees with live supervision. *Family Process, 17,* 225–230.

Hardy, K. (1993). Live supervision in the postmodern era of family therapy: Issues, reflections, and questions. *Contemporary Family Therapy, 15,* 9–20.

Heath, A. (1983). The live supervision form: Structure and theory for assessment in live supervision. In

B. Keeney (Ed.), *Diagnosis and assessment in family therapy* (pp. 143–154). Rockville, MD: Aspen.

Liddle, H. (1991). Training and supervision in family therapy: A comprehensive and critical analysis. In A. Gurman & D. Kniskern (Eds.), *Handbook of family therapy, Vol. II* (pp. 638–704). New York: Brunner/Mazel.

Liddle, H., Davidson, G., & Barrett, M. (1988). Outcomes of live supervision: Trainee perspectives. In H. Liddle, D. Breunlin, & R. Schwartz (Eds.), *Handbook of family therapy training and supervision* (pp. 183–193). New York: Guilford Press.

Liddle, H., & Schwartz, R. (1983). Live supervision/consultation: Conceptual and pragmatic guidelines for family therapy training. *Family Process, 22,* 477–490.

Lowenstein, S., Reder, P., & Clark, A. (1982). The consumer's response: Trainees' discussion of the experience of live supervision. In R. Whiffen & J. Byng-Hall (Eds.), *Family therapy supervision: Recent developments in practice* (pp. 115–129). New York: Grune & Stratton.

Montalvo, B. (1972). Aspects of live supervision. *Family Process, 12,* 343–359.

Piercy, F., Sprenkle, D., & Constantine, J. (1986). Family members' perceptions of live observation/supervision. *Contemporary Family Therapy: An International Journal, 8,* 171–187.

Schwartz, R., Liddle, H., & Breunlin, D. (1988). Muddles in live supervision. In H. Liddle, D. Breunlin, & R. Schwartz (Eds.), *Handbook of family therapy training and supervision* (pp. 183–193). New York: Guilford Press.

Wright, L. (1986). An analysis of live supervision "phone-ins" in family therapy. *Journal of Marital and Family Therapy, 12,* 187–190.

Zarski, J., Sand-Pringle, C., Greenbank, M., & Gibik, P. (1991). The invisible mirror: In home family therapy and supervision. *Journal of Marital and Family Therapy, 17,* 133–143.

Live Supervision as a Window

An Interview with Braulio Montalvo

STORM: You are the author of the now classic paper on live supervision (Montalvo, 1973).

MONTALVO: When I wrote that paper, I was proposing live supervision as a supplement to other supervision methods. It was developed because we were looking for other windows for viewing therapists' work. Our original intention was to find a way to get closer to the therapy when our supervisees were needing our help. I am surprised it has become such a single tool. It has been perverted and for many is now the only way.

STORM: So, do you believe other methods of supervision are valuable?

MONTALVO: Live supervision should not be the only tool used in supervision but used with others. Supervisees learn different skills from what I call *synoptic supervision,* supervision in which supervisees summarize several of their therapy sessions with a case, than from live supervision. There is tremendous value in contrasting what is learned through synoptic supervision with live supervision of a case. It is the contrast between "talking about" or abstracting from the "raw stuff" and "seeing in the real world" that provides supervisors with something to work on with supervisees. Each method is a window to help supervisors and supervisees gain information to

Note: Reprinted by permission of the American Association for Marriage and Family Therapy from the Spring 1992 *Supervision Bulletin, 5*(2), 1–2.

understand families and to refine the tools of the therapist. Supervisors should think about using a variety of methods. Sometimes seeing less is seeing more. Observing every other therapy session enables supervisors to see broad patterns. Many supervisors get too wrapped up in one or two themes because they get too close and miss the bigger picture. All windows are needed. Synoptic supervision taps what therapists think, live supervision accesses what they do and once a month sporadic supervision shows their overall professional development.

STORM: You state in your article that the relationship between the supervisor and supervisee is "vertical" yet "a model of mutual consent and collaboration" (p. 344).

MONTALVO: I was focusing on the nature of the supervision contract. The relationship is vertical by consent. If you are going to be responsible for shaping a profession by facilitating appropriate use of abilities, those with experience must lead the way. I believe assuming supervisors and supervisees are on equal footing is unethical. In fact, I even believe that the relationship of supervisor and supervisee should not be too isomorphic to the relationship of the therapist and family. Without differentiation of form and function it is hard to work.

STORM: Probably the major criticism of live supervision is that therapists can become "puppets," dependent on their supervisors, and fail to develop as unique professionals.

MONTALVO: Robotization is a honest pitfall of the method. Live supervision can lead to the flat-footed supervisor who continuously interrupts and detracts from the autonomy of the supervisee. This method was developed based on the model of the good attending physician who helps you over the hump. He or she leaves you standing, in control. Therapists who have supervisors who misuse the method to exhibit their expertise or to gain control are crippled by live supervision and should escape. However, this can also happen from other methods of supervision such as when supervisees "sit in" with their supervisors. This method too can fail to produce the agile, flexible supervisees we aim to train.

STORM: Do you have any advice for supervisors to prevent robotization?

MONTALVO: Live supervision is an art. My model was Haley, who by the way encouraged me to write that paper. He could say three words and you would know just what to do. Supervisors should be cryptic and economical in their comments, have an unobtrusive way of operating, and leave their supervisees standing on their own. Thus, good live supervisors do not interrupt constantly and allow themselves the flexibility to *not* intervene.

STORM: Some supervisors have "taken the mirror down" and supervision occurs in the presence of families and with input from clients. Do you have any reactions to these new developments?

MONTALVO: I have seen variations on this method. I am not sure whether what I have seen is the method or the method not used well. I was called in recently to disentangle a case in which this method resulted in a disaster. Each member of a team of therapists shared their views with a family based on the idea that therapy is a democratic smorgasbord of ideas and that all participants, clients and professionals, are equal. It seemed that everyone was afraid of leaving someone out, which resulted in confusion. I question the outcome of therapy with this method. In this particular case, no one seemed to be concerned about the adolescent's continuing truancy and drug use. I believe responsible hierarchy is essential in therapy and to learning therapy. People, whether clients or therapists, come to us because we are "humble" experts and we should respond with a direction, even if the direction is "I don't know."

STORM: Does it surprise you that your paper has had so much influence in the field?

MONTALVO: I see live supervision, when used carefully, as a symbol of family therapy's strong traditional respect for the immediacy of the family's presenting problem, for what's observable and has to be empirically addressed in order to be helpful. Live supervision, despite its flaws, helped us to move one step closer to the ground of family work, and away from philosophic and ideologic cobwebs, which abound in our field's explanations of what it does.

STORM: What changes do you see occurring in the process of supervision?

MONTALVO: Attention to helping supervisees become open and respectful of contribu-

tions from members of surrounding institutions such as the school, health-care providers, and so on. Supervision must occur at these interfaces. Skill in problem solving with strictly intrafamilial issues is seldom enough in dealing with the complex problems we see. Supervisors must help therapists to enhance their skills at dealing with the interfaces.

In the next article, new guidelines are offered for supervisors practicing live supervision that adapt the method to today's times in which supervision is viewed as a vulnerable commodity (Raggio, 1994).

REFERENCES

Montalvo, B. (1973). Aspects of live supervision. *Family Process, 12,* 343–359.

Raggio, S. (1994). Supervision and business: A nonreimbursable, yet valuable commodity. *Supervision Bulletin, 7,* 3.

Live Supervision: Restrained and Sequence-Centered

Braulio Montalvo

Part of the job of the supervisor is providing the therapist with ideas that will help guide the direction of the healing work. Ideas also help develop a method for handling a particular situation, and/or provide a means of clarifying the nature of the problem.

Note: The author wishes to thank K. Greenstein, D. Bennahum, C. Roche, L. Moll, E. Monaghan, C. García, D. Harmon, and C. Fishman for sharing their clinical experiences.

Those who take therapists as apprentices—in modern times referred to as *supervisors*—have told them throughout centuries, and in many different cultures, to find rituals and objects that will assist them in obtaining ideas and increasing their healing power. For example, an Indian curandera is told by her mentor to light a candle and then read the wax dropping at the base of the candle to obtain insights about the nature of the patient's attachment to the problem.

Another therapist was told by a supervisor to have an undecided man, who was obsessing about whether or no to commit to a love relationship, consult with the moon. An old popular Spanish song, *La Luna Me Miró* by Pepe Jiménez, underscores this advice: "I was about to love you, but I held back. The moon looked at me, and I understood. She told me that your love would not make me happy, that you were going to leave me, because that's how you are." The moon—like the curandera's wax dropping; an African medicineman's throwing and reading of bones; or other healer's use of tarot cards, oracles, or prayer—provides a vehicle for accessing problem-solving ideas and realizations.

MODERN LIVE SUPERVISION

Except for beginners in graduate programs and training institutes, among today's most ritualized vehicles for finding problem-solving ideas is the case conference or team meeting. For experienced therapists based in clinics, reviewing a case with colleagues who listen to their comments and respond to questions remains a main source of ideas for orienting and managing a case. What is new is that the help may come, not only in terms of obtaining colleagues' professional advice, but also in terms of actually recruiting from the conference an ally who joins the work for a while, starting the process of live supervision. Such live supervision may involve observation through a one-way mirror or actual participation in meetings with the patient and family. By noting features of the situation that the therapist may have viewed as incidental or not worth pursuing, the person recruited into the live supervision task contributes to the process of problem modification. In this kind of live supervision, the interpersonal situation has become the unit of observation and intervention. As noted by Minuchin (1974), it has evolved toward philosopher Ortega y Gasset's concept: "I am myself plus my circumstances." The unconscious intrapersonal aspects of the person in the situation are no longer considered more important than the immediate interpersonal circumstances (Auerswald, 1968). The unit of observation consists of both aspects. The person is observed within the context of the sequences of interpersonal interaction (Haley, 1976). To better prepare therapists to address interpersonal circumstances, the supervisor employs various eclectic and noneclectic methods (Liddle, 1982). The format of live supervision can be used flexibly at the service of different therapeutic ideologies and techniques.

Combined Supervisory Methods

Therapists tend to benefit most from live supervision if they have developed the use of synoptic skills in conventional supervision (Montalvo & Storm, 1992). The exercise of synoptic skills entails inferring which redundant patterns of interaction are maintaining maladaptive behaviors. It also includes the use of the imagination to see possibilities of changing them. Mastery of these basic skills allows therapists to experience live supervision as a window to new sources of information that contrast sharply with those available in conventional supervision.

Live supervision looks at interpersonal sequences as the person's most immediate circumstance. To discuss how it looks at less immediate, but powerful circumstances, would take us far beyond its main concern (Compher, 1989; Van Deusen & Lappin, 1993). Live supervision's main concern is more with having visual access to the actual unfolding of decision-making sequences than with the content and narrative employed in conventional supervision. Both windows, when used in combination can supplement and complement each other. Each offers a unique source of clinically useful information.

Before presenting brief examples of how a therapist is joined by a supervisor in live supervision to diagnose and block certain sequences of interaction, and to initiate and maintain others, this chapter first offers examples that illustrate supervisory restraint. This is done to demonstrate that certain requests for live supervision can be productively evaded by making economical use of conventional supervisory approaches to promote the therapist's independence.

Supervisory Restraint of Live Supervision

By examining, via active listening and exploratory support, the influence of the therapist's own personal and educational development and unrecognized feelings, a supervisor may render unnecessary the request for live supervision. Consider this situation created by the interface between a family and a health clinic.

_____

A doctor at the clinic is working with a single-parent family, a mother with AIDS whose baby also has the disease. This mother had been a drug addict, and is now requesting a stronger pain killer to help with her chronic arthritis. The doctor is uneasy about the request, especially after the baby's pediatrician tells the doctor clearly that, because of the mother's past drug-seeking behavior, her request should be denied. His suggestion matched the strong cautions the doctor learned in her medical education. Still, in this case, the doctor felt some intuitive resistance to the coercive wisdom of her medical training, and even to the advice of her pediatric colleague. She decided to request a second opinion, and to get live supervision to assist in the session in which she was to deny the patient's request for stronger pain medication.

When the doctor asked for live supervision, the supervisor saw signals of ambivalence and distress, and asked, "Are you sure you want to do this?" The supervisor questioned the doctor's reaction because it was uncharacteristic of her. Usually any hint of inappropriate drug use led to

a clear decision. Based on the supervisor's experience of this physician as responsible and responsive to patients, the supervisor decided to intervene by supporting the therapist's reluctance to deny the patient's request. The doctor was surprised at her own explosive response: "Hell, no, I really feel sympathetic to this mother, and I don't want to get into a battle with her over shifting pain killers, which I think I could get her to control adequately." The doctor decided right there and then that she did not need the live supervision support after all. She was going to trust the patient's capacity to employ the drug judiciously without impairing the care of the baby.

_____

At first, this doctor had minimized her empathy for the patient and her self-confidence in her ability to assess the situation. She had tried to ignore those feelings until the supervisor's question brought them to the surface.

This doctor went on to contract firmly with her patient, making it clear that if the baby's care were compromised in any way by the misuse of the new pain killers, the arrangement was off. The patient complied with the doctor's directives and close monitoring; in fact, her pain relief enhanced her ability to care for her baby. In this case, the doctor trusted the patient and the supervisor needed to trust the doctor's decision to challenge conventional wisdom. The supervisor needed to refrain from being protocol-bound by the larger system and to be sensitive to the reactions of the supervisee. Supervisors must refuse the inherent seduction of live supervision to do more than is necessary. The supervisory job is to help supervisees to gain confidence and to be independent.

Deferred Live Supervision

Another interface of a family and a hospital involves a woman trying to help her elderly husband who is suffering from terminal congestive heart failure with serious renal complications.

The wife is observed at her husband's side day and night. The man has been wavering for weeks between comatose states and semilucidity. Despite the best pharmacological efforts of his medical providers, he is generally uncomfortable. The initiative for change in his situation comes from the man's circumstances in the hospital. His medical providers pleaded with the wife, "Please, you have to help him to let go." A therapist is assigned to help her, but finds her holding on tight: "I just cannot tell him to let go. I just can't." Soon, the therapist requests a supervisor to come into the next session and help, because he is not making any headway. The supervisor replies, "Before we do that, check to see what she does with him when she is here in the room, and what they used to do in better days when they were together." The supervisor adds, "See if she has a friend or relative who can tell her how to tell her husband to let go, without saying it straight out."

Soon the woman tells the therapist that whenever she visits her husband she waits for periods of lucidity to reminisce with him about their golfing trips. After the last session the woman took the therapist's advice and called her cousin who gave the following suggestion: "Keep talking about those golf trips, and when he is fully into it, play golf with him, and take him to the last hole." The wife began to sit on the bed next to her husband, and when she felt he was connected to her words, she would gently take him to the final hole.

The therapist's contribution became that of helping her make the message more concrete. He asked her to bring a golf ball with her, put it in her husband's hand, and make sure he could hold it. At the end of their reminiscing, the wife was to say to him, "It's time to go home now. Let go of the ball, I will take good care of it for you."

The live supervision request was deferred indefinitely. The wife found all the help she needed in her own social network resources, drawing on support and a metaphoric tool to assist her husband in a good death.

Limited Live Supervision

The modulation of feelings in the session is a natural focus in live supervision as it tries to protect coping efforts from being derailed. The following case demonstrates the interface of family and school.

A therapist feels she needs help in dealing with the wounded and puzzled feelings of parents whose mentally retarded adolescent recently attempted to overdose. The parents had been struggling to find out what had contributed to the girl's feeling of devaluation and depression. The therapist had requested live supervision for a special session with only the parents because she felt the injured parents were not really acknowledging any responsibility for their daughter's behavior. The live supervisor offered to observe the session and call in only if necessary.

The therapist skillfully helped the parents appreciate that for a long time the teachers in school had been treating the girl as a disappointment Right after that, as expected, the parents started considering that perhaps they, too, had something to do with the overdosing. For weeks they had been ridiculing the girl, constantly finding fault in her performance of chores around the house. As the parents began to acknowledge they had something to do with the daughter's actions, nonverbal cues of sadness and anger began to increase. They were rapidly on the way to being inundated with guilt, and painfully puzzled at how, just a few days before overdosing, the girl had responded to their criticism by becoming "super good."

At that point, the supervisor called the therapist to say, "Watch it! These parents may now swing completely the other way Reassure them They do not have to carry all the responsibility for this." The therapist told them, "Now you are about to say that you had everything to do with the problem. Let me tell you, your daughter is very good at making you feel like taking all the blame." The parent's reaction of immediate relief from excessive guilt was clear. "Yes, we had a lot to do with it, but it's true. She makes us feel like taking all the blame."

Prevented from feeling overwhelmed, the parents then participated in a sober, productive discussion. They moved on to moderate not only their own perfectionistic demands on the girl but those of the school.

One limited supervisory call had helped the therapist learn how to modulate the fluctuations of feelings in the session, adjusting the allocation of blame without disrupting the flow of constructive work. This experience immediately affected the therapist's work with other cases.

ENTERING LIVE SUPERVISION

What the therapist learns from the supervisor's involvement in the session goes beyond having a model of how to implement specific approaches to help a family. When the live supervision is effective, the therapist has opportunity to learn to do the following:

1. Modify interpersonal sequences that uphold maladaptive behavior.
2. Initiate sequences that may solve the problem.
3. Recognize that determining who starts, who upholds, and who finishes interpersonal sequences is not always obvious, although these factors have significant consequences.
4. Block certain sequences in order to surface the unseen influence of decision making that curtail the problem-solving process.

5. Protect the new decisions and the productive sequence that follows.
6. Motivate the unfolding of problem-solving sequences away from the session, encouraging participants to change inflexible positions, loosening rigid situations.

The brief cases that follow exemplify these points. The first case arises from the interface of a family and a nursing home.

THE VENDETTA

A man has severe circulatory problems, dementia, and out-of-control diabetes. His wife, though witnessing his prolonged suffering, will not agree to "do not hospitalize" and "do not resuscitate" orders. The medical providers and the therapists have been explicit and patient with her. Although her husband's poor quality of life requires that she carefully reconsider her decision, she continues to insist that she wants everything done.

In a case conference, the therapist presents the case to his colleagues. One doctor in the group notes that the therapist describes the woman's reaction as being like a "wall." This doctor listens carefully as the therapist explains that the woman's reaction probably emerges from strong wishes to pay her husband back. When he was a younger man, he had brutally abused her. Toward the end of the description of the woman's possible motivation, the doctor listens to the therapist's afterthought: 'The sons' wishes don't help either." By exploring the therapist's afterthought, the supervisor helps solve the case.

The doctor is invited to participate as a live supervisor in the therapist's next session with the family. Perhaps he can help find a way that this woman will consent to change her decision, or at least to clarify what family processes reinforce her stubbornness in wanting "everything done." The woman, her adult daughter and three sons come in. The invited supervisor quickly sees that the mother looks to the sons after every utterance, and suspects this is a basic circuit of decision-making in this family. He begins to be less impressed with the hypothesis of this woman's motivation being a personal vendetta as he observes that the mother seems to be at the mercy of her sons. The doctor also notes the alert and dismayed expression of the daughter who seems to have the respect of the sons.

The doctor proceeds to initiate a sequence in which the daughter is to explain further the father's situation to her brothers. When she begins, "We are prolonging our father's misery . ." it is clear that she is including herself, and that her brothers will respond to her arguments. As the compassionate older sister, she gains their attention. Soon after, one of the brothers says, "I sure don't want him to suffer." Another one joins in, "I did not know it was that bad." Seeing the result of the doctor's intervention, the therapist rapidly moves to protect this new sequence. He encourages them to ask questions. After not too long, their mother changes her mind. This change clearly hinges on the sons' releasing her from their push to save their father at all costs; this occurred after his daughter intervened.

The therapist learned to value carefully his incidental afterthoughts for clues on how to solve problem situations. The following case underscores that understanding of the course of decision-making can generally be helpful but is not always easy.

MOTHER ALONE

At the interface between a geriatric clinic and a family, a doctor attending an elderly woman consults with a therapist after seeing the patient overwhelmed with aches and lethargy as a result of depression. Besides meeting the needs of her severely demented husband, the woman has recently been facing the threatening behavior of an adult schizophrenic son. "He has guns and has us in a constant upheaval," the woman declared to the doctor. The therapist rapidly checked on the plight of the son and dis-

covered that, after his last hospitalization, he had been designated to go to a halfway house but never got there. The doctor suspected a family process underlay the situation. Perhaps the woman's other sons were trying to get her to shelter the schizophrenic son; he found out differently, however. The hospital provider told him that, "All four siblings think he should go into a halfway house, and away from his mother. Mother is the one who does not like the halfway house arrangement."

This discovery ended the doctor's concern with the family. "If my patient is sabotaging herself, then there is nothing I can do to relieve her depression, except to medicate," was the doctor's conclusion. Actually, the therapist discovered that the other sons had simply decided to get out of the way, leaving the son's problems to their mother. They claimed they supported sending their brother to a halfway house but offered no help with the burden of care, with the upholding of routines for safety, the removal of weapons, or the transition to the halfway house. The therapist's request for a family session with live supervision to work on disengaging the mother from her son by involving his siblings more was ignored. This was considered unnecessary because the doctor had determined that the mother's decision alone was sabotaging change. In time the schizophrenic son's intimidation increased, and so did his mother's depression. Soon, the son's agitation, and the dangerousness of the situation, required that he be hospitalized again. Mother and son enmeshed further as siblings stayed out of it. Probably the son will return home for the cycle to start again.

If a live supervision session had occurred, the physician would have had first-hand contact with the ways in which the rest of the family was invested in keeping the problematic son glued to the mother. The therapist and physician then could have challenged the family to help mother and son in their disengagement process. Other forms of supervision leave the door open for just commenting on the disengagement, perhaps even facilitating further enmeshment by the lack of challenge on the part of the therapist. In addition, if the therapist and the physician were not involved in the live session, possibly they would have worked at cross purposes with one another because the physician's and the therapist's view differed.

Live supervision is most rewarding for the family and the therapist when it brings out previously unseen decisions that are crucial to the resolution of conflict.

_____

PLEASE DO IT

A clinician was working at the interface of the family and an elementary school when a husband and wife brought in their two children, ages eight and ten. The eight-year-old was overactive, with a diagnosis of attention deficit hyperactive disorder. During class he could barely stay in his seat. His older sister whined often and habitually visited the nurse's station with frequent vague somatic complaints. When the couple entered the room, it was immediately evident that they were constantly bickering. The therapist felt that the youngsters escalated their display of symptoms in the session to interrupt the angry exchanges between mother and father. The mother concentrated on consoling the children, and the husband criticized her for so doing. She counterattacked, "If you want to help me, stop criticizing me, and put your arms around our daughter." He shouted back, "I am not allowed to do it, I have been trying, and I am not allowed."

The supervisor decided that this redundant drama was overwhelming the mother. He entered the room and announced to the mother, "I came to support you." The mother started crying, and immediately the daughter moved over to comfort her and the boy was about to follow her. The live supervisor quickly told the husband, "Your daughter is taking on your job." The man answered, "She has always had it." The girl was still in motion, reaching out to her mother when the supervisor shouted, "Don't let her do it."

There was some effort on the man's part to reach out, but then he pulled back. Just at this moment the wife covered her face with her hands and uttered a despairing cry, "Please do it, do it." Finally, her husband moved toward his wife and hugged her. As they embraced, the girl was about to move between them and displace the father but the supervisor distracted her, protecting the new sequence. "Look Jane, this is strictly for mom and dad. . . . What kind of games do you like to play?" The girl stopped whining, and flowed into age-appropriate activities. The therapist followed the supervisor and engaged the boy in playing games while his mother and father kept embracing and talking softly to each other.

_____

The live supervisor had plunged into the rapids of interpersonal interaction, aware that the children needed to be blocked before they interfered with the efforts of the husband to reach out to help his wife (Fishman, 1993). But neither the therapist nor the supervisor had any awareness of how necessary to the resolution of conflict it was for the husband to receive an explicit invitation from the wife. After her decision to invite him, the adults' closing of ranks became much easier, and the children's symptoms lessened.

Supervisors cannot guarantee that therapists will feel supported when intervening by joining in the sessions, but they can consider several factors when stepping in. These include the nature of the problem in therapy, the degree to which the perception of the seriousness of the problem is shared, and the history of the relationship between supervisor and supervisee. If a supervisee feels temporarily disconcerted, and the superpervisory relationship is one of trust and caring, the supervisor's interventions are likely to be welcomed. If, as in this case, clients accommodate to the new input and supervisees can become active participants in the intervention rather than observers, the supervisory input will become a learning experience.

Live supervision is well suited to deal with situations characterized by impasses among family members. In these situations, the supervisor's emphasis is on activating, but also restraining, the participants who must select certain sequences over others in order to resolve the impasse.

THE DEAD FATHER

An old man who suffered from Alzheimer's disease dies; his death brings up conflict between his daughter and son. His daughter wants to have an autopsy performed because she is afraid she or her children could suffer from the same disease some day. Her brother refuses to consent, saying he does not want his father's body touched. This impasse occurs at the interface of the hospital and the family as the brother, sister, and her children meet with the doctor. To the doctor, it reflects an impaired sibling relationship of long standing, which is now about to worsen.

The doctor wants to do preventive work because he sees the conflict building into a major family rift that could damage all surviving relatives. He spends three hours with them, explaining that it is unlikely they will learn much from the autopsy, because the forensic study usually agrees with clinical opinion regarding Alzheimer's. This argument supports the son's position and increases the daughter's determination. She insists, "At least, I must know whether it was multi-infarct dementia or Alzheimer's." Her brother states, "I could never forgive myself if I allowed a defiling of my father's body."

Realizing at last that his rational arguments were getting him nowhere, the doctor decides to get help. He recruits a family therapist as a live supervisor/collaborator in a case conference. After working together for half an hour, the impasse looks worse until, without warning, the live supervisor begins to impersonate the dead father. Addressing the son, the supervisor says, "You know, it's OK for her to want whatever she wants. She took very good care of me during the last days of my life." The son is about to reply but is interrupted by a question addressed to the daughter, "How old are my grandchildren now?" "Five and seven," she replied. "What do they think of their uncle?" was his next question. She answered, "Though they do not see each other too much, they have good feelings for him." Before she had a chance to add anything else, the supervisor, still acting as the dead father, asks the son, "Do the kids like you?" "I guess so," was his reply. Immediately came the next question, "Wouldn't it be good to know for sure what could happen to them when they get old?"

Before the son had a chance to answer, the doctor collaborates, expounding on the unreasonable costs of exhuming a body for an autopsy, and on the money that lawyers will likely take if the family has to go to court. The dead father speaks with annoyance, "Don't you think my grandchildren would enjoy a trip to Disney World more than spending all that money in court? This fight has nothing to do with me, it has to do with your rivalry." The son interrupts, "I would not forgive myself if I allowed an autopsy." The dead father breaks the son's self-hypnosis, using the same self-directives, "Would you forgive yourself if you deprived the children of their uncle's friendship? I know you wanted to do more for me, and you couldn't." Just then, the doctor throws in his powerful time bomb, which unifies the family in a race against the morgue. "The freezer people at the morgue are about to have their way. If the two of you don't make up your minds in the next ten days, your father will be buried as an indigent in a mass tomb." Both the doctor and the live supervisor then stood up to exit, increasing the impact of their warning with hasty goodbyes.

Three days later, the dead man's daughter called to inform the doctor that her brother had agreed to allow the autopsy. She had helped him decide by providing him with all the information she had carefully collected on the Alzheimer's family tree. It is not clear whether her brother yielded before or after she offered him the information.

The supervisor's enactment of the dead father is reminiscent of the formal trance or religious healing rituals used in various cultures such as in Brazil (Richeport, 1984). The device stirred up guilt as motivation for change. The impersonated father's voice mobilized constructive guilt in the daughter, who became remorseful about alienating her children from their uncle, just after they had lost their grandfather. It also elicited guilt in the son who had been competing with his sister to demonstrate that he too had a place of importance in decisions pertaining to their father. Yet the enactment of the dead father recognized the son as wanting to share in the burden of care, which his sister had abrogated. Perhaps this last message prompted the sister to give him, for the first time, an opportunity to share in decisions pertaining to their father. Allowing the autopsy may have been the brother's way of reciprocating.

In this particular instance of live supervision, the doctor started by assisting and observing the supervisor's intervention with the family. As the doctor observed the supervisor's interventions, he experienced the impasse differently, and added his own creativity to the intervention. When he added the "time bomb," he joined the supervisor and they marched with the family in unison. This was a collaborative moment. When supervisees take the initiative and expand the work being done, supervisors must fade. Supervisees can then leave the session feeling confident and competent.

CONCLUSION

Live supervision continues to be used by therapists at the interface of the family and its surrounding institutions. It has become a form of brief apprenticeship and can be used with restraint and with other supervising methods to help therapists find and reinforce family strengths (Montalvo, 1987). Live supervision remains especially useful for diagnosing and blocking maladaptive sequences, for initiating productive sequences, and in maintaining their actualization. Live supervision serves well for modulating affective fluctuations that impede problem solving, for surfacing and changing decisions that curtail resolution of family conflict, and for prompting impasse-breaking sequences among stalemated family members. Among today's trends in live supervision are found attempts to have it more focused on crucial sequences, and given by a collaborative colleague recruited from the case conference or team meeting, rather than from a staff's permanent teaching hierarchy. This trend and its implications deserve further study.

REFERENCES

Auerswald, E. (1968). Interdisciplinary versus ecological approach. *Family Process, 7*, 202–215.

Compher, V. (1989). *Family-centered practice: The interactional dance beyond the family system.* New York: Plenum Publishing.

Fishman, C. (1993). *Intensive structural therapy: Treating families in their social context.* New York: Basic Books.

Haley, J. (1976). *Problem-solving therapy.* San Francisco: Jossey-Bass.

Liddle, H. (1982). On the problems of eclecticism: A call for epistemologic clarification and human-scale theories. *Family Process, 21,* 243–250.

Montalvo, B. (1987). Family strengths: Obstacles and facilitators. In M. Karpel (Ed.), *Family resources: The hidden partner in family therapy* (pp. 93–115). New York: Guilford Press.

Montalvo, B., & Storm, C. (1992). Live supervision as a window: An interview with Braulio Montalvo. *Supervision Bulletin, 5,* 1–2.

Ortega y Gasset, J. (as quoted by Minuchin, S.) (1974). *Families and family therapy.* Cambridge: Harvard University Press.

Richeport, M. (1984). *Macumba, trance and spirit healing.* New York: Filmmakers Library Inc.

Van Deusen, J., & Lappin, J. (1993). Supervising systems. *Supervision Bulletin, 6,* 3–4.

21

Dismounting the Tiger
Using Tape in Supervision

Howard Protinsky

A supervisee once related an Asian proverb, "He who chooses to ride the tiger will not easily dismount" to capture her experience with a marital therapy case. She described herself as along for the ride, unable to interact with the couple in such a way that might alter the rigid patterns of interaction in the therapeutic ecosystem. In a discussion with her supervisor, she was able to identify the internal and interpersonal manifestations of this experience. She was then asked to review the videotapes of her last five sessions with this couple and find those portions of each session when she felt like she was "riding the tiger." Those sections of videotape then became the focus of the next several supervision sessions. By reviewing this process with her supervisor, she was able to discover how her family-of-origin themes were being reenacted in the therapy sessions and, then, to devise new therapeutic stances to implement in the coming sessions.

This example of the use of videotape in supervision is but one way to illustrate the tremendous changes technology has stimulated in marriage and family therapy (MFT) supervision. In the 1940s, Earl Zinn's recordings of psychotherapy sessions on wax Dictaphone cylinders were seen as *the* innovative tool in the study of the psychotherapeutic process (Gill, Newman, & Redlich, 1954). In the 1950s, it was generally agreed that Carl

Rogers was most influential in the use of electronic recording of the psychotherapy session. During the late 1960s and early 1970s, the use of video as a supervisory tool mushroomed at least in part because of the technical revolution in that industry (Heilveil, 1981).

Today, the use of audio- and videotapes for supervision of MFT has become commonplace. Tapes have been used within the context of supervision for teaching therapy techniques, family dynamics, and family assessment, as well as contributing to self-awareness and the therapeutic use of self. Despite such widespread use, there is relatively little written about the use of tape modalities in MFT supervision. One notable exception is the work of Breunlin et al. (1988) in which a model for the use of videotape supervision was developed using second-order cybernetics as the organizing theory. Second-order cybernetics was chosen because it connects interactive and internal processes and is an improvement over first-order cybernetics, which neglects the internal process of the therapist. In this model, the focus of the videotape supervision becomes the therapist–family system rather than the client system. The purpose of this chapter, however, is not to place audio- or videotape MFT supervision within any particular theoretical framework. Rather, examples of using tape in supervision are presented from various frameworks in an effort to develop an enriched description of its application.

GENERAL CONSIDERATIONS

Prior to the use of audiotape, supervisees were limited to their recollections of previous therapy sessions. The information about the therapist–client interaction was less than optimal. Because the supervisor was not able to hear or see the client, she or he was deprived of valuable information and perhaps was led to focus more attention on the supervisee than the client. By listening to an audiotape, however, both supervisor and supervisee are able to have a greater access to the therapy process, not only to the words exchanged but also to the emotional tone of the conversation. In addition, nonfluencies in speech, tonal shifts, and the verbal interaction patterns of the therapist and client can be ascertained.

Audiotape supervision may be the preferred mode of supervision depending on the MFT model being used. For example, live or videotape supervision might be preferred for structural therapy with its emphasis on nonverbal as well as verbal processes. However, with the focus on verbal interaction in the session and the development of between-session homework tasks, historically, the MRI group has relied on audiotape for supervision.

Keeney and Ray (1992) make the argument that perhaps sight has been unfairly privileged over sound in the supervision process. Instead of super*vision*, they offer the idea of super*audition* in which there would be an emphasis on the technology of sound. Thus, the qualities of spoken language, such as pitch, loudness, and rhythm, would be highlighted. Supervision interventions might then focus on changing the resonance of spoken words. Keeney and Ray make the case that a variety of unique therapeutic strategies could be developed that em-

phasize the auditory such as the use of percussion instruments to underscore talk or a voice synthesizer to transform voices.

The use of videotape, of course, adds much more data to the supervision process through access to nonverbal behavior. With videotape, for example, clues to *coenesis* (interactional synchrony), in which one person in the room moves in rhythmic synchrony with another without awareness, may be discovered. Both types of tape supervision have certain advantages over live supervision. Tape playback can freeze time so that a session may be studied in detail—small sections can be selected or the general flow of the entire session can be experienced. A recap of months of therapy can take place through the serial viewing/listening of sections of tape; a Sartrean metaphor of what one has become as a therapist can be developed through time as therapists select multiple portions of tape that create self-portraits. Through the use of tapes, alliances in the therapeutic ecosystem can be more obvious. In the same way, distances within the therapist–client system can be perceived by ignoring the auditory channel or by observing forms of nonverbal behavior. Also, the use of tape may have the advantage of producing some professional distance from the emotional process of the session. Such space may be conducive to gaining a different perspective by both supervisor and therapist.

SPECIFIC UTILIZATIONS

Therapeutic Use of Self

Tape playback might be understood as a form of self-confrontation (Heilveil & Muehleman, 1981). The words and/or images played in the supervision process can have profound effects on the supervisee as she or he views what Karen Horney (1950) refers to as *the* significant aspect of neurosis—the gap between a person's idealized image and real self. The emotional distance afforded by the tape playback allows the supervisee to be less defensive concerning this gap and, thus, offers a unique opportunity for new perceptions with subsequent ability to practice new behaviors. In cases where supervisees experience an uncomfortable degree of emotional reactivity and describe themselves as "stuck," a study of the patterns of interaction in which this emotional process is embedded can be useful.

After returning from a workshop on the use of paradox in psychotherapy, a relatively inexperienced marriage and family therapist decided to take the plunge. He was working with a couple whose presenting complaint was the frequency of their arguments. The therapist was in private practice but was able to audiotape his sessions for supervision and selected the section of tape in which he attempted the paradoxical intervention. He described the session as having gone poorly, and he felt he had become emotionally reactive to the couple as his intervention was falling flat. In listening to the tape, it was easy to hear that the husband reacted negatively to the therapist's suggestion that he and his wife schedule fights. As the husband became angry and challenged the therapist, the supervisor noticed a subtle change in the tone of the therapist's voice. This section of tape was played several times with the supervisor asking the therapist to listen carefully to his reaction to the husband's challenges. At first, the therapist only noticed that he responded to the husband with what he believed to be the appropriate therapeutic words; however, after listening during the third playback, he was able to hear his subtle anger and, then, to listen to the effect his anger had on the couple. This awareness led to a discussion of a family-of-origin theme for this supervisee concerning his relationship with his father and their style of dealing with anger. The supervisee was then asked to review other tapes in order to listen for this theme in his work.

Another therapist described herself as being confused and anxious concerning her work with a certain couple. She presented sections of videotape of several of her sessions that, to her, were a good illustration of her confusion and anxiety. The pattern that emerged from observing these tapes was one in which the therapist was having difficulty handling intense, in-session, verbal fighting by the couple. She felt immobilized at first; then, when she would intervene actively, she was ineffective in changing the interaction. As parts of several sessions were reviewed, the supervisor noticed that an alliance seemed to have been formed between the wife and therapist. When asked about her feelings of closeness and distance with each member of the couple, the therapist indicated that she believed she was in a somewhat neutral stance. Indeed, in listening to the conversation in the session, there were no overt examples of side-taking on the part of the therapist. The supervisor then asked the therapist to replay several of the taped examples again, but without the sound. The supervisee was asked to observe her body posture and movements only. As visual portions of the tape were replayed several times, a dance emerged in which the therapist and wife moved in a type of interactional synchrony. The supervisee was able to see this and also to observe the movements of the husband that seemed to indicate his exclusion. Next, this pattern was played with the audio. By using the tape in this way, the therapist was able to perceive the discrepancy between her verbal and nonverbal communications with the couple.

Teaching Theory and Technique

The use of taped sessions for supervision may actually be superior to live supervision if the goal is learning to implement specific therapeutic theory or technique. For example, one can analyze a tape at a microlevel, stopping and starting multiple times to process small chunks. The therapist can discuss a theoretical rationale for each specific sequence being examined. Minute details of family interaction patterns, as well as those of the therapist and the family, can be studied. This micro-analysis is especially useful in assisting the new marriage and family therapist to move from a linear to a circular approach.

Tape replay greatly enhances the ability to perceive how each part of the therapeutic system contributes to a certain chain of events and how punctuation may be understood as arbitrary. For example, Whiffen (1982) suggests a useful exercise in which the supervisor asks the therapist to select the starting point for a sequence of interaction on a tape. Then, the supervisee is to look at that sequence again but start the tape a little earlier. In this way, a new perspective emerges from a new punctuation.

One supervision goal that therapists often have is to learn how to implement a specific therapeutic intervention. Obviously, the content of this type of supervision will depend on the specific technique being learned. The teaching of many of the techniques that are consistent with popular MFT models, such as structural and strategic, are greatly enhanced by tape supervision. In the previous example concerning the use of paradox, the supervisor was able to analyze the tape on a microlevel in order to enhance technique. For example, the therapist had attempted to use the intervention without constructing a meaningful rationale for the couple. The construction and delivery of the paradoxical intervention were listened to in detail, and suggestions were made for their improvement.

Multiple Realities

In the postmodern MFT world, there is an awareness of reality as a social construct. Many find it difficult to defend the position that family therapy theories represent truth. Rather,

these theories and models are understood as constructions that may be both useful and, at the same time, limiting. It may be helpful to involve multiple viewpoints when constructing a therapeutic problem and a therapeutic process. For example, the traditional approach to audio- or videotape supervision is for the therapist and supervisor to review the tape with the supervisor clearly being at the top of the hierarchy. Less traditional is for the supervisor and supervisee to exchange their views of the case and attempt to co-evolve a therapeutic plan. Yet another experience can be attained by having the supervisor, therapist, and client review the tape together with each having a voice concerning the meaning of a particular therapeutic session.

In a supervision session attended by the client, a single parent, the therapist, and a supervisor, an audiotape was played of the last session. A fifteen-minute section was reviewed with the participants giving their views of the therapy process. In this particular case, the client was asking for help with the handling of her seven-year-old son's misbehavior. She saw herself as being in a power struggle with him. The therapist had many ideas he deemed useful for the client; however, she never seemed to follow through. As often happens, there was a parallel process taking place between the therapist and supervisor. The therapist would ask for suggestions on how to handle the case. The supervisor would offer several, the therapist would agree, and then proceed not to use the ideas.

After this particular section of tape was listened to, the client expressed her perspective that the therapist's tone of voice seemed to say he was upset with her for not using his ideas. The therapist acknowledged her perspective and related that he indeed felt frustrated with her. Then, the discussion focused on how interesting it was that the client seemed frustrated with her son in the same way the therapist was frustrated with her. They were both able to process these feelings and describe a better understanding of these two levels of relationships. As the supervisor listened to this conversation, he became aware of the next level of the parallel process, his frustration with the supervisee. This perspective was openly discussed with the client and therapist. As they each reacted to the audiotape, the three participants co-constructed a new view of the therapy process and were able to evolve into a different system of interaction.

One method of teaching multiple realities involves the use of videotape in group supervision. Traditionally, group observation of a taped therapy session allows group members to talk about their perceptions of the case and to contribute their ideas concerning the therapeutic process. Another way is to ask each member of the group to observe the tape from the viewpoint of one of the therapy session participants. That is, as they view the tape, each member is to attempt to become one of the participants and to experience the session from that perspective. For example, for a family, one group member would experience the videotape playback from the position of the father, one from the mother, one from the son, and so on. By participating in this activity, an enriched description of the therapy process can be attained. More information becomes available to the therapist from these multiple perspectives.

One such group supervision process involved a therapist who was perceiving various family members in ways that highlighted their aversive behaviors toward him. In the session, he experienced the mother as dependent and complaining, the father as overly aggressive, and the child as uncooperative. The members of the supervision group agreed that it would be easy to describe these family members in that way. However, a discussion soon arose as to how a different perception might lead to a different and perhaps more effective way of engaging the family in the therapeutic process.

The four members of the supervision group then observed the video, with three of them taking the perspective of each of the family members, and one taking the perspective of the therapist. After viewing the tape in this way, a lively conversation resulted in which multiple views were expressed. For instance, mother's representative spoke of the hurt she experienced from her perceived rejection by her husband and son. She talked of feeling small and inadequate and, as a female, being left out of this male-oriented family. Father's representative spoke of the stress he experienced for having to overfunction for his wife and son, while the son's representative spoke of his feeling of being alone. The therapist's representative talked about feelings of inadequacy in his relationship to this family. As these and many other perspectives were presented, the therapist was able to see himself and the family in new ways—multiple perspectives that aided him in future sessions.

Reflecting Team Supervision

The concept of the reflecting team was developed by Andersen and colleagues (1987) to enhance therapy, especially when a therapeutic impasse seemed to be present. A bilevel process was used in which a group of therapists observed a therapy session from behind a one-way mirror. During a break, the therapist and clients switched places with the observation/reflecting team. The clients and therapist then observed the team reflect on their observations of the therapy process. This process can also be used in audio- and videotape supervision. A supervision reflecting team may observe the tape of a supervision session between therapist and supervisor. The team then discusses their observations of the supervision session. These observations are recorded on tape and made available to the therapist and supervisor to watch separately or together. With such a process, multiple viewpoints about the therapy and supervisory sessions are made available.

Reflecting team supervision also can be used within the context of a particular model of therapy. For example, one supervisee was using a solution-focused approach to MFT, and her supervisor was using solution-focused principles in the supervision sessions. That is, while the therapist was orienting her therapy around the principles of goal setting, amplifying exceptions to the problem, and the use of scaling questions, the supervisor did the same with the supervisee concerning her therapeutic work in the session. She asked the supervisee to play videotape of the most therapeutic aspects of each session, amplifying each one. The solution-focused reflecting team then discussed their viewing of the supervision tape from the same perspective. In their discussion, they reflected on such issues as, "I wonder what would have happened in the therapy session if the therapist had stayed with her efforts to try to find exceptions to the problem?" or, "I wonder what the experience of the supervisee would have been like if her supervisor had focused more on her strengths with this family?"

The use of such curious questioning by the supervisory team while they viewed the tape created and allowed room for amplification of positives and the complimenting of the supervisor and supervisee. For example, the team indirectly complimented the supervisor by posing questions like, "I wonder how she kept herself on track?" Observing the tape and noticing the change in language from observational statements to questioning had a reported positive effect on the therapist and supervisor. Both agreed that the curious questioning opened new possibilities and ways of thinking.

This particular supervisee and supervisor believed that having the team's discussion on videotape was a distinct advantage over watching such a discussion from behind the one-way mirror. They were able to watch the tape in a relaxed atmosphere and to dialogue with one another about their reactions. This leisurely processing of the reflecting team discussion helped to decrease some of the anxiety associated with the process. The fears concerning evaluation seemed to be replaced by the discovery of resources and an expanded view of the therapy and supervisory processes.

Evaluation Process

The use of audio- and videotapes are especially valuable in the evaluation process. Depending on the goals of supervision, tapes can be used to evaluate therapist, supervisor, and the supervision process. If supervision has focused on the developing of certain skills within the framework of one particular model, then tapes that illustrate the skill enhancement of the therapist within that model can be kept throughout supervision. For example, as one therapist was learning the solution-focused model in supervision, the supervisor saved on tape the best efforts of the supervisee during each session. At the point of evaluation, these sections of tape were played for the supervisee to demonstrate her progress. On the other hand, the supervisee could be asked to keep her own tape recordings of her progress to play during the final evaluation. Of course, tapes can be kept to illustrate aspects of the therapist's work that need improving also.

If the focus of supervision has been on the self of the therapist, then sections of tape might be accumulated that illustrate the therapist's strengths and areas that need improvement. On a larger scale, the therapist may review her taped work over time and select examples that best illustrate her therapeutic self-portrait; that is, finding those moments in therapy that really indicate who she is theoretically and pragmatically in the therapy context.

It is also useful to tape supervision sessions. Therapist and supervisor can review some of these tapes, either separately or together, and select those elements of the supervision process that seem most meaningful to them. It is often the case that the therapist and supervisor have differing views on the most meaningful aspects of supervision. This discrepancy can be an important discovery that enhances the supervision process.

Problems and Pragmatics

Breunlin et al. (1988) remind us that a common pitfall of the use of tape in supervision is the loss of focus during the supervision session. Because of the abundance of stimuli offered by the use of tape, goals should be agreed on in order to focus the supervision. Such goals are often derived from the MFT model being used and guide the therapist and supervisor in the selection of which segments of the tape to use. Based on those goals, then, the supervisee reviews the tape and selects those sections to use in supervision that are congruent with agreed-on supervision goals. This process helps to counter the possibility of inadequate preparation for either audio- or videotape supervision because of time constraints experienced by the therapist and supervisor.

Research has shown that the supervisee's experience of confronting self through tape supervision can create anxiety and defensiveness (Holzman, 1969). Also, the supervisee's performance anxiety and concern about supervisor approval can create additional anxiety which can interfere with the learning process. When supervisors are aware of this possibility, they can process these feelings with their supervisees to create a context that is more conducive to learning. Breunlin et al. (1988) also discuss a problem with tape supervision from the perspective of too little arousal, which may create a context in which there is a lack of interest in learning through supervision. For example, if a tape is played for a long period of time without interruption, a trancelike state might develop accompanied by a certain degree of boredom. By having a clear contract with mutually agreed-on goals that inform tape segment selection, the potential for low arousal can be decreased.

On a very pragmatic level, a problem arises when a supervisee is unable to obtain permission from his or her employer to tape clinical sessions. It can be helpful for the clinical supervisor to meet with the agency supervisor to discuss the merits of tape supervision. Therapists also need to be sensitive to clients' reactions to the process of being taped. In addition to discussing the benefits of taping sessions for supervision, the fears and anxieties of clients need to be worked through.

TAPE SUPERVISION AND RESEARCH

There is little published research concerning the MFT supervision process. The literature on supervision has generally focused on the issue of how to do supervision, not what happens during the supervision process (Liddle et al., 1984). Thus, there is very little known about the "lived" experience of MFT supervision.

One research strategy, which can easily become a part of the supervision process, is the analysis of significant events. This qualitative approach has been used by Elliott and Shapiro (1992) to study the therapy process. *Significant events* are defined as those portions of the supervision session that the supervisee and the supervisor experience as most meaningful. These significant events then represent important supervision factors as reflected by the momentary private experiences of the supervisee and supervisor.

Elliott and Shapiro (1992) maintain that psychotherapy research has been too dominated by hypothesis testing and that there is a need for qualitative, discovery-type approaches. Certainly, then, supervision research could greatly benefit from a more discovery-oriented approach. Tape supervision lends itself to this research strategy. For example, one methodology would be for the supervisee to describe the most significant event in a recent supervision session. The supervision tape would be played until that event was located. The supervisee would then be asked to describe the event itself, its meaning, and its effect; the same process could be used by the supervisor. Discrepancies in their perceptions would be discussed. In this way, a research process, which would provide important information for the supervisor and supervisee at hand, could be implemented while at the same time offering a rich description of the supervisory process.

A recent qualitative study, which focused on an in-depth description of a specific therapeutic relationship (West, 1994), offered some findings that were related to the use of videotape in supervision and could apply to audiotape supervision just as well. The researcher, writing from a narrative perspective, offered the idea of not separating the therapeutic conversation from the supervision conversation. When such a separation is emphasized, as in traditional supervision, the therapist and supervisor tend to focus on the therapist's version of the client's narratives and the therapist's views of the therapy relationship. The client is often left out of this supervisory conversation which also means that the client's understandings of what would be helpful may also be excluded. Thus, the researcher concluded that the separation of the therapeutic and supervisory conversations impoverished all the participants—client, therapist, and supervisor.

West (1994) suggests that all participants might benefit from what he terms an "augmentation conversation," which does not exclude anyone from the process. Sessions in which the client, therapist, and supervisor come together to review a taped session would be useful. In addition, he proposed having the client and therapist either listen to audiotapes or view videotapes in an effort to help the supervisor, while the supervisor and client might listen to or view tapes in order to help the therapist. In this way, tapes could be used to help all three act as "co-augmenters."

In West's study, the client expressed some viewpoints that have important implications for the use of tape supervision. For example, this client indicated that the practice of the therapist taking the tape into a supervision session with his supervisor might yield a rather "emotionally sterile analysis" of the therapy session if it is without the input of the client. He also experienced this process as rather demeaning, feeling that his life was being handled by way of videotape—"like a soap opera." The client had many ideas about how the tapes should be analyzed by all the participants to bring about the richest description possible. This particular client felt empowered by the process of reviewing the tapes of some of his sessions with his therapist and the researcher. Through the use of tapes, he was able to have a chance to reevaluate what he was saying, thinking, and feeling during the therapy session. He was able to listen to the others' narratives and add his own to them. The client took a more reflective position in relation to his own therapy as did the therapist in relation to his conduct in the sessions. This process was also experienced by the supervisor in a positive way. He was able to be less of a hierarchial supervisor and more of a "curious facilitator." The supervisor experienced less of a demand to provide some outstanding insight or change-producing directive.

A recently completed four-year qualitative research project in the MFT Program at Virginia Tech (Keller & Protinsky, 1996) focused on understanding the process of MFT supervision. Videotapes were chosen as the primary data source for the opportunities they provided to examine a range of nonverbal cues. Each taped supervision session was analyzed for themes and patterns of interaction by a team of researchers.

Although many supervision themes were discovered in this project, of particular interest was a theme labeled "hierarchy." In these tapes, it was relatively easy to notice that supervisees related to supervisors in a hierarchial manner with accompanying anxiety over their performance. However, thanks to repetitious viewing of the tapes, another aspect of hierarchy was discovered. Supervisees seemed to show their power by using various methods to control the supervision session such as changing an uncomfortable topic, controlling the use of the videotape, excessive social discussions, and challenging the supervisor overtly. Thus, the hierarchy was not as clear as originally presumed. There was more of a reciprocal hierarchy in operation. Although there were many other findings in this particular project, the ones mentioned here tend to underscore the importance of the use of videotape in the research process. Only through careful and repeated viewing of the tapes were researchers able to deconstruct the supervision sessions.

ETHICAL CONSIDERATIONS

The use of tapes for supervision presents some special ethical concerns. It is not unusual in training programs for the taping of therapy sessions to be a requirement. Often, to minimize possible client objections, the discussion between the client and therapist concerning taping is kept to a minimum. However, clients should be given a thorough orientation to the taping process. For example, they need to understand the rationale for taping, who will view the tape, where the tape will be stored, and when the tape will be erased. In those cases where legal involvement might be a possibility, a clear contract needs to be made concerning the use of tapes in court. Perhaps these elements could be a part of a contract between therapist, client, and supervisor. For those in

private or agency practice, the issue of the safe and confidential transporting of a tape to supervision should be discussed and agreed on.

Addressing the issues here may successfully deal with many of a client's anxieties; however, time should be taken to explore other concerns the client may have about being taped. For example, there may be performance issues present. Some clients may perceive the process of being reviewed on tape as demeaning. It is important for clients to feel they have a sense of power concerning whether to be taped or not. In academic and training programs, clients may have to choose to be taped to receive services. However, clients can decide to seek treatment elsewhere; that decision should be made at the initial session and not after treatment has been started.

For some clients, it may not be appropriate to have any sessions taped. One example would be survivors of child pornography. Taping may recreate their original traumas. Clients with paranoid delusions may have their anxiety raised to an unmanageable level by the taping process Other clients may have different, yet important, negative experiences with either audio- or videotaping. Therefore, it is important to gather history in this area before deciding on whether to tape.

It may be beneficial to both the client and the therapist to keep tapes of multiple therapy sessions. Such tapes provide data for treatment progress and content. Although both the client and therapist may gain from reviewing past sessions, the opportunity afforded by taping sessions can also provide safeguards concerning certain of today's legal issues. For example, if hypnosis is being used for the treatment of past abuse, a tape of the session may be useful in demonstrating that false memories have not been implanted through the hypnotic process. It may also be useful in other sessions to ascertain if the therapist used leading questions or statements in the assessment process.

Another example of such "defensive" use of taping might occur with clients who could possibly present a risk to the therapist, such as an accusation from a client of sexual misconduct within the session. Legally, it should be noted that tapes can be useful to demonstrate that unethical behavior did not occur. However, many legal experts say that tapes probably are not useful for the prosecution of behaviors such as child abuse. That is, even though a child within a session may reveal on tape that his father is abusing him, the tape probably would not be admissible in court. This varies from state to state, however. It is important for therapists and supervisors to be aware of the possible legal uses of taped sessions in their states.

CONCLUSION

The advances in technology that have created the ability to use taping in supervision have revolutionized the supervision process. Now, more than ever before, the supervision process can be more richly developed, implemented, and studied. MFT theory and technique can be taught in a more meaningful way. The therapist's use of self can be ascertained and thoroughly examined. Multiple realities can lead to enriched descriptions because clients can be brought into the supervision conversation through the shared listening/viewing of tapes. Time can be "frozen" so that therapeutic and supervisory processes can be understood and improved. Used within ethical guidelines, taping will continue to be instrumental in the enrichment of the MFT supervision process.

REFERENCES

Andersen, T. (1987). The reflecting team: Dialogue and metadialogue in clinical social work. *Family Process, 26,* 415–428.

Bernard, J., & Goodyear, P. (1992). *Fundamentals of supervision.* Boston: Allyn and Bacon.

Breunlin, D., Karrer, B., McGuire, D., & Cimmarusti, R. (1988). Cybernetics of videotape supervision. In H. Liddle, D. Breunlin, & R. Schwartz (Eds.), *Handbook of family therapy training and supervision* (pp. 194–206). New York: Guilford Press.

Elliott, R., & Shapiro, D. (1992). Client and therapist as analysts of significant events. In S. Toukmonian & D. Rennie (Eds.), *Psychotherapy process research* (pp. 163–186). Newbury Park, CA: Sage Publications.

Gill, M., Newman, R., & Redlich, F. (1954). *The initial interview in psychiatric practice.* New York: International Universities Press.

Heilveil, I., & Muehleman, J. (1981). Nonverbal clues to deception in a psychotherapy analogue. *Psychotherapy: Theory, Research, and Practice, 18,* 329–335.

Holzman, P. (1969). On hearing and seeing oneself. *Journal of Nervous and Mental Disease, 148,* 198–209.

Horney, K. (1950). *Neurosis and human growth.* New York: W. W. Norton.

Keeney, B., & Ray, W. (1992). Shifting from supervision to superaudition. *Supervisor Bulletin, 5,* 3.

Keller, J., & Protinsky, H. (1996). The process of clinical supervision: Direct observation research. *The Clinical Supervisor, 14,* 51–64.

Liddle, H., Breunlin, D., Schwartz, R., & Constantine, I. (1984). Training family therapy supervisors: Issues of content, form, and context. *Journal of Marital and Family Therapy, 10,* 139–150.

West, C. (1994). An investigation of second-person narratives: The construction of "you" and "I" in a family therapy case study. Unpublished dissertation.

Whiffen, R. (1982). The use of videotape in supervision. In R. Whiffen & J. Byng-Hall (Eds.), *Family therapy supervision: Recent developments in practice* (pp. 39–46). New York: Grune & Stratton.

22

Case Consultation
Stories Told About Stories

Kenneth Stewart

The case consultation mode of supervision is a common method of supervision because of the constraints of time, equipment, space, and personnel. Therapists present cases they are currently working with to supervisors, and together they discuss them at some length. During the conversations, therapists present what they think are key facts about a case: particular problems encountered in their therapy relating to specific aspects of clients problems, particular strategies or interventions used, and feelings therapists may have about their clients or vice versa. In response, supervisors ask questions; offer various forms of advice, strategy, or conceptual ideas for therapists to consider; and may address therapist–client relationships. After some discussion, they move on to the next case until their time is up. This usually happens in one of two formats: a group setting or a setting with a supervisor and one or two therapists.

In contrast, case presentations usually have the goal of presenting information about the status of a particular case's treatment more than one of getting specific ideas about therapy. Therapists present to their colleagues: case demographics, diagnoses, medications, a brief social history, an account of the current course of treatment, and any dilemmas currently encountered. Participants ask questions or make comments relating to what has been done or how the patient's care might be managed bet-

ter. A plan is formulated, or the current treatment plan is approved or modified, by adjusting medications or by trying another form of treatment modality such as group therapy. Supervision using this model is often a search for what other treatment modalities might be tried. Case presentations of this kind frequently occur in group settings in agencies.

Although both formats are commonly used, this chapter focuses on supervision in the case consultation, rather than the case presentation format, for several reasons. First, the case consultation method is aimed more specifically at the development of therapists' competencies, which is a primary goal of supervision. Second, although both formats are concerned with clients receiving the services they require, the case consultation method tends to address the nuances of therapy while the case presentation method tends to emphasize changing or endorsing a treatment plan. In supervision, therapists frequently cite their goal to be improving and/or increasing their abilities to conduct ongoing therapy. Finally, case consultation formats are more conducive to focusing on therapists' resources and solutions to dilemmas than the case presentation method. The case presentation format can easily move from a discussion of "What is wrong with the patient?" to "What is wrong with the therapy?" because of the emphasis on managing the case better.

ADVANTAGES AND LIMITATIONS OF CASE CONSULTATION

Since the advent of one-way mirrors and videotape technology many supervisors incorporate "raw data," observation of therapy, or taped clips of therapy into supervision. Given this, one might conclude that case consultation is quickly becoming a thing of the past. However, in a national survey on supervision, a third of the sample said they do not use live supervision primarily because the facilities are not available (McKenzie et al., 1986). In this same survey, case consultation was the second most frequently used method of supervision; however, only 8.5% thought this method to be very effective. I will argue that this need not be the case. There are certain advantages to this method, although not readily apparent, that can be creatively put to use for therapists.

In a recent article, McCollum and Wetchler (1995) suggest that the case consultation form of supervision has a number of advantages over live supervision or video- and audiotaped supervision. They argue that while live or video- and audiotaped supervision can capture the therapeutic moment and provide a view into the actual therapy process, it cannot accomplish other important things. Live supervision does not allow time to discuss the assumptions of the therapist (at least at much length), nor does it have the luxury of discussing the larger political, social, and cultural context of the therapy (or supervision, for that matter) because of the immediacy of the format. However, in the more languid atmosphere of case consultation, there is time to discuss the *architecture*—how the therapy is constructed—as well as the contextual elements defining the therapeutic endeavor. The experience of watching a movie versus reading the book on which the movie is based are quite different experiences, both of which provide something the other cannot.

Beginning therapists often appreciate case consultation because the less immediate format gives them an opportunity to discuss other issues, such as the structure of their jobs, relationships with co-workers, or other contextual concerns, affecting their work. Often, these concerns occupy more of the therapist's attention than their direct clinical work. Case consultation also allows them a chance to cover a variety of questions and/or concerns that may arise about their caseload, but do not require in-depth supervisory attention. Supervisors can take the time to ask about other aspects of therapists' caseload, for which they are responsible, in order to spot any red flags or issues of concern. More experienced therapists often seek out case consultations because they offer them the opportunity to consider several alternative approaches simultaneously. This format further allows them to thoughtfully select one of a combination of intervention strategies discussed during supervision. Experienced therapists frequently report that their goal for supervision is the integration of their preferred ideas, beliefs, and methods from several therapy models into their unique approach to therapy.

Case consultations do have limitations that become apparent when compared to live or video- and audiotaped supervision. When supervisors have access to the raw data of the therapy session, subtle dynamics between therapist and client are more easily seen. Facial expressions, body movement, and other nonverbal nuances, which might go unnoticed or unreported, can be readily observed and discussed. The tone of voice, syntax, and rhythm of the conversation are more easily captured live than after the fact. The unfolding of the story, line by line, is much less apparent when reconstructed later. For these reasons, case consultations can never fully substitute for live or video- and audiotaped supervision because it cannot capture or reveal all the important details that provide color and richness to the story of therapy. But, as mentioned before, the experience of watching a movie is quite different than reading a book; both tell stories in different ways, each providing something the other cannot.

SUPERVISION CAN BE LISTENING TO STORIES

Like therapy, supervision in the case consultation format can be thought of as a narrative event where stories are told about events by therapists to supervisors with whom therapists have cast their hopes for growth. Supervisors and therapists hope the outcome of supervision is a change in therapists, their abilities, and relationships with clients. Therapists' stories are not simply taken in by supervisors as "received texts" that are unquestioned and unaltered. There are always presuppositions and assumptions guiding therapists' recollection of events and the selection of certain memories. Supervision can unpack or "deconstruct" these guiding presuppositions in order to more clearly situate the therapy. Rarely are stories told with such clarity or completeness that these additional questions can be set aside. Hence, questions are asked by supervisors that take the story further than originally intended by therapists. In this way, supervision parallels therapy in the ways in which it opens space and generates alternatives. In the context of supervision, therapists become more effective therapists than they were before. Future therapy will be different as a result of the "re-storying" and meaning-making venture of supervision.

Exploring Embedded Contexts

It is possible to conceive of the stories being presented as one in a series of *embedded frames*—contexts that contain and define events—much like those hollow Russian dolls that contain a series of ever smaller dolls (*cf.* Keeney, 1990). These frames are the social, political, and economic factors, as well as beliefs and assump-

tions, that influence particular points of view. The story the therapist tells the supervisor is embedded within a whole host of other stories that frame, or are framed by, other stories and contexts that can be addressed in supervision (see Figure 22.1). For example, one of the larger (not the largest) dolls or "frames" might be the supervisory context of supervisor and therapist.

Context includes the supervisor's context, such as a private practice, agency, educational or hospital setting, and the therapist's position in relation to that context: visiting outsider, intern, graduate student, resident, employee, subcontractor, and so on. Within each of these contextual frames are the individual stories of training, family history, and personal experiences of both supervisor and therapist. Linked to the therapist's frames are the contextual frames of various stories told by family members, including the presenting problem, and how the family has organized itself around the problem.

No story that is told to supervisors exists in isolation from other stories that frame and are framed by it. One of the tasks of supervision is for the participants to become increasingly aware of the ways in which the particular frames of stories—beliefs and assumptions that construct particular points of view—shape and reshape the ways in which they understand their work and their clients' concerns.

Interpretation

Understanding how points of view construct the interpretations of events is a venture into *hermeneutics*—the science of interpretation (Steele, 1986). One of the central tasks of supervision is for the supervisor and therapist to play with these frames, essentially to offer "reframes" of stories. During their conversations, different frames can be offered that suggest different interpretations for therapists and subsequently for different therapy. The give-and-take of this conversation crafts a "meta-theoretical framework" for the evaluation of

FIGURE 22-1.   The overlapping stories of supervision

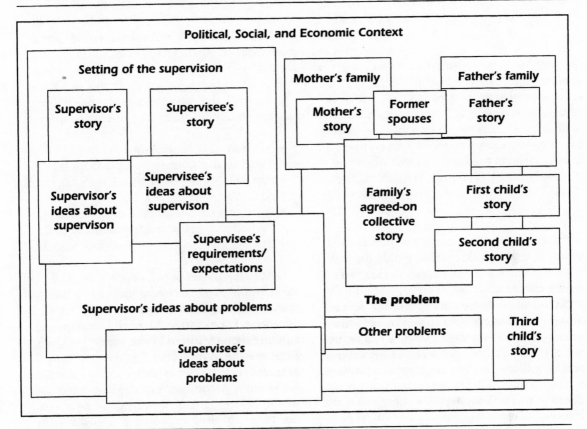

various therapeutic narratives. In this post-modern "universe of stories" (Parry, 1991) in which we find ourselves, no one point of view can achieve a perch outside history to become the final point of view.

A hermeneutic metaposition critiques the temptations of certainty of any text claiming to be the only text. It is our hope that we can illustrate that the "certainty" of the various frames are rendered more permeable through supervisory dialogue. Through the conversation between supervisor and therapist, unquestioned beliefs about the meaning of persons, contexts, and events are questioned and can become less rigid. In other instances,

particular frames become more substantial, predictable, or visible. For example, in the instance of an emerging identity of a therapist's or client's strength, supervisors can encourage beliefs about these inner resources. Still, this illustration only hints at the complexity of the storied contexts of supervision.

GETTING THE MOST FROM CASE CONSULTATION

In case consultations, even though supervisors have to rely on the accounts given by therapists, this very limitation can be used to supervisors' advantage to explore the perceptions, assumptions, and predispositions constraining therapists. Access to raw data may be nice because it eliminates one filter from the account of what happened in therapy; but when this is not possible, case consultation offers supervisors the opportunity to explore, take apart, and reconstruct therapists' accounts of events. Consequently, supervisors hope to expand therapists' future therapeutic possibilities, which can result in a more rewarding story. The following sections present areas that supervisors can explore with therapists to reach that goal.

Describe the Context

Although the context of supervision is often taken for granted, the setting where the therapy takes place is an important contextual element that should be taken into account in supervision. A large county human service center will likely evoke different responses from clients and therapists than, say, a family medical clinic, a hospital, a church, or private practice office suite. The geographical location of the facility determines, in part, who the clientele are and may say something about the values or mandates of the overall clinical practice. A United Way supported walk-in counseling center in the inner city is quite different from a suburban private practice twenty miles from the city center. Contextual descriptions should also include the cultural and political setting:

- Does the neighborhood have a concentration of certain ethnic groups that the clinic serves?
- What is the clinic's reputation among its neighbors?
- Is it known as a good place to go, or is it seen as cold and indifferent?
- Is it known as responsive to its setting or does the clinic ignore the people in its neighborhood?

- What difference might that make to therapists and therapy?

Likewise, the physical appearance of clients may evoke certain responses that, although not mentioned, may nevertheless play an important part in the therapy. Asking therapists to physically describe the appearance of clients can give supervisors some idea of what therapists see:

- Are they neat or slovenly?
- Considerably overweight or underweight?
- Slouching or on the edge of their chairs?
- Animated or stiff?
- What conclusions do therapists draw from the body language and appearance of their clients?

At times, even the physical appearance of the therapist can evoke responses from clients that impact the therapy and are topics for supervision. For example, Manijeh Doneshpour, a family therapy intern I once supervised, is a Muslim woman from Iran. She wears a "hijab" or scarf over her head as is the custom for Muslim women. According to Manijeh, this is done to emphasize the intelligence of women and not their physical appearance. However, in Minnesota where she had her internship, Muslim women wearing hijabs are fairly uncommon and evoke certain responses from others. Each time she met a family for the first time she would explain her traditional dress and answer any questions they had. Having lived in the United States for ten years helped her understand our culture, but she did not take for granted that her clients would know this. (Actually, she found her ethnic and religious background was more of a hinderance among her professors and professional colleagues than with her clients.) Supervision needs to address the degree to which the appearance of clients (or therapists) creates a situation in which the client (or the therapist) is seen as the "other"— someone distinct and apart (not like us), and therefore marginalized and accorded a lower status. Supervisors who help therapists pay attention to these contextual constraints help to ensure that therapy is contextually sensitive beyond the therapy room and help therapists highlight contextual variables within therapy when necessary.

Note Key Words and Phrases

Supervision and therapy are languaging processes in which words are used in constructing stories to make sense of things. Paying close attention to key words that summarize or define persons or events is a central aspect of supervision and therapy (*cf.* White, 1995). Supervisors can listen for key words and phrases therapists use in describing their clients This is especially helpful with therapy jargon such as "co-dependent," "passive-aggressive," "abusive" or with other words—"damaged" or "unaware"—that describe persons. Instead of taking these words for granted, supervision can carefully explore the particular meanings therapists attach to these words, the history of those phrases in the therapist's experience, and the effects of using those words on the therapist and the therapy.

Even though words like "co-dependent" may have commonly understood definitions, just what they mean in relation to this particular client can be useful for the therapist:

- Is there a history of this behavior in the therapist's life that informs the current use of the term?
- Are there degrees of this behavior, times when the behaviors strongly manifest themselves and times when they are barely apparent?
- If that is the case, what words could be used to more accurately describe this continuum of behavior?

Similarly, words like "damaged" are sometimes used in describing child victims of abuse.

Detailed inquiry into the meaning this word has for this therapist might reveal the extent to which the therapist believes there is permanent damage to this child or damage that might be healed in the course of therapy. Therapists might be reifying their clients and succumbing to a certainty that might seize up therapy and reduce therapeutic flexibility (*cf.* Amundson, Stewart, & Valentine, 1993).

Disclose Feelings: Overcoming Disconnection

Most forms of supervision pay attention to feelings evoked in therapists, but in the case consultation format, time can be taken to explore a variety of meanings attributed to these feelings and what they might signify about the connection between therapists and clients and between supervisors and therapists. Some supervisors highlight the examination of feelings evoked within therapy as the *sine qua non* of supervision. Hence, when a therapist finds a pattern of getting stuck with various kinds of families, it may point to a parallel of unfinished business in the therapist's family of origin (Aponte, 1992, 1994). Assuming that when feelings are experienced in therapy they relate in some way to deeper unresolved issues within therapists might pathologize the process instead of merely informing it. If therapists find themselves becoming angry, sad, or anxious at specific times during the interview, it may just say something about the intensity of the moment (Miller & Stiver, 1993, 1994). It can mean that when clients are telling their stories, something has been triggered within therapists at that moment that represents, at the very least, a significant connection between them and their clients. The emotional reaction evoked within therapists connects therapists to clients during the interview and may move the therapy to greater depths. Instead of only inquiring about possible unfinished issues within the therapist, supervisors might inquire how therapists might share this experience with their clients in subsequent interviews.

Miller and Stiver (1993, 1994) suggest that clients can only risk change in themselves when they feel the therapist is moved by their experiences. They suggest that therapeutic change begins to happen when clients begin to give up some of their strategies of disconnection and make risky new connections with therapists and with significant others. Supervisors can inquire about emotional reactions therapists have during their interviews with clients and discuss what those reactions might mean in terms of their connections to clients. These reactions may suggest new connections to clients and a breaking through of clients' usual strategies of disconnection. They might also discuss how the therapist can tell the difference between emotional reactions that signify unfinished business in the therapist's life from new and deeper connections to the client during the interview that signify a change in the therapy. In my supervision of Manijeh, this aspect of supervision has been one of the most rewarding for her as a beginning therapist. Her therapy with adolescents, who had initially been distant and guarded, has changed dramatically when connections have been established in this way. Supervision has focused on her remaining open to her clients in such a way that when she begins to have an emotional reaction to their story, she can share those feelings in a way that strengthens a connection and validates their story. We have spent time discussing how she can disclose her feelings to her clients so that she does not overwhelm them, yet is genuine and caring.

Review the Received Definition of the Problem

Supervisors can explore various definitions of problems to expand the parameters of therapy. They can help therapists avoid the traps of specifying only one definition or understanding of problems. There are as many ways for therapists to understand problems as there are schools of therapy, and probably more, because each school of therapy usually has several ways to address particular problems. Supervisors can ask therapists:

- How have you arrived at a definition of the problem?
- If the client says it is one thing and you think it might be something else, how have you negotiated this difference?
- If there have been competing definitions between spouses or other family members and one definition has been adopted, has it been to the exclusion or detriment of someone else in the family?
- Have you attempted to consolidate them into one global definition; or have competing definitions been acknowledged while attempting to work with each of them?

Definitions and understandings of problems can be fluid and evolve throughout the course of therapy as the story unfolds. Paying attention to this process in supervision can assist therapists in widening the focus of discussion in future interviews.

This can be extended even further into the emerging identity of therapists. Do therapists see themselves in a singular, essentialistic manner? Or, is there room for multiple descriptions of the person of the therapist? Not *just* interns, *just* students, *just* structuralists, *just* narrativists, *just* any one thing. Gergen (1991) suggests that we are "saturated selves" with many attributes, some inconsistent with others. If there are many aspects to the person of the therapist, self-understanding is a process of inclusion as well as choice and responsibility. It is not a *fait accompli*—decided once and for all.

The Politics of Therapy

Competing definitions of what is wrong and needs changing often allude to wider political issues in therapy. By political issues, we are referring to how the therapeutic context is not exempt from the politics of gender, class, race, or culture. The context of the therapy room is fraught with politics and often can be complicit with the dominant social order regarding ideas about men, women, social class, and ethnicity. There are also hierarchies of knowledge that privilege professional knowledge over the "local" knowledge of clients. These hierarchies of knowledge include ways in which persons are objectified, and sometimes defined only by their problems, resulting in "totalizing" definitions of persons (White, 1995). When certain "knowledges" are imposed on persons by others more powerful than they are, it often results in overpowering the persons being defined. This is especially so when those being defined eventually accept these definitions of themselves. Spouses defining their partners as "losers" or parents defining their children as "problems from day one" are good examples of this kind of local politics. When these definitions are gradually accepted as true or inevitable by these spouses or children, their own "knowledges" are forsaken for the certainty of their more imposing and intimidating spouses or parents, leaving them overwhelmed and overpowered.

In some therapeutic contexts, political issues regarding definition and representation may show themselves in medical/psychiatric definitions of symptoms versus wider systemic definitions. Problem definitions compete between individuals being "depressed/anxious/alcoholic/borderline"—primarily associated with diagnostic categories from the *Diagnostic and Statistical Manual of Mental Disorders* (APA, 1994)—versus terms, such as "enmeshed family" or "dysfunctional family" or "chaotic family," used to describe the whole family. In either case, supervisors can ask therapists to pay attention to the terms used to describe the problem among professionals. Each of these definitions suggest a certain set of assumptions and, hence, a certain kind of story about clients and therapy.

For therapists, supervision can highlight the process of "stepping into" various story frames without being aware of it and operating from those frames or definitions to make sense of and retell the story of therapy and the story of clients. Supervision can raise questions about these terms, often used as a shorthand between professionals in such a way that they reduce complexity. What are the effects of reducing complexity and relying on shorthand in this way? Do they call forth or overpower alternative stories? What attempts are made to contextualize the problem within economic or political contexts? In other words, is the economic, cultural, or political context referred to only in the opening remarks within the intake process and then forgotten? Or, are attempts made to highlight these larger influences more frequently?

Likewise, if therapy takes place within the territory of a managed-care provider, often, therapists must adopt a problem-focused view in order to have their prior authorizations approved. If so, do therapists attempt to translate these terms to clients, or do therapists attempt to sidestep problem-focused discourse in favor of discourse more congenial to solutions and resources?

All therapy takes place within a number of political contexts. The challenge is to pay attention to these contexts, how they may compete with each other, and the effects of each contextual definition on therapy and supervision. Therapists may wish to be collaborative instead of hierarchical, but sometimes the rest of the world may not want to go along with these ideas. If therapy is bristling with competing certainties, each hoping to define the territory in question, supervisors can ask therapists:

- Is it possible to let these two (or more) descriptions of clients sit side by side without either one defining the whole?

- What would be the effects on clients if we adopted one definition of the problem over that of another?
- Could clients sit in on our discussion of therapy and feel empowered by our discussions?
- Or, would we change in some way our discussion if clients were present?

Discuss Limitations of Particular Theoretical Frameworks

Just as the political context helps to define the problem and what is needed for help, so too does the theoretical framework being employed frame all observations about therapy and supervision. Recently, Rosenblatt (1994) and Stewart (1995) suggest that the particular set of metaphors one adopts will tend to highlight certain things and obscure others. For example, a structural framework will highlight family boundaries and rules, while obscuring the fact that boundaries and rules are artifacts that are not physical entities and are observer-dependent. They do not necessarily represent actual boundaries or actual rules, but artifacts that are constructed in the mind of the observer are limiting. Bowenian metaphors will encourage therapists to look for distance-regulating strategies, cut-offs, triangles, and intergenerational patterns. The MRI brief therapy model uses metaphors that frame stories around attempted solutions, and ways in which these contribute to the problem. A Milan systemic model may employ metaphors that refer to the function of symptoms across generations, family secrets, and circular patterns within the family or larger system. An object relations framework may use metaphors that refer to ways in which persons have identified with objects during development or ways in which persons have contained or failed to contain anxiety, anger, or sadness during crucial developmental periods.

Each of these frameworks have their preferred way to think about normal and pathological development, family structure, family communication, and so forth. They each suggest various steps to take in therapy. Supervision with this understanding asks therapists to highlight their theoretical and process assumptions from time to time so that therapy and supervision do not get bogged down with a singular point of view. If supervisors and therapists happen to prefer different metaphors, they can spend time discussing what each group of metaphors highlights and what each obscures.

Rosenblatt (1994) also points out that there are certain entailments with the use of any metaphor. These entailments lead us in certain directions and away from others. If we begin using identity metaphors, we are invited to think of a constellation of traits, personality, self-understanding, or character. The use of functional metaphors entails not only the use or nonuse of some activity or thing, but of purpose or intent as well. In the early 1970s, it was not uncommon to hear family therapists speak of symptoms serving certain functions within families (e.g., the "acting out" child deflects attention from the strained marriage). Attributing intent to certain behaviors of family members entailed the maintenance and homeostatic functions of behavior. And, this entailed a specific way to understand systems theory, which entailed assumptions made from a position that would later come under criticism by second-order theorists as an epistemological error. What Rosenblatt (1994) and Lakoff and Johnson (1980)—from whose work Rosenblatt cites—suggest we pay attention to are the ways metaphors structure and subtly frame our attention. Therefore, examining what metaphors highlight and what they obscure can open up discussions in supervision to areas previously taken for granted.

Play with Alternative Frameworks

One way supervisors and therapists can avoid the essentialism or the singular views of these frameworks is to play with them much as an author might play with various voices or viewpoints in constructing a story (Stewart, 1995). Supervisors might ask therapists what kind of story is being told if a strategic framework is used to describe what happened in therapy. If the focus is on particular strategies, a discussion may occur regarding how offering directives to clients differs from asking reflexive questions (*cf*. Tomm, 1988). If therapists tell clients to do a certain thing, it will have different effects than asking questions that invite clients to reflect on their behavior or the intentions of others. Similarly, a focus on the structure of the family (the family rules or generational boundaries) suggests normative comparisons of family functioning. Supervisors can discuss with therapists who defines the range of what is "normal or functional" and how it is subsequently discussed with families. The dominant white culture of many therapists and social workers may likely define normality and functionality different than families from Hispanic or African American cultures. Middle-class persons will define these differently than lower- or poverty-class persons; or blue-collar men may have definitions quite different from middle-class, educated women therapists.

If we understand case consultation as a discursive process of storytelling and re-telling, then paying attention to the ways in which therapists' "editorial rules" shape the telling can be a key feature of supervision. Recently, postmodern critiques (Anderson & Goolishian, 1992; Hoffman, 1990; Lowe, 1991; White & Epston, 1990) suggest that it is not the "truth" of stories that is acknowledged so much as the relative effects various story con-structions have on relationships. Although supervision can raise questions about the implications of defining or framing things one way instead of some other way, such an appeal to the diversity of perspectives does not mean that all principles and ethics are sacrificed on the "altar" of postmodernism. The aesthetic visions of unity that our theories suggest are constantly held in creative tension with the diversity that postmodernistic appreciation for multiple perspectives suggests (*cf*. Ravn, 1991). Furthermore, the pragmatics of ethical codes of conduct for professional behavior represent "special status certainties" we do not so easily "deconstruct" (Stewart & Amundson, 1995).

Outline Directions Therapy Could Take

Supervisors can ask therapists what are several directions they think therapy might take the next time they meet with clients. Any ideas or suggestions that evolve in supervision are, for the most part, only for consideration; they do not always provide an unwavering direction therapy must go. Although agencies may require that treatment plans get completed along with specific behavioral criteria for termination, attention can be paid to other agendas carried by therapists. Is the plan for therapists to carry out some kind of therapeutic strategy not shared with clients or are more general values guiding the therapy, such as staying connected and curious? For therapists to stay closely connected to clients, supervisors can ask that they keep in mind whether they have goals for families, if they match with the families' goals, or who in the family might disagree with these goals. Finally, supervisors can ask therapists to consider the degree of hope versus pessimism carried about a particular family and how this affects their work.

CONCLUSION

Supervising therapists' work in case consultation is not necessarily a limitation. Case consultation can be a time to explore many defining aspects of therapy that might go undiscussed within an audio- and videotaped or live supervision format. Let us conclude with these remarks from Manijeh; it is important that ideas about her experience with case consultation be shared.

As a therapist, having a sense of connection with my supervisor has been a very important part of my professional development. It is helpful because I feel safe to talk about my sense of confusion or to express my concerns about whether I am going in the right direction with a family. This sense of connection is also important because it makes it easier for me to ask questions and to discuss my point of view. It often happens that I prefer one therapeutic approach and my supervisor suggests another. This sense of connection helps us to have an interesting discourse about our different viewpoints. If at the end I choose my supervisor's approach, I understand the process very clearly.

When I present a case to my supervisor, the way we discuss the case gives me the freedom to ask for specific step-by-step feedback or to request some general therapeutic strategies. This flexibility is important for a therapist who is sometimes striving for a specific direction and at other times needs only some general guidelines.

As a therapist who is from a different culture, it has been an interesting challenge and struggle to feel accepted in the field of family therapy. Experts in the field often express their concern that I am not from this culture and I might not know enough about American culture and families. It took me a long time to realize that each family is unique and we often do not know much about them anyway. The only advantage for me, however, is that I know that I do not know, and I know that I need to ask. Often, Americans do not ask, assuming they already know, and they should ask. Therefore, the advantage for me is my sense of curiosity and my willingness to learn about families. These points were not clear to me until I discussed them with

my supervisor and he made me realize that I can perceive my cultural differences as a strength not as a weakness, and I can use my cultural differences and my religious outlook to help families.

REFERENCES

American Psychiatric Association (APA). (1994). *Diagnostic and statistical manual of mental disorders*, 4th edition. Washington, DC: Author.

Amudson, J., Stewart, K., & Valentine, L. (1993). Temptations of power and certainty. *Journal of Marital and Family Therapy, 19*, 111–123.

Anderson, H., & Goolishian, H. (1992). The client is the expert: A not-knowing approach to therapy. In S. McNamee & K. Gergen (Eds.), *Therapy as social construction* (pp. 25–39). Newbury Park, CA: Sage Publications.

Aponte, H. (1992). Training the person of the therapist in structural family therapy. *Journal of Marital and Family Therapy. 18*, 269–281.

Aponte, H. (1994). How personal can training get? *Journal of Marital and Family Therapy, 20*, 1–15

Gergen, K. (1991) *The saturated self*. New York: Basic Books.

Hoffman, L. (1990) Constructing realities: An art of lenses. *Family Process, 29*, 1–12.

Keeney, B. (1990). *Improvisational therapy*. St. Paul: Systemic Therapy Press.

Lakoff, G., & Johnson, M. (1980). *Metaphors we live by*. Chicago: University of Chicago Press.

Lowe, R. (1991). Postmodern themes and therapeutic practices: Notes toward the definition of 'family therapy': Part 2. *Dulwich Centre Newsletter, 3*, 41–52.

McCollum, E., & Wetchler, J. (1995). In defense of case consultation: Maybe "dead" supervision isn't dead after all. *Journal of Marital and Family Therapy, 21*, 155–166.

McKenzie, P., Atkinson, B., Quinn, W., & Heath, A. (1986). Training and supervision in marriage and family therapy: A national survey. *The American Journal of Family Therapy, 14*, 293–303.

McNamee, S., & Gergen, K. (1992). *Therapy as social construction*. Newbury Park, CA: Sage Publications.

Miller, J., & Stiver, I. (1993). A relational approach to understanding women's lives and problems. *Psychiatric Annals, 23*, 424–431.

Miller, J., & Stiver, I. (1994). A relational model of psychotherapy. Conference presentation at Department of Psychiatry and Psychology, Mayo Clinic, Rochester, MN, October 28–29.

Parry, A. (1991). A universe of stories. *Family Process, 30*, 37–54.

Ravn, I. (1991). What should guide reality construction? In F. Steier (Ed.), *Research and reflexivity* (pp. 96–114). Newbury Park, CA: Sage Publications.

Rosenblatt, P. (1994). *Metaphors in family systems theory.* New York: Guilford Press.

Steele, R. (1986). Deconstructing histories: Toward a systemic criticism of psychological narratives. In T. Sarbin (Ed.), *Narrative psychology: The storied nature of human conduct* (pp. 175–256). New York: Praeger.

Stewart, K. (1995). At play in the fields of memory: A novel approach to training. *Journal of Systemic Therapies, 14*, 32–38.

Stewart, K., & Amundson, J. (1995) The ethical postmodernist: Or not everything is relative all at once. *Journal of Systemic Therapies, 14*, 70–78.

Tomm, K. (1988). Interventive Interviewing: Part III. Intending to ask circular, strategic, or reflexive questions? *Family Process, 27*, 1–16.

White, M. (1995). The politics of therapy. In M. White (Ed.), *Re-Authoring lives: Interviews and essays* (pp. 41–59). Adelaide: Dulwich Centre Publications.

White, M., & Epston, D. (1990). *Narrative means to therapeutic ends.* New York: W. W. Norton.

23

Selecting and Constructing Supervision Structures
Individuals, Dyads, Co-Therapists, Groups, and Teams

Charles D. York

Education and supervision are often understood as separate processes (Piercy & Sprenkle, 1986). Supervision is frequently referred to as a continuous relationship, in a real-world work setting, which focuses on the specific development of therapists' skills as they gain practical experience (Saba & Liddle, 1986). In contrast, education is often defined as the transmission of conceptual and clinical knowledge usually within a classroom setting (Piercy & Sprenkle, 1986). However, it is misleading to assume that education is not an integral part of the supervision process. Once application of theoretical concepts begins, in the world of clinical practice, a new educational frontier is discovered by supervisors and supervisees.

This frontier is a learning environment significantly influenced by the type of supervision structure selected. The most common supervision structures are: individuals, dyads, co-therapists, groups, and teams. To promote optimum learning, supervisors as educators negotiate with supervisees the type of supervisory structure; however, supervisors and supervisees do not live in a vacuum. There are many critical factors to be reviewed before making a choice. This chapter discusses a matrix of interrelated factors that play a role in the outcome of this decision.

When thinking about which structure to offer, supervisors are influenced by the supervision system and the larger context in which the supervision is embedded. In the following sections, external and internal factors, which influence the choices supervisors make (see Table 23.1), are explored. Although these factors are not descriptive of all influences, they represent the most common ones. Internal factors are defined as influences stemming from the supervision system consisting of the supervisor, supervisee, and client. External factors refer to distinctive characteristics of the larger context that influence the supervision system. At times there can be a blurring of these factors, whether they are internal, external, or simultaneously both. The key is for supervisors to consider the factors as a whole. When they do so, the factors form a decision tree for the selection of supervisory structures.

Any time someone proposes a list (i.e., factors) as a composite of a suggested reality one quickly invites attack. On the other hand, the following factors and principles have the potential of helping beginning supervisors process the complexity of selecting a supervisory structure. As an educator in a university setting, I am consistently confronted with supervising beginning therapists and repeatedly observe their expected anxiety and confusion as they commence with the "real thing." I have come to value the need to offer them some elementary guidance to begin with, accompanied by a large dose of en-

TABLE 23-1. Factors That Influence the Selection of a Supervision Structure

Internal Factors	External Factors
• Epistemologies of supervisors and supervisees*	Supervisors' position in the institution (teacher, clinician, etc.)
• Supervisees' professional development	Practice context (agency, private, etc.)
–Supervisees' theory competence level	State laws (licensure, legal accountability, etc.)
–Supervisees' therapy competence level	Ethical codes (state, professional, agency, etc.)
–Supervisees' experience level	Resources context (financial, etc.)
• Supervisors' developmental model for supervision	Selection of supervisees
• Homogeneous/heterogeneous groupings	Culture and gender of practice context (community, agency, etc.)
Supervisors' and supervisees' structure preference	
Supervisors' competence level	
Cultural and gender sensitivity of supervisors/ supervisees	
Clientele characteristics (symptom presentation, family structure, etc.)	

Internal and external factors need to be observed as a whole in the selection of supervision structures.
*The bullets designate the internal "core" factors.

couragement. I have also trained supervisors, and observed a similar phenomena as seasoned therapists begin the transition into the new territory of being a supervisor. My own training as a supervisor could initially be characterized by the proverbial feeling of "What am I going to do now!" A cookbook outlining the basics would have helped; but, as one becomes a chef, the art and knowledge to create goes beyond the book. I hope what is offered here will be viewed as a cookbook, not the final dish nor the sum of the chef's creativity.

INTERNAL CORE FACTORS: INITIAL SUPERVISORY DECISIONS

The internal core factors of supervisors' and supervisees' epistemologies, supervisees' professional development, supervisors' de-

velopmental models for supervision, and homogeneous/heterogeneous groupings are beginning decisions for supervisors. As assessed by supervisors, these internal core factors are key in determining the structure for supervision and are central to the goals of supervision. Experience shows that the closer supervisors organize supervision structures to these core factors the more effective supervision and supervisees' therapy becomes. Supervisors begin with these core factors and move outward by considering the influence of the other internal and external factors in formulating the final choice of structure. The following sections discuss each of the core internal factors.

Supervisors' and Supervisees' Epistemologies

The supervisory structure, whether it is individual, dyad, co-therapy, group, or team, is generally more effective if supervisors follow this suggested principle:

> Supervisors who operate from a theory with supervisees practicing the same theory in the context of therapy, more easily produce isomorphic patterns that improve therapy and the competence of supervisees.

The literature consistently points out the isomorphic relationship between supervision and therapy (Haley, 1976; Liddle, 1982; Liddle, Breunlin, & Schwartz, 1988; Liddle & Saba, 1983; Liddle & Schwartz, 1983). Liddle (1988) describes isomorphism as a phenomena of patterns being replicated across subsystem boundaries. When supervisors, supervisees, and families join along the lines of worldviews, theory of change, and problem description then isomorphic patterns are replicated across subsystem boundaries that positively support supervision and therapy. In contrast, if a supervisor focuses on intergenerational patterns and a supervisee prefers a model of therapy that is behavioral and present-focused, theoretical confusion within the supervision relationship may parallel the confusion within a family. Isomorphism, which jeopardizes therapy and supervision, is created. Many supervisors assume that supervisees and supervisors must mirror each others' theories of change to more easily meet the goals of supervision. This inference can be overlooked by supervisors and supervisees initially without careful attention to the theoretical match between the two.

Suggesting that supervisors and supervisees make an epistemological declaration of their assumptions about therapy (Liddle, 1982), as part of their contract for supervision, is the obvious first step. As White (1989/90) notes, a matching of expectations is a more direct route to comfortable interaction. Although a Bowenian supervising someone practicing structural family therapy could be an interesting experience, it is potentially confusing for clients and therapists participating in supervision and therapy processes.

As supervisors assist their supervisees in making an epistemological declaration, at times they become educators. Because one goal of supervision is to increase the competence of supervisees, this cannot be accomplished without ensuring that supervisees are operating from a consistent clinical theory, whether that theory is integrative or a specific model. Recognizing this as an ongoing process, supervision often requires a linkage to education (Everett & Koerpel, 1986), as supervisees learn therapy skills related to the application of theory.

Assuming supervisees' competencies are consistent with their understanding of a theory and its application, based on conceptual, perceptual, and executive skills (Cleghorn & Levin, 1973), one must concomitantly assume supervisors are knowledgeable about the theories utilized by their supervisees. The necessary theoretical match between supervisors and supervisees in individual supervision is easily accomplished. This match may be even more important in individual supervision because this structure allows for a more intense focus on a single supervisee that is not as possible in multiple member structures. However, this is a more complicated exercise when you consider forming multiple member structures such as dyads, groups, or teams of supervisees.

The challenge for a supervisor is twofold. First, is the supervisor proficient with all of the theories being practiced by supervisees? Second, can the supervisor involve all supervisees in the supervision process if a variety of theories are being practiced? It is more difficult to keep members included in the dialogue of learning when some may not be well versed on the theory being applied during a specific case discussion. As will be discussed later, it may require different supervision skills and a more advanced group of supervisees to manage different theories within the same multiple member grouping. Creative diversity of thought is valued and desired by accomplished and experienced professionals as an expected part of professionalism and theory building.

Supervisees' Professional Development

The next factor is supervisees' professional development, their theoretical competence, therapeutic competence, and experience level. The terms *experienced* and *competent* are not viewed as necessarily the same. Competence refers to a level of theoretical knowledge and therapeutic skills, while experience implies a length of time spent as a therapist. For example, an experienced supervisee may or may not be highly competent with a particular theory. An inexperienced supervisee may be more competent in understanding the theory but limited in her or his repertoire of responses to clients.

In supervision groupings, frequently the less experienced and less competent members defer to the more experienced and more competent. Sometimes problems arise because the less experienced are not necessarily the less competent. The supervisory challenge is to help these supervisees speak up and to assist the more experienced supervisees to appropriately recognize their own learning needs. Similarly, the less competent supervisees may occupy too much group time in comparison to the needs of the more highly competent members. Multiple member supervision structures, which consist of members with a similar level of experience, therapy, and theoretical sophistication, are more easily supervised and create an environment for cooperation and challenge between equals. Therefore, a suggested principle is:

To more easily ensure effective supervision, bring together members with similar theories, levels of theory and therapy competence, and length of experience.

Supervisees are by level of competence and experience, particularly beginning therapists, in a process of learning theory and its application, a complex learning task that initially requires a focus in supervision rather than confusion and persistent theoretical debates. In regard to theory, supervisors and supervisees are dealing with similar questions at different levels of the system. Supervisors are processing: How is the theory of therapy utilized by supervisees being supported by my supervision? Similarly, supervisees are asking: Is my theory of therapy consistent with my operations within the therapy room? These two subsystems must be answering these questions from the same reference point, a recognition and knowledge of the same theory of practice. Given the complexity of this learning task the principle here is offered as a global solution. There are other solutions to be discussed later in the chapter (see section on Mixture and Sequencing of Structures).

Supervisors' Developmental Models of Supervision

It is important for supervisors to have a scheme in mind regarding how they supervise beginning, middle, and advanced supervisees. According to Liddle (1988a,b), supervisees learn and practice from an increasingly complex set of theoretical concepts and related interventions over time. This requires supervisors to modify their supervision as supervisees develop their competency. A helpful concept for supervisors is the idea of developmental stages for supervision as the competency of the supervisees increases. It is suggested that how a supervisor uses supervisory structures can help with this developmental process. Consequently, a suggested principle is:

Supervision that attends to the application of theory and its increased complexity as the experience and competence of supervisees grows may have greater success. Therefore, supervisors can utilize different groupings and combinations of supervisory structures to support this developmental process.

An example of a supervisor's scheme for helping supervisees increase their competence in stages follows. Supervisees' developmental level determines whether supervision should begin with a specific theoretical approach, their own integrative model, or by selecting specific models according to client problems. Because beginning therapists value support and specific technical direction (Brock & Sibbald, 1988; Heppner & Roehlke, 1984; Wetchler, 1989), they may become more confident and competent by beginning with a specific therapy model. Middle-level supervisees are ready to become competent with more than one specific marriage and family therapy (MFT) theory. This requires supervisors who provide training in more complex and dynamic views of change (Worthington, 1984). The final level, although never totally completed in one's professional career, is advanced supervisees' ability to conceptually support their theoretical position and related interventions to colleagues and supervisors. This ability to provide a rationale for their work may take the form of advocating one specific theory, integrating a theory of their own, or selecting a specific theory to use with particular client problems. This is an experienced and competent supervisee's epistemological declaration.

In supervision with one supervisee the sequence of stages described here is more easily accomplished. But in multiple member structures, juggling several supervisees at different developmental stages can be challenging. Group members can split into subgroups based on level of experience or competency and/or theoretical preferences. Group discussions regarding case material can become overwhelming for supervisees, especially for beginners, because of the multitude of ideas and approaches taken. Co-therapists with different levels of experience and competence, or theoretical preferences, can become involved in a confusing tug-of-war. This is not a process that easily enhances beginning clinicians' abilities to develop clear theoretical positions and skills for practice when it occurs. One preventive step is to observe the previously stated "principle of similar members." For more advanced supervisees, in which the focus is to support their personal formalizations and declarations of theory and practice, multiple member groupings may be a more invigorating and creative environment. For these supervisees, a heterogeneous member structure (along theoretical lines) can offer multiple perspectives and valuable feedback.

Homogeneous and Heterogeneous Groupings

Kagan (1983) and Nichols (1979) express reservations about supervisees who observe more experienced clinicians, believing that beginning therapists need to develop their own styles and not imitate others. This may be a matter of degree, but their concern indicates supervisors must carefully design and utilize structures to ensure the growth of all supervisees within multiple member structures. This points out the value of supervisors being clear about their developmental model for supervision as it strongly relates to this factor of homogeneous and heterogeneous groupings.

Some of the advantages of homogeneous groupings for supervision have already been noted in the previous suggested principles of similar theory and competence level supervisees. In sum, there are fewer risks or factors to worry about when, like a marriage, the members of dyads, co-therapists, groups, and teams consist of equals in competence and experience. They can even be viewed as collegial mentors. However, supervisors are often in situations where implementing a choice of homogeneous or heterogeneous structures is not easily accomplished. The decision can be shaped by situational factors yet to be covered such as, the practice context, resources, or a supervisor or a supervisee's preference for certain structures for supervision. As a consequence, a suggested principle is offered to help forge a decision that can work:

> *In groupings of dissimilar members, it is useful to design a mixture of supervision structures to accommodate the different learning needs and levels of supervisees.*

A mixture of supervision structures may help supervisors who are confronted with a situation of supervising dissimilar supervisees. For example, in a group structure, supervisors can arrange for similar level supervisees to practice co-therapy together. Or, in a group, several treatment teams can be formed along theoretical lines according to their preferred models of therapy. This provides an opportunity for similars or equals to enjoy the support of peers while perhaps taking advantage of input from more advanced supervisees or theoretically different members by participating in a dissimilar multiple group structure.

OTHER INTERNAL FACTORS THAT INFLUENCE STRUCTURE SELECTION

As a result of situational circumstances, the remaining internal factors may become primary considerations in the selection of supervisory structures. Although they are not designated as being core factors, they are not to be minimized.

Supervisors' and Supervisees' Structure Preference

It is not uncommon for supervisees or supervisors to prefer one type of structure. In a private practice situation, this is more easily accomplished because supervisors and supervisees can find a fit based solely on their own negotiations. However, settings such as institutes, universities, and agencies may constrict the range of choice because of financial restraints,

state laws, institutional requirements, and a host of other external factors. For example, state laws may have specific requirements regarding what type of supervision structure can be used in the process of becoming eligible for certification or licensure.

Supervisors' Competence Level

As noted by Liddle (1988b), there is little known about the characteristics of quality supervisors. It is reasonable to assume that most beginning supervisors are more comfortable with fewer supervisees. However, some supervisors may be more skilled in including all members' voices and viewpoints in groups and teams. This makes sense when viewing the magnitude of the supervisory job. First, supervisors must consider the supervision relationship. Second, supervisors must ensure that all supervisees are providing quality therapy. Third, supervisors must learn and develop their supervisory roles and strategies with single and multiple member groups. Fourth, supervisors need to develop the ability to conceptualize parallel patterns (isomorphism) across the multiple systems in supervision. Supervisors' increasing level of development, however, can be viewed as a potential advantage for institutions, agencies, and the profession. Supervisors may need to begin with smaller membership structures in order to build toward a greater complexity of conceptual skills related to team and group structures.

Culture and Gender Competence

The factors of culture (Fallcov, 1988) and gender (McGoldrick, Anderson, & Walsh, 1989; Wheeler et al., 1985) are central to the understanding and treatment of client systems. For instance, in an agency serving an Asian population, it may be necessary to educate a group of supervisees, no matter what their competence or experience level, to be culturally informed about this population. The most efficacious method in this situation may be a group structure. Multiple member structures, in general, offer the advantage of supervisees learning from a diversity of worldviews during supervision.

These factors also offer opportunity for growth in the supervisory relationship. Supervisors and supervisees can gain invaluable experience by having supervisors and supervisees of different genders and backgrounds in an atmosphere that promotes the learning of different experiences and points of view. However, supervisors need to be observant and sensitive to patterns of quiet voices in dyads, groups, and teams. This can be particularly relevant if it is a minority member or supervisee of a different gender who feels uncomfortable or not well connected with the supervisor or other group members. In such a situation, a change in the supervision structure may be a potential solution. I recall a minority woman in one of my supervision groups who said very little, but was known by me to be an eager beginning therapist. Fortunately, the situation allowed for a mixture of structures. In a dyad structure, she was very verbal about therapy concepts and practice. On sharing this observation with her, she noted that in the group she felt less sure of herself. Our conversation created an opportunity for us to discuss in the group how our backgrounds (i.e., culture, ethnicity, and gender) influence us as therapists. From that time on, each group member shared equally as each was now defined as a therapist with a previous history that can shape their therapy. What I learned is that for some minority individuals, a smaller supervision structure may be a more appropriate or comfortable starting point for supervision. (Please refer to Chapters 3 through 10 in the Context part of this book to learn more about how supervision is influenced by these factors.)

Clientele Characteristics

A clientele of a particular characteristic may indeed be critical to structure selection. For example, in a university setting where there is ongoing research or training regarding a specific client characteristic, such as single parent families or families with a depressed adolescent, a team structure may be useful. Teams can work together observing and treating the same case(s) and offer invigorating exchanges of information regarding their observations. Co-therapy structures can also offer a similar advantage.

EXTERNAL FACTORS

External factors (see Table 23.1) relate to the larger context of supervision and tend to be viewed as outside of the holon of the supervisors, supervisees, and clients. However, they often have an immediate effect on the internal factors and the ultimate structure selection in a myriad of idiosyncratic ways too complex for complete discussion here.

Requirements of professional organizations, the context of practice, the supervisor's position in the institution, laws and legal responsibilities, ethical codes, and resources available are powerful pragmatics and usually prominent in the selection of structures. They can also interact to shape the selection of supervisees. For example, an agency primarily treating sexual dysfunctions may be very sensitive to selecting a balance of male and female supervisees. Or, in a Native American community, the selection of supervisees already knowledgeable about gender roles and ethnic values characteristic of this population can be critical to the mission of an agency.

Sometimes the supervisor's role or position in an agency, or institution, is the key external factor. For instance, university professors have influence over curriculum development in the education and supervision of marriage and family therapists and must select the supervision structure that best fits the curriculum's goals. In contrast, most supervisors in private practice do not have a relationship with a larger institutional mission. Therefore, other external factors (e.g., financial, state laws) may have greater influence on shaping their selection of a structure.

STRUCTURES: A CHALLENGING CHOICE

Each structure of supervision has a set of advantages and disadvantages. However, what is seen as a characteristic disadvantage may rapidly change to a strength based on supervisors' assessments of what the core and major factors are in their decision tree for structure selection. For example, it is understandable to expect groups of beginning supervisees to have more questions and anxiety about their cases, which makes supervisor availability very important. While groups are resource effective, supervisors' time can become stretched if they are responsible for several groups whose members are beginning therapists. However, in educational settings where a priority exists for students to learn theory and beginning therapy skills, the institution often devotes resources to ensure a larger proportion of individual or dyad supervision. If the combined goal is education and supervision, the disadvantages of increased supervisory costs and time becomes acceptable. The advantages and disadvantages discussed are those typically found by supervisors.

The Individual Supervision Structure

Individual (one-to-one) supervision offers an intimate supervision experience, and begin-

ning level supervisors do not have to deal with the complexities of group or team processes. Supervisees receive the sole attention of supervisors, which allows for a closer observation of cases and patterns that develop in supervisees' therapy. Some supervisees may be more comfortable and open to critiquing their work with an individual supervisor they trust. This structure can be offered to supervisees who may temporarily need individual attention to expedite their learning curve or empower a member who, for a number of reasons, may be overwhelmed in a multiple member structure. At one time I had a group member who literally became physically sick to her stomach just before her therapy sessions with a couple who verbally battered each other during their time together. As a result, the supervisee began to believe she might have chosen the wrong profession. She and I worked out a solution based on what she needed. Live individual supervision for only a few sessions offered her supervisory support and encouragement, as well as an opportunity for her to be open about her parents' angry divorce when she was a young adolescent. She had the "right stuff" to become a therapist; the solution was just temporarily using the benefits an individual structure can provide.

With time this relationship may run the risk of becoming a closed system, which can negatively affect supervision. For example, supervisors and supervisees can experience a lack of new ideas. Variation in ideas, gender, culture, and values are important experiences in both participants' professional development.

Individual supervision can be a powerful learning experience, but it is perhaps best if mixed or sequenced over time with supervisees' participation in other multiple member structures of supervision. This may become particularly true when realizing the increased resource expenditure for such a structure.

The Dyad Supervision Structure

The "principle of similar members," unless both members are advanced, is useful when supervising dyads. This principle promotes a dialogue between equals, creates learning through listening to colleagues, and prevents one partner from being left out of the interaction.

There are similar advantages to the intimacy of individual supervision when supervision is done in dyads. There is also a decrease in the comparative disadvantages to the individual structure. With two supervisees, the development of a closed system is less likely and a diversity of views is more probable. This structure requires supervisors to expand their viewpoint of the system. There is an addition of two subsystems requiring the attention of the supervisor (i.e., the supervisors' relationship to each supervisee, and the supervisees' relationship). With dyads, a supervisor's skill in maintaining the involvement of both supervisees may resemble techniques used in marital therapy. This expansion is further tested when dealing with groups and teams. A dyad I supervised developed a pattern where one very verbal therapist occupied most of the time talking about his therapy cases while the other therapist quietly listened. I formally alternated weeks and had each supervisee present a video or live case for supervision as a way to interrupt this pattern. This balanced the level of involvement for each supervisee.

If the two supervisees are widely disparate on the competence factor, it may prove more difficult to offer both the same opportunity for growth. It is certainly more arduous for a less advanced supervisee to feel confident during supervision discussions if coupled with someone with greater skills. As noted earlier, two supervisees who are both advanced but operating from different systemic theories may in fact complement each others' growth because of the sophistication of the feedback available to one another. This also applies to the following multiple member supervision structure.

The Co-Therapy Supervision Structure

Although there is little evidence to support the efficacy of co-therapy (Gurman & Kniskern, 1981), it is an often used structure in supervision. Therapists join together in co-therapy teams for many different reasons, such as learning to do therapy, fulfilling affirmation needs, or collaborating on studying a phenomena or theory; these reasons may influence supervision (Storm, York, & Sheehy, 1990). The comments here are limited to the co-therapy members who join for the purpose of learning to do therapy in the context of supervision.

Co-therapy can be a mutually rewarding and supportive arrangement. Both partners are learning by treating the same clients and therefore both are intensely involved in the treatment and supervisory case discussions. This is a clear advantage over other structures. Co-therapy also helps subside the anxiety experienced by beginning therapists, and if their supervisor is their co-therapist (Connell, 1984; Latham, 1982), they can learn by doing therapy with a more advanced clinician.

In contrast, some disadvantages exist (Storm, York, & Sheehy, 1990). If the co-therapists are of different levels of competence and/or experience, or in a situation in which the supervisor is acting as a co-therapist, a permanent complementary relationship may result. Therapists who are in the one down position may feel discomfort and repeatedly defer to their partner. If there is a covert lack of respect for each other's skills, or theory of practice, a covert symmetrical struggle may ensue, leading to competitiveness rather than collaboration. Therapists can also risk a lack of autonomy, and a high degree of mutual dependency and admiration can lead to a closed system. Several years ago I supervised a highly enmeshed co-therapy team. They were exclusionary of input by other student colleagues in the agency. To intervene I told them it was time to graduate onto solo therapy because they were now entirely advanced enough to do so. I used the idea of solo practice as being a logical extension of the type of practice that would be expected once they had graduated from their master's program. Rather than being closed and reticent they viewed this change as an opportunity and the shift was easily made.

The Group Supervision Structure

Group supervision offers a greater complexity of relationships and experiences of anxiety and competitiveness, as well as distinct opportunities for supervisee growth (Cohen, Gross, & Turner, 1976; Tucker & Liddle, 1978). Groups also provide an opportunity to connect group process and experiential exercises with the interactions of families. A major advantage for groups is that they require fewer resources in terms of supervisors' time and cost.

A group can create a rich context of different viewpoints. The possibility of peers learning from each other may be equally desirable to what supervisors can offer. Group interaction builds professional colleagueship and confidence. The classic notion that "two heads are better than one" certainly applies to groups. Several authors suggest that in groups the experience level of supervisees (Wendorf, 1984) and the level of competence (Rabi, Lehr, & Hayner, 1984) are central to a successfully functioning group. These ideas support the principle of "similar members" and perhaps a goal of greater collaboration in supervision (Fine, 1993). Without the effects of these factors being considered, the probability is greater that there will be impediments to the group process. Too great a disparity of members across core factors will limit the growth of individual members

and the advantages of a group. The group process will become the constant focus rather than supervisee growth and effective therapy.

Never being married to my own suggested principles, one supervision group of mine consisted of three beginning level therapy students and three advanced, more competent students. After two meetings it became quite clear that the advanced students were in a sense "showing off" what they knew and how comfortable they were in designing interventions for difficult cases. The beginning students became clearly one down and were reticent to participate and share their ideas. As an intervention, I began to make pointed observations and comments to the beginning students regarding how I appreciated their slow pace at learning to be precise with the theory they were practicing, and how when they designed interventions they were clearly theory-based. This intervention allowed the beginners to feel more competent and led the advanced students to once again realize that they were also learning a new theory.

A final disadvantage is that members usually rotate case presentations, whether live sessions, audio, or video. This provides less continuity for following the development of the therapy related to a specific case and supervisee. Therefore, supplemental individual supervision may be needed.

The Team Supervision Structure

Teams typically place one or two of their members in session with families while the remainder of the team observes. The observing members assess and discuss possible interventions. Teams can be expanded into reflecting teams (Prest, Darden, & Keller, 1990) and collaborative teams (Roberts, 1983). (See Chapter 24 on teams for additional information.)

A unique quality of this structure is that all members are responsible for the therapy (Heath, 1982). Assisting a team to work together is a primary task for supervisors. Supervisors must attend to the functioning of teams, while being cognizant of the therapy the team is performing. Although supervisors typically are reluctant to utilize authority as a means for decisions, supervisors must determine what is important to focus on in relation to the client's welfare versus supporting a team's therapeutic decisions. This is a dilemma that must be carefully weighed or teams will become too submissive to supervisors and lose their spontaneity and cohesion.

However, at times it is appropriate for a supervisor to intervene into the team process. One team I supervised was seeing a couple in the midst of deciding to separate. Part of the team thought they should continue to see them as a couple interspersed with individual sessions for each spouse. The remainder of the team felt they should just see the wife because it was the husband who was going to move out of the home; if he wanted further therapy, they could refer him to another therapist. My intervention was to ask the team, "Who is the client system?" This encouraged a dialogue that led the team into discussions about isomorphism. Because the team was now also separated, was this reflective of the marriage? Further team dialogue touched on gender when I asked them, "Why wouldn't they just see the husband and refer the wife to a new therapist?" In this case they decided a separation is still a relationship, and they would see both partners. As can be seen, a supervisor may have to help a team process a decision and even shape it, but the goal is to let the team receive input and create their own dialogue about a decision.

Teams have the advantage of all supervisees working with the same clinical cases. Teams also have some of the same advantages as groups (e.g., multiple viewpoints and observers, peer learning, and so on). Yet members receive less individual feedback. Because of the latter, it is proposed that teams will accomplish more supervisory goals if the members are sim-

ilar within the supervisee developmental factor. A group of team members, heterogeneous in experience, theory, and competence, can be detrimental to both the supervision and therapy. Supplemental structures may be necessary.

A Mixture or Sequencing of Structures

It is possible to mix or sequence structures to support supervisors' rationale for their model of supervising clinicians at differing developmental levels. For example, a group structure can be organized to have beginning therapists practice in co-therapy. This offers a nice arrangement to match "similars" and help reduce anxiety for beginning therapists. Also, a mix of structures might be to have clinicians in group supervision be joined as co-therapists according to their interest in a specific theory or client phenomena and periodically receive supervision as co-therapists. In sum, structures can be supplemented to strengthen supervision goals.

Sequencing of structures can also be utilized to support supervisors' developmental models. For example, if a supervisor matches supervisees along core factors, it is possible to begin with individual, dyad, or co-therapy supervision for beginning supervisees. This offers supervisees more individual time and supervisory attention. It also provides supervisors with a greater ability to follow through on case progress from week to week. As these beginners become more confident and competent, they can advance to groups and teams of supervisees. They now have the advantage of a greater diversity of viewpoints and theoretical ideas. A group or team also diminishes supervisors' depth of awareness of all supervisee cases. But, supervisees may begin to accurately perceive supervisors' trust in their competence as they graduate to a more autonomous level of practice. The designs for using a mixture, sequencing, and/or supplemental supervision structures are exhaustive. The key is for supervisors to have a rationale based on the advancement of supervisees' competence as therapists.

FACTORS THAT INFLUENCE THE SELECTION OF A STRUCTURE

In a perfect world, the best structure would be chosen based on a thoughtful review of the factors. For example, a structure of supervision with few members, such as individual or dyad supervision, would perhaps best fit the beginning supervisee and beginning supervisor. The needs for time and proximity to the supervisor are more likely to be met. However, resources, context of practice, clientele served, and other noted factors may significantly influence the structure selected. For instance, in an agency or unit of an agency that primarily serves a clientele where spousal abuse is of concern, a supervisor may have to weigh the advantages of having individual versus group supervision. The influence of the gender factor may be critical because most abused spouses are women. In terms of support and sharing of ideas, the advantages of a group are obvious. However, individual, co-therapy, or dyad supervision offer more access to the supervisor, particularly in light of a clientele that may be known to have significant emergencies related to safety. Thus, a supervisor could conclude that as a result of the severity of client problems and the beginning level of supervisees, "one-to-one" or dyad supervision could be the best move to ensure client safety and change for the client system. Supervising beginning therapists in groups may increase the risk to clients with intense safety needs because of time limitations for each group member. However, administrators could determine this to be too expensive. At this point, the supervisor and administrators may be at a crossroad of determining what is of

priority amongst the noted factors: to provide the best supervision possible for beginning supervisees, to honor the supervisor's preferences, or to use the structure that would best serve client needs.

Several factors must be considered simultaneously. First, services to the clientele must be within the standard level of practice (i.e., practice context, state laws, and ethical code factors). Second, administrators must be able to serve the most people with as few resources as possible (i.e., resources and practice context factors). Third, supervisees must feel confident in serving their clientele (i.e., structure preference and supervisee professional development factors). This includes their confidence in the support and guidance of their supervisor (i.e., supervisor competence factor).

Not all possible factors are readily exposed in this example, but several possible solutions exist. For example, when resources are a major factor, it is beneficial for the supervisor to go to an "if then" position. "If" resources are thin, and the clientele is a high safety risk, and the supervisor is lower in the hierarchy of power for decision making, "then" the supervisor could present to the agency the following solutions: (1) select supervisees who are homogeneous with theory and therapy competence, or (2) select advanced supervisees who are heterogeneous theoretically but demonstrate therapy competence. Group supervision can be provided in solution (1) or (2) while staying within resources available. A supervisor would need to ensure that supervisees are knowledgeable about gender and culture, in general. Although other solutions are possible, supervisors utilizing the factors consider multiple influences in their decisions and develop a rationale.

The practice context is often a major factor, as opposed to an internal core factor, in the selection of a supervision structure. The missions of various practice contexts may strongly influence what is a major factor in selecting a structure, but supervisors will benefit by considering internal core factors, as noted, because they are central to the goals of supervision.

CONCLUSION

Without presuming to know all combinations and possibilities, it is reasonable to assume that supervisors can begin with the internal core factors to establish which structure to select. It is suggested the next step is to work outward to the remaining internal and external factors as possible major influencers on the structure selection. The interdependence of internal and external factors, taken as a whole, forms the decision matrix. I might add that the factors and principles offered here are only a touchstone for those you may develop in your work. Nothing can replace a supervisor's intimate knowledge and experience of their own context for challenging and developing new factors, principles, and ideas.

REFERENCES

Brock, G., & Sibbald, S. (1988). Supervision in AAMFT accredited programs: Supervisee perceptions and preferences. *American Journal of Family Therapy, 16*, 256–261.

Cleghorn, J., & Levin, S. (1973). Training family therapists by setting learning objectives. *American Journal of Orthopsychiatry, 43*, 439–446.

Cohen, M., Gross, S., & Turner, M. (1976). A note on a developmental model for training family therapists through group supervision. *Journal of Marriage and Family Counseling, 2*, 48–76.

Connell, G. (1984). An approach to supervision of symbolic-experiential psychotherapy. *Journal of Marriage and Family Therapy, 10*, 273–280.

Everett, C., & Koerpel, B. (1986). Family therapy supervision: A review and critique of the literature. *Contemporary Family Therapy, 8*, 62–74.

Falicov, C. (1988). Learning to think culturally. In H. Liddle, D. Breunlin, & R. Schwartz (Eds.), *Handbook of family therapy training and supervision* (pp. 335–357). New York: Guilford Press.

Fine, M. (1993). Collaboration in supervision. *Supervision Bulletin, 6*, 1, 7.

Gurman, A., & Kniskern, D. (1981). *Handbook of family therapy*. New York: Brunner/Mazel.

Haley, J. (1976). *Problem-solving therapy*. San Francisco: Jossey-Bass.

Heath, A. (1982). Team family therapy training: Conceptual and pragmatic considerations. *Family Process, 21*, 187–194.

Heppner, P., & Roehlke, H. (1984). Differences among supervisees at different levels of training: Implications for a developmental model of supervision. *Journal of Consulting Psychology, 31*, 76–90.

Kagan, N. (1983). Classroom to client: Issues in supervision. *Counseling Psychologist, 11*, 69–72.

Latham, T. (1982). The use of coworking (cotherapy) as a training method. *Journal of Family Therapy, 4*, 257–269.

Liddle, H. (1982). On the problems of eclecticism: A call for epistemological clarification and human scale theories. *Family Process, 21*, 243–250.

Liddle, H. (1988a). Developmental thinking and the family life cycle: Implications for training family therapists. In C. Falicov (Ed.), *Family transitions: Continuity and change across the life cycle* (pp. 449–466). New York: Guilford Press.

Liddle, H. (1988b). Systemic supervision: Conceptual overlays and pragmatic guidelines. In H. Liddle, D. Breunlin, & R. Schwartz (Eds.), *Handbook of family therapy and supervision* (pp. 153–171). New York: Guilford Press.

Liddle, H., Breunlin, D., & Schwartz, R. (1988). Introduction. In H. Liddle, D. Breunlin, & R. Schwartz (Eds.), *Handbook of family therapy and supervision* (pp. 13–16). New York: Guilford Press.

Liddle, H., & Saba, G. (1983). On context replication: The isomorphic relationship of family therapy training. *Journal of Strategic and Systems Therapies, 2*, 3–11.

Liddle, H., & Schwartz, R. (1983). Live supervision/consultation: Conceptual and pragmatic guidelines for family therapy trainers. *Family Process, 22*, 477–490.

McGoldrick, M., Anderson, C., & Walsh, F. (1989). *Women in families: A framework for family therapy*. New York: W. W. Norton.

Nichols, W. (1979). Education of marriage and family therapists. *Journal of Marital and Family Therapy, 5*, 19–28.

Piercy, F., & Sprenkle, D. (1986). Supervision and training. In F. Piercy & D. Sprenkle (Eds.), *Family therapy sourcebook* (pp. 288–321). New York: Guilford Press.

Prest, L., Darden, E., & Keller, K. (1990). "The fly on the wall" reflecting team supervision. *Journal of Marital and Family Therapy, 16,* 265–273.

Rabi, J., Lehr, M., & Hayner, M. (1984). Study group II: The peer consultation team: An alternative. *Journal of Strategic and Systemic Therapies, 3,* 66–71.

Roberts, J. (1983). Two models of live supervision: Collaborative team and supervisor guided. *Journal of Strategic and Systemic Therapies, 2,* 68–78.

Saba, G., & Liddle, H. (1986). Perceptions of professional needs, practice patterns and initial issues facing family therapy trainers and supervisors. *American Journal of Family Therapy, 14,* 109–122.

Storm, C., York, C., & Sheehy, P. (1990). Supervision of cotherapists: Cotherapy liaisons and the shaping of supervision. *Journal of Family Psychotherapy, 1,* 65–74.

Tucker, B., & Liddle, H. (1978). Intra- and interpersonal process in the group supervision of family therapists. *Family Therapy, 5,* 13–28.

Wendorf, D. (1984). A model for training practicing professionals in family therapy. *Journal of Marital and Family Therapy, 10,* 31–41.

Wetchler, J. (1989). Supervisor's and supervisee's perceptions of the effectiveness of family therapy supervisor interpersonal skills. *American Journal of Family Therapy, 17,* 244–256.

Wheeler, D., Avis, J., Miller, L., & Chaney, S. (1985). Rethinking family therapy training and supervision: A feminist model. *Journal of Psychotherapy and the Family, 1,* 53–72.

White, M. (1989/90). Family therapy training and supervision in a world of experience and narrative. *Dulwich Centre Newsletter, Summer,* 27–38.

Worthington, E. (1984). Empirical investigation of supervision of counselors as they gain experience. *Journal of Counseling Psychology, 31,* 63–75.

24

Reflecting Processes and "Supervision"

Looking at Ourselves as We Work with Others

Janine Roberts

Marchella, the supervisor, asked Nate, a supervisee, "Do you feel ready to do the reflection for the family now?"

"Yes," said Nate, "Let me turn on the tape recorder."

Marchella began, "It seems that the family is working very hard to sort through what it meant all those years after their father's death to live with the stories about what a great person he was, when their own experience inside the family with his alcoholism was very different. I'm impressed with how they acknowledge the ways in which those mythical positive stories helped the grandparents deal with the loss of their son, but at the same time talk about the price they paid not to have a more realistic picture of their dad as a human being with his own problems"

"It gave me a sense of hope to hear them say that," added Nate. "The ways in which they can understand different people's needs and positions is very powerful" Marchella and Nate went on to share several more of their reflections about the last session Nate had conducted with the family. Nate then took the audiotape to their home for their next therapy meeting and played

it for the family. He asked them to comment on which of the ideas stood out for them, which seemed irrelevant, and which they wanted to pursue further; Nate used their responses to focus the session.

After Raul presented his thoughts on help he wanted with his case, the four therapists and supervisor launched into the reflecting team format they had devised for their bimonthly supervision group. "I appreciated how Raul was trying to make space for more of the mother's experience to come into the family to strengthen her relationship with the three kids. Given that she has so few of her extended family here and is so far away from Cambodia (her country of origin), I wondered what it might be like to have her share stories about her life in Cambodia at the kids' bedtime, especially about before she had to flee, as it seems so many of those stories have been lost with the trauma of the escape story"

"I like that idea because the kids and family have much more contact with their father's relatives who all live around here. I was also curious about what it might be like to have the father, Tom, find out more from his wife, Chin, about her thoughts on how to bring up children, values she learned from her culture, so that her voice is heard more. It also might be a way to

Note: With much appreciation to Cheryl Storm, Ph. D., and Carey Dimmitt, M.Ed., for their thoughtful edits on this chapter, as well as to the various supervisory groups with whom I have worked. You have taught me a great deal.

communicate to the children, who often do not listen to her, about the importance of her ideas." After each person in the group presented an idea or two, the supervisor proceeded to interview Raul about which of the suggested ideas he might want to discuss more before trying them out in his next session with the family.

_____

_____

After three months of doing live supervision with a reflecting team format, the group wanted to look at their dynamics. Each person was asked to comment on what was working well, not so well and what they might want to change or modify about their work together. They began by talking about what was going well.

Eileen, a supervisee, noted: "I have been struck by our capacity to work out with each family what kind of relationship they want with the team. With Sarah and Daniel, it is clear that it is easier for them to have the therapist and the reflecting team in the room for each session. With the Wilson family, our written reflections have been a creative way to respond to the intrusiveness they were worried about if team members came into the room. And, for a couple of the other families, it seems to be working out with them letting us know when they are ready for a reflection." After all group members commented on areas they felt had gone well, each person was asked to comment on areas of concern, including in their comments ideas for how things might be done differently.

Zhang, the supervisor, began: "I have a concern that with the two lesbian couples we have been working with that we have not always asked some of the more difficult questions that may have been appropriate. It feels like our own investment of wanting each of them to make it as a couple might be getting in the way. It's hard for me to even bring this up here. I'm afraid I won't say it in the right way or it will somehow be seen as politically 'incorrect.'"

Using the same ground rules for discussion that they used for reflections for families (see Other Strategies section of this chapter), the group went on to evaluate their work and shape a new course for their next few months together in supervision.

_____

What do all three of these vignettes have in common? In each situation, supervisors and supervisees were using the basic tenets of reflecting team work: open dialogue with a chance for all to be heard; protected listening space (where one does not have to respond immediately to a conversation); a positive, exploratory frame where the person(s) asking for help have the last comments and these comments are taken as key feedback to refocus the work. Reflecting strategies used for therapeutic work with families can be used in a wide range of supervisory situations to make rich feedback loops between supervision time and the therapy session with clients, within the group to generate new ideas, and to examine supervision group dynamics with an eye to seeing how the group is functioning. This chapter explores a range of ways in which reflecting processes can be used in supervision[1] to meet

_____

[1]The word *supervision* can be separated into two main parts: *super* carries the meanings of "beyond, besides, and above"; *vision* comes from *videre* (to see) and has its roots in signifying "something that appears to be seen otherwise than by ordinary sight and seeing something not present to the eye" (*Oxford Dictionary of English Etymology*, 1983, p. 983). If you think about visionaries, they are people who look beyond the day-to-day routine.

There has sometimes been too much focus on the *above* meaning of *super* in supervision. The supervisor is viewed as someone who is higher than the supervisee in the hierarchy and therefore knows better. In supervising, she or he then hands down to the supervisee this "better" knowledge. This does not hold a sense of learning that helps people put together information in new ways and discover things themselves. I prefer to emphasize the *beyond* and *besides* meanings of *super*, and think about supervision as *extraordinary vision*. Thus, the supervisor's role is to facilitate an exploratory and expansive view for all in supervision (Roberts, 1994, p. 185).

the unique individual needs of supervisees while providing a structure that is attentive to group learning, with a focus on the best therapy possible for families. But how did I get to this place? Just as we often ask families to tell the story of how they came to find themselves meeting in therapy, I want to briefly share my sojourn with supervision.

THEMES AND THREADS LEADING TO REFLECTING SUPERVISION

In watching intersession discussions behind the one-way mirror with a Haley style supervisor-guided team in the late 1970s, a number of times I observed a supervisor handwrite, in his words, an intervention that the supervisee was to take back into the therapy room and read to the family (Roberts, 1983a). When the supervisee returned to the session, he or she read it, often with little affect and looking down trying to figure out the words. Many times, the families did not give much response, and it was hard to know what sense they made of it. The fact that there was not a direct conversation going on between the person who had put the ideas together and the family seemed to flatten the interchange.

I observed a strikingly different process while viewing another training team working with a Milan style collaborative supervision model (Roberts, 1983a). There, in intersession discussions, supervisees were expected to thread together thoughts and ideas from multiple comments of other team members and supervisors, and to share them with families in their own words. They were seldom written down in a formal manner; rather, supervisees might make a few notes to themselves, and then return to the families to share them. It was not always as eloquently stated as it might have been if the supervisor had written it down, but supervisees were engaged in trying

to communicate the ideas and feelings they had pulled together with families, and the families usually responded with interest and queries and engaged in the conversation with therapists. If there was a point that team members felt the therapist had not made clear or needed more elaboration, then the phone was used to call the therapist or a family member and reiterate the idea. The therapists were speaking with more of their voices, and the communication was somewhat more direct. Yet there were still lines drawn between the family and team members speaking face-to-face to each other.

What further piqued my interest over a year's observation of the two teams is that people did not comment on the different ways in which the therapists, families, and/or team members spoke directly or indirectly to each other. As neither team had structured the time and/or a format to look at their own group processes, opportunities did not arise to reflect on their dynamics.

In the 1980s, Cecchin and Boscolo of the Milan school developed a variation of their team supervision model where they divided the team behind the mirror into two parts: the T or treatment team which worked with the family, and the O or observing team which watched the T team do their presession, phone-ins, intersession discussions, final intervention to the family, and then postsession. After the therapy session was over, the O team commented on what they had observed. A structure was created to examine group processes but, as Boscolo and Cecchin (1982) describe it, the observations focused primarily on the therapeutic work, not the dynamics of the supervisory group. As I did more supervision, I adopted the T and O team model to look at the myriad levels involved in the supervision process: good therapy for the family; skill development of the supervisee in the room; supervisor-supervisee relationships; group learning environment; the supervisor–group relationships

(Roberts, 1983b), as well as the fit between families and their views of change and health, and the various models clinicians had to offer them (Roberts, 1986; Roberts et al., 1989). I also devised strategies to be used in supervision and training to look at practice through particular lenses, such as gender (Roberts, 1991), as a way to highlight often unspoken values and beliefs that influenced therapy and supervision.

While the T and O team format provided a way to step back and comment on therapy and supervision practice, it still did not address the issue of more direct dialogue between the family and members of the supervisory group. Information was communicated to the family primarily through the therapist who was working with them in the room. When team members came into the session, it was usually with a preplanned strategy, which may have come out of the meta-observing, but these kinds of observations were not openly shared in front of the family.

With the development of reflecting teams (Anderson, 1987, 1990) in which team members no longer use intersession discussions as a primary conduit to shape input to a family, but rather share their ideas openly in front of the family (either face-to-face or, as in the opening vignette, record their comments in some way to share with families) and then invite the family to ask about and comment on them, new possibilities for supervision modalities were opened up (Davidson et al., 1990). Supervision began to be seen as more of a reflexive process in which, just as in therapy, clients' feedback is central to the work; supervisees' ideas are invited and integrated into the structure of supervision as well. Hoffman (1991) talks about reflexivity as a folding back of a part on itself. The roots of the word *reflect* come from *refle*—throwing back of heat or light. In this "throwing back," White (1995) talks about the importance of transparency—therapists make it clear to clients where their ideas are coming from whether it be from their own life experiences,

conceptual models or from their experiences in talking and working with families.

REFLECTING SUPERVISION

So what does supervision look like within a reflecting team frame? Structures and stances that support reflecting work are brought centrally into supervision:

- Make sure that each person has input into discussions
- Ask clients to focus their comments in a resource frame concentrating on strengths and using everyday language
- Invite transparency in which people share the reasons why they are thinking of an idea or a story
- Set up formats in which people do not respond right away to ideas but have protected space to hear a range of thoughts
- Invite the person(s) asking for the help to comment on them once ideas for help are generated.

These comments are then used as a central focus for further dialogue and work. An essential role that the supervisor takes on is that of facilitator and protector of these kinds of structures and stances. As described in the opening vignettes, one does not need to be doing reflecting team work in the therapy hour to do this kind of work in supervision. In fact, doing reflecting work in supervision can be a good way to practice and learn reflecting skills so that they can then be used with families. Also, supervisees can get feedback on their reflections and incorporate suggestions about their work before they do reflections in sessions.

Often reflections are offered in the spirit of questions, or possible areas to explore. In that vein, four questions undergird the rest of this chapter. These questions have emerged as I have done supervision in mental health agencies, schools, university clinics, and with teams doing in-home family therapy. The following questions emphasize central areas to explore as we learn more about doing this kind of work:

1. In supervision, what skills need to be particularly developed to do work with reflecting teams? For example, what supports supervisees learning to do reflections and then processing them with families?

2. How does one do supervision that is congruent with therapeutic work that is less hierarchically organized and more relationally focused, in which the boundary between therapy and supervision is much more diffuse?

3. How can the interchange between families, therapists, and teams be kept lively, responsive, and focused without overwhelming people with too much information or the logistics of the work becoming too complicated?

4. In what ways does supervision need to be done differently if one is working with reflecting team ideas about transparency and self-disclosure on the part of therapists to clients?

There is not *a* way to do reflecting team supervision, because this runs counter to the idea of bringing the voices of each member of a supervision group into the conversation. Rather, processes to develop reflecting team supervision formats are explored in this chapter. Yet, with all structures, the guidelines in Table 24.1 are used to create a reflective framework.

I have also found the need to clarify with various supervisees that reflections do not mean only presenting a contemplative frame. Quite active interventions can be suggested in a reflection, even though they are described in an exploratory manner: "What might happen if a family member or supervisee tried this?" or "Does the family think this might be a useful idea to experiment with?"

TABLE 24.1. Guidelines for Reflections for Supervision

- Comments are formed as positive or logical connotations as opposed to negative attributions or blaming
- Ideas are presented tentatively with qualifiers such as "I was wondering," "perhaps," "possibly," "it's just an idea," and/or presented in an inquiring hypothetical frame: "what might happen if . . ?"
- Reflections attempt to present both sides of a dilemma, moving from an either/or position to a both/and or neither/nor position
- Emphasis is on presenting ideas versus "correct" interpretations two or more ideas are usually presented
- Comments are kept brief so as not to overwhelm listeners with too many ideas (reflectors often speak no more than one or two times in a reflection)
- Language and metaphors of the clients and supervisees are used—avoid psychological and diagnostic terms

- Questions and comments are raised that the interviewer did not or contextually could not say in the interview
- Comments may be presented as stories or metaphors
- Information is given in reflections that help locate how comments from team members may be similar or different, this can link or distinguish ideas, cohere reflecting comments, and prevent them from being too fragmented
- Reflections are often around 5–10 minutes (nonverbals from the family and/or supervision group can be important here)
- The impact of the size of the team on a family or supervision group is taken into account (reflecting groups that are more than 3–4 members can sometimes offer too many ideas)
- Careful attention is paid to nonverbals of the reflecting group to make space for each to speak, and to begin and end the group comments with grace

From Lax and Lussardi (1994), and expanded on by the author.

DIFFERENT WAYS TO SET UP REFLECTING TEAM SUPERVISION

Just as there are a range of ways to structure reflecting team work (e.g., with the team in the room all the time; the team behind the mirror; co-therapists turning to each other to do a reflection; when teams reflect they speak directly to family members, or, they keep a boundary between them), there is variability in supervision formats that adhere to a reflecting stance. In this section, the intent is to provide a sense of the possibilities as well as the parameters to pay attention to in setting up these kinds of structures. A central role of the supervisor is to facilitate the creative exploration of different structures, as well as keep an open dialogue going about what is working and not working in supervision.

Live Supervision of Reflecting Teams

Supervisory presessions are often more focused on the working relationships of the team than they are on describing family dynamics. Supervisee–supervisor discussions might include inquiries about when reflections could be useful to bring into the session and in what way, if it might be supportive to have more than one reflection, specific skills the supervisee would like help with, and/or whether to have an intersession discussion. In addition, when reflecting teams are supervised live, the technologies of the one-way mirror, phone-in, and videotaping capacities provide an array of choices about how to do supervision that needs to be negotiated. Supervisor–supervisee agreements can be made with each person on the team about how to use these different components, including elements such as whether the supervisee wants to have call-ins or not, who will do them if the phone is being used, ways to

structure phone-ins (Wright, 1986), as well as particular ways to videotape the session (for instance, a lot of close ups so nonverbal facial expressions are highlighted, or wide-angle shots so everyone can be seen simultaneously).

ARE WE WORKING TOGETHER HERE OR NOT?

In her presession supervision time, Fran talked with her supervisor about the frustration she felt in the first two sessions with a family because she thought she had not joined well with all the family members and they seemed to have widely disparate ideas about whether they wanted to be participating or not. Fran asked for help in clarifying her relationship with the family and how they might work together. The other three supervisees were listening to this discussion between Fran and the supervisor.

After they had talked for about ten minutes, the three supervisees reflected on what they had heard and shared their ideas. They proposed asking the family if they could come in near the beginning of the session to reflect on some of the different positions family members seemed to be taking, things they were curious about, as well as wonderings about what would happen if members shifted their positions. Fran was then asked what she thought of the idea. She commented that she thought it would be helpful, especially if they would be willing to reflect as well about her own concerns about joining with the family. The presession focus was on working out the details of how they might work together that session, knowing, of course, that modifications would be made once the family was actually there.

Given the range of choices available with live supervision, my bias is that I expect to see variability from session to session (e.g., the use of the phone for some sessions, little or no use of it for others; or, sometimes a team might have an intersession discussion behind the mirror, and at other times the team reflects in the room, or the family might be asked if they would like to do a reflection). The family might be invited to join an intersession discussion or to have their own at the same time as the team is meeting, with the family and team then coming together to share their two separate discussions. Team and family members might do a reflection together, or they might move a reflection into the future by enacting a reflection they imagine themselves doing at the last session when therapy is coming to a successful close. When the structure supports variations, creative possibilities for "news of a difference" are accessible.

MAKING TRANSITIONS ON MY OWN

One supervisee, Van, thought he was becoming too dependent on phone-ins to help him make transitions from one part of a session to another. He wanted to try a couple of sessions without any phone-ins so that he could further develop his linking skills. Before his next session, he asked other team members to reflect on and share the strategies they used to help them do this.

The supervisor, Patricia, talked about coming into sessions with two or three "panels" of ideas (e.g., themes or issues) she had organized based on previous sessions. Patricia then held these panels lightly in reserve as possible areas to explore when she found that an area she was exploring with the family was not fruitful. Tom, another team member, shared his strategy of checking in with families at the beginning of sessions about what they thought might be useful to discuss that day. Then, Tom kept these ideas in the back of his mind for interweaving during the discussion.

Felice, another supervisee, described phrases she used to facilitate transitions such as asking, "can we switch gears to. . . ." or, "I'm curious to

see how these topics might be connected." She also explained that she tried to make summary kinds of statements about a topic area before she moved on, thus bringing some closure to them for the time being.

Having this kind of discussion helped team members articulate and name what they were doing as well as gave Van ideas. After working on managing the transitions himself, Van requested that his colleagues ask him some questions to help him reflect on and process what he tried out. Van described himself as less anxious in the room because he had several strategies to use.

CAN WE COME INTO THE ROOM?

Sarah, Michelle, and Pete, three supervisees working as a reflecting team on an intense case that included a teenage daughter hospitalized recently for cutting her wrists, felt that when they came in to reflect they were missing a lot of the affect in the room because they were behind the one-way mirror. They asked the therapist and the family if they could sit in the room for a couple sessions because they thought it might help them better understand and respond to the range of emotions people were experiencing. The family members agreed to it even though the father felt it was somewhat intrusive. Sarah, Michelle, and Pete were in the room for three sessions. Ultimately the father described it as generating a feeling of extra support for the family—"additional people we can lean on " As things began to be on a more even keel for the family, the supervisees went back behind the mirror.

Other Strategies to Use in Live Supervision of Reflecting Teams

Often a good place to start in thinking about the next therapy session is with the family's reactions to whatever occurred at the end of the previous session. This can help build a bridge to what happened in the prior session as well as keep the focus on the family and their dilemmas. Different strategies to do this are looking at the videotape of the end of the session, reading from any notes recorders may have made,[2] or asking the therapist and team members to recall comments and reactions from family members. Other ways to start include asking therapists who were in the room with the family to reflect on what stood out for them in the session, especially "sparkling" moments (White, 1989/90); moments when they had questions and/or concerns about what was going on; their responses to watching the video of the session; and/or what help they would have liked in this session.

When supervisees behind the mirror know that they may go into the room to reflect, or they are responsible for phone-ins or videotaping in a particular way, they seem to become more connected to the family, more attentive to what is happening in the session, and to remember more of the details about the family and previous sessions. Because they are directly contributing to the treatment conversation, they have a different kind of involvement with the case.

To finish sessions that are supervised live, a variety of strategies can be used including affirmations to each other for work well done, reflecting on what seemed like key juncture points in the session, giving feedback to each other regarding the team work, highlighting what seemed to help the family and the team to be hopeful about possibilities for change, and noting things that people want to be sure to remember for next session.

Post Hoc Supervision: Bringing the Cases Back Home

In this situation, a different kind of structure is needed because people are sharing cases they have worked on alone or with someone else away from the supervisory group. Because the participants in the group do not have the common experience of seeing the session together, other strategies are needed to introduce information to members as well as send it back to the family. Because members have not observed the session, much of the supervision time can be used up in presenting details of the case. This can result in little time or space for reflecting on the therapy or family. Some ideas to prevent this from happening include preparing a genogram ahead of time so that central family information can be scanned quickly, drawing up an ecomap or structural map that introduces key members of the family and larger systems that may be involved with them, or doing a brief case write-up.[3]

Many therapists, however, do not always have time to prepare this kind of information, so another strategy is to have the supervisor or other member of the supervisory group interview the supervisee in a structured manner. For instance, using questions, such as the ones in Table 24.2, that emphasize a resource, solution-oriented stance focuses the discussion on a workable frame and avoids getting bogged down in too many details of the case, especially

---

[2]For a thoughtful description of a variety of team roles that members may choose to take on, including the recorder role, see Bernstein et al. (1984).

[3]In keeping with the narrative focus of reflecting team work, supervisees should be encouraged to use headings and subheadings that break from the usual case write-up headings (e.g., "Formulation of the presenting problem," "Structure of the family," "Treatment plan"). Some sample headings: "Brief history," "Musings about what has been helpful and what has not been helpful in therapy," "Wonderings about where to go from here," and "Who has gathered together?" If necessary, these can be transferred back to traditional headings for final reports.

TABLE 24.2. Case Sharing: A Resource Frame

- When have you felt most successful with the case?
- When and in what ways has the family (client) felt most hopeful?
- How can you build on these successes/feelings of hope?
- What gets in the way of feeling like you are being of help now?
- What are you learning by working on this case—about yourself, about other people, about larger systems (clinics, schools, social service agencies, the court system)?
- What kind of help would you like from this support group?
- If you were to speak to this group in one or more of your clients' voices, what kinds of things might you say?
- What have you tried with this case that has not been helpful that you do not think would be useful to do again?
- What helps you to be hopeful about this family (client)?

---

minutiae about things that have not been of help. After 5 to 10 minutes of this, everyone else in the group forms a reflecting team and each member shares any reflections they have about the conversation they have just heard and the case. This makes a protected space for people in the group to really be able to listen to the case (without immediately jumping in with their questions and ideas), and provides a way for all to share other perspectives (not just the most vocal members). Then the therapist who is presenting the case reflects on what is said by the supervision group and shapes the dialogue in regard to what he or she wants to talk about—what would be most helpful to him or her.

I'M NOT GOING NEAR THAT SCHOOL

In supervision, Vikram, an experienced school counselor, asked for help with a boy, Tom, and his family whom he had worked with off and on for over a year. Vikram described Tom as doing poorly in school academically. Small and thin for his age, he was physically aggressive to teachers and other children, especially on the playground. To shift the focus from defining Tom primarily in problem behaviors, the supervisor interviewing Vikram about the case began to ask questions from the list in Table 24.2 that highlighted strengths of Tom, his family, and Vikram A different picture emerged. Vikram noted that Tom did well in math and that in the afternoon when he was in the multi-aged classroom, which had a less "academic" and more hands-on, relaxed, learning focus, he did quite well. Vikram also shared that Tom was not verbally aggressive and that it seemed hard at times for him to communicate verbally what he wanted. The relationship between Tom's mother and the school was described as up and down. A school–family journal that Vikram had recently helped Tom's teacher and his mother start, which focused on things that were going well with Tom, seemed to be improving relationships between the school, Tom, and his family.

Vikram did not have a relationship with Tom's father. He had recently found out from Tom's mother that her husband said a number of times, "I'm not going near *that* school," because he had had a run-in with them a number of years earlier. Apparently, the school had called the family and asked them to discipline their other son, Joseph, because he had cut some classes. The father grounded him, and when he tried to leave the house, he grabbed Joseph, leaving a mark on his arm. The school then reported the father to social services because of the mark on Joseph. The father felt double-crossed by the school and did not trust them.

Vikram asked the supervision group for help with the case. First, each person contributed an idea or two. People commented on how Tom seemed to respond when people validated him and they wondered about the possibility of Tom perhaps tutoring other students in math Another idea was that he might be given some fun and helpful responsibilities at recess, such as helping the teacher on duty set out play equipment. Other people wondered what would happen if Vikram met with Tom's father and shared with him that he knew about his prior experience with the school and that he was proposing a different kind of school–family relationship. Finally, there were ideas about providing nonverbal safe ways for Tom to express emotion, as well as perhaps documenting the small shifts in Tom as he began to take on a new school identity.

Vikram then commented on which ideas he wanted to pursue further, including looking into Tom's tutoring others, trying to restructure recess time for him, and going to the house to talk to the father. The supervisor had facilitated a process whereby there was a resource focus on the case, an opening up of new ideas with a chance for everyone to be heard, and then a refocusing by the therapist involved in the case on some particular suggestions and perspectives.

Another role that supervisors might take on includes encouraging supervisees to expropriate some of the technologies of live supervision into their in-home and office settings that do not have one-way mirrors. The creative use of videotaped and/or audiotaped messages and reflections, and/or written reflections that are sent to a family can all be introduced into post hoc supervision and provide flexibility for reflecting formats. With the Blake family, who were struggling with the seizure disorder of one of the children, the supervisory group (with the family's permission) looked at part of the videotape that had been made of the last session in the home. They then sent their videotaped reflection on that session back to the family for them to watch at their next meeting. Although not as condensed in time as a reflection done on the spot in a session, it helped the supervisee introduce new ideas to the family. The family especially liked it because before

the group members had been "faceless" to them and known only by name. Now they felt like they at least knew who they were.

Transferring the Skills to the Therapy Hour

Similar to the ideas presented in the earlier section on live reflecting team supervision, supervisees can also be helped to work on specific skills and goals in sessions. Given that members from the supervision group will not be with them when they are actually trying to implement them, attention should be paid to supportive ways to inspire the therapist. One group chose a common theme of "trying out new skills." Each person, including the supervisor, identified an area they wanted to work on such as including young children as active participants in sessions and trying out new techniques such as psychodrama. Knowing that they were all stretching themselves to learn fledgling skills facilitated a spirit of camaraderie and support for risk-taking. In another group in which supervisees were all in situations in which they could not videotape their sessions, they brainstormed ways to create other records of the session such as doing journal notes to themselves, having a sheet for each member of the family and the therapist to take a few minutes to jot down highlights just before the end of the session, audiotaping sessions with the help of children in the family, and/or bringing in headlines and subheadings on large sheets of paper that identified key segments of the therapy hour.

In another group, after people found they were putting low amounts of energy into new goals they had set for themselves, the supervisor brought in brightly colored pieces of paper and asked each of them to write out with colored markers (coded to the content if they wished), all the reasons they could think of that would stop them from applying themselves to what they had said they wanted to do. With humor he encouraged them to embellish and exaggerate these somewhat. Strategies like the ones here can help to individualize supervision while providing group support to each member.

Another arena, which needs special attention paid to it in post hoc supervision, is clarity about guidelines for therapists when they do any personal story sharing (either of stories from their own life or other clients). In live supervision, the supervisor and other team members are there to help therapists talk through what stories might or might not be useful to tell to clients. In reflecting team work, the power of sharing everyday life experiences has been clearly identified, but it needs to be done in a way that keeps the focus on the clients and indicates that the therapist is in no way looking for particular responses to their telling. Table 24.3 contains some important guidelines to discuss, elaborate on, and explore.

Supervisors and group members can ask therapists to think about whether a story that comes to mind is appropriate to share with clients by asking questions such as the following: What would it be like for you to share that story with the family? For the family? For co-therapists or other people working with you on the case? Why do you want to share it? Has the family seemed interested in hearing your stories or have they seemed irrelevant and/or intrusive? (See Roberts, 1994, for a more extended discussion of stories, transparency, and therapy.)

CREATING AN ARENA FOR INQUIRY

Regardless of how reflecting supervision is structured, the work can be facilitated with attention to group building and awareness of the variety of ways in which people are learning. Team building can create connections and trust between members and increase their comfort level in working with the unknown and the unexpected. Strategies that encourage self-reflection about cases can enhance the preparedness of individuals when they come to supervision meetings. Sharing readings together and blocking out time to discuss key concepts, or try out new ideas in the protective environment of role-plays, can invigorate the group. Creating spaces to check-in and rework group processes can provide ways to surface and address any difficulties and to change aspects of the structure that are not functioning well.

Group Building

Activities that help to link members and create a sense of trust in and responsibility to the group are both important early on in group supervision as well as throughout the time the group is together. Echoing the kind of information often gathered from the family in reflecting team work, the story of how they came to therapy, supervision can begin by asking people to share the story of how they came to the group. On one team, Donald shared that he had actually requested another team that met for less time than the one he was participating in and that he had mixed feelings about being on it. Knowing this up front helped the supervisor to rethink and restructure his time with

---

TABLE 24.3. Guidelines for Transparency and Story Sharing

- Therapist/team member telling the story is responsible for their own emotional reactions.
- There are no expectations that a story will be responded to in a particular way.
- Story sharing is brief and to the point with a focus on what the client might wish to pick up on from it (if anything).
- Therapist/team member is cognizant of what level of disclosure is comfortable for him or her.
- Think through carefully what pieces/parts of stories to share—focus is not usually on a solution to complicated dilemmas.

the group so that it met both his needs and the needs of the group. Recounting the stories of how people came to their names can also be a good introductory exercise (Roberts, 1988). As information is shared about one's family of origin, ethnic and/or geographical and religious roots, and family dynamics, different links are often made between people. On one team, two women found that they were both twins, something they had not known before. On another, several people on the team found out they shared the experience of having a name that had been handed down through the family from father to son.

Doing an exercise together, such as open-ended sentences on *super-vision* (Table 24.4), can help to begin a dialogue about the meaning it has taken on in people's lives. For instance, for some people supervision has a very *evaluative* cast. For others, supervision may imply a supportive learning *environ-ment*. Sharing the responses to these sentences can create a conversational space to comment on the significance of supervision to each person and on ways they would like supervision to work in this new situation.

This kind of exercise can also be designed with a particular population in mind. With a group of school psychologists and guidance counselors all in different schools who were just starting a supervision group, open-ended sentences focused on sharing what was working and not working in people's jobs. This helped bring forth information to understand the varied school contexts for each person as well as strategies they employed that worked for them (see Table 24.5). One group found the ideas people had about advice so helpful that they asked to have the advice quotes put together on one sheet in order to be able to refer to them frequently. Some of the advice they wrote to themselves included: "Real change takes more time than you thought. A little success is still a success. You can't do everything so just do what you can well."

TABLE 24.4. Making Meaning of Supervision: Open-Ended Sentence Exercise

- Supervision is . . .
- When I was a child, supervision was . . .
- To my parents (guardians), supervision . . .
- In my first job, supervision . . .
- In school, supervision . . .
- Supervision in mental health . . .
- When supervision is problematic, . . .
- When I am being supervised, I . . .
- When I am a supervisor, I . . .
- When supervision works well, . . .

From Roberts, 1994, p. 186.

An activity that can be done later on that can support group building is asking members to bring a found symbol (something you pick up in your living space, the outdoors, where you work, or somewhere else) that represents where each person sees herself or himself in relation to the group. For instance, in one supervision group of six people, Masha brought in a photo of a yellow chrysanthemum in the middle of a bunch of red-purple peonies. She identified herself as the chrysanthemum and described how she felt herself as in the garden with the team but also quite different in that she often brought in ideas she felt were outside of the usual ideas presented by others. Following

TABLE 24.5. Reflections on Work in Schools

- Sharing my work is . . .
- The hardest part of my job in schools is . . .
- The most rewarding part of my job is . . .
- One piece of advice I wish I'd had when I started . . .
- Advice I give to myself that I find hard to follow is . . .
- A structural change in how my work is organized that might enhance it is . . .
- What supports me most in this work is . . .

up on the symbolism of the photo, she was able to hear from others in the group how they did experience her ideas as unique, but very enriching—that she brought new colors, textures and smells into the garden.

Bringing in food to share can also provide group nurturance. Small rituals of affirmations and appreciations—things we often forget to do for ourselves as we work to help others— can be introduced. Toasts to the work done together, words of thanks written out to share, or a few moments at the end of a working session for each to give an appreciation can keep the group centered on what is working.

Strategies to Support Self-Reflection

Reflecting team work involves a continuous flow of ideas in and out from the primary therapist who is in the room and other team members. Enhancing each individual's capacities to examine their work will contribute to their skill development and to the team's capacity to work together. Outside of group supervision time, supervisees can be encouraged to look at videotapes of their sessions and note what stands out for them, including "sparkling moments"; intriguing sequences; parts of the session they have questions about; and responses of family members to their questions, ideas, and thoughts shared by reflecting team members. Videos of sessions can be watched with the sound off so that people can focus on nonverbal communication. Clips from the videotapes can be chosen to share with the family and/or the team as a way for all to reflect on the sessions. Often, it is also helpful to watch videos in dyads so the supervisee can have a chance to talk through what she or he is observing as well as hear another person's interpretation.

Notes to oneself can sometimes help facilitate reflective distance (Roberts, 1994). Supervisees have found it useful to make notes as they watch a video about what they remember they were thinking and feeling during key parts of the session. Writing down dialogue can help the supervisee to look at language patterns. Sharing stories that come to mind when thinking about a case, having the supervisee sculpt the relationship to a family or to the team, making relationship maps, bringing in symbols that exemplify something about the case all can be ways to creatively look at therapeutic process.

Looping Back on Ourselves

It is also important to have ways in place to make any needed changes in supervisory processes. Given the complexities of doing therapeutic and supervisory work at the same time, these strategies need to be focused, short and not too time consuming so that they do not detract from the primary focus of the development of therapeutic skills. Supervision meetings and intersession discussions can be videotaped so that people can look at their own team dynamics. As described earlier, O team type reflections can be set up, or a person observing from outside the group can share his or her reflections. For instance, in doing supervision of supervision, I was asked to reflect with the supervisor what I had observed in team meetings. I commented on the ways in which everyone on the team seemed so polite with each other that it seemed as if they never got to some more direct comments. It was as if they were overusing all the rules about doing reflections in front of families to the point that they could not speak about some of the more difficult parts of their work. After hearing this reflection, members of the team were relieved. They had wanted to be more open with each other but were afraid that somehow they might be breaking the rules of how one was supposed to do this work. Phone-ins can be audiotaped and listened to, allowing supervisors to think about the ways messages are conveyed to supervisees in the room, when phone-ins are made into the session, and the impact they seem to have on the session (Gorman, 1989).

Any kind of evaluative feedback needs to be done in a webbed fashion—in which everyone comments on each other's work—rather than in the traditional hierarchical structure in which the supervisor evaluates the supervisee and the supervisee has no input into evaluating the supervisor, and no information is gathered from families. Feedback can be given to supervisors by supervisees, all can evaluate the team work, information can be gathered from each family about what has been helpful and not helpful in therapy. Key to this process is including the family's voice in any written reports about the work.

STRENGTHS AND PITFALLS OF WORKING IN THESE WAYS

Supervision using the reflecting stance incorporates feedback loops to keep the dialogue going between clients, supervisees, and supervisors. Space is made for multiple voices to be heard. Time is taken to listen to a range of ideas and thoughts. Reflecting conversations can be used at many different interfaces of the work: to share ideas with families, to invite clinicians to explore new possibilities, to examine dynamics of the supervision group, and to look at supervisor–supervisee relationships. There are many possibilities to individualize supervision even while in a group setting because the structure invites people to bring up their varied points of view and there is not an assumption that there is *a* correct interpretation of familial dynamics, or *a* way to do supervision.

Reflecting team work also offers the potential to pull supervisees quickly into the center of the work. Even before they take on cases as primary therapists, they can contribute as part of the team in numerous ways. Skills can be deliberately practiced in supervision that are directly applicable to the therapeutic process. When supervision brings in and engages multiple voices and viewpoints, there is important modeling of ways this can be done in therapy. The protected space for inner talk that is built into reflecting processes also highlights the importance of listening in therapy, an area that has been underemphasized in family work.[4] Reflecting team supervision, with its respectful resource focus that is collaborative and less hierarchical, provides a supervisory model that is syntonic with the directions the family therapy field has been moving.

On the other hand, this kind of work can feel unwieldy and cumbersome, especially if people are strapped for time. When sessions run over and crises in therapeutic work come, it can be hard to block out and find the time needed to keep this kind of fluid structure going. There is also the danger that because the hierarchy is flattened, people will not be as attentive to its existence or to the various power differentials within the group. Supervisors usually have evaluative power over supervisees and this can influence the comfort level supervisees have about stating all that they are thinking.

Reflecting team supervision adds another layer of work to an already complex process. Ultimately I think it is worth doing because it builds in ways to look at how we are learning and how that then influences what we do. It can keep us curious and asking questions. What we envision and practice in supervision and how we treat each other is at the core of communicating what we think is important in therapeutic work.

_____

[4]See pp. 150–154 in Roberts (1994) for some training exercises and examples of ways to work with listening in a familial context.

REFERENCES

Anderson, T. (1987). The reflecting team: Dialogue and meta-dialogue in clinical work. *Family Process, 26,* 415–428.

Anderson, T. (Ed.) (1990). *The reflecting team: Dialogues and dialogues about the dialogues.* Kent, UK: Borgmann Publishing.

Bernstein, R., Brown, E., & Ferrier, M. (1984). A model for collaborative team processing in brief systemic family therapy. *Journal of Marital and Family Therapy, 20,* 151–156.

Boscolo, L., & Cecchin, G. (1982). Training in systemic therapy at the Milan Center. In R. Whiffen & J. Byng-Hall (Eds.), *Family therapy supervision: Recent developments in practice* (pp. 153–165). London: Academic Press.

Davidson, J., Lax, W., & Lussardi, D. (1990). Use of the reflecting team in the initial interview and in supervision and training. In T. Anderson (Ed.), *The reflecting team: Dialogues and dialogues about the dialogues* (pp. 134–156). Kent, UK: Borgmann Publishing.

Gorman, P. (1989). Family therapy in an agency setting: An analysis of moments-of-interaction (doctoral dissertation). University of Massachusetts at Amherst, Microfilm #8119 (1990).

Hoffman, L. (1991). Personal communication.

Lax, W., & Lussardi, D. (1994). Adapted from Anderson (1990) and Lax, W. (1989). Systemic family therapy with young children in the family: Use of the reflecting team. In J. Zilbach (Ed.), *Children in family therapy* (pp. 55–74). New York: Haworth Press.

Roberts, J. (1983a). Two models of live supervision: Collaborative team and supervisor guided. *Journal of Strategic and Systemic Therapies, 2,* 68–84.

Roberts, J. (1983b). The third tier: The ignored dimension in family therapy training. *Family Therapy Networker, 7,* 30, 31, 60, 61.

Roberts, J. (1986). An evolving model: Links between the Milan approach and strategic models of family therapy. In D. Efron (Ed.), *Journeys: Expansion of the strategic/systemic therapies* (pp. 150–173). New York: Brunner/Mazel.

Roberts, J. (1988). Rituals and trainees. In E. Black, J. Roberts, & R. Whiting (Eds.), *Rituals in families and family therapy* (pp. 387–401). New York: W. W. Norton.

Roberts, J. (1991). Sugar and spice, toads and mice: Gender issues in family therapy training. *Journal of Marital and Family Therapy, 17,* 121–132.

Roberts, J. (1994). *Tales and transformations.* New York: W.W. Norton.

Roberts, J., Matthews, W., Bodin, A., Cohen, D., Lewandowski, L., Novo, J., Pumilla, J., & Willis, C. (1989). Training with O (observing) and T (treatment) teams in live supervision: Reflections in the looking glass. *Journal of Marital and Family Therapy, 15,* 197–214.

White, M. (1989/90). Family therapy training and supervision in a world of experience and narrative. *Dulwich Centre Newsletter, Summer,* 27–38.

White, M. (1995). Commentary on "From stuck debate to new conversation on controversial issues: A report from the public conversations project." *Journal of Feminist Family Therapy, 7,* 165–167.

Wright, L. (1986) An analysis of live supervision "phone-ins" in family therapy. *Journal of Marital and Family Therapy, 12,* 187–190

25

The Use of Genograms in Supervision

Shirley Braverman

There is an old saying that a picture is worth a thousand words; so it is with the genogram. A map depicting the family tree of three generations, the *genogram* records information about family members and their relationships (McGoldrick & Gerson, 1985). It is a concrete, pictorial method of seeing family patterns and tracing them across generations. For clinicians, a genogram is a useful tool in making links among events, assessing the quality of interpersonal relationships, and seeing the possible development of problems or illnesses in a family. Clinicians use genograms as aids in hypothesis building (Guerin & Pendergast, 1976; McGoldrick & Gerson, 1985; Wachtel, 1982), as a way of involving family members in therapy (Beck, 1987; Hartman, 1978; Woolf, 1983), in working with the elderly (Bannerman, 1986; Erlanger, 1990), in dealing with sexual problems (Hof & Berman, 1986; Rekers, 1985), and in family therapy training (Braverman, 1984; Kelly, 1990; Wells et al., 1990).

Although the genogram grew out of Bowen's (1978) ideas about the transmission of relational patterns across generations and the importance of therapist differentiation, it was later used as an experiential vehicle by those therapists who emphasized personal growth in therapy (Framo, 1979; Satir & Baldwin, 1983; Whitaker & Napier, 1978). Initially therapists used genograms to collect and to intellectually analyze data. There is now greater interest in the reaction of clients when doing the genogram. The client's affect offers important clues to help therapists understand the meaning of data and formulate hypotheses.

The changing use of the genogram in therapy led to their becoming an increasingly useful tool in supervision by supervisors of many theoretical orientations (e.g., Forman, 1984; Kuehl, 1995; Protinsky & Keller, 1984). Some supervisors help supervisees use client genograms to teach systemic thinking, the organizing of large amounts of data into patterns, systemic assessment of cases, and systemic interventions (Braverman, 1984). Other supervisors use them to assist supervisees in raising cultural awareness and increasing cultural sensitivity (Hardy & Laszloffy, 1995). Those supervisors who take a more problem-solving approach to supervision use genograms as a conceptual aid in supervision to help their supervisees organize data prior to focusing on solutions (Kuehl, 1995). Some supervisors also assist supervisees in using client genograms to secure client cooperation initially and throughout therapy.

Those supervisors who believe that the person of the therapist is critical to therapy (Bowen, 1974; Liddle, 1988; McGoldrick, 1982; Mendelsohn & Ferber, 1972) ask supervisees to share their genograms. Many of these supervisors use their supervisees' genograms to assist in increasing supervisees' differentiation. This approach is emphasized by experiential, Bowenian, and intergenerational supervisors who focus heavily on supervisees' use of self: they believe that experiential techniques are particularly well suited to illustrate process. Their guiding premise in supervision is: experience first and conceptualize later (Mendelsohn & Ferber, 1972). The genogram is an ideal tool to link the person of the supervisee and the person of the client in supervision. Those supervisors who emphasize process and affect can also use supervisees' genograms as experiential tools to address supervisees' learning blocks. The next sections highlight ways supervisors can use genograms in supervision to teach systemic thinking, to secure client collaboration, to increase supervisee differentiation, and to promote resolution of supervisees' learning blocks.

GENOGRAMS TEACH SUPERVISEES SYSTEMIC THINKING

Supervisors of novice supervisees need technical aids to teach a systemic way of thinking. Conceptual skills can be taught didactically in the classroom; helping supervisees apply theory to particular cases is the task of supervisors. The client genogram is an ideal technical aid in accomplishing this task. A three-generational map can quickly clarify a mass of family data. Drawing the family composition in each generation, indicating the close relationships with straight lines, and the conflictual ones with jagged lines depicts the quality of relationships at a glance. The squares represent males, the circles, females. Crosses represent deaths.

After depicting the dyadic relationships, the next step is to understand and draw important triangles in the family as a prelude to plan-

ning intervention. Refer to McGoldrick and Gerson (1985) for complete symbol representation. Genograms can be used in the beginning phase of therapy as part of assessment in every case. With supervisees whose systemic thinking and hypothesizing skills are weak, routine use of the genogram as part of assessment enhances learning in this area.

Genograms can be useful for supervisees practicing all theoretical orientations. For example, in the genogram in Figure 25.1, what becomes instantly clear is that mothers have been important attachment figures while the fathers have been either conflictual or distant figures. By carefully looking at the dates and ages on the genogram, one can make links among certain events and speculate about the quality of the relationship between family members.

_____

Mr. Jones, who had a distant relationship with his father, was very close to his mother. He married Mrs. Jones the year after his mother died. They had a conflictual relationship. Was Mrs. Jones a replacement for his beloved mother? Jane was born a year later. Mrs. Jones had a distant relationship with her father. Did she have a child so soon after the marriage as a way of creating distance between herself and Mr. Jones? Jane's relationship with her father is a distant one. Is it because Mr. Jones felt disappointment at losing a wished-for closeness with his wife or Mrs. Jones' lack of encouragement to her husband to get involved with their child? In any case, Mr. Jones seems shut out of the family. The Jones' six-year-old son's presenting problem, dressing in girls' clothes, could be understood in the light of the negative position that men have had on both sides of the family. Women were the beloved ones, the good ones, therefore being male might mean joining the team of outcasts—not an appealing role model for a young boy.

_____

FIGURE 25.1. The Jones family's genogram

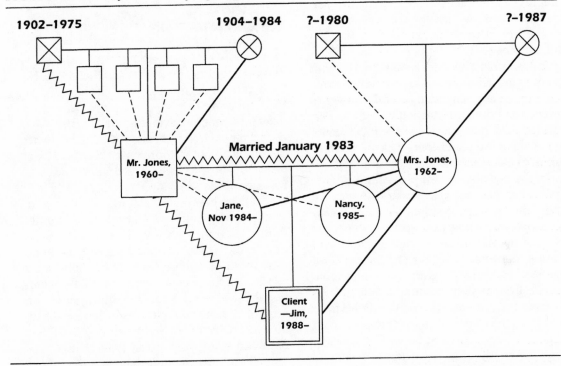

□ = males; ○ = females; ✕ = died.

The genogram does not offer specific interventions but can be a basis from which supervisees can create strategies or encourage interactions that aim for changes in the system consistent with their theoretical models.

GENOGRAMS HELP SUPERVISEES SECURE CLIENT COLLABORATION

In models of therapy that consider clients' awareness of dysfunctional behaviors and relationships necessary to produce change, the genogram can be used to assist supervisees in developing relationships with clients and in stimulating their clients' interest in the transmission of patterns of relating across genera-

tions. For example, in the case of the Jones family, Mr. Jones was an extremely reluctant participant in family therapy until the supervisor suggested to her supervisee that having him do a genogram of his family might be a way of reaching out to him empathically. The supervisee was pleasantly surprised at Mr. Jones' collaborative response. The second surprise came when the use of the genogram helped the supervisee join with the wife. Mrs. Jones became tearful after the supervisee commented to Mr. Jones that it must have been hard for him not to have his mother present at his wedding, given the close relationship he had had with her. Mrs. Jones stated that she was identifying her husband's loss with the loss of her mother and felt sad for him and for herself.

At a later point in therapy, the supervisor encouraged the supervisee to stimulate Mr. Jones' interest in the family transmission process. The supervisee commented that despite his sensitivity, he appeared to be following in his father's footsteps, being a kind but distant figure in the family. Would he like to examine the genogram more carefully to try to understand how that had happened? He responded with interest, as did the other members of the family, and there followed a very fruitful phase of therapy.

In the postassessment phases of therapy, supervisors can suggest supervisees use a genogram if therapy does not seem to be making progress. Genograms enlarge the focus from the nuclear to the extended family and provide an opportunity for supervisees and clients to temporarily gain some emotional distance from anxiety-producing material. As Mr. Jones became more involved with his family, Mrs. Jones became more hopeless and began to talk of dropping out of therapy. Mr. Jones, confused, appeared ready to accede to his wife's wishes. The supervisor suggested a change of focus from the family interaction to Mrs. Jones' genogram. The supervisor's reasoning was twofold. First, because Mrs. Jones was losing an exclusive relationship with her children now that her husband was getting more involved with them, having the supervisee focus on her in a nonthreatening way would provide her with the attention and support she sorely needed. Second, changing the focus would also give the supervisee an opportunity to explore with Mrs. Jones the familial roots of her mistrust of men. With this shift of focus in therapy, the supervisor demonstrated that genograms can be used as a way of slowing down the process of change in the family. It helped the supervisee assist Mrs. Jones in some cognitive restructuring, based on her understanding of the family transmission process.

GENOGRAMS ASSIST SUPERVISEES' DIFFERENTIATION

Bowen (1974) espoused the goal of a well-differentiated self for clients and therapists. He believed that the intellect was the locus of control of mature behavior; the more people are driven by emotion, the less control they have over their environment and the more likely the development of symptoms or dysfunctional behavior. Bowen encouraged supervisees to focus on understanding the client family system rather than on developing techniques to change it. He believed that when the family thinks differently and understands the functioning of its own system, the members themselves will find other ways of handling their relationships. "Some resolution of the emotional problem of a relationship system can occur if at least one person can achieve just a little more detachment and neutrality than they have had in the past" (Kerr, 1984, p. 16).

When Bowen found that his supervisees, who were applying his ideas about differentiation of self to their own families of origin, were making greater progress in their clinical work, he began to focus more and more on that aspect in his training of therapists. There was a shift of focus away from the client. As a result, the training and supervision of Bowenian family therapists focuses on supervisees' work in their families of origin (Guerin & Fogarty, 1972). The goal is therapists' awareness of the difference between their intellectually and emotionally determined functioning, and for them to have some choice about their behavior. Thus, supervisees' behavior is guided more by their own needs and wishes than by the needs and wishes of others with whom they are close. Well-differentiated therapists do not project responsibility for their emotions onto someone else. Bowen saw intimacy as a quality of relationship in which each individual was capable of emotional closeness without loss of autonomy (Becvar & Becvar, 1993).

In this model, the genogram is used in supervision to identify triangles in the supervisees' families of origin. According to Bowenian theory, the triangle is a three-person emotional system created when anxiety in a dyad is sufficiently high to cause discomfort. Over time, triangulation patterns in families become repetitious and predictable. Supervisors, or supervisory groups, then help therapists devise strategies to break up this pattern of relating. These might include increasing contact with one peripheral family member while decreasing contact with the dominant one, revealing secrets to certain family members or the extended family to destroy family myths, increasing sibling contacts and decreasing parental contacts, and so on. When the client family triggers anxiety in therapists, they are likely to react with the same patterns of triangulation that existed in their families of origin. Understanding and changing these patterns in their own families will help supervisees remain more objective with client families.

Bowen's theory influenced a number of therapists who use family-of-origin approaches with their supervisees (Framo, 1979; Kramer, 1980; Protinsky & Keller, 1984). Munson (1984) discusses problems that can arise for supervisees when too much attention is paid to the person of the therapist, without a practical link to the client family and problem. These include losing sight of the goal of therapy, which is to improve clients' functioning, and blurring the boundary between therapy and supervision, which can have a disorganizing effect on supervisees. Teaching family therapy by focusing exclusively on supervisees' families of origins is, I believe, taking a good idea to an illogical extreme. The person of the therapist is an important part of the therapeutic system; however, it is not the only one. Therapists need to have a variety of perspectives about human development and pathology as well as a variety of techniques to deal with human problems.

GENOGRAMS AID RESOLUTION OF SUPERVISEES' LEARNING BLOCKS

The genogram can be particularly useful for supervisors who are dealing with persistent learning blocks. McGoldrick (1982) believes that persistent blocks that therapists have with client families are the result of negative emotional reactions stemming from experiences in their families of origin (i.e., countertransference feelings). Ideally, these feelings should have been resolved prior to supervision, either through normal maturation or through therapy. In fact, because we are human, we cannot resolve all conflictual issues from our families of origin. Because family therapy is so emotionally powerful, it does tend to stir up old conflicts in spite of their apparent resolution.

There are four stages in supervision that supervisors should go through with supervisees before considering a focus on countertransference problems. First, supervisors can help supervisees clarify their systemic hypotheses about cases. Second, supervisors can assist supervisees in understanding how presenting problems are being perpetuated by the behaviors and attitudes of family members. Third, they can teach supervisees techniques for changing the family interaction. Finally, supervisors can discuss their supervisor–therapist relationships to see whether supervisees' inabilities to be effective learners are related to some suppressed negative feelings about their supervisor.

The Double Genogram Approach

Once the aforementioned supervisory stages have been passed to no avail, supervisors can then describe the following family-of-origin approach to supervisees and invite them to try it to resolve the learning impasse. This is never imposed on supervisees because it involves sharing aspects of their personal history with supervisors (and supervisory groups, if supervision is done in a group). If supervisors use this approach, including it in the learning contract from the start avoids any unexpected or threatening surprises for supervisees. If, after giving it some thought, a supervisee declines, the supervisor must respect the decision and then suggest that the supervisee consult a therapist to discuss the issue. This approach is recommended particularly if learning blocks are sufficiently serious to hamper a supervisee's professional development.

If supervisees decide to go ahead with a family-of-origin approach, supervisors ask them to make two genograms: one of the client family and one of their own family. The quality of the relationships in each genogram is depicted (Figure 25.2) and discussed. The aim of these sessions is to uncover possible emotional links between the two families that are creating a learning block for supervisees. Because of the task-oriented attitude of supervisors and supervisees plus time-limited supervisory sessions, supervisees' affect does not become intense as may happen when doing genograms with clients. Supervisees have more cognitive control than they would have if supervision were part of an all day or weekend session devoted to the exploration of families of origin.

Both genograms are put side by side. Supervisees are then asked whether there is any similarity between the relationships portrayed in the two genograms. The genogram helps supervisees gain some distance from the material and, in a Bowenian sense, use an intellectual process to master some emotional reactivity. Patterns quickly emerge. Supervisees tend to see client family members who remind them of a conflictual relative as more disturbed and rigid than they are in reality, tending not to see their strengths as clearly as those of other family members. Supervisees cannot recognize certain client behaviors as defensive and are therefore unable to get to that individual's fear, even though they had been able to do so with other family members. Conversely, supervisees tend to have some blind spots for those clients who are similar to an idealized relative; seeing how that person can be manipulative and self-serving can be particularly difficult. It is, therefore, important to explore the positive relationships in the client families as well as to link them to supervisees' idealized relationships in their families of origin. Supervisees' negative dyadic relationships, as well as their triangulated position in their families of origin, must be addressed when they contribute to a learning block.

A Double Genogram Case Example

The following case example illustrates a situation in which family-of-origin work, utilizing the double genogram approach, was used as part of ongoing supervision. Although the pur-

FIGURE 25.2. The meaning of genogram symbols

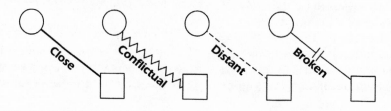

pose of the work was to have a direct effect on the supervisee's performance in this specific case, it is hoped that the beneficial effects will carry over to other cases.

The Learning Block

Eric was a forty-year-old social worker who was having a great deal of difficulty with the Tanner family in which the presenting problem was a ten-year-old boy, John. The child was having increasingly violent temper tantrums which terrorized his mother and seven-year-old sister. The client father, Mr. Tanner, was an intelligent and articulate man. A school principal, he was also heavily involved in extracurricular community activities and was rarely home. The client mother, Mrs. Tanner, was a submissive, gentle person who could not tolerate confrontation; she either withdrew or developed physical symptoms in the face of any expression of anger. She was always home, available to the children and her husband, and never complained about her lonely life. The other child was obedient, an excellent student, and frequently helpful to her mother—a model child. The children were not close. Both parents expressed satisfaction with their marital relationship. Mrs. Tanner spoke of her husband with great respect, and said she felt his loyalty and support even though he was so busy outside the home. Mr. Tanner described his relationship with his wife as very close and said it was because of her support that he had been able to achieve so much in his profession and his community. John, their son, had always been a bright, achieving child but had temper tantrums from a very early age. In the past year, they had increased in frequency and intensity so that they could no longer be ignored, as they had been in the past.

Eric's perception of Mr. Tanner was that he was a self-centered man whose needs superseded those of any other family member. His need for praise and recognition was enormous; he exploited his wife and children, using

their interest and caring as support for his fragile self-esteem without responding to their needs in any way. Eric saw Mrs. Tanner as an all-giving, kind, and devoted woman controlled by her stronger, charismatic husband. He saw John's temper tantrums as a reaction to the neglect he was experiencing as a result of his father's absence.

In supervision Eric was able to identify the mother–father–John triangle and was able to see John's symptom as a way of getting his father's attention in the family in a way that his mother could not. He understood John's temper tantrums as an unsuccessful attempt to provoke his mother into taking some initiative with her husband, her children, and in her extrafamilial life. He saw John as being unable to bear his mother's passivity or her loneliness. Despite his understanding of the dynamics and the supervisor's suggestions about how he might change the interactions among family members, Eric was not able to follow through. His anger at John and Mr. Tanner and his sympathy for Mrs. Tanner paralyzed him.

The supervisor focused on the supervisor–supervisee relationship. She discussed her feeling that even though they had a good relationship to date Eric was beginning to see her as a demanding, critical authority. She noted this as a problem for both of them. Eric agreed, expressed frustration at feeling stupid, and annoyance at the supervisor's demands. No conclusion was reached after this discussion. The supervisor's stance was to listen and agree that she could feel Eric's frustration; she would be prepared to hear any other thoughts he had about the case. The supervisor left it for a week to see whether anything would change in Eric's handling of the case after this discussion. Nothing changed.

The supervisor then suggested the possibility of the two genogram family-of-origin session as a way of resolving Eric's learning block in this case. She clearly conveyed that this was not mandatory and that there was no certainty it would work, but it had been helpful to other therapists who had encountered serious learning blocks in the course of their clinical work. Because Eric sensed that if he did not do something quickly the family would drop out of treatment, he decided to try the family-of-origin session. He was asked if he preferred to do this in private with the supervisor or in the presence of his supervisory group. Eric chose the group.

The Client Family Genogram

In preparation for the session, Eric gathered more information from the client family about the parents' families of origin for the genogram (Figure 25.3A). The client mother came from a family in which women were submissive, serious, and took the major responsibility for the family's cohesion and functioning. The men were seen as aggressive, superior, and controlling all family resources. Mr. Tanner came from a large, poor, rural family in which he had little emotional support from his overburdened parents. The nonverbal message to Mr. Tanner from his mother was that education and achievement were the only way out of their poverty. The children who did achieve were given nonverbal recognition from their depressed mother. Mr. Tanner adapted to this depriving environment by investing in an objective rather than in an interpersonal relationship: achievement brought him emotional rewards that intimate relationships never had.

The Supervisee's Genogram

Eric's genogram (Figure 25.3B) showed the primacy of his mother and her side of the family in his life. His father's family lived in another country and he had no contact with them before they died. Eric was the oldest of three children, he had two younger sisters. His father was a very preoccupied, successful businessman who was distant from the family. Eric had the closest relationship in the family with his mother and maternal grandmother. Both were warm, kind women but whereas his grandmother was an energetic woman his mother was lethargic and suffered from periodic bouts of depression. His grandmother died when he was nine. Eric remembered greatly missing her cheerful, energetic presence. His mother's first serious depression, during which she took to her bed, was when Eric was ten. His father left his wife and children to deal with each other as if the family was not his domain. At the beginning of their marriage, his wife took care of the children with the support of her mother. Later, when her mother died and her depressions incapacitated her, it was the children, mainly Eric, who took care of their mother.

Resolving the Learning Block

In describing his family, Eric readily expressed exasperation with his father's preoccupation with business to the exclusion of his family. He felt he was a disappointment to his father, otherwise his father would have shown more interest in Eric. Nevertheless, he was able to express admiration for his father's intelligence, energy, and initiative. On the other hand, Eric was very positive about his mother's warmth and caring. He expressed no negative feelings about her. When the supervisor asked if there was anything about her he had ever wished were different, he was thoughtful for a long time. Slowly, he admitted that sometimes he wished she were cheerful and energetic. It had been hard, at times, to have a depressed mother; he wished there had been more lightness and pleasure in his home. He missed his grandmother terribly because she had brought that dimension into their family life. He realized he had put all the blame for their muted family life onto his father; he resented his father for not taking part in the family because he was a cheerful and energetic person. It appeared to Eric that his father had given up the task of livening up his depressed wife and left the children with her as their burden. In fact, Eric did

FIGURE 25.3 Genograms for a client (A) and his therapist (B)

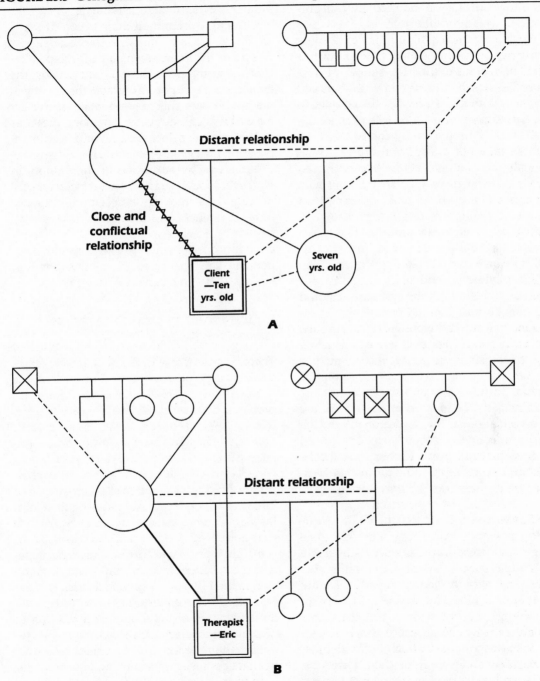

A

B

admit that his mother was very hard to cheer up; he knew because he had tried. Livening his mother up was a full-time job!

Eric's awareness of his ambivalence about his mother made him realize how protective he had been of his client, Mrs. Tanner. He recognized that he had identified with John and was angry with him for having the courage to fight (i.e., to have severe temper tantrums to involve his father in the family and to shake his mother out of her passive withdrawal). John was only ten years old yet he had not given up; Eric, however, had given up long ago. When asked to draw the most significant triangle in his family of origin, Eric drew his mother, his father, and himself. The cross-generational coalition between him and his mother became clear. He realized that his father had contributed to, and reacted against, his closeness to his mother by withdrawing and becoming the marginalized parent.

Eric was touched emotionally during the session, but it was not primarily an emotional experience for him. The genograms seemed to help Eric use his intellect to distance from his client family as well as his own. Interestingly, once Eric could be touched affectively during the presentation of his family of origin, the genogram became an integrative tool; it allowed him to use his emotion and his intellect so that he could develop more empathy for the key individuals in the genograms. It freed him as a person and as a therapist in relation to them.

This session seemed to unblock Eric's difficulty, not only in dealing with his male client's aggression, but also with his own. He was gradually able to become more confrontive in his work with the submissive Mrs. Tanner and the marginalized Mr. Tanner. His inability to challenge the homeostatic balance in the Tanner family was because it so closely resembled the balance in his own family. With time, Eric began to understand the complicated nature of ambivalence. The genogram session

helped him not only with this particular family but in his general therapeutic style.

The most important information depicted on the genogram during supervision is the quality of the interpersonal relationships. Factual data, given verbally, is not put on the genogram so as not to obscure the relational map. Although this method was inspired by the Bowenian model, the supervisor's questions or comments to the supervisee come from an integration of an object-relations and systems theory model. The resolution of the session, in which no specific suggestions for treatment are made, comes from the expectation that emotional awareness and intellectual insight may free the supervisee to behave in a therapeutically appropriate way. Directives from the supervisor are not necessary at this point. If needed, they can be given at a later time.

Ethical Issues in Using the Double Genogram Approach

There is controversy in the field as to whether the learning blocks mentioned here should be dealt with in supervision or whether these are problems best dealt with in individual therapy (Horn, 1982; Munson, 1984; Storm, 1991; Tomm, 1993). When learning problems are impeding supervisees' progress, they do not always get dealt with quickly enough in their personal therapy to have an effect on cases or to influence supervisees' evaluation on their jobs. Insight alone does not necessarily lead to change in therapy (Guttman, 1982) or supervision. Therapists who do not have rigid defenses can benefit from having some attention paid to their personal problematic issues in supervision. The double genogram approach has the advantage of moving from a position of helping supervisees gain insight into past familial patterns to a practical approach which actively encourages their seeking new behavior with their clients. Insight does create a climate of awareness and openness which facilitates supervisees' abilities to use their supervisors' practical suggestions in a way that had not been possible before.

Regarding the issue of psychotherapy for supervisees, some supervisors believe that it is sufficient to identify dysfunctional psychological structures leaving supervisees free to address or not to address what has been uncovered (Kantor et al., 1992). I believe that this can only occur when clients are not being unduly affected. Our primary professional responsibility is to the public we are serving and only secondarily to our supervisees. We cannot allow unlimited freedom of choice to our supervisees if their problems are interfering with their work. They can be strongly advised to go into psychotherapy, but whether they do so or not, it is a supervisory responsibility to monitor the quality of clinical work. If supervisees' work is below par, harmful to clients, or not showing any improvement within a reasonable length of time, supervisees should be advised not to continue in the field at that time. It is a delicate balancing act for supervisors to respect supervisees' privacy, to serve clients effectively, and to help supervisees overcome learning blocks.

The supervisory responsibility of maintaining confidentiality about the personal information gleaned in the family-of-origin approach is a *sine qua non* of this work. The question arises whether supervisors' evaluations are influenced by personal information about their supervisees. Because evaluation is skill-based and not personality based, supervisors need to assess supervisees' functioning in a variety of cases (e.g., different cultures, different ages, different genders). When supervisors have concerns about supervisees' potential biases or fragility in certain areas, they should assign supervisees cases that test that vulnerability. For example, a supervisee, a single mother who lost the custody of her son in a bit-

ter battle with her ex-husband, was given a case of a single mother with two children in which one of the problems was that the seventeen-year-old son was struggling against his mother for more freedom. In this case the supervisee not only had to address the mother–son issue but had to have several family sessions in which she had to address the separated spouses' roles as parents in a way that would secure the father's collaboration. She was successful despite her anger at her ex-husband. This demonstrated her skill; her anger at her ex-husband and possible disappointment in all men because of her particular history did not affect her work with men or boys. All therapists have biases, unresolved conflicts, vulnerabilities. If they are not affecting supervisees' clinical work, they are not relevant to the evaluation. A supervisor's judgment about a supervisee's work must be performance-based.

Effective Use of the Double Genogram Approach

The following recommendations (Braverman, 1984, 1994) are made for those supervisors who consider it within their function to help therapists with their family-of-origin related learning blocks:

1. Other supervisory interventions should be tried first; using family-of-origin genograms to deal with learning blocks should be a last resort.
2. The purpose should be clear and case-related. Using two genograms, the client's and the supervisee's, helps to keep the session case-related.
3. The double genogram approach should not be imposed on supervisees.
4. Sessions should be time-limited so that the focus can remain on supervision and not on therapy; one-and-a-half to two hours for double genogram sessions seems adequate.

5. Supervisors should be available to supervisees after sessions to process any unforeseen supervisee reactions.

6. Responsibility for conducting family-of-origin supervisory sessions belongs with supervisors. If it is done in the presence of a group, there can a short time period allotted to the group at the end for discussion of the process. The group does not interact with the supervisee presenting the double genograms about any of the material.

There is a certain emotional momentum that builds between supervisors and supervisees in the double genogram process. Experience shows that allowing group members to interact with supervisees defuses that momentum and detracts from supervisees' learning. The session then becomes a more intellectual exercise because supervisees must block off any feelings that were aroused and must limit their introspection to respond to questions from the group. This puts a premature closure to the process. By having supervisors answer questions for group members, the focus becomes teaching rather than the use of the double genogram for understanding the impact of supervisees' familial experience on their work. We wish to avoid, at all costs, group members "therapizing" supervisees with clinical comments no matter how relevant they are.

If supervisors are sensitive to supervisees, maintain the focus on learning, and are available for follow-up contacts by supervisees if necessary, the double family-of-origin genogram can be used as an important resource in the supervision of family therapists. Referral to another therapist, if needed after sessions, is part of the responsibility of the supervisor. Generally, this has not been necessary as long as safeguards are employed. Learning takes place in the context of a relationship between supervisor and supervisee. When that relationship is not nour-

ishing or supportive, it hinders the learning process.

THE TRIPLE GENOGRAM IN SUPERVISION-OF-SUPERVISION

The triple genogram is an interesting tool for teaching supervisors how their family-of-origin issues influence what they will pick up to focus on with their supervisees. This approach has two parts to it. In the first part, supervisors-in-training (SITs) use the double genogram with supervisees while being observed by their supervisors. Then supervisees leave the room. In the second part, SITs add their own genogram to the others, using the same technique as previously described, to indicate the quality of the relationships. The supervisor then makes any connections between SITs' interventions and their family-of-origin experience. The emphasis here is on teaching supervisors that we are not neutral observers: supervisors, teachers, and therapists see the world in the context of their own life experiences. The triple genogram is a powerful, experiential learning tool.

It has been suggested that supervisors share their genograms with their supervisees. This procedure is not recommended for two reasons. First, supervisees need to concentrate on their own learning. It is complicated enough to keep track of all the data contained in a double genogram; it would be excessively confusing to supervisees to be confronted with yet another mass of data to integrate as well. Second, the procedure upsets the hierarchy. For learning to take place, especially with less experienced supervisors, the learning structure needs to be supportive and clear. Blurring the boundaries between supervisees' and supervisors' issues can be very upsetting. For advanced supervisees or supervisors this may be an interesting experience, but it is best to use sharing of supervisors' genograms in supervision-of-supervision situations.

CONCLUSION

The genogram is a tool and like every tool it depends on how the artisan uses it. It can be used bluntly or delicately: a genogram can be a distancing device, an intellectual exercise, an experiential one, or a balance between the last two. Depending on the stage of supervision and the level of development of supervisees, genograms can be used in any of the ways mentioned in this chapter, including as an information gathering device in the assessment phase, which is useful for hypothesis building; as a basis for strategies in problem solving; for increasing client collaboration during a period of resistance; and for unblocking supervisees' learning problems that are family-of-origin based. The relationship within which a genogram is used will dictate whether it will be an effective tool or not.

REFERENCES

Bannerman, C. (1986). The genogram and elderly patients. *Journal of Family Practice, 23*, 426–428.

Beck, R. (1984). The supervision of family of origin family systems treatment. In C. Munson (Ed.), *Family of origin applications in clinical supervision* (pp. 49–60). New York: Haworth Press.

Beck, R. (1987). The genogram as process. *American Journal of Family Therapy, 15*, 343–351.

Becvar, D., & Becvar, R. (1993). *Family therapy: A systemic integration.* Boston: Allyn and Bacon.

Bowen, M. (1974). Toward the differentiation of self in one's family of origin. In P. Lorio & F. Andres (Eds.), *Georgetown Family Symposia 1* (pp. 70–86). Washington, DC: Department of Psychiatry, Georgetown University Medical Center.

Bowen, M. (1978). *Family therapy in clinical practice.* New York: Jason Aronson.

Braverman, S. (1984). Family of origin as a training resource for family therapists. In C. Munson (Ed.), *Family of origin applications in clinical supervision* (pp. 37–48). New York: Haworth Press.

Braverman, S. (1994). The integration of individual and family therapy. Plenary address, Twentieth Anniversary Conference of the Ontario Association of Marriage and Family Therapy, London, Ontario, May.

Erlanger, M. (1990). Using the genogram with the older client. *Journal of Mental Health Counseling, 12*, 321–331.

Forman, B. (1984). Family of origin work in systemic/strategic therapy training. In C. Munson (Ed.), *Family of origin applications in supervision* (pp. 81–85). New York: Haworth Press.

Framo, J. (1979). A personal viewpoint on training in marital and family therapy. *Professional Psychology, 10*, 868–875.

Guerin, P., & Fogerty, T. (1972). Study your own family. In A. Ferber, M. Medelsohn, & A. Napier (Eds.), *The book of family therapy* (pp. 445–457). New York: Science House.

Guerin, P., Jr. & Pendergast, E. (1976). Evaluation of family system and genogram. In P. Guerin, Jr. (Ed.), *Family therapy: Theory and practice* (pp. 450–464). New York: Gardner Press.

Guttman, H. (1982). Transference and countertransference in conjoint couple therapy: Therapeutic and theoretical considerations. *Canadian Journal of Psychiatry, 27*, 92–97.

Hardy, K., & Laszloffy, T. (1995). The cultural genogram: Key to training culturally competent family therapists. *Journal of Marital and Family Therapy, 21*, 227–238.

Hartman, A. (1978). Diagrammatic assessment of family relationships. *Social Casework, 59*, 465–476.

Hof, L., & Berman, E. (1986). The sexual genogram. *Journal of Marital and Family Therapy, 4*, 9–15.

Horn, D. (1982). Family of origin technique. *Canadian Journal of Psychiatry, 27*, 616.

Kantor, D., Mitchell, E., Pillemer, J., & Slobodnik, A. (1992). Letter to the editor. *Supervision Bulletin, 5*, 2.

Kelly, G. (1990). The cultural family of origin: A description of a training strategy. *Counselor Education and Supervision, 30*, 77–84.

Kerr, M. (1984). Theoretical base for differentiation of self in one's family of origin. In C. Munson (Ed.),

Family of origin applications in supervision (pp. 3–47). New York: Haworth Press.

Kramer, C. (1980). *Becoming a family therapist: Developing an integrated approach to working with families.* New York: Human Sciences Press.

Kuehl, B. (1995). The solution-oriented genogram: A collaborative approach. *Journal of Marital and Family Therapy, 21,* 239–250.

Liddle, H. (1988). Systemic supervision: Conceptual overlays and pragmatic guidelines. In H. Liddle, D. Breunlin, & R. Schwartz (Eds.), *Handbook of family training and supervision* (pp. 153–171). New York: Guilford Press.

McGoldrick, M. (1982). Through the looking glass: Supervision of a trainee's "trigger" family. In R. Whiffen & J. Byng-Hall (Eds.), *Family therapy supervision* (pp. 17–37). London: Academic Press.

McGoldrick, M., & Gerson, R. (1985). *Genograms in family assessment.* New York: W. W. Norton.

Mendelsohn, H., & Ferber, A. (1972). Is everybody watching? In A. Ferber, M. Mendelsohn, & A. Napier (Eds.), *The book of family therapy* (pp. 431–444). New York: Science House.

Munson, C. (1984). Uses and abuses of family of origin material in family therapy supervision. In C. Munson (Ed.), *Family of origin applications in clinical supervision* (pp. 61–74). New York: Haworth Press.

Protinsky, H., & Keller, J. (1984). Supervision of marriage and family therapy: A family of origin approach. In C. Munson (Ed.), *Family of origin applications in clinical supervision* (pp. 75–80). New York: Haworth Press.

Rekers, G. (1985). The genogram: Her story of a woman. *Women and Therapy, 4,* 9–15.

Satir, V., & Baldwin, M. (1983). *Satir step by step.* Palo Alto: Science and Behavior Books.

Storm, C. (1991). Drawing the line: An issue for all supervisors. *Supervision Bulletin, 4,* 1.

Tomm, K. (1993). Defining supervision and therapy: A fuzzy boundary? *Supervision Bulletin, 6,* 2.

Wachtel, E. (1982). The family psyche over three generations: The genogram revisited. *Journal of Marital and Family Therapy, 8,* 335–343.

Wells, V., Scott, R., Schmeller, L., & Hillman, J. (1990). The family-of-origin framework: A model for clinical training. *Journal of Contemporary Psychiatry, 20,* 223–235.

Whitaker, C., & Napier, A. (1978). *The family crucible.* New York: Harper & Row.

Woolf, V. (1983). Family network systems in transgenerational psychotherapy: The theory, advantages, and expanded applications of genograms. *Family Therapy, 10,* 119–137.

26

Teaching Therapists to Become Supervisors

Cheryl L. Storm

There are several excellent resources for designing comprehensive supervisory training programs (Breunlin, Liddle, & Schwartz, 1988; Constantine, Piercy, & Sprenkle, 1984; Heath & Storm, 1985; Liddle et al., 1984). A primary goal of supervision training is for supervisors to develop a personal philosophy of supervision. There are usually three steps to doing so. First, supervisors-in-training (SITs) are helped to identify their preferred ideas, methods, and style of being a supervisor. This process is based on a review of marriage and family therapy (MFT) supervision knowledge, literature, and research. Second, they are assisted to develop their personal supervision philosophy. A philosophy of supervision incorporates a set of ideas regarding (1) the process of change in the therapeutic and supervisory system, (2) supervisee learning, and (3) appropriate methods that are consistent with SITs' underlying assumptions and personal styles. The philosophy has to fit a changing field, apply to diverse supervisees and settings, and uphold legal and ethical responsibilities. Third, SITs are supervised in the implementation of their supervision philosophy via the practice of supervision and supervision-of-supervision. As they practice, their philosophy is tested, refined, and expanded. Overall, SITs develop a professional identity as a supervisor in addition to that of a therapist (Liddle et al., 1984).

Most supervisory training includes didactic and supervised practice components. This chapter focuses on the didactic or supervision course component, which can be an academic class, a seminar with a small group of SITs, or a tailored independent study course. Supervisors, acting as teachers, accomplish the first two steps defined here with therapists interested in becoming supervisors by using the ideas and methods described in this chapter in their courses. (See Chapter 27 for a discussion of supervision-of-supervision.)

CHALLENGES OF TEACHING THERAPISTS TO BECOME SUPERVISORS

Seduction of Doing Therapy Rather Than Supervision

A major challenge for instructors is to help SITs fight the everpresent seduction of doing therapy rather than supervision. As Breunlin et al. (1988) state: "supervisors supervise—they do not conduct indirect therapy" (p. 212). Because most individuals become supervisors because they feel clinically competent and are excited to pass their expertise on to the next generation, when beginning supervisors discuss their work they frequently find themselves focusing on what they would do if they were the therapists working with the cases. Supervisors-in-training must switch from thinking about their way of doing therapy to thinking about how they can use their philosophy of supervision to assist their supervisees to use their own ideas, abilities, or styles to proceed with their cases. They must further shift their thinking from the family system to the therapeutic system or family plus therapist, planting supervisees squarely into their equation (Liddle et al., 1984). All skilled supervisors proactively intervene to develop supervisees' conceptual, perceptual, executive, and interventive competencies. Even supervisors who are highly case focused consider supervisees' learning and development as they discuss particular clients.

Instructors, fighting the seduction to do therapy rather than supervision, persistently and consistently pose questions about supervision that help refocus SITs' attention. "As a therapist, you would ———, but how would you help your supervisees develop their ability to decide what course of action to take?"

Intellectual Stimulation of Adult Learners

A major challenge for instructors is to create a learning context that stimulates adult learners. Supervisors-in-training are experienced therapists with years of professional employment who usually have some quasi-supervisory experience. Less experienced colleagues may be seeking their input and/or they may be fulfilling supervisory roles in their work settings. Frequently, they are supervising without the title or the education. Some SITs may be concurrently supervising therapists and receiving supervision-of-supervision. Thus, participants are adult learners with a wealth of professional, practice, and life experiences.

If research on adult learners serves as a guide (Zemke & Zemke, 1981), instructors will take the following findings into account when developing their courses. Adult learners are interested in the cheapest, fastest, and most efficient way to learn material that is oriented toward application. Structuring the course with this in mind probably means avoiding prime practice hours, providing class materials that SITs have at their fingertips, and requiring assignments that have a practical bent.

Adult learners prefer active participation. Supervisors-in-training enjoy and demand opportunities to contribute their unique expertise. Just try and hold the floor for more than fifteen minutes without interruption with a group of SITs! Acknowledging and using SITs' experiences are critical to include via active teaching methods, such as exercises, role-plays, debates, and so on, which require SITs to apply ideals to "real-world" supervision situations. With adult learners, instructors must balance the presentation of new material and interaction with the clock, orchestrate discussions to protect minority opinions, make connections between various opinions and ideas, and constantly underscore that there are many ways to supervise.

Adult learners prefer self-directed learning in which they can take personal responsibility for their education. Instructors attending to this preference offer opportunities to SITs to help design their experience. If there is mutual respect among participants, SITs can learn from extensive dialogue with their peers.

Finally, adult learners take criticism more personally and take fewer risks. Instructors may have to wrestle with creating a learning context in which all feel comfortable participating because classes tend to be highly diverse in terms of professional experience. However, everyone can participate because SITs have been supervisees at some point in their history. Instructors' willingness to be challenged and to challenge participants to consider alternative ideas, methods, and styles can set an important tone for the course, perhaps serving as an invitation for those hesitant to join in.

Examination of Strongly Held Beliefs

A major challenge is to help SITs discover the way their therapy model "fits" as a supervision model. Supervisors-in-training come with predetermined, strongly held beliefs about change and therapy. The isomorphic nature of supervision and therapy allows these ideas to be transferred from the therapy context and applied to the supervision context (Liddle & Halpin, 1978; Liddle & Saba, 1983). However, isomorphism does not mean *the same as*, rather it means *similar to* (Storm & Heath, 1985). Supervision and therapy are similar processes of facilitating change, but they are not the same endeavors. Any model is judged according to its usefulness in fostering action and further thought (deShazer, 1984). Determining the fit requires critical exploration and reflection on where therapy ideas are useful in supervision and where they are not. For example, Storm and Heath (1991) found that the brief therapy model fit the context of supervision better when supervision customers presented problems with their cases than when noncustomers were required by an outside body to chalk up supervision hours. Supervisors-in-training must be enticed to discover the ways their models must be altered, refined, or expanded to be useful as their philosophy for supervision.

COURSE LEARNING OBJECTIVES AND TEACHING PEDAGOGY

Most courses are designed to meet the learning objectives set by the American Association for Marriage and Family Therapy (AAMFT)—the only standard-setting body that exists for supervisory training. This section outlines these learning objectives (AAMFT, 1991b) and the material usually covered to meet them. Note that the learning objectives and the accompanying teaching pedagogy can be modified to fit supervision practices in other mental health disciplines.

Familiarity with Supervision Models

Supervisors-in-training are to be familiarized "with the major models of MFT supervision, in terms of their philosophical assumptions and pragmatic implications" (AAMFT, 1991b, p. 3). Comparing supervision practices based on the major models of MFT on the following criteria underscores the differences in philosophical assumptions and the pragmatic implications: goals, supervisory relationship and methods, and typical interventions. *Goals* refers to the major assumptions about the primary purpose of supervision. For example, some models assume supervision is skill-building (Mead & Crane, 1978) while others view it as aimed at personal growth of supervisees and supervisors (Connell, 1984). *Supervisory relationship* refers to the quality of the interaction between supervisor and supervisee. Is it teaching (Colapinto, 1988), coaching (Papero, 1988), an apprenticeship (Connell, 1984), or a relationship of co-authors (White 1989/1990)? *Supervisory methods* refers to standard formats for supervision and structures of supervision. Would supervision typically be done via case presentations, audiotapes, videotapes, or live? For example, most psychodynamic supervisors observe therapy but rarely intervene during sessions (Nichols, 1988); structural therapists prefer live supervision (Colapinto, 1988). Will supervision usually occur with therapists individually, in groups, or as co-therapists with supervisors? For example, Milan supervisors prefer supervising teams of therapists (Pirrotta & Cecchin, 1988); experientialists conduct therapy as co-therapists with their supervisees (Connell, 1984). *Interventions* are the typical ways supervisors intervene to help their supervisees become more effective as therapists. Supervisors practicing strategically regularly give directives (Mazza, 1988), post-modern supervisors listen with a curious, not knowing attitude (Anderson & Swim, 1995). For more information, see Liddle et al. (1988) and Part II of this book for a discussion of supervision practices of the major models.

One of the most revealing exercises is when SITs are randomly assigned a model other than their own to practice in a supervision role-play. Supervisors-in-training quickly find their own preferences and biases, and realize that assumptions suggest certain methods and interventions that greatly influence supervision.

There are many reasons for SITs to be familiar with the major models. First, SITs who are knowledgeable about MFT supervision models are better prepared to work with supervisees practicing from a variety of models. Few supervisors have the luxury of supervising therapists who practice from a "purist" theoretical orientation or of supervising in settings in which only one therapy approach is practiced exclusively. Second, familiarity with the differences in the supervision models aids SITs in defining their "scope of supervision practice." Supervisors frequently must decide if they will supervise therapists who have different ideas about therapy than they have (Kaslow, 1986; Storm, 1994; White, 1989/1990). Will supervisors staunchly require supervisees to practice from their preferred approach? Will they adapt to supervisees' models? Or, will they refer supervisees to another supervisor? Some supervisors limit their supervision practice to a particular model of therapy while others determine a range of practice models they feel comfortable with supervising. Third, because advanced supervisees tend to have development of their own integrated model as their supervision goal (Mead, 1990), SITs who are familiar with a range of therapy ideas will find it easier to facilitate integration. Finally, reviewing the major MFT supervision models for their assumptions and pragmatic implications helps SITs identify ideas and methods

they prefer and is a step toward articulating their own models of supervision.

Articulation of a Model of Supervision

Ultimately, SITs "articulate a personal model of supervision, drawn from existing models of supervision and from preferred styles of therapy" (AAMFT, 1991b, p. 3). In my experience, this learning objective is the most challenging for SITs—perhaps because developing a philosophy seems like a formidable task to them. Instructional methods are critical that assist SITs to identify; expand; and articulate their preferred ideas, methods, and styles.

Exercises are useful to uncover SITs' existing beliefs and highlight areas in their philosophy still needing to be developed. Asking SITs to respond to a series of forced choice statements regarding the assumptions underlying the various models of supervision can assist in identification of existing beliefs and areas for development (Liddle et al., 1988). For example, SITs choose between statements like "the supervisory relationship should be egalitarian" and "the supervisory relationship is hierarchical," or "changes in supervisees' personal attributes and personality are the goal of supervision" and "supervisees need only learn a set of skills or way of thinking about therapy." The questions posed by Liddle (1988) or Piercy and Sprenkle (1986) can also aid in this process. Sample questions suggested by Liddle (1988) include: What constitutes success in supervision? To what extent do I believe therapists are born not made; and conversely, to what extent do I believe all individuals can develop the skills of a therapist? Using the concept of isomorphism, SITs can be asked to explore the ways their therapy model fits the supervision context (Storm & Heath, 1985). This involves consciously applying and critically examining theoretical ideas and methods drawn from SITs' models of therapy and using them as a guide in supervision. In what ways are therapy and supervision similar and in what ways is each a different process? All of these exercises can be responded to in small groups beginning with the "supervisors epistemological declaration" (Liddle, 1988, p. 157) or articulation of their philosophy.

Because many supervisors combine several supervision models (Piercy & Sprenkle, 1986), Lebow's (1984, 1987) guidelines for integration can be useful to participants. Most courses require a written supervision philosophy with a case study illustration as part of their requirements.

Structuring and Intervening in Supervision

Supervisors-in-training "structure supervision, solve problems and implement supervisory interventions within a range of supervisory modalities (for example live and videotaped supervision)" (AAMFT, 1991b, p. 3). The supervision of individuals, dyads, co-therapists, groups, and teams each have advantages and disadvantages, promote specific types of learning, and are consistent with certain sets of ideas. For example, individual supervision has the advantage of allowing significant attention to the unique needs of supervisees but limits therapists' exposure to ideas. Groups provide the learning context for expanding supervisees' repertoires of ideas and interventions. For postmodern supervisors, teams of therapists, who can participate in reflections with clients and each other, fit with notions of multiple ideas as critical to change. Discussions comparing these structures familiarize SITs with dyad and group supervision, which are the most commonly practiced structures, while highlighting those supervision arrangements SITs gravitate to because of their assumptions about supervision.

Case consultation, review of audio- and videotapes, and live supervision are considered similarly. Discussions comparing these methods, although useful, are best coupled

with class simulations or the actual experience whenever possible. Supervisors-in-training can experience case consultations by pairing up in dyads with one assuming the supervisory role and the other presenting a case. The importance of contracting becomes evident as some pairs experience tension as a result of differences in their expectations while others fit together well. While watching a videotaped therapy session, SITs can pretend they are supervising the therapist. Assuming the supervisory role, they signal when they want to stop the tape, provide their rationale, and make supervisory interventions. This exercise quickly illustrates the existence of a diversity of supervisory assumptions and methods in the field. A role-played live session demonstrates the complexity of live supervision and the multiple levels of interaction that must be considered (Liddle & Schwartz, 1983). Whether focusing on the supervisory structure or method, instructors stress the importance of selecting the best one for the learning situation and for the supervisee's needs.

Facilitation of Supervisory Relationships

Supervisors-in-training must be able to "facilitate the co-evolving therapist–client and supervisor–therapist–client relationships" and "to evaluate and identify problems in therapist–client and supervisor–therapist–client relationships" (AAMFT, 1991b, p. 3). This learning objective addresses the initial formation of a supervision contract to the final evaluation. Supervisors-in-training enthusiastically endorse assignments of developing a supervision contract (see Chapter 19) and evaluation procedures because initially these promote their conceptualization of supervision and then have a long life as they are implemented into their supervision practices.

Supervision involves the added dynamic of supervisee development and socialization to the therapy process. To illustrate the complexity of the supervisory relationship system, a brief videotape clip of a supervisee discussing a "stuck case" can be shown, followed with these questions developed by Heath and Todd (1989): How would you describe your hunches about the therapist–client system? What else do you need to know about the client(s) to proceed as a supervisor? About the therapist? Why? How would you describe the therapist-supervisor system? What else would you need to know about the supervisory context or the relationship? Why?

Typical supervision case examples of difficulties that may occur in supervision and challenge even the most experienced supervisors can be given to small groups with the assignment to devise a supervision plan to resolve them. For example, SITs can be asked how they would proceed with a supervisee who always agrees with them or a supervisee who seems only interested in gaining hours so rarely comes to supervision prepared and often seems uninterested in supervisory input (see Chapter 17).

Supervisors usually are responsible for an initial evaluation of supervisees' knowledge of MFT and their readiness to practice, for ongoing assessment of the progress of supervisees and the supervision process in reaching supervision goals, and for evaluations at the end of supervision. Supervisors-in-training must consider which of the two major philosophies of evaluation they will use. Traditionally, supervisors measure supervisees' abilities against what is believed as essential to know (Figley & Nelson, 1989, 1990; Nelson, Heilbrun, & Figley, 1993; Tomm & Wright, 1979). More recently, Turner and Fine (1995) propose an alternative view of evaluation as supervisors measuring supervisees against what has been "agreed upon through dialogue as currently important regulatory criteria" (p. 60). Mead (1993) suggests SITs consider: Who should evaluate supervision? What should be evaluated in su-

pervision assessments? Where should supervision evaluations be done? Plus, when and how should supervision be evaluated?

Because SITs vary in their comfort with their evaluative role, discussions about what constitutes too little versus too much evaluation; various methods from informal supervisory conversations to evaluation instruments; and purposes of the initial, ongoing, and final evaluations can lead to SITs developing their own evaluation process. Reviewing an array of evaluation forms and instruments used by supervisors is helpful for SITs interested in developing a formalized, written procedure. (See *Resource Guide* for examples of forms and instruments.)

Exposure to the key literature reviewing research findings (Avis & Sprenkle, 1990; Kniskern & Gurman, 1988) and issues of MFT supervision contribute to SITs' evaluation of their philosophy and supervision practice. Supervisors-in-training can use the "Supervisory Styles Inventory" (Long, Dotson, & Lawless, 1994) to assess their own styles of supervision.

Sensitivity to Contextual Influences

Supervisors should be "sensitive to contextual variables such as culture, gender, ethnicity, and economics" (AAMFT, 1991b, p. 3). Because many SITs were educated before contextual variables were emphasized in MFT education, instructors have the dual role of helping them consider the influence of these variables on the process of therapy and supervision simultaneously. Many SITs easily acknowledge that in certain cases such factors shape therapy significantly and delve into discussions about this influence. The more difficult territory is focusing on ways to help SITs consider the ever-present influence of these factors. Supervisors-in-training frequently ask questions such as the following. If I am a white, middle-class male who supervises males just like me, how are contextual variables an influence? In response, instructors assist SITs, whether they are supervising the same or opposite sex supervisees, consider: How does the gender constellation affect the learning process? If they are from the same or a different cultural group than that of their supervisees, how does their own and their supervisees' participation in the majority or minority culture influence therapy and supervision? How do they ensure that their supervisees are prepared to work with a heterogeneous clientele? Overall, what are their own beliefs and methods for assisting their supervisees develop a deeper sensitivity to these contextual influences?

During the course, SITs can practice some of the methods suggested for increasing contextual sensitivity. Roberts (1991) suggests coding the process of therapy, individual, or group supervision for the gendered ways participants may communicate with one another. This includes noting the number of times, the amount of talk, who talks after whom, who responds to whom, body language, and whether content is relational or instrumental. Reviewing a supervision tape and discussing questions, such as the following ones, promotes the awareness of SITs' gender values, assumptions, and gendered reactions and responses. How does the supervisor's and supervisee's gender influence their responses to each other? The language used? The nonverbal communication? How does gender influence the difficulties whether the supervisee's frustrations or the clients' presenting problem, being discussed? Roberts (1991) suggests considering questions about the influence of gender in the work context as a useful exercise. Supervisors-in-training can review a supervision tape by using an altered version (i.e., change all references to clients to supervisees) of the Feminist Family Therapy Checklist (Chaney & Piercy, 1988) to underscore the many opportunities for intervention in gendered interaction. They can use the Feminist Family Therapy Checklist (Black & Piercy, 1991) to assess their conceptualizations about the influence of gender in family life and therapy.

For other contextual influences, SITs can determine their own multiculturalism by identifying their contextual backgrounds (McGoldrick, 1982; Preli & Bernard, 1993), through identifying their race, ethnicity, socioeconomic status, religion, generation, gender, region of country lived in, type of community resided in, and family structures. Then, SITs can determine ways they can convey their multiculturalism to supervisees. A supervision tape can be reviewed with the following types of questions in mind: How have the similarities and differences in the contextual experiences of supervisor and supervisee influenced the supervision? In what ways have they enhanced supervision? Created challenges for both? If you were the supervisor, how would your contextual background shape the supervisory interaction? How could the supervisor help the supervisee to decide whether to intervene with clients in a way that would contribute to change in the larger sociopolitical, economic, and historical context? Supervisors-in-training can be presented with scenarios in which supervisees may unknowingly make sexist or racist remarks, and asked for their supervisory responses.

Knowledge of Professional Issues

Supervisors-in-training are to "be knowledgeable of ethical and legal issues of supervision" (AAMFT, 1991b, p. 3). This involves a review of the ethical standards that apply specifically to the process of supervision and the recognition of the new legal responsibilities they are assuming by becoming supervisors. Resources include the AAMFT's Code of Ethics (1991a), the standards and responsibilities of AAMFT Approved Supervisors (AAMFT, 1991b), and state laws. In their work with supervisees, supervisors must learn to consider the ethical and legal implications of their supervisees while also ensuring that they are always behaving as an ethical and responsible supervisor.

A standard teaching method is to present SITs with ethical dilemmas (such as those in Chapter 3) for them to discuss. The trick is to describe scenarios in which supervisors find themselves in dilemmas where they are balancing competing ethical standards of supervision rather than ethical therapy situations. These are in addition to situations in which they formulate supervisory responses that help supervisees develop their ethical reasoning and decision making. For example, in the first type of situation, a supervisor may have to weigh supervisee confidentiality with the responsibility to ensure clients are receiving at least adequate treatment if a supervisee has shared some personal information that could affect the supervisee's ability to practice. In the second situation, it may be clear to a supervisor, for example, that a therapist must report child abuse, but still be challenged with how to assist the supervisee to draw the same conclusion.

Supervising Supervisors

In the not so distant future, SITs may find themselves training supervisors; thus, they need to learn "to address the distinctive issues that arise in supervision of supervision" (AAMFT, 1991b, p. 3). There are several differences in supervising supervisors rather than supervisees, including: (1) increased collaboration in supervisory relationships, (2) increased emphasis on SITs' ideas, and (3) increased responsibility for creating a learning context that is comprehensive because supervision-of-supervision frequently only occurs under one supervisor. Managing the additional complexity of the added level of supervision-of-supervision requires an expanded view of the supervision system, focusing on the process of supervision and leaving the process of therapy up to SITs, keeping a re-

spectful distance from supervisees, and maintaining an organizational perspective. Chapter 27 discusses these distinctions in depth. Because course participants usually are currently engaged in supervision-of-supervision, their experiences—both positive and negative—can create stimulating discussions and be a basis for designing supervision training experiences for several fictitious therapists wishing to become supervisors.

THE IDEAL SUPERVISION TRAINING EXPERIENCE

Probably, the ideal educational experience is for SITs to simultaneously take a course like the one described in this chapter when they are beginning to supervise. This enables SITs to apply theory to practice and to experiment with differing ideas and methods. The most comprehensive and richest training is when SITs (1) gain experience supervising therapists at differing professional development levels in a diversity of settings with a variety of personal characteristics (gender, race, culture, and so on); (2) have opportunities to supervise live, review audio- and videotapes, and consult about cases in their work with alternative supervisory arrangements; and (3) supervise therapists who have goals of credentialing as well as solely professional growth. Likewise, a supervision-of-supervision experience is the most comprehensive and rich when it incorporates the experiences identified here.

REFERENCES

American Association for Marriage and Family Therapy (AAMFT). (1991a). *AAMFT Code of Ethics.* Washington, DC: Author.

AAMFT. (1991b). *AAMFT Approved Supervisor designation: Standards and responsibilities.* Washington, DC: Author.

Anderson, H., & Swim, S. (1995). Supervision as collaborative conversation: Connecting the voices of supervisor and supervisee. *Journal of Systemic Therapies, 14*, 1–13.

Avis, J., & Sprenkle, D. (1990). Outcome research on family therapy training: A substantive and methodological review. *Journal of Marital and Family Therapy, 16*, 241–264.

Black, L., & Piercy, F. (1991). A feminist family therapy scale. *Journal of Marital and Family Therapy, 17*, 111–120.

Breunlin, D., Liddle, H., & Schwartz, D. (1988). Concurrent training of supervisors and therapists. In H. Liddle, D. Breunlin, & D. Schwartz (Eds.), *Handbook of family therapy training and supervision* (pp. 207–224). New York: Guilford Press.

Chaney, S., & Piercy, F. (1988). A feminist family therapist behavioral checklist. *American Journal of Family Therapy, 18*, 305–318.

Colapinto, J. (1988). Teaching the structural way. In H. Liddle, D. Breunlin, & R. Schwartz (Eds.), *Handbook of family therapy training and supervision* (pp. 17–37). New York: Guilford Press.

Connell, G. (1984). An approach to supervision of symbolic-experiential psychotherapy. *Journal of Marital and Family Therapy, 10*, 273–280.

Constantine, J., Piercy, F., & Sprenkle, D. (1984). Live supervision-of-supervision in family therapy. *Journal of Marital and Family Therapy, 10*, 95–98.

deShazer, S. (1984). Fit. *Journal of Strategic and Systemic Therapies, 3*, 34–38.

Figley, C., & Nelson, T. (1989). Basic family therapy skills, I: Conceptualization and initial findings. *Journal of Marital and Family Therapy, 15*, 349–365.

Figley, C., & Nelson, T. (1990). Basic family therapy skills, II: Structural family therapy. *Journal of Marital and Family Therapy, 16*, 225–239.

Heath, A., & Storm, C. (1985). From the ivory tower to the institute: The live supervision stage approach for teaching supervision in academic settings. *American Journal of Family Therapy, 13*, 27–36.

Heath, A., & Todd, T. (1989). Presentation at the AAMFT meeting, San Francisco, October.

Kaslow, F. (1986). Seeking and providing supervision in private practice. In F. Kaslow (Ed.), *Supervision and training: Models, dilemmas, and challenges* (pp. 143–158). New York: Haworth Press.

Kniskern, D., & Gurman, A. (1988). Research. In H. Liddle, D. Breunlin, & D. Schwartz (Eds.), *Handbook*

of family therapy training and supervision (pp. 368–378). New York: Guilford Press.

Lebow, L. (1984). On the value of integrating approaches to family therapy. *Journal of Marital and Family Therapy, 10*, 127–138.

Lebow, L. (1987). Developing a personal integration in family therapy: Principles for model construction and practice. *Journal of Marital and Family Therapy, 13*, 1–14.

Liddle, H. (1988). Systemic supervision: Conceptual overlays and pragmatic guidelines. In H. Liddle, D. Breunlin, & D. Schwartz (Eds.), *Handbook of family therapy training and supervision* (pp. 153–171). New York: Guilford Press.

Liddle, H., Breunlin, D., Schwartz, R., & Constantine, J. (1984). Training family therapy supervisors: Issues of content, form and context. *Journal of Marital and Family Therapy, 10*, 139–150.

Liddle, H., Breunlin, D., & Schwartz, R. (1988). Introduction. *Handbook of family therapy training and supervision* (pp. 13–16). New York: Guilford Press.

Liddle, H., & Halpin, R. (1978). Family therapy training and supervision literature: A comparative review. *Journal of Marriage and Family Counseling, 4*, 77–98.

Liddle, H., & Saba, G. (1983). On context replication: *Journal of Strategic and Systemic Therapies, 2*, 3–11.

Liddle, H., & Schwartz, H. (1983). Live supervision/consultation: Conceptual and pragmatic guidelines for family therapy training. *Family Process, 22*, 477–490.

Long, J., Dotson, D., & Lawless, J. (1994). Assessing your supervisory style. Presentation at AAMFT, Chicago, October.

Mazza, J. (1988). Training strategic therapists: The use of indirect techniques. In H. Liddle, D. Breunlin, & R. Schwartz (Eds.), *Handbook of family therapy training and supervision* (pp. 93–109). New York: Guilford Press.

McGoldrick, M. (1982). Ethnicity and family therapy: An overview. In M. McGoldrick, J. Pearce, & J. Giordano (Eds.), *Ethnicity and family therapy* (pp. 3–30). New York: Guilford Press.

Mead, D. (1993). Assessing supervision: Social validity and invalidity of evaluation. *Supervision Bulletin, 6*, 4, 8.

Mead, D., & Crane, D. (1978). An empirical approach to supervision and training of relationship therapists. *Journal of Marriage and Family Counseling, 4*, 67–76.

Nelson, T., Heilbrun, G., & Figley, C. (1993). Basic family therapy skills IV: Transgenerational theories of family therapy. *Journal of Marital and Family Therapy, 19,* 253–266.

Nichols, W. (1988). An integrated psychodynamic and systems approach. In H. Liddle, D. Breunlin, & R. Schwartz (Eds.), *Handbook of family therapy training and supervision* (pp. 110–127). New York: Guilford Press.

Papero, D. (1988). Training in Bowen theory. In H. Liddle, D. Breunlin, & R. Schwartz (Eds.), *Handbook of family therapy training and supervision* (pp. 62–77). New York: Guilford Press.

Piercy, F., & Sprenkle, D. (1986). *Family therapy sourcebook.* New York: Guilford Press.

Pirrotta, S., & Cecchin, G. (1988). The Milan training program. In H. Liddle, D. Breunlin, & R. Schwartz (Eds.), *Handbook of family therapy training and supervision* (pp. 38–61). New York: Guilford Press.

Preli, R., & Bernard, J. (1993). Making multiculturalism relevant for majority culture graduate students. *Journal of Marital and Family Therapy, 19,* 5–16.

Roberts, J. (1991). Sugar and spice, toads and mice: Gender issues in family therapy training. *Journal of Marital and Family Therapy, 17,* 121–132.

Storm, C. (1994). Defensive supervision: Balancing ethical responsibility with vulnerability. In G. Brock (Ed.), *Ethics casebook* (pp. 173–190). Washington, DC: AAMFT.

Storm, C., & Heath, A. (1985). Models of supervision: Using therapy theory as a guide. *The Clinical Supervisor, 3,* 87–96.

Storm, C., & Heath, A. (1991). Problem-focused supervision: Rationale, exemplification and limitations. *Journal of Family Psychotherapy, 2,* 55–70.

Tomm, K., & Wright, L. (1979). Training in family therapy: Perceptual, conceptual, and executive skills. *Family Process, 18,* 227–250.

Turner, J., & Fine, M. (1995). Postmodern evaluation in family therapy supervision. *Journal of Systemic Therapies, 14,* 57–69.

White, M. (1989/1990). Family therapy training and supervision in a world of experience and narrative. *Dulwich Centre Newsletter, Summer,* 27–38.

Zemke, R., & Zemke, S. (1981). Thirty things we know for sure about adult learning. *Training, 18,* 115–117.

27

Supervising Supervisors

Cheryl L. Storm, Thomas C. Todd, Teresa McDowell,
and Tim Sutherland

Supervisors who turn eagerly to the literature for guidance as they begin the task of supervising a supervisor-in-training (SIT) will find themselves disappointed. Most readings in this area focus predominantly on the teaching/training of supervisors rather than supervising them (Breunlin, Liddle, & Schwartz, 1988; Heath & Storm, 1985; Liddle et al., 1984). This is unfortunate, because it is clearly a different task than supervising therapists. This chapter addresses this lack by focusing on the distinctive differences of supervising supervisors versus therapists including: creating collaborative supervisory relationships, managing multiple levels, highlighting gatekeeping responsibilities, and developing supervisors' theories of supervision. The distinctions are based on the authors' combined experiences. The authors differ significantly in professional background and credentials, and degree of supervisory experience. Because the two first authors had been supervisors for many years, it seemed useful to obtain a firsthand account from two supervisors who had been SITs fairly recently and who could therefore offer a fresh perspective on this experience. The third author, Teresa, became a supervisor five years ago, allowing her to reflect on the preparation she had for her supervision practice after supervising for a period of time. The final author of this chapter, Tim, recently completed supervision-of-supervision and offers the perspective of a beginning supervisor.

CREATING COLLABORATIVE SUPERVISORY RELATIONSHIPS

Overall, supervising supervisors is an interaction between near equals who are colleagues within the field. Supervisors-of-supervision are assisting their colleagues to add to and diversify their professional abilities. Thus supervision-of-supervision relationships tend to be more symmetrical or collaborative than complementary or hierarchical for two reasons (Constantine, Piercy, & Sprenkle, 1984; Fine & Fennell, 1985). First, SITs have a great deal to contribute to supervisory relationships. Although they may know little regarding supervision, they have significant therapy and professional experience within the field on which to draw during their supervision-of-supervision training. Second, they have more in common with supervisors than with their supervisees (Constantine et al., 1984). Supervising therapists, particularly beginners, involves assisting partially trained professionals to become fully qualified colleagues. Supervisees are usually beginning a new training experience, learning a new body of knowledge, and entering a new professional community. In contrast, supervisors and SITs have already had relatively similar training experiences, have a common knowledge base, and participate in the same professional community.

When viewed over time, relationships between supervisors and therapists and eventually between supervisors-of-supervision and SITs become increasingly collaborative. Liddle (1988) distinguishes between three phases of supervision, describing an increase in collaboration at each stage. During the initial phase, supervisory relationships are negotiated and collaboration begins as therapists and supervisors set out to accomplish shared goals. Mutual trust develops and the collaborative nature of relationships increases during the middle phase. During the final phase of supervision, the hierarchical nature of relationships is further reduced, with autonomy and career development becoming a primary focus. When relationships are taken a step further and experienced and autonomous therapists return to supervisors for supervision-of-supervision, this established collaboration becomes the starting point for their relationships. It is important for supervisors-of-supervision to enter and structure supervisory relationships in ways that will nurture this collaboration. Some supervisors have even recommended encouraging the collaborative or symmetrical aspects of supervision relationships by having SITs supervise supervisors-of-supervision (Fine & Fennell, 1985; Woodside, 1994).[1]

Cocreating a Learning Experience

When deciding to become a therapist, interested individuals find a set of prescribed steps. A master's degree in family therapy or the equivalent curriculum is spelled out with specified post-master's practice and supervision requirements delineated by credentialing bodies. Although requirements to become a supervisor are also defined by credentialing bodies, such as the American Association for Marriage and

Family Therapy (AAMFT) and some state laws, there are many more programs training therapists than supervisors. Few universities offer courses in family therapy supervision, and supervised practice experiences for SITs rarely exist in structured ways. Thus, potential SITs frequently are in the position of creating with their chosen supervisors-of-supervision a learning experience that entails a supervision course, supervision of therapists, and supervision-of-supervision (see Chapter 26 for a discussion of the components of a supervision course). This shared responsibility for creating a learning program immediately sets a collaborative context for their work together.

Supervisors-of-supervision can structure collaborative relationships in numerous ways. The initial contract for supervision-of-supervision can be cocreated by requesting information from SITs about how they would like to arrange their training experiences. "What training experiences are most important to you for your development as a supervisor?" and "How will you let me know what you need as we proceed in this experience together?" are examples of questions that might encourage SITs to be active participants in the training process. Training goals, a supervision plan, and the unique needs of SITs can be included in the contract and tracked throughout the relationships.

TERESA'S EXPERIENCE: INCREASED RESPONSIBILITY FOR LEARNING

Teresa has a marriage and family therapy (MFT) degree and practiced for four years at two mental health agencies and a private practice before beginning her supervisory training. She had considerable experience in providing training, consultation, and supervision to community agencies. She took an active and responsible role in her development as a supervisor by identifying the areas she wanted to work on, by contracting with ther-

---

[1]See Fine and Fennell (1985) for specific instructions for maximizing the effectiveness of this procedure.

apists who worked in a variety of settings and had different degrees of training and experience in family therapy, by supervising individually and in groups, and by maximizing the use of videotape and live sessions. She and Cheryl, her supervisor, worked together to secure opportunities and to plan supervision in a way that met those needs.

During her supervision training, Teresa supervised therapists in a group at a mental health clinic, a group of family reconciliation counselors, an MFT private practitioner, and several MFT student therapists. Cheryl helped create collaboration and involvement by encouraging Teresa to evaluate her training needs throughout their work together, incorporating Teresa's ideas into supervision, and working together to establish goals and identify strengths as well as areas for potential growth. It was extremely helpful for Teresa to have Cheryl structure meetings and keep the focus on skill development. This allowed Teresa to think through the role she played and the interactions involved in the various systems she was working in while exploring abilities she was developing across systems. Cheryl also invited her into a more collegial relationship with other supervisors by encouraging her to submit some of her ideas for publication, welcoming her into supervisory meetings, and so on.

Because of the experience level of SITs, they are able to practice supervision more independently than most therapists receiving supervision of their therapy. Supervisors-of-supervision must trust in their SITs' abilities and professional judgment to a greater degree because there is usually considerably more time between meetings of supervisors and SITs than supervisors and therapists. Consequently, SITs have to attend to a wide array of experiences to decide on issues that need attention. For example, between supervision sessions Teresa struggled to encourage theoretical adherence in a group of therapists just learning family therapy, had an ethical issue regarding

confidentiality arise with a supervisee she was seeing individually, and felt stuck in a repetitive pattern with a co-therapy team. Supervisors-in-training must be able to examine their work, develop and recognize potential solutions to problems that arise, notice reoccurring areas of difficulty, and prioritize issues to prepare for supervision sessions.

Supervision-of-Supervision: A More Heuristic Process

Because of the degree of sophistication of SITs' knowledge, supervisors-of-supervision and SITs seem to share an understanding of the process of supervision that is occurring for SITs, which creates more collaboration. Supervisees tend to be much less aware of the larger supervisory system and of interventions supervisors make to help them change in relationship to their work. Supervision-of-supervision relationships become more transparent with more open discussion of the intentions of supervisors-of-supervision in intervening with SITs. There is a greater need for agreement regarding interventions during supervision-of-supervision for them to be effective, and there is more emphasis on the development of SITs' preferred ideas and ways of working.

TIM'S EXPERIENCE: SHARED LEARNING IN SUPERVISION-OF-SUPERVISION

Tim, a graduate of an MFT master's program, works in conjunction with evangelical Christian churches to provide on-site counseling to their communities and has recently completed supervisory training. His supervisees are recruited primarily through his professional and personal contacts in the churches with which he works. His own training in therapy took place in training centers where specific models of therapy were taught and there was an emphasis on acquiring specific skills within each model. However, in supervision-of-supervision, even though Tom, his supervisor, is well known for his work as a strategic therapist, there was no emphasis on learning Tom's model of doing supervision. What Tim found most beneficial in his supervision was not learning a specific model, but the consistent emphasis on thinking through the potential implications and ramifications of doing supervision from his own narrative and solution-focused perspective. Tim also appreciated a comprehensive approach to the practice of supervision including discussion of legal issues, liability concerns, contracting for supervision, and other aspects that most would consider more general to the practice of supervision.

Because Tim began supervision as a novice, the attention paid by Tom to more general concerns in doing supervision was understandably warranted: he clearly needed supervision of "the basics" of doing supervision. Tim's supervision meetings included another SIT Tom treated their years of doing therapy as a significant knowledge base for doing supervision, and both were free to ask questions or give input to the other at any time. Because of this emphasis by Tom, Tim found supervision as a supervisor to be more heuristic than the more didactic supervision he received as a therapist.

MANAGING MULTIPLE LEVELS

If supervision adds a new level of complexity compared to conducting therapy, consider the complexity of supervision-of-supervision. In addition to the level of individual client, couple or family, there is the level of the therapist, the level of the SIT, and the level of supervisor-of-supervision. Even if each level is uncomplicated by interaction with other systems (an unlikely possibility!), managing this complexity is a formidable task. It "requires the ability

to evaluate relationship systems at multiple levels simultaneously" (Wright & Coppersmith, 1982, p. 218).

Expanded View of Interactional System

The first step in managing the complexity for supervisors-of-supervision is to expand their views to include all levels of interaction. One of the most significant challenges in becoming a supervisor is learning to think and act on many different levels of interaction. For SITs, it is like going behind the scenes and discovering that a lot more is going on than simply focusing on cases while considering the development of supervisees' therapy skills. The client–therapist system continues to be in front of the screen, while the relationship between supervisor, SIT, therapist, and family becomes the expanded focus of attention. Wright and Coppersmith (1983) suggest that when supervisors-of-supervision do not keep the various levels clearly in mind: (1) supervisors-of-supervision may focus more on therapy content rather than facilitating the process between SITs and supervisees, (2) dysfunctional triads may erupt, (3) the mirroring of relationship processes from one level of the system to the next may evolve, and/or (4) a lack of clarity regarding goals for supervision-of-supervision may occur. Supervisors-of-supervision have the role of continually assisting SITs to clarify their focus and their targeted level of interaction.

Supervisors-of-Supervision Join the System

The second step for supervisors-of-supervision is to position themselves appropriately within the system and to respect the role of SITs. This requires supervisors-of-supervision to maintain a focus on the process of supervision, leaving the process of therapy up to SITs. Being several levels removed from the clinical case diminishes the tendency to offer interventions based on "If I were the therapist . . ." (see Chapter 26). However, a recent study of beginning supervisors found they commonly felt confused regarding how supervisors should intervene with supervisees (McColley & Baker, 1982). Thus beginning supervisors may steer supervision-of-supervision toward clinical content rather than the process of supervision in an effort to reduce their confusion.

In supervision-of-supervision, there is a parallel temptation to offer guidance in the form of "If I were the supervisor . . ." Beginning supervisors can feed into this by asking, "What would you do if you were the supervisor?" It is not necessarily a sin to ask such a question, but on this level, self-sufficiency also should be the goal (see Chapter 2). It is harder to use client welfare as a justification for taking over supervision, compared to therapy, because supervision is being conducted by experienced clinicians who might trample on the feelings or autonomy of supervisees but are unlikely to harm clients. Breunlin et al. (1988) discuss direct intervention as a necessary option in some situations, but suggest that in most cases it should be avoided. Hopefully experienced supervisors who are performing supervision-of-supervision have well-developed theories of supervision and of therapy that will help them to organize and reduce this complexity. No particular theory has an inherent advantage, but supervisors-of-supervision need some method of reducing the potentially huge amount of information.

It is also important for supervisors-of-supervision to maintain a respectful distance from supervisees, even though this can be a challenge in some circumstances. Supervisors-of-supervision often are well-known, respected, and established supervisors and trainers within their community. In contrast, SITs are often comparatively unknown in this professional arena. Supervisees are frequently interested in the perspective of supervisors-of-supervision about their work, progress, and

clinical cases. Questions to SITs, such as "What does your supervisor think about . . . ?" are not infrequent. This, of course, can detract from the credibility and confidence of SITs. Consider the following case example.

A SUPERVISOR-OF-SUPERVISION UNDERMINES A SUPERVISOR-IN-TRAINING

After a supervision session with a therapist who seemed to question Teresa's ability as an SIT, Cheryl, her supervisor, benignly intervened to offer information to the therapist. Later they considered how this might escalate a pattern that could decrease Teresa's confidence and the confidence the therapist had in her while fostering a relationship with Cheryl as the expert. By watching Cheryl examine her impact on the system and recognize when her actions might become part of a problematic pattern, Teresa was able to begin considering her participation in the supervisory system in a much more active and flexible way.

Although supervisors should avoid unwittingly undermining SITs, both parties should acknowledge situations that have the potential for reinforcing the "supervisor-of-supervision as expert" dynamic. This can result from the supervisor-of-supervision having an important faculty role with supervisees, as is often true for Cheryl. Specific areas of expertise held by supervisors-of-supervision can also contribute, as was the case when Tim supervised a therapist conducting family therapy with substance abusers. Tim recommended Tom's book to help his supervisee conceptualize cases, but this made Tim and the supervisee more sensitive to the knowledge that Tom was listening to their supervision tapes. Supervisors-of-supervision can minimize the potential for undermining SITs by discussing their respective roles with them and encouraging them to do so with their supervisees.

Additionally, this phenomenon can be exacerbated when supervisors-of-supervision serve as matchmakers by referring potential supervisees to SITs who do not have their own supervisees. These may be supervisees who have approached supervisors-of-supervision for supervision or may be students within a training institution where supervisors-of-supervision play a training role. In such cases, supervisors-of-supervision often have inside knowledge about supervisees and are invested in their overall training. Hearing concerns or criticisms raised by SITs can be difficult for supervisors-of-supervision. Dilemmas about dealing with "insider information" also may surface.

A SUPERVISOR-OF-SUPERVISION STRUGGLES WITH INSIDER INFORMATION

Karen, a supervisee working with Barbara, an SIT, was a graduate of the MFT program where Cheryl, the supervisor-of-supervision, was the director. Karen, an informed consumer of supervision, was excited that she found cost-effective supervision, and that her previous graduate program supervisor would still be involved, however indirectly, in her training. She willingly consented to Cheryl sharing information about her capabilities with Barbara. The dilemma for Cheryl was how much to share. Karen's abilities were considered adequate, but not particularly strong by supervisors within the program. Should she allow Barbara to conduct her own assessment and form her own opinion? Or should she convey full information to her? If she were silent, would Barbara feel free to express concerns if they should arise, since Karen had been a supervisee of her supervisor-of-supervision? Is she preventing Karen from experiencing the best supervision she could get if Barbara is not fully in-

formed? If she gives full disclosure, is she predisposing Barbara to see weaknesses?

Supervisors-of-supervision who share previous knowledge may find themselves inadvertently in a coalition with their SITs, perhaps even pathologizing supervisees so they can both have a supervision problem to work on, thereby increasing their feeling of usefulness. As Liddle (1988) notes:

> Supervisors [and supervisors-of-supervision] are not immune to the destructive therapeutic stance of deficit detective. . . . It is sometimes difficult to implement their "search for strengths" and "resource mobilization" principles with trainees (p. 167, parenthesis added).

In our experience, supervisees frequently assume (we hope appropriately!) that supervisors-of-supervision and SITs have their best interests at heart. However, they also trust that discussions of them and their work in supervision-of-supervision are positively oriented, and are focused more on the development of SITs as supervisors than about the deficits of supervisees! One of us has occasionally been asked to audiotape supervision-of-supervision sessions for playback by the supervisee. Not only has it been useful to tape sessions, but it has also been a good mental discipline to imagine that supervision sessions are always being recorded so that there is no tendency to criticize supervisees behind their backs.

Maintaining an Organizational Perspective of the Supervision Context

Supervisors who have an organizational perspective will find it easier to position themselves appropriately within the larger context and assist their SITs in engaging in their new roles. Supervisors-in-training are fulfilling a broader role than supervising a therapist or two, a role that they often fail to appreciate fully at first. An organizational perspective can help supervisors-of-supervision assist SITs in understanding the role supervision fulfills within agencies and the work environments of their supervisees. It can also result in supervisors-of-supervision encouraging SITs to negotiate or renegotiate mutual understandings of their responsibilities as supervisors with the agencies their supervisees are employed by or the organization they contract with to provide supervision.

Part of becoming a supervisor involves learning to enter and contract with many different systems. It is important for supervisors to assist SITs to develop the ability to recognize therapists as part of larger systems and to consider how to join and intervene in those systems in a way that will allow supervision to be successful.

DISGRUNTLED SUPERVISEES REQUEST SUPERVISION

During Teresa's training, a group of therapists who were disgruntled with the lack of supervision they were receiving at their agency, approached her to establish a contract for outside supervision. Because during supervision-of-supervision sessions, Cheryl and Teresa had discussed various ways Teresa could contract with community agencies and develop a supervisory role within the organizations, Teresa carefully considered her response. She felt she could be in dangerous territory if she were to contract with them without the agency's blessing or if she were to "go to battle" for them by approaching the agency director herself. She felt her first intervention as a supervisor was to respect the agency's hierarchy and to join as close to the top as possible.

Teresa recommended that the therapists talk to their clinical director, discuss supervision with him and offer the option of contracting with her. Several weeks later she received a call from the clinical director and they met to establish a contract. This allowed them the opportunity to discuss the agency's philosophies, policies and procedures, and to review any concerns he had in allowing an outsider to influence therapists' work. They were also able to agree on how to support each other and what to do should problems arise.

Being well joined at the top allows supervisors to develop a more specific contract with therapists that fit agency parameters. It also prevents inadvertently teaming up with therapists in a way that would eventually undermine supervision. Supervisors can facilitate the ability of SITs to maintain an organizational perspective by reminding them of the importance of the contracting process and assisting them in clarifying their relationships. Frequently, SITs are so excited about having opportunities to supervise they forget to contract carefully.

GATEKEEPING RESPONSIBILITIES

Supervisors-of-supervision need to remain aware that they are training future gatekeepers of the profession. It is tempting to focus on the technical and theoretical aspects of doing supervision, which is a challenging enough task, as well as often being less conflictual than exercising responsibility for evaluation and other gatekeeping functions. Supervisors-in-training, who are comparatively inexperienced or unfamiliar with supervising toward licensure or AAMFT membership, may fail to appreciate the importance and complexity of this function.

Recognizing the Power Embedded in the Supervisory Role

As Chapter 16 documents at length, supervisees are well aware of the power inherent in the supervisory role. Even SITs report being surprised at their level of anxiety over having their supervision and writing exposed to close scrutiny, no matter how long they have been MFT practitioners. Although the degree of "jeopardy" may vary, the awareness of the power differential is virtually universal from the lower level of supervisees or SITs.

A SIMPLE BUT COMPLEX FOUR-WORD QUESTION

Tim was supervising Maria. Tim thought he and Maria had a very productive 90-minute conversation and audiotape review of a solution-focused brief therapy case. Maria came well prepared to present the case, they discussed both the theory and practice of solution-focused therapy, and the client seemed to be reaching the goals he had set for himself with Maria's help. When they finished talking about the case, Maria gathered together her notes, her tape player, and her books. But as she stood up to leave, she stopped, cocked her head to one side, and with a rather discouraged look on her face asked, "Am I doing okay?" Tim asked her what she meant and she said she couldn't tell how well she was doing in her own development as a solution-focused therapist.

Maria's question enabled Tom and Tim to focus on the power Tim automatically assumed by virtue of becoming an SIT. Tim was reminded supervisors need to identify positive and productive therapist behavior based on the goals that are set by therapists (Selekman & Todd, 1995), and the question reinforced for him how easily supervisors can get caught up in their own criteria for success of supervision. Tom was struck once again with

the need for him to help SITs recognize the inherent power in the supervisory role, power that he and supervisees tended to appreciate more readily than SITs. Tim noted that working collaboratively, which was important to him, included recognizing and cooperating with supervisees' expectations and perceptions. Having the supervisor stress collaboration and flattening the hierarchy was important, but this would not work automatically, especially when a beginning supervisee expected and desired a more hierarchical relationship.

As supervisors, we would often like to minimize this power by flattening the hierarchy and demonstrating our empathic skills. Some movement in this direction is desirable, as several chapters in this book have argued. As the case example illustrates, it is a mistake, however, to believe that it is ever possible (or even desirable) to eliminate hierarchy altogether in view of the gatekeeping expectations of credentialing bodies, the public, and even supervisees.

The Importance of Developing an Evaluation Process

Beginning supervisors often approach supervision as they do therapy, in the sense that they proceed on a session-by-session basis to work toward supervisees' goals at that moment in time. Supervisors-of-supervision generally are the ones who must introduce a dose of external reality into this process by reminding participants that SITs will need to make an evaluation at a future point in time that will compare supervisees to some presumed standard of the profession. Left unchecked, a narrow focus on session-by-session progress often results in rude awakenings later, when SITs are uncomfortable with the overall progress of a supervisee and are unwilling to recommend the supervisee as being ready for licensure, employment, or independent practice. The obvious remedy is to develop an evaluation process that is clear from the outset of supervision. Not only will this spell out training goals, but it will also address the issue of expectations for meeting credentialing or Clinical Membership requirements. This information can be used by supervisors-of-supervision to help SITs to evaluate their work with supervisees on an ongoing basis.

A SURPRISING EVALUATION

Tim had been supervising Larry, a therapist, for a little over six months when Larry decided to relocate to another state. They agreed to use the last session to mutually review and evaluate the experience. When Tim asked Larry what had not been helpful about supervision, Larry expressed some dissatisfaction that Tim had not given him "enough direction" on some of his cases. Larry shared that he expected supervision to be more of a question-and-answer session where Tim told him what to do. Tim asked him if he remembered going over the part of their written contract for supervision where they had discussed at length that Tim was not interested in doing supervision that way. Larry said he did recall that, but he thought the contract was "just a formality." When Tim asked him where he got the idea that supervision was a process of the supervisor supplying the therapist with exactly what to do in certain kinds of cases, Larry replied that he assumed so because that was how all his other supervisory relationships had been. Though they had talked about his previous supervision, Tim had failed to ask Larry how this experience might affect their work together. When Tim processed this in supervision with Tom he found that this incident was pivotal in helping him see the "big picture" of supervision. Up to this point, Tim had tended to supervise on a session-by-session basis. He realized that he had considered contracting an isolated activity that supervisors performed early in supervision, rather than an ongoing process that carried throughout the lifetime of supervisory relationships. Tim now asks more detailed questions about supervisees' expectations of supervision and remains alert to changes in supervisory contracts over time.

Many supervisees tend to put very little stock in the contract for supervision. Thus, mutual evaluation of supervision needs to take place on an ongoing basis. As noted earlier, in our experience, it is easy for SITs to become so case-focused that they assume supervision is going well and infrequently ask supervisees for their input.

Supervisors-of-supervisors should be modeling similar behavior in supervision-of-supervision. Thoroughly discussing all parties' expectations of the supervisory relationship and paying special attention to potentially conflicting ideas about hierarchy and collaboration is important. Once this has been done, it is critical to co-evaluate the supervision relationship regularly to check on how each person sees the relationship unfolding, compared to their original expectations. The usefulness of any evaluation process can be increased by regularly identifying signs of progress based on the goals of SITs, liberally conveying this progress to SITs, and asking for their feedback frequently. Supervisors-of-supervision should also make expectations clear for designation as an AAMFT Approved Supervisor or other credentialing processes.

Relationship to Credentialing Bodies

Ultimately supervisors-of-supervision are responsible for ensuring that all parties are aware of their relationship to appropriate credentialing bodies to avoid surprises at a later date. Usually this includes some explicit discussion of precise requirements for licensure, Clinical Membership, and so on. Two common situations have often contributed to difficulties in this area. On the supervisee level, it may be unclear what the ultimate purposes of supervision will be. Supervision may begin with no notion of AAMFT Clinical Membership; for example, when the initial purpose is different, such as staff supervision or a training program. Problems can arise if a supervisee later wishes credit for the supervision for another purpose, because this was not clear at the time. Supervision may not have been set up to meet these other requirements optimally; for example, not using tapes or live supervision or not keeping a careful distinction between MFT cases and other cases.

According to AAMFT policy, potential Approved Supervisors need not have previously been Clinical Members of AAMFT, even though they must meet equivalent standards. This has often meant that SITs have had little organizational experience with AAMFT so that they are unaware of requirements for Clinical Membership, do not fully appreciate the importance of access to primary clinical data, or have not thought about the definition of what constitutes an MFT case. Supervisors-of-supervision need to help such supervisors quickly realize the importance of these issues.

DEVELOPING A PHILOSOPHY OF SUPERVISION

Thus far the discussion of supervising supervisors has pertained to all supervisors, whether those being supervised are novice supervisors or are experienced supervisors seeking new credentials. Both categories of supervisors present some distinct challenges, especially regarding their development of a philosophy of supervision, so guidelines differ for them.

The Inexperienced Supervisor: Using Therapy Theory as a Guide for Supervision

The present book offers many examples of supervisors who apply specific models of therapy to the supervision context and who supervise radically differently from one another (see Chapters 11–15). Because most therapists have a theory of therapy that is a unique mix of their values, styles, and preferred ideas from several established models in the field, it can be difficult to develop a supervision approach that is based on one model of therapy. Therefore, beginning supervisors must develop their own conceptualization schema that reflects their ideas about change, learning, auspices under which supervision is taking place, the type of authority and locus of evaluation, techniques and methods, and roadblocks to effective supervision (Olsen & Stern, 1990). Supervisors-of-supervision can make major contributions to this process.

Supervisors-of-supervision can encourage beginning supervisors to consciously adapt and use their theories of therapy as an initial guide in developing their supervision philosophy (Liddle, 1982, 1988; Storm & Heath, 1985). Turning to their therapy model makes good sense because beginning supervisors have developed guiding principles and accompanying techniques for facilitating change that they can use (Storm & Heath, 1985). For example, if therapists tend to focus on boundaries in therapy, it is highly likely that as supervisors they will attend to proximity in their supervisees' relationships with clients and in their supervisory relationships. However, using one's theory of therapy as a guide for supervision requires beginning supervisors to find where their therapy models fit the context of supervision and where they do not.

Supervisors-of-supervision can facilitate this process in several ways. First, when SITs express confusion about what to do in supervision, they can assist SITs in accessing their models of therapy as useful guides for supervision by asking: "How would your model of therapy suggest you proceed?" Second, supervisors-of-supervision can gently push their SITs to find the limits of their therapy models for the context of supervision by asking them to articulate the similarities and differences between change in therapy and change in supervision. Finally, supervisors-of-supervision can help SITs conceptualize their learning by discovering their beliefs, knowledge, and values regarding ways individuals learn. For example, do they value a particular style of learning? How will they work with supervisees with an alternative style?

In the following reprinted case example from Storm and Heath (1985), a supervisor (S) coaches an experienced therapist (T), who was a novice supervisor, to use her model of therapy as an initial guide in developing her philosophy of supervision.[2] This edited transcript illustrates the process involved when supervisors adapt their therapy theory for use in supervision and discover areas of correspondence and difference.

A SUPERVISOR COACHES AN INEXPERIENCED SUPERVISOR

T Let me make sure I understand you. You are suggesting that I use my theory of therapy to guide my work as a supervisor

S: Right.

T: All right, but where do I start?

S. Well, you start by clarifying your own ideas about therapy Liddle (1982) argues that therapists should declare their basic beliefs about therapy at regular intervals. The clearer you are about your own ideas about problems and problem resolution, the more consistent you will be as a thera-

pist I think your ideas about therapy, your own personal therapy theory, will become increasingly clear as you articulate your beliefs

T· Thanks Actually I consider myself to be a strategic therapist.

S: Fine. I'm not sure what you mean exactly by strategic therapy, but what is important is that you use a set of clearly defined ideas consistently

T: I think I do. So what do I do next? Where do I begin when I supervise?

S· You start just as you would with a client. When you begin work with a new client, what do you do first?

T. I ask clients to state their problem, and I try to use their language.

S Okay, what would you do first in supervision, then?

T. Ask the therapist what her problem is? I don't think that would go over well with therapists

S Okay, so how could you ask your opening question in the therapist's language?

T Well, I could ask her what she would like to accomplish in the next session, or ask what difficulty or concern she has with the case

S: I bet either of those approaches would work. The point is to define a problem focus in supervision just as you would in therapy, and to do so in the therapist's language. Now, what do you do in therapy once a problem is defined?

T I contract with clients to help them solve the presenting problem Then I gather information on the behavioral sequences that maintain the problem. Sometimes I do this by asking clients what they have done to try to solve their problem.

S. So what could you do in supervision that would parallel your work in therapy?

T: I could contract to help the therapist reach her goal and then gather information about how the therapist has tried to solve her problem.

S· Watch your language!

T. Okay. I could ask what she has done to resolve her difficulties with the case, or ask what she has done to develop new skills or whatever. Then I could agree to help her reach her goal So you are suggesting that supervisors should accept their therapists' definition of their difficulties and goals, and then contract to help them.

S: No, actually I'm not suggesting that. Your theory of therapy guides you in that direction If you

_____

[2]Reprinted by permission of Haworth Press from *The Clinical Supervisor,* 3(1), 91–95, 1985. Minor changes have been made to update the material.

had a different therapy theory, you would be guided in a different direction. For example, if you practiced experiential therapy, you would probably focus more on how you experience your relationship with the therapist

T: But what about the difficulties seen by supervisors? Surely supervisors know more about the requisite skills of therapy than do their therapists.

S. Good point. There seems to be two possibilities here. One is that your strategic therapy theory does not completely fit the supervision context. That is, maybe strategic therapy is an imperfect model for supervision. On the other hand, as a strategic therapist you may identify different problems than your clients, but believe for change to begin you must work on the one your client reports. With success, according to the theory, you trigger a virtuous cycle of change. If you don't begin with your clients, they may be dissatisfied and possibly drop out of therapy. Perhaps the same ideas apply to therapists. If this is so, strategic theory fits the supervision context after all.

T: If it does fit and I continue with this line of thought, I would end most supervision sessions by designing interventions, usually including tasks, to help the therapist with her concern.

S Yes You've got the idea.

T: But should I really assign homework to therapists?

S: That sounded odd to me at first, too But now it seems obvious that if you believe tasks are important techniques for facilitating change, then you should assign tasks to therapists. Of course, the tasks should be clearly related to your supervisory goals just as therapeutic tasks are related to your therapy goals.

T: So you're saying that whenever I'm unsure about what to do in supervision, I should ask myself what I would do in therapy

S Yes That's how you use your therapy theory as a supervision model

T: But, are there instances when my therapy theory will be unable to guide my supervision?

S· Perhaps. I've thought of three instances when therapy theory fails to prove useful in supervision. First, a supervisor may discover a gap in her understanding of her therapy theory In fact, I guarantee that by using your therapy theory as a guide you will discover the limits in your comprehension of your theory These gaps can be filled

by turning to the writings of the master therapy theorists. Second, a supervisor may stumble into an actual hole in her therapy theory. Your new supervision theory can be only as good as your therapy theory. Third, there may be differences between the contexts of supervision and therapy that prevent or limit the usefulness of therapy theory as a guide in supervision For example, strategic theory seems to leave little room for teaching. Especially when supervising beginners, the easiest way to facilitate a behavior change may be to offer a mini-lecture

T: But even a lecture can be strategically timed and delivered in the therapist's language

S· Right. That's consistent with your thought.

T· Thanks, but I'd like to take your example one more step. I think of supervisors as teachers of therapy Consequently, don't supervisors, as educators, have a responsibility to discuss their thinking with supervisees while therapists do not have that obligation to clients? In fact, I never explain therapy theory to clients, but I have discussed it with therapists.

S Yes and no. Supervisors usually do talk with therapists about therapy theory, but they don't necessarily talk to them about their supervision theory. Again, how much explanation you give for your interventions should depend on your supervision theory. If your theory says understanding and insight are important ingredients for change, then you will explain your thinking to clients and to supervisees But if your theory doesn't emphasize understanding and insight, then you should primarily concern yourself with behavioral change, providing a rationale only when necessary.

T: Then should supervisors only supervise therapists who have theoretical orientations similar to their own?

S: Not necessarily, but it is much easier to work with a therapist who shares your basic theoretical assumptions . . .

T: So you and your supervisee speak the same language.

S: Right Unfortunately it's not always so easy Supervisors often work in settings where they are required to supervise therapists working from a variety of theoretical orientations. At other times therapists may ask for supervision in a therapy that the supervisor doesn't practice. In either case, a broad-based understanding of the principles and techniques of various family therapy theories will prove invaluable.

T: Then perhaps I should tell therapists my preferred theoretical orientation and any other family therapy theories that I understand.

S: Good idea. I also think it is important to know your limitations. For example, I find it difficult to think psychodynamically. I would not be a good supervisor for a therapist working from that orientation. But the point I'm leading up to is that no matter what your therapist's theoretical choice is, you can use your own theoretical orientation to guide your supervision.

T: So if you supervise me and your personal choice of therapy theory is structural family therapy, you can use structural therapy theory as a guide while supervising me as a strategic therapist?

S: Yes, but it's complex so I would have to think through the ways I could use structural principles to help you be a better strategic therapist.

T: Whew! You'd have to think about two theories at once.

S: Right. One in the context of therapy and one in the context of supervision.

T: Okay. But I'm curious, what would a structural supervisor actually do?

S: What do structural *therapists* do? Think about it and then go reread Montalvo (1973).

T: You know, as we've talked, I've become increasingly aware that to be an effective supervisor one must have a consistent supervision theory which requires a good grasp of therapy theory. In addition, it helps to be knowledgeable about family therapy theories other than your own.

S: Exactly. So in essence we are back to the first step. Declare your therapy theory and then use it to declare your new supervision theory.

From a Constructivist Model of Therapy to a Model of Supervision

In this section, Tim describes his experience in adapting his collaborative social constructivist perspective model of therapy to supervision.

As a therapist Tim typically found clients receptive to attempts to engage in conversations where the therapist operates from a position of "not knowing" and the client can be "the expert" (Anderson & Goolishian, 1990). Tim rarely had the experience of clients insisting that he tell them what to do or that he hand out solutions to their difficulties as if he had some reservoir of objective knowledge from which to draw. In doing therapy, collaborative conversations seemed to come fairly easily.

In supervision, however, Tim found that all but one of the first five therapists with whom he worked adhered to "stories" about supervision that consistently included hierarchical supervisory relationships and supervisors as possessing expert knowledge. Although Tim attempted to clearly indicate and explain his commitment to collaboration and social constructivism in the contracting process, therapists regularly insisted that he tell them exactly what to do as well as what was "really going on" with the couples and families with whom they became stuck. This presented a challenging paradox: How could he work with therapists from a collaborative/constructivist perspective when the therapists' own constructions of supervisory reality dictate that the relationship be predominantly hierarchical and that it draw extensively on the supervisor's objective knowledge of how to do therapy? Tim was challenged to find a way to either adapt or expand his model to fit the context of supervision. In response, he used his idea of collaboration. Tim finds it helpful to simply share his discomfort with supervisees when it seems to him that they are wanting him to take the position of "the knower." He now asks them how they think he can be respectful of their expectations of supervision without abandoning his own interest in collaboration as a supervisor. Together they discuss a way of working together that is comfortable for both.

The second challenge to doing supervision collaboratively came from one of his stories about therapist competence. He found himself consistently prodded by the idea that therapists should be able to clearly and consistently elucidate their models of therapy and the philosophical underpinnings thereof. Tim regularly found himself "crusading" with therapists for what some in the field of supervision have called a "big picture" epistemology for doing therapy (Liddle, Breunlin, & Schwartz, 1988). He found it ironic and challenging that his own experience of the usefulness of theoretical clarity and consistency in collaborative/constructivist therapy presented a hindrance to doing supervision collaboratively when therapists did not express any interest in any particular models of therapy. As a therapist, he felt no pressure to impose the need to develop any particular theory for dealing with problems on his clients; yet as a supervisor, he found it difficult not to impose on therapists his belief in the necessity of having a well-developed theoretical approach to doing therapy.

Tim began to wonder if his collaborative model fit the context of supervision or if he was applying the ideas inconsistently. Tim turned to writers who write about collaboration in therapy. O'Hanlon and Wilk (1987) suggest that every therapy room have a couch in it so that if a hypothesis should enter the therapist's head during a session, the therapist can lie down until it goes away. When he feels the temptation to crusade for theoretical clarity and consistency with supervisees, he thinks of his beliefs about the importance of models and theories in therapy as a hypothesis that might best be allowed to go away to make room for more of supervisees' criteria for success.

The Experienced Supervisor

Experienced supervisors have developed by necessity some framework for conducting supervision. Depending on their degree of formal training, such supervisors are not always especially proud of their rudimentary models.

Indeed they often have a quality of "home-brewed" eclecticism and may be functional but be far from elegant. Often the situation is even worse, as SITs have reflected, in that they may be quite experienced at offering advice and clinical wisdom but have thought little about their model of supervision.

Regardless of the degree of elegance and sophistication of their supervisory thinking, it rarely seems appropriate to assume a top-down teaching stance when supervising experienced supervisors. Although they may be self-conscious about their models, experienced supervisors all seem to value help in articulating and developing their own ideas, rather than being expected to be clones of supervisors-of-supervision. Such teaching will occur in the supervision course (see Chapter 26), and many senior clinicians report gratitude for being brought up to date in their reading. In supervision-of-supervision, however, it is most appropriate to focus on their emerging models of supervision.

EXPERIENCED TRAINERS SEEK SUPERVISION TRAINING

Tom was asked to supervise four individuals who had been training family therapists for over ten years. Until recently there had been no reason for them to obtain supervisory credentials. However, their supervisees increasingly were requesting that they be designated AAMFT Approved Supervisors because their work together was not counting toward supervisees' required supervision hours for membership in AAMFT. The individuals, as experienced supervisors and trainers, met the criteria for AAMFT's "Advanced Track." According to the structure for this track, Tom could serve more as a facilitator than a supervisor-of-supervision, in recognition of the candidates' experience. Even though this initially appeared as a situation whereby hierarchy in the relationship and the differential between

Tom's expertise and the SITs' were minimized, Tom's supervisory knowledge was sought and valued. This seemed to arise from several factors: (1) The individuals had never received formal training in supervision. (2) They felt out of touch with the current literature, especially related to supervision. (3) Although they were experienced clinicians and even trainers in the field, they had not necessarily given much thought to their model of supervision. (4) Because there is no requirement that candidates for Approved Supervisor be previous members of AAMFT, they were relatively naive about the structure and expectations of the organization and their gatekeeping responsibilities.

As can be seen, even experienced supervisors typically seek guidance in the areas cited here and function like other SITs. In other more clinical areas, they function autonomously and it is easy to trust that they are conducting supervision skillfully and managing cases responsibly. The supervision group can be much more collaborative and nonhierarchical, and all participants, including the facilitator, can have a rich learning experience.

READINESS TO SUPERVISE SUPERVISION

If supervising supervisors is a challenging, complex process requiring an understanding of its distinct differences from supervising therapists, and supervisors-of-supervision must be able to establish more collaborative relationships while managing multiple levels and being gatekeepers to the profession, then how do supervisors know when they are ready to become supervisors-of-supervision?

Supervisors-of-supervision are ready when they are interested in the supervision process itself. They must be able to acknowledge that SITs are the experts who are attending to ther-

apy while supervisors-of-supervision are attending to the supervision system. Essentially, supervision is in the foreground with the therapy in the background. Closely linked to this is the commitment of supervisors-of-supervision to professional development of SITs. There must be an investment in preparing SITs to become competent supervisors and to assume greater leadership roles in the field.

Supervisors-of-supervision must have a wide repertoire of supervisory knowledge and methods to help supervisors develop; expand; and explore their preferred ideas, values, and methods. Otherwise supervisors-of-supervision cannot easily fulfill their responsibility of assisting their SITs to apply their philosophy of supervision in practice.

Just as therapists need experience doing therapy before becoming supervisors, SITs need experience doing supervision before training others to supervise. Supervisors-of-supervision who have a breadth of experience with different supervisees at different levels of professional development are able to recognize expected levels of competency. For example, recently Cheryl was supervising an SIT who became concerned that a therapist did not have adequate background in research information about working with divorcing couples. Because Cheryl has supervised clinicians with a wide array of experience, she was able to help her SIT place her concern in context. Most practicing clinicians are not current on recent research in specific clinical areas unless they specialize in them, thus the issue became how to expand the supervisee's knowledge base in this area rather than defining this lack of information as a deficit.

Without experience with clinicians at different levels of experience, it can be difficult for SITs to place supervisees within the wider context of supervisees in general. Experience also helps supervisors-of-supervision to be comfortable in their supervisory roles. What once required significant attention, such as looking for isomorphic patterns between family, therapist, and supervisory systems, becomes "second nature" over time. This allows supervisors-of-supervision to be freer to concentrate on managing multiple levels of interaction.

Experience in supervising, with its concomitant evaluation component, prepares supervisors-of-supervision to lead SITs in their gatekeeping responsibilities. Although similar in many respects, evaluation conducted within the privacy of the supervision relationship that is aimed at professional growth has different repercussions than evaluation that is required by outside licensing and credentialing bodies, employers, and so on.

When supervisors see themselves and are seen by others as "ready" based on their interest in supervision as a distinct process in and of itself, knowledge of supervision theory and methods, and experience in practicing supervision, becoming supervisors-of-supervision is a natural career step. At this point, experienced supervisors may be prepared to answer a new "call" (Heath & Storm, 1983) as supervisors-of-supervisors.

REFERENCES

Anderson, H., & Goolishian, H. (1990). Supervision as collaborative conversation: Questions and reflections. In H. Brandau (Ed.), *Von der supervision zur systemischen vision*. Salzburg: Otto Muller Verlag.

Breunlin, D., Liddle, H., & Schwartz, R. (1988). Concurrent training of supervisors and therapists. In H. Liddle, D. Breunlin, & R. Schwartz (Eds.), *Handbook of family therapy training and supervision* (pp. 207–224). New York: Guilford Press.

Constantine, J., Piercy, F., & Sprenkle, D. (1984). Live supervision-of-supervision in family therapy. *Journal of Marital and Family Therapy, 10,* 95–97.

deShazer, S. (1991). *Putting difference to work.* New York: W. W. Norton.

Fine, M., & Fennell, D. (1985). Supervising the supervisor-of-supervision: A supervision-of-supervision or hierarchical blurring? *Journal of Strategic and Systemic Therapies, 4,* 56–59.

Heath, A., & Storm, C. (1983). Answering the call: A manual for beginning supervisors. *Family Networker, 7,* 36–39.

Heath, A., & Storm, C. (1985). From the ivory tower to the institute: The live supervision stage approach for teaching supervision in academic settings. *American Journal of Family Therapy, 13,* 27–36.

Liddle, H. (1982). Family therapy training: Current issues and future trends. *International Journal of Family Therapy, 4,* 87–97.

Liddle, H. (1988). Systemic supervision: Conceptual overlays and pragmatic guidelines. In H. Liddle, D. Breunlin, & R. Schwartz (Eds.), *Handbook of family therapy training and supervision* (pp. 153–171). New York: Guilford Press.

Liddle, H., Bruenlin, D., Schwartz, R., & Constantine, J. (1984). Training family therapy supervisors: Issues of content, form, and context. *Journal of Marital and Family Therapy, 10,* 139–150.

Liddle, H., Bruenlin, D., & Schwartz, R. (1988). *Handbook of family therapy training and supervision.* New York: Guilford Press.

McColley, S., & Baker, E. (1982). Training activities and styles of beginning supervisors: A survey. *Professional Psychology, 13,* 283–292.

Montalvo, B. (1973). Aspects of live supervision. *Family Process, 12,* 343–359.

O'Hanlon, B., & Wilk, J. (1987). *Shifting contexts.* New York: Guilford Press.

Olsen, D., & Stern, S. (1990). Issues in the development of a family therapy supervision model. *The Clinical Supervisor, 8,* 49–65.

Selekman, M., & Todd, T. (1995). Co-creating a context for change: The solution-focused supervision model. *Journal of Systemic Therapies, 14,* 21–33.

Storm, C., & Heath, A. (1985). Models of supervision: Using therapy theory as a guide. *The Clinical Supervisor, 3,* 87–96.

Woodside, D. (1994). Reverse live supervision: Leveling the supervisory playing field. *Supervision Bulletin, 7,* 6.

Wright, L., & Coppersmith, E. (1983). Supervision-of-supervision: How to be "meta" to a metaposition. *Journal of Strategic and Systemic Therapies, 2,* 40–50.

Index

0-595-26133-7

1150356

Made in the USA